The First Zionist Congress in 1897 –
Causes, Significance, Topicality

... in Basel habe ich
den Judenstaat gegründet

The First Zionist Congress in 1897 – Causes, Significance, Topicality

... in Basel habe ich den Judenstaat gegründet

... in Basel I have founded the Jewish State

Edited by
Heiko Haumann

In co-operation with
Peter Haber, Patrick Kury, Kathrin Ringger, Bettina Zeugin

190 illustrations, 1997

Basel · Freiburg · Paris · London · New York
New Delhi · Bangkok · Singapore · Tokyo · Sydney

This book was produced under the patronage of the Canton Basel-Stadt and made possible through the generous support of the Berta Hess-Cohn Foundation

In addition, the following foundations and companies helped to share the production costs:
Anne Frank Fund
Lucien and Reine Bloch Foundation
Ruth and Paul Wallach Foundation
S. Karger Publishers

Translated from German by
Wayne van Dalsum and Vivian Kramer, Munich

The original German version appears under the title:
'Der Erste Zionistenkongress von 1897 – Ursachen, Bedeutung, Aktualität' published by S. Karger AG, Basel
ISBN 3–8055–6491–0

Library of Congress Cataloging-in-Publication Data
The First Zionist Congress in 1897: Causes, Significance, Topicality / edited by Heiko Haumann in co-operation with Peter Haber ... [et al.].
Includes bibliographical references and index.
1. Zionism – History.   2. Zionist Congress (1st: 1897: Basel, Switzerland) – Anniversaries, etc.   I. Haumann, Heiko, 1945 –   II. Haber, Peter.
DS149.F496   1997   320.54'095694 – dc21
ISBN 3–8055–6544–5 (softcover; alk. paper)

All rights reserved. No part of this publication may be translated into other languages, reproduced or utilized in any form or by any means, electronic or mechanical, including photocopying, recording, microcopying, or by any information storage and retrieval system, without permission in writing from the publisher.

© Copyright 1997 by S. Karger AG, Postfach, CH–4009 Basel and the Canton Basel-Stadt
Printed in Switzerland on acid-free paper
by Reinhardt Druck, Basel
ISBN 3–8055–6544–5

Contents

Ueli Vischer
IX   Prefatory Remarks
Basel and the First Zionist Congress

Heiko Haumann
XI   Foreword

1   Introduction

Heiko Haumann
2   Judaism and Zionism
22   The Basle Program
Approved at the First Zionist Congress in Basel in 1897

23   Preconditions and Beginnings of Zionism

Simone Berger
24   Jewish Messianism

Chris Kaiser
29   Early Zionism – Messianic Redemption and Jewish Nation

Peter Haber
32   Josef Natonek: A Forerunner of Herzl from Hungary

Alex Camel
34   Christian Hopes of Zion: Palestine in the 19th Century

Alex Carmel
42   William Hechler: Herzl's Christian Ally

Alex Carmel
46   Impressions from Palestine
46   The Basler Johannes Frutiger
46   Sir Moses Montefiore
46   The Swiss Samuel Gobat
47   The 'Lämel School' in Jerusalem
48   'Mount Hope': A German-American Settlement Near Jaffa
48   The 'Rothschild Hospital' in Jerusalem
49   Bishop Michael Solomon Alexander
50   Mikveh Israel – 'Hope' or 'Gathering of Israel'

Catherine Schott
51   The Change of Jewish Patterns of Life in Poland and the Reorientation of Jewish Self-Image

Stefanie Middendorf
58   'My Shtetl Is the People Who Live in It, Not the Place ...'

Almut Bonhage
64   Jewish Individuality in the Eastern European Shtetl: Sholem Aleichem's 'aisnbangeschichtess'

Sabine Strebel
69   '... from the Gan Eden, the Paradise of Frankfurt, to Gehenna, the Hell of Galicia ...'

Heiko Hauman
74   'Present-Day National Work' in the Shtetl: The Beginnings of Zionism in Galicia

Desanka Schwara
79   'Lo se haderech!' – 'This Is Not the Way!' Eastern Jewish Zionists and Palestine

Valerii Yulevich Gessen
85 Yulii Gessen: A Jewish Historian and His Forgotten Connection to Zionism

Erik Petry
87 The First Aliyah (1882–1904)

Gillian Cavarero
91 The General Jewish Workers' Union in Lithuania, Poland and Russia

Milorad Andrial / Heiko Haumann
96 The Jews of Prague in Search of Their Self-Image, and the 'Prague Line' in Zionism

Martin Trančik
101 Between Old and New Land: The Steiner Family in Pressburg

Peter Haber
106 'The Castle of Zion Shines Far down the Banks of the Danube'
The Difficult Beginnings of Hungarian Zionism

Peter Haber
110 Zionism in Austria

Erik Petry / Anatol Schenker
112 Preconditions and History of Zionism in Germany

Patrick Marcolli
117 Between Tradition and Modernity: Two Jewish Worlds in England

Chris Kaiser / Patrick Kury
121 Zionism and Anti-Semitism in France

Peter Haber
124 'Vamos a la Palestina': Zionism among the Sephardim in the Ottoman Empire and in the Balkans

127 The First Zionist Congress in Basel in 1897

Yaakov Zur
128 The 'Protest Rabbis'

Nadia Guth Biasini
131 Basel and the Zionist Congress

Bettina Zeugin
141 Three Days in Basel

Nadia Guth Biasini
149 Theodor Herzl

François Guesnet
155 The First Interview
The First International Zionist Congress as the Turning Point in the Jewish Reform Movement of Congress Poland, and Its Reception in the Warsaw Newspaper 'Izraelita' in 1897

Nadia Guth Biasini / Patrick Marcolli
161 The Dream of Modernity
Literary Treatments of Zionist Ideas in the Oeuvres of Israel Zangwill and Theodor Herzl

Portraits of Zionist Personalities

Erik Petry
166 David Wolffsohn

Nadia Guth Biasini
167 Max Nordau

Nadia Guth Biasini
168 Arthur Cohn, Rabbi of Basel's Jewish Community

Simone Berger
169 David Farbstein: A Pioneer of Swiss Zionism

Verena von Planta
171 Ahad Haam

Almut Bonhage
172 Nathan Birnbaum

Patrick Marcolli
173 Israel Zangwill

175 Jews in Basel and the Region: Their Situation and the Beginnings of Zionism

Werner Meyer
176 Jews in Medieval Basel

Nadia Guth Biasini
181 The Jewish Community in Basel

Patrick Kury
185 'First the Return Home, Then the Conversion'
Christian Zionism and Philo-Semitism in Basel at the Time of the First Zionist Congress

Patrick Kury
191 The Other Side of the Coin: Anti-Semitism in Basel at the Turn of the Century

Patrick Kury
197 'Foreign and Backward': Eastern Jews in Basel around 1900

Bettina Zeugin
202 The Beginnings of Zionism in Basel and in Switzerland: 1897–1918

Dominique Shaul Ferrero
206 Chaim Weizmann and Switzerland

Dominique Shaul Ferrero
208 Henri Dunant and Zionism

Patrick Kury
211 Veit Wyler

Patrick Kury
213 Wladimir Sagal and Benjamin Sagalowitz

Heiko Haumann
216 Samuel Scheps

Nathalie Meyrat
218 From the City to the Country: Jews in the Alsace

Barbara Lüthi / Sabine Strebel
221 Rural Jewry in the Alsace: Stories of the Past?

Daniel Gerson
224 Zionism in the Alsace

Astrid Starck
227 Alfred Elias

Ulrich Baumann
228 Zionism and the Changes in the Patterns of Life in the Rural Jewry of Southern Baden around 1900

Manfred Bosch
231 '... and I Said to Myself, There Is Something Great in Zionism'
On the Reception of Zionism in Rural Alemannic Jewry, Based Largely on the Example of the Poet Jacob Picard

Ariane Dannacher Brand
236 The Acceptance of Zionism among the 'Rural Jews'
Three Examples

Ruben Frankenstein
239 Zionism in Freiburg im Breisgau

243 The Consequences of the First Zionist Congress up to the Founding of Israel

Bettina Zeugin
244 The 22 Zionist Congresses before the Foundation of the State of Israel
A Brief Summary

Patrick Marcolli / Erik Petry / Bettina Zeugin
250 Trends in Zionism

Erik Petry
257 Martin Buber

Monika Häfliger
258 Zionism in the USA

Monika Häfliger
262 Henrietta Szold

Barbara Lüthi
264 One's Personal Traits in Another Person: First Encounters of Zionists with the Arab Culture
Reflections on Zionism and the Arabs Seen in Historical Perspective Based on a Book by Yosef Gorny

Erik Petry
268 Immigration Movements from 1904–1948

Kathrin Ringger
272 'An English Adventure': Diplomatic Efforts for a Home for the Jewish People 1897–1922

Kathrin Ringger
282 The Palestine Mandate 1923–1948: The Institutionalization of the Conflict
A Chronology

Attila Novák
286 'There Is a Community of Interests Here ...'
Contacts between the Hungarian and Zionist Diplomacy in the Thirties

Heiko Haumann
289 Shoah and Zionism

Priska Gmür
292 'It Is Not up to Us Women to Solve Great Problems'
   The Duty of the Zionist Woman in the Context of the First Ten Zionist Congresses

Ruben Frankenstein
297 Zionism: Only Something for Men?
   The Forgotten Contribution of Zionist Women: The Example of Betty Frankenstein

Claudia Prestel
299 'Strong, Courageous Women and Loyal Jewesses!'
   Image and Role of Women Zionists in the Early Years of the Building-Up of Palestine

Simon Erlanger
303 The Zionist Youth Movements

Inka Bertz
308 Culture and Politics in the Zionist Movement

Erik Petry / Kathrin Ringger
312 Iconographic Aspects of Zionism

Jerzy Malinowski
316 A Jewish National Art
   The Ideas of Zionism in the Art of the Polish Jews

Monica Rüthers
320 'Muscle Jews' and 'Effeminate Jews'

Anatol Schenker
324 Zionist Press and Publishing Houses in German-Speaking Countries
   A Survey from the Beginnings up to the Second World War

Silke Schaeper
328 'From Zwickau to Jerusalem': The Cultural Zionist Salman Schocken

Heiko Haumann
331 'A Jewish Switzerland Built on Shares?'
   Inner Jewish Opposition to Zionism

335 Zionism Today – An Outlook

Michael Hagemeister
336 The 'Protocols of the Learned Elders of Zion' and the Basel Zionist Congress of 1897

Moshe Zimmermann
341 Zionism and Anti-Semitism

Daniel Gerson
346 Zionism, Anti-Zionism, Anti-Semitism

Patrick Kury / Kathrin Ringger
349 Unsolved Questions

Sumaya Farhat-Naser
353 One Hundred Years of Zionism – Associations of a Palestinian Woman

Christian Hofer
358 The Use of Historical Myths in the Creation of the State of Israel

Barbara Lüthi
362 The Variability of History: Israel's Historian Debate

Simon Erlanger
367 Topicality of Zionism

375 Appendix

Desanka Schwara
376 Glossary

Silke Schaeper
384 Library and Private Archive of Salman Schocken
   The 'Schocken Institute for Jewish Research' in Jerusalem

385 Selected Bibliography and Further Reading
395 Acknowledgement of Illustrations
396 Index of Persons
401 Acknowledgements and Thanks

Prefatory Remarks
Basel and the First Zionist Congress

One hundred years ago, at the end of August 1897, Basel played host to the more than 200 participants of the first Zionist Congress. Thanks to the assistance of Jewish and Christian citizens, a good infrastructure was ensured. The city made the music auditorium of the Stadtcasino available for the gathering, as well as a further conference room in the Burgvogtei and an office in the Freie Strasse. The president of the city council at that time, Prof. Dr. Paul Speiser, took part in some of the Congress negotiations with great interest. Theodor Herzl expressed his thanks to 'this hospitable city, which has received us with such benevolence, this administration, which has given us several signs to show its acceptance of our cause' at the end of the Congress.

This openness towards a Jewish movement remained in the time following. The government repeatedly expressed its respect for the efforts which the movement was making. In 1901 the chairman of the canton council, Dr. Heinrich David, said, on the occasion of the Fifth Congress, that Zionism was 'something honourable' and that he was happy that 'this great and beautiful idea had found a home in Basel'. Of the 22 congresses which took place before the founding of the state of Israel, ten were held in Basel, including the last one in 1946. To that day, no other city had been host to this event more often. The close relationship of Basel to the Zionist movement and Israel has, up until today, been shown in many other ways too.

At the time, Basel itself was in a period of profound change. The population exploded towards the end of the 19th century, new buildings sprang up and construction quickly expanded beyond the city walls. The streets within the city were broadened, the marketplace was redesigned. In 1895 the first streetcar drove through Basel and a few years after the First Zionist Congress, the wooden bridge across the Rhine, as it can still be seen in the famous photograph of Theodor Herzl, was replaced by a stone counterpart. These changes did not go unnoticed among the population. There were considerable tensions and even anti-Semitic voices could be heard. In 1893, within the scope of the citizens' initiative against the Jewish ritual slaughtering practices, the marketplace was turned into the forum for an anti-Jewish demonstration. It was all the more important that the canton council proved its liberal stance, by distancing itself from such tendencies and applying pressure to succeed in making Basel the location for the Congress of the Zionist movement.

Zionism wanted to give the Jewish people a new self-confidence and provide them with – as the 'Basle Program', which was passed at the first Congress, expressed – a 'homestead in Palestine secured by public law'.

Numerous aims and hopes from 1897 were not fulfilled. Most noticeable was the failure to maintain this homestead in a peaceful way. Much spilling of blood and misery accompany the history of Zionism. Similarly unsuccessful were the hopes of being able to save the Jews threatened by anti-Semitism in time. Quite on the contrary: it was only the genocide attempted by the German

National Socialists that was able to convince the great powers of the necessity of a state of Israel. In many countries, including Switzerland, things were done and have failed to be done, that accompany us today as severe responsibility with regard to the persecuted Jews.

The centenary offers the opportunity to take stock of occurrences. The council of the Canton of Basel was happy to take over patronage of the corresponding activities, including the exhibition and this publication 'The First Zionist Congress in 1897' which should serve to inform an interested public of the causes, significance and topicality of the first Zionist Congress. A wide range of authors approached – under the auspices of a team from the Historical Seminar of the University of Basel – an even wider range of aspects which point out to us the background of the Zionist movement, the effects of the Congress, from 1897 to the present day, as well as the role which Basel, the region and Switzerland played in this process. This book can deepen the impressions which are offered by the exhibition, give us the basis for and spur us on to critical confrontation with the history of Zionism. I hope this book will find many interested readers.

Ueli Vischer
President of the City Council of the Canton Basel-Stadt

Foreword

The first Zionist Congress was held in Basel exactly one hundred years ago in 1897. On October 14, 1992, I proposed to the government of the Canton Basel-Stadt that this centenary be commemorated with an exhibition, a publication and an international conference. After a number of preparatory meetings and a rough outline of the project, which was submitted by Dr. Katia Guth-Dreyfus of the Jewish Museum of Switzerland in Basel, Prof. Dr. Ekkehard Stegemann and myself on December 15, 1993, these plans were included as the contribution of the university to an overall programme for the jubilee which was prepared by the Canton Basel-Stadt under the auspices of Dr. Ueli Vischer, member of the city council. Since then, Dr. Vischer has accompanied our activities with great dedication and a high degree of personal interest. I would like to take this opportunity to express my thanks to him. The organization committee chaired by Dennis L. Rhein also deserves our thanks for co-ordinating all the activities, ensuring that the financial means were available and answering any questions that arose.

Ekkehard Stegemann took on the management of the Academic Congress and I offered to take over the administration of the exhibition and the accompanying book, which was also to be the commemorative publication. From the very beginning it was clear that this was a project for the Historical Seminar of the University of Basel and it also fitted nicely into its educative scope. In the winter semester 1993/94 I held two seminars: 'The beginnings of Zionism' and 'Jews between village and city in the Upper Rhine Area'. At the same time, I organized a regular colloquium: 'Study group for the History of the Jews / Zionism'. A number of interested students of this study group along with further collaborators formed a team to prepare the exhibition and the book with me. Later on, a number of external advisors and authors joined the team. Then, in regular meetings and sometimes heated debates, we elaborated the concept of the exhibition. Smaller groups discussed projects and the intensive research of several subjects began. Archives in Israel, New York and Eastern Europe had to be consulted in the search for sources and objects.

In my eyes, the goal of the project has been achieved. The participants were not only able to work independently on historical matters within the team framework, but they also gained inestimable experience in dealing with organizational problems, conveying academic knowledge via an exhibition, writing and editing texts, negotiating loans, and discussing with the organization committee and public authorities. The obstacles that we were faced with when looking for a suitable location for the exhibition will remain unforgettable, but this is another story. Fortunately, the Kunsthalle was kindly made available to us by the Kunstverein and the curator – my special thanks go to Mrs. Soiron and Mr. Pakesch. Of course, there were 'frictional losses' while preparing an exhibition in this way, tension was inevitable in view of the long period of time and the often complex problems, but I also considered it to be an important part of this project to learn how to deal with these factors. And I am convinced that even with a 'more effective' hierarchical structure the results could not have been better. For me this collaborative work in a team was a particularly motivating component of the project and an enjoyable experience that I would not want to have missed.

The foundations of the organizational structure of our team were formed by a committee which, apart from the external people, was largely identical with the authors of this book. This committee discussed the basic questions, made decisions, listened to guest speakers and discussed the individual topics of the project at regular colloquiums and special meetings. For the channelling of the work, the committee elected a 'core group' which co-ordinated the detailed tasks: the members of the 'exhibition concept group' were – some on a temporary basis – Almut Bonhage, Nadia Guth Biasini, Heiko Haumann, Chris Kaiser, Patrick Kury, Barbara Lüthi, Anatol Schenker, Catherine Schott, Martin Trančik; the 'publication group' consisted of Peter Haber, Heiko Haumann, Patrick Kury, Kathrin Ringger and Bettina Zeugin. The initial administrative responsibility was held by Simone Berger and Chris Kaiser and then, subsequently, during the 'intensive' work as the manuscripts were made ready for printing, by Almut Bonhage and finally by Jacqueline Weber. In urgent cases, the other team members also lent a helping hand. The contacts to Poland, from where we received many exhibits which had never before been made available to the public, were upheld by Catherine Schott. Patrick Kury was responsible for the assistance and project co-ordination, and in the last months Erik Petry, who also participated intensively in the editorial work, joined him in this capacity. During the course of this project, all often placed other interests in the background and worked with unique devotion and creativity.

A team of American artists, Michael Clegg & Martin Guttmann, was recommended to us by the Kunsthalle for the realization of our results and concepts. In co-operation with the Basel designers Christian Stauffenegger & Ruedi Stutz, the representatives of the Kunsthalle – Peter Pakesch, Andrea Vegh, Madeleine Schuppli and Klaus Haenisch – as well as our team, developed the design concept; the details of the exhibition were produced by the entire team. Together with students, Erhard Klöss provided the film equipment. My thanks to all of these persons. I am also indebted to all those who graciously loaned us exhibits – as their representatives I would like to mention Yoram Mayorek and his colleagues of the Central Zionist Archives in Jerusalem – to all those who supported and sponsored the exhibition and the book, to the staff of the Historical Seminar and not least to Karger-Publishers, especially Dr. h.c. Thomas Karger and Steven Karger, Rolf Steinebrunner, Alexander Geraets, Robert Grünig and Iris Ruf, whose dedicated attention to the book has been of a rarely seen high quality. Of course I extend my special thanks to the authors.

Editorial responsibility for the English translation was assumed by Barbara Lüthi, Erik Petry, Kathrin Ringger and Jacqueline Weber. Readers of the translation were Andrea Shaw-Schneider and Marie-Louise de Stachelski. Footnotes and references are given according to the German way of citation. Whenever possible Hebrew names and expressions were spelled according to the *Encyclopedia Judaica*.

It goes without saying that the final decision about the quality of the publication and the exhibition lies with the visitors and the readers. We would all be happy to hear their comments.

Heiko Haumann

Professor at the Historical Seminar of the University of Basel

Introduction

Heiko Haumann

Judaism and Zionism

Theodor Herzl was much too exhausted during the First Zionist Congress between August 29 and 31, 1897, in Basel and also during the journey home to entrust details to his diary – except for a brief note on the morning of August 30. Not until he had arrived back in Vienna did he resume recording his thoughts on September 3. The initial reactions at the Congress had shown him

'that our movement has gone down into the annals of history. If I were to summarize the Baseler Congress in a few words, words that I would never say out loud, I would say this: in Basel I have founded the Jewish state. If I were to be overheard I would become a laughing stock, but maybe in five years' time, or at least in fifty everyone will understand.'[1]

Herzl was to be proved right. The Zionist movement grew after humble beginnings to become a factor of historical importance, and little more than fifty years had passed as, on November 29, 1947, the United Nations General Assembly agreed to the foundation of a Jewish state – and the splitting of Palestine. On May 14, 1948, David Ben Gurion read out Israel's declaration of independence. Basel played an important part here. The diary entry also bears witness to Herzl's overconfidence, which was fed by his narcissism and depressions, and which had already given rise to numerous unfortunate failures on his part. Nonetheless, his fire, his inexhaustible activity, his emotive rhetoric and his unassailable belief in the inevitably approaching realization of the Zionist ideal helped the movement to find its breakthrough and gave it the strength to be able to overcome all obstacles in its path.

The Zionism connected to the name Herzl has always been controversial, ever since its inception and right up to this day, both within and outside the Jewish community. It meant a radical break: for a people strewn all over the world, which considered itself in the Diaspora, in exile and which did not fit into the accepted concept of a political unit, the claim had been voiced to have the right to be a nation and to be allowed to base this 'homestead' in Palestine.[2] Despite this break, Zionism saw itself as part of the Jewish tradition, wanted to finally realize the dream of the return to Zion and the Messianic liberation.

The longing to return to Zion goes back as far as the destruction of the Temple in Jerusalem in the year 70 and the gradual dispersion of the Jewish people to all corners of the world. 'Zion' was originally the term for a hill in Jerusalem, the fortress on which was called the 'City of David' after being conquered by David. With the expansion of this area, the term Zionism also expanded to include the Temple Mount and its shrine. Later, Zion came to stand for all of Jerusalem and even for the country of Israel. The hope of one day

---

[1] Theodor Herzl: Tagebücher. Vol. 5, 3 September 1897. In: Central Zionist Archives (in the following CZA), HII B2 5/H 75, pp. 49–50. Published e.g. in Theodor Herzl: Briefe und Tagebücher. Ed. by Alex Bein et al. Vol. 2. Berlin, Frankfurt a. M., Vienna 1983, pp. 538–539.

[2] As in 'Baseler Programm'. Draft in: CZA, DD A 2/1/1/1, final version: Zionisten-Congress in Basel (29, 30 and 31 August 1897). Officielles Protocoll. Vienna 1898, pp. 114, 119.

1 Jerusalem as seen from Mount Scopus, 1907. Photographer: American Colony.

leading the Jewish people back to Erez Israel stayed alive, was expressed in prayer formulas like 'Next year in Jerusalem!' and was strongly connected to the Messianic ideal that said that as soon as the Jews were united back in Israel, the Messiah would appear, rebuild the Temple and the Jewish kingdom and bring peace and freedom to the Jewish people and the entire world.

Especially in times of change the belief was widespread that the return of the Messiah was imminent or that he had already appeared and that he would soon complete his work of redemption: for example David Rubeni between 1520 and 1532, Shabbetai Zevi [1626–1676] and Jacob Frank [1726–1791]. Time and time again believers would sell all of their belongings to return to the Promised Land and wait for the Messiah. A small Jewish community always existed in Israel, that had been called Palestine since 135, Jews could be found in Jerusalem, Hebron, Safed und Tiberias. For religious Jews this meant the fulfilment of a lifelong goal to be able to travel to Israel where they could see the holy places, perhaps even to be buried there, but at the very least to take a small pouch of earth back home with them. However, this was not connected to a desire for a mass exodus, or even the wish to liberate the Jews from the Diaspora by founding a new Jewish home in Erez Israel, thus giving rise to the redemption through their own actions. This would have contradicted the religious ideal that mankind must not try to force the will of God.

Thus the numerous projects for a 'Jewish state' that have been undertaken since the Middle Ages were mostly not born of a religious movement in Judaism. In general, these were simply the adventurous plans of individual people. The Christians wanted to bring the Jews together in this way and to form some kind of a mass ghetto, or simply to get rid of them. If a Jewish person had a similar idea it was because he wanted relief from oppression or persecution. Only very seldom was the aim to pave the way for the Second Coming of the Messiah by forming a Jewish state.

This began to change after the end of the 18th century. In the movement based around the 'False Messiah' Jacob Frank, the 'True Jacob', not only the desire for a crossing of the boundaries

Judaism and Zionism

set by belief and tradition, or even – less well defined – for a radical change of the societal conditions was expressed, but also the idea that the redemption could be forced. Frank taught, in an exaggerated continuation of Kabbalist theories and the movement of Shabbetai Zevi, that people must suffer sin down to the deepest part of their being in order to overcome evil from within and thus give rise to the redemption, which he said would come during the exile of the Jews. This standpoint expressed, in an extremist manner, the activist trend in Judaism, which spread its influence just as much to the Haskalah – the Jewish 'enlightenment' –, to reform Judaism, the way to assimilation and secularization, to the turning away from the religion as it did to national Judaism and Zionism.

Of course the turnaround did not come unprepared: there was – not least of all in the Kabbalah – a tradition of freeing oneself from the bonds of the authorities. But now, in the second half of the 18th and the beginning of the 19th century, a trend towards the outside grew out of this. Even the Hassidim got involved. Hassidism – the 'movement of the orthodox Jews' – had been founded by Israel ben Eliezer [1700–1760] in the Poland of that time. Baal Shem Tov – the 'Master of the Divine', that is God's 'Name' – had taught that redemption is to be found in each individual and that the inner turnaround is the most important factor for redemption. A mass movement of new devoutness was the consequence, but even the Baal Shem Tov had supposedly already tried to force God to redeem the world through the power of his prayers. This desire became even stronger after the French Revolution and during the terrible wars which followed it. The opinion was widespread that the end was nigh. The patterns of life were overturned for many people, they sought orientation in this social crisis that would give meaning to their lives. Particularly among the Hassidim the belief grew that Napoleon's crusades were the precursor of the coming of the Messiah as prophesied in the Bible. Three of the most influential Zaddikim of the time decided to force God to send the Redeemer at once by uniting their prayers. However, they died before they could carry out their plan. There were those who viewed their deaths as a punishment from God. The will to actively accelerate the salvation process was, however, unmistakeable and went hand in hand with the profound changes in economy and politics and in the way people thought and behaved. These tendencies grew more intense during the 19th century: the consequences of the enlightenment, the secularization, the approaches for the legal emancipation of the Jews, the industrialization and the social changes which they caused did not take place without leaving their mark on the Jewish people itself and on the posture of the non-Jewish environment towards it.

The question of a legal equality of the Jews was often connected to the idea that it should only be given to them if they gave up their Jewish culture and independence. In the image of 'civilization' and its corresponding human being of that time, the Jewish culture was considered, however, as old fashioned, shaped by superstition and prejudice. The awaited assimilation thus also meant a 'colonialization' of the traditional patterns of life.[3] This process gave rise to many new Jewish state projects out of varied motivations. Those who considered the Jews to be not 'civilizable' and integrateable wanted to drive them out of their places of residence and put them all together in a new, independent state.

Other ideas were founded on messianic hopes. If it should prove possible to reunite the Jews in their original homeland, the redemption of the world would finally come about. Interestingly enough, the Polish Messianism – which as the poet Adam Mickiewicz [1798–1855] formulated most strongly, saw the liberation of Poland as a prerequisite for the liberation of mankind –

---

[3] For a definition see Jürgen Habermas: Theorie des kommunikativen Handelns. Vol. 2. Frankfurt a. M. 1988, p. 293.

associated itself with such concepts. Christian groups too supported the project of a Jewish state. Some of these efforts were associated with thoughts of a Jewish mission, for example at the 'London Society for Promoting Christianity among the Jews' or at the 'Basel Mission' and the 'Verein der Freunde Israels' (Society of the Friends of Israel): once the longing for Zion, the expectation of the Messiah was so strong among the Jews that they would unite to form their own state in Israel, it would be much easier to convince them that Jesus was the Messiah. Others based their thoughts on the biblical prophecy that a certain number of Jews had to be reunited in Israel, then the Day of Redemption would dawn. All of these ideas gave rise to serious colonization plans in Palestine. The concept of a Jewish state was in the air.

And the Jewish people itself began planning more projects which stemmed from the insight that the 'misery of the Jews' could not be improved or even solved with purely philanthropic means. A Jewish state was necessary – in Palestine or elsewhere – in order to solve the problem. In the USA, Mordecai Manuel Noah [1785–1851] proclaimed, in various different attempts between 1818 and 1844, an 'independent and free Jewish state',[4] in Germany the businessman Bernhard Berend asked the Frankfurt banker Mayer Amschel Rothschild [1773–1855] in 1832 to buy an area of land in North America and to found a colony there which could become the Jewish state. Rothschild – as well as a number of other people whom Berend appealed to – declined to do so and as Berend arranged a personal meeting with him in 1845 Rothschild ended the discussion with a brusque 'Schtuss', which roughly translates to 'nonsense'. In Rothschild's opinion the Jewish people had to bear the fate sought out for them by God with patience. This stance showed the expectation that the 'Jewish question' would take care of itself via the legal emancipation and assimilation.[5] Orthodox rabbis such as Judah ben Alkalai [1798–1878], Zevi Hirsch Kalischer [1795–1874] and Josef Natonek [1813–1892] pushed for the return of the Jews to Erez Israel in influential writings and for the colonization of the country. The socialist Moses Hess [1812–1875] predicted the failure of the emancipation in his work 'Rome and Jerusalem. The Last Question of Nationality'. The only way out which he could see was in a national self-contemplation and the formation of a Jewish national state. However the time was not yet ripe.

Thus, on the one hand there was the hope for emancipation and assimilation or acculturation – the abandonment of one's own culture by adapting to another or joining with the other with the aim of finding a new synthesis – religiously spoken the attitude to trust in God's guidance. On the other hand, there was the growing will to change the fate of the Jews by way of a radical political solution and the knowledge that the 'Jewish misery' had reached a stage which had made drastic measures necessary. Of course the Jewish people had not previously simply accepted all the tribulations. The 'advocates' – the Shtadlanim – attempted to influence those at the source of power, and in critical situations the Jewish community often turned to unusual methods in order to save what could be saved. Via the self-administration organizations, an active policy was followed and it was not at all out of the question that they would turn to weaponry to defend themselves. In Eastern Europe, especially in the kingdom of Poland-Lithuania, this posture was much more widespread than in Western Europe, probably because the situation of the Jews here had been better for a long time. However the political posture fundamentally depended on the situation. The

---

[4] N.M. [Nathan Michael] Gelber: Zur Vorgeschichte des Zionismus. Judenstaatsprojekte in den Jahren 1695–1845. Published in cooperation with the executive of the Zionist World Organization. London, Vienna 1927, pp. 62–84, quotation p. 84.

[5] Gelber: Vorgeschichte des Zionismus, pp. 85–90; Karl Cohen: Ein Judenstaatsprojekt vor 100 Jahren. In: Jüdisches Gemeindeblatt Mannheim 16 (1937) 6, p. 4 (my thanks to Manfred Bosch for pointing out this source).

Jewish people saw itself drawn into a conflict and had to make a decision, had to act, could also defend itself – all this was God's will. But they did not get involved in any long-term politics, planned no projects for the future – that would have been an attempt to anticipate God's plans. This attitude, therefore, began to slowly change among parts of the Jewish people, on the one hand under the impression of the existential disruptions of the 17th and 18th centuries and their consequences for the faith and way of thinking, and then ever-increasingly under the impression of the 'misery of the Jews'. This term referred to the social and economic effects of the industrialization which was taking place – and which made paupers of numerous Jews – as well as to renewed anti-Jewish actions that were turned against the emancipation and that stamped the Jewish people as the whipping boy for crises the causes of which were obscure. More and more Jews began to doubt that assimilation was the right way which would lead all Jews to freedom.

In Germany and the rest of Central Europe, the tendency toward assimilation and acculturation was so dominant that all other proposed orientations were only met with minimal response. The roots for a radical change were laid in Eastern Europe. Among the Jews in the Polish-Lithuanian empire in the 18th century a consciousness of a 'complete cultural personality' developed, triggered by the previous fundamental changes in their situation, for which the concept of Eastern Jewry later became common.[6] During the 19th century, the patterns of life of these Jews changed profoundly. The partitions of Poland between 1772 and 1815 tore the previous, largely unified state allocation of this settlement area apart. The rule of West Poland was usurped by the Prussians; the Jews there slowly adapted the Western Jewish life style. On the other hand, there was a strengthening of the individuality of the patterns of life of the Jews who lived in the Austrian and Russian section of Poland – Galicia and Congress Poland – as well as Russia itself – in the 'pale of settlement' which had previously largely belonged to Poland – or who had immigrated from other areas of Eastern Europe to Hungary and Romania due to political or economical conditions.

Furthermore, a major agricultural crisis at the beginning of the 19th century interrupted the traditional economical circulation between town and country, between aristocratic land owners, peasants, rural and urban craftsmen, merchants and entrepreneurs, where the Jews functioned as the middlemen. The pressure which was used to try to drive the Jews out of the villages caused their numbers in the towns to rise rapidly. A tough competitive situation arose between the established Jews and the newcomers for the few jobs available in handicrafts and trading. The 'expulsion' from the former professions and residential areas, combined with the industrialization, led to a lasting socioeconomic 'restructuring'. Most of the Jews became impoverished and lived under unimaginable living, working and income conditions. The overcrowded situation, especially in the different handicraft professions created numerous 'Luftmenschen' (air people) who had to worry daily if they would get food from somewhere and often only lived on the air that they breathed. Retail replaced handicrafts as the most important source of income. On the other hand, a few Jews succeeded in rising to positions as bankers or industrialists. This sharp social polarization gave rise to a number of consequences for the inner structure and the coexistence of the people in the Jewish community.

At the same time, the growth in the share of Jewish people in the population, who was concentrated in certain streets and quarters – ghet-

---

[6] M.A.: Polnische Juden. In: Der Jude 1 (1916/17) pp. 561 f., quotation p. 561. As early as the First Zionist Congress Nathan Birnbaum speaks without reservation of the East Jews with their own culture in his address (Zionisten-Congress, pp. 82–94) and refers to them subsequently as their 'own cultural community', 'filled with inner power, rich in history, strong in their present and full of future' (Was sind Ostjuden? Zur ersten Information. Vienna 1916, p. 15).

2 Cheap lunch in front of the market hall in Vilnius.

tos – gave rise to new forms of anti-Jewish attitudes. The rising non-Jewish bourgeoisie entered into a competition of displacement with the wealthy Jews who were moreover subject to the hatred of other parts of the population, also from the workers, who saw them as 'capitalists' in the most negative sense of the word. Similar procedures could be observed in the retail industry which often escalated into boycott movements. The anti-Jewish sentiments combined with nationalist trends amongst the Polish, who forced the Jews out of the national union and declared them to be the enemy. It became obvious in a number of riots just how quickly nationalist feelings and problems with socioeconomical changes could be vented on the Jews. The bloody pogroms subsequent to the assassination of Czar Alexander II in 1881, for which the Jews were held responsible against the background of growing social and religious contrasts, gave the last push to the search for fundamentally new ways of alleviating the 'Jewish misery'.

The worsening of the relationships between Jews and non-Jews basically brought an end to the attempts of the Jewish enlightenment – the Haskalah –, to reach complete integration of the Jewish people into the existing society, to fit them into the worldly education system and to make them abandon their obsolete way of life. A number of Jews in the Russian empire began to reflect on Judaism. Students joined together in 1882 to form the group 'Bilu'. They selected the initials of the Hebrew 'Beit Yaakov Lekhu ve-Nelkhah' – the word from Isaiah 'House of Jakob, come ye and let us go!' – not only to organize a national resistance to the pogroms but they also wanted to initiate an emigration to Erez Israel. In Rishon le-Zion which was among the first new Jewish colo-

3 Jewish retail dealers in front of their shops in Lida.

nies, the Bilu worked together with the 'Hovevei Zion' – the 'lovers of Zion' – in the movement 'Hibbat Zion' – 'love of Zion'. However, the initial successes of this 'First Aliyah' – the 'ascent' to Zion – never fulfilled the hopes that had been placed in it. All in all the desire for self-emancipation, 'Autoemancipation' as Leon Pinsker [1821–1891] had put it in 1882, was stronger among the Eastern Jews: they were forced to see that an emancipation from the 'outside' could not be expected in the foreseeable future, especially considering that the non-Jewish community itself was not emancipated either.

The answers to the question regarding where the new place in society should be varied greatly. Only a small part – most of all from the very small upper class – chose to continue with assimilation. Many emigrated to seek better living conditions elsewhere. Socialism was well received, the internationalist workers' movement, which, by eliminating the class structure, also wanted to overcome national borders. It is no coincidence that the 'Bund' – the 'General Jewish Workers' Union in Lithuania, Poland and Russia' – was founded in the same year as the World Zionist Organization. Numerous Jews, especially the less wealthy, sought protection, safety and orientation in the religious community, particularly in this time of radical change. In addition to the rabbinical orthodoxy the mystical Hassidism remained alive. And another path led to the understanding of a national Judaism and to Zionism as a political movement; this was a nationalist answer to the nationalist movement of the non-Jewish environment, but it was also much more than this.

There were similarities with other nationalist movements, such as that in the initial phase the intellectuals constructed, 'invented' the nation. Also in the conceptualization, in the symbolism, the method of analysis and interpretation of the situation, similarities can be found. But differences are also apparent. Despite mutual foundations in the history and culture of all Jews, which did indeed give rise to a feeling of belonging

4 A 'parliament'. Jews in the Krasiński park in Warsaw, 1930. Photographer: Moshé Raviv-Vorobeichic (Moï Ver).

together, a kind of 'people's consciousness', there were many individual differences between the various countries in the Diaspora. Furthermore there was no area in which at least a large portion of the nation lived and there was no mutual language – even when one concedes that German initially served as the common language, even at the Zionist congresses, and Hebrew subsequently prevailed. What is more, it must be seen as a special exception that the Jews were already defined as a nation by the rest of the world and as such were already seen as outsiders before they even saw themselves as a national movement. The national consciousness which existed and which was largely thrust upon them had now to be replaced by a new consciousness which was to be independent from the subjective self-conceptualization and 'objective'. This also made some Zionists receptive to the biological argumentation of 'racial anthropology' which was subject to intense discussion in the sciences at that time. With this reconstruction of the nation, the 'national rebirth of the Jewish people' could once again be discussed, with reference to the religious Zionist tradition.

Of particular importance for the development of Zionism was the perception of the differences between Eastern and Western Jews. Due to the different conditions in Eastern and Western Europe there were varying conceptions of the aim and the way to achieve it, although the roots were essentially the same. For most Eastern Jews, their established cultural tradition meant that Zion was connected exclusively with Erez Israel. Above and beyond this the state as an aim was generally regarded as less important than the tangible aid for the threatened and impoverished Jews of Eastern Europe through help in their efforts to colonize and emigrate. One of the reasons that they found Zionism attractive was because it combined a radical solution – which was desperately necessary – with the traditional beliefs. In connection with this it aimed to improve the position of Jews in their native countries, right up to their recognition as an autonomous national minority. Here, the Eastern European Zionists met with representatives of other groups, from autonomists and national Jews through to liberals and the Bund. For the Western Jews this did not represent a solution to the problems of Jewry: the legal equality and socioeconomic improvement had already been achieved in Western Europe. The varying roles which the state played in the political concepts of the Zionists in Eastern and Western Europe may also have had something to do with the experiences of the respective environments. The Eastern-Jewish cultural group had become known along with the growth of the national consciousness of the different peoples in Eastern Europe which was originally closely related to a political liberation movement. Even as this visibly developed into an aggressive nationalism which excluded other nationalities, something of the former concept of a peaceful coexistence of various nationalities in the same state-territory remained in the minds and lives of many Jewish people. The Western Jews, on the other hand, much more torn in their cultural characters, lived to a large extent in countries which participated in the international imperialist partition of the world as powerful national states. This had a marked influence on their understanding of the terms nation, nationalism and international politics. Thus they sought the path of rapidly constructing a state by exploiting the international power struggle, even employing the future state as a power factor. All things considered, it was no wonder that 'cultural misunderstandings' arose between the Eastern and Western Jews.

In retrospect of the First Zionist Congress, Alexander Hausmann from Lemberg accused the Western Jews – and thus also Herzl whom he actually admired – of forgetting the 'national present-day-work in the Golus', that is, in the Diaspora, above and beyond the aim of establishing a Jewish state.[7] Several reports confirm that there were repeated tensions between the Eastern and Western Jews at this Congress, as well as on many other occasions, because they knew so little about each other. Herzl himself is a good example of this. Initially enthusiastically greeted by the Eastern Jewish Zionists, because he seemed to bring their hopes to fruition as well, he quickly lost popularity because he often reacted to their problems with a lack of understanding. This was not simply because Herzl knew little about the life of the Jews in Eastern Europe and had not even read the earlier Zionist writings, the deeper reason is to be found in the fact that he 'always remained convinced of their inferior position' despite all the tactical admissions which he made because he realized very quickly that Zionism would not succeed without the mass movement among the Eastern Jews. Many Russian Zionists took offense in the fact that in 1903 he met with Pleve the czarian minister of the interior who they considered to be responsible for the terrible pogrom in Kishinev just a few months previously. Although Herzl managed to achieve a facilitation of Zionist activities in the Russian empire, he also heeded the minister's argument that the Zionists should particularly take those Jews to Palestine who were disagreeable to the government. In the conflict surrounding the 'Uganda Scheme' in 1903/04 Herzl's 'prejudices' against the Eastern Jews, which he shared with many 'cultivated' Western Jews, became particularly apparent.[8]

In Palestine this affected the actions of Edmond de Rothschild [1845–1934]. He treated the settlers from Eastern Europe in the colonies which he financed – in 1903 these were 19 of a total of 28 – like 'beggars', who he thought should accept his help as alms, and he fought against the 'exaggerated activism of the Zionists of Eastern Europe'. This was fueled by the 'self produced stereotype of the Eastern European Jew' who was incapable of running a farm independently and under his own steam and who first had to be 'educated'. The idealism of many humiliated settlers disappeared quickly, many settlements and projects could only be kept alive – if at all – with great difficulty and alterations to their character. With-

---

[7] Berliner Büro der Zionistischen Organisation (ed.): Warum gingen wir zum Ersten Zionistenkongress? Berlin 1922, p. 47.

[8] Yossi Goldstein: Herzl and the Russian Zionists: The Unavoidable Crisis? In: Peter Y. Medding (ed.): Studies in Contemporary Jewry 2 (1986) pp. 208–226, quotations pp. 215, 221.

out Rothschild's conduct, the rebuilding of Palestine would have been achieved 'with less sacrifice and less misery'.⁹

Zionism is effectively an expression for the crisis of the Jewish self-image in the 19th century. It is based on the tradition of Judaism and is part of that dealing with this crisis, which, in addition to many other directions, caused the Jewish people to turn to an activist posture in the world. Zionism was an answer to the fact that the Messiah had not yet come again but that the 'Jewish misery' desperately required relief; it was an answer to secularization and tolerance, to emancipation and liberalism, to industrialization and impoverishment, to the change in the patterns of life. One could speak of a worldly messianism, while observing that Zionism in many aspects adopted the religious tradition in Judaism and continued it. The increase in anti-Semitism and nationalism was closely related to these intellectual, political and socioeconomic changes. They accelerated the formation of the Zionist movement, making the time ripe for their organization to be taken seriously as a power. Herzl's 'Jewish State' of 1896 and the First Zionist Congress in Basel came just at the right time.

Theodor Herzl [1860–1904], who came from an assimilated Jewish family in Budapest and who lived in Vienna, had, a long time previously, seen his calling as that of a writer and had already composed successful feature articles and plays. In Vienna and subsequently in France, where he worked as a correspondent for the 'Neue Freie Presse', he was confronted with a growing anti-Semitism. He came more and more to the conviction that the anti-Jewish feeling would not disappear and that the only solution was to form a state for the Jews as a people. The last push was given by the atmosphere full of hatred that arose among the people of Paris in connection with the legal case against the supposed German spy Captain Dreyfus in 1894. In the space of a few months Herzl recorded his thoughts in the work 'Der Judenstaat. Versuch einer modernen Lösung der Judenfrage' (The Jewish State. An Attempt to Find a Modern Solution to the Jewish Question) which was published on February 14, 1896. In this work, he did not yet commit himself to a place where such a state could be founded – it should quite simply be some 'portion of the globe'. However, Palestine, as the 'ever-memorable historic home' would

'attract our people with a force of marvellous potency [...] We should there form a portion of a rampart of Europe against Asia, an outpost of civilization as opposed to barbarism.'

As a neutral state they would remain in contact with Europe and safeguard even the sanctuaries of Christendom. All those of different religious persuasions should be treated with tolerance and enjoy equality.¹⁰

The enthusiasm that Herzl had understood the subject perfectly and expressed this in a work which was capable of convincing and leading people, caused many national Jews to put pressure on Herzl to take over the leadership of the movement. Herzl, being very sure of himself, created his own Zionist weekly magazine 'Die Welt' (the world), the first edition of which was published on June 4, 1897, in Vienna and which was printed on yellow paper in order to transform that with which the Jews had been branded in the Middle Ages into a badge of honour. Most of all, Herzl aimed all his efforts and organizational talent at creating a meeting of representatives of Zionist groups. Nathan Birnbaum [1864–1937],

---

9 Yoram Mayorek: Zwischen Ost und West: Edmond de Rothschild und Palästina. In: Georg Heuberger (ed.): Die Rothschilds. Beiträge zur Geschichte einer europäischen Familie. Sigmaringen 1994, pp. 133–150, quotations pp. 136, 146, 149.

10 Theodor Herzl: Der Judenstaat. Versuch einer modernen Lösung der Judenfrage. Leipzig, Vienna 1896, quoted here from the English version of New York 1988, pp. 92, 96.

5   The old bridge across the Rhine in Basel. Photographer: Varady.

who had coined the term 'Zionism' as the name for the new movement in his newspaper 'Selbst-Emancipation' (self-emancipation) in 1890, had never managed to achieve more than a preliminary conference in 1894. Now, the enthusiasm of being able to achieve the breakthrough overcame all previous resistance. Even the right location was found, after initial difficulties: Basel. Here the anti-Semitism was not as prevalent as in Vienna, there were no protests by orthodox rabbis or by the Jewish community as in Munich, no colony of revolutionary Russians as in Zurich who would cause the Zionist delegates from Eastern Europe to fear that the czarian secret police would be monitoring them and cause problems for them. Instead there was a good infrastructure available in Basel, the government of the canton was receptive and helpful, the orthodox Rabbi Arthur Cohn lent his assistance for the preparations although he was still rather sceptical, as did the 'Christian Zionists' – even if not totally selflessly. All in all the atmosphere was liberal and open in a way that would have been difficult to find elsewhere. Even the obvious anti-Jewish tendencies or inner problems of the Jewish community – for example how they referred to the Eastern Jews who were immigrating into the area – could not change the positive atmosphere.

The First Zionist Congress convened in the Stadtcasino which was decorated festively. The participants appeared – all but one – in tails and the ladies in equally elegant attire. As one of the delegates inquired whether the women had the right to vote, Herzl, who had been voted president, answered:

'The ladies are of course very honoured guests but will not take part in the vote.'¹¹

Nonetheless, at the Second Congress which again took place a year later in Basel they were allowed to vote. Theodor Herzl, with his calm, impressive address, in which he represented the aims of Zionism, became the undisputed figure of integration for the movement. Max Nordau [1849–1923], the vice president, touched the listeners with his analysis of the situation of the Jewish people and anti-Semitism and urged them to change these circumstances. David Farbstein [1868–1953] gave reasons for the necessity of Zionism based on the economic development, and Nathan Birnbaum dealt with the cultural

¹¹ Zionisten-Congress, p. 115.

6   Third Zionist Congress in Basel, 1899. Photographer: Emil Buri.

background. He drew attention to the differences between the Eastern and Western Jews which had to be taken into account and his speech was followed by individual reports on the situation in the different countries.

The participants of the Congress decided to form the Zionist Organization. In addition, the foundation of a Jewish national fund and a bank were considered in order to be able to buy land in Palestine. Due to the limited time available, the questions regarding Hebrew, literature and education, as well as that of a future Hebrew tertiary education institution could only be dealt with superficially. The most important occurrence was the agreement on the 'Basle Program', which remained valid until the formation of the state of Israel on May 14, 1948. Its slogan was:

'Zionism seeks to establish a home for the Jewish people in Palestine secured under public law'.

This core statement was a compromise, just as was the entire programme. By using the term 'home' instead of 'state', the statement was designed to accommodate those Jews for whom the settlement of the country was more important than a 'Jewish state' and those who did not wish to force God's will. At the same time, the Sultan of the Ottoman Empire was not to be slighted; which is why the expression 'secured under public law' was chosen instead of 'secured under international law', although a restriction to 'under law', as was originally proposed, was considered to be too weak a guarantee. With the planned means of achieving the aim, they endeavoured to integrate different schools of thought within the movement equally: those in favour of colonization, the assimilated Jews, those who wanted to work in their own native lands, the national Jews and the cultural Zionists, for whom the 'strengthening of the Jewish feeling of unity and consciousness as a people' was the focus. Herzl's influence can be seen when the 'winning of the government's approval' – that is, diplomatic activity – was considered necessary in order to achieve this aim.

After the Congress, Zionism found considerable acceptance in Basel but also in the rural Jewish communities of the Alsace and South Baden, as well as among Jewish students at the University of Freiburg im Breisgau. Zionist organizations were founded. The Freiburg group then served as the basis for meetings of delegates from Eastern Europe, namely from the 'Democratic Fraction' who discussed their strategy for opposing the 'Uganda Scheme' here. Switzerland played an important role for the Zionist movement: most of the congresses were held here up until the founding of the state of Israel, the Swiss constitution was often taken into consideration for the future organization of the Jewish state, and important Zionist personalities were active here.

Herzl was right: although there were still negative reactions all over the world, with the success of the First Congress the Zionists went down in history as a societal movement. At the presentation of the organization principles, Max Bodenheimer [1865–1940] was very well aware of the ground on which the Zionists stood:

'So may a spirit of unity, the spirit of the Rütli also preside over our meeting of new Swiss confederates.'[12]

Perhaps Herzl and his closest allies had hoped to have unified the movement so that it would present a united front in the future, however, this proved to be an illusion. Shortly after the Congress, the old existing contrasts developed again and additional new differences also arose which led to several splits.

Thus, the general direction which developed within the World Zionist Organization was not without opposition and controversy. The 'synthetic Zionism' as proposed by Chaim Weizmann [1874–1952] in 1907 attempted to combine the 'practical' Zionism, aimed at settling Palestine, with the 'political', which placed the emphasis on the diplomatic activities and the formation of a state. This was a solution which the religious Zionists, who had organized to form the 'Mizrachi' movement in 1902, could associate with. There was also regular cooperation with the rather more socialistically oriented forces, the Zionist workers' movement. This movement broke down into different groups ranging from the Marxists through to milder, social democratic-minded organizations which then regrouped to form political parties but never had a completely unified ideology. Ber Borochov [1881–1917], the Marxist and theoretician of the 'Poalei Zion' – the 'workers of Zion' – founded in 1901, answered the non-Zionist Jewish socialists, who considered Zionism to be a kind of 'bourgeois' nationalism, by saying that the Jews needed Zion as a territory in which the class struggle could develop. He went on to say that the Arabian proletariat would be the ally of the Jewish workers. On the other hand, Nachman Syrkin [1868–1924], who also had great influence on the workers' movement, distanced himself from the fixation on Palestine in the context of the 'Uganda debate'. During the 1920s, the class struggle perspective became weaker and weaker in favour of a more nationalistic way of thinking.

These 'blocs' were faced with alternatives that were to be taken seriously. The 'Territorialists' of Israel Zangwill [1864–1926] did not want to be bound to Erez Israel as their future state. They searched for other possibilities to find a place where Jews could live according to their wishes and needs. Because of irreconcilable differences with the majority of the Zionist organizations in

---

[12] Zionisten-Congress, p. 130.

the 'Uganda issue' they formed the independent 'Jewish Territorial Organization' in the 'Safranzunft' in Basel in 1905. To a certain extent, the Soviet Union accommodated these efforts by trying – unsuccessfully – to give the Jews a 'homestead' in the 'Jewish Autonomous Region of Birobidzhan'. It was officially founded on May 8, 1934, after a corresponding resolution had been made in 1928. This was met with little response on the part of the Jewish people. Those who settled there never represented more than a distinct minority in the country. The experiment was poorly prepared. In the wave of terror surrounding the 'great purification' in the thirties – and subsequently again after 1948 – a considerable number of the Jews lost their lives. The remainder was used by the central leadership to economically develop the country. The beginnings of a Yiddish culture were unmistakeably discernable; there were Yiddish newspapers and magazines and even a Yiddish university was planned.

The other extreme of the spectrum in this context of political Zionism was represented by the 'Zionist Revisionists' who formed in the twenties under the leadership of Zeev Jabotinsky [Vladimir Zhabotinskii, 1880–1940] and who wanted to enforce the concept of the state of Israel, uncompromisingly and with any and all means necessary, including armed conflict. This group was the expression of an exaggerated nationalism, so it comes as no surprise to learn that Jabotinsky was an admirer of Mussolini.

Ahad Haam [Asher Ginzberg, 1856–1927] considered the Jewish state to be an unachievable castle in the air and was instead for turning Palestine into a new spiritual centre of Judaism with the aim of triggering off a renaissance of the Jewish people in the Diaspora. This 'cultural Zionism' was then further developed by Martin Buber [1878–1965] and his followers. In 1901 they presented an exhibition of 'Jewish art' at the Fifth Congress in Basel. In many varied activities they wanted to cause people to reflect on 'Jewishness', not least of all taking the Eastern Jewish roots into account. The emphasis on the special Jewish culture was also connected to the recognition of the Arab culture, which meant that a strong basis can be found in this movement for an attempt to find a common ground with the Arabs. In the analysis of the situation and in the conclusions drawn from it, that the Jews had to see themselves as a people and a nation and act accordingly on a political level, this movement of 'national Judaism' was very close to the ideology of Zionism. But even more than many of the Eastern-European Zionists, the national Jews wanted to attain an autonomous status within the country in which they lived. Their most important representative was the historian Simon Dubnow [1860–1941], who founded the Jewish People's Party in Russia in 1906.

In their efforts to find a solution to the social changes and the threats to Jewishness, many Zionists internalized the 'Zeitgeist' (spirit of the times) to a certain extent – this too is part of the crisis of their self-image. So they entered into the discussion surrounding the 'Arian' and 'Semitic' race and Max Nordau coined the term 'degeneration' in Judaism with his culturally critical book which was published in 1892. In order to combat the cliché of the 'effeminate' Jew – the academic, pale, impractical and physically weak man – the Zionists propagated the concept of the 'muscle Jew', the strong, 'manly', 'productive', active man. Max Nordau, who had tossed the term 'muscle Jew' into the debate, compared him to the 'dumsy, lanky, coughing, pitiable dwarf of the Eastern ghettos'.[13] As a consequence, there were repeated attempts to select only suitable 'men' for the colonization of Palestine. Furthermore, this had consequences for the attitude towards sexuality or the role of man and woman. For the Zionist women, this meant that they were certainly then in a position to build a bridge between tradition and the modern, they could uphold their

---

[13] Max Nordau: V. Kongressrede (Basel, 27. Dezember 1901). In: Zionistisches Aktionskomitee (ed.): Max Nordau's Zionistische Schriften. Cologne, Leipzig 1909, pp. 112–139, here p. 132.

7 Farm workers – Halutzim on their way to work. 'Hachsharah' in Baranowicz (Poland), 1937: Training pioneers for agricultural work in Erez Israel.
Photographer: Moshé Raviv-Vorobeicic (Moï Ver).

Jewishness and nevertheless become publicly active: in the modern social and education system, in the agricultural work, for example in the Jewish colonies of Palestine, but also politically. Taking this into consideration, it is no coincidence that women were given the right to vote at the Second Zionist Congress in 1898. But at the same time the image of the 'muscle Jew' led quickly to multiple burdens, role allocations and identity problems which neutralized the new scope for action.

Furthermore, this image of masculinity was accompanied by a despising of the alleged cowardly, passive behaviour of most Jews when faced with their opponents, especially in Eastern Europe. The 'manly' Jew, who saw himself as part of a nation, was supposed to offer resistance. Resistance was, in certain situations, reconcilable with the beliefs of religiously orthodox Jews, such as armed self-defence as had been shown during the persecutions in medieval Western Europe or the wars in Poland. But the armed action was not seen as a virtue. Normally, the answer to violence should be tolerance.

'The apparent cowardliness of the Jew, who does not react to the stone thrown at him by the little boy and who tries to ignore the derogatory names he is called, is in truth the pride of one who knows that he will one day triumph and that nothing can happen to him if it is not God's will and that no defence protects as wonderfully does God's will.'[14]

Some Zionists exhibited little understanding for the human dignity which lay in this faith in God, in this self-confidence and in the knowledge of the stupidity of violence. When – for example – Josef Trumpeldor [1880–1920], a man who organized self-defence units and who was killed fighting the Arabs, was made into a hero and stylized into a figurehead, reservations were certainly justified as to whether his was the right approach: did that not simply give rise to more violence?

The masculine ideal, the emphasis on the national and civilizational successes of the Jews, the taking up of the concept of race, even 'racial elements'[15] among some Zionists had an effect on the attitude toward the Arabs. If these were looked down upon, categorized as culturally inferior, this was understandable against the background of the 'Zeitgeist', but it laid the foundation

---

[14] Joseph Roth: Juden auf Wanderschaft (1927/1937). In: Joseph Roth: Werke. Ed. by Hermann Kesten. Vol. 3. Cologne 1976, pp. 293–369, here pp. 308–309.

[15] cf. George Eisen: Zionism, Nationalism and the Emergence of the Jüdische Turnerschaft. In: Leo Baeck Institute Year Book 38 (1983) pp. 247–262, especially p. 259; Joachim Doron: Rassenbewusstsein und naturwissenschaftliches Denken im deutschen Zionismus während der wilhelminischen Ära. In: Jahrbuch des Instituts für deutsche Geschichte 9 (1980) pp. 389–427.

8 Special edition on the occasion of the tenth anniversary of the workers newspaper 'Davar', Tel Aviv, June 1935. Photomontage from five negatives by Moshé Raviv-Vorobeichic (Moï Ver).

stone for a disastrous conflict which still today has not been solved. Of course there were also other opinions, attempts to enter into dialogues with the Arabs as equal partners, to come to an agreement and live as neighbours, but the historical development only promoted the confrontation. Due to the mutual lack of knowledge about the customs and traditions of the other people 'cultural misunderstandings', and even physical conflicts about the acquisition of land already arose between the first Zionist colonialists in Erez Israel and the Arab settlers. There were, nevertheless, repeated efforts made towards a successful cooperation. Not until after the First World War did the relationship between the Arabs and the Jews escalate into an open confrontation due to the international background – not least of all because of the imbalances in the British political stance towards Arabs and Jews – and the growing nationalism on both sides.

Two occurrences in the twenties were decisive turning points in this relationship. The assas-

Judaism and Zionism

sination of the politician of the orthodox 'Agudat Israel', Jacob Israel de Haan, on June 30, 1924, by two Zionists under the order of the self-defence organization 'Haganah', signalized that some Zionists were willing to employ any and all means to hinder a settlement from being reached between the Jews and the Palestinians and to combat Zionist efforts. In 1929, after an incident at the Wailing Wall in Jerusalem, there were bitter and bloody disturbances, within the course of which Arab groups attacked numerous Jewish settlements. Especially the massacre of unarmed Jews in Hebron, which claimed the lives of over 60 people, triggered off a shock, the effects of which are still felt today. If any hope had still existed of reaching some kind of agreement between Jews and Arabs, these were now destroyed, once and for a long, long time. The hope of a peaceful coexistence of these two people was now very distant.

Against the background of the Arab-Jewish conflict there were also strong differences of opinion both within the Zionist movement as well as between it and their opponents in the Jewish world. The extremist Zionist Revisionists fought with increasing ardour against the centristic school of thought within the movement because it was too moderate and not aggressive enough for them. On June 16, 1933, Chaim Arlosoroff [born in 1899], one of the leaders of the Zionist Workers' Party, endeavoured to find an agreement between Jews and Arabs while at the same time being concerned about saving the German Jews, was assassinated. Much pointed to the probability that members of the Zionist Revisionist movement may have been responsible for the murder, even if the suspects had to be declared innocent due to a lack of evidence. Criticism was also directed at the official Zionist politics by those Zionists who were in favour of reaching a level of understanding with the Arab population of Palestine. The 'Berit Shalom' founded in 1925/26 – the 'Peace Alliance' – and the succeeding organization 'Ihud' – the 'Unity' – which was formed in 1942 advocated a binational state of Palestine with equal rights for Jews and Arabs. Although many of the followers of this direction had official functions within the Zionist movement, their ideas pushed them towards the outside limits of Zionism. After all, not only those Zionists who wanted not only a joint development with the Arabs, but whose aim it was to realize a socialist utopia were affected by the development of their movement. Arnold Zweig [1887–1965] saw his concept of the future joint system threatened which was to be like a 'leftist Switzerland' – pacifist, classless, multicultural, a shining example for the peoples of Europe who were trapped in their nationalist mania and capitalist class divisions.[16]

What had developed very strongly was the alienation between Zionists and their opponents in religious Judaism. From the very beginning the Hassidim in Eastern Europe had been against the Zionist efforts as they had become visible after 1881. As they saw it, this would strengthen the worldly tendencies in Judaism, and thus delay the coming of the Messiah. Numerous orthodox Jews in Eastern and Western Europe reacted just as negatively. This could be seen in 1897 in the 'protest' of the 'Allgemeine Rabbinerverband' (General Association of Rabbis) of Germany, a group of liberal and orthodox rabbis who were against the convening of the Zionist Congress, and afterwards in the 'Agudat Israel' – the 'Union of Israel' – founded in 1912, which was strictly religiously orientated. They were of the conviction that only God could end the banishment of the Jews in exile and lead them back to Israel. Rabbi Arthur Cohn of Basel also joined this group, a man who during the First Zionist Congress had become a Zionist, and ensured that the front of rejection of the orthodox Jews began to crumble. He now thought that the Zionist policy no longer seemed to be reconcilable with the religious prin-

---

[16] cf. Arnold Zweig: Das Neue Kanaan. Eine Untersuchung über Land und Geist. Berlin 1925.

ciples. The Agudat Israel attempted to join all orthodox groups in Eastern and Western Europe against Zionism. It became politically active in the different countries and strived for recognition as an independent Jewish community. In Palestine the ultra-orthodox concept had been gaining more and more influence since the 1920. As the belief in the Torah excluded anything new, Zionism – just as emancipation, enlightenment and assimilation – is considered to be deadly for Judaism.

In fighting Zionism, the orthodox Jews often joined up with those for whom they actually only felt contempt, with liberal Jews prepared to assimilate. As the 'protest' of the Rabbis of 1897 had already made very clear, they were afraid that their integration into the existing state would be in danger. They did not want to cause their 'national reliability' to be placed in doubt and to have to accept the accusation – which is still raised today – of 'dual loyalty' between their native countries and the Zionist world movement or the State of Israel. The literature critic Anton Bettelheim had already referred derisively to Herzl's concept of a 'Jewish state' in 1896 as being a 'founder's prospectus' of a 'Jewish Switzerland in shares'.[17] The sociologist Ludwig Gumplowicz [1838–1909] who came from a reform Jewish family living in Crakow wrote to Herzl on December 12, 1899, that he should stick to his features and poems, as Zionism was evidence of an unparalleled 'political naiveté'.

'You want to found a state without the spilling of blood? Where have you ever seen that done before? Without any force or trickery? With absolute openness and honesty – in shares?'[18]

Furthermore, assimilated Jews criticized the demagogy and the authoritarian style of leadership of Herzl and other Zionists.[19]

Many Zionists had no problem whatsoever in reconciling the desire for a 'Jewish state' with their feeling of belonging to the state in which they lived. Nor was it Herzl's aim that all Jews should emigrate to the future state. His major concern was to find a sanctuary for persecuted and economically suffering Jews. This was also how the majority of the German and Swiss Zionists initially thought. When the radical wing of the Zionist movement represented its opinion that an integration of the Jews in a non-Jewish environment was not possible, this conviction was happily picked up by devout anti-Semites. They even went as far as to commend and praise this posture, because it partially supported their demand that the Jews should leave their 'host countries'. So it is not surprising that contact and negotiations even arose between Zionists and anti-Semites.

This was how it came to be that on August 11, 1933, the sociologist Arthur Ruppin [1876–1943], who as the head of the 'Palestine Office' since 1908 had organized the colonization of the country and as a member of Berit Shalom was an advocate of the concept of a binational state, even met with the national socialist ethnogenist Hans F.K. Günther [1891–1968] for a scientific discussion. Günther 'was very kind' and agreed with Ruppin 'that the Jews were not inferior, but rather merely different and that the Jewish question should be settled in a respectable way'.[20] If a misjudgement of the national socialist mode of thought would seem to be apparent here, negotiations between

---

[17] Anton Bettelheim: Der Gründerprospect einer jüdischen Schweiz. In: Beilage zur Allgemeinen Zeitung (Munich) No. 52 from 3 March 1896, pp. 4–6. My thanks to Dr. Edith Schipper of the Bavarian State Library in Munich, for making the article accessible to me and for the research work of the employees of the Munich State Archive and the Austrian National Library in Vienna.
[18] Herzl: Briefe und Tagebücher, vol. 5, Frankfurt a.M., Berlin 1991, pp. 601–602 (note 4), quotation p. 602.
[19] An example: Victor Klemperer: LTI. Notizbuch eines Philologen. 13th ed. Leipzig 1995, pp. 213–227 (chap. XXIX: Zion).
[20] Arthur Ruppin: Briefe, Tagebücher, Erinnerungen. Published by Schlomo Krolik. Königstein 1985, p. 446, cf. 422.

Zionists and representatives of the Third Reich were unavoidable in order to clarify the conditions for the departure of the Jews out of Germany.

That despite the contact points between Zionists and anti-Semites, anti-Semitism and anti-Bolshevism became a synonym for anti-Semitism and hatred of Jews in certain situations is another matter altogether. An almost infamous role in the fight against Zionism – as well as Judaism as a whole – was played by the 'Protocols of the Learned Elders of Zion'. These documents which were probably forged by the czarist secret police which supposedly had documented a meeting in the sourrounding of the First Zionist Congress served as proof of the centrally controlled conspiracy of the Jews for seizing power over the entire world. Neither a legal process in Bern in the thirties, nor other evidences that the documents were fakes changed the fact that they are, to this very day, repeatedly published in new editions and put onto the market.

In many respects, Zionism did not attain its goals, or at least not in the way which the first Zionists had imagined. The diplomatic-political efforts did not, as Herzl had hoped, lead to a rapid success. Only gradually did the required finances flow. The spilling of blood and violence could not be avoided, just as little could the Jews threatened by anti-Semitism be saved in time. The positive posture toward Zionism remained restricted to a relatively small group for a long time. Put briefly, one could say that the Shoah was the first experience that bound all Jews together and made the foundation of the state of Israel a necessity and a generally accepted requirement. Collective experience also led to a

'levelling out of different forms of Jewish consciousness and self conceptualization which up till this time had been prevalent. The result: the history of the Jews had transformed itself to a Jewish history.'[21]

[21] Dan Diner: Zweierlei Emanzipation. Westliche Juden und Ostjuden in universalhistorischer Perspektive. In: Neue Zürcher Zeitung No. 22 from 27/28 January 1996, p. 17.

However, the experience of the Shoah triggered off processes of suppression among many Jews. The feeling of perhaps not having done quite enough to save the endangered Jews, despite considerable efforts, surfaced in accusations: why did they not emigrate, while there was still time or why did they not offer more resistance, as well as disdain for non-Zionist patterns of life. Zionist myths of the heroic struggle of the Jews – in Massada against the Romans as well as in the Eastern European ghettos during the time of the Nazis or in founding the state of Israel – required the new conception of history. After the victory in the Six-Day War of 1967, through which the holy places came into the possession of Israel, a point of view found increasing numbers of followers for whom an abandonment of those regions could no longer be considered. It linked up to a movement in orthodox Judaism which had always been open to Zionism right from its inception: it connected Zionism to the religiously determined longing of the Jews for their ancestral land, out of which they had been driven by the Romans. To strengthen Judaism and to trigger the return to Zion, they considered that a national congregation of all Jews and a strengthening of the Jewish national consciousness were necessary. Zionism, they felt, would also contribute to returning those to the faith who had distanced themselves from it. The recovery of the holy places was interpreted by this reinterpretation of Zionism as a sign from God that the Messianic deliverance could not be far away.

The conflict with the Palestinians was heightened by this and it became more difficult to find a solution. On the other hand, the Zionist myths had then been critically discussed, the history of Zionism reworked and the dialogue with the Palestinians sought. The consolidation of the state of Israel and the possibility of overcoming its isolation in a hostile environment and also starting a long-term peaceful coexistence with the Palestinians lead to the question of whether Zionism has not fulfilled its task after Israel has become a 'normal' state, or whether it should not at least reorient itself. Equally the relationship between the Jews in Israel and the Jews in the Diaspora as well as that of the religious Jews to the non-religious Jews should be redefined.

The remembrance, the consideration of the past, plays an important role in this search for orientation. Zionism never was a closed, unified movement and ideology. It changed Judaism and nevertheless – in accordance with the different directions within the movement – has its own place in its tradition. It was and is still changeable in itself. The Shoah did bring with it a 'levelling out' of the different forms of Jewish self-conception, but eventually the diversity and the differences have remained. This is why the Jewish history still continues to be a history of the Jewish people themselves.

The Basle Program

Approved at the First Zionist Congress in Basel in 1897

'Zionism seeks to establish a home for the Jewish people in Palestine secured under public law. The Congress contemplates the following means to the attainment of this end:

(I) The promotion by appropriate means of the settlement in Palestine of Jewish farmers, artisans, and manufacturers.

(II) The organization and uniting of the whole of Jewry by means of appropriate institutions, both local and international, in accordance with the laws of each country.

(III) The strengthening and fostering of Jewish national sentiment and national consciousness.

(IV) Preparatory steps toward obtaining the consent of governments, where necessary, in order to reach the goal of Zionism.'

1 Handwritten draft of the 'Basle Program'; in the final version 'under public law' was added.

Preconditions and Beginnings of Zionism

Simone Berger

Jewish Messianism

'Jewish messianism [...] is a belief in God's ultimate responsibility for the Exile of the Jews and in the certainty that God, through a redeemer, will restore His people to greatness, inaugurating a new era in accordance with biblical prophecies.'[1]

The saviour will be the Messiah, his coming will initiate the return of the dispersed to the Holy Land, the rebuilding of national independence and the house of King David and the reconstruction of the temple in Jerusalem.

The hopes of deliverance reflected in the Messianic idea accompany the Jews throughout their history in exile. The historical origin of the hopes lies in the descent of the Jewish empire after the golden age of King David and Solomon whose glory is documented in the Old Testament and its interpretations in the Talmud and Midrash literature. The hopes of deliverance not only include the pure rebuilding of the former conditions of political independence, but also ideas of a Messianic condition of the world which has never before existed. Yes, 'the very new includes elements of the very old, but the old itself is not the real part, but something transfigured by a dream, touched by the beam of an utopia'.[2]

Land and the Longing for Zion

The connection to the Holy Land existed not only in the time of the fulfilment of the Messianic utopia, but through all the time of exile. In the weekly Bible readings at the religious services, the Jews regularly heard the story of Abraham and his descendants, to whom God promised the land of Canaan in an eternal covenant:

'To you and your children I give all Canaan, the country in which you live as a stranger, to be your own forever and I will be their God' (Genesis 17:8).

God and the people were inseparably united with this land by this covenant. Just as important were the biblical passages that prophecied a return to the land of Palestine. The Jewish people read Ezekiel, who had prophecied while in exile in Babylon:

'I shall take the Israelites from those peoples to whom they were forced to go; I shall gather them from all sides and bring them to their land' (Ezekiel 37:21).

The Babylonian Talmud, which was written in exile and was finished in 500 C.E., and which every male Jew in later generations had the duty to study all his life, discusses the question of whether a Jew has to live in Palestine. It is even written that every Jew living abroad is comparable to an idolater.

The longing for the return to the land that had been promised to Abraham and in which the Royal empire of King David and Solomon had been built, at the same time meant the longing for

---

[1] Jody Elizabeth Myers: The Messianic Idea and Zionist Ideologies. In: Jonathan Frankel (ed.): Jews and Messianism in the Modern Era: Metaphor and Meaning. New York, Oxford 1991, pp. 3–13, here p. 4.
[2] Gershom Scholem: Zum Verständnis der messianischen Idee im Judentum. In: Gershom Scholem: Judaica I. Frankfurt a. M. 1986, pp. 7–74, here p. 13.

the city of Jerusalem, referred to in poetry as 'Zion'. At the same time Zion referred to the Temple-Mount in Jerusalem, where the first and second temples stood. In the 12th or 13th century a supposedly German Bible interpreter, using the Midrash literature as his source, maintained that Isaac's sacrifice had taken place on this hill, thus setting a traditional link between the most ancient past and the present. Zion with its temple district represented the centre of the holiness of God, and the city of Jerusalem the 'axis mundi', the holy centre of the world. This longing for Zion expanded to these visionary centres and the entire holiness of the land of Palestine.

No matter how long the exile lasted, reports of emigrations to the Promised Land did exist, such as the journey of the most famous Hebrew poet in the Middle Ages, Judah Halevi. Still living in Andalusia he wrote poems to the city of Zion, expressing his desire in a style full of pain:

> 'My heart is in the East and
> I am at the edge of the West.
> Then how can I taste what I eat,
> how can I enjoy it?
> How can I fulfil my vows and
> pledges while Zion is in the domain of Edom,
> and I am in the bonds of Arabia?
> It would be easy for me to leave behind
> all the good things of Spain;
> it would be glorious to see
> the dust of ruined Shrine.'[3]

In the famous work 'Kusari' by Judah Halevi, the rabbi explains to the Prince of the Khazars the chosen nature of the Land and its connection to the chosen people. Martin Buber takes seven principles from 'Kusari', the last of which states, 'that the act of those moving to the Holy Land with a willing soul will have its effect on the country of Israel, on the community of Israel and on the redemption'.[4] Judah Halevi followed his longing for Zion, and started on his way to Palestine between 1135 and 1140, but he was not to reach his aim before he died in 1141.

'It is no coincidence that the idea of Jewish Messianism is often considered a utopia by many academics and scientists.'[5] This emphasized the fixation on a destiny that was unattainable in the foreseeable future. The utopia of Jewish Messianism does indeed aim at a distant goal, but the realistic basis is by no means lacking: it refers to a historical fact and to a 'tangible point on the Earth [...], the land of Israel'.[6]

Messiah and Deliverance

Deliverance will be initiated by the arrival of the Messiah. Originally 'Messiah' was the term for King David and stood for nothing more than 'God's Anointed'. Not until the eschatological transfiguration did the Messiah become the figure that was supposed to lead the Jewish people out of exile to deliverance. As the image of the perfect King, the longings and hopes expressed in the Messianic ideal were bound closely to it.

The real Messiah has to be a descendant of David's lineage. He is not excluded from history, but is rather a historical personality in the world, a tool of God. The following tract from the Babylonian Talmud shows impressively that the Messiah is dependent on God's orders, but also that deliverance can happen anytime and that daily waiting for the Messiah is worth it:

In front of the cave of Rabbi Simon bar Jochai, Rabbi Jehoshua meets Elias: 'He asks him: When will the Messiah come? – He replies: Go and ask him yourself. – Where is he? – At the gates of Rome. – How can I recognise him? – He sits between the poor and sick: all of the other unwrap their wounds all at once and bandage

---

[3] Jehuda Halevi: My Heart is in the East. In: The Penguin Book of Hebrew Verse. Ed. by T. Carmi. Harmondsworth, New York, Ringwood et al. 1981, p. 347.
[4] Martin Buber: Israel und Palästina. Zur Geschichte einer Idee. Munich 1968.
[5] Jacob Katz: Zwischen Messianismus und Zionismus. Frankfurt a. M. 1993, p. 22.
[6] Ibid.

1 Contemporary engraving of the coronation of Shabbetai Zevi.

short-termed apocalyptical interpretations of the present, to longer-term forecasts. And always misery, need, desolation and disaster were considered to be signs that deliverance was not far away. So the popularity of the Messianic movement surrounding Shabbetai Zevi in the 17th century can be only explained as the consequence of the deep crisis in Judaism which was triggered off by the expulsion of the Jews from Spain in 1492 and the massacre of Jews due to the revolt in the Ukraine in 1648.

An activism broke out among the Messianic movements that pushed for 'the End' and tried to speed up the process of deliverance. This contradicted the classical attitude of rabbinical Judaism, the faith in patiently waiting for the Messiah, until God sends Him to the people. 'He will come suddenly, without warning, and just when He is least expected or when hope has long been lost'.[8] The leading belief in the Messiah by rabbinical Judaism held tightly to the interpretation of exile as being a punishment from God.

Zionism

The religiously based, patient expectation, which considered the collecting of all those spread throughout the world in the Holy Land to be the duty of Messianism, was an obstacle for the development of Zionism. Until this very day there is a minority of Jews in Israel who does not acknowledge the state on religious grounds.

Rabbi Abraham Isaak Kook [1865–1935] succeeded in unifying religious and wordly aspects by taking the belief in the Messiah as the basis for the co-operation with Zionism. He emphasized the importance of earthly Jerusalem and Palestine, to where every Jewish person had to return. 'The hope for the Redemption is the force that

them up again, but he unwinds his bandages one at a time and rebinds them individually because he thinks: perhaps I will be called for, and I don't want there to be any delay when I am asked for.'[7]

Again and again during the exile it was discussed when the Messiah and – with him – deliverance would come. The answers varied from

---

[7] Quoted in: Yosef Hayim Yerushalmi: Zachor: Erinnere Dich! Jüdische Geschichte und Jüdisches Gedächtnis. Berlin 1988, p. 36.

[8] Scholem: Verständnis, p. 27.

sustains Judaism in the Diaspora; the Judaism of Eretz Israel is the very Redemption [...]'⁹ The settling of Palestine, carried out by non-religious Jews was also, in his opinion, in the service of God. For Rabbi Kook the Zionist process is one step towards true deliverance. His Messianic interpretation of Zionism built a bridge to rabbinical Judaism.

For Gershom Scholem too, Zionism was within the tradition of Jewish Messianism, 'by taking on one of its most important aspects, even if in secular form, namely the utopia which the biblical Prophets referred to as "the leading home of the dispersed" and the rebuilding of the national sovereignty'.¹⁰ Zionism arose as a social and national movement in the 19th century, a time, in which the legal emancipation of Jews had already been achieved in many countries. Like the Messianist movement, Zionism was an answer to a profound crisis in Judaism, a crisis of the Jewish identity, which came into existence on their way to equality, but was also caused by political, economical and cultural changes of the time.

For the non-religious Jews, the belief in the Messiah was certainly a topic of interest. Theodor Herzl was aware of the conflict between Zionist activism and waiting for the Messiah. He hoped, 'that the orthodox would understand that there was nothing contrary to God's will in taking one's fate into one's own hands'.¹¹

Most important for Herzl's work was not Messianic hope however, but the national drive, the 'vigilant and active personality of the people'.

In his novel 'Altneuland' (Oldnewland) he assigned the longing for the Messiah to those 'poor, dark times', as 'our people' was not yet capable

2 Henryk Glicenstein: Sleeping Messiah. 1903–1906, bronze sculpture.

of 'reflecting upon itself'.¹² This was possibly also a reaction to remarks made since the First Zionist Congress, which praised him as the longed for Messiah himself.

⁹ Quoted in: Shlomo Avineri: The Making of Modern Zionism. The Intellectual Origins of the Jewish State. London 1981, p. 191.
¹⁰ Stéphane Mosès: Der Engel der Geschichte. Franz Rosenzweig, Walter Benjamin, Gershom Scholem. Frankfurt a. M. 1994, p. 168.
¹¹ Theodor Herzl: Altneuland. In: Julius H. Schoeps (ed.): Wenn ihr wollt, ist es kein Märchen. Kronberg im Taunus 1978, p. 78.
¹² Ibid.

Herzl's worldly Zionism and the religious Rabbi Kook have one very obvious thing in common through which both can be considered as Messianist thinkers: their sense of mission. 'All the civilization of the world will be renewed by the renaissance of our spirit', Rabbi Kook writes. 'All quarrels will be resolved, and our revival will cause all life to be luminous [...]'[13] and Herzl's 'Judenstaat' (Jewish State) ends with the words: 'The world will be freed by our liberty, enriched by our wealth, magnified by our greatness. And whatever we attempt there to accomplish for our own welfare, will react powerfully and beneficially for the good of humanity.'[14]

---

[13] Quoted in: Avinieri: Making, p. 195.

[14] Theodor Herzl: The Jewish State. New York, 1988, p. 157.

Chris Kaiser

Early Zionism – Messianic Redemption and Jewish Nation

In 1839 in England a series of articles appeared in the pro-government 'Globe' about the possibility of a Jewish state. The main participants in this debate were Lord Palmerston, who later would become prime minister, and Anthony Ashley Shaftesbury. Lord Shaftesbury took up Palmerston's suggestion about creating a state in the regions of Syria and Palestine for the Jewish people. For Shaftesbury such an undertaking represented the opportunity to offer 'reparations' to the Jews for all the injustices done to them during the past centuries.

Although the endeavours to realize this idea led to debates in Parliament and even reached Queen Victoria, there were no concrete results. However, from then on the idea of a Jewish state was placed on the foreign-affairs agenda of the great powers, even though for different reasons. At the Paris Conference of 1856, at the end of the Crimean War, the diplomats present were largely agreed that it was time to go ahead with the Jewish colonization of Palestine. In his book 'La nouvelle question d'Orient', published in 1860, Ernest Laharanne, private secretary to Napoleon III, made the intentions of the Western powers clear, by viewing a Jewish state especially as a bulwark against the Arabs.

The aspirations of the European powers coincided with a newly awakened interest in Palestine in Christian circles, with the humanitarian plans of Moses Montefiore [1784–1885] to lease land there and have it colonized by Jewish settlers, and went along with Jewish endeavours to no longer simply wait passively for the coming of the Messiah. Thus, in 1840 an anonymous Jewish author, in an article which appeared in the magazine 'The Orient', called for his fellow Jews to return to Palestine and initiate the redemption. Perhaps it was the series of articles in the 'Globe' that had induced him to do this, but it also might have been a particular incident which occurred at that time and caused a sensation. In February 1840, a Capuchin monk disappeared from Damascus. Witnesses giving false testimony accused Jews of having killed him in a ritual murder. One of the accused Jews was forced to make a confession under torture. Only through the intervention of the Western European powers was it possible to get the authorities in Damascus to release the falsely accused man.

In any case, this incident became the turning point for Judah ben Alkalai [1798–1878], the Rabbi of Semlin (Zemun in Slavonia, situated across Belgrade). As many other scholars before him, he prophesied the appearance of the Messiah on a particular date: he expected this to happen in the year 1840. From the incident in Damascus, he drew the conclusion that the persecutions of the Jews had always represented God's punishment, because the Jewish people had never made the decision to return to Palestine of their own accord.

From then on, he concerned himself more and more intensely with returning home to the Holy Land. In 1852, he called for the Jewish community to convene an assembly in order to urge all the Jews in the world to emigrate to Palestine. Alkalai's idea was, however, not to create an indepen-

1 Zevi Hirsch Kalischer [1795–1874].

2 Moses Hess [1812–1875].

dent Jewish state, but rather it concerned the role he had in mind for his fellow Jews, which was that of becoming subjects of the Turkish Sultan. Later Alkalai, who himself moved to Palestine in 1871, participated in establishing societies whose aim it was to colonize Palestine.

The rabbi in the Polish city of Thorn, Zevi Hirsch Kalischer [1795–1874], argued in a similar way, especially from a religious point of view. In his view, the redemptive process of the Jewish people was divided into four periods, the first two of which – the cultivation of the land in Palestine by Israelite colonists, as well as the erection of an altar in Jerusalem – required the active participation of Jewish men and women. In order to fulfil these conditions, Kalischer urged Amschel Rothschild as early as 1836 to buy land in Palestine.

He propagated Jewish self-help, travelled about a great deal and paid visits to influential politicians, persuading them to participate in setting up colonization societies. In 1860 he became member of the first Jewish Colonization Society of Germany, founded by Chaim Lorje [1821–1878] in Frankfurt a.d. Oder. In his paper 'Derishat Ziyyon', published in 1862, Kalischer urged the active colonization of Palestine. In his view, poor Jewish settlers from the Eastern part of Europe should first move to Palestine. The task of financing the purchase of land in Palestine would fall to those affluent Jews who remained in the Diaspora. The time for their return to the land of Zion would come with the reappearance of the Messiah.

In his book 'Rome and Jerusalem. The Last Nationality Problem', published in 1862, Moses Hess [1812–1875] cited lengthy passages from the writings of Zevi Hirsch Kalischer and Ernest Laharanne. He did not believe that the hopes of the Jews, which were linked to legal emancipation, would be fulfilled. He regarded efforts to assimilate as a mistake. For him both the Jews as a nation and the religion of the Jews were an expression of the 'national spirit'. The Messianic redemption of humanity would be initiated by establishing a Jewish national state.

Theodor Herzl, who did not read 'Rome and Jerusalem' until 1901, found in the book a major part of his own reflections and described Hess as an immediate precursor and pioneer who paved the way for Zionism. Nevertheless, Hess's work elicited hardly any response, even in Jewish communities. The main reason for this was because up to then Hess had become well known particularly through his socialist writings – in which he also supported Messianic ideas – and through his collaboration with Karl Marx and Friedrich Engels. In spite of the disillusionment which in the meantime he had begun to experience about them, many of his contemporaries viewed the 'communist rabbi' (Arnold Ruge) with suspicion. Moreover, his way of life – he married a Christian woman after living with her for several years – provided ample points of censure for orthodox Jews, in whose eyes the transformation from Saul to Paul lacked credibility.

Hess also lacked the élan to generate enthusiasm in others for his ideas. He was convinced that the socialistic component was already present in the faith of the Jewish people. This would then come into force in the liberation of mankind brought about by the establishment of the Jewish state. Perhaps Hess sensed that the time was not ripe for this kind of thinking. He continued to occupy himself with Jewish issues only for a short time, and then, together with Ferdinand Lassalle, he addressed himself again to the plight of the working class.

The question, however, of the Jewish self-image remained alive. Peretz Smolenskin [1842–1885], just as Hess, was of the opinion that the Jews were a nation. For him their peculiar characteristic lay in the cultural and intellectual sphere, especially in the Hebrew language and in the Messianic hope. He had been the editor of the magazine 'Ha-Shahar' – 'The Dawn' – since 1868, which emphasized the idea of a nation and the Jewish traditions, and was quite influential.

Only few years later, a new phase began, which was reflected especially in the person of the physician Leon Pinsker [actually Judah Leib, 1821–1891] in Odessa. For many years, Pinsker supported the view that Jewish men and women in Russia should assimilate. It was not until the pogroms in 1871 that he began to change his opinion. Ten years later, when after the murder of the Czar thousands of Jews once again fell victim to the pogroms, he became active. In 1882 he anonymously published the brochure entitled 'Auto-Emancipation', which he described as a 'warning from a Russian Jew to all his religious brothers'. His thoughts were not necessarily focused on the 'holy' land of Palestine, but rather on a land 'of their own', and for him the place itself played a subordinate role. In contrast to his earlier views, he now regarded assimilation as something impossible to achieve, because wherever the Jews were found, they remained foreigners, and even legal equality would not increase the degree of respect accorded to them by other peoples. With the emancipation granted to them, the Jews would continue to assume the role of objects. But only through self-emancipation would a change to being an active subject take place. Pinsker thought about initiating this national rebirth of the Jews through a congress of prominent Jewish people. As one of the leaders of the 'Hovevei Zion' – a movement which actively promoted the idea of settling Palestine – he convened three large conferences in the eighties. A common programme, however, did not emerge. At the second conference in 1887 Pinsker, under pressure from powerful religious groups, was forced to accept a weakening of his position. These groups resented the fact that he considered religion a hindrance to developing the idea of a nation. Pinsker can definitely be viewed as a link to two other early Zionists: Nathan Birnbaum, whose work for the student's association 'Khadimah' he strongly supported and Ahad Haam, who joined the Hovevei Zion in Odessa – then under the guidance of Pinsker – but later argued that first of all Palestine should become a spiritual centre of Judaism.

Peter Haber

Josef Natonek: A Forerunner of Herzl from Hungary

One of the forerunners of Herzl who has fallen into oblivion was Josef Natonek. He was born in Kömlöd, in the Hungarian-Slovakian border area, in 1813 and died in 1892 in Bátor, in the Comitat Heves. During his education he lived in Zagreb and in Nikolsburg in Moravia. He received his rabbinical diploma in Pozsony (Bratislava) at the Yeshiwa of Chatam Sofer (other sources indicate in Nikolsburg). Between 1854 and 1860 he was the Rabbi in Jászberény. He was then forced to withdraw from his position under the pressure of the Hungarian authorities, after he had preached that the Hungarian Jews did not need the emancipation, because their home was not Hungary but Palestine. The government considered this statement to be unpatriotic and hindered him in his office.

Natonek moved from Jászberény to the large community of Székesfehérvár (Stuhlweissenburg). But he did not stay there very long either: already in 1867 he voluntarily resigned from his position in order to completely dedicate his time to the resettlement of Palestine. Today, Natonek is seen as one of the First 'Zionists', although this term did not yet exist in those days. Living in Jászberény he had already shown himself to be a fighter against Jewish assimilation. In 1861, using the pseudonym Abir Amieli, he published the script 'The Messiah or an Essay about Jewish Emancipation'[1], advocating the national independence of the Jews. The Hungarian authorities

1   Josef Natonek [1813–1892].

---

[1]   Abir Amieli [József Natonek]: Messiás, avagy értekezés a zsidó emancipációról. Buda 1861.

prohibited this script, which, for a long time, was considered to be lost.

In the middle of the sixties, Natonek travelled to Western Europe with the purpose of promoting his ideas. He was in contact with Zevi Hirsch Kalischer and Moses Hess, both of whom felt attracted to his plan and supported him as much as possible. Natonek also went to Paris, where he tried to arouse interest for his ideas at the 'Alliance Israélite Universelle', which was founded in 1860. After an initially positive reaction, the Alliance withdrew in 1867. Meanwhile Natonek aspired to negotiate with the Sublime Porte in Constantinople about a Jewish colonization of Palestine. He succeeded in getting a reference letter from the Ottoman ambassador in Vienna, with which he then started his adventurous journey. Although he was kindly received in Constantinople, he failed to convince the Sultan. Natonek returned exhausted and sick from Constantinople.

In May 1872 Josef Natonek published a magazine in Pest entitled 'Das einige Israel' (The United Israel), but this project had very little success and its publication had to be discontinued after only few issues. Natonek retired and it seemed as if he had accepted the fact that he was powerless to counter the assimilation tendencies in society. During his remaining years, he published several scripts dealing with the relationship between science and religion. He died in 1892 and was soon forgotten.

Alex Carmel

Christian Hopes of Zion: Palestine in the 19th Century

When in 1516 the Ottomans conquered their fellow Moslems and rulers of Egypt, the Mamelukes, and took the Holy Land from them, they were at the peak of their power. They concentrated on first rebuilding the country, for example by building the walls around Jerusalem that still exist today, and on establishing order. The strength of the Turks was not enough, however, to secure stable sovereignty over Palestine. This land, which during 400 years of Turkish sovereignty had never been an independent province, became a place of countless armed skirmishes and was slowly driven to ruin. The population decreased drastically and the inhabitants became impoverished. At the end of the 18th century no more than some 200,000 people lived in the territory known as Palestine, 90% Arab Moslems, the rest Arab Christians and Jews.

European pilgrims and travellers who dared to visit the Holy Land under these circumstances, spoke of the curse that obviously lay upon the biblical land of milk and honey. Nowhere in the Holy Land, they would say, is there regulated public life except in Akko. At the same time the people started to hate the 'Franks' – the Europeans – because these 'unbelieving' Christians – especially Russia – put pressure on the Ottoman Empire. For nearly all Europeans, Palestine was a closed country which was not opened up again until the 19th century.

The French expedition in 1799 brought about the turning point. The French left Palestine after a short time, but Europe now realized that is was possible to take the Holy Land from the 'unbelieving' Moslems. European powers began taking an interest in Palestine. Even Protestant states, which had until then not shown much interest in the cult of holy sites, suddenly started enthusiastically promoting the 'Return of the Jews' to Palestine. In January 1826 the Dane John Nikolayson travelled from London to Jerusalem as a representative of the large and influential 'London Society for Promoting Christianity amongst the Jews' with the distinct objective of securing a strong domicile for the Church of England in the Holy City. Founded in 1809 the aim of this society was to convert the Jewish masses and direct them towards Palestine ('the restoration of the Jews'). This would then bring about the return of Jesus and the establishment of the kingdom of God on Earth.

Initially he was not successful. The situation changed, however, when the Egyptian ruler Muhammed Ali freed himself from the Ottoman Empire, becoming virtually independent and his son Ibrahim Pasha conquered Palestine in 1831/32. Allied with France, the Egyptians organized a modern administration. To placate the other European countries, Muhammed Ali demonstrated extremely liberal attitudes towards the non-Moslem population and foreigners in Palestine. The gates were open for Europeans and in 1833 John Nikolayson was able to settle in Jerusalem with his Anglican Jewish mission.[1] His activities soon caused the Catholic and Greek Orthodox

---

[1] John Nikolayson: Mitteilungen für eine Skizze der Geschichte der englischen Mission und des evangelischen Bisthums zu Jerusalem. In: Zions-Bote 1, no place 1852.

1 At the Jaffa Gate in Jerusalem, around 1900.

Churches to give a new direction to their work in Palestine as well. Their foreign policies reflect the rivalry which existed between France, Russia and England, which established the first consulate in Jerusalem in 1839. This conflict of interest formed the background to the politics which governed European relations until the beginning of the First World War.

The 'oriental crisis' of 1839/40 showed up the animosity existing between the interested parties when the Turkish Sultan was because of the support of England, Austria, Russia and Prussia able to regain control of Palestine against the will of France. But then the powers could not agree about their influence in Palestine: France claimed a privileged position in the Holy Land on the basis of its former rights in the Orient, the discrimination of their Egyptian federal companions and the protection of Catholic interests. This claim, however, was contested by Austria, who, seeing itself as the 'real' protecting power of Catholicism in Palestine, wanted to weaken the political position of France. Russia rejected every suggestion which did not concur with its wishes as its people had a particularly close religious relationship to the Holy Land. Russian pilgrims far outnumbered those from the entire rest of the Christian world and its Greek Orthodox protégés represented, with about 90% of all Arabian Christians, the largest Christian community in Palestine. Prussia's primary objective was to make sure that Protestant Christians in Palestine were respected and protected. In 1841 Helmuth von Moltke, former military adviser of the Turkish Sultan and later Prussian, then German military chief of staff, suggested proclaiming a German Duke as ruler of Palestine. He thought that a Prussian administration would be most capable of finally establishing law and order in Palestine, without giving rise to too much envy among other Christian powers.[2] The English had no ancient claims which they could bring into their argument except for their navy fleet which had forced the Egyptians to retreat. But Palmerston, the foreign minister, resorted to a special tactic which improved England's position and which had far-reaching ramifications and moral implications. He supported the emigration of Jews from Europe to Palestine and presented himself as the protector of this minority.

The Ottoman Empire had no choice but to keep Palestine open for the Europeans. In 1841 it had to endorse the Prussian demand, made by the Prussian King Friedrich Wilhelm IV, to found a Protestant diocese in Jerusalem. This was supported by England.

This institution had enormous influence on the subsequent development of Palestine in the 19th century. The diocese provided vital support for the Protestant Mission, which went about its business with energy and talent. These activities urged on the missionary work of the Catholic and Greek Orthodox Churches in Palestine. For the first time since the crusades the seat of the Latin Patriarch of Jerusalem was filled through an appointment of the Vatican. Russia started to choose suitable people for the clergy in Jerusalem, to compete on a religious and political level with the Catholic and Protestant representatives. In a place where missionary work had been practically impossible, suddenly innumerable church representatives began operating. Huge amounts of money poured into the Holy Land from all over the world to support missionary work and to stimulate the economy.

The Turks reacted to this development with increasing hostility. For them it was an insult that 'unbelievers' should be able to interfere in Palestine and were becoming increasingly demanding and critical of the administration of the country. They also realized that the Christian powers were simply waiting for an opportunity to drive them out of the Holy Land and to further weaken their empire. In the middle of the century such a situation arose. As the conflict between Catholics and

---

[2] Vermischte Schriften des General-Feldmarschalls Grafen Helmuth von Moltke. Vol. 2. Berlin 1892, pp. 279–289.

2 The Jaffa Gate in Jerusalem from the inside, around 1900.

Greek Orthodox about the holy places came to a head, their protectors, on the one hand France, on the other Russia, threatend the powerless Turkish Sultan with war if he would not agree to their respective demands. England though, who wanted to prevent the Russian advance in the Mediterranean region, allied itself with the Ottoman Empire. During the 'Crimean War' between 1853 and 1856, Russia was bitterly defeated by the allied powers. In return for this help, the Sultan announced extensive reforms, which improved the position of Christians and Jews in the empire.

'Thirty years ago an American missionary, an Italian physician in the employ of Mehemed Ali, a so-called Baron Müller, a German gardener and a French drum major were together with me in Jerusalem, and today what number of Franks, what capital of their intellectual activity. The peaceful crusade has begun. Jerusalem must become ours.'[3]

These words were written by the Swiss physician Titus Tobler, one of the most important explorers of Palestine of the last century, after his forth visit to the Holy Land in 1865. His prophecy was never to be fulfilled: Tobler was counting on the Protestant Church in particular, but although the church was enormously helpful in rebuilding Palestine, in the end it was the Jewish influence that changed the fate of this country. Since the seventies, and especially since the first 'immigration wave' of 1882, Jewish activities began to surpass Christian activities. Tobler had already passed away at this stage. His prophecies were based on proceedings he had witnessed in the years between 1835 and 1865. Out of almost nothing the European Christian communities had developed in Palestine and built churches and monasteries, schools, hospitals, orphanages, businesses and hostels for pilgrims and tourists. The number of Christians increased from a tiny group to hundreds and then thousands. The increase in population had no demographical effects, but it changed the landscape of Palestine and its appearance and saved it from further decline.

The first visible sign was the 'Christ Church' opposite the Citadel in the old city of Jerusalem, which John Nikolayson, the pioneer of the Protestant mission in Palestine, opened as the first Protestant Church in the Ottoman Empire in 1849. The mission among the highly religious Jews in Palestine was a failure, despite the enormous amounts of money which were invested in it. The widespread belief that the kingdom of God was nigh gradually subsided. Even the appointment of a baptized Rabbi, Michael Salomon Alexander, to the position of the first bishop of the English-Prussian diocese in 1841 did not change the situation. The sudden death of the young bishop was just as unexpected as was his lack of success. In contrast, his successor, the industrious Swiss Samuel Gobat, a pupil of the Basel Mission, served as the second bishop in Jerusalem for 33 years starting in 1846. Gobat learned from the bitter experience of his predecessor how difficult missionary work was among Jews. As the Turks had forbidden any missionary activity among the Moslems, the bishop's activities slowly concentrated on the Christian Arabs of Palestine. The success that the English, and to an even greater extent the much more numerous German Protestants, mainly from Württemberg, had among the Greek Orthodox and the Catholic Arabs, also moved the other religious communities to take a greater interest in their charges in Palestine. Usually these activities were supported by the various European states. Even the Jewish world was motivated to build hospitals, orphanages, schools and other institutions for the impoverished Jewish population of the country, so that their fellow believers would not be at the mercy of the Christian missionaries. Through this rivalry, Jerusalem and the entire Holy Land developed to an extent which had not been seen in Palestine for centuries. The Holy Land, which in 1799 was still a lifeless desert, became one of the most progressive areas in the Ottoman Empire by 1914.

---

[3] Titus Tobler: Nazareth in Palästina. Berlin 1868, p. 322.

3   The St. John's Hospice in Jerusalem, around 1900.

4 The Wailing Wall in Jerusalem, around 1900.

Thanks to the now improved standard of living, many people emigrated there from neighbouring provinces in search of work. This caused the Arab population of the country to treble during this time. The number of Jews rose from around 5,000 to almost 100,000, and the European Christians from a few dozen to about 5,000. Among these were approximately 3,000 Germans, most of whom were settlers from Württemberg and followers of the 'Temple community' who had been immigrating to Palestine since 1868 'to build the kingdom of God on Earth in Jerusalem'.

Perhaps the best indication of the size of the Christian contribution to the modernization of Palestine during the last decades of Turkish rule were the seven flourishing 'Templer colonies'. The German settlers were the first to introduce horse-drawn wagons and started up a regular passenger service between Jaffa and Jerusalem, Haifa and Akko and from Haifa to Nazareth and Tiberias, where they had had first of all to make the road passable at their own expense. In the agricultural industry they made use of modern methods which had never been seen in Palestine before, and they did the same with respect to other trades, commerce and industry. Various academic professions also came to Palestine. The settlers battled with malaria by planting eucalyptus trees, sowed the seeds of the forests on the Mount Carmel and constructed the first settlement on the mountain. But most of all they were the founders of seven exemplary colonies in Haifa, Jaffa, Sarona, Jerusalem, Wilhelma, Bethlehem Galilee and Waldheim, which were without equal in Palestine.

Another example of the extraordinary efforts of the Europeans was the initiative of Christian Friedrich Spittler who was – among other things – the founder of the Basel Pilgrim Mission, regarding the construction of the Syrian orphanage in Jerusalem in 1860 that had become the largest Protestant mission institution in the Middle East by 1914. Under its auspices, thousands of Arab children received an education as craftsmen. As early as 1846, Spittler had sent Conrad Schick of Württemberg to Palestine, where he became the most important surveyor and builder in the Holy City, finally becoming the city engineer. Another envoy, Johannes Frutiger of Basel, succeeded in expanding Spittler's 'Mission Trading House' in Jerusalem in such a way that he finally became the most successful banker in Palestine. Even the country's first railway which was opened in 1892 between Jaffa and Jerusalem was due to his initiative and financing, not to mention numerous other works including the construction of Jewish housing districts.

In 1914 the Holy Land already had 40 Jewish colonies. In the rapidly growing cities the Jewish influence had become increasingly important, especially in Jerusalem, Jaffa and in Haifa. Here the 'German-Jewish Technical College', the first technical university in the Ottoman Empire, was built. Tel Aviv was founded in 1909 as a Jewish suburb of Jaffa, and constructed according to the plan of a municipal building reform as a garden city. Its name – 'hill of spring' – harks back to the Hebrew translation of Theodor Herzl's novel 'Altneuland' (Oldnewland) and expressed the hopes of the settlers in a time in which Jewish immigration found itself faced with serious problems.

Alex Carmel

William Hechler: Herzl's Christian Ally

A critical look at Herzl's diary reveals something unusual. The three most frequently mentioned people are Christians: A missionary – Reverend William Henry Hechler –, a prince – Grand Duke Friedrich of Baden – and an emperor – Wilhelm II.[1] Today they are seldom mentioned in publications of the Zionist movement. They are, so to speak, 'passé'. The most astonishing is the disappearance of William H. Hechler, one of Herzl's dearest friends and supporters.

'For today', Herzl wrote in his diary on April 16, 1896, 'the plan [of the Jewish state] has possibly taken a historically memorable step towards its realization. Reverend Hechler, who travelled to Karlsruhe to win over the grand duke and through him the Kaiser, has telegraphed that I should be prepared to come to Karlsruhe.'[2]

Recently, an Israeli journalist interested in history searched the city maps of the country in vain for a 'Hechler street'. Neither in Tel Aviv, Haifa, Jerusalem nor elsewhere could he find 'my poor Hechler', as Herzl called him in his diary on June 15, 1896,

'although in the cities of Israel, leading personalities of the Zionist movement are so often remembered in this way, even Zionists whose character one could have reason to doubt'.[3]

One hundred years after the First Zionist Congress, the time has come to honour all of Herzl's numerous Christian friends, especially Hechler.

Sometimes the ways of history are strange. In 1841 Friedrich Wilhelm IV, king of Prussia, laid the foundation for the special relationship between the house of Hohenzollern and the Holy Land by supporting the foundation of the German-Protestant Diocese in Jerusalem. In 1869, his brother and successor, King Wilhelm I ordered his son, Crown Prince Friedrich Wilhelm, the later Emperor Friedrich III, on his way to the opening ceremony of the Suez Canal, to acquire a location in Jerusalem for the Prussian Crown. Later the Church of Redemption was to be built on this place in the name of the English-Prussian community of Jerusalem. On the day he purchased the ground, the crown prince mentioned his aspiration that his son should consecrate this church. In 1871 Wilhelm I was proclaimed German emperor. In the Hall of mirrors of the castle of Versailles his son-in-law Friedrich I, Grand Duke of Baden, placed the Kaiser's crown

---

[1] Cf. index of Herzl's Tagebücher. Vol. 3. Berlin 1923.
[2] Theodor Herzl: Tagebücher. Vol. 1. Berlin 1922, p. 29. Herzl wrote this on a piece of paper on 16 April 1896, and his 'dear father' was to write it into his diary, ibid. pp. 28–29.

[3] Yinon, Jakob: In: 'Dvar hashavu'a', the weekly insert of 'Dávar', 9 July 1993. In view of this, David Pilaggi – not accidentally a Christian with missionary tendencies – is a delightful exception with his article 'Vicarious Zionist' (The Jerusalem Post, 8 November 1988).

on his head. Kaiser Wilhelm I died in 1888. A few months later, Friedrich III – the former Jerusalem pilgrim – died after a long illness. Wilhelm II, who was supposed to consecrate the church in Jerusalem, now became Kaiser.

His uncle, the Grand Duke of Baden, established a special relationship to Jerusalem in another way. In this case, William Henry Hechler, born in 1845 in Benares, India, was his contact. His father Dietrich Hechler from Vögisheim near Müllheim in Baden, a student of the 'Basel Pilgrim Mission', was working there for the English administration. Back in Europe he then worked for the 'Jews' Mission of London', while William studied theology in Tübingen and London. In 1874 he was asked to come to Karlsruhe, to become the private teacher of the children of the Grand Duke of Baden.

Soon Hechler succeeded in winning over the grand duke – a religious and very liberal man who despised any kind of anti-Semitism – for the idea of the 'return of the Jews', which at the time was mainly popular in England. The close connection to Friedrich I continued even after Hechler returned to London. As the bloody pogroms against the Jews were taking place in Russia and Rumania in 1881, Hechler pleaded to high English circles for the resettlement of persecuted Eastern Jews to Palestine. In 1882 Hechler went to Russia to encourage Jews to set off to the Promised Land and to negotiate with the leaders of 'Hibbat Zion' – 'Love of Zion'. In 1884 he published the brochure 'The Restoration of the Jews to Palestine According to the Prophets'. Queen Victoria is said to have given him a letter for the Turkish sultan, to facilitate the immigration procedures. The Grand Duke of Baden even suggested to Kaiser Wilhelm to appoint Hechler as Protestant Bishop of Jerusalem. The right time had not yet come. In 1885 Hechler had to be content with the position of chaplain of the English embassy in Vienna.

Ten years later, 'Moses' appeared, who, according to Hechler's biblical calculations, should lead the children of Israel back to the Promised Land in 1897/98. In 1895 Theodor Herzl started to elaborate his idea of the 'Jewish State'. In February 1896 his revolutionary book was published in Vienna and immediately became the 'talk of the town', as Herzl wrote in his diary on February 23, 1896. A few days later, on March 11, 1896, he noted:

'Rev. William H. Hechler, chaplain of the English embassy here visited me. A pleasant, sensitive person with a long, grey prophet's beard [...] He has calculated, from a prophecy of [Calif] Omar's era (637/8), that after 42 prophetic moons, that is 1,260 years, Palestine would be given back to the Jews. This would mean 1897/98. As he had finished reading my book, he hurried immediately to the [English] ambassador [Sir Edmund] Monson and said to him: The forecast movement has come! Hechler declared my movement to be a "biblical" one, although I proceed rationally in all. He wants to pass on my book to a number of German princes. He was the preceptor in the house of the Grand Duke of Baden, he knows the German Kaiser personally and believes that he can procure me an audience with him.'

Herzl visited Hechler already on the following Sunday.

'After Colonel [Albert] Goldsmid [1846–1904, an English officer who converted to Judaism, a follower of Herzl at the time] the most curious person I have ever met in this movement [...] [Afterwards] he played the organ and sang a Zionist song of his own composition. From my English teacher I heard that Hechler was a hypocrite. I consider him myself to be much more a naive dreamer with a mania for collecting. But there is something delightful in his naive enthusiasm which I felt particularly strongly as he sang his song.

Afterwards we came to the core of the matter. I said to him: I have got to establish a direct, obvious connection with a responsible or irresponsible member of the government, that is either a minister or a prince. Then the Jews will believe in me, then they will follow me. The most suitable would be the German Kaiser. I need help if I am to succeed in completing this work. Until now I have been fully occupied with overcoming obstacles which take up my strength. Hechler announced his willingness to travel to Berlin immediately to speak with the court preacher [Ernst von Dryander, 1842–1922], and with Prince Günther and Prince Heinrich. [...] He thinks

1 Kaiser Wilhelm II with his suite in Jaffa on October 27, 1898. Photographed by G. Krikorian.

that we will travel to Jerusalem very soon and showed me the pocket of his coat where he would put his great map of Palestine when we travel together in the Holy Land. That was his most naive and convincing feature yesterday [March 15, 1896].'[4]

On the floor of a room at Schiller Square in Vienna two strange people started a lifelong friendship. On one side the journalist, strictly speaking a half Jew, half Hungarian, on the other side the missionary, half German, half English. Their plan: to found a Jewish state in Palestine preferably with the help of the German Kaiser. Hechler kept his promise. He introduced Herzl to the Grand Duke Friedrich, who was very enthusiastic about the plan. His only honest reservation was that his support of the plan of an emigration of Jews to Palestine could be interpreted as a hidden wish to get rid of them. With the help of Hechler and the benevolent Grand Duke, Herzl was able to meet with the Kaiser – who was not opposed to the idea – and to convince him to intercede with the Sultan in favour of the plan. Philipp Count of Eulenburg, the German ambassador in Vienna at the time and close confidant of the Kaiser, also supported Herzl's intention. On November 2, 1898 Herzl met with Kaiser Wilhelm in Palestine. And yet – despite Herzl's and Hechler's unceasing and major efforts – all was in vain. The sultan refused. The First World War was

[4] Theodor Herzl: Tagebücher. Vol. 1. Berlin 1922, pp. 357–358.

needed to free Palestine from Turkish sovereignty and the Second World War – and the Shoah! – to convince the Christian world of the necessity of a Jewish State.

The idea of those two friends from Schiller Square in Vienna finally had its day. For good reason Herzl can be celebrated as a visionary and the spiritual father of the state of Israel. But Hechler too, the man who served him to the last, who opened all conceivable doors, who stood at his side at all the congresses and who accompanied him tactfully – as a Christian missionary – to Palestine also deserves a place of honour in the history of Zionism. Impoverished, abandoned and almost forgotten, Hechler died of old age at the age of 85, on January 30, 1931 in 'Midway Memorial Hospital' in London. Herzl at least ensured that his dear friend, who had remained active in the Zionist movement for many years, received a pension, but he expected another fate for his dear friend.

Alex Carmel

Impressions from Palestine

1   Johannes Frutiger in 1867.

The Basler Johannes Frutiger

In 1858 Johannes Frutiger [1836–1899] was sent to Jerusalem by Christian Friedrich Spittler [1782–1867] to the 'Handelshaus der Basler Pilgermission' (Trading house of the Basel Pilgrim Mission) as an assistant. When Basel gave up this firm in 1873, Frutiger took over the bank, and later on, the whole business. As the most distinguished banker in Palestine he was mainly involved in building and supporting Christian and Jewish projects. Due to his efforts and his generous financial sponsorship, the country's first railroad – from Jaffa to Jerusalem – was opened in 1892.

Sir Moses Montefiore

Between 1827 and 1875, the English statesman and philanthropist Sir Moses Montefiore [1784–1885] travelled seven times to Palestine to support his Jewish co-religionists. With his second journey in 1839, Montefiore tried to 'raise the productivity' of the Jews of Galilee, Jaffa and most of all Jerusalem with different activities. His attempts were not very successful in the beginning. In 1860, he built the first Jewish quarter outside the walls of Jerusalem. Until the second half of the 19th century, most of the Jews of Palestine had to rely on the 'Halukkah', the distribution of money collected from all over the world.

The Swiss Samuel Gobat

Samuel Gobat [1799–1879] was brought up at the Basel Mission. From 1825 he worked for the English 'Church Missionary Society' mainly and pioneeringly in Abyssinia. From 1846 until his death in 1879 he succeeded Michael Solomon Alexander as protestant bishop of Jerusalem. He transferred the missionary activity of the Anglo-Prussian diocese from the Jewish people to the Arabic – mostly Greek-orthodox – Christians of Palestine. He was responsible for the foundation of several schools, hospitals and other charitable institutions, thus moving other churches, governments and also the Jews of Europe to actively support Palestine in similar ways. In this way, Gobat indirectly made a major contribution to the rebuilding of Palestine in the 19th century.

2 Samuel Gobat at old age.

The 'Lämel School' in Jerusalem

Elise Herz, the Viennese daughter of Simon Edler von Lämel [1766–1845], wanted to use her father's fortune to found the first modern Jewish school of Palestine. Its purpose was to provide a counterpart to the Christian mission schools and, for the first time, offer Jewish students the possibility of a worldly education. To this end she sent the famous poet Ludwig August Frankl [1810–1894] to Jerusalem in 1856. His efforts met with strong resistance from the strictly orthodox Ashkenazic community. So, initially, the 'Lämel School' served mainly the Sephardic Jews. The school moved out of the Old City and found its final home in 1903 in the magnificent construction by the architect Theodor Sandel located in New-Jerusalem.

3 The 'Lämel School' in Jerusalem, inaugurated in 1903.

Impressions from Palestine

4 'Mount Hope', today in the area of Tel Aviv, around 1900 (has been demolished in the meantime).

'Mount Hope': A German-American Settlement Near Jaffa

In the middle of the 19th century, the first attempts by a few Germans and Americans were made to rebuild Palestine via agricultural settlements involving the Jews. The massive 'Return of the Jews' was to precede the resurrection of Jesus and thus accelerate the arrival of 'The Kingdom of God'. On a hill near Jaffa, now in the centre of Tel Aviv, they acquired an estate. Full of hope, they called it 'Mount Hope' and worked hard on it. Clorinda Minor [1806–1855], an American, and the brothers Friedrich and Johann Steinbeck from Wuppertal, whose grandchild was the American author John Steinbeck, were the leaders of this first attempt to colonize Palestine. In 1858 neighbouring Arab criminals set a cruel end to their efforts.

The 'Rothschild Hospital' in Jerusalem

In order to prevent Christian missions from holding the field in Palestine, the director of a bank in Paris at the time, James Jacob Rothschild [1792–1868] supported Jewish charitable institutions in the Holy Land. In 1853, the Rothschild Hospital was founded in the Jewish quarter in the Old City of Jerusalem. It provided 18 beds. Rothschild's son Alfons [1827–1905] made every effort to extend the hospital. In 1888, the 'Hôpital Israélite Mayer Rothschild', named after Mayer Amschel [1743–1812] of Frankfurt, founder of the Rothschild dynasty and father of James Jacob, moved to a large modern new building outside the Old City. Some years later, the English and the German hospitals also moved to the then 'elegant' neighbourhood of the Rothschild Hospital, to the present 'Street of the Prophets'.

5   On the right the Rothschild Hospital in Jerusalem of 1888. Photo taken around 1980.

6   Original plate from 1888.

Bishop Michael Solomon Alexander

Born as the son of a rabbi in Schönlanke (Poznań) in 1799, he went to England as a youth where he started off being a rabbi but soon converted and became a reverend in Ireland in 1827. The 'London Jewish Mission' made use of the services of the talented young former rabbi who was to become a professor for Hebrew and rabbinical literature at the highly esteemed King's College in London in 1832.

Alexander was the obvious choice as in 1841 England appointed the first bishop of the new founded Anglo-Prussian diocese in Jerusalem. He could serve as the best example for his former co-religionists in Palestine and thus for the earliest possible Second Coming of Jesus. In 1842 the bishop arrived in Jaffa with a British warship, but once in Jerusalem he aroused fear and aversion, which to this very day have not been forgotten, amongst the Jews of Palestine who were particularly pious at that time. Under these conditions,

7   Bishop Michael Solomon Alexander.

Impressions from Palestine

his missionary attempts totally failed. The premature death of the first 'Christian rabbi' while on a journey to Egypt in 1845 brought the mission which had started with such high hopes to an end.

'Mikveh Israel' – 'Hope' or 'Gathering of Israel'

In 1870 Charles Netter [1826–1882] from the Alsace founded the first Jewish agricultural school in Palestine near Jaffa on the way to Jerusalem. This school was the 'Mikveh Israel' and it was founded in the name of the French-Jewish 'Alliance Israélite Universelle'. This splendid facility was designed by the templar architect Theodor Sandel from Heilbronn [1845–1902] who was at this time living in a German colony near Jaffa. The first, eventually disappointing, meeting between Theodor Herzl and Kaiser Wilhelm II in Palestine, took place at the gates of the Mikveh Israel. The school was to serve the expected development of Palestine by training specially educated Jewish farmers and at the same time by strengthening French influence in the Orient. In the time of the founding of the Mikveh Israel approximately 20,000 Jews were living in Palestine supported mainly by alms that were collected from their brethren in Europe. The core of the 'Old Jewish Community' (Ha-Yishuv ha-yashan) of the country was formed by the orthodox inhabitants of the four Holy Cities Jerusalem, Hebron, Safed (Zefat) and Tiberias.

The Mikveh Israel was designed to improve 'productivity'. In 1870, the first signs of such 'productive' Jewish life were already noticeable elsewhere such as Jaffa and Haifa. But the success was so rarely visible and so limited, that even Charles Netter came to the conclusion shortly before he died that the solution to the 'Jewish question' had to be found in America and not in Palestine.

Only the massive Jewish waves of immigration starting in 1882 and the foundation of several agricultural colonies gave fresh impetus to Mikveh Israel. Today 1,500 students are enrolled and at the same time it is the seat of the national bureau for the preservation of historical monuments.

8   Porch of the 'Mikveh Israel' on the road from Jaffa to Jerusalem.

Catherine Schott

The Change of Jewish Patterns of Life in Poland and the Reorientation of Jewish Self-Image

A strong and lively Eastern-Jewish culture developed in Poland over the course of the centuries. When the Jews were persecuted and driven out of Western Europe in the Middle Ages, they were admitted to Poland where they augmented the Jewish community which was already established there. Their professional skills, crafts, and their capital were welcomed by the Polish rulers, who granted them special rights and protection in return. The communities were under the authority of the 'Kahal', a self-governing body which had both political and religious power. As a result of this privileged legal position, the Jews were able to generate a brisk economy, which gave them a secure position as middlemen between the classes as well as between the urban and rural populations. These favourable conditions, even if they were not positive in all cases, promoted the development of a culture of high standing. Thus rabbinical literature was held in high esteem far beyond the borders of Poland. The 16th century, characterized to a large extent by political stability and a cultural flourishing, is considered to be the golden age not only in the history of the Polish Jews, but of Poland itself too.

However, the position of the Jews deteriorated rapidly from the 17th century onwards. In the Polish aristocratic republic, which was weakened by wars and internal tension, the former tolerant attitude towards the Jews changed into increasing hostility. The great revolt of the Cossacks and peasants against the Polish rulers in 1648 also claimed numerous victims amongst the Jewish population, and represented a catastrophe for the Jewish communities in Poland. Their economic and financial foundation was partly ruined, their cultural establishments destroyed, and their self-governing bodies weakened. Added to this the landed gentry tried to force the Jews out of their existing position by driving them out of their villages and by marginalizing them economically. Their difference, expressed above all in their appearance and in the use of their own language, Yiddish, but also by a lifestyle governed by religious laws, all culminating in the Eastern-Jewish 'cultural personality', was less and less accepted. Instead of recognition, anti-Jewish prejudice and stereotyped images were revived. Long-established certainties no longer held true. New solutions were sought to the crisis, among which were the Messianic movements, such as the followers of Shabbetai Zevi [1626–1676] in the sixties of the 17th century or of Jacob Frank [1726–1791], but above all the mass movement of the 'Devout' – the 'Hassidim' – which emerged and spread in the first half of the 18th century. Based on the teachings of Israel ben Eliezer [1700–1760], influenced by the Kabbalah, the 'Baal Shem Tov' (Master of the Holy Name) a popular piety developed which was at the same time deeply mystic, enthusiastic and cheerful. Later the Hassidim split up into numerous schools and rallied round their 'Zaddikim' – the 'righteous men' – some of whom were venerated as miracle rabbis. They created real dynasties and laid claim to power. This led to violent conflicts with the supporters of Orthodox Jewry, the 'Mitnaggedim' – the 'opponents' – not least for leadership of the communities. The 'Maskilim' – the 'Thinkers' – as supporters of the Jewish enlightenment – the 'Haskalah' – initially found little support. They were contemptuously called 'Berliners' on account of their spiritual origins. In the meantime, the context had fundamentally changed once more.

In 1772, 1793 and 1795, Poland was partitioned between Russia, Austria and Prussia. From then on, the situation of the Polish Jews in each of the three divided territories was different and followed a different path, depending on the policy of the respective power and not least on the attitude of the Poles towards them. The Congress of Vienna in 1815 confirmed the final partition and allocation of Poland among the three powers, Prussia, Austria, and Russia. The Jews in West Poland, now under Prussian control, mostly assimilated with the Western Jews. On the other hand, in Galicia, which came under Austrian domination, and in the territories controlled by the Russian Empire, the Jews maintained their traditional cultural identity. From the belt of land which had been incorporated from the former Kingdom of Poland-Lithuania, Russia had created the 'pale of settlement' 'cherta osedlosti evreev' that reached from the Baltic to the Ukraine and the Black Sea which the Jews were only allowed to leave in exceptional cases. The Kingdom of Poland – also called Congress Poland, as a result of its creation at the Congress of Vienna – had a special position in some respects, it was in personal union with Russia and will be the focus of attention in the following. Somewhat more than 200,000 Jews lived within its borders. By the end of the 19th century, the Jewish population of Congress Poland had grown by a factor of six, whereas the total population had only tripled.

The 1815 constitution of Congress Poland only granted Christian inhabitants civil and political rights; the Jewish population was excluded from these rights. The economic marginalization and legal restrictions initiated against the Jews were upheld and gradually expanded until the mid 19th century under the rule of Alexander I, and in particular, his successor, Nicholas I. Jews were not allowed to hold public office. Likewise they could not become members of the craft guilds. Town privileges already in force 'de non tolerandis Judaeis' were confirmed. A decree in force since 1822 allowed the towns to establish Jewish quarters, outside of which only a few wealthy Jewish families were allowed to reside. Furthermore, ritual foodstuffs and utensils were subjected to special taxes. The Kahal was abolished in 1821 and replaced by the 'Supervisory Body for Synagogues', whose powers were now restricted to religious and charitable matters. Codes of dress which forebade the wearing of Jewish traditional costumes in public were repeatedly imposed and the introduction of national service for Jews in 1843 was meant to counteract their different exterior appearance and interfere with their lives, that were dominated by religious traditions. At the same time, the legislation overall aimed at maintaining the special position of the Jews and as a result confirmed the difference for which they were reproached. However, the legal provisions were not read in the same way by local administrations and were often interpreted in the respective interests of the towns and landed gentry. Thus, under the rule of Nicholas I, Jews also settled in rural areas.

Reform projects for the improvements of the lot of the Jews and their integration into the Polish society which had been drafted by Polish and Russian members of parliament since the partitions of Poland assumed their 'civilization', their assimilation – retaining their Mosaic faith. Significantly, this was to be achieved with the same legal restrictions and with the maintenance of the special taxes. Only if the Jews lay aside their traditional clothing, and spoke Polish or Russian, and not Yiddish anymore, and could prove that they had a secular education would they be granted civil rights or even equal rights. The representatives of the Jewish population were of the opinion that only if these rights were granted would it be possible for the Jews to be integrated into the Christian society. Repeated requests that the legal restrictions and heavy special taxes be rescinded were however unsuccessful.

In addition to the political and legal context, the economic and social conditions also changed fundamentally. The increasing hostility of the landed gentry who – as a result of their financial problems – no longer wished to avail themselves of the middleman function exercised by the Jews, the resultant attempt to exclude Jews from the hostelry trade, the prohibition of establishing in villages, and restrictions on their trading drove the Jews into the towns, where they mostly worked as craftsmen and shopkeepers. The offer quickly exceeded the demand in these trades, leading to merciless competition and unimaginable misery. Industrialization which gradually developed in the first half of the 19th century, exacerbated the situation, since traditional crafts waned into insignificance. So, in addition to losing their former homes and hereditary trades, all their personal circumstances were turned upside down. Large parts of the Jewish population were rapidly reduced to poverty. The Warsaw 'Supervisory Body for Synagogues' brought these conditions to the attention of the government in 1856, and pleaded for the annulation of the legal restrictions:

'The life and the opportunities for gainful employment in the cities, to which the Jews are condemned, do not make it possible for all family members to earn an income. The head of the family alone has to provide for the sustenance of the entire household with his business or trade. And the wife together with their children awaits the return of her husband and their father with his earnings, which barely guarantees them the scantiest of fare. This gives rise not only to the poverty of the Jews, followed by neglected clothing and homes, but also to the decline of the younger generation which has no avenues leading to useful and practical work, and which sacrifices its youth to spiritual education by studying religious works. In contrast, life in the country provides all kinds of ways of earning a living for people of all classes and ages and has a positive effect on the development of physical strength of the individual.'[1]

All these aggressions on the living conditions had consequences regarding mentality and behaviour. The traditional family structures were broken up, the power of the parents increasingly came to be questioned. The roles of husband and wife as well as the relationship between them began to change. The previous Jewish self-image began to falter. Once again many sought new answers to the changes that had occurred, they sought a realignment of their beliefs, support and a place in the society. The great majority, the poorer classes in particular, continued to seek protection in the religious community – rabbinical Orthodoxy or Hassidism. However, a growing proportion tried to break out of their traditional patterns of life, possibly influenced and encouraged by the emerging 'activist turning point' in the 18th and early 19th century: Trends had become visible in the Messianic movements as in Hassidism that the arrival of the Messiah and thus salvation were not simply to be passively awaited, but were to be brought about by life-style and action. Why should it not be possible to improve the situation by worldly action?

The representatives of the Haskalah – the Maskilim – stressed the need for internal Jewish reforms and acculturation to the dominant society in order to improve the situation of the Jews. On the other hand, those who advocated assimilation were in favour of leaving the traditional Jewish patterns of life behind – mostly while retaining the Jewish faith – and tried to immerse themselves in the Polish culture. They began to

---

[1] Letter from the 'Supervisory body for Synagogues' (Dozór, Bożniczy) of the Warsaw district to the Administrative Board of the Kingdom of Poland dated 27 December 1856. In: Zofia Borzymińska: Dzieje Żydów w Polsce XIX wiek. Warszawa 1994, p. 39.

1 The Tlomacki reformed synagogue in Warsaw, inaugurated in 1878 and destroyed during the Second World War.

send their children to Polish schools. As in Vilnius (Vilna), secular subjects were also taught in the reformed rabbinical school in Warsaw founded in 1826. Reformed synagogues were created with a modified cult and sermons in Polish. In Warsaw there existed a small but influential Jewish upper class which belonged to the Polish upper bourgeoisie and was not only economically and politically active in Congress Poland, but also played an important role in the assimilation movement. Some of these well-to-do people even went one step further and converted to Catholicism or Protestantism.

In the early 1860s, the problems in Congress Poland aggravated. After the failure of the November revolt in 1830 against the Russian domination, rumours of another revolt circulated. Part of the Jewish population also hoped that a better life would be in store for them in an independent Poland. This is why Dov Berush Meisel, Chief Rabbi of the Warsaw community, fuelled with patriotism and close ties to Poland, called on the Jews to take part in the Polish struggle for independence. The patriotic demonstrations in Warsaw in 1861 became the symbol of a 'Jewish-Polish' fraternization. One year later, under the pressure of the revolutionary atmosphere, equal rights were formally conceded to the Jews in Congress Poland on the basis of the reforms worked out by Aleksander Wielopolski, which emphasized the benefits brought to the national economy by the Jews. However, some of the restrictive laws remained in force. Nevertheless, the assimilation movement was now given new impetus. When the January revolt broke out in Warsaw in 1863, numerous young assimilated Jews fought for Polish independence. Many Jews – including those who had converted – helped, passing on information, providing money, food, weapons and uniforms. Others lent support to the Russian troops. All in all, however, less Jews were involved in the revolt than in 1830. After its repression a policy of rigorous russification was implemented. In Poland itself a new way of thinking set in. More and more people began to think that economic success as a symbol of national power was better than a new uprising. Primarily those Jews who were willing to assimilate and played an active part in the economy were regarded as allies.

The assimilation movement, filled with new hopes, can be regarded as the first Jewish political movement in Poland by virtue of its ideology and its programme. It was mainly based in Warsaw, but was also present in some larger towns, whereas in the provinces it hardly exerted any influence at all. The assimilated Jews – Poles of Mosaic belief, as they already called themselves – felt that it was their mission to deliver the Jews living in accordance with religious traditions from their conventional patterns of life, and to integrate them into Polish society. In Lodz, established as an industrial town in 1820, where many manufacturing companies belonged to German Jews, the attempt was primarily made to assimilate into German culture. Education and information were supposed to make social advancement and integration into Polish society possible, and thereby remove the material misery of the masses. The objective was to support 'productive work' amongst the Jews to work against their concentration in business and thus achieve an adaption to the employment structure of the non-Jewish society.

The main organ of the assimilated Jews was the weekly newspaper 'Izraelita', written in Polish, which appeared in Warsaw from 1866 to 1915. However, because of the language barrier, it did not reach the broad masses who also did not want to have anything to do with the assimilated Jews. The 'Ha-Zefira' – 'Dawn' – newspaper, written in Hebrew, took its lead from the Haskalah tradition, and was likewise published in Warsaw, with interruptions, from 1862 to 1931. It became very popular, even beyond the borders of Congress Poland. Mendele Mokher Seforim and Sholem Aleichem ranked amongst its authors for a while. Nahum Sokolow established the modern Hebrew journalism with his brilliantly written feature supplements and editorials in 'Ha-Zefira'. From 1897 onwards the paper supported the Zionist movement and in the 20th century it finally became the voice of the Polish Zionists.

While the industrialization of Poland was in full swing, the migration of the Jewish population went from the North East to the South West, to the developing industrial centres, which attracted workers and craftsmen. In 1865, 91.5% of the Jews in Congress Poland already lived in towns, mostly in small shtetls. In the textile industry town of Lodz, the Jewish population grew from 5,633 inhabitants in 1862 to 98,677 in 1897, and in Warsaw from 42,639 to 219,141 inhabitants.[2] In the following years the increase speeded up. To some extent, this may be ascribed to the higher birth rates compared to non-Jews, but above all to the low infant mortality. But also the immigration authorization for Jews from the pale of settlement to Congress Poland in force from 1868 onwards and the pogroms in Russia in 1881 that triggered off an inflow of 'Litvak' Jews contributed to this rise. Amongst Polish Jews this name was applied to all Jews who had immigrated from Russia, not only those from Lithuania. It is difficult to ascertain their numbers, but at least between 60,000 and 100,000 are supposed to have settled in Warsaw. Rich businessmen and entrepreneurs were amongst the 'Litvaks' who settled here. This represented economic competition for the indigenous Jews. Moreover, they tended to have an advanced outlook and spoke a different Yiddish or even mastered Russian. In the eyes of Polish Jews and non-Jews, they were considered to be supporters of Russian culture and were therefore shunned. Many Jews even feared that they would promote anti-Semitism in Poland. To this extent they remained in Warsaw, a group that was admittedly not completely isolated, but nevertheless segregated.

In addition to the assimilated Jews, the growing Jewish working class gradually began to become secularized. The representatives of Jewish Orthodoxy and Hassidism led a bitter struggle against these trends. But for all its multiplicity

---

[2] Ignacy Schiper: Dzieje handlu żydowskiego na ziemiach polskich. Warsaw 1937 (Reprint 1991) p. 493; Najnowsze dzieje Żydów w Polsce w zarysie (do 1950 roku). Pod red. Jerzego Tomaszewskiego. Warsaw 1993, pp. 25, 28.

2 Jewish Bazar in Warsaw around 1880.

and all the struggles to redirect the development of Jewry, a movement emerged which incorporated almost all Jewish trends. This movement rediscovered traditional Jewish culture and did not scorn the Yiddish language, but turned it into a tool instead. The newspapers written in Yiddish were able to reach a far larger audience than those written in Hebrew or Polish. Tradition and revival combined to become a specifically Jewish culture, a Jewish self-consciousness. It was impossible to ignore the demands for unity within Jewish society, aptly expressed by the journalist Mordechaj Spektor: 'Oh Jews, Jews! When will the good times come when all Jews will call themselves the same, namely "Jews", and not "Litvaks", "Polish Hassidim", "Poles of Mosaic belief", "Mitnaggedim", "Sadigerer", "Palestinian", "Talner", "Argentines", "Gerer" '[3].

The attitude of Polish society towards the Jews became increasingly hostile. Large Jewish entrepreneurs and their wealth were envied. Above all, the middle-class bourgeoisie feared Jewish competition. The wave of pogroms which also spread from Russia to Poland in the 1880s – resulting in riots at Christmas 1881 in Warsaw, in

[3] Mordechaj Spektor: 'Wegs-lajt'. In: Der Hojz Frajnd 4 (1894). The supporters of the settlement of Palestine or emigration to Argentina were known as 'Palestinian' and 'Argentines'. The Hassidic followers of the Zaddikim of Sadagóra, Tałno and of Góra Kalwaria are meant by 'Sadigerers', 'Talners' and 'Gerers'. Quote in : Alina Cała: Asymilacja Żydów w Królestwie Polskim (1864–1897) Postawy, Konflikty, Stereotypy, Warsaw 1989, p. 113.

1892 in Lodz – marked the external turning point. As a result, the discriminatory regulations of the czarist government were also tightened up. More and more supporters of assimilation realized that their road was not leading to the hoped for solution, but to a dead end. It was not leading them away from economic and social problems, but poverty and destitution became more pressing for most Jews. A growing number of them lived as 'Luftmenschen' (air people), without a regular job and income. More than a million Jews emigrated from the Russian empire between the 1890s and the First World War, to run away from poverty and persecution. In addition, the growing anti-Semitism dashed hopes that assimilation could easily lead to integration into Polish society. The 'National Democratic Party', formed in 1897, whose manifesto was essentially based on anti-Semitism, was able to exert an increasing influence on Polish politics. Even as early as 1916, two years prior to the re-establishment of the Polish state, Joshua Heshel Farbstein – the brother of the Zurich Zionist David Farbstein – saw the future clearly: 'What can we expect later on, if an independent Poland was actually to be proclaimed?'[4].

3   Leopold Kronenberg II, Jewish industrialist [1849–1937].

The new Jewish self-consciousness offered a way out of the crisis. In the Jewish society which in the meantime had become more differentiated it was possible to turn again to the pattern of life of the Orthodox and Hassidim, or to become involved – without giving up secularization – in the socialist workers' movement, namely in the 'Bund' and in political Zionism.

---

[4] Farbstein to the Central Zionist Office in Berlin (November 1916). Quoted in: Frank Golczewski: Polnisch-jüdische Beziehungen 1881–1922. Eine Studie zur Geschichte des Antisemitismus in Osteuropa. Wiesbaden 1981, p. 163.

Stefanie Middendorf

'My Shtetl Is the People Who Live in It, Not the Place ...'[1]

The shtetl has become the symbol of a whole culture – the culture of the Jews in the small towns and the municipal districts in Eastern Europe. At the same time this term stands for an actual place in which Polish, Russian or Galician Jews lived as a majority or a strong minority and were able to develop and preserve their own tradition until the beginning of this century. Life in this geographical space was governed by a number of demographic, social and legal circumstances; it was marked by poverty and hopelessness, cramped conditions and isolation. The reality of the shtetl must not be veiled over by nostalgic and melancholic admiration for a 'strangely idealized world of wittiness and wistfulness'[2]; the wretchedness of Jewish life in Eastern Europe was one of the reasons why Zionist, socialist and assimilatory endeavours and their search for new prospects emerged.

The World of the Shtetl

'A shtetl was not the appendage of a Christian community within the precincts of a town, not a foreign body, an object of discrimination, inside a higher civilization, but, on the contrary, a sharply defined autonomous community, consolidated in its fundamentals, with a culture of its own – and this in the midst of poverty and ugliness and encircled by enemies of the Jewish faith.'[3]

The pressure from without and the insular situation within non-Jewish surroundings long prevented internal differences from breaking out in the Jewish community and allowed a specific shtetl world to develop. Poverty and the daily chase after 'parnosse' – 'the livelihood' – determined the Jewish population's everyday life. Limited by government decrees in their economic activities, many inhabitants of the small Jewish centres lived in a miserable, in many cases completely insecure, situation. Often the differences in the social spectrum were only those between the poor and the hopelessly poor. The Jewish beggars as well as the so-called 'Luftmenschen' (air people), people who lived – without capital, without any specific training and without any regular work – on air, so to speak, and from poorly paid casual jobs have become the symbol of this destitution. In his 'Experiences of a Jewish Statistician in Poland' Isaac Leib Peretz describes his encounter with such a person:

'And what sort of a business have you got now?' – 'Who's got a business?' – 'What do you live on?' – 'Oh, that's what you mean? One kind of lives.' – 'But what

---

[1] Mark Zborowski and Elizabeth Herzog: Das Schtetl. Die untergegangene Welt der osteuropäischen Juden. 3rd ed. Munich 1992, p. 44.
[2] Leon Brandt (ed.): Abschied von Tewjes Welt. Lebensbilder aus dem jiddischen Stätel. Cologne 1981, p. 30.
[3] Manès Sperber: Die Wasserträger Gottes. All das Vergangene ... Vol. 1. Vienna 1974, p. 25.

on?' – 'On God, praise be to Him! When He gives, one has.' – 'But He doesn't throw it down from heaven.' – 'Yes, He does, He really does. How should I know what I live on?'[4]

As this shows, Jewish occupational and social structures in the shtetl cannot be readily ascertained statistically. Most people had more than one area of activity; the most important line of business, although completely overcrowded, was small trade. That is why the market was the heart of the shtetl on weekdays. This bustling scene of buying and selling, running and dealing, standing and discussing, personified the function of the Jews as mediators between town and country, the mutual dependence of Jews and non-Jews, but also the fierce competition between the Jews themselves.

The importance of the craft trades gradually declined as a result of measures taken by the authorities and the onset of industrialization. Manual work was not approved of anyway. Cobblers and tailors were right at the bottom of the social scale. But the structure of the shtetl, everyday life, was less determined by the professional situation of each and every one than by religion. For this reason that is what the status criteria were based on. Religious scholarship and the observance of all the religious commandments – the 'mitzvot' – met with highest esteem. Wealth, 'yichus' – respect derived from descent and one's personal achievements – and social conduct ranked only second. Material prosperity was not sufficient for a high status; only in conjunction with religious education and a charitable use of one's own possessions could it lead to respect.

The highest esteem in society was enjoyed by the 'schejnen Jidn' – the 'fair Jews' – in other words: the scholarly and socially very competent Jews. These were, firstly, the rabbis and the Hassidic rebbes, who saw their activity in the community as a vocation and therefore did not practise a secular profession; to these were added the officials of the Jewish local administration. In addition, those Jews who combined their education with a certain prosperity and professional success also belonged to the highest class. There was thus frequently a merger of religious and economic power, a tension between the ideal of a spiritual renunciation of the world and the real-life influence of everything material and secular. With the advent of modern times, wealth increasingly threatened to take over the position of scholarship; at the same time the 'Kahal' partially became the instrument of an internal Jewish exploitation.

At the other end of the social scale was the large mass of the 'prosten Jidn' – the poor and uneducated Jews. All classes were, however, connected by their ideals and their religiousness. Even the poorest Jew tried to acquire a certain religious education by studying and to incorporate this into his day-to-day communication by means of quotations and allusions. The poorer Jews practised numerous mystical and magic customs. They provided most of the supporters of Hassidism and of its leaders, so that it was possible for whole dynasties to form around a 'zaddik'. Representatives of various religious movements, who in some cases fiercely opposed one another, therefore often lived inside one shtetl. The 'Crown Rabbis', appointed by the state, were, on the other hand, unpopular and enjoyed hardly any authority.

The whole education system was geared to the ideal of religious scholarship of the men. Every Jewish boy passed through the 'heder' up to about the age of twelve, then he could enter the 'Bet ha-Midrash' – the public study house – and, if especially gifted and backed by the necessary financial means from family members or patrons, he could attend the 'yeshiva' – the institute for higher Talmud learning. Thus a large section of the Jewish population acquired at least a small mea-

---

[4] Isaak Leib Perez: Erlebnisse eines jüdischen Statistikers in Polen. In: Ulf Diedrichs (ed.): Dein aschenes Haar Sulamith. Ostjüdische Geschichten. Düsseldorf, Cologne 1981, p. 69.

1 Interior of the Temple of the miracle Rabbi of Sadagóra.

sure of education, and illiteracy was rare; but the exclusively religious instruction of the male shtetl population was unable to impart practical training that could be applied to the world of work.

Women were largely excluded from the study of the Holy Scripture. This fact determined their life in the shtetl. Girls learnt to read and write a little bit of Yiddish and acquired some basic knowledge of Hebrew at their 'heder'. Women were denied a deeper religious education. Thus they could not attain a high status as an individual but only as the wife of a husband who was as learned as possible. Their activities were restricted to the social and economic areas, and at the same time it was their major duty to safeguard the religious life in the family. Often the concern about earning a living was the sole responsibility of the wife if she wanted to enable her husband to pursue his religious studies.

The girls, however, were given access to state schools at an earlier date than the boys. Around the middle of the 19th century it was to a large extent the more secular education of the girls and women which made it possible for enlightened and emancipatory ideas to find their way into the world of the shtetl, whereas the boys could only deal with them secretly in their religious schools.

Early marriage and the patriarchal family model had – although frequently ignored in practice – a central function as the guardian of tradition and established structures within the shtetl society. The family also became the mirror image of the change in the Jewish patterns of life:

'All the nuances of the people are represented in this image: the old grandfather, a preacher, admonishes and urges his people only to abide by the ancient faith, for everything, he says, goes the way marked out by the Lord. The father, a shopkeeper, is only worried about his business. One of his sons is a Zionist and urges everyone to return to the Promised Land, another believes in assimilation and preaches the merger and integration with other peoples. One is a socialist and believes that only his ideals are capable of liberating poor and oppressed people.'[5]

Contact between the shtetl population and the Christian environment was mostly limited to the business area. Now and then also closer personal relations were formed. The relationship to non-Jews was strongly marked by the Jewish minority's own definition of themselves as the 'chosen people', who perceived themselves as being in the proximity – timeless and without history – to a redeeming future, and thus could look down on the 'Goiim' in pity and without any missionary zeal:

'We thought they were in a very unhappy situation. They had no pleasure ... no Sabbath ... no holidays ... no fun.' 'They drank a great deal, and one could not blame them for that, their life was so wretched.'[6]

Each individual saw himself in the light of the expectations of the shtetl and linked his personal fate with the life and suffering of all the Jews. In this way a collective consciousness evolved which asked for a certain measure of internal responsibility for living together and became the vehicle of the shtetl's culture – of Yiddishness. The shtetl's way of thinking was moulded by the spirit of Talmudic training and influenced by deductive logic and dialectical analysis, which manifested itself in the Yiddish language, so full of allusions. In this culture, with its strong linguistic expression, words were more than a means of communication; they embodied substance. In the study of the Holy Scripture feelings were transformed into thoughts, and emotions were expressed in sophisticated theoretical formulations.

Yiddish literature and music were a reflection of life in the Jewish shtetl and the change in Eastern European Jewish ways of thinking. In their jokes, which, in retrospect, were interpreted to be

2 Jewish beggar.

a specific form of amusement and irony in the shtetl, the Jews treated each other self-critically and turned their experience into practice. The jokes had their origins in bitter reality:

'This humour was the heroic attempt to counter historical reality with a religious optimism, to cling to a reassuring mystification, which became a genuine support in the elemental struggle for life.'[7]

The Awakening and Change in the Shtetl

At the end of the 19th century, this mystical hope could no longer offer any prospect for life to the younger generation and a large number of the shtetl inhabitants who were being reduced to poverty. Those who broke out of the shtetl life

---

[5] Alexander Granach: Da geht ein Mensch. Roman eines Lebens. 3rd ed. Munich 1994, p. 213/214 (on the presentation of a Russian Jewish family in a play by David Pinsky).
[6] Zborowski: Schtetl, p. 40.
[7] Claudio Magris: Weit von wo. Verlorene Welt des Ostjudentums. Vienna 1974, p. 11.

3 Prayers in the home of a deceased in Lida.

became the vehicles of change in Jewish society in Eastern Europe. After many had only secretly spent a lot of time with 'secular' ideas, mainly young people, often the pupils of the yeshivot, were now openly and actively seeking the way out. Isrulik, a central figure in the novel 'Die Mähre' (The Mare) by Mendele Mokher Seforim, expresses their doubts and hopes:

> 'I shall remain a "Luftmensch", a force without content – that means: I shall feel the force within me to do something, without having the chance or the energy to express it, to make use of it, to be useful, and unfortunately there are many such people among us Jews.' 'We Jews, who are eternally in dire straits, pressed to the point of suffocation on all sides, for us there is no other way to escape misery than to acquire scholarship [...] or some other profession.'[8]

In the second half of the 19th century, more and more children – at first mainly from families that tended to be assimilated and more prosperous – were sent to a secular school parallel to their training at the heder, so that emancipatory and modern ideas entered the religiously structured shtetl society. At the same time, Zionist and socialist youth movements became fertile soil for activating the shtetl youth politically and socially.

Towards the end of the 19th century the impoverishment of the Jews had reached such proportions that it could no longer be mitigated by existing family nor by religious structures and charitable organizations. As a consequence of the political, economic and social upheavals, many Jews left the shtetl to find work in the larger towns. In the working-class areas in the towns, traditional and religious ties lost their influence. Thus not only the young intelligentsia but also the Jewish proletariat that was emerging became supporters of the new endeavours.

Secular – especially German – education and contact with the culture of the respective country

---

[8] Mendele Mojcher Sforim: Die Mähre. Stuttgart 1984 (= Die Bücher der goldenen Pawe 1), p. 23 and p. 20/21.

seemed to be ways out of the ghetto. But most universities remained closed to Jews. For this reason, academic societies were founded in which the intellectual energy that had earlier on been devoted to religious studies was turned towards dealing with party programmes, modern research and enlightening ideas. Thus a mixture of traditional and modern thinking arose as the basis of the new movements. Workers, too, organized themselves into study groups, and trade unions formed places for Jewish political activities.

In rural areas, however, the traditional shtetl society and the authority of Orthodoxy continued to exist until far into the 20th century. The world of the shtetl did not break up until the Shoah. Prior to this, especially after the First World War, its inhabitants had no longer simply rejected the departure to the 'outside', as it was expressed in socialism and Zionism, as being godless. They accepted that the efforts to improve the living conditions and not to just wait for redemption were necessary. Part of the Jewish workers' movement and in particular also Zionism tried to link up the social and national challenge with the tradition and cultural identity of Eastern Jewry. In this respect it was a question of 'outstripping the Messiah'.[9]

---

[9] Zborowski: Schtetl, p. 129.

Almut Bonhage

Jewish Individuality in the Eastern European Shtetl: Sholem Aleichem's 'aisnbangeschichtess'

The 'aisnbangeschichtess' (Train Stories) are twenty individual stories that together make a whole. The narrator is a travelling salesman, a frequent traveller on the railway from Odessa to Baranovich and from Kiev to Pereshchepene. He advises emphatically against travelling first class:

'I ask you with all honesty, how can anybody find it appealing to travel completely alone without saying a word to anyone? You could, God forbid, forget how to talk!'[1]

And the second class is not much better; full of snobs and society mesdemoiselles. He is only satisfied in the third class:

'Ah, but when you travel third class, it's just like being at home! Or even worse, because there are no other passengers in the third class carriages than scores of the children of Israel, you even feel a little too much at home! It is true, third class is not as comfortable, you have to fight resolutely for a seat, there is turmoil, a muddle, a hurly burly! You don't know where you are or who your neighbours are. But you make their acquaintance very quickly. It doesn't take long before everyone knows who you are, where you are going and what you do, and you know who they are, where they are going and what they do. You don't bother trying to sleep at night, because there is almost certainly someone there who wants to have a conversation with you. And if you don't feel like talking, the others most certainly will and they won't let you get any sleep anyway! And why of all things try to sleep on the train? It makes much more sense to talk with someone, because when you converse, something good always comes out of it.'

For the reader, these twenty highly amusing and witty stories give an insight into the themes of the many different aspects of poverty and distress of those populating the 'pale of settlements'. The author of these stories was born in the Ukrainian Perejaslav in 1859. He knew the Eastern Jewish world from the inside. However, during the different stages in his life he was confronted by very different forms of Jewish self-conception and various approaches to solving Jewish problems. His parents, strongly influenced by the Haskalah, gave him the opportunity to go to a Russian high school after having attended a heder. This was a privilege considering the restricted admission of Jews at the time. He earned his living as a private teacher of a rich squire. Later he became a rabbi. He wrote stories in Russian and Hebrew. His first Yiddish story was published in 1883. Later, fleeing from creditors, he went to Vienna, Paris, Czernowitz and Odessa. After having experienced a brutal pogrom in Kiev he decided to emmigrate to the USA. In 1907 he returned to Europe. He died in New York in 1916.

In spite of being able to write in Russian and Hebrew, Sholem Aleichem chose Yiddish as the language for his narratives and novels. Although he had travelled the world he remained true to

---

[1] All quotations from: Scholem Alejchem: Eisenbahngeschichten. Ed. by Gernot Jonas. Frankfurt a. M. 1995.

1 Jew at a station in Volhynia looking for a job.

one topic, the shtetl. So he is not merely by chance through his background an author of the shtetl, but he chose the cultivation of the Yiddish language and the culture of shtetl to be his life's work. This is also shown in the 'Jiddische Folksbibliotek' (Yiddish People's Library), a magazine which published only Yiddish authors.

The main concern of Sholem Aleichem and other contemporary Yiddish authors was to create a specific literature dealing with the life in the shtetl and to give it a permanent place in the world literature. In the 19th century, Yiddish appeared to be a dying language. For Moses Mendelssohn [1729–1786] Yiddish was an annoying 'jargon', and many 'progressive' Jews of the Haskalah shared his opinion. In his view, Yiddish underlined the special religious and cultural position of the Jews in Germany, and thus represented an obstacle on the way to emancipation and acculturation. Mendelssohn supported the use of 'High German'. At the same time others who strove to enlighten the people rediscovered Hebrew: they wanted Hebrew, which had till then been solely the language of religion and erudition, to become the living language of the people and indeed the modernized Hebrew experienced an enormous boost in Eastern Europe. Poets used the language and newspapers were published in Hebrew. In 1881 Eliezer ben Judah [1858–1922], born in Lithuania, emigrated to Palestine and soon managed to get the majority of the Jews in Palestine to speak Hebrew, and an intensive academic study of this language started.

In order to reach the masses, the 'Maskilim', the 'enlightened', resorted to an alternative strategy after initial, unsuccessful attempts to appeal to a larger circle of Hebrew readers in Eastern Europe. They made use of the 'jargon' as a temporary evil to approach a broad audience with enlightening literature, short novellas, satires, parables and dramatic works. They hoped that the people, once enlightened and liberated from the 'narrowmindedness' of the traditional way of thought would also abandon Yiddish and turn to the more dignified Hebrew.

2 Sholem Aleichem (pseudonym for Shalom Rabinowitsch) [1859–1916].

Instead of this Yiddish had a revival, for which Hassidism was largely responsible. It emphasized the dignity of the 'simple' people and at the same time the dignity of their language. The new language consciousness was part of the Eastern Jewish 'cultural personality' which had been growing since the 18th century. Emerging from the traditional Hassidic themes with mystic, religious visions, a literary language slowly developed.

The 'grandfather' of modern Yiddish literature, responsible for its breakthrough to acceptance, was Mendele Mokher Seforim [1835–1917]. Although writing in Hebrew he invented his own personal Yiddish style enriching written Yiddish with the treasures of the spoken language. Together with Isaac Leib Peretz [1851–1915] and Sholem Aleichem they were the triumvirate of the 'Hassidic' epoch of the new Yiddish literature which reached its pinnacle between the eighties of the 19th century and the First World War. Along with the Yiddish literature the entire Jewish culture flourished in Eastern Europe: numerous Yiddish theatres opened, Jewish music found new ways of expression, a variety of Yiddish newspapers were published.

This culture was part of a growing Jewish self-confidence – the comprehension of 'Jewishness' and nation. Thus, Yiddish can be viewed as the national language of the Eastern Jews. At the same time the foundation was laid in Eastern Europe – often by the same people – for Hebrew to become the national language of Erez Israel. It is only logical that this was then closely related to Zionism. Nathan Birnbaum [1864–1937], who turned his attention away from political Zionism and concentrated on the Jewish culture in the Diaspora, was concerned with the question of the national language, whether it should be Yiddish or Hebrew. His commitment to Yiddish reached its peak in 1908 when he organized a language conference in Czernowitz with Peretz as the president.

Sholem Aleichem's 'aisnbangeschichtess' are to be seen in this context. The stories, just as the anecdotes and jokes and narratives as a whole, represent the Eastern Jewish world. Sholem Aleichem's stories certainly do not claim to be documentary, but neither are they pure imagination. He takes his inspiration from a personal wealth of experience, as organized information about realities, creating testimonials of an era.

In the Eastern European culture, stories are not an end in themselves, they always accompany other activities. The stories always fill a very special place in a conversation, sometimes even in an argumentation. The story is a tool that has to be used properly, whether to lighten the atmosphere while studying in the heder, to emphasize an opinion, to make use of the time between the afternoon and the evening prayer, as a relief from strenuous work, or, as in this case, when travelling. A narrative has its own course which can, of course, vary. Each story must be introduced, blended into the current debate, interpreted if necessary and, maybe, given a moral or a teaching.

3 Jewish fire brigade in Baranovich.

Regarding his themes Sholem Aleichem uses not only the problems and relevant topics of his time and age, he also masters a Jewish tradition with his method of telling a story. He always refers to the situation in a discussion into which the story fits, to a person who told him the story. Often, this person did not have first-hand experience of the events told but heard the story on a particular occasion. The framework of each story, however, not only serves to lend authenticity to the storyteller or to relieve him of the responsibility for it, but rather it gives the story its strength, as regards the objective mentioned above: each story has a function, be it as an argument, a way of passing the time or as a lesson.

And this also explains why Sholem Aleichem chose Yiddish as the language of his stories. Only the language oriented toward the spoken word is suitable to retell the spoken culture and to exactly pinpoint the tone of the interaction between people. In the dialogues it is precisely these detours, metaphors, examples and excursions that turn a simple telling of a fact into an entire cosmos of Jewish individuality.

'Travel third class!' is what the travelling salesman recommends. Sholem Aleichem has written everything down for those who can no longer follow this advice. We simply have to open the book and the world of the third class carriage is right there before our very eyes.

As an example, story number three 'Baranovich Station' is quoted here. The narrator is, as always in the Train Stories, the travelling salesman:

'On that day we weren't more than a few dozen people and we sat, quite cosily, in the third class car. That is, strictly speaking, only those who had managed to find a seat quickly enough were seated. The others stood, leaning against the walls, but they were just as involved in the discussion as those with a seat. Our chat was most animated. Everyone was talking at the same time, the way these discussions are [...] Everybody tried to tell their latest news, happenings that everybody quite simply had to listen to, but no one managed to make the people stick to one subject.' And it goes on like this until one man speaks up, 'one of the passengers who hadn't found a seat but who hung over us somewhere holding on to the partitions [...] I liked him immediately. I liked his generous build. His unusual accent also appealed to me and that he quite simply called all of us a herd of cattle [...] Now the people in the train were initially somewhat baffled as the man from Kaminke compared them to this somewhat less dignified horned beast. [...] But they soon regained their composure, looked at each other and then said to the man from Kaminke: "You are waiting to be asked? Alright, so we'll ask, why not? But tell us, we really would like to know what happened to you in Kaminke! Come, why are you still standing up? Take a seat! You don't know where? Come on everybody, shift a little closer together!" [...] And the passengers, who are pretty well squeezed together as it is, all shuffle along and actually manage to find room for the man from Kaminke. The man from Kaminke seats himself with great dignity and strikes a pose (as if he were holding the child at circumcision festivities and it is the moment when the shammes calls to him: "Godfather!", and the child is carried in). He pushes his cap up off his forehead, rolls up his sleeves and begins to tell his story in his broad way of expressing himself.' The story that follows is full of cunning and treachery and does not only keep the passengers on the edge of their seat but also the readers. When the storyteller interrupts his story to enjoy a cigarette, everybody waits impatiently until he begins again. But in Baranovich the storyteller stops in the middle of a sentence and says that he has to get off the train. The crowd of people protest vociferously: "Unthinkable, no sir, that is not possible! We will not just let you go! You have to tell us the end of the story. How does it finish?" "The end? But that was just the beginning! Let me go! Should I miss my next train because of you? [...]" And before we can do anything, our man from Kaminke has disappeared without a trace. To the devil with Baranovich station!'

Sabine Strebel

'... from the Gan Eden, the Paradise of Frankfurt, to Gehenna, the Hell of Galicia ...'

This sentence was written by Bertha Pappenheim in 1904 in an account of her travels entitled 'On the Situation of the Jewish People in Galicia'.[1] During this five-week journey, which was followed by several others, she wanted to get her own impression of the social conditions there and to work out suggestions about how to combat prostitution and the white slave trade. Together with Sara Rabinowitch she undertook the journey on behalf of the 'Frankfurt Israelitic Relief Organization' and the 'Hamburg Branch of the Jewish Committee to Fight White Slavery'.

The hell of Galicia? Is not this dramatic expression simply an indication of the Western perspective of the observer? Bertha Pappenheim made her own viewpoint a central theme. She often spoke of the differences between East and West as well as of the danger of applying a 'plane made by Western culture' in Galicia. The problems of Western social work were addressed: 'People [women in Galicia, S.St.] gave me personally to understand that my expectations were so high because I had come from the Garden of Eden, the Paradise of Frankfurt, to Gehenna, the hell of Galicia.'[2] Pappenheim called for help from outside, from the West, but also from the women of Galicia itself. In the reports she wrote, the Western, middle-class standards that influenced her observations and interpretations showed through again and again. Thus, in reference to Galicia she used terms such as 'land of non-culture', 'depravity', 'dilapidation' and 'caves for dwelling and instructing'. This, however, did not prevent her from analyzing her own views repeatedly or from striving to understand more. She emphasized the fact that she was describing things from a woman's point of view and was making no claim to be objective.

Bertha Pappenheim [1859–1936] – born in Vienna, her father was from Pressburg, her mother from Frankfurt – also became known as the co-founder of the 'Jewish Women's Alliance' in Germany and the first president of the 'International Alliance of Jewish Women'. She translated not only important writings for the women's movement – such as Mary Wollestonecraft's 'A Vindication of the Rights of Women' – but also the women's bible and the popular 'Maasse' Book from the Middle Ages, in order to revive the female Jewish tradition.

Why, however, did a woman who was raised in the orthodox manner concern herself with white slavery and Jewish prostitution of all issues? Why did she spend numerous weeks travelling around Galicia on the train, often alone? Until the second half of the 19th century, Jewish prostitution as such was slight and practically unknown. The white slave trade, which today is referred to as trafficking in women and children or migrational prostitution, reached a climax between 1880 and 1914. This was related to the

---

[1] Bertha Pappenheim: Zur Lage der jüdischen Bevölkerung in Galizien. Reiseeindrücke und Vorschläge zur Verbesserung der Verhältnisse. In: Helga Heubach (ed.): Bertha Pappenheim, die Anna O. Sisyphus: Gegen den Mädchenhandel – Galizien. Freiburg i. Br. 1992, pp. 43–106.

[2] Pappenheim: Zur Lage, p. 61.

1 Bertha Pappenheim [1859–1936], after a drawing made in 1934 by Joseph Oppenheim.

spread of the industrial society, the increasing migration from Eastern Europe to the West and the rise of mobility. In view of the growing hostility toward Jews and the enthusiastic reception given these ideas by anti-Semitic circles, Bertha Pappenheim stressed the necessity of dealing with the problems from a Jewish point of view and of making them a central issue:

'We know that a large number of young Jewish women are involved in the business of freelance prostitution; – we know that Jewish women can be found in every brothel in the world and that in the white slave trade both the traffickers and the female merchandise are for the most part Jewish – and we also know that family life today is no longer what it once was, because the men – the fathers and the sons – can no longer keep themselves and their homes free of the filth that cannot be washed away by the tears of the deceived and ruined women. It is terribly difficult to have to express what I have just said – but it is better to admit the danger and enter into a bond of friendship in order to fight it than to stick our heads in the sand and live on credit given long ago until we go bankrupt.'[3]

Various studies had shown that the proportion of Jewish prostitutes, male and female pimps and traffickers, especially from Galicia, was large.

With the knowledge of this situation Bertha Pappenheim went to Galicia. Even before, while she was in Frankfurt, Bertha Pappenheim had been involved in an association called 'Women's Welfare Services', which had been especially established for Jewish women immigrating from Eastern Europe and particularly from Galicia, whose lives were 'ruined'. She encountered what in other reports had already been described as the causes for white slavery and prostitution: the economic and social plight of the Jewish population, the high unemployment, a one-sided educational system and the deplorable situation with regard to housing and mass emigration.

In her descriptions of the employment situation and working conditions, she battled against the anti-Jewish notion implying that Jews were living in affluence at the expense of Christians. Although there were a small number of prosperous merchants, the majority of the Jews in Galicia involved in trade and commerce were, however, among the poorest members of the proletariat in the world.

'The total livelihood of those Jews, who in the jargon of the anti-Semites are referred to as 'vampires, who suck the blood of Christian farmers', is such that no Christian farmer or workman need have the feeling of envy with regard to them. They are professional starvers [...]'[4]

[3] Zur Sittlichkeitsfrage. Lecture by Bertha Pappenheim at the 2nd Delegates' Conference of the Jewish Women's Alliance. Frankfurt a.M. 2 and 3 October 1907. Hamburg 1907, p. 19 (reproduced in abridged form in: Heubach: Pappenheim, pp. 107–117, here p. 110).
[4] Pappenheim: Zur Lage, p. 66.

Bertha Pappenheim saw the most important cause, however, in the particular difficulties that stemmed from Jewish law and which affected women and children.

'Intelligent, often very beautiful, but lacking self-reliance in a state of oriental dependency, brought up by men mainly to be sexual beings, with no education or professional training, these Polish (meant are Galician, S.St.) Jewish women lead a life of idleness. It is then not surprising at all when they seize every opportunity to leave the squalor of their villages, however improbable, fabulous or absurd the pretext to do so might be, as only secret agents and white slave traders are able to devise.'[5]

Thus, Bertha Pappenheim was pointing to a central problem: the subordinate role of women in Jewish culture, which resulted in the view of women as simply sexual beings. She pointed this out clearly using education as an example. Boys were taught religion in the heder, 'schools in which [...] a terrible, one-sided, mental drill was conducted.' With the girls, 'according to customary views considered inferior creatures', the orthodoxy had no religious objections to allowing them to attend public, i.e. Christian-Polish state schools.[6] On the one hand, the girls acquired a knowledge of the national language there, but were nevertheless not capable of getting a good position. On the other hand, they were no longer under the authority of religion and the family. Since the girls grew up in a Christian environment, they became alienated not only from their cultural-religious heritage, but also from their mothers, whose task it was to pass on to them the Jewish traditions. Bertha Pappenheim recognized that because of the inferior value placed on girls and the inadequate degree to which they were rooted in religion and traditional culture, prostitution offered the possibility of earning money and thus served as a way of getting out of the hopeless situation on Galicia. In addition, this also provided the freedom to escape from orthodox religion, which was often simply a strict but empty form:

'She wants to get out of the cramped confines of the little room, which she shares with ten or more other people, out of the dreary monotony of the main street in the village. A page from a newspaper, a letter from America, a third- or fourth-hand story told by a girlfriend, the circumstance that she is superfluous, the drive to live and not to vegetate chases her out into the world.'[7]

This had consequences for the relationship between the sexes and the structures within the family, and thus also for the state and Jewish culture.

As a further example, Bertha Pappenheim cites the position of the 'agunah', a woman whose husband has disappeared and according to Jewish law cannot remarry until a Jewish attestant certifies that the husband is dead. In this period, above all men emigrated in large numbers, while many women stayed behind with no standing in the society and no possibility of changing their situation. After the First World War the problem worsened: thousands of indigent widows whose husbands had disappeared in the war were left on their own with no prospects of remarrying according to religious law. These women experienced such deprivation that they got mixed in accepting promises of falsified divorces and of better opportunities abroad.

Pappenheim thus attacked not only the rigid rabbinical and Hassidic orthodoxy in Galicia, but she also called for a new evaluation of the status of women in general and a new image of the Jewish woman in particular. As an independent person, she should assume responsibility in the state and in the Jewish community:

'The morality of Jewish women and girls, this pillar on which our people's indestructible endurance and power of regeneration is based, is indeed being threatened – but not only by the women from Galicia.'[8]

---

5   Bertha Pappenheim: Zustände in Galizien (1908). In: Heubach: Pappenheim, pp. 119–128, here p. 124.
6   Pappenheim: Zur Lage, pp. 50, 52.
7   Pappenheim: Zustände, p. 124.
8   Bertha Pappenheim: Die 'Immoralität der Galizianerinnen' (1901). In: Heubach: Pappenheim, here p. 19.

2 'Adorn Marushka,
  adorn the girl,
  adorn the child
  for the white slave trader!'
  Rumanian folksong. Caricature
  by Pascin from 'Simplicissimus'
  [from Eduard Fuchs: Sozialgeschichte der Frau. Die Frau in der Karikatur. Munich 1928].

It had to become the responsibility of women to become 'an isho chashuwo – a moral woman.'[9]

Bertha Pappenheim supported the ideals of the bourgeoise women's movement in Germany. She transferred their demands for equal opportunities in education and for political equality for women to the Jewish situation:

> 'And what about women as "guardians of the family", where are they [...] the thinking woman of today must be even more conscious of the fact that, apart from the values of the individual's personality, which are developed and tended to within the family, the family is the central element of the state and the nation. The modern woman is therefore confronted from all sides with tasks designed to preserve the state and the nation.'[10]

Pappenheim considered Zionism a 'liberating and invigorating' power, though at the same time it was limited and did not keep its promises. 'The Zionists are poor builders. Their castles in the air have no foundations.' Certainly there were positive signs, such the reformed heder, the reading societies and libraries as well as the fostering of sociability. Ultimately, however, the Zionists despised the practical petty activities and the education of the people, and instead preached slogans and theories. This was also true of the Zionist women. It was, of course, commendable for the Zionists to turn to the women for their cooperation 'for the salvation of a people', but this activity remained limited. 'Do they [the Zionist women, S.St.] explain to women and girls what beyond the limits of their intellect is no longer a women's *question* but a women's *movement?*' Just as with men, there was a 'propaganda of words without a propaganda of deeds'. The Zionists would have to work towards educating 'modern women' with 'characteristics and strengths, who adapting to the stage of today's social development are capable of following the rapidly moving current'. Nevertheless: despite their modesty, the ideas of Zionism might be able to win over the youth.

---

[9] Bertha Pappenheim: Zur Sittlichkeitsfrage. In: Heubach: Pappenheim, p. 114.
[10] Bertha Pappenheim: Über die Verantwortung der jüdischen Frau (1910). In: Heubach: Pappenheim, pp. 137–144, here p. 143.

'Perhaps some day history will recognize the mission of Zionism as the fanfare that awakened the sleeping spirits, so that the Jews would rouse themselves and keep pace with other peoples in the performance of their duties and in claiming their rights. Then Zionism would have achieved a great purpose, even if the creation of a Jewish state remains a utopia.'[11]

Bertha Pappenheim recognized that the causes of Jewish prostitution and the white slave trade lay not only in the social conditions, but that they were related to the inferior position of women in society. '[...] in the eyes of Jewish law a woman is not an individual, not a personality [...]', but rather only serves 'the purpose of reproduction'.[12] The insights she acquired as a result of observing the conditions in Galicia proved to be a problem affecting all Jews. With her views she set off a bitter debate among Jews, and had to endure not only charges of exaggeration and ignorance of the law, but also of 'denigrating Judaism' and inflicting 'moral damage'.[13] Although non-Jewish groups used her writings for spreading anti-Jewish propaganda – as the National Socialist smear sheet 'Der Stürmer' was to do in 1935 – Bertha Pappenheim was convinced that only addressing the problem openly could help eliminate its causes and this would be the best means of confronting anti-Semitism.

---

[11] Pappenheim: Zur Lage, pp. 81–84.
[12] Bertha Pappenheim: Zur Sittlichkeitsfrage. In: Heubach: Pappenheim, pp. 111–112; Heubach: Zur Lage, p. 52.
[13] Heubach: Pappenheim, pp. 115, 116.

Heiko Haumann

'Present-Day National Work' in the Shtetl: The Beginnings of Zionism in Galicia

Galicia remained a centre of Eastern Jewry even after the partitions of Poland. The legal situation proved to be a little more favourable for the Jews under Austrian rule than in the Russian Empire, although they were obliged to accept a number of restrictions to their way of life which were intended to 'civilize' them. They were accorded an equal legal status in 1867. The economic conditions tended to be worse than in Congress Poland, for example, so that the impoverishment of the Galician Jews assumed even larger proportions. This process was intensified by the fact that the Jews, as mediators between town and country, between landowners and peasants, were not only caught up in growing social and economic conflicts but also stood between all the fronts in the national and religious differences of the Poles, Ruthenians and German Austrians, Catholics and Russian Orthodox adherents (as well as members of the Uniate Church) which were coming to a head.

Most of the over one million Jews who lived in Galicia and in the Bukovina before the First World War – about eleven per cent of the total population – belonged to the Hassidim. Numerous Zaddikim dynasties gathered their supporters around them. Besides this, rabbinism also preserved its force. Life in the shtetl was characterized completely by religion and tradition. The fact that the world of the Galician shtetl remained alive is due in no small measure to a rich literary legacy. One only needs to mention as examples: Leopold von Sacher-Masoch [1836–1895], Karl Emil Franzos [1848–1904], Hinde Bergner [1870–1942?], Samuel Joseph Agnon [1888–1970], Alexander Granach [1890–1945], Bruno Schulz [1892–1942], Joseph Roth [1894–1939], Soma Morgenstern [1896–1976], Manès Sperber [1905–1984], and Rose Ausländer [1907–1988].

But again and again this world with its difficult material conditions and its circumstances which were often felt to be restrictively rigid challenged its inhabitants to break out. Messianic hopes of redemption as well as the Haskalah both found their centres here, and after 1867 the enlightment movement strengthened, especially since the relatively well-developed education system offered a favourable basis for it. Part of these Jews then identified themselves with the German culture, another with the Polish, and a third saw the future not in acculturation but in recalling on national Jewry.

Against this background and in view of the nationalistic atmosphere that had been aroused, it is not surprising that Zionist ideas caught on at an early time. In 1883 in Lvov the first national Jewish organization, the 'Mikra Kodesh' society – the 'Holy Assembly' – was founded, which principally supported Jewish students and soon changed its name to 'Sjon'. In 1887 a 'Hovevei Zion' group followed in Drohobycz – the centre of oil production with a strong Jewish proletariat. Along the lines of the Vienna students' fraternity 'Kadimah', in the foundation of which Galician students in particular also participated, similar groups formed in Lvov and other towns. New pro-

1 Jewish market trader selling textiles to his Polish countrymen.

fessional associations laid emphasis on Jewish history, culture and the national idea, especially among young people. The 'Sjon' group called for an improvement in the material situation, an expansion of education – here first and foremost of Judaic learning – tuition in Hebrew and aid for the Jews in the Russian Empire and in Romania, so that they could emigrate to Palestine. The national idea provoked the fierce opposition of those willing to assimilate, especially since they felt threatened in their positions by the considerable political activities of the young national Jews – also in the religious communities – and they feared new conflicts in Galicia's nationalities struggle.

At first the attitude of the 'Sjon' towards an independent Jewish state in Palestine remained equivocal. The majority of its members were probably thinking in the first place of a cultural-national identity. That gradually began to change, after Alfred Nossig [1864–1944], who was also to play an important role as an artist, joined up with the society at the end of the 80s. He had originally worked for an acculturation with Polish society, and only at the beginning of the 80s – continuing the Polish-Jewish symbiosis marked by Messianism, especially represented by Adam Mickiewicz – had praised Poland as the reborn Israel. Disappointed by the growing anti-Semitic tendencies, he then turned to national Jewry, however. Now he clearly set as his aim a Jewish sovereign state in Palestine and became the major theorist of Jewish nationalism in Galicia. As early as 1886, he clearly stated that the conflicts between Jews and non-Jews could only be eliminated if the Diaspora was ended and the majority of Jews created a state in their former home. Nossig's radical views were, however, controversial, even among Zionists. The prevailing opinion aimed at resettling the poorer and endangered Jews in Palestine as colonizing farmers and at cultivating a national existence in Galicia itself. The national idea was thus also to be developed in the very country in which one lived. This is what constituted the specific characteristic of Zionism in Eastern Europe and was connected

2   Street scene in a small borough.

with the development of a new self-esteem and solidarity in Eastern Jewry.

The two schools of thought appeared even at the First Zionist Congress in Basel. The Galician Jews were represented by a strong delegation. Abraham Salz [1864–1941], the delegate from Tarnów, was elected Second Vice President of the Congress – a clear sign of the importance that was attached to this group. He also gave a report on the situation of the Jews in Galicia and vividly described their 'plight' and the 'attempt to expulse' them. The 'enormous poverty' was confirmed by Mayer Ebner [1872–1955] from Czernowitz, who talked about the Bukovina. To redress these grievances, Salz advocated intense political activity in the religious communities. Moreover, he called on the Jews from the Western countries to give help in their own interest to contain emigration from Galicia to their countries.¹ There was no mention of Palestine, of a Jewish state. Salz was concerned solely about improving conditions.

The appeal to the Jews of Western Europe is remarkable: this is possibly an indication of the conflict, or at least of the distance, between the two Jewish cultural societies. Alexander Hausmann from Lvov, 18 years old and thus the youngest Congress member, on looking back, still very strongly felt 'the struggle of views' which broke out between the Western and Eastern Jewish delegates. He counted Herzl, whom he actually admired, among the Western Jews and accused him, with his aim of a homestead in Palestine, of having forgotten the 'present-day national work in the Golus', i.e. in the Diaspora.² On the other hand, Herzl read out a petition sent to Congress by the Galician 'Society for Colonization' in which the signatories declared their readiness to settle

---

¹   Zionist-Congress in Basel (29., 30. und 31. August 1897). Officielles Protocoll. Vienna 1898, pp. 21–28, quotations p. 27 (Salz), pp. 56–61, quotation p. 59 (Ebner).

²   Warum gingen wir zum Ersten Zionistenkongress? Ed. by the Berliner Büro der Zionistischen Organisation. Berlin 1922, pp 45–47, quotations pp. 46, 47.

3 Jewish girls working as embroideresses.

in Palestine if constitutional and material guarantees were given. For this purpose they had even collected money.³

Both lines converged in that the emigration to Palestine was generally supported. As early as 1892, Salz had set up the first Galician colony there – 'Machnajim' – of which Sigmund Bromberg-Bytkowski became the director. Later there was to be a severe conflict with Herzl about the colonization projects. At the same time, however, there was active involvement in politics. At the beginning of the 90s, the 'Jewish National Party' was founded to enable them to present themselves independently in Galicia. The national Jews, concentrated particularly in Lvov, considered the Zionist movement in Galicia to be the strongest and perceived themselves as not being adequately represented by the Vienna Zionists. But the latter did not want to tolerate a split in the organization and in 1893 followed suit by forming

the 'General Austrian Jewish National Party' in Cracow. By recognizing the decisions of the Galicians they managed after all to create a common organization. In 1895, with the 'Political Society', they created for themselves a body in order to improve the co-ordination of the country's policies. Their efforts were directed towards achieving equality, as a people and a nation, with the other peoples in Galicia and in the whole Habsburg Empire as well as national autonomy. This attitude of most of the Galician national Jews, for whom the 'homestead' in Palestine did not have top priority, repeatedly encountered the sharp criticism of the 'pure' Zionists. The concrete proposals to reduce poverty among the Jews, to promote economic activity and to raise standards of education and culture resulted, on the other hand, in substantial support by the Jewish population. The influence of national Jewish thought in the workers' movement was also considerable. In the Austrian parliamentary elections of 1900/1901, for the first time, the Zionists won a seat in the Galician constituency of Brody. In 1907, in the

³ Zionisten-Congress, pp. 109–110.

4 Jewish and Ruthenian stands at the market of Kolomea.

first general and direct elections for the House of Representatives of the Imperial Council, four Jewish politicians from Galicia and the Bukovina were elected and formed the 'Jewish Club'. It was now difficult to imagine political discussions in the Habsburg Empire without recognizing Jewish nationality and national autonomy – with Yiddish as a language of its own. In the end it could not be achieved: the Austrian government feared a weakening of German culture and civilization if the Jewish population formed a separate nationality. Nevertheless, this right was conceded for the Bukovina in 1910.

In the elections of 1911, the Zionists and national Jews sustained a defeat, however. This was due to the efforts of the assimilated and orthodox Jews to prevent them by all means from scoring another victory. They entered into alliances not only mutually but also with Polish parties. An analysis of the election results shows, however, that the supporters of the Zionists among the Jews were still surprisingly numerous. In the shtetls they met with vehement rejection from the population, which was influenced by the rabbis or Zaddikim. Although the colonization of Palestine was supported, only the religious Zionists of the Mizrachi managed to score any successes. Besides this, those who were beginning to free themselves from traditional ties frequently voted for the Zionist candidates. An indication of the strength of the Zionists is also given by the report from Galicia on the Tenth Zionist Congress in Basel in 1911, which mentions 103 societies and 13 youth organizations with a total of 10,000 members.

Desanka Schwara

'Lo se haderech!' – 'This Is Not the Way!'

Eastern Jewish Zionists and Palestine

The Beginnings

In the course of the 19th century it became more and more apparent that many Jews, especially the enlightened, were no longer willing to accept the terrible living conditions and injustices which they had suffered as 'God's will'. Enlightening ideas and efforts made in order to be assimilated on the one hand and denial of equality, 'civilization' efforts and oppression on the other, led, almost inevitably, in a time in which thoughts of 'national awakening' were omnipresent, to the idea of Jewish nationalism. Zionism began to become established in Eastern Europe. For the first time, the idea was voiced that the Jewish people also had the intrinsic right and the obligation to demand rights.

The realization of this idea was supported by older thoughts of finding a place for the Jewish people, as well as early Zionist writings as produced by Judah Leib Gordon, Eliezer ben Judah, Peretz Smolenskin, Moses Leib Lilienblum and Judah Leib (Leon) Pinsker. Under the pressure of the pogroms of the years 1881 and 1882 in the Russian Empire, the already Russianized Jewish youth began to find its way back to Judaism. In some cities small groups of followers of the Zionist idea formed. They called themselves 'Hovevei Zion'- 'Lovers of Zion'- and their movement 'Hibbat Zion'- 'Love of Zion'. Their aim was the emigration to Palestine, to Erez Israel.

With the aid of the Hovevei Zion, Jewish students had been able to settle in Palestine in 1882. Due to the persecution in Russia their decision was reflected in the name of their group, which they then put into action: 'Bilu', 'Beit Yaakov Lekhu ve-Nelkhah' – 'Arise house of Jacob, let us go!'. As early as 1888 the English-Jewish lawyer E.N. Adler noticed the strong presence of Eastern Jews in Palestine and particularly in Jerusalem: 'Half of the Jews [...] are Russians [...] and they have managed to impress their individuality on their surroundings very strongly.'[1]

Pinsker and other early Zionists joined the Hovevei Zion. Attempts were made to join the existing groups together and to organize the colonization in Palestine. At the beginning of the eighties, groups started up in Bialystok, Warsaw, Vilnius, Brest, Moscow, Kharkov, Minsk, Kovno, Libau, Kiev, Poltava, Saint Petersburg and Riga. Further groups were founded in Romania and Galicia. In Russia itself the work in the Hovevei Zion soon encountered major political difficulties. Nevertheless, the second conference of the Hovevei Zion, which was largely concerned with the question of the legalization of the Palestine company, took place in Eastern Europe ten years before the First Zionist Congress in Basel. One year later the third conference was held. In 1890 the statutes of the 'Gesellschaft zur Unterstützung jüdischer Ackerbauern und Handwerker in Syrien und Palästina' (Society for the Support of Jewish Farmers and Craftsmen in Syria and Palestine) of the Odessa Committee were endorsed by the Russian government.

---

[1] E.N. Adler: Von Ghetto zu Ghetto. Reisen und Beobachtungen. Stuttgart 1909, p. 26.

1 Polish and Jewish orphans in the streets of Vilnius.

Ahad Haam, one of the major Eastern Jewish Zionists, had visited Palestine in the meantime and criticized the colonies there. In his work 'This Is Not the Way!' – 'Lo se haderech!' he came to the conclusion that Palestine, as a country, could not solve the Jewish problem, but it could solve the problem of Judaism as a cultural unit. He directed heavy criticism at the Western Jewry. In his essay 'Outward Liberty and Inner Slavery' he wrote that the emancipated Western Jews thought themselves to be free citizens but were in actual fact slaves who in the process of assimilation had given up the freedom to have their own people's identity for the sake of their 'host peoples'. Because they feared being suspected of inadequate love for the fatherland, they denied the unity of the Jewish people and its connection to Palestine. The consciousness of the national belonging and the longing for a national rebirth had to be awakened within the people itself by way of a 'reanimation of their hearts'. As a consequence, the 'Bnai Moshe', the 'sons of Moses', founded in Odessa in 1889, began their cultural work in the Diaspora under the leadership of Ahad Haam. Not until Herzl's 'Judenstaat' (Jewish State) and the Zionist Congress in Basel did the impetus arise to merge the different Zionist organizations in Eastern Europe and to join them together with the Western Jewish associations in common pursuit of political goals.

Persecution by the Authorities

The Russian authorities equated the Zionists with socialist movements and persecuted all such political groups without pity. They pursued every tip-off and allegation, most of which were anonymous. Propaganda material in particular from the 'Poalei Zion'- the 'Workers of Zion'- the Socialist Zionist Movement founded in 1906, and other socialist groups was confiscated. They prose-

2 Jewish inhabitants during the fire in Szawle.

cuted the authors and distributors of brochures and stored copies of the documents in police files. As a result it is possible to find the calls of the Poalei Zion to the Jewish population to emigrate to Palestine or at least to pay into the fund for colonization or, for those who could not afford this, to work for it instead. Appeals were made to the Jewish proletarian ideals of the working class.[2] And in fact many poor Russian Jews spent their last ruble to at least purchase a share of the 'Jewish Colonial Trust' or to participate in the illusion of helping to rebuild the homeland by paying the 'shekel'. The secret notes of the police are evidence of the attempts to monitor the Zionist organization and to keep those people who had been identified as Zionist sympathizers – and this included numerous women – under control.

The Habsburg monarchy was not more positively inclined to the Eastern Jewish Zionists than the czarian empire. Those police files from Galicia which still exist prove that politically active Jews, regardless of whether they were being pursued for their connections with Zionism, socialism or anarchism, usually were accused of being spies. The supposition that the Galician Jews wanted to be reunited with their fellow believers in the Russian empire was the basic reason for the persecution, so it is not surprising that they were then accused, after the start of the First World War, of being pro entente.

Zionism wanted to rebuild and strengthen the self-confidence of all Jews, including those in the Diaspora. This was the main reason why the Russian Minister of the Interior, Pleve, voiced criticism and tried to justify the merciless persecution of the Zionists. By his account he advocated Zionism as long as its goal was to make the Jewish population to emigrate from Russia. Ideological

[2] Archiwum Państwowe Lublin, Zand. Pow. Bialsk. Sign. 124, pp. 1–3. All translations from Russian: D.S.

Zionism, on the other hand, was in his view based on the national feelings of the Jewish population and such a development stood in conflict with the interests of Russia.

The regional police administrations in Russia received strict orders on several occasions about not allowing the establishment of 'any Zionist organization'. In 1911 on the occasion of the World Conference of the Poalei Zion in Vienna, a confidential enquiry went out to all those who were responsible for 'political investigations' asking who had taken part in this conference as a Russian delegate and inquiring about the conclusions the conference had arrived at.[3]

In 1913 another confidential circular was sent to all police administration departments within the government. In this it was stated that a new conference of the Poalei Zion was planned, this time in Cracow, but the programme was not known. 25 delegates were expected from Russia, and others would come from other countries. Directly afterwards, additional meetings were planned to be held in Vienna. In all the cities of Russia collections had already been organized. Special stamps were being sold to this end, on which Palestine was pictured with the heading: 'Eternal Issue for the Jewish People'. The police were requested to find the delegates, to observe them up until their reaching of the border and to search them upon their return to Russia. After this they should be arrested and interrogated. 'If enough material evidence could be gathered, these persons should be arrested for their affiliation to a revolutionary political party.' Full stop. This was followed by the signatures of those responsible. It does not go on to state what the ensuing procedure should be in such cases. Apparently, whether on purpose or by accident, the police administrations were then free to do as they saw fit.[4]

In September 1913 the Russian authorities finally had the report on the final objectives of

[3] Lublin: pp. 16, 19, 20.
[4] Lublin: p. 37.

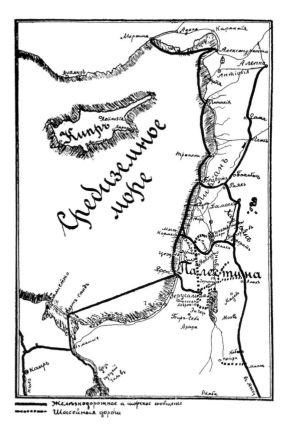

3   Map of Palestine from one of the several brochures for Eastern European emigrants. Not the state frontiers, but rather the traffic routes are marked in order to show the potential of the country for development.

Poalei Zion. One of the things that must have alarmed the Russian secret service were probably the statements calling for mass meetings and the political education of the people. These lines are underlined in the files. The reports of the Poalei Zion regarding pogroms and anti-Semitic legal processes were noted with great interest, as was the joint front which resulted from alliances with other socialist groups such as the 'Bund'. 'Thus a vicious circle was created: those Jews who were persecuted most terribly by the old regime were forced into the freedom movement, for which black Russia avenged itself via the pogroms, which only caused the Jewish population to become even more revolutionary.'[5]

In addition the innumerable brochures which kept the Russian Jews informed as to the events at the Zionist congresses are also evidence for the Zionist propaganda activities. The statements of the most famous Russian Zionists, usually arguing the necessity of 'practical' Zionism and criticizing a hesitant passive 'political' approach, were printed. Information for emigrants gave further details about Palestine. The 'Society for the Support of Jewish Farmers and Craftsmen in Syria and Palestine' published several scripts such as 'Jewish Colonies in Palestine', 'Palestine from a Sanitary-Medical Point of View', 'Palestine Studies. Second Zionist Congress. Critical Summary' and reports about Jewish settlements in Palestine or collections of letters of the first settlers could be found in Russian.

The Particular Situation of the Eastern Zionists

The differing patterns of life would appear to be the reason for the decisive points of controversy between the Western and Eastern Zionists. The reason why the Western Jews were prepared to proceed with diplomatic means and to come up with political solutions was because in view of the Eastern Jews they were already too assimilated and not threatened tangibly enough by their environment. Ahad Haam criticized Herzl because he placed too little emphasis on Jewish culture and because he made too many concessions to the 'European states with their cult of the governing nationality'.[6] One section of the Hovevei Zion fought Herzl, especially the section from Galicia, because he wanted to stop the colonization in Palestine until such time as a Jewish state was legally secured. Despite the national states in Europe which had been formed shortly beforehand, nobody at the time ever thought that in the Middle East people could one day also call themselves 'nations' to validate mutual claims to the countries that they lived in. The only thing that had to be done, or so they thought, was to come to an agreement with the ruling powers.

Due to the diversity of cultural traditions and differing perceptions of the purpose of Zionism, it is hardly surprising that the delegates from Eastern Europe reacted with rejection, even indignation to suggestions that a country other than Palestine could become the 'homestead' for Jews. This conflict reached its peak during the Uganda project between 1903 and 1905.

The Zionist Eastern Jews saw the idea of abandoning Palestine, even if it was to be for only a short time, as an unforgiveable betrayal. Not even the pogroms and dangers which most of the Russian Jews were subject to, and an end to which was not in sight, changed their devotion to Palestine. A Jewish state, they said, could only be founded in Palestine for historical and spiritual reasons.

At the time of the Seventh Zionist Congress in Basel in 1905, Herzl had already died, not only was the Uganda Scheme rejected, but a compromise was arrived at which allowed for the 'systematic development of our position in Palestine' alongside the diplomatic-political activity in accordance with the demands of the opposition under the leadership of Menahem Ussishkin [Usyshkin, 1863–1941] and Chaim Weizmann [1874–1952]. The practical Palestine work of the Hovevei Zion was reinforced and the Odessa committee led by Ussishkin was reorganized. After the Russian Revolution in 1905 many young people, especially those with socialistic ideas, left for Palestine and founded the workers' movement there. The method of colonization up to that time, by which the Jewish colonists as owners of the land had Arab workers work the soil, was considered to be in contrast to the Zionist principle

---

[5] Simon Dubnow: Weltgeschichte des jüdischen Volkes. Von den Uranfängen bis zur Gegenwart. 10 Vols. Berlin 1925–1929, vol. 10, p. 592.
[6] Dubnow: Weltgeschichte, vol. 10, p. 331.

4 Jewish women on their way to the synagogue.

which stated that the ground of the homeland was to be tilled by the work of their own hands. The Zionist youth movement 'Hashomer Hazair', founded in 1913 in Galicia and in the Russian Empire, associated the Zionist ideology with revolutionary tendencies. After the First World War, the demand was made, particularly by the youth, to actively work for the realization of Zionism by moving to Palestine. In 'Halutziyyut', in being pioneers, national and socialist elements joined which shaped the kibbutz movements. Controversy about the 'practical' and the 'political Zionists', in whose hands the financial power rested, continued to occur for quite some time, however.

The ideas of Ahad Haam increasingly influenced the political and cultural activity, even in the Diaspora. The realization dawned that a large number of the Jews would remain in exile and attempts were made to maintain and strengthen ties with Jewish people in all countries through policial, social and cultural work. Ahad Haam was of the opinion that the rebirth could only be a gradual, organic process and that every hasty move destroyed the important values of the movement and placed the issue itself in great danger. Palestine should become the 'spiritual centre' of Judaism. This was also an approach to the movement of national Jewry which was widespread in Eastern Europe and which did not place emigration to Palestine in the foreground but instead demanded protective rights for minorities as well as cultural and even territorial autonomy in the countries they lived in.

Valerii Yulevich Gessen

Yulii Gessen: A Jewish Historian and His Forgotten Connection to Zionism

Yulii Gessen was born in Odessa in 1871 as the son of a businessman. His father was engaged in building up the shipping on the Dnjestr river. For his efforts he was given the hereditary rank of honourable Citizen of Russia.

Yulii Gessen's literary and scientific work began in 1895 with the publication of stories and poems based on Jewish subjects. In the following year he moved to St-Petersburg, where he started publishing articles and books about the history of the Jews in Russia in 1898. He became famous with his 'History of the Jewish People in Russia' in two volumes and as publisher and author of many articles in the 'Jewish Encyclopedia', which was published between 1908 and 1913 in 16 volumes and which remains a standard reference work.

So far not many details of Gessen's connection to the Zionist movement were known. He himself made no comments on this between 1917 until he died in 1939, because he was afraid of repressions of the Bolshevic government. Still there is a close connection. Presumably, he already participated in circles in Odessa which occupied themselves with Palestine and he met Leon Pinsker and Ahad Haam. In 1899 Gessen participated in the Third Zionist Congress in Basel. We know this from letters of his friend Sergei L. Cinberg [1873–1939]. He writes that Gessen had travelled to Basel privately where he intended to write several articles about his impressions for the Russian newspaper 'Rossija'. On August 5th, Cinberg wrote, that his friend 'following his heart, had accepted Zionism and was not secretive about it'. Later he reported that he received a postcard from Gessen with the message that he had already met Herzl. Another hint of Gessen's connections to Zionism is a postcard, sent from Karlsbad on July 16, 1907, to Gessen's father-in-law. On the back there is a photograph of Yulii Gessen and his wife Adel' Iosifovna together with Ahad Haam and the Zionist Aleksandr I. Braudo [1864–1924] who possibly were on their way to the Zionist Congress.

As early as 1898 Gessen published his translation of Leon Pinsker's brochure 'Auto-Emancipation' in St-Petersburg. Gessen commented on this pamphlet as follows:

'But just this necessity of having to overcome such difficulties [on the way to emancipation] moved a group of scholars to burn the ship behind them, to extinguish within themselves the smallest spark of the old belief in the brotherhood of people [...] The people's consciousness has awakened. The ambitious ideas of the 18th and 19th centuries have not gone unnoticed, even in our people. We do not only feel our identity as Jews, we also feel that we are human beings, we want to live like humans, we want to be a nation just like all others. And if we really do wish for it, we have to free ourselves from this yoke and be courageous. But to do so it is absolutely essential that we entirely want to help ourselves.'[1]

Inspired by the 'Society for the Spreading of Education among Russian Jews', Gessen published his extraordinary work about Judah Maccabee. Under his leadership Jerusalem was reconquered in 167 B.C.E. and the temple 'purified'

---

[1] Yulii I. Gessen: Istorija evreev v Rossii. St-Petersburg 1914, p. 340f.

1   Aleksandr I. Braudo, Ahad Haam, Yulii Gessen and his wife Adel' Iosifovna.

of the desecrations of the Pagan cults. In its memory, Hanukkah is still celebrated today. Gessen's book obviously had Zionist motives.

'Our – distressing and happy – past is a great teacher, which teaches us to live, to suffer and to hope; it teaches us about our spiritual property, the traces of our forefathers, to appreciate it and not to swap it for deceptive prosperity. [...] Judah died for the future and for the spiritual ideal in whose name the Jews courageously accepted the worst sufferings for 2000 years. Since this time they have never stopped living this national life by drawing their moral heritage from the past.'[2]

[2]   Yulii I. Gessen: Iuda Makkavej. Istoričeskij očerk. St-Petersburg 1901.

Erik Petry

The First Aliyah

(1882–1904)

'Aliyah' is the Hebrew expression for the emigration to Erez Israel and means 'Rise' or 'Ascend'. Ascending to read the Torah in the synagogue, which is a great honour for all those who are called upon to do so, is also called Aliyah. The choice of this word shows that the Jewish emigration to Erez Israel has a unique position and is connected with a rise of personality.

Following the pogroms which broke out at Easter 1881 in several cities of Southern Russia nearly a million (by 1914) Eastern European Jews emigrated mainly to the USA, via Western Europe. However, between 20,000 and 30,000 Jews decided to emigrate to Palestine, whereto the main immigration waves took place between 1882 and 1884 and also between 1890 and 1891. Carried by the ideas of the Hibbat Zion, Jews came alone or as members of the settlement societies that were founded in Eastern Europe in 1881/82, first of all to the city of Jaffa, which was not at all prepared for so many people and whose infrastructure and social structure were soon submerged. Because of these conditions only 10,000 immigrants remained in Palestine; disappointed by the conditions they found, the others soon left the country again. By 1904, 5,500 of the remaining immigrants had decided to live in the cities of Palestine. This was the traditional way of immigration until 1882. Somehow, these citizens also belong to the First Aliyah. But in view of the ideas and effects of these 22 years, the term 'the First Aliyah' includes mainly the 4,500 Jews who settled in the new colonies, because they arrived in Palestine oriented towards the future, with Zionist ideas: they wanted to found self-supporting agricultural areas where Jewish life could be reorganized, just based on an economic and social order. Attempts to realize these ideals led to the setting-up of cooperative systems in the colonies of Rosh Pinnah and Rishon le-Zion.

Rural colonization was seen as the only rescue from the still existing anti-Judaism and the increase of violent anti-Semitism in Europe. They wanted to make Eastern European Jews aware of the threat and at the same time renew the entire Jewry. All immigrants were convinced that the reform could only start from Erez Israel. The main pillar was to form the self-confident Jewry, that turned the settlement in Erez Israel into a religious obligation. Most of the colonists were orthodox Jews with no interest in building up political state structures. Only the small group of Biluim – that in its prime never consisted of more than 27 persons in Palestine – differed from most of the other immigrants by emphasizing socialistic aims and rejecting any theocratic tendencies in the colonies.

The realization of these sublime colonization plans, however, confronted the immigrants with unexpected problems. In November 1881, fearing a Jewish national movement in Palestine, the Turkish administration surprisingly interdicted the immigration of Jews from Eastern Europe. In addition, several laws on land ownership should make it impossible for Eastern European Jews to settle in Palestine. However, the working methods of the Turkish administration and corruption made it possible to overcome these regulations.

1 A view of Rosh Pinnah.

This can be clearly seen by the large number of immigrants and the foundation of 17 colonies until 1904.

When buying land, which was made by private persons or representatives of the Eastern European settling societies, the immigrants could not be too selective and they often had to settle for ground of inferior quality, especially since their financial means were limited. The biggest obstacle for building up an agricultural economy was that the immigrants lacked any agricultural experience. They could not judge the quality of the ground, did not know what to cultivate and had no idea what agricultural products were suited to be produced in Palestine. Most of the immigrants had enormous problems with the climate, especially in connection with illnesses unknown to them, among which the life-threatening epidemic malaria was most feared. Not to mention the problems the Jewish immigrants had with the Arab population in Palestine: prejudices and misunderstandings on both sides as well as the imported ignorance and arrogance of the European immigrants towards the Arab culture often caused problems in all areas of daily life – from the joint use of a watering place to buying and selling agricultural products right through to the protection of the colonies, which was carried out by Arab watchmen for the first few years.

The colonization movement can be classified into three phases: until 1884 seven settlements were founded and one, Petah Tikvah, which had been founded as early as 1878, was deserted one and a half years later, was resettled. The second immigration peak provided the conditions for another five settlements and finally, between 1896 and 1898, four more colonies were established. Geographically also three centres can be determined, which, however, do not correspond to the foundation phases: the Judean land between the outskirts of Jaffa and Jerusalem, the area between Tiberias and the lake of Hula as well as the area of the Shefela plain south of Haifa.

From the beginning, all the difficulties hindered a thriving development of the colonies. And as the financial resources that had been set aside for emergencies were soon used up, the first colonies got into such a severe economic crisis in 1882, the very year of their foundation, that the

2 Vintage in Petah Tikvah.

leaders of the colony Rishon le-Zion had to rely on support from the outside in order to survive. Originally, they had refused this Halukkah from the Diaspora, which was already common for the population in the cities. The emissary who was sent to Europe and who initially begged for financial support in Germany in vain, was able to meet Baron Edmond de Rothschild [1845–1934] in Paris in October 1882 and to win him over for the colonization. Rothschild, a grandson of the banker Mayer Amschel Rothschild from Frankfurt, was a bel esprit, not a broker or banker. He had had a traditionally Jewish education which enabled him to identify with the idea of a colonization in Erez Israel.

Rothschild was willing to become involved in Palestine, but only under his conditions: concretely, he urged the establishment of a French administration in the colonies he subsidized, planting fruits selected by this administration, which meant that the cultivation of wine became predominant and that the settlements became disconnected from the market prices as Rothschild bought the products at a fixed price.

Although he was only actively involved in founding two settlements, he eventually supported nine settlements out of 17 completely. Hibbat Zion and the Bnai B'rith Lodge of Jerusalem also gave money to the settlements, but these organizations too were linked up economically with Rothschild.

The rigid enforcement of his conditions meant that at the end of the 19th century, Rothschild virtually ruled all the settlements. The Rothschild administration was not only involved in economic concerns, but also interfered with all social concerns of the colony as it thought appropriate. His subsidies saved the colonies from inevitable ruin and they earned him the honorific title of 'Father of the Yishuv'. Rothschild paid millions of French francs for the administrations of the colonies, and they had to give up their Zionist ideas in return. In the eighties of the 19th century, minor revolts against the strict administration occurred, but they fizzled out without any effect. The initial enthusiasm of the emigrants of when they arrived in Erez Israel then turned from fatalism to apathy. In 1898 the Zionist Leo Motzkin visited Palestine and wrote in his diary: 'The humanity, the beauty, the greatness of the struggle for independence, for human dignity and self-help were destroyed with one blow.'[1] There was not even the thought of an autarkic agriculture or of the reform of Jewry anymore. The settlers became executing planters, '[...] a herd of subordinate sheep'[2], as one critic cynically remarked in 1903, who, with few exceptions, were only busy trying to secure their own standard of living. One almost has to speak of an ambivalent development of the colonization project: although the economic situation recovered, achieved respectable results and created stability, the idealism of the settlers, that had led them to Palestine and not to the USA since 1881, was exhausted.

---

[1] Leo Motzkin: Eine Fahrt nach Galiläa (from his diary), 24 July 1898. Central Zionist Archives, A 126/22.
[2] J. B. Sapir: Der Zionismus. Brno 1903, p. 75.

Gillian Cavarero

The General Jewish Workers' Union in Lithuania, Poland and Russia

Only a few months after the first Zionist Congress in Basel in July 1897 another Jewish organization – The General Jewish Workers' Union in Lithuania, Poland and Russia (Allgemeiner Jüdischer Arbeiterbund von Litauen, Polen und Russland) – was founded in Vilnius. Even though there was presumably no direct connection between these two occasions their timing was not a coincidence. The Jewish 'Bund' like Zionism was an answer to the changes in the 19th century: the enlightenment and emancipation, social and economical changes, secularization of Messianic hopes of redemption, disbanding of traditional bonds, the crisis of the Jewish self-image, increasing anti-Semitism and the building up of self-defence. Unlike the Zionists the Bund thought that erecting a Jewish nation was not a solution to the problem. As socialists their thoughts were internationalistic. They thought that the proletariat would execute the revolution in Russia and elsewhere. They wanted to create a classless society, regardless of the religious or national background or the social, political and legal differences. Nevertheless, they came to the conclusion of regarding the Jewish people as an independent group because of their special social conditions and culture. So the Bund and the Zionists were a part of the new consciousness of Jewish mutuality, even nationality, which developed towards the end of the 19th century. On the spectrum of reactions to the new conditions the Jewish Workers' Bund can be seen as an alternative pole to the Zionists.

This context did not exist from the beginning. Although economic changes and the industrialization in the czarian empire drastically worsened the Jewish poverty, there were too few factories in the pale of settlement in which they could find work. For this reason, the 'Jewish proletariat' mainly consisted of craftsmen. Slowly an increasing number of workers joined these craftsmen. Therefore, the first Jewish socialists and revolutionaries directed their attention to the overall Russian situation.

The Beginning of the Revolutionary Movement

In the seventies the first revolutionary circles appeared in the pale of settlement. These were founded by students who, studying in tertiary education institutions, had come into contact with revolutionary illegal literature. Dissatisfied with society and the political system they met to read forbidden authors such as Nikolai Chernyshevskij, Aleksander Herzen and Dimitri Pisarev. These circles were founded by – among others – Aaron Samuel Liebermann [1845–1880] – who is viewed the intellectual father of the Jewish Workers' Union, Jakub Finkelstein and Aaron Cundelevich. In 1875 Liebermann fled the country, fearing arrest. In London he founded the Hebrew Socialist Union to continue spreading socialist ideas.

During the eighties of the 19th century a change took place in political sympathies. The industrial working force became the centre of political-revolutionary work. The intelligentsia saw its main task in convincing the workers of their importance in a possible revolution. Thus the circles were turned into night schools, where students first learned Russian so they could read the works of Marx and Engels.

The revolutionary circles worked very isolated and neglected the Jewish craftsman proletariat. Not until the beginning of the nineties did they recognize that the proletariat had a strong class consciousness and that it was organized in so-called 'Hevrot' – 'brotherhoods' much more efficiently than the non-Jewish proletariat in Russia. In 1890 they founded the Vilnius Group. 10–15 independent circles were merged together in this group which was the immediate forerunner of the Bund. It was no coincidence that Vilnius was the centre of the movement. The city was the capital of Jewish rationalism and in the centre of Jewish culture. The Jews were the biggest section of population. Here, the Christian rivalry was no threat to the Jewish proletariat.

A new impulse was given by the Polish revolutionary movement which placed more emphasis on the agitation of the masses. Initially the Jewish socialists were against this method. The cancelation of the Russian lessons and night schools would destroy an important possibility of education of the proletariat. Mainly women were against disbanding the circles. Furthermore, the agitation of the masses had to take place in Yiddish because most Jewish workers did not speak Russian. The new method was accepted despite the opposition. The time had come to turn to more active means: participating in strikes, joint 1st of May celebrations, where both political and economical aims were to be be formulated. In 1894 the pioneering works of Arkadii Kremer [1865–1935] 'Ob agitacii' (About Agitation) and Samuel Gozhanskii 'A briv tsu agitatorn' were published. Both authors were co-founders of the Bund.

Integration of 'Jewishness' into the Revolutionary Movement

Until this time, the revolutionary movement in the Russian empire had not dealt separately with the 'Jewish question'. Because of their education most of the Jewish socialists were assimilated. They spoke Russian among themselves not Yiddish. Up to a certain point they were alienated from the shtetl. They even partly despised their roots and everything connected with Judaism. Some had strong assimilatorial tendencies. Their aims included the entire Russian proletariat. They saw their work in the pale of settlements as a preparation for the revolutionary activity with the proletariat in the central industrial areas. In their training circles they prepared cadre for the Russian revolution.

This change in their orientation came about not least of all because of the decision to declare Yiddish as their language of propaganda. In order to procure the missing written material in Yiddish the socialists turned to the 'semi-intellectuals' for help. Most of these were Yeshiva students or autodidacts who spoke and wrote Yiddish fluently. Their job was to draw up the pamphlets. They were the connection between the intellectuals and the work force. One outstanding representative of the 'semi-intellectuals' was A. Litvak [actually Chaim Yankel Helfand, 1874–1932]. He started to assemble small libraries so the workers could have access to the copious works of Jewish authors from the 19th century. This discovery of Yiddish culture and literature strengthened the consciousness of the Jewish proletariat giving it a broad social basis for the Bund to be founded later. In the middle of the nineties authors such as Isaac Leib Peretz and David Pinski started to write about the Jewish workers. At the same time in 1896 and 1897 the socialist workers' newspapers 'Der Jiddischer Arbeter' (The Jewish Worker) and 'Di Arbeter Schtime' (The Voice of the Worker) appeared for the first time in Yiddish.

Founding the Bund

In the middle of the nineties the foundation of a Russian social-democratic workers' party seemed to be approaching. The Jewish socialists decided to found a party in order to make use of the well-organized Jewish proletariat. Taking strict precautions the foundation took place in Vilnius between the 25th and 27th of September (according to the Russian calendar). From outside Vilnius only members of the groups from Warsaw, Minsk and Bialystok were officially invited. Altogether thirteen socialists participated in this meeting but they never met all at the same time. They had not worked out an actual programme. The Vilnius Group dominated the meeting. The participants decided to join the Russian party as an autonomous section once this party had been founded. The Bund planned to especially represent the interests of the Jewish workers. The members of the central committee would be mainly from the Vilnius Group: Arkadii Kremer, Nahum Mendel Levinson [1867–1941, under the pseudonym Kosovskii] and Abram Mutnikovich [1868–1930, alias Gleb or Mutnik].

The name of the new organization was a cause for discussion. Of the two suggestions, 'The Alliance of the Jewish Social Democratic Groups' and the 'Jewish Workers' Union', the latter was preferred. They feared that the workers could be disturbed by the words 'social democratic'. Founding the Bund was not an alternative to the first Zionist Congress in Basel. Although Zionism was regarded as a possible rival it was not discussed at all in Vilnius. In 1901, at the fourth meeting of the Bund, they criticized Zionism for the first time as a utopia and a reaction of the bourgeoisie to anti-Semitism.

1 The synagogue in Vilnius.

The Bund, Lenin and the Russian Social Democratic Workers' Party

Because the Bund saw itself as a part of the Russian Workers' Party it acted as host as in March 1898 when the first convention of the Russian Social Democratic Workers' Party took place in Minsk within the pale of settlement. The Congress guaranteed the Bund complete autonomy on concerns of the Jewish workers. Some time later the police broke up the party. Many revolutionaries were arrested, among them many members of the central committee of the Bund. The Jewish socialists recovered from this incident rapidly however. They elected a new committee and continued their activities. The new activists all spoke Yiddish which increased their popularity among the masses.

2 Members of the Socialist-Zionist party's self-defence group, bearing arms and posters, Dvinsk, Latvia, 1905.

However the desire of the Bund to represent only the Jewish proletariat and to organize the party as a federation of national groups in accordance with the demand made in 1901 and to integrate the Jewish people into the Russian empire in a future federation of nationalities with complete cultural autonomy led to a conflict within the Russian Social Democratic Workers' Party. For the Bund this link to the consciousness of the masses was necessary to support the common class interests in the long term and to repeal national contradictions. At the second convention in 1903 the majority of the party rejected this proposition. They thought that nationalist – and anti-Semitic – tendencies among the workers could be encouraged and furthermore the unity of the proletariat and the party alike could be endangered. The representatives of the Bund left the convention due to this decision and declared their withdrawal from the organization. This decision had enormous consequences. The group around Martov [actual name: Yulii O. Zederbaum, 1873–1923] which strived for a decentralized democratically structured party of the masses and actually sympathized with the Bund except for the idea of a federative structure was weakened and became the 'minority' (Mensheviki). Lenin and his followers, approving a strictly centralized hierarchical organization under illegal conditions in the czarian empire, became the 'majority' (Bolsheviki).

The Jewish workers gave more and more respect to the Bund, among other reasons because it armed itself and opposed the pogroms which had been organized by the government. The peak of the Bund's popularity was reached during the revolution in 1905 with 35,000 members. In 1906 they reunified with the Russian Social Democratic Workers' Party. They did not approach the question of national-cultural autonomy and it was not endorsed until 1912 after the Bund joined the now independent Menshevik party.

The February Revolution achieved general political and cultural freedoms, which were, however, restricted again after the October revolution. The Department for Questions on Nationalities which was led by Stalin and – which had a separate 'Jewish Department' and the 'Jewish Section' – within the Bolshevik party exerted pressure to force the Jewish organizations to give up their independence. By 1920 the Bund had largely dissolved into the communist party. In 1921, after initial autonomy, the dissolution of the Bund was announced, however, it continued to play an important role in Poland and Romania and among the emigrants.

Milorad Andrial
Heiko Haumann

The Jews of Prague in Search of Their Self-Image, and the 'Prague Line' in Zionism

Prague was venerated by the Jews as 'mother Israel'. The Jewish community in Prague was at times the largest and most respected in Europe. Prague had one of the real medieval 'Jewish cities', a ghetto, located in the centre of the old part of the city. The improvement of the sanitary conditions in the Prague ghetto took place between 1893 and 1905.

The legislation enacted under Emperor Joseph II changed the living conditions of the Jews: the 'Toleranzpatent' (Edict of Toleration) of 1781 improved the situation of the Jews, and put an end to the humiliation of wearing the Star of David. It officially permitted them to establish and run factories as well as to lease land, but not to own land that could be inherited. In their business or trade, however, Jews were not allowed to employ Christians, nor could they hold a public office, and they were denied civil rights. The enlightened absolutism of the emperor also resulted in the controlled germanization of the Jews, the introduction of compulsory military service and the strict regulation of the educational system. With this toleration edict, Jews were no longer forced to live in the ghetto, which was abolished in 1852. Nevertheless, many Jews, especially the poorer people, continued to live there. Only the richer Jews gradually left the ghetto. It was not until 1867 that the Jews of Prague were considered equal citizens with the same rights as everyone else.

This initiated an upswing in many areas of Jewish social and economic life. The expression often heard was that of a Jewish 'economic miracle': Jews began to dominate in banking and finance, and they occupied a leading position in the wholesale and retail business, in the textile industry as well as in the press and the theatre. They also made up a considerable share of those working in professions. Because of the increasing attraction, more and more Jews moved from the country to the city. At the beginning of the twentieth century they represented roughly 6.5 percent of those living in urban areas, while their share of the population in all of Bohemia was only 1.5 percent. The improvement in their economic situation was accompanied by a stronger urge for academic education. Altogether the Jews played a significant role in the cultural field. Our present impression of the 'Jewish Prague' is still influenced by the works produced at that time and the published recollections of that period.

At the same time the situation of the Jewish religious community also began to change. The Jews did no longer depend on it because of economic or personal reasons. Many stopped participating in religious activities or even converted to one of the Christian denominations.

All of these changes tore the Jews from their traditional way of life and upset the way they viewed themselves. The radical transformation they experienced became even more intense through the fact that they were drawn into the growing differences which developed between Germans and Czechs. The German-speaking minority in Prague belonged almost exclusively to

1 The 'Altneuschul' and the Jewish city hall, around 1900.

the upper class, and even during the period of accelerating industrialization it occupied the best positions. This class, however, increasingly saw itself having to face competition from an aspiring Czech bourgeoisie. More and more this social 'competition of displacement' was interpreted as a fierce national struggle. Many Czechs regarded the Jews as Germans, especially since a greater part of them were actually closely bound to the German culture, and the affluent Jews considered themselves as belonging to the German middle class. In the second half of the 19th century, the conflict escalated. In order to mobilize the masses, Jews and Germans, and Jews and capitalists were often treated as being the same, and hatred for Jews was stirred up.

Czech writers contributed to this by publishing anti-Semitic documents. Thus in 1870 the distinguished poet Jan Neruda published a brochure entitled 'Fearing Judaism', in which ideas appear about an international Judaism that has its marionettes dancing in all the countries of the world. Another important Czech poet, Svatopluk Chech, wrote a satirical poem in 1882 entitled 'The Wandering Jew'. For him the Jew was the usurer and exploiter, the villain, who only wants to become

2 Pinkasova ulice (Pinkas Street) in Prague with a 'matzoh-bakery', around 1905.

rich and in addition even takes the side of the nation's adversary. In the same way Petr Bezruch linked social and national motives in his 'Songs of Silesia.' Therefore the fact that in crisis situations the pent-up anger would explode in outbreaks of violence against the Jews time and again is not surprising. At the end of 1897 this developed to such an extent that in Prague the military had to be called in and martial law imposed.

The anti-Jewish atmosphere was aggravated even more by a trial for ritual murder, in which the accused person was actually convicted by the judges, first in 1899 and once again in 1900.

Only few prominent Czech figures expressed their support for the Jews in public. Among these were the writers Joseph Svatopluk Machar and in particular Jaroslav Vrchlický with his poetic work 'Bar Kokhba'. Staunch opponents of anti-Semitism also included the Czech Social Democrats and the philosophy professor and future president of Czechoslovakia, Tomáš Masaryk. He spoke out emphatically against the ritual murder trial and as a result had to temporarily discontinue his teaching activities.

For some of the Jews, namely those from the middle class, this position gave cause to draw closer to the Czechs – and especially to the ideas of the Social Democrats. A factor that contributed to this was the anti-Semitism that was spreading even throughout the German bourgeoisie. The German University in Prague in particular developed into a stronghold of enmity toward Jews. German students and their organizations played in this regard an especially ignominious role. In 1871 the German August Rohling, a German and a Catholic theology professor, who taught in Prague, published a book entitled 'The Talmud Jew', in which he used partly falsified passages from the Talmud in an attempt to prove that ritual murder has its roots in the Jewish religion. Although the forgery was revealed in a trial, the alleged proof remained popular and even in the 20th century was referred to again and again by anti-Semitic groups.

The Jews' attempt to seak the support of the Germans or the Czechs failed to bring them a secure place in the society. The abortive efforts to assimilate and the degrading behaviour of some Jews who acted more German and more anti-Semitic than the Germans themselves, produced a feeling of 'self-hatred' among Jews of the younger generation. Franz Kafka is an excellent example of this. Others found a direction in socialism and sought the essence and origin of Jewishness in Eastern Jewry.

In this search for orientation, Zionism too increased in popularity. After beginning in a modest way in 1897, some of its supporters joined together in the students' organization 'Bar Kokhba'. The writer and philosopher Max Brod [1884–1968], the historian and political scientist Hans Kohn [1891–1971], the journalist Robert Weltsch [1891–1982] and his cousin, the philosopher Felix Weltsch [1884–1964] as well as the philosopher Hugo Bergmann [1883–1975] were among its most prominent members. The most important thing for them was above all to discover Jewish culture; the creation of a Jewish state in Palestine was actually of secondary importance for them and only later moved to the foreground. As a guest of the organization, between 1909 and 1911 Martin Buber recited his famous 'Three Speeches on Judaism' and thus left his mark on the cultural Zionism of the 'Prague line'. The writings of Ahad Haam also exerted a great influence. The sympathizers of political Zionism were concentrated in the students' association called 'Barissia.' Little by little interconnections developed especially via the magazine 'Selbstwehr' (Self-Defence), which began to appear in 1907.

Mainly at the urging of Hans Kohn, the cultural Zionists in Prague began quite early to concern themselves with the concrete circumstances in Palestine, and for this reason they often had to accept the accusation of 'heresy'.[1] In an essay written after the First World War, Kohn made the unequivocal observation that 'Palestine today [...] is actually an Arabic country'. He disagreed with the basis for their endeavours, namely that the Jews had a historical right to this land. Only the fact that there had always been Jewish colonies there and that now many Jews for the love of Erez Israel felt drawn to it, was a justification for immigration.

'Although this does not give the Jews the right to take the land away from the Arabs, it does indeed give them the right to settle down on unoccupied land next to the Arabs.'

He emphasized the following with great insistance:

'We are dependent on a relationship in peaceful and friendly harmony with the Arabs.'

By no means may we proceed in a 'chauvinistic-imperialistic' manner and feel like 'a dominating, stately people'.

'Would not all our pathos against our oppressors be ridiculous if we – no longer oppressed but now in power – were to endeavour to deprive the Arabs of their rights and their national identity?'

---

[1] Robert Weltsch, quoted in: Wilma Iggers (ed.): Die Juden in Böhmen und Mähren. Ein historisches Lesebuch. Munich 1986, p. 239.

He protested vigorously against the arrogance of those who considered themselves the 'owners' of the land – be they Jewish or Arabic.

'No land belongs to a particular people; it belongs to those who live and work there peacefully – and in Palestine this will always not only be Jews, but also Arabs.'[2]

As a logical development, in 1926 Kohn was among those who founded 'Berit Shalom' – the 'Peace Alliance' – in Palestine, which supported the idea of a binational state consisting of Jews and Arabs. He condemned the development in Zionism which in his opinion was going to bring on disaster.

The 'Prague Line' in Zionism was highly significant in the search for a Jewish identity and in the development of Jewish self-awareness. It was not a coincidence that it was Robert Weltsch who called out to the German Jews on April 4, 1933, 'Wear it with pride, the yellow patch!'[3] The idea of emigrating to Palestine, on the other hand, met with no response among the majority of the Jews in Prague. In spite of all the hostility directed toward them, they felt at home in the 'Jewish atmosphere' of Prague, in 'their' city. There was a joke that circulated widely at that time:

'What is Zionism? Zionism, that's when one Jew persuades another one to donate money so that a third one can pay for the trip to Palestine.'[4]

---

[2] Hans Kohn: Zur Araberfrage. In: Der Jude 4 (1919/20), pp. 566–571; as quoted in Wilma Iggers (ed.): Die Juden in Böhmen und Mähren, pp. 232–237.

[3] Jüdische Rundschau, 4 April 1933, as quoted in: Konrad Kwiet and Helmut Eschwege: Selbstbehauptung und Widerstand. Deutsche Juden im Kampf um Existenz und Menschenwürde 1933–1945. Hamburg 1984, p. 219. Later Weltsch expressed the opinion, however, that it would have been better to have caused them to emigrate immediately instead of encouraging an attitude of defiance.

[4] Iggers (ed.): Die Juden in Böhmen und Mähren, p. 226.

Martin Trančik

Between Old and New Land: The Steiner Family in Pressburg

In the 19th century and until the Second World War, around four to five percent of the Slovakian population was Jewish. They did not concentrate in one big city to such an extent as the Jews in Bohemia in Prague for example, but lived in numerous villages and small cities in the Slovakian provinces. The Jewish Slovakia can be seen as stronghold of orthodoxy. Although during the 19th century several modern secularized forms of life were adopted, the religion in its orthodox form remained a determining element of the Jewish life in Slovakia until the time between the two world wars.

The most important Jewish community was in Pressburg (Slovakian: Bratislava; Hungarian: Poszony). Here, at the beginning of the 19th century, Rabbi Moses Schreiber – better known as Chatam Sofer [1763–1839] – founded his world-famous Yeshiva. He was an uncompromising supporter of traditional Judaism and opposed to any kind of reform. During the revolution in 1848 the Jews in Pressburg were given the right of free choice of domicile and their segregated living area outside the old city walls was abolished. The emancipation of the Jews in the entire Habsburg realm in 1867 was followed by legal equality for the Pressburg Jews as well. Shortly afterwards, they split into an orthodox community and a small reformatory one, called 'neological' – a course of events that in similar ways could be observed in the Hungarian part of the Dual Monarchy.

As Germans, Hungarians and Slovakians the inhabitants of Pressburg belonged to the three different nationalities. Between about 1850 and 1945 each one of these nations succeeded in shaping the city more than the two others at one stage or another. Although the Jewish population nearly found itself between the fronts it could also keep its identity in this multinational society without being placed under the pressure to adapt by an omnipotent group. The story of the Pressburg family Steiner can thus be seen as an example of a family in which there were both orthodox Jews as well as Zionists.

The Steiner family had resided in Pressburg since about 1840. Sigmund Steiner [1821–1907] was the first of the family to move from Kojetein in Moravia to the city. He and his wife, the widow Josephine König-Bendiner [1814–1890], ran a library that was linked to an antiquarian bookshop. Their son Hermann [1849–1926] learned the trade of bookseller in Leipzig after passing his Abitur (secondary school diploma). After his return from Leipzig, he extended the antiquarian bookshop of his parents to a book and music shop, which became the most significant in the city. In 1877 he married Selma Goldberger [1856–1924] who came from Galicia. They had ten children. At the turn of the century, the Steiner family had already an esteemed position in the German-Jewish bourgeoisie of their hometown. Of course the family spoke German, but it did neither assimilate to the German nor to one of the other two nations in Pressburg. Hermann Steiner was a much more enthusiastic supporter of the neo-orthodoxy, in accordance with the ideas of Samson Raphael Hirsch [1808–1888] who – in contrast to Chatam Sofer – tried to bring together a life

1 The Steiner family around 1900, three generations. From left to the right, standing at the back: Siegfried, Moritz, Max, Wilhelm (with a mustache), the bookseller Hermann Steiner and Margit. In the middle, standing: Nelly and the bookseller's wife Selma Steiner. Sitting in the middle, with his youngest grandchild Josephine on his lap, the teacher and bookseller Sigmund Steiner. On his left and his right in school uniforms, Gustav and Józsi Steiner.

strictly governed by the Torah, with a secular education.

In the year of the First Zionist Congress in Basel, a new 'Shiur' – a Talmud class – for young businessmen was founded in Pressburg. From this course a local branch of Pressburg Zionists, 'Ahavath Zion', emerged in winter 1899. Hermann Steiner and his three oldest sons joined this association: the bookseller Wilhelm [1878–1948], the high school teacher Moritz [1880–1942] and the lawyer to be, Dr. Siegfried Steiner [1883–1942].

Like his son Moritz, Hermann Steiner was temporarily chairman, and he represented the association at the Seventh Congress in Basel in 1905. One year before, in summer 1904, the First World Congress of the religious, Torah-faithful Zionists, the 'Mizrachi', had taken place in Pressburg. Hermann Steiner participated as a member of the board for educational questions, his son Siegfried wrote the shorthand minutes of the meetings. The religious Zionists tried to unite Jewish religion with Zionism. But within the scope of Zion-

2 The synagogue of Pressburg at the Fischplatz, in the back the Coronation Cathedral, around 1900.

ism they were never more than merely a small minority. The Steiners, however, remained dedicated to Mizrachi.

Wilhelm Steiner was a delegate of the 'Ahavath Zion' at the Eighth Zionist Congress in 1907 in The Hague. After his return, he held an enthusiastic speech in front of the association, the closing thoughts of which were:

'Oh, and again we can hear the terrible pogrom cry from Russia – the water is rising – let us at least save the future for the sinking race! Standing proud let us teach them to fight and not to beg! We bring them the greening twig of hope – determined Zionist work has already fashioned the rescuing ark which should lead us out of the Golus! Arise! Arm yourselves for the journey! [...]'[1]

In the first place, emigration should be made possible for people like the Steiners, but their efforts were spent on those Jews whose life was in immediate danger. Wilhelm Steiner, however, had never seen Palestine.

Little is known about other Zionist activities of the Steiner family before the First World War. None of the Steiners had ever been a 'professional Zionist'. Their Zionist activities were done in addition to their profession. This included a family visit to the Pressburg city theatre on Hanukkah 1899 to watch a staging of Herzl's play 'Das neue Ghetto' (The New Ghetto) which was shown during the first Maccabi celebration. The Steiner family probably also participated in the Hebrew literature association that was founded in the same year.

After the First World War the new Czechoslovakian republic came into being with Pressburg as the most important city. In this restless time of the transition from Hungary to Czechoslovakia, Jewish soldiers, returning from the war, founded their own guard, to protect the Jewish population of the city from riots. But then they integrated quickly into the democratic state and social order of Czechoslovakia.

In the time between the wars, Hermann Steiner's children started their own families and persued their own careers. His three sons Wilhelm, Max [1887–1942] and Józsi [1895–1942] became booksellers, Siegfried became a lawyer and Gustav [1893–1944] became a physician. His daughters Margit [1889–1929], Nelly [1891–1944] and Josephine [1899–1944], a pharmacist, married a jeweler, a constructional engineer and an accoun-

---

[1] Wilhelm Steiner: Referat im Ahawat-Zion-Verein über den 8. Zionistenkongress. Bratislava 1907.

tant, respectively. When Hermann Steiner died in October 1926, the 'Pressburger Zeitung' referred to him as a 'genuine', a 'veritable Pressburger'. The city already had become the intimate, native 'old land' for the family. But even now the Steiners remained actively involved in Zionism. The family members joined the local branch of the Mizrachi in Pressburg, which by now was separated from the 'Ahavath Zion'. Siegfried Steiner even became their chairman and between 1919 and 1939 he held several honorary functions for the Czechoslovakian Mizrachi Zionism.

What did it mean to be a Zionist? Siegfried Steiner and his brothers and sisters had a cousin in the city Moravian Ostrau, the lawyer Dr. Rudolf Goldberger [born in 1910]. In the twenties and thirties he was a dedicated Zionist himself and is living today in Kiriat Motzkin in Israel. He comments on the Zionist activities in the Diaspora in the time between the wars, as follows:

> '[...] but just as Zionism at that time was defined in a spiteful joke: a Zionist is someone, who collects money from B, so that C can emigrate. And that's just the way it was. But it had not obliged anyone to anything. The Steiners gave and supported [...] I don't wish to say that we were simply enjoying the feeling of clubbiness. There was some of that perhaps, but it was also a statement, it was solidarity [...], but all things being equal, I should today be a lawyer in Moravian Ostrau. I mean, this is purely hypothetical, but that's how I had pictured it for myself. I will continue to be a very active Zionist for another 20 or 30 years and help those from Poland – for it was always like this: the poor Polish Jews cried out that they wanted to emigrate. We have to help them and the Carpathian Russians (Ruthenian), who were as poor as church mice, we have to help them. We don't need help, we are safe and secure here [...] Sure, there were Fascists. But we did not have any reason to be afraid, we had the feeling of being at home here [...]'[2]

In a world such as that of the bookseller family Steiner in Pressburg it was still not a logical consequence that being active in Zionism meant moving to Palestine. Zionists should collect money and even give donations to support different development projects in Palestine – schools, agricultural or handicraft production facilities – and to make emigration possible for others. This also included acquiring exit and entry permits. In this respect Diaspora Zionism was also an expression of charity towards poor Jews and towards those who were threatened with persecution in Poland, Ruthenia or Russia. This combined with the cultivation of the national identity and – in the Mizrachi – also the religious identity. So the children of Siegfried Steiner and of his brothers and sisters in Pressburg joined the youth organization of the religious Zionists – the 'Bnai Akiwa' – where they among other things learned Hebrew. That is what Theodor Herzl must have thought, when he wrote in his 'Jewish State': 'The poorest will go first to cultivate the soil.'[3]

At a later time, that was his plan, the more prosperous should follow. In the Steiner family there was an enormous interest in Palestine. In 1935 the bookseller Max, his wife Lily and the physician Gustav Steiner traveled for one month to the Promised Land and stayed there for Pessah. So they probably came closer to the rising Zionist 'New Land' than others of their fellow Zionists. Today the members of the family say that at that time they even considered purchasing real estate in Palestine.

After the 'Münchner Abkommen' (Munich Agreement) in 1938 and fully after the formation of the Fascist Slovakian state in March 1939, life for Jews in Slovakia completely changed. Anti-Semitism became a part of the official policy. After Hanukkah in 1938 Max Steiner wrote to a friend in Palestine:

> 'Now what chances do you think a public library has in Jerusalem or Tel Aviv these days, a music shop [...], in what language do the people there read their novels?'

---

[2] Interview with Dr. Rudolf Goldberger, Kiriat Motzkin, 23 April 1994.

[3] Theodor Herzl: Der Judenstaat. Versuch einer modernen Lösung der Judenfrage. Quoted here from the English edition New York 1988, p. 93.

Max Steiner knew that above all agricultural and skilled trades were needed:

'I would feel most comfortable in the countryside near a larger city, so that after a certain time, maybe later, I could spend part of the day in the city practising my original profession.'[4]

The British authorities scrutinized the emigration to Palestine closely. At that time Max Steiner was 52 years old and had no experience in agriculture or any trade. He had almost no chance of receiving an entry certificate.

Max Steiner's brother Wilhelm had a daughter named Reline [1922–1942]. In February 1939 she received such an entry certificate. She was even exempted from the actually compulsory preparation camp – the 'Hachsharah'. But her father Wilhelm did not want to let her go. Reline's brother David Sigmund, who is today living in Jerusalem, explains his father's reaction as follows:

'But my dear sweet father did not want to let her out into the world alone on any conditions. He said: "You don't send a girl alone into the world."'[5]

Here we can clearly see the position once again between 'old and new land'. Without any doubt Wilhelm Steiner felt deeply affiliated to Zionism and sent Reline to the religious Zionist youth movement like her brother David Sigmund. But their daily life was equally determined by the attachment to family and home, by the expectation of finding security in the place where one had lived for a long time. Reline was more able to free herself from traditional ideas and saw the future much more clearly as can be seen in a letter to her parents in February 1939: 'I know that a father wants what is best for his child, but what do you consider the best? The circles are getting smaller and more restricting until, God forbid, they are tight around one's neck.'[6]

The life of the Steiner family, having been active in Zionism in Pressburg for nearly 40 years, was interrupted by the extermination machinery of the Nazis and their accomplices. In both deportation waves in 1942 and in 1944/45 in which the Slovakian Jews were killed, numerous members of the Steiner family were to be found. Reline Steiner died in Auschwitz. Selma, daughter of the bookseller Max Steiner, joined a group of partisans as a nurse during a revolt against the Fascist Slovakian government. She was probably arrested, interrogated and shot in November 1944. Wilhelm Steiner survived the war and died in Pressburg in 1948. Between 1945 and 1949 most of the surviving family members emigrated to Erez Israel.

---

[4] Max Steiner's letter to his wife Bella, undated, but written after Hanukkah 1938. Private archive of Zevi Steiner, Jerusalem.
[5] Interview with David Sigmund Steiner, Jerusalem, 14/15 April 1994.
[6] Reline Steiner writing to her parents Wilhelm and Josy Steiner, 21 February 1939. Private archive of David Sigmund Steiner, Jerusalem.

Peter Haber

'The Castle of Zion Shines Far down the Banks of the Danube'

The Difficult Beginnings of Hungarian Zionism

Only seven delegates from Hungary participated in the First Zionist Congress in 1897, and none of them came from the capital Budapest. At first these two facts seem astonishing given that at the turn of the century not less than 830,000 Jews were living in Hungary, which represented nearly 5% of the population. In Budapest as much as a fifth of the population at that time was Jewish.[1]

One look at the varied Hungarian-Jewish history of the 19th century may explain why Zionism received hardly any positive reaction in Hungary during these decades, but had rather to contend with hatred and mockery.

Since the 18th century many Jews had immigrated from Moravia, Poland and from Galicia, which had become Austrian. They largely found positions as intermediaries between city and country, and had strong connections to the aristocracy, which had already agitated for their equality in the first half of the 19th century. Some Jews succeeded in improving their social status. They then normally moved to Budapest and merged with the established Jewry. They overtly looked upon the Hassidic and orthodox Eastern Jews from the country as a 'strange' element, capable of disturbing their harmonious co-existence with the Magyars. In 1849 the Hungarian National Assembly decided to grant the Jews equality in political and religious matters. This resolution was, however, postponed and after the Habsburg Empire had put down the Hungarian revolt, the imperial military government blocked the Jewish emancipation. Only after the Austrian-Hungarian agreement in November 1867 did the Hungarian parliament grant legal and political, but not religious equality to the Jews. Not until 1895, after the so-called Reception Law, did the Hungarian Jewry gain confessional equality.

In the meantime the Hungarian Jewry had quarreled so bitterly at a congress in 1868/69 that they split into three groups: the reform-oriented neologists, the orthodox and the so-called 'status-quo-ante' group, who wanted to preserve the situation which had existed before the congress. The neologists made up the largest group.

By the end of the 19th century most of the Hungarian Jews were assimilated into the Magyarian culture: In the census of 1890, 63.8% of Jews declared Hungarian to be their native language. Many Jews even converted to Christianity. This relatively quick assimilation, which was not hindered even by occasional incidents of anti-Semitism, had great consequences for the further development of Hungary. In the second half of the 19th century, several Jewish entrepreneurs influenced the economic development of Hungary. In 1910, for example 85% of self-employed and 42% of employees in the banking and finance industries considered themselves to be Jewish.

---

[1] Gyula Zeke: Statisztikai mellékletek (1735–1949). In: László Bányai, László Csorba et al.: Hét évtized a hazai zsidóság életében. 2 Vols. Budapest 1990 (= Vallástudományi tanulmányok 4/5), pp. 185–199, here p. 188.

1 Herzl's birthplace in Budapest on the left beside the big synagogue of the Dohány utca.

Jews also represented a disproportionately large number of the country's lawyers (45%), doctors (49%) and journalists (42%). Another sign for the Hungarian-Jewish symbiosis was the high number of Jews who were elevated to the nobility: between 1800 and 1918, 346 Jewish families were awarded this status, most of them at the beginning of the 20th century.

This environment was accordingly difficult for the development of Zionist ideas. Additionally, in 1896 Hungary celebrated the so-called 'acquisition of land' a thousand years earlier. This millenial celebration also occupied the Hungarian Jews. Dr. Samuel Kohn, chief rabbi of the neologst community of Budapest and one of the most influential Jewish persons of the time, published a theory in 1884 about the descent of Hungarian Jews. According to this publication, Hungarian Jews were descendants of the Khazaric tribe of the Kharbars who, according to Kohn, had come to their present home together with the Hungarians. Consequently, the Hungarian Jews were descendants of the Khazars that had converted to Judaism, and were not descendants of the Jews who once lived in Erez Israel. This thesis was readily accepted by many historians at the time since it corresponded to the Hungarian government's magyarization policy, which aimed to integrate the Jews with the Hungarian majority. The idea of a national Jewish movement and a return to Palestine became a threat to the assimilated and magyarized Jews.

This is why parts of the Jewish Hungarian press reacted with great irritation when it was announced that a Zionist congress would take place in Basel:

'We have our blessed Hungarian homeland, we do not seek another. Here we are free and legally emancipated. We are integrated into public life, [...] we are surrounded by love and respect; and we too love and respect the nation as a whole with its individuals, who have freely accepted and acknowledged our religion, this much hated, persecuted, slandered religion, as one of the Hungarian religions.'[2]

For the assimilated Jews in Hungary there was no doubt whatsoever where their homeland was:

'Where our God is with us, that is our homeland, that is where our Temple is.'[3] And: '[...] The King of Jerusalem has become our King and the lights of the castle of Zion shine far down the banks of the Danube.'[4]

But other voices were also raised in the Hungarian Jewish press, although only seldom. The 'Hungarian Weekly' for example wrote:

'Finally Zionism has succeeded in being heard here in Hungary as well. Not that it has laid a foundation here or conquered the hearts of the Jewry or even of a small number of them; no this is still not the case. However, it is quite sufficient and an inestimable gain for Zionism that the Jewish people in Hungary are speaking of it and giving vent to its goals and desires.'[5]

János Rónai, a lawyer from Balázsfalva in Transylvania, was one of the seven Hungarian participants in the First Zionist Congress in Basel. He reported there about the situation of Hungarian Jews:

'In Hungary, an independent and strong state, liberty and justice are as unshakeable as a rock.'[6]

For him too, who was probably the most important Hungarian Zionist of that time, there was no chance for the new movement in Hungary:

'Taking this into account, I can only assume that active Zionism has no ground beneath its feet in Hungary.'

He went on to say, however, that educational work was necessary. Only Zionism, he pointed out, can solve the problems of immigration in the East of Hungary while at the same time observing that Zionism and patriotism do not necessarily have to be mutually exclusive.

But even this was already too much for the newspaper 'Egyenlöség' – 'Equality' – the most important newspaper of assimilated Jews in Budapest:

'The two hundred people who attended the Basel Congress represent two hundred people, no more and no less. Or does anybody know if, for example, even the tiniest little community actually sent Dr. János Rónai of Balázsfalva, so that he could speak about our situation at the meeting in Basel?'[7]

On the other hand the newspaper 'A Jövö' – 'The Future' – published articles by Rónai. Several times it let the belligerent Zionist state his piont of view:

'I can report that I have come to the conclusion, through discussions with my colleagues at the congress, that orthodox and progressive Jews all over the world see the Jews of Hungary as their brothers and sisters who have become unfaithful due to their arrogance, who are short-sighted, devoid of feeling and allegiance and for whom they feel contempt and bitterness.'[8]

---

[2] Adolf Silberstein: A sionizmus. In: Egyenlöség 16 (1897), No. 28, pp. 1–2.
[3] Adolf Silberstein: Mennyiben lehetünk mi sionisták. In: Egyenlöség 16 (1897), No. 37, pp. 1–2.
[4] Silberstein: A sionizmus.
[5] M. Dornbusch: Wie sollen sich die ungarischen Juden dem Zionismus gegenüber verhalten? In: Ungarische Wochenschrift 3 (1897), No. 24, pp. 2–3.
[6] János Rónai: A czionista kongresszus befejezése. In: A Jövö 1 (1897), No. 35, pp. 3–4.
[7] Miksa Szabolcsi: Álláspontunk a sionizmussal szemben. In: Egyenlöség 16 (1897), No. 36, pp. 2–3.
[8] János Rónai: Értsük meg egymást! In: A Jövö 1 (1897), No. 36, pp. 1–2.

2 The first Hungarian edition of the 'Judenstaat' was published probably around 1919 in Budapest.

At this time there was no organized Zionist movement in Hungary. But after the Congress, the first local groups appeared: in Pozsony (Bratislava), Kolozsvár (Cluj), Nagyszombat (Trnava), Kassa (Košice), Szabadka (Subotica) and even in Budapest. One year after the First Congress there were approximately 30 Zionist groups in the entire Hungarian Kingdom.

Not until after the turn of the century in 1902 was the provisional National Committee of the Zionist movement in Hungary founded in Pozsony. Among the members of the Committee were János Rónai, Samuel Bettelheim (Pozsony) and Béla Oesterreicher (Boldogasszony). All three were re-elected at the First Zionist Congress in Hungary in 1903, where also the 'Magyar Cionista Szervezet' (Hungarian Zionist Union) was founded of which János Rónai became the first president.

In the same year the Zionist students' association 'Maccabi' was founded. 'Maccabi' became one of the most important institutions of the Hungarian Zionist movement with 1,000 members in 1913. During the First World War there were no activities, because nearly all leading members were drafted into the army.

Even Theodor Herzl, having been born in Budapest in 1860 and having lived there for the first 18 years of his life, knew that Hungary was a difficult place for the Zionist movement. In 1903 Herzl wrote a letter to the Hungarian publicist Ernö Mezei. The sentences he wrote became cruel reality in the Shoah, a few decades later:

'I could do without the Hungarian Jewry if I knew that its patriotism would protect it from the plague of anti-Semitism. I do not wish to speculate on misery, but destiny will catch up with the Hungarian Jews too, the more brutal and harsh, the longer it takes, the more influential they are, the further they will fall. There is no escape.'[9]

---

[9] Letter of Herzl of 10 March 1903. In: Theodor Herzl: Letters and Diaries. Ed. by Alex Bein et al. Vol. 7. Frankfurt a.M., Berlin 1996, p. 77.

Peter Haber

Zionism in Austria

The history of Austrian Zionism is virtually identical to the history of Viennese Zionism. At the end of the 19th century, the capital of the Habsburg multinational state was an important intellectual centre, where not only literary, philosophical and artistic movements, but political groups likewise – such as Zionism – had their origins.

In Vienna, in May 1882, the first Austrian Palestine colonization association was founded: the 'Ahavath Zion'. Its aims corresponded to those of the 'Hovevei Zion' associations in Eastern Europe. The ideals of the association were written in the statutes: 'The association will support Israelite colonialists in Palestine to the extent of its means.'[1] In 1881 the persecution of the Jews that started in Russia gave rise to the foundation of 'Ahavath Zion'. Among the main founding members were Nathan Birnbaum, Ruben Bierer and Peretz Smolenskin. It was also Birnbaum who coined the term Zionism in 1890.

'Ahavath Zion' existed for only one year. The tension between the Orthodox and the 'Enlightened' quickly became critical and the orthodox Rabbi Salomon Spitzer withdrew from his position as president. Many orthodox members left the association together with him.

A circle of non-orthodox members of the 'Ahavath Zion' based around Nathan Birnbaum, Bierer, Smolenskin and other active Jewish students founded a Jewish national students' fraternity in autumn 1882. In March 1883 the authorities approved the foundation of this fraternity. The first orderly plenary meeting of the 'Kadimah' took place in Vienna on May 5, 1883. This step was a reaction to the exclusion of Jewish students from German national student associations. The motto of the Kadimah was to 'fight assimilation, encourage Jewish self-confidence and colonize Palestine'.[2] After Herzl's 'Judenstaat' (Jewish State) was published, the Kadimah collected thousands of signatures, to persuade Herzl to become the leader of the Zionist movement. Several years after the foundation of the Kadimah, they decided to become a duelling fraternity. This was a pattern for many Jewish national student fraternities which were founded in several European cities within a very short time. They were a reaction by the Jewish students to the increasing anti-Semitic enmity of their Christian fellow students.

After the large upswing of the Zionist movement in the last years of the last century Vienna became the true capital of Zionism. Herzl, who had lived in Vienna since he was a young boy, based the most important offices of the movement in his adopted country: for example, on June 3, 1897, the first edition of the newspaper 'Die Welt' (The World) was published in Vienna and remained 'central publication of the Zionist

---

[1] Quote: Adolf Gaisbauer: Davidstern und Doppeladler. Zionismus und jüdischer Nationalismus in Österreich 1882–1918 (= Publications of the Commission of Modern History in Austria 78). Vienna 1988, p. 40.

[2] Quote: Adolf Böhm: The Zionist movement up until the end of the World War. Tel Aviv 1935, p. I/136.

1 Theodor Herzl with Viennese Zionists in the Café 'Louvre' in the First district. Photograph from 1896.

movement' until the outbreak of the First World War.³

In addition, the 'Keren Kayemet Le Israel' – 'Jewish National Fund' – and the 'Action Committee', which had been instituted at the First Zionist Congress in Basel, also had their headquarters in Vienna. In 1909 two dozen Zionist fraternities already existed, most of them in Vienna. They were organized in the 'Zionistische Landesverband' (Zionist State Association). In 1913 the Eleventh Zionist Congress was held in Vienna. Nevertheless, after the death of Herzl in 1904, Vienna lost its significance again because the important Zionist institutions were transferred to Cologne.

³ Böhm: The Zionist Movement, p. I/179.

Erik Petry
Anatol Schenker

Preconditions and History of Zionism in Germany

During the century of emancipation legislation between 1780 and 1871, the idea of the return to Erez Israel lost its meaning for the German Jews. The legal equality made an economic rise into the middle class possible. Still existing limitations in state administration, army or education were seen as anachronistic phenomena which would disappear with time. German Jews, often in an exhibition of exaggerated patriotism, tried to gain respect in the German society as 'German citizens of Mosaic faith', by engaging in nearly every social-cultural and political field. But in 1871, after the foundation of the Reich, a very exclusive German-Christian society developed which refused Jewish citizens the right to 'be German'. Furthermore, theologically based anti-Judaism turned into racially defined anti-Semitism, which determined the supposed 'foreignness' of Jews as natural and unchangeable.

Jews in Germany were thus forced to redefine their identity. During the difficult and lengthy process, several alternatives appeared. One part of the Jews reacted to the hostility by assimilating, which often ended in their abandoning the Jewish faith. Others searched for an internal-Jewish new orientation and became religious. The neo-orthodoxy attempted to combine the faithfulness to the Torah and to the traditional interpretation of religion with a large degree of secular education. Alongside with the move into the socialist movement for which the Jewish question was less important than the class question and which could be solved with a world revolution, Zionism represented a further alternative. Until the end of the 19th century, Zionism did not manage to improve its status beyond that of a minor movement, although early Zionist projects had already been propagated for quite some time. All attempts to convince the German Jews of the idea of agricultural colonization of Palestine or to acknowledge the Jewish nation, remained just as unheard as the warning voice of Rabbi Hile Wechsler in 1881 as he called the colonization of Palestine the only protection from deadly anti-Semitism.

This development only started to change in 1882. The colonies founded in Palestine were in a bad financial situation and had to search for sponsors in the early autumn of 1882. The settlers had in mind the influential and prosperous Jewish community in Germany, which they paid respect to and admired in a somewhat naive way. However, most of the German Jews were not interested in supporting the colonies. They did make donations to the cities of Erez Israel, but ignored settlements as they had the reputation of being Jewish nationalist. Only a few were willing to support the settlements. Several organizations were founded to this end with the Hibbat Zion aim of advancing the settlements but partly also with political aims. But all of these groups except for the 'Esra', founded in 1884, soon disappeared.

The first concrete Zionist activities started in Cologne. In 1890 the lawyer Max Isidor Bodenheimer [1865–1940] published his 'Vision – eine grosse zionistische Dichtung' (Vision – A Major Zionist Poem). In 1891, followed by the brochure 'Wohin mit den russischen Juden' (What to Do with the Russian Jews?), which made him popular among the Zionists practically overnight. Bodenheimer was the son of a family from Stuttgart. Despite his totally assimilated upbringing, he adopted the ideas of Hibbat Zion at a very early age. So he remained closely linked to the issues of 'colonization' and 'Jewish nation', even after 1891. He published several articles and became acquainted with the Hovevei Zion organization in Berlin before he finally founded the 'Verein behufs Förderung der jüdischen Ackerbaucolonien in Syrien und Palästina' in 1894 (Association for the Promotion of Jewish Agricultural Settlement in Syria and Palestine) together with David Wolffsohn.

1 Max Isidor Bodenheimer [1865–1940].

Also David Wolffsohn [1856–1914], born in Lithuania and having had a strict traditional upbringing, came into touch with Hibbat Zion very early, mainly because of his studies under Isaak Rülf [1831–1902] and his acquaintance with David Gordon [1856–1922], a pioneer in the new Hebrew press. Bodenheimer and Wolffsohn met for the first time in Cologne in 1892. There they found that they had corresponding ideas and started to propagate their own Zionism.

In Berlin, federations with Zionist goals were also founded from 1890 onwards, such as 'Jung Israel' (Young Israel) and the 'Jüdische Humanitätsgesellschaft' (Jewish Humanitarian Association). Gradually a dialogue between all Zionists spread all over Germany started and had become so widespread by 1896 that plans of organizing a congress, to overcome dissipation and disharmony were contemplated. In February 1896 this plan was given enormous impetus, when Herzl's brochure 'The Jewish State' was published. Wolffsohn unconditionally followed Herzl immediately, visited him in Vienna and became one of his closest advisers. Meanwhile Bodenheimer and his companions worked on concepts for a national Jewish association which already contained elements which later became the main point of the 'Basle Program':

'[...] thus, the final solution of the Jewish question can only be found in the foundation of a Jewish state [...]'.

The Cologne association subordinated itself to Herzl's claim to leadership, while the Berlin group, on which Herzl had placed great hopes for the spreading of his ideas, had no common position. Because of the negative attitude of the Hovevei Zion, who saw the existing colonies endangered by Herzl's ideas, Herzl decided to declare Cologne as the 'capital of German Zionism', whereby he sowed the seed for rivalry between Cologne and Berlin Zionists.

The majority of German Jews remained sceptical about Zionism. For the assimilated Jews it seemed too paradox, too dangerous to connect Jewish nationality with German citizenship. Zionism in Germany developed to a very active, but small and quite elitist movement. After the

First Zionist Congress, the Cologne association changed its form to become the 'Zionistische Vereinigung für Deutschland' (Zionist Association for Germany), chaired by Bodenheimer and representing all German Zionists. The first years of its existence were characterized by internal fights, while German Zionists, such as Bodenheimer and Wolffsohn, helped to form the World Zionist Organization. With the foundation of the 'Jüdische Rundschau' in 1902 and the takeover of the 'Jüdischer Verlag' in 1907, two institutions had been created, which were known far beyond the borders of Germany.

But the conflict between Berlin and Cologne intensified. The Cologne leaders were increasingly accused of being incapable of turning Zionism into a mass movement. This merely led to a compromise at the Seventh Delegates' Meeting in 1907: an additional central office was to be opened in Berlin. It was the task of this office to implement the decisions made in Cologne by way of a 'managing committee'. The geographical separation of the 'executive' and 'legislative' branches of the Zionist organization in Germany inevitably led to problems which lasted for many years. More and more the office in Berlin took over the leading position and showed, through its impressive preparations for the Ninth Congress in Hamburg, that the Berlin office had become the leading power of the Zionist Association for Germany. The conflict between Wolffsohn and Bodenheimer in Cologne and the Berlin office was once again aggravated. At the delegates' meeting in Frankfurt in 1910, Bodenheimer resigned from his position as chairman. The headquarters were then officially moved to Berlin. Five Berlin members were elected to the managing committee with the lawyer Dr. Arthur Hantke [1884–1955] as the first chairman. Hantke remained in this position until 1920 and proved to be one of the strongest, integrating and most important personalities in German Zionism although he is not well known today. Since the mid twenties, Hantke lived in

2   Arthur Hantke [1884–1955].

Jerusalem where he worked in leading positions in several organizations of the 'Jewish Agency' until his death.

Despite the considerable success of the Zionist movement in Germany in the years before the outbreak of the First World War, bitter debates about the right direction still took place. In 1912, the 'Posener Resolution' proved to be a victory of the 'practical' over the 'political' line. This demanded that every Zionist should have the aim of emigrating to Palestine to realize the Zionist ideal. In a time of increasing nationalism, the fight with the 'Centralverein deutscher Staatsbürger jüdischen Glaubens' (Central Organization of German Citizens of the Jewish Faith) founded in 1893 which rejected Zionism and supported assimilation, started again. In 1913 the Zionist Association for Germany adopted a constitution which prohibited a double membership in both the Centralverein and the Zionist Association of Germany. This conflict led to the foundation of the 'Reichsverein deutscher Juden' (Reich Union of German Jews) with the aim of developing a defence against anti-Semitic attacks, just as was the aim of the central organization. Due to this and other similar developments, the Zionist Association for Germany ran the risk of segmenting its power and possibilities. The 'language debate' caused bitter discussions in the 'Jüdische Rundschau', the 'Welt' and several pamphlets. The question whether the official language at the newly founded Technion in Haifa should be German or Hebrew threatened to split the Zionist movement in Germany down the middle. But there was more behind this question: Should Hebrew become the official language of the New Yishuv? The victory of the Zionist Association for Germany in 1914, in having the Hebrew language adopted, was one of the biggest successes of Zionism in Germany, and strengthened and unified the Zionist Association for Germany.

The outbreak of the First World War in August 1914 cast the Zionist movement, and consequently also the Zionist Association for Germany, into a deep crisis all over the world. On August 7, 1914, a proclamation was published, that the Jewish people should arm themselves, just like every other country that was going to war. The debate among several groups and directions in Germany had not subsided by any means but was masked by the roar of patriotic articles in the Zionist Press. It took several months until the leaders were brought to their senses. Heinrich Loewe's slogan proposed in September 1914: '[...] – in German matters German – in Jewish matters Jewish [...]' was generally followed during the entire war. There was no way of realising the 'Posener Resolution' until after the end of the war. The 'Balfour Declaration' of 1917 opened new perspectives, which were, however, only rarely exploited. Between 1919 and 1933 less than 2,000 Jews emigrated to Palestine. This confirms the persistent dissensions within the German Jewry in a time of new chances and testifies to the relative weakness of Zionism in Germany.

The years of the Weimar Republic were shaped by intensifying defence against increasing fascism. Meanwhile the conflict between the Centralverein and the partly newly founded, na-

3 Front page of the monthly 'Altneuland'.

tionally oriented Jewish organizations continued. The influence of the Zionist Association for Germany within the World Zionist Organization diminished strongly. Although it was successful in gaining political acceptance for Zionism, under the chairmanship of Felix Rosenblüth, this union was still unable to become a mass movement up to 1933. The advent of the National Socialists in January 1933 totally changed the situation: The Zionist Association for Germany and the affiliated 'Palästina-Amt' (Palestine office) became the great hope for all those who wanted to emigrate and it succeeded in helping many. At the same time, the Zionist organizations in Germany intensified their youth work and information policy, which was initially tolerated by the Nazis, but then increasingly hindered by them. Publications such as the 'Jüdische Rundschau', which was able to be published in Berlin until 1938, testify to the courageous engagement for the remaining rights. After the November pogrom in 1938, the Zionist Association for Germany was prohibited and dissolved. The 'Palästina-Amt', responsible for emigration, finally had to be closed down in 1941.

Patrick Marcolli

Between Tradition and Modernity: Two Jewish Worlds in England

In many respects the last century represents a turning-point in the history of the Jewish people in England. After a long period of political ostracism and persecution – first and foremost the expulsion of all Jews from England towards the end of the 13th century – the Jewish community succeeded in firmly re-establishing itself in the English society, particularly in the first years of Queen Victoria's reign, which lasted from 1837 to 1901.

A date that is referred to again and again in the integration process of the Jews into Victorian society is the year 1858. At that time Lionel de Rothschild was the first person of Jewish faith to enter the House of Commons as an elected Member of Parliament. The debate about his election – particularly the abolition of the Christian preamble in the parliamentary oath – largely reflects the lines of reasoning as they can be applied to the entire emancipation of minorities in early Victorian England. They usually ran along the party political boundaries between the Conservatives and the Liberals. On behalf of Jews only a few wealthy families intervened. The Jewish community's stance was passive, as their vital interests were not affected by the emancipation campaigns. Around the middle of the century the legal equality of the Jews had virtually been achieved.

In view of the changing patterns of life this process of political-legal emancipation was accompanied by a debate on a religious reform, in which the communities were far more interested. Back in the twenties first attempts were made to renew the organization of the synagogues and the religious service. The intention was to adapt Jewish traditions to the new age. A further aim, however, was to somehow combine or even unite the interests of Judaism with those of the state. A significant role – particularly in the external representation towards non-Jewish England – was played by the organization of the communal representation and the internal power structure. This was the background of the founding of the 'West London Synagogue' in 1842. At that time the general observation of religious regulations and practices was at a low: in 1851 only 24 percent of London Jews attended the Sabbath service. The founders of the synagogue sought to remedy this situation. They went on to reform the religious contents of the services. For the first time the use of the English language was introduced to the synagogue. In political terms, the founders' aim was also to increase their influence. Their activities meant a serious challenge both to the representative authority, the 'Board of Deputies' with its almost monopolistic position, as well as the rabbinate. The ensuing conflicts became a touchstone for the English Jews of the early Victorian period.

But the greatest challenge of the century was still to come. Between 1880 and 1914 approximately 150,000 Eastern Jews – originally intending to emigrate to the United States – settled permanently in England, the vast majority of them in London. Around 1876 the Jewish community in England comprised only about 50,000 people.

These plain figures alone can by no means illustrate the full potential for conflict. Immigration led to a social and intellectual-religious crisis among the Jewish people in England, a crisis mainly hinging on the different social structures of the long-established Anglo-Jewry and the new arrivals. Whereas the majority in the Jewish 'Establishment' were members of the upper middle class, largely secularized and integrated into the political-social system in England, most of the refugees from Eastern Europe belonged to the lower classes. Their appearance, customs and habits seemed strange, and in their faith they usually were strictly orthodox. The boundary between the wealthy London West End and the proletarian Jewish East End mainly characterized by trade was virtually a symbol of the gap separating these two Jewish ways of life.

It was from here that the problems quickly spread. Owing to the high numbers of immigrants, harsh competition soon developed that led to exploitation practices such as the 'sweating system', tantamount to a cottage industry allocating labour via a middle man, characterized by very low wages and long working hours. The massive concentration of immigrants living in the various parts of the East End led to acute housing problems and stirred up strong feelings of anti-Semitism.

Contemporary commentators – even those that were Jewish – often referred to the Eastern Jewish immigrant – although there was no truth in the matter – as the model of the 'economic man', a human being living morally and materially on such a level that most people never had been able to reach or never would, and thus consciously dodging their standard of living with the sole purpose of rapidly climbing the social and material ladder.

The reaction of English Christians to the waves of mass immigration followed similar lines as they can also be found in contemporary debates on immigration: opponents of the bourgeoisie believed that the Christian spirit of the nation was at risk and the workers feared for their economic position. These debates were also constantly used for political purposes. The conservative governments of the time which opposed immigration – often focused on this problem in order to detract attention from other – more pressing – problems. Openly anti-Semitic reactions – despite all the sabre-rattling – were relatively rare. In 1904 the hard-liners, however, finally gained the upper hand in Parliament: the 'Aliens Act' radically tightened up immigration legislation. Curiously enough, a part of English Zionists welcomed or at least tacitly tolerated this measure: they regarded Jewish integration into a non-Jewish society as impossible – just like certain forces in English society who were hostile to foreigners.

Generally, there was little enthusiasm about the immigration of the Eastern European Jews in the Jewish West End. The influx fundamentally threatened the long-cherished image of a progressive, well-adapted Judaism practised by patriotic English Jews. And yet there was a willingness to help. On the whole, the upper class of Anglo-Jewry reacted as compassionate Jewish fellow brethren and at the same time as part of the English bourgeoisie. They set up a network of charity institutions to demonstrate their philanthropical – and financial – responsibility for the needy immigrants. The idea was that the new arrivals who had no means should not be a burden for the English society as a whole and its welfare system. The English Jews were afraid of losing their social achievements and stirring latent feelings of anti-Semitism.

Consequently, the repatriation of the immigrants was promoted. The 'Jewish Board of Guardians' and the 'Russo-Jewish Committee' energetically supported the repatriation of a total of over 30,000 refugees to Eastern Europe between 1881 and 1906. The attempts to prevent Jews from emigrating from the countries in Eastern Europe in the first place, however, were largely ineffective. The chief Rabbi Nathan Adler sent a pamphlet to

1 Jews fleeing.

his colleagues in Eastern Europe in 1888, stating:

'There are many in your countries who believe that all the cobblestones of London are precious stones, and that it is a place of gold. But alas, it is not so!'[1]

Initially, the immigrants from Eastern Europe were not represented within the communal Anglo-Jewish structures, which meant that social forces went to waste. They had to be controlled and correctly channelled, if the danger of burgeoning 'subversive' movements – such as socialism – was to be countered. That is why Sir Samuel Montagu, a wealthy banker of orthodox faith in the Anglo-Jewish ruling class, set up the 'Hevrot Bnai Israel' – 'Federation of Synagogues' – in 1887. Unlike the 'United Synagogue', which was not suitable for most immigrants because of its high membership fees and its progressive reforms of the religious service, it was the intention of Montagu and those that shared his faith to set up a synagogue based on strictly orthodox ideas. The immigrants addressed were thus able to practise a kind of religious self-determination without leaving the existing structure of the communal organization – the Federation remained under the administration of the rabbinate and became the most effective instrument of social control by the Anglo-Jewry.

These conditions were indeed not very favourable for creating an influential Zionist movement. In fact, the organization did not have any great influence before 1917, when Chaim Weizmann became chairman of the 'English Zionist Federation' founded in 1899. Up to World War I only six percent of the whole Jewish population in England openly supported the Zionists. Many probably thought that the Zionist ideas were unrealistic. But what was again more important was the internal scission between the East End and the West End. The established and philanthropi-

---

[1] Quoted from: Geoffrey Alderman: Modern British Jewry. Oxford 1992, p. 114.

2 Jewish families returning to their native countries.

cal Jewry had strongly supported the 'Hovevei Zion' movement with large sums of money and thus contributed to the colonization of Palestine. But an open commitment to Zion with a national background went too far for these influential people. They saw themselves as citizens of the United Kingdom. In the East End of London the Zionist movement was able to gain a foothold, but it contained every faction possible, ranging from socialism to religious orthodoxy. This explains why externally it often seemed to be divided.

In the first few years of the 'English Zionist Federation' a Zionist leading class emerged, which was eager not to allow the movement to fall into the hands of the Jewish proletariat, seeking to prevent the danger of a social revolution under the guise of Zionism. Consequently, the very forces that had prepared a triumphant reception for Theodor Herzl – and thus for his movement – in the middle of the nineties were kept away from the reins of power of the organization. Besides, the sole concern of the Federation's leading officials was often only to challenge the Anglo-Jewish oligarchy ruling the communities. As a result, most energy was wasted in intercommunal disputes and power struggles, the origin of which can be traced back to the 'pre-Zionist age'. This did not change until World War I when the discussions about the Jewish State were given more priority.

Chris Kaiser
Patrick Kury

Zionism and Anti-Semitism in France

The Dreyfus affair is commonly seen as an important milestone in the development of political Zionism. Theodor Herzl saw this as the confirmation of his change from being an assimilated Jew to a national thinking Jew, giving him strength to pursue his idea of a 'Jewish state'. Generally the affair positively influenced the acceptance of his plan, which finally led to the First Zionist Congress in Basel. Herzl later explained that this affair turned him into a Zionist and many others suddenly realized that the 'Jewish question' could not be solved by assimilation.

Not necessarily the arrest of the Alsatian Jewish officer Alfred Dreyfus [1859–1935] on October 11, 1894, his being accused of selling military secrets to the German Reich, his sentence on December 22, 1894, and his subsequent deportation were decisive reasons for this change of mind. From the beginning, neither Herzl nor other Zionists were fully convinced of Dreyfus' innocence. Rather the fanatic anti-Semitic mood of the demonstrating masses, shouting and demanding 'death to the Jews!' was what shocked them all. This shock increased after it became clear that the evidence against Dreyfus was faked and the real spy was tried and acquitted and Dreyfus was again sentenced in 1899, although he was later 'pardoned'. And all this happened in a country that was the first to legalize Jewish emancipation in 1791, a country thought to be modern and civilized, where the social integration of Jews seemed to be the most advanced of all.

Nonetheless, this anti-Semitic mass hysteria did not come out of the blue. One clear sign could be recognized when in 1886 Edouard Drumont published a book in two volumes 'La France juive. Essai d' histoire contemporaine', which became a bestseller despite its voluminous size. In it, the author tried to prove that Jews had used their legal equality to economically take over France and to increase their control in political life. Drumont was trying to fight the existing order and trends of this time and he had obviously recognized the popularity of anti-Semitism and used it to his own ends. In doing so he made use of the common clichés of traditional Christian anti-Judaism as well as economic and racial-national-oriented anti-Semitism with reference to other authors.

Political insecurity after the defeat in the German-French war in 1870/71 and the abolition of the monarchy, anti-republican tendencies within the army, an economic depression in the eighties and scandals – the bankruptcy and collapse of the Panama Canal Trading Company in 1892, which was blamed on Jewish bankers – were a perfect foundation for anti-Semitic slogans. The contemporary comprehension of the 'Jewish question' can be seen in early Zionist scripts, which, however, cannot be seen as an answer to rising anti-Semitism.

In 1860, the historian of religion Joseph Salvador, published a study called 'Paris, Rome, Jérusalem ou la question religieuse au 19ème siècle', in which he advocated the idea of the return

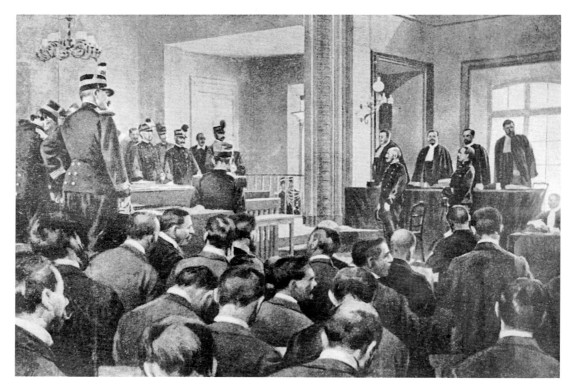

1 Alfred Dreyfus during his retrial at the courthouse in Rennes in 1899.

of the Jews to Palestine. At the same time the author and private secretary of Napoleon III, Ernest Laharanne, published a book, 'La nouvelle question d'orient. Empire d'Égypte et d'Arabie. Reconstitution de la nationalité juive', in which he came to the same conclusions. In 1864 Lazar Lévy used the same argumentation in his study 'Rétablissement de la nationalité juive'.

Growing anti-Semitism, the preparation of a Jewish-national consciousness, the shock of the Dreyfus affair, which called into question the status of Jews in France, should, or so one would think, have been the best conditions for effecting Zionist ideas in the country. But the reactions of Herzl and others were not typical and the Zionist movement was not at all successful in France. So it is remarkable that among the 94,131 emigrants to Palestine between 1919 and 1926, there were only 105 French.

Perhaps the annexation of Alsace-Lorraine by the Germans between 1871 and 1918 played an important role for the weak position of the Zionist movement in France. The Alsace was the home of the biggest Jewish community so here one would have found the biggest potential for a young Zionist movement. The main reason, however, was that the French Jews quite simply did not need Zionism. The adaptation of traditional Jewish values to republican-egalitarian values was far advanced. The term 'israélites' symbolized the successful synthesis of nation and long-established Judaism. The majority of the Jews felt integrated into the social, cultural and political life. The Dreyfus affair was merely seen as a passing episode. Dreyfus' rehabilitation in 1906 and, the separation of church and state carried out one year previously strengthened this perception as did the election of several Jewish scholars to public or prestigious positions. The teaching position of the sociologist Emile Durkheim [1858–1917] at the Sorbonne and the election of Henri Bergson [1859–1941] to the Académie Française are examples which deserve a special mention. French Jews also held political positions from very early on. During the Second World War this evaluation turned out to have been a mistake. The behaviour of the Vichy regime towards Jews made it obvious that anti-Semitism in France was more widespread than the assimilated French Jews had ever been prepared to acknowledge.

Peter Haber

'Vamos a la Palestina': Zionism among the Sephardim in the Ottoman Empire and in the Balkans

In the Holy Scriptures 'Sepharad' is used to describe a country which was later identified with Spain. Sephardim was therefore the name originally given to the descendants of those Jews who had once lived on the Iberian peninsula. Today the oriental Jews of the Middle East and the Jews of the Maghreb in North Africa are usually called Sephardic Jews as well. According to this wide-ranging definition, at the beginning of the 19th century about 40 percent of the world's 2.5 million Jews belonged to this group. However, the proportion changed radically in favour of the Ashkenazim (Hebrew name of the Jews of Central and Eastern Europe) up to the Second World War, when only about 8 percent of the 16 million Jews were Sephardic. Today roughly one-fifth of all Jews belong to the Sephardim.

Until the 15th century, 'Sepharad', the Iberian peninsula, was an important cultural centre in which Jews, Moslems and Christians lived more or less peacefully together. After the Reconquista, the reconquest of this territory by the Christians, the new rulers drove out the Jews: from Spain in 1492, and from Portugal as well in 1496. The fugitives – their number was estimated at 150,000 – settled in other Mediterranean countries; some of them made their way to the Netherlands and northern Germany.

An important place of refuge was offered to them by the Ottoman Empire, since Sultan Bayezid II [1481–1512] invited the Jews to settle in his empire. He was hoping first and foremost for economic gain: the Sephardim had centuries-old experience in trade and were familiar with many new technologies. Thus as early as 1494, they set up the first printing press in the Ottoman Empire. In Constantinople, Salonika, Adrianople and Safed, major Jewish centres had been coming into being since the 16th century. The Jews benefited from the comparatively great tolerance of the Moslems towards those of other faiths. As they had been called by the Sultan, they lived relatively safely in the empire. However – like all non–Moslems – they had to pay a special poll tax and observe certain rules regarding their clothing. The Sephardim living outside Palestine cultivated close contacts with Erez Israel. Numerous Jews went on pilgrimages to the Holy Places there.

As the Ottoman Empire began to weaken, the influence of the Christians grew in the 19th century: while Salonika and Macedonia remained under Ottoman rule until 1912, the southern part of the Greek peninsula became independent in 1830. In the course of the century, other areas were able to extend their autonomy – although formally under Ottoman sovereignty. As a consequence, tensions arose between Jews and Christians and anti-Semitism intensified. Thus in the 19th century, for example, numerous charges of ritual murder were levelled against the Jews. At the same time, great social inequalities and the growing impoverishment of broad strata of Jews led to conflicts within the Jewish community.

In the last quarter of the 19th century the Jewish population of Salonika grew to 75,000 people. The Jews dominated the economic life of the town: on the Sabbath, for example, the harbour remained closed, and the colloquial language was – and not only in the harbour – 'Judeo-Español' – 'Jews' Spanish'. The Sephardim had taken this with them in 1492 when they had to leave the Iberian peninsula. 'Judeo-Español' consists basically of the Castilian language of the 15th century, but in the course of time was enriched with numerous Turkish, Hebrew and Slavic elements. Unlike 'Judeo-Español', which still lives on in numerous variants, 'Ladino' originally referred to the language of the divine service, which had its origin in the literal Bible translation and was not used in everyday life. Today, however, the everyday language of the Sephardim is also frequently called 'Ladino'.

Until the Shoah, a large number of Sephardic Jews also lived 'on the fringe' of the Ottoman Empire, for example in Bulgaria, the territory of the former Yugoslavia and in large areas of the Habsburg Empire. Vienna, for instance, was for a long time an important cultural and journalistic centre of the European Sephardim.

As in Western Europe, towards the end of the 19th century the first signs of a comprehensive societal upheaval began to emerge among the Eastern European Sephardim as well. More and more Jewish children could attend state schools, Jewish delegates were also sitting in the Turkish Parliament now, and the literary life was flourishing. But this period was not to last long: the participation of some Jews in the rebellions of the 'Young Turks' in 1908 and the occupation of Salonika by the Greeks meant that life became more difficult for the Sephardim. Many of them left the Ottoman Empire and the Balkans and settled in Western Europe, in America and also in Africa.

Incidentally, the new leading power of the 'Young Turks' was – like their predecessors – opposed to the Jewish settlement of Palestine and

1 With the returns of the theater group, the Zionist Organization 'Max Nordau' financed its cultural and sporting activities in Salonika.

especially to this country's independence. Thus the upheaval of 1908/09 by no means meant an upswing in Zionism. The Zionist movement attained greater importance especially in Salonika, where there had been appropriate groupings since 1898. It is from there that one of the few Zionist songs in Jews' Spanish from these times comes:

'Kon un trapo i un handrajo
yo a ti te va tomar.
Vamos a la Palestina, aman
Ayi 'sta muestro mazal.'[1]

[1] Personally recited by Aron Saltiel (Vienna) in Budapest on 30 November 1996: 'Even in rags and shreds [as a dowry] / I take you [to be my wife] / Oh, let us go to Palestine / For our happiness is there' (Translation: Ursina Fäh).

Zionist life between the wars was extremely diverse in Salonika, now a Greek city.

'Every suburb, every settlement, immediately had its Zionist club [...] In addition to these organizations of general [...] Zionism there were others with special political tendencies.'[2]

In Turkey, on the other hand, the cultural rights of the Jews living there – like those of other minorities – were strongly curtailed as part of Kemal Atatürk's 'turkicization policy' from 1923 to 1938. Zionist activities were officially banned, as was tuition in Hebrew.

In Bulgaria, which had become independent of the Ottoman Empire in 1878, the Zionist idea and Theodor Herzl had found enthusiastic supporters very early on. Joseph Marcou Baruch [1872–1899] already founded a Zionist grouping in Sofia in 1895. Baruch, who was born in Constantinople, tried, while studying in Berne, to convince his fellow Jewish students of the senselessness of assimilation. In 1893 he went to Vienna, where he joined the Zionist student association 'Kadimah'. When Herzl travelled to Constantinople in summer 1896, enthusiastic Zionists received him while he was making a stop in Sofia:

'In Sofia a moving scene awaited me. In front of the platform at which the train arrived there was a crowd – who had come for my sake [...] There were men, women and children there, Sephardim and Ashkenazim, boys and old men with white beards.'

Several welcoming addresses were read out in honour of Herzl.

'In these and the speeches that followed I was celebrated as the leader, as the heart of Israel and so on in effusive terms. I believe I stood there completely taken aback, and the passengers of the Orient train stared at the strange scene in amazement.'[3]

Several Bulgarian delegates attended the First Zionist Congress in Basel. Marcus (Mordechai) Ehrenpreis [1869–1951], later to become chief rabbi of Sofia, also took part in the congress. At Herzl's request, he had translated the invitation to the congress into Hebrew. In 1898 the first national conference of the Bulgarian Zionists took place in Plovdiv, the major Zionist centre in the country. Very soon the Zionists were in the majority in most of the communities. Although their great success provoked the opposition of the assimilated Jews, who tended to be members of the 'Alliance Israélite Universelle', these forces were not as strong in Bulgaria as in other countries in the region. In the period between the wars a varied Zionist life emerged in Bulgaria. The number of people who paid their 'shekels' was relatively large. During and immediately after the Second World War the Bulgarian Zionists played an important part in organizing illegal immigration operations to Palestine.

---

[2] Michael Molho (ed.): Israelitische Gemeinde Thessalonikis in memoriam gewidmet dem Andenken an die jüdischen Opfer der Naziherrschaft in Griechenland. Essen 1981, pp. 35ff.

[3] Theodor Herzl: Briefe und Tagebücher. Ed. by Alex Bein et al. Vol 2. Frankfurt a.M., Berlin, Vienna 1984, p. 358.

The First Zionist Congress in Basel in 1897

Yaakov Zur

The 'Protest Rabbis'

In 1896, for the first time, a group of orthodox rabbis joined the 'Allgemeiner Rabbiner Verband in Deutschland' (General Association of Rabbis in Germany) which had been founded in 1884. They wanted to form a joint front against 'external enemies', to fight the increasing anti-Semitic powers. Two prominent orthodox Rabbis, Selig Auerbach [1840–1901] and Marcus Horovitz [1844–1910], were elected to the five-headed board. The first important action, however, was not against the 'external' but against the 'internal enemy': against Zionism, which represented a threat to the emancipatory achievements of German Jewry. As a reaction to the announced Zionist Congress, the board published its 'protest' on July 6, 1897 (see box).

The still extant correspondence between the members of the board reveals the differences of opinion between the liberal and the orthodox rabbis with regard to the growing Zionism.[1] One major point of contention is the question of Messianism which was evoked in the first paragraph. The orthodox Rabbi Auerbach had suggested the following version:

'The efforts of the Zionist organizations to found a Jewish national state in Palestine are in contradiction to all the statements made in the Holy Scripture and subsequent religious sources about the form and the tasks of a rebuilding of the Jewish state and sanctuary foreseen for a time in the future.'

---

[1] Central Archives for the History of the Jewish People [CAHJP], M 4/1, 11 June 1897–6 July 1897. The quotes hereafter stem from this source.

'Declaration

Due to the Zionist Congress that has been called and the publication of its agenda, such confusing perceptions of the teachings of Judaism and about the endeavours of its followers have been spread that the board of the Association of Rabbis in Germany signed below, considers it to be necessary to make the following declaration:

1. The efforts of the so-called Zionists towards the foundation of a Jewish national state in Palestine contradicts the Messianic prophecies of Judaism, as they stand in the Holy Scripture and in subsequent religious sources.

2. Judaism obliges its followers to support the fatherland to which they belong, with all devotion and to serve its national interests with all their heart and all their power.

3. The honourable intentions which relate to the colonization of Palestine by Jewish farmers do not stand in contradiction to this obligation because they have no relationship whatsoever to the foundation of a national state.

Thus, religion and love of the fatherland oblige us to ask all those who have an interest in the well-being of the Jewish people not to become involved in the aforementioned Zionist efforts and especially in the congress which is still supposed to take place despite all the warnings.

Berlin, July 6, 1897.

The managing board of the
Association of Rabbis in Germany
Dr. Maybaum (Berlin), Dr. Horovitz (Frankfurt), Dr. Guttmann (Wroclaw), Dr. Auerbach (Halberstadt), Dr. Werner (Munich)'

This formulation was untenable for the liberal reform rabbi and chairman of the association Siegmund Maybaum. He attempted to find a diplomatic solution:

'The efforts of the Zionist associations of founding a Jewish national state in Palestine contradict the Messianic hopes of Judaism.'

He justified his proposal as follows:

'In this general version, this hope is not defined more precisely. Thus this statement fits *every* standpoint. Auerbach's version on the other hand, is only suitable for *one* standpoint and could, therefore, not be accepted by followers of the other party.'

We see here an example of a deliberately unclear formulation designed to accommodate all directions. Orthodox religionists who refused to join the General Association of Rabbis and Zionists alike, thus confronted this paragraph with sharp criticism and ridicule.

The most important and controversial passage was the second paragraph in which patriotism is dealt with. Here Rabbi Werner took the initiative. Obviously, the rabbi from Munich, in whose city the Congress was originally to be held, was particularly sensitive. He feared that the Zionist efforts could lead to a questioning of the Jewish love of the fatherland. On these grounds he wrote:

'2. Judaism obliges its followers to belong to the nationality of the people in whose midst they live and to love the fatherland with all their heart.'

Rabbi Marcus Horovitz did not agree with this version. He said that a Jew could not renounce his nationality,

'what should, for example, Austrian Jews do then?'

So he demanded:

'The notion of nation should be replaced by that of fatherland.'

His proposed change to the controversial paragraph was as follows:

'Judaism obliges its followers to serve the fatherland to which they belong with all their devotion and to support its national interests with all their hearts and ability.'

Thus Horovitz did not want to deny Jewish nationality but he nevertheless emphasized that the Jews, as patriots, were obliged to be true to the state in which they lived. In this view, he agreed entirely with the German Zionists of the time.

The fundamental differences between the orthodox and the liberal rabbis cannot be ignored, and again only the deliberately vague formulation, which allows different interpretations, enabled them to come to an agreement. This was facilitated by the fact that at the time, terms such as 'nation', 'nationality' or 'people' were largely unclear. In the second half of the 19th century this terminology changed fundamentally. This allowed a certain 'juggling' with the words. Thus 'nation', with which originally an ethnical, culturally emotional substance was associated, became a state and political term. With the term 'people' it was exactly the contrary. However, just how inconsistent one was in 1897 is proven by the following sentence which the Zionist Rabbi Isaak Rülf wrote in the 'Welt' of July 30, 1897:

'In fact we German Jews do not belong to the Germanic nation, but we certainly are a part of the German people. We are not Germanic but we are German.'

The consequences of this multi-meaning terminology can also be seen in Theodor Herzl's brusque answer to the 'Declaration' of July 6, which he wrote on July 16 in the 'Welt'. He entitled this article 'Protest Rabbis' – a term which then became the accepted name for the group. Herzl reacted particularly strongly to the second paragraph in which he saw a virtual denunciation. He ridiculed:

'Incidentally, one can also see that Mr. Maybaum's cradle did not stand in Germany [...] A German would never write: "the fatherland to which I belong", he would say "my fatherland" [...] You do not belong to a fatherland, it belongs to you [...] it is by no means a sophistry in the view of the Zionists: that everyone should serve his fatherland just as much as the nation to which he belongs – here, this word is correct [...]'.

Not knowing how the formulation had come to be, Herzl basically agreed with Horovitz' standpoint, but he accused the rabbis' Declaration of having a liberal point of view. With his interpretation he heightened the differences of opionion, which Horovitz had wanted to avoid. This irony of history proves that often the intention of a document is less important than the accepted interpretation. Herzl's understanding – and not the clever formulation – became the 'historical truth' in the eyes of his contemporaries and of history.

The same applies to the third point, by the way, which Herzl also ridiculed, without knowing the background and without considering that many orthodox rabbis – notably Horovitz – were themselves active in the colonization associations. With the compromise formulation, Horovitz had succeeded in avoiding the attempt of the liberals to separate colonization and nationality. For the orthodox, the work in Palestine was indeed associated with Jewish nationality, but they refused the foundation of a state, as this was dependent on God's will. This was most certainly a major difference to the attitude of the Zionists, but Herzl made the distance to the orthodox even wider than it really was with his – considering the preceding history – undifferentiated interpretation. One must say, however, that the inaccurate formulations of the 'Declaration', which were also criticized by a group of rabbis who joined together in 1885 to form the 'Free Association for the interests of orthodox Judaism', contributed to this. The Basler Rabbi Arthur Cohn finally attempted to bridge the gap between the orthodox and the Zionists with his speech at the First Zionist Congress. The significance of the religious element and the attitude toward the foundation of a state was, however, to remain controversial. In any case, the coalition between orthodox and liberal rabbis which had led to the 'protest' had not achieved its aim and proved to be untenable.

Nadia Guth Biasini

Basel and the Zionist Congress

From Munich to Basel

On March 7, 1897, in Vienna, while preparing for the First Zionist Congress, the action committee had decided that the convention should be summoned in Munich. However, the Jewish community in Munich and the spokesman for the orthodox communities and the reform rabbis in Germany voiced intense opposition to this suggestion. Consequently a decision had to be made within very short period of time, as to whether the Congress could meet in Zurich as had already been considered earlier. Theodor Herzl wrote to David Farbstein in Zurich and asked him to immediately inquire whether Zurich would be a possibility or

'which place in Switzerland would be suitable in every respect for the holding of the Congress'.[1]

Herzl's attention had been drawn to Farbstein after he had discussed Herzl's 'Judenstaat' in the magazine 'Ha-Shiloah' in 1897. David Farbstein, who came from Warsaw, was in the process of starting his career as a lawyer in Zurich after having completed his legal studies. Herzl continued in his letter to Farbstein:

'While impressing upon you the need to reply urgently to this letter, I would also like to ask you to investigate whether the holding of the Congress [would meet with opposition] on the part of the Swiss government, the Zurich municipal authorities or the Jewry of Zurich.'[2]

Farbstein advised Herzl to steer clear of Zurich and proposed Basel as the place to hold the conference. Basel seemed to be more suitable to him, as Zurich was considered to be a centre of Russian revolutionaries by the czarist government. He feared that the Russian participants in the Congress could experience difficulties due to this. As Farbstein also recalled, Herzl sent him

'letters to well-known Christian friends of Zion in Basel. In Basel Paul Kober-Gobat and his wife, both honourable, good-hearted, noble people, helped a great deal in the preparations for the Congress. My study looked like a secretariat until the opening of the Congress.'[3]

Who it was who directed the inquiry to the Basel cantonal authorities is not indicated in those files which remain extant. The board of the Jewish community had obviously not been included in the negotiations. On July 22, Herzl noted in his diary while travelling by train to Ischl:

'The most interesting event since the last time I made an entry while travelling in a coupé has been the transferral of the Congress from Munich to Basel that has become necessary. I wasn't overly happy about going to Munich, which had always seemed unsuitable to me, and which I had only accepted in obedience to the majority vote of the preparatory commission. This is why I used the pitiable patriotic protests of the president of the community in Munich to move the Congress to Switzerland. Basel was chosen after research made by a new, courageous colleague Dr. Farbstein of Zurich.'[4]

---

[1] Theodor Herzl: Briefe und Tagebücher. Ed. by Alex Bein et al. 7 vols. Frankfurt a. M., Berlin 1983 ff. Here vol. 4, pp. 287, 288, Vienna, 9 June 1897. Subsequently abbreviated as BTB.

[2] Ibid. In the original letter, the last lines are smudged and no longer legible. What is meant can, however, be deciphered.

[3] David Farbstein: Aus meinem Leben. In: Schweizerischer Israelitischer Gemeindebund. 1904–1954. Festschrift. Zurich 1954, p. 200.

[4] BTB 2, p. 532, 22 July 1897.

1 Probably the best-known photograph of Theodor Herzl on the balcony of the hotel 'Drei Könige' with a view of the Mittlere Rheinbrücke (Rhine bridge), photograph taken by E.M. Lilien, 1903.

Thus we can see that the thought of holding the Congress in Switzerland had appealed to Herzl from the very outset. Obviously the city of Basel proved to be a good location for the Congress, since five of the six congresses which took place during his lifetime were held there. In 1905, one year after Herzl's death, the Zionist delegates gathered once again in Basel, elected their new president, David Wolffsohn of Cologne, and finally decided on Palestine as their objective. As early as 1898, Herzl had planned to erect a 'Congress House' in Basel. Apparently he was convinced that the city was particularly suitable for a Jewish parliamentary building and for a symbol of this kind.

'The Jewish house in Basel will be a curiosity of Switzerland, but most of all a symbol for Jewry.'[5]

Because he was not convinced by the design produced by the architect Oscar Marmorek, Herzl sketched his own idea of a Congress house in Venetian style in his diary.

There is no doubt that Basel has been closely linked symbolically to Zionism since 1897. If we consider just individual links there is, for example, the Herzl postcard, in the background of which the 'Rheinbrücke' (one of the bridges

[5] BTB 2, p. 594, 10 July 1898.

> Fasse ich den Basler Congress in ein Wort zusammen — das ich mich hüten werde öffentlich auszusprechen — so ist es dieses: in Basel habe ich den Judenstaat gegründet.

Wenn ich das heute laut sagte, würde mir ein universelles Gelächter antworten. Vielleicht in fünf Jahren, jedenfalls in fünfzig wird es Jeder einsehen. Der Staat ist wesentlich im Staatswillen des Volkes, ja selbst eines genügend mächtigen Einzelnen (l'état c'est moi Ludwig XIV) begründet. Territorium ist nur die concrete Unterlage, der Staat ist selbst wo er Territorium hat immer etwas Abstractes. Der Kirchenstaat besteht auch ohne Territorium, sonst wäre der Papst nicht souverän.

Ich habe also in Basel dieses Abstracte u. darum den Allermeisten Unsichtbare geschaffen. Eigentlich mit infinitesimalen Mitteln. Ich hetzte die Leute allmälig in die Staatsstimmung hinein u. brachte ihnen das Gefühl bei, dass sie die Nationalversammlung seien.

2 Excerpt from the diary entrance by Theodor Herzl of September 3, 1897.

Basel and the Zionist Congress

133

3 The Freie Strasse in Basel, where the government had provided an office for the participants of the Congress.

crossing the Rhine) in Basel can be seen, Herzl's comment on September 3, 1897 that 'in Basel I have founded the Jewish state', the group photo of the participants of the Basel Congress and the 'Basle Program'. Mainstream Zionism between 1897 and 1903 was incidentally characterized by Ahad Haam in his magazine 'Ha-Shiloah' as 'Basle Zionism'.[6]

Of the 15 congresses in the years between 1907 and 1946, a further four took place in Basel, including that of 1946, which was the last to take place outside of Israel. Since the foundation of the state, the congress meets in Jerusalem. As no other city can lay claim to more than two congresses, Basel can be seen as the one city outside of Israel which is most closely connected to Zionism.

The Basel City Council and the Congress

The Basel City Council placed two congress centres at the disposal of the Congress, the 'Burgvogtei' and the music hall of the 'Stadtcasino', as well as an office in the 'Freie Strasse'.[7] The general meetings of the Jewish community had already taken place on a number of occasions in the Stadtcasino in the nineties. Dr. Paul Speiser, the liberal-conservative president of the City Council of the Canton Basel Stadt at the time, presumably attended the opening session of the Congress. This formal gesture and the reports in the leading newspapers, the 'National-Zeitung' and the 'Basler Nachrichten', as well as the entry into the city book of Basel point to the fact that the Congress was met here with unusual openness. Perhaps this arose from the clarity of the situation in Basel. Also the economic and demographic changes taking place at that time as well as the distinctly federalistic attitude of the city might

---

[6] Encyclopaedia Judaica. Berlin 1928–34, vol. 1, p. 685, article 'Ahad Haam'.

[7] See BTB 4, p. 335, 8 August 1897; Basler Nachrichten of 28 August 1897, p. 2.

have contributed to the fact that the demand for self-determination by a group with its own identity was met with understanding. Herzl expressed his gratitude at the end of the Congress to

'this hospitable city, which has received us with such goodwill, the government which has given us various signals of its sympathy'.[8]

However, the Basel City Council did not send an official welcoming letter until the occasion of the Fifth Congress in 1901:

'Dear Mr. Pres. Dear Sirs. As the Zionist Congress has elected to hold its congress this year once again – for the fourth time – in Basel, the CC [city council] is pleased to take this opportunity to sincerely welcome the congress and to express its great respect for its efforts. Please convey our regards to the assembly as well as our sincere wishes for the fruitfulness of your negotiations.'[9]

Also for the first time in 1901, the government received Herzl as the representative of the Congress. Dr. Heinrich David, the head of the government at the time, pointed out, as Herzl recalled that

'[...] Zionism was something illustrious. He was very happy that this great and excellent idea had found a home in Basel.'[10]

Herzl wrote expressing his thanks on January 7, 1902:

'The proclamation of the Basel City Council has left a deep impression on those attending our meeting and has further intensified the feelings of sincere gratitude which the Zionists of the entire world feel for the celebrated City of Basel.'[11]

In 1903 the president of the government, Dr. Zutt, welcomed the Sixth Congress with the following words:

4   Paul Speiser [1846–1936], president of the City Council of the Canton Basel Stadt. Presumably he was present at the opening session of the First Congress.

'If you have succeeded, through your annual meetings in Basel, to promote your ernest efforts and if this year's Congress can further strengthen these efforts and brings you another step closer to achieving your aims, this is also a source of great satisfaction for the city authorities who were able to offer hospitality to the congress.'[12]

In the same year, the Zionist organization passed on a donation of 2,000 francs to the city as a contribution to the poor.

Upon Herzl's unexpected death on July 3, 1904, the government wrote a letter of condolence to the Swiss Zionist Organization and to the Action Committee in Vienna in which it described Herzl as the 'outstanding leader of the Zionist movement'.

8   Zionisten-Congress in Basel (29., 30. und 31. August 1897). Officielles Protocoll. Vienna 1898, p. 191.
9   Staatsarchiv Basel-Stadt (StABS), Kirchenakten Q1, 28 December 1901.
10 BTB 3, p. 324, 25 December 1901, written on 5 January 1902.
11 StABS, Kirchenakten Q1.

12 Stenographisches Protokoll der Verhandlungen des VI. Zionistenkongresses in Basel. 23., 24., 25., 26., 27. und 28. August 1903. Vienna 1903, pp. 10ff.

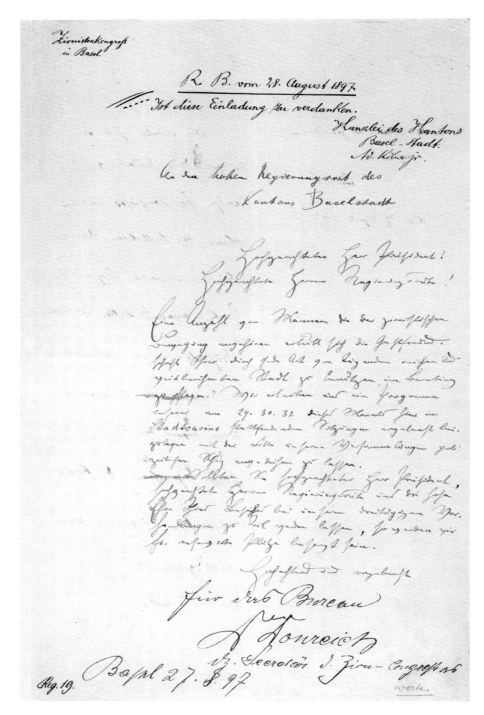

5   The official invitation of the Zionist Congress to the Basel City Council of August 27, 1897.

6   Paul Kober-Gobat [1842–1898], Basel publisher, supported the Congress participants.

The Christian Zionists and the Congress

Herzl possibly heard about the Christian Zionists in Basel via Reverend William Hechler. Paul Kober-Gobat, a representative of the evangelical publishers, was married to the daughter of the Protestant bishop of Jerusalem. This married couple and the 'Society of the Friends of Israel' played an important role in the organization of the Zionist Congress in Basel. As early as 1840, Samuel Preiswerk, professor for Old Testament Exegesis at the University of Basel expressed in his magazine 'Das Morgenland' – probably following Judah ben Alkalai – the notion 'of a reconstitution of the Jewish nation' and wrote that the Jews were a people with a 'right' and a 'claim [...] to the land and heritage of their forefathers' in Palestine.[15] Since then pietistic circles in Basel had occupied themselves with the concept of a return of the Jewish people to Palestine. This is why several public figures were already familiar with the aims of the Zionist movement well before the beginning of the Congress. Herzl expressly referred to the Christian Zionists in his vote of thanks but did not mention any of the members from Basel by name.

Immediately after the First Congress, Carl Friedrich Heman, who taught philosophy and pedagogics at the University of Basel, published a script called 'Das Erwachen der jüdischen Nation' (The Awakening of the Jewish Nation).[14] In it he speaks enthusiastically of the Zionist movement in which 'the Jewish people are trying to find a solution to their problem through their own efforts'. Although 'the awakening of the Jewish sense of ethnic identity' was judged by many as being 'inappropriate and dangerous' it was 'not to be undone'. Aims, organization and individual spokesmen were carefully introduced. As there was still a long way to go before the aims of Zionism would be achieved and the 'honourable, heavenly order of the world, the eternal law of the world', would still be valid, there was not even reason for concern about the Christian communities in Palestine. That Heman himself had kept his distance from the Congress can also be ascertained from this script. In a lecture delivered twelve years later the same author dealt exclusively with the conversion of the Jews which was supposed to originate from the person of Jesus Christ, and he no longer discussed the theme of the Jewish state.

The Jewish Community and the Congress

Upon receiving Herzl's letter, David Farbstein established contact with the rabbi of the Jewish community, Arthur Cohn. When asked 'how he would feel about holding the Congress in Basel' he was told, by Cohn, that 'he had nothing against

---

[13]   Die Juden und ihr Vaterland. In: Das Morgenland. Altes und Neues für Freunde der heiligen Schrift. Basel, August 1840, No. 8, pp. 241–256.

[14]   Friedrich Heman: Das Erwachen der jüdischen Nation. Der Weg zur endgültigen Lösung der Judenfrage. Basel 1897. Introductory address of October 1897. In the following pp. 3 and 112 are quoted.

7 The Basel Stadtcasino around 1900. Here the first Zionist congresses took place.

Basel as the Congress city'.[15] He probably also influenced the president of the community to give his corresponding consent. During the preparations for the Congress, the Basel rabbi liaised with the community on Farbstein's behalf. On July 3 he wrote to Cohn requesting him

'to pass on to him the addresses of those localities which he considered to be suitable for the Congress. The location must accommodate 200–300 participants and have a gallery. With Zionist greetings'.[16]

There is no further information on the proceedings of the rabbi apart from one note that the restaurant 'Braunschweig' in the 'Spalenvorstadt'

was under the supervision of the rabbi and that the hotels 'Basler Hof', 'Wilder Mann', 'Deutscher Hof' and 'Hotel Krafft' were possible accommodation locations for the participants of the Congress.[17] Although the Jewish community did not send an official representative to the Congress, Rabbi Cohn kept a close and interested eye on the meetings. After the Congress he published an enthusiastic article in the magazine 'Der Israelit', the 'Central Organ for Orthodox Jewry', from which the editorial office of the magazine distanced itself in a series of subsequent articles.[18] In contrast to his orthodox colleagues in the

---

[15] Marcus Cohn: Erinnerungen eines Baslers an den ersten Zionistenkongress. In: Schweizerischer Israelitischer Gemeindebund. 1904–1954. Festschrift. Zurich 1954, p. 227.
[16] CZA, K 12, 3 July 1897.

[17] CZA, H V A 7–751.
[18] Der Israelit, 6 September 1897.

region and also in various German cities, this rabbi continued to work for Zionism until 1911, and was motivated to a large extent by his enthusiasm for Herzl.

Moreover towards the end of the First Congress Arthur Cohn in the name of the Swiss rabbis asked Herzl the question of whether he could promise that the religious regulations – such as Sabbath – would be upheld in Palestine. Herzl answered:

'I would firstly like to thank Rabbi Dr. Cohn for speaking out so loyally as our former opponent and for the frankness of his question, which I most certainly shall not answer in detail. I can ensure you that Zionism does not intend to do anything which could hurt any movement within overall Jewry.' (Loud applause)[19]

At the beginning of his speech, Arthur Cohn had described his impression of the Congress:

'You have provided me with unforgettable hours. When I reflect on the speeches of Dr. Herzl and Dr. Nordau, my heart swells with enthusiasm. The speech of Dr. Nordau could be signed by any orthodox Jew, word for word, sentence for sentence.'

Rabbi Cohn's appearance in the stand was greeted by the Congress with overwhelming applause which he himself immediately referred to as unjustified. This applause was presumably because of his independent position with respect to the orthodox rabbis of Western Europe, in particular because of his position as a representative of the Jewish community in Basel, which had kept its distance from the Congress. Theodor Herzl wrote to Rabbi Cohn after the Congress:

'The great sincerity of your behaviour at the Basel Congress will never be forgotten by any of us. Without having made unworthy concessions we have found a way to meet each other and this is perhaps one of the greatest achievements of these times, which are a part of Jewish history.'[20]

On the Saturday before the Congress, Herzl had attended the service in the synagogue. Marcus Cohn states that his father, the rabbi, had welcomed the Congress on this occasion.[21] Herzl himself wrote in his diary about this visit to the synagogue shortly after the Congress:

'I went to the temple on the Saturday before the Congress to give some thought to those doubting for religious reasons. The leader of the community called me up. I had the brother-in-law of my friend Beer from Paris, Mr. Markus from Meran, drum the Broches into me. And as I approached the altar I was more nervous than in all of the days of the Congress. The few words of the Hebrew Broche made me more apprehensive than my opening and closing speeches and the entire leading of the proceedings.'[22]

As participants from Basel, we can find entered in the various Congress lists, in addition to rabbi Cohn: Miss Elsa Bloch, student – Julius Dreyfus-Brodski, financier – S. Drujan, head cantor – H. Feinberg, medical student – M. Jacobsohn, businessman – Oscar Meyer, synagogue employee – J. Pickard, businessman – M. Swidrichsen – Joe Weil, student – B.L. Wittes, student. The Jewish community initially kept its distance, despite the rabbi's gesture. In the files, the minutes of the meetings of the community and the minutes of the board, there is no mention of or entry about the Congress during the years 1897, 1898, 1899, 1901 or 1903. In 1903 the community seems to have welcomed the Congress officially,[23] but this was, strangely enough, not mentioned in the files.

This distanced stance in relation to Zionism is also expressed in the relationship to the Zionist association. It had been founded in November 1897 and turned to the community in 1898 with the request to extend the list of recipients for possible donations in the synagogue by adding a cat-

[19] Zionisten-Congress in Basel, p. 190.
[20] Herzl's letter from Vienna of 18 September 1897, is represented in: Rabbi Dr. Arthur Cohn: Of Israel's Teachings and Destiny. New York 1972 (after p. 239, last page of illustrations). See also: BTB 4, pp. 347f.
[21] Cohn: Erinnerungen, p. 235.
[22] BTB 2, pp. 544, 545, after 6 September 1897 'Eine Baseler Erinnerung'.
[23] Stenographisches Protokoll der Verhandlungen des VI. Zionistenkongresses in Basel. 23., 24., 25., 26., 27. und 28. August 1903. Vienna 1903, p. 339.

8 Theodor Herzl during his opening address to the Second Zionist Congress, 1898.

egory 'for Zionist purposes'. After the board first rejected this request, it was adopted all the same in a renewed application on May 24, 1898. Thus Basel became the first Jewish community in Switzerland to allow donations to be made for the Zionist organization. On the other hand, the board of the Basel community decided, on August 21, 1898, not to make a financial contribution to the reception of the delegates at the Second Congress. In 1904 it was still not possible to agree on a joint funeral ceremony for Herzl. In 1905, at the Seventh Zionist Congress, however, the representative board of the community did allow the synagogue to be used for a commemorative celebration. The reason why the community responded with such reserve to the Zionist movement can be found in the fact that – only 30 years after political and legal emancipation – it was still striving to be accepted by society in Basel and Switzerland. These efforts seemed to be endangered by Zionism with its national aims. However, there were no protests against the Congress in Basel – as was the case in a number of the German communities. The fact that the first congresses were able to convene in Basel is more likely to be the result of the political and economic climate which prevailed there at the turn of the century than the result of any interest taken by the board of the community.

Bettina Zeugin

Three Days in Basel

As the Zionist Congress was opened on Sunday August 29, 1897 on a hot summer morning in the Basler Stadtcasino, representatives of the Jewish people from the most varied Jewish movements and from innumerable countries met for the first time in centuries. Above the door of the congress building, a board with the inscription 'Zionistenkongress' was affixed which was visible from far and wide. Above it was the Star of David, the old national symbol. Next to the board a white flag with blue stripes and a Star of David in the middle was waving. Many visitors thought it was the Jewish national flag, but it had been made especially for the Congress by David Wolffsohn.

On the invitation Theodor Herzl had required that the participants come in white tie and tails. By doing so he wanted to emphasize the significance of this event. As Max Nordau appeared in a frock-coat, Herzl insisted that he returned to his hotel and changed his clothes. Only Aron Markus, a mystic from Cracow, supposedly succeeded in being allowed to enter in his long coat. The few ladies present also came in elegant clothing.

The Basler Stadtcasino, which was chosen as the venue of the congress, was a concert hall with bare, grey walls. The committee was seated at a long, green table on the podium. A higher chair was provided for the president. The stand was decorated with green cloth and there was a separate table for the stenographers and the representatives of the press. Herzl was very impressed by

1 Theodor Herzl on Barfüsserplatz, beside him Oscar Marmorek, in the background Israel Zangwill and Max Nordau. The picture cannot be dated exactly.

the decoration of the hall: as he put it, he was first disturbed and had to leave the room for a while in order to gather himself. And the hall must have made an even greater impression on the participants who had come from afar.

Anybody could participate in the Congress, under the condition that he agreed to the ideals of Zionism, had registered with the preparatory committee by the middle of August 1897 and

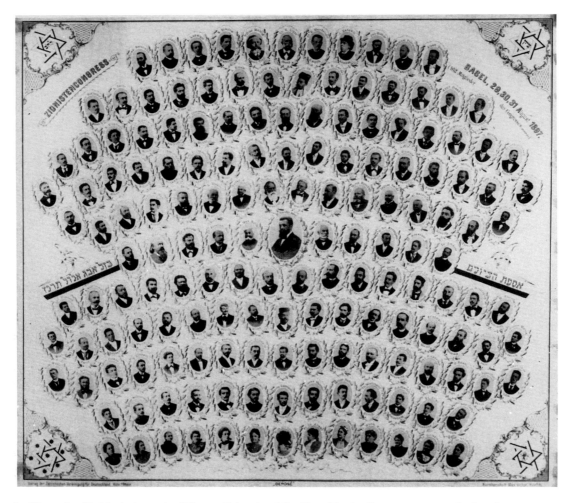

2 The only official photograph of the participants of the First Zionist Congress, prepared after the congress, however.

had been accepted by this committee.¹ These principles probably did not apply to women. According to the information from Haiyim Orlan, of 246 participants, 21 were women, and on the official attendance list attached to the minutes, of the 196 delegates, 14 were women. The women, however, did not have the right to vote but were merely admitted as guests. When asked by Dr. Kornblüh whether the women would be allowed to vote, Herzl replied in his position as president:

'The ladies are of course very honoured guests but will not take part in the vote.'²

[1] Cf. 'Arbeitsprogramm' and 'Geschäftsordnung des Zionisten-Congresses'. Central Zionist Archives (CZA), Jerusalem, Z1 36.

[2] Zionisten-Congress in Basel (August 29, 30 and 31, 1897). Officielles Protocoll. Vienna 1898, p. 115. The total number of participants is unknown.

3   The later Hotel 'Spalenbrunnen', around 1880.

And that was that.

Both convinced and hesitating Zionists had come to Basel from sixteen different countries; similar numbers came from Eastern and Western Europe. At this Congress the participants were not actually delegates yet. They often came on their own initiative or were sent by a Zionist-oriented group. Nor is it obvious whether these people were actual participants or whether they were simply observers of the event. Rabbi Arthur Cohn of Basel, for instance, who made a speech on the third day, was not mentioned on the list of participants. Eventually, even the official list of the participants prepared by the Congress bureau was declared invalid.

The expectations and hopes of those Jews who had travelled to Basel were very varied. Herzl noted in his diary:

'Congress members arrive at Restaurant Braunschweig [today Spalenbrunnen], where the food is very poor, with every incoming train from the most varied regions, covered with coal dust, sweaty from the trip, full of intentions – most of them with good ones, some of them with bad ones.'[5]

Herzl was particularly uncertain about the attitude of the Hovevei Zion members from Russia. These were concerned about the fact that the events at the congress might split the people even more, which would make the Palestine work harder. They also feared that hasty comments at the congress could even worsen the already miserable situation of the Jewish population in Russia.

[5]   Theodor Herzl: Briefe und Tagebücher. Ed. by Alex Bein et al. Vol. 2. Berlin, Frankfurt a. M. 1983, p. 537.

In addition to the large number of congress members, a large audience had also gathered in the stand. They also waited anxiously to see what would happen at the 'Congress of the Jews'. Among them were Jews who did not want to, or could not take part in the congress themselves, including numerous Jewish students as well as citizens of Basel who were interested in Jewish issues or who simply did not want to miss this great event. Dr. Karl Speiser, president of the governement of Basel, sat in the stand during the opening ceremony.

The participants had only three days to get organized for the continued work and to agree on a common programme. To ensure that things went smoothly, a commission had established a 'work programme' and a 'standing order' which had been sent to the participants before the beginning of the congress. These documents specified among others that points not mentioned on the agenda could not be discussed. Reports should not exceed half an hour, speeches, ten minutes. The official language of the congress was German. For Hebrew, Russian and English, secretaries had been hired.

In addition to the opening ceremony, the first day of the congress was dedicated to the situation of the Jewish peoples in the different countries. After the opening address of the president of the elders Dr. Karpel Lippe [1830–1915], Theodor Herzl, who had been awaited impatiently, stepped up to the podium. He spoke for the first time in front of a large audience in Basel and his welcoming address deeply moved many of those present. Immediately at the beginning of his address, he clarified the objectives of the congress:

'We want to lay the foundation stone of the house which will one day be the home of the Jewish nation.'

He explained that Zionism was the best instrument to solve the 'Jewish question'. In well-chosen words he outlined his further aims, spoke of the situation of the Jewish people and appealed to the Jewish feeling of unity. He was conscious of the worldwide significance of the congress and called on the participants to act with the required carefulness:

'The news of our discussions and our decisions will go forth to distant countries in the next hour, across the oceans of the world. Therefore, explanation and reassurance should emanate from this congress. All over the world people should see what Zionism, which has been held for a kind of chiliastic terror, really is: a civilized, legal, humanistic movement in accordance with the ancient goal of the longing of our people. What we have written or said until now as individuals could be ignored, in contrast to what emanates from the congress. So may the Congress, which from now on is master of its debates, be a wise master.'[4]

Herzl considered it to be very important to clear up prejudice about Zionism and to pave the way for a mass movement. He often pointed out that the first important step in this direction was the creation of a strict organization.

'A storm of applause' followed his address. Many believed Herzl to be the 'King of the Jews'. According to the statements of witnesses, the enthusiasm for his person would seem to have been extraordinary. Just like the Jewish participants of the Congress, the Christians were also particularly curious as to Herzl's person. His imposing appearance and his address gave rise to trust and admiration. Marcus Cohn reports that Maria Kober-Gobat, a religious woman from Basel from the Christian Zionist group and daughter of the Protestant bishop of Jerusalem, who took part in the Congress as a guest, declared to his father, Rabbi Arthur Cohn, that she saw in Herzl the Messiah.[5] The enthusiasm which his person evoked among most participants helped him to become the integration figure of Zionism. After his address, Herzl was elected president by the

---

[4] Zionisten-Congress, pp. 4–9. The following quotes are also taken from the protocol and are therefore not further documented.

[5] Marcus Cohn: Erinnerungen eines Baslers an den ersten Zionistenkongress. In: Schweizerischer Israelitischer Gemeindebund, Festschrift zum 50-jährigen Bestehen 1904–1954. Basel 1954, p. 228.

4 Membership card of the First Zionist Congress.

plenum following a proposal of the pre-conference.

Max Nordau, who had previously been elected vice president, followed as the second main speaker. In impressive words he presented the general situation of the Jewish people,

the 'Jewish misery' – 'a particular misery which the Jews suffer, not as people but as Jews and to which they would not be subjected if they were not Jews.'

In the foreground was the material misery:

'[...] a large proportion of the Jewish people originate from outcast beggars.'

Furthermore the expectations of the emancipation had not been fulfilled. Many Jews who had placed their trust in it, he said, were now uprooted.

'That is the moral Jewish misery [...].'

And the growing anti-Semitism heightened this problem. He went on to say that Zionism now offered a way out of this predicament, to once again find

'security in a society', 'a benevolent society, the possibility to use all of its organic power to develop its real nature [...].'[6]

Nordau's moving speech and the subsequent reports to the various countries, which showed that these were largely subject to poverty, anti-Semitism and persecution, and which, for the first time, showed an overall picture of the Jewish people at the end of the 19th century, caused the majority of those who had not yet made up their minds for the cause, to cast off their doubts and dedicate themselves to Zionism. They could see themselves as even more encouraged as Nathan Birnbaum and David Farbstein then gave their reasons for the necessity of Zionism. Both men emphasized that it was by no means merely a 'defence against anti-Semitism'. Farbstein explained how economic reasons demanded the 'systematic emigration of the Jews to Palestine'. He described in detail the over-population, the misery, the innumerable poor who 'lived on the air that they breathed', in Russia, whose condition, due to political considerations, was not dealt with in a sep-

6   Zionisten-Congress, pp. 9–20, quotations pp. 9, 17, 18.

arate lecture so that the Jewish population would not be endangered additionally. In order to give rise to a fundamental

'modification of the economic way of life of the Jews, to make an agricultural and industrially active people out of the independent dealers and craftsmen'

an own territory was absolutely necessary. As past experience had proven, he said, the colonization of Palestine would only be successful if guarantees be given on an international legal level. So in this respect, Zionism was, as he put it, an 'act of self-help'.[7]

Birnbaum concluded that Zionism was simply a mandatory result of the development of the 'Jewish nation'. With the 'exit from the ghetto culture' the Jews had lost their original 'national culture', but without taking on the nationality and culture of another people. Attempts to live as citizens of the world, he went on to say, and at assimilation, had not succeeded, inner disunion and lack of orientation were the consequences, made worse by anti-Semitism. What had long been established in the 'Western civilization' was now clearly appearing among the 'jargon Jews of Eastern Europe' with their own 'national individuality', their 'Eastern-Jewish culture'. The 'Eastern Jews' were also leaving their ghetto and moving into the 'European civilization', so that the 'anomaly' of its existence had also become apparent among this largest part of the Jewish people. For this reason the masses were now looking for a way out which Zionism offered them: an 'own country', 'the earthly homeland'. This, he maintained, was imperative for the further development and could be found in Palestine. Elsewhere there were too many restrictions for the Jews and Palestine also brought with it the 'Zion feelings'. Here they could also be the 'mediator between the East and the West', because they were influenced by European civilization. Thus, this speech, quite apart from its interesting justification of the Jewish nation, is an informative example of the perception between Western and Eastern Jews and also of the conditions in Palestine as seen by European Jews.[8]

The first day demonstrated the feeling of unity of the Jews. Under the pressure of the 'Jewish misery' and the anti-Semitism in Eastern and Western Europe, only a joint path seemed to be able to provide a solution. The multitude of petitions and telegrammes which arrived from all over the world underlined the feeling of unity and gave the Congress moral support for its further proceedings.

After this opening, the summary of the situation of the Jewish people and the justification of Zionist aims, the second day had to be used to take concrete steps. In the focus of the debates were the discussions about the programme which the Congress had to pass. A preparatory commission had drafted a programme which, in the opinions of Herzl and Nordau, should have been unanimously agreed to without any changes: this would, they said, demonstrate the unity at the Congress and there would be enough time to deal with further problems. Despite these hopes, there were, however, discussions about the first sentence of the draft programme. It read initially:

'Zionism seeks to establish a home for the Jewish people in Palestine secured by law'.

What was under dispute was how the homestead was to be guaranteed. Nordau warned:

'We should emphasize everything that unites us and put behind us all that separates us'.

Some of the Congress participants, on the other hand, felt that this urging bypassed their democratic rights. Leo Motzkin [1867–1933] from Kiev proposed to demand 'international legal' assur-

---

[7] Zionisten-Congress, pp. 14–108, quotations pp. 94, 95, 104, 106.

[8] Zionisten-Congress, pp. 82–94, quotations pp. 83, 84, 85, 87, 88, 92.

ance. Finally, Herzl's suggestion was accepted which proposed the expression 'public law'. The outbreak of further differences of opinion was avoided. The Congress passed 'by acclamation' the 'Basle Program', which was to determine the aims of Zionism for a long time. The statements in the programme were deliberately formulated vaguely. As many inner Jewish movements as possible should be able to identify with it. Nor did the Congress go as far as to demand a sovereign Jewish state, in order to avoid international legal problems.[9]

Already in the course of the second day, the discussion about the further organization of the movement was addressed. Max Bodenheimer from Cologne held an introductory lecture about the Zionist Organization. He too called on the participants to overcome disunion. To this end he referred to the Swiss Rütli myth:

> 'May the spirit of unity, the spirit of the Rütli also preside over our meeting of new confederates.'[10]

On the third day of talks, August 31, it became quite obvious that there were completely varying ideas about the organization of the movement. For instance, would all Zionists in the future be allowed to take part in the congress, or only delegates? They agreed to the use of the 'shekel' as the general contribution to the organization but the amount of the contribution that could reasonably be expected from the poorest of the poor was unclear. The congress agreed to only deciding on the fundamental structure of the movement and to allow the board, which was to be elected, to work on the details. This decision was taken notably because in many countries the Jewish population was forbidden to belong to international organizations. The structure and the hierarchy, therefore, were to be left to the individual countries.

[9] Zionisten-Congress, pp. 113–119, quotations pp. 114, 116, 118, 119.
[10] Zionisten-Congress, pp. 119–130, here p. 130.

The assembly then defined the congress as the legislative organ of the Zionist movement. Only selected representatives, actual delegates were allowed to be members. The leadership during the rest of the time was to be taken on by an action committee based in Vienna. The decision to found a Jewish national fund which should purchase land in Palestine remained a particularly significant issue. The details of its organization were to be clarified later on.

In the afternoon of the third day, various lectures about the situation in Palestine followed. In 1897, most of the participants, including Herzl and the rest of the leaders of the movement, still had a very imprecise picture of Palestine and the living conditions there. Thus the discussions were often based on assumptions which later proved to be inadequate. Marcus Ehrenpreis [1869–1951] wanted the Hebrew language and literature to be promoted as intensively as possible. To this end, a literature commission was elected.

As an extension of the Congress had not been planned for, many speeches and votes had to be shortened or were left out altogether. Nevertheless, with the constitution of its organization and the 'Basle Program', the First Congress managed to lay the foundations of the Zionist movement. Western and Eastern Zionists united organizationally and politically. The Hovevei Zion now also accepted political Zionism.

At the end of the Congress, Herzl was satisfied with what had been achieved. Although the Congress had threatened to fall apart numerous times, it managed to disprove the stereotype that Jews were too quarrelsome and undisciplined to find solutions together. They were united in their wish to fight against oppression, to gather the powers of Jewry to find a new path and in the age of nations to appear as a politically acting nation. The demand for an own homestead in Palestine – at the time there were no other countries in question – was to secure the existence of the people and to raise the Jewish nation among the other nations as an equal partner with its own territory.

This common ideal supported the feeling of unity of the participants. This was aided by the fact that at the First Congress, there were no sub-groups yet with diverging political or religious tendencies which would lead to fragmentation and conflicts at subsequent congresses. With the congress and its programme, the Zionist movement had, for the first time, announced its claim to Palestine to the world community and thus shaken it up, as the local and international media showed.

Theodor Herzl had become an internationally known personage. On September 3, 1897, he wrote in his diary:

'If I were to summarise the first Congress in one word – which I would be wary of uttering in public – I would say this: In Basel I founded the Jewish state. If I said this aloud today, I would be the laughing-stock of the whole world. Perhaps in five, at most in fifty years, everyone will see.'[11]

---

[11] CZA, H II B2 5/H. 75, pp. 49–50.

Nadia Guth Biasini

Theodor Herzl

Theodor Herzl was born in Pest on May 2, 1860. During the years of his childhood, the Hungarian Jews gained constitutional equality, which however, was not to be joined by religious freedom until the nineties. Herzl's home can be characterized as 'economically secure, religiously enlightened, politically liberal and culturally German'.[1] The liberal attitude towards religion included visiting the synagogue every Sabbath and on holidays with his father; Herzl's mother was the reason for the enthusiasm about German culture. After graduating in 1878 in Budapest, he received his doctorate in laws in Vienna in 1884. He spent one year in court in Vienna and Salzburg. After that he turned away from law and justice and decided to become a writer and playwright.

Herzl discovered his liking for writing during his youth and followed this passion during his years of university study. Presumably, winning the first prize in a writing competition of the 'Wiener Allgemeine Zeitung' for the feature 'Das Alltägliche' on May 27, 1885, while he still worked at court, eased his decision to become a writer. In the coming years Herzl received some attention. In 1887 the drama 'Tabarin' was staged with success in New York with the 'Burgtheater' actor Friedrich Mitterwurzer. The feature 'Emmelfey' was also very well received in Vienna. In the following years the Vienna Burgtheater successfully staged a number of Herzl's comedies 'Der Flüchtling' (The Refugee), 'Die Wilddiebe' (The Poachers) and 'Die Dame in Schwarz' (The Lady in Black) – all three were written in co-operation with Hugo Wittmann. All in all Herzl wrote – in addition to his articles in the 'Neue Freie Presse', his Zionist scripts, diaries and his letters – 19 plays, mainly comedies, and one novella.

In the middle of 1889 he married Julie Naschauer, the daughter of a businessman as well. She bore him three children. At the beginning of October 1891, the 'Neue Freie Presse' asked Herzl if he was prepared to go to Paris as their France correspondent. He accepted the challenge and for nearly four years he wrote articles about the political, economical and cultural events in France for this, the most distinguished liberal newspaper in Austria.

Theodor Herzl would have preferred to be seen as celebrated author of the city of Vienna. However he became known as chairman of the Zionist organization, the basis of which he created himself with the political work 'The Jewish State. An Attempt to Find a Modern Solution to the Jewish Question', published on February 14, 1896. Herzl wrote this manifesto in a state of obsession within six months. This obsession was not to leave him until he died at the age of 44. Even while still writing this book, he tried to attract prosperous members of the Jewish community to his cause. Still living in Paris, he visited Baron Maurice de Hirsch, with the intention of convincing him to stop his philanthropic project

---

[1] Jakob Allerhand: Messianische Elemente im Denken und Wirken Theodor Herzls. In: Norbert Leser (ed.): Theodor Herzl und das Wien des Fin de Siècle. Vienna 1987, p. 67.

1 Frontpage of the first edition of the «Jewish State», 1896.

in Argentina in which he had invested 400 million francs, and to support the plan of a Jewish state.

With his 'Address to the Rothschilds' which he wrote between June 13 and 15, 1895, he tried to win over the Rothschild family for his 'Judenstaat' project. This 'Address', of over 90 diary pages and multitudinous notes, can be seen as an outline for the 'Judenstaat'. Many of its aspects were dealt with in depth in this address. Obliged to the political spirit of his generation, Herzl's idea was based on the fact that the 'Jewish question' was a national question and needed a political solution. The book by Moses Hess 'Rome and Jerusalem', published in 1862, and of which Herzl was not aware it existed, already defined the Jews as a nation. Herzl finally referred to a future peaceful co-existence of national states, according to Messianic nationalism, as could be found in connection with Giuseppe Mazzini, a leader of the Italian liberation movement.[2] On the one hand, the script unfolded the theoretical basis for the political reconstruction of the Jewish nation and therefore the frame of a future Jewish state, but in addition to this, Herzl presented a detailed programme of how this state could be constructed. In addition to the constitutional and economical framework, he also gave several organizatorial suggestions on practical questions such as emigration, immigration, buying land and the real estate market in the new country. The 'Jewish misery', which he said still existed in society despite the emancipation, had become an anachronism if one considers the technical achievements of the century. This idea was one which he was to turn into his novel 'Altneuland' (Oldnewland).

Just as in the 'Address to the Rothschilds', Herzl's outline of a utopian state showed a high grade of tolerance towards other religions and nationalities. The author refers particularly to Switzerland, as an example of a 'federal state of different nations'.[3] In his outline Herzl did not take into consideration that the population of Palestine or the adjoining powers could be against the new Jewish state. All in all, Herzl attached great importance in 'Judenstaat', to the size of the movement, which had the aim of founding a Jewish state:

'The idea depends only on the number of its followers.'[4]

---

[2] Giuseppe Mazzini: Scritti editi ed inediti. Edizione nazionale a cura di Mario Menghini. Imola 1906–1943, vol. 46, p. 219, vol. 59, p. 121.
[3] Theodor Herzl: Briefe und Tagebücher. Ed. by Alex Bein et al. 7 vols. Frankfurt a.M., Berlin 1983ff. Here vol. 2, p. 190f. Abbreviation: BTB.
[4] Theodor Herzl: Der Judenstaat. Versuch einer Lösung der jüdischen Frage. Leipzig, Vienna 1896. All quotations are taken from the preface.

2 Herzl and the Zionist delegation in front of the old city wall in Jerusalem, 1898. From the left: Max Bodenheimer, David Wolffsohn, Theodor Herzl, Moses Schnirer, Joseph Seiderer.

Without referring to any of the possible forerunners, which he presumably had not read, Herzl called his outline a 'combination' and 'construction', all elements of which and their drive – the 'Judennoth' – already existed 'in reality'. In this way he distanced his programme from being defined as a 'utopia' and 'fantasy'.

How did he undergo the change from being a writer to being the leader of the Zionist movement? From his personal diary in 1882, we know that he dealt intensively with the anti-Semitic script of Eugen Dühring of 1881 'The Jewish Question as a Racial, Moral and Cultural Question. With a Historical Answer'. One year later he declared his withdrawal from the German national student association 'Albia', after it had participated in a large anti-Semitic rally on the occasion of a Wagner memorial celebration. In the following ten years, until he moved to Paris, there are no more indications that he concerned himself intensively with anti-Semitism. The first public and comprehensive statement of Herzl was published on August 31, 1892, in the 'Neue Freie Presse' in the form of an article about anti-Semitic activities in France. Anti-Semitism became more and more his theme. He wrote several letters to the editorial office of his newspaper and held a meeting with the editors in which he sought possible solutions to the 'Jewish question'. Moreover his thoughts about the future of his son Hans Herzl – born in June 1891 – appeared to increase his preoccupation with anti-Semitism. In the beginning of the nineties Herzl was obviously still convinced that there was a 'solution to the Jewish question' within the European society. In 1893 he described the most spectacular suggestion to Moritz Benedikt, the publisher of the 'Neue Freie Presse' in the form of a daydream, in which some aspects become apparent that should also prove characteristic for his later leadership of the Zionist movement: the public procedure, the tendency to stage and dramatize, the preparedness to take measures of unexpected, even shocking consequence, the effort to find a lasting and complete solution to the

'Jewish question' and the respect for the concept of honour of the fin de siècle culture.

A public baptism of the entire young, Jewish generation in the Stephansdom, which the Pope and the Austrian clergy had agreed to, was to solve the Jewish question in Austria. All children that were too young to decide for themselves should be baptized. Herzl and his generation would remain Jews. Thereby a 'move of great honour will lift the entirety'.[5]

As baptisms occasionally were performed that suggestion was by no means unfounded.

In the following years Herzl took a decisive step forward. In 1894 he ended the play 'The Ghetto', dealing with problems of Jewish existence in contemporary society after the legal and political emancipation. Herzl saw the baptism much more sceptically now. The physician Bichler, who was in favour of it, did no longer view baptism as a solution. In 1897 Herzl changed the title into 'The New Ghetto' – possibly because of impressions he received at the Dreyfus trial in Paris, which he reported on for the 'Neue Freie Presse'. The anti-Semitic campaign in France which the court case aroused, the act of demoting Captain Alfred Dreyfus on January, 1895, Dreyfus' attitude and the anti-Semitic mood of the masses left a lasting impression on Herzl, for he had always seen France as the country of human rights, solidarity and emancipation.

The immediate reactions to Herzl's 'Judenstaat' were extraordinarily varied, ranging from devoted support to bitter disapproval. The well-known culture critic of the eighties and nineties Max Nordau supported Herzl's plan and was convinced totally after two days. But Moritz Benedikt, the publisher of the 'Neue Freie Presse', had a 'hot discussion' with his editor – who had returned from Paris and been in charge of the features editorial office for several months – ten days before the 'Judenstaat' was published. On the one hand, Benedikt told him, the brochure was not yet ready to be published and required improvements, on the other hand he warned Herzl not to start the ball rolling, which could lead to the Jews having neither a fatherland nor their own state. Herzl writes, Benedikt wished, 'that I [Herzl] should refrain from publication.'[6] The 'Neue Freie Presse' would not let Zionism get a word in until Herzl died on July 3, 1904. Even in Herzls' obituary they did not mention his efforts for Zionism. The Rabbi of Vienna Moritz Güdemann, whom Herzl respected as a great authority on Judaism, greeted him with the following words:

'You look to me like Moses [...] Don't change! Maybe you are God's Chosen.'[7]

3   Contemporary caricature of Theodor Herzl.

---

[5]   BTB 2, 4 February 1897, p. 46f.
[6]   BTB 2, 4 February 1897, p. 294f.
[7]   BTB 2, 18 August 1895, p. 242f.

4 The Seventh Congress, 1905, under the impression of Theodor Herzl's death.

Shortly after the publication appeared however, the rabbi dissociated himself from Zionism and became one of the leaders of the opposition, defining Judaism as religion and disapproving of a national movement. Orthodox Jews reacted intensely to the 'Judenstaat', which, for them, was inconsistent to the tradition of waiting for the Messiah. But also the liberal and assimilated Jews, who had freed themselves from Messianic expectations, were against Herzl. They felt their integration into the European societies being at risk. On the other hand, the large Jewish population of Eastern Europe which received Herzl on his visits like their liberator and king was impressed by his plan.

Disappointed by his meeting with Baron Edmond de Rothschild on July 19, 1896, in Paris, whom he wanted to convince to increase his commitment to the idea, Herzl decided to start 'organizing the masses now.' This led to the formation of committees in London, Paris and Vienna, the result of which was the first Zionist Congress in Basel and the Zionist Organization.[8]

Herzl based his efforts on the concept of building up the Jewish state on a diplomatic level. Even after the forming of the Zionist movement, the diplomatic negotiations with different powers that could have an influence on Palestine such as the German Reich, Turkey, Great Britain and Russia remained the main concern of Herzl. This caused Martin Buber to characterize him as a 'statesman without a state'. All efforts were ini-

[8] BTB 2, 21 July 1896, p. 413.

tially largely in vain. In March 1902 Herzl's invitation to speak by the newly established 'Royal Commission on Alien Immigration' can be seen as the first political acceptance of Zionism by a government. However, as in August 1903 Great Britain suggested a Jewish settlement in East Africa, Herzl was barely able to prevent a splitting of the movement. At the Seventh Congress in 1905 – one year after Herzls death – the 'Uganda Scheme' was refused. On the occasion of his funeral it became obvious that he had become a symbol for many Jews and even for his opponents inside the Zionist movement. The seemingly endless funeral procession with mourners from east and west, north and south remained unforgettable for those who participated. Herzl had succeeded in finding the right words for thoughts and feelings which had for so long remained unspoken and arousing the interest of a broad public for Zionism.[9]

---

[9] Shlomo Avineri: The Making of Modern Zionism. The Intellectual Origins of the Jewish State. London 1981, p. 100.

François Guesnet

The First Interview

The First International Zionist Congress[1] as the Turning Point in the Jewish Reform Movement of Congress Poland, and Its Reception in the Warsaw Newspaper 'Izraelita' in 1897

1 Nahum Sokolów [1859–1936].

The journal 'Izraelita', which was founded in 1866 and was at that time the only Jewish weekly in the Kingdom of Poland (or Congress Poland) written in Polish, viewed itself as an organ which was committed to the enlightenment and acculturation, the 'Europeanization' of the Jewish population in Poland. Although with this attitude the editorial staff clearly represented a small minority of the Jewry in Congress Poland, they nevertheless exerted an enormous influence because of their wealth and education. After the death of Samuel Zevi Peltin [1831–1896], the founder of the paper, Nahum Sokolów [1861–1937] took over the position of 'literary director' of the publication, which remained the property of Peltin's widow, Salomea Peltinova.

Under Sokolów's direction, 'Izraelita' improved its image considerably, both in terms of content and political position. The number and quality of the reports from the various communities throughout the Kingdom of Poland increased, and in various articles, columns and editorials Sokolów even dealt critically and openly with controversial topics relating to Jewish life. Thus, it was not surprising that he showed a great deal of interest in the preparations for the 'First International Zionist Congress'. The Basel Congress, however, was not just one topic among others. In many respects, the role it played was a very special one.

In retrospect, the Basel Congress represents a turning point also for the Jewish political culture in the Kingdom of Poland. A new generation of Jewish politicians had appeared on the scene. Sokolów emphasized this by employing a journalistic method of treating subject matter, which up to then had never been used in 'Izraelita': an interview, which he conducted with Theodor Herzl in Vienna immediately after the Basel Congress.[2] The unusually large amount of space taken up by the reports of the Basel Congress in general in 'Izraelita' and by this interview in particular suggests that Sokolów shared Herzl's convictions even before the Basel Congress.

This change in the behaviour of the new Jewish political elite in the Kingdom of Poland coin-

---

[1] This was how the Congress was referred to in the first detailed article of 13/25 June 1897, by Nahum Sokolów: Za wiele hałasu o nic. No. 25, p. 241.
[2] Ibid. No. 41–43, 10/22 October, 17/29 October, 24 October/11 November 1887, p. 391f., p. 403f., p. 415f.

cided with a series of profound changes in the situation of the Jewish people living there. The success of Hassidism put the rabbinical orthodoxy on the defensive. A reform-oriented Jewish religious policy – which Zionism was also considered to be – could benefit somewhat from this. The clearly noticeable deterioration of Jewish-Polish relations around the turn of the century was certain to foster political approaches that strove to find inner Jewish solutions to social and material problems. The involvement of the Jewish men and women who had immigrated from Russia since the 1860s and had settled down in many of the communities of the kingdom was eventually of considerable importance. They played a key role in the development of new organizational forms and were the first to spread the idea of a Jewish nation in the Kingdom of Poland. As a result of the government's official Russian policy after Nicholas I, which was so disastrous for the formation and the perception of the Jews as a community, it was no longer possible to take political action at this level. The Jewish workers' movement, which formed up the 'Bund' in the year of the Basel Congress also showed signs of the same kind of new orientation. And finally a generation of prominent Jewish notables left public life, people who as no others before or after them had tried to serve the cause of a Jewish-Polish rapprochement as dedicated 'liberals'. But also the death of an orthodox 'Klal-tuer', that is, a person engaged to take care of general matters concerning the Jewish population in a particular area, reflected this change of generations. In an obituary of one of them, Liber Korngold from Warsaw, who died in 1896, Nahum Sokołów wrote the following:

'There was a pleasant touch about these old men: a remarkable connection to the city and to the community, a "being at ease with oneself" (Pol. "swojszczyzna"), a feeling of pride to be here at home and to use these standards to measure everything: "civis romanus sum".'[5]

---

[5] Nahum Sokołów: Z tygodnia. In: Izraelita 32 (1897) 1 (20 December 1896/1 January 1897), p. 7.

There were various occasions when Herzl expressed himself in a very positive way about Sokolów, as in 1902 at the celebration of the author's twenty-fifth anniversary as a journalist:

'A figure like Sokolów must be completely incomprehensible to Western European Jews, who have degenerated in their attempts to imitate other nationalities. Here stands a modern human being, nourished by all the knowledge of the present age, in motion and pursuing the events of the day, a journalist in the best sense of the word – and the day about which he writes is a Jewish day. In Sokolów I honour one of those who have helped to create the free exchange of public opinion among the Jewish people. His views are certainly not always the same as my views, but this is precisely the reason why I enjoy reading and benefiting from what he writes. He has a difficult task, and he performs it with courage, talent and wisdom. And I am convinced that in the times ahead he will be an unforgettable figure in this Jewish renaissance, which we are now struggling and suffering through.'
In Żydzi w Polsce odrodzonej. Vol. 1. Warsaw 1932, p. 524.

It was precisely in this Kingdom of Poland, where the tradition of community autonomy had remained in the consciousness of the people to a much greater degree, that a political movement that had chosen 'general human qualities' in its 'European' definition as the measure of all things – what Theodor Herzl in his interview was never tired of emphasizing – had to represent the break not only with the ideology of assimilation, but also with the central, traditional points of reference of Jewish political culture: the community and its concerns.

Sokolów was not a delegate to the First Zionist Congress but worked as a correspondent reporting from Basel. From that time on, the news coverage changed from being cautious and critical to clearly supporting the plans of Herzl. The extraordinary nature of the event and the excitement with which Sokolów awaited the opening of the Congress were expressed in a short letter he sent to his wife Regina. He wrote it on stationery from the 'Hôtel des Trois Rois' on the day after his arrival in Basel, which was at the eve of the Congress:

> 'I don't have a single free minute. We arrived [...] yesterday. First we had to look for a hotel; after finding one [...], I went to town. Crowds of people I know at every step. I'm moving all the time and can hardly think. Running about, interviews, articles on the Congress – never ending. The Congress officially begins tomorrow. I'm going to finish this letter now, because I'm exhausted and hungry, and I'm writing this between two sessions.'[4]

In later years, Sokołów played an exceptionally great and mostly underestimated role in Polish Jewry, and held leading positions in international Jewish organizations, finally as president of the Zionist Organization from 1931 to 1935. Even before the Basel Congress, he underwent a development process which his son and biographer described in the following manner:

> 'When he was still a young man, my father turned away from the cosmopolitan Haskalah and toward a spiritual Zionism; Hebrew was at that time his most important medium of expression. Until he finally became a political Zionist in 1897.'[5]

At the beginning, he apparently endeavoured not to antagonize the readers of 'Izraelita', who were striving for a Jewish-Polish rapprochement and therefore disapproved of a Jewry that would act in a politically independent manner. He thus avoided conveying the impression of being an uncritical follower of Herzl, and stressed the financial and technical obstacles involved in implementing the idea of a Jewish state. Even in these texts, however, he emphatically referred to the honourable and almost charitable objectives of the Zionists. Two months before the Zionist Congress, when there was still a plan to hold it in Munich, Sokołów, in an editorial, took a reserved even mocking position:

> 'Mr. Herzl had not even thought once about his "Jewish state" when millions in donations were already pouring in to support the colonists; what still must be done will happen even without holding a Congress and totally independent of any papers that are going to be read there in Munich [...] It seems that if in the end Mr. Herzl is simply a copy of Baron Hirsch, and a bad one at that [...] The "Munich Congress" will not be helpful. And not because the Jews cannot work; on the contrary, the Jewish skill and zest for action go beyond the boldest expectations, but rather because the artificial creation of a colony, *due to the nature of it*, is an extremely difficult thing.'[6]

Two weeks later, he wrote a sarcastic article about the organizational difficulties in Munich:

> 'Well there is indeed "much ado about nothing". Not only does Mr. Herzl have no place to carry out his plans for the establishment of a Jewish state, he does not even have a place for his Congress. Because of the protests of the Jewish community in Munich, who are against his endeavours, Mr. Herzl will namely have to reconsider his intention to have the conference take place in this city. This shows how unripe the whole matter is.'[7]

Despite this rather malicious presentation, 'Izraelita' reported in detail and in short intervals on how the planning of the Congress was developing, such things as on the new location for the conference in Basel and the preparations with regard to content, which was now treated with an unmistakably positive attitude:

> 'It is a worthy goal to endeavour to acquire by constitutional means a not too densely populated portion of a region in order to settle Jewish emigrants who wander about the world without a place of their own – who would not approve of such a goal? Whether the plan succeeds, this is the big question, but who will doubt that this is a subject worthy of discussion?'[8]

---

[4] Unpublished letter of 26 August 1897, written in Polish, CZA, by Nahum Sokołów, sign. A 18 574.
[5] Florian Sokołow: Nahum Sokołow. Life and Legend. London 1975, p. 68ff.
[6] Nahum Sokołów: Za wiele hałasu o nic. In: Izraelita 32 (1897) 25 (13/25 June 1897), p. 241.
[7] Nahum Sokołów: Odgłosy. In: Izraelita 32 (1897) 27 (27 June/9 July 1897), p. 266.
[8] Op. cit.: Odglosy – Kongress w Bazylei. In: Izraelita 32 (1897) 31 (25 July/6 August 1897), p. 303.

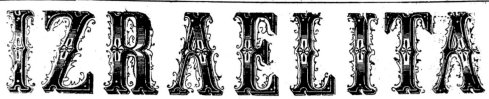

2 Editorial by Nahum Sokołów in 'Izraelita' concerning the First Congress in Basel, 1897.

In the last issue, which Sokolów was responsible for before he departed for Basel, he contributed an editorial entitled 'The Conference Lovers of Zion' as well as the complete programme of the Congress and the qualifications required to attend it. He underlined the urgency of Jewish poverty as the key motive for a Jewish colony in Palestine. He viewed political Zionism as an ideological movement which stood closer to the needs of the 'Jewish people' than 'liberalism':

'A strong popular spirit breathes through this "Herzliade"; not that our people would know a lot about Herzl and his plans, but in contrast to the Jewish liberals, who are self-satisfied with their attitude of superiority and can but look down on the people like an arrogant Juno aloof on her proud summit among the clouds, a spirit is flaring up which, as it is related and friendly to the people, is close to them.'⁹

This article clearly shows that the editor of 'Izraelita' did not first experience a kind of conversion at the Basel Congress, but rather had already sympathized earlier with the political idea of establishing a Jewish state in Palestine. It was precisely under the conditions of czarist censorship that he stressed in an astonishing way his personal political priorities by using formulations such as 'our people'. He later characterized the Congress in a similar way, in his 'History of Zionism':

'This gathering will one day be surrounded by a mythical radiance. There were approximately 200 delegates of Jews who had been called together for the first time since the exile of the Jewish people. The excitement was indescribable. In spite of their being scattered throughout the world, for the first time the Jews felt united through the bonds of nationality and through their common history and suffering.'¹⁰

Sokolów reported on the Basel Congress itself in a three-part series of long editorials. The tone of these articles corresponds to the author's high spirits described at the beginning:

'Herzl conducted the sessions with dignity and impartiality, with energy and tact, in a manner which was neither curt nor arrogant [...] The appearance of Herzl on the platform was accompanied by a storm of applause, and the gigantic hall literally shook under the ovation.'¹¹

In the subsequent issues, the editorial office documented the great speech made by Max Nordau and published a two-part article on results and initial reactions to the Congress. The author of this résumé observed that for the majority of the foreign Jewish publications the results of the Congress were negative, and he himself considered that the plan for establishing a Jewish colony in Palestine was to be welcomed, however, not the plan for establishing a Jewish state. Since the author, known by the abbreviation 'Cor.', regularly published articles in 'Izraelita', it can be assumed that not the entire editorial staff of the weekly publication shared Sokolów's views.

The most remarkable document, however, with which 'Izraelita' conveyed an impression of the Congress to its readers, is an account of an interview that Sokolów conducted with Theodor Herzl in Vienna after the conclusion of the Congress. The historical significance of the event as well as the interlocutor was thus emphasized by a new medium: the first interview ever printed in the weekly, with which the editor tried to give the impression of immediacy and authenticity. In his introduction and summary, Sokolów distinguished the ideologies of assimilation from those of Zionism and formulated his own position. He endeavoured to achieve a balance, but nevertheless supported Herzl's views. Thus he rejected the claims to leadership put forward by supporters of integration, those representing Jewish 'liberalism', and acknowledged the pressing need for helping the 'Jewish masses'. For Herzl and for Sokolów, the masses were the basis for a Jewish popular thought. In a way both men reproduced the paternalism with respect to the needy Jewish population in Eastern Europe – something for which they reproached the 'liberals' with their 'philanthropy' – by calling for the necessity of bringing about the 'social' or 'moral' improvement, the instruments for achieving this they intended to control. This argumentation linked them firmly to the milieu from which they came, the Jewish bourgeoisie living in large European cities, which economically was basically secure and no longer educated only in the Jewish tradition. The younger generation was no longer satis-

---

9 Nahum Sokołów: Zjazd miłośników Syjonu und Odgłosy – Szczegóły kongresu syonistów. In: Izraelita 32 (1897) 32 (1/13 August 1897), p. 309 and p. 312.
10 Nahum Sokołów: Geschichte des Zionismus. 2 vols. e.g. Vienna et al. (no year), p. 277.
11 Izraelita 32 (1897) 36–38, pp. 341, 349, 361. Quotation p. 342.

fied with the promises of the integrationist ideology. This clearly indicates once more that presumably even before the Basel Congress Sokolów must already have been closer to the ideas of political Zionism. Now, after the Congress, the appearance, form and definition of the position could be put forward in a decidedly more specific and self-confident manner.

From Theodor Herzl's Interview in Warsaw's 'Izraelita'

The term 'Zion' [...] does not have the aim of stirring up the people and inciting them to emigrate. Our goal is merely to create a legally politically secured homestead for those Jews who consider themselves to be forced to emigrate even without our intervention. [...] The colonization has to find its way out of the diapers of philanthropy. The winding and laborious path of carefully creeping into the country has outlived itself [...].

We know the backwardness of this people, we know its poverty, its helplessness, but the moment will come when a feeling of dignity will awaken in it instead of roaming about the Ghettos of London and America. It will show the world that it is capable of helping itself through its own work on its own soil. It should and must find that motivating force and that power through which it can rise to the level, not of the 'chosen people' – such an idea is unknown to us – but much more of a people like every other [...] We do not turn to those who can and who want to live in the countries of their birth. It would be naive of us to try to move in this direction. Those who are contented, those who have associated themselves with the culture of their country do not search for new directions [...] We only turn to those who are forced to emigrate against their will, who would emigrate without us as well, but who emigrate without cohesion, without a goal and represent, wherever they do end up, the kindling used for anti-Semitic fires. In the bosom of nature this people which has lost its way can rediscover its youth and cast off the stigma of dilapidation, here it can find its original appearance again which has been lost during centuries of wandering, its Israelite appearance! And we can but support this movement of rebirth [...] Can there be a goal that would be more worthy of joint efforts, than to form the homestead of a modern culture on the ruins of an ancient civilization? For it is obvious that what will be created in Palestine will have to be modern and – with all tolerance for varying religious directions – progressive. There the Jewish culture shall be creative, founding, there it will prove itself in its most elementary form [...] So what is Zionism? It is the eternal faith of our people, reinforced by philosophical spirit and fanned by the burning enthusiasm of action. All Jewry should rejuvenate and go the way of the world's culture, but without losing its essence. But here, Zionism has only a stimulating effect. I cannot show you a programme, for I myself have only approached the soul of our people a very short time ago. You, the disseminators of Jewish enlightenment, you, who know the situations in your respective countries, work on the moral and material improvement of our people. For a work such as this cannot be done without indigenous, intelligent powers which come from the people and which belong to it with all their heart and soul.

Excerpts from: Izraelita 32 (1897) No. 41–43 from 10/22, 17/29 October and 24 October/5 November 1897, p. 391f., 403f., 415f. Translated from Polish by François Guesnet.

Nadia Guth Biasini
Patrick Marcolli

The Dream of Modernity

Literary Treatments of Zionist Ideas in the Oeuvres of Israel Zangwill and Theodor Herzl

Zangwill's relatively extensive literary oeuvre comprises works based on Jewish and non-Jewish themes. Very rarely among his more important 'Jewish' works is there any direct discussion of Zionism and its aims and ideas. In fact, in his novels and plays Zangwill pursues the lines of thought he devoted himself to with the greatest consistency throughout his life. The spiritual-philosophical element meant more to him than his political activities as a Zionist and territorialist – which admittedly were always founded on these ideas – were able to convey. His favourite issues were those of orthodoxy, assimilation, renewal of Judaism in the light of modernity as well as the guiding role of the Jewish people in the unification of mankind. To illustrate these issues Zangwill uses as his mouthpiece either historical figures – as in 'Dreamers of the Ghetto' which he wrote in 1898 – or makes use of contemporary times, giving the issues he addresses topical significance by describing the Jewish patterns of life in Victorian England, as in 'Children of the Ghetto', written in 1892, 'The King of the Schnorrers' in 1894 and 'Ghetto Comedies' in 1907. While issues of Zionism frequently arise in his essays and letters, his short stories and novels contain only a few passages on the topic. One chapter in 'Children of the Ghetto' deserves special attention because of its historical Zionist perspective. Zangwill caricatures a meeting of the Hovevei Zion movement in London in his title 'The Holy Land League' with a constant ironical undertone. He makes fun of their debates and activities. The chairman of the Hovevei Zion movement is a greengrocer in whose shop the meeting takes place:

'He was a tall, loosely built man, with a pasty complexion, capable of shining with enthusiasm. He was dressed shabbily, and in the intervals of selling cabbages, projected the regeneration of Judah.'[1]

In a second passage, couched in a completely different tone, Zangwill expresses his position on Zionism. In the chapter 'Dreamers in Congress' in his work 'Dreamers of the Ghetto' published in 1898 Zangwill reveals his first impressions of the First Zionist Congress in Basel, Switzerland, where he had a kind of observer status.[2] He praises the Congress as being a 'modern Moses in an abstract-concrete form'. He is extremely enthusiastic about Herzl, particularly the latter's rhetorical abilities appealed to Zangwill. He describes the congress atmosphere as

'stern, [...] the speeches little lightened by humor, the atmosphere of historic tragedy too overbrooding for intellectual dalliance'.

The seriousness of the situation could be seen on all the faces there, be it the German student's, the swarthy Egyptian's, the blond Hungarian's or the small Pole's. And Zangwill once again disassociates himself from the colonization projects preceding Zionism:

---

[1] Israel Zangwill: Children of the Ghetto. London, Toronto 1930, pp. 194ff.
[2] Israel Zangwill: Dreamers of the Ghetto. London 1898, pp. 391ff.

'Let not his movement be confounded with those petty projects for helping Jewish agriculturists into Palestine'.

However, he was not (yet) quite convinced of Herzl's Zionism, either:

'Even our open-eyed Jewish idealist has been blest with the ignorance of the actual. But, in his very ignorance of the people he would lead and the country he would lead them to lies his strength [...] Of the real political and agricultural conditions of Palestine he knows only by hearsay. Of Jews he knows even less.'

According to Zangwill, Herzl's strength therefore lies in his idealism and lack of knowledge about certain matters:

'He stands so high and aloof that all specific colourings and markings are blurred for him into the common brotherhood.'

And at this point the author himself reveals some enthusiasm for the cause:

1 Theodor Herzl, Israel Zangwill and Herzl's mother in front of the Casino in Basel.

'States are the expression of souls; in any land the Jewish soul could express itself in characteristic institutions, could shake off the long oppression of the ages, and renew its youth in touch with the soil. Yet since there *is* this longing for Palestine, let us make capital of it.'

Finally, Zangwill launches into a eulogy of the intellectual abilities of the congress participants present and finishes the chapter with the following, almost memorable passage, in which he again points out that for him a renewed religion is just as important as the national restoration:

'The world in which prophecies are uttered cannot be the world in which prophecies are fulfilled. And yet when – at the wind-up of this memorable meeting – the Rabbi of Bâle [...] ascending the tribune amid the deafening applause of a catholic Congress, expresses the fears of the faithful, lest in the new Jewish State the religious Jew be under a ban; and when the President gravely gives the assurance, amid enthusiasm as frantic, that Judaism has nothing to fear – Judaism, the one cause and consolation of the ages of isolation and martyrdom, – does no sense of the irony of history intrude upon his exalted mood?'

Herzl himself did not focus on Zionist issues in his literary essayistic production until 1902. In his only novel 'Altneuland' (Oldnewland) Herzl described how he imagined the Jewish state once it had been internationally recognized. This work, which formally belongs to the literary genre of 'utopia' and created a vehement controversy, unfurled that Jewish state to the readers which he mapped out on the basis of 'Der Judenstaat' (The Jewish State) and his journey to Palestine. The motto of the novel 'If you will, it is no fairy tale' takes up the idea of 'Der Judenstaat', according to which the success of the movement would depend on the Zionism supporters' will to 'create a state' and on their number. The framework story allows the reader to keep a certain ironical detachment from the emphatically described 'New Society', especially as Herzl modeled it on barely concealed major figures of the Zionist movement. It introduced two friends, an elderly Prussian aristocrat and a younger Viennese Jew. Disappointed by the human race, both withdrew from western society for a period of twenty years to spend their days together on a yacht and an island. After they had visited the 'Holy Land' for the first time in 1902, that is the year the book was published, the Prussian Kingscourt expresses the view that the Jews might

'undertake to set up the pilot plant for mankind, a better world over there, where we've just come from, a new land on the old soil'. But the young Jew from Vienna heard this only in his dream: '... and dreaming, sailed on through the Red Sea into the future.'[3]

Twenty years later, in 1923, the two of them managed to get to the Near East again, where they were in fact guided around a newly instituted state by David Littwak, who would be elected president of the new society towards the end of the novel. They landed in Haifa:

'A beautiful city had been built close to the deep-blue sea [...] the safest and best port in the Mediterranean. Vessels of all shapes and sizes, of all nationalities lay at peace here. Kingscourt and Friedrich were dazed. Their twenty-year-old sea-chart showed no habour here at all – and now here it was, magically brought into being.'[4]

This description includes several elements of 'Der Judenstaat': 'The safest and best port' represents Herzl's demand that the Jewish state should be founded on contemporary technical achievements. If the harbour of Haifa is to afford the ships of all nations safe shelter, this image seems to match the Messianic nationalism of Giuseppe Mazzini [1805–1872], who assumed peaceful coexistence between the national states.[5] The paraphrase 'magically brought into being' is derived from Herzl's deterministic view that the Jewish state constitutes a necessary element in the system of national states.[6]

The political system of the new country seems to be closer to a democracy than Herzl had suggested in 'Der Judenstaat', in which he declared an oligarchy and a constitutional monarchy to be more suitable than a republic. His remarks on the political domain are however rather brief, mainly restricted to the election of the new president of 'Altneuland', the final outcome of which falls back on a gentlemen's agreement. In remarkable detail, the novel describes economic aspects of the new state. Herzl had already been introduced to the plans drawn up by Utopian socialists such as Charles Fourier [1772–1857] and Franz Oppenheimer [1864–1943] in 1901 in his Zionist organ 'Die Welt'. In 'Der Judenstaat' Herzl had already implied that not only capitalism but also socialism should be represented in the new society. David Littwak describes to his two friends an economic order that is based on the system of co-operatives, but at the same time protects private property and in which the level of wages corresponds to the work performed. Moreover, the investment of foreign capital by both Jewish and non-Jewish entrepreneurs is encouraged. Whereas 'Der Judenstaat' is ultimately based on an urban population, 'Altneuland' devotes lengthy passages to agriculture and life in the country. The subject of technology receives the author's special attention. Technological innovations had already thrilled Herzl in his youth. In 'Der Judenstaat' he therefore declared the Jewish question to be obsolete, as 'technological achievements' such as steam power and electricity – and not the postulates of the Enlightenment' – had made it an anachronism. The utopian novel completely documents Herzl's fasci-

---

[3] Theodor Herzl: Altneuland. 4th ed. Leipzig 1903. Quoted from the English version: Theodor Herzl: Oldnewland.Tel Aviv 1960, p. 38.
[4] Ibid, p. 46.
[5] Guiseppe Mazzini: Scritti editi ed inediti. Edizione nazionale a cura di Mario Menghini. Imola 1906–1943, con appendici fino al 1986. Vol. 46, p. 219, vol. 59, p. 121.
[6] Theodor Herzl: Der Judenstaat. Versuch einer Lösung der jüdischen Frage. Leipzig, Vienna 1896, quoted here from the English version of New York 1988, Preface, p. 72: 'The Jewish state is essential to the world; it will therefore be created.'

2   Herzl and the Zionist delegation on the ship to Jaffa, 1898.

nation about technology. Electricity, the engine and contemporary research made a considerable contribution to the building up of the new economy and society of 'Altneuland'. In the novel the 'electrical plough' was introduced from America, which was later to be tested in Soviet Russia. The building up of industry and agriculture was organized by a body of directors and its 'general manager', who actively supported the optimal use of water power.[7]

The feuilleton entitled 'Das lenkbare Luftschiff' (The Dirigible Air Ship), published just a few months after 'Der Judenstaat' on May 31, 1896, also focuses on the subject of technology. The inventor of this dirigible air ship, which was to undertake its maiden flight in 1900 as the 'Zeppelin', decided to destroy his trailblazing invention, as mankind was not worthy of such inventions. The metaphor of the 'air ship', also used in 'Altneuland', apparently goes back to an ironical remark made by Herzl's friend Friedrich Schiff, who described his condition and appearance after the writing of the 'speech to the Rothschilds' as follows: 'I look as if I had invented the dirigible balloon.'[8] In the novel 'Altneuland' David Littwak again adopts the image of the 'air ship', describing the utopias of Bellamy and Hertzka as 'beautiful dreams, or if you like air ships only they are not dirigible'.[9] Besides the image of the 'dirigible air ship' from the field of technology, employed by Herzl to delimit his concept of a state from such utopias based on the idea of a free and sensible individual, Herzl uses another metaphor from the field of technology in his preface to 'Der Judenstaat'. The 'Judennoth' (Jewish Misery) is introduced as steam power 'powerful enough to propel a large engine and to move passengers and goods' and ultimately to found a state. Towards the end of the text, however, he described power despite its progressive function as the cause of unhappiness for many people employed in industrial production 'squeezed together' and subject to the crises of this form of production.[10] Thus the driving power

---

[7]   Herzl: Altneuland, pp. 225ff., 239 and 217ff. Quoted from the German version: Altneuland, 4th ed. Leipzig 1903.

[8]   Theodor Herzl: Briefe und Tagebücher. [BTB] Ed. by Alex Bein et al. 7 vol. Frankfurt a. M., Berlin 1983ff. Here vol. 2, p. 134.
[9]   Herzl: Altneuland, p. 165.
[10] Herzl: Judenstaat, Introduction.

3 Herzl and the Zionist delegation at the Suez Canal, 1898.

used in 'Altneuland' was mainly electricity gained from waterpower.

On the occasion of his journey to Palestine that he embarked on with a delegation after the Second Basel Congress, Herzl expressed his enthusiasm for the technical achievement in his diary entry on the Suez Canal, ascribing a metaphysical dimension to the construction:

'In Port Said I very much admired the Suez Canal. The Suez Canal, that shimmering water line stretching beyond infinity, impressed me far more than the Acropolis [...] but still the colossal will-power that realized the simple thought of digging up sand deserves admiration.'[11]

The shimmering 'water line, the edge of heavens' was already mentioned in a feuilleton entitled 'Emmelfey' he had written ten years before in March 1887, which had been a great success with the readers. In this essay Herzl counters the more or less attractive Amalfi with the magic word 'Emmelfey', coined by a young English beauty. Besides, 'Emmelfey' lingered at the place where

'the view is lost – at the water line, at the confines of heavens [...] And no other folly is as blissful as this: staring at Emmelfey, unreachable and remote.'

In many of his feuilletons before 1895, Herzl contrasted a mixed or even unpleasant outside world with a dream world. 'Das Alltägliche' (The Ordinary) of 1885, 'Neues von der Venus' (News from Venus) written around 1887 and 'Warum schreiben Sie keine Theaterstücke' (Why don't you write plays) of 1895 are based on the irreconcilability of the outside world and the interior dream world. In its framework story 'Altneuland' initially falls back on this structure of earlier essays. The centre of the novel is however the new society, in which society plans, dreams and daydreams influence the creation of the outside world and in which technological progress is applied for the benefit of the whole population.

[11] BTB 2, p. 674, 27 October 1898.

Erik Petry

David Wolffsohn

1   David Wolffsohn [1856–1914].

The Zionist Heinrich Loewe writing about Wolffsohn, Theodor Herzl's successor as president of the Zionist World Organization, states that 'Wolffsohn was loyal to Herzl. As a result his political views are clearly circumscribed',[1] and thereby endorsed the established view of Wolffsohn which had been passed down by historiography and which did not do justice to Wolffsohn.

Wolffsohn, who grew up in a religious, Eastern European family, attended the Talmud Torah school of the Rabbi Isaak Rülf [1831–1902], who inspired his enthusiasm for Zionist ideals at a very early age. After trying his hand at several different professions he lived as a wholesale wood merchant in Cologne from 1888, where he met Max Bodenheimer. Together they founded an 'Association for Colonizing Palestine' in 1894 and the 'National Jewish Association of Cologne' in 1896. Wolffsohn became intersted in the political realization of forming a state in Palestine and therefore soon became Herzl's advisor and friend after the publication of the work 'Der Judenstaat'. Although he was largely in agreement with Herzl's aims, he was not an uncritical follower. He tried to keep the high-flying plans at a realistic level and was, more than anything, a mediator of Herzl's ideas to Eastern European Jewry.

After Herzl's death, Wolffsohn was elected his successor in 1905, but his presidency was not blessed with good fortune. Wolffsohn's personality and his liberal attitude meant that he sought to conclude agreements, and was consequently searching for compromises, for solutions that would satisfy all sides and draw the different strands of Zionism within the organization together and to steer them towards a mutual aim. However, the conflicts about the location for the headquarters – Cologne or Berlin – and the intense arguments between 'practical' and 'political' Zionists which came to a head at the Ninth Congress in 1909 crushed him. In the end he became the focus of animosity from all sides and was seen as a symbol for a Zionism that was merely trying to survive. Wolffsohn was aware of the ambivalence of his position but fought it in vain, until he gave up and resigned in 1911 due to poor health.

Wolffsohn's work for the Zionist movement, his efforts for the development of the Jewish Colonial Bank and the Jewish publishing house and his successes in Eastern Europe were quickly forgotten after his death in 1914. The cliché of Herzl's loyal servant remained, and meant that Wolffsohn was to remain one of the most underestimated and misjudged figures of Zionism.

---

[1]   Heinrich Loewe: Sichronoth, chap. David Wolffsohn, p. 1. Central Zionist Archives, A146/6/2.

Nadia Guth Biasini

Max Nordau

Nordau was born in Pest in 1849. As the son of Rabbi Gabriel Südfeld he received a traditional Jewish education. Aged 15 he turned away from his parents' way of life and changed his name to Nordau. In 1880, after having worked as a physician for some years, he moved to Paris together with his mother and sister, where he worked as physician, psychiatrist, journalist and author. He became known in 1883 by publishing a critical book 'Die conventionellen Lügen der Kulturmenschheit' (Conventional Lies of Cultural Mankind). Like the script 'Entartung' (Degeneration), published in 1892, it had a great influence on the thinking of his times. He criticized the contemporary society, which was – in his eyes – dominated by convention, stagnation and decline. He was actively involved in researching the culture of the 'fin de siècle' and its representatives.

Nordau first came into contact with Zionism during a conversation about the book 'Der Judenstaat' with Herzl in Paris in November 1895, the time when Herzl was writing it. Herzl noted in his diary that Nordau seemed to have been 'fully convinced of the idea' within two days. Presumably Herzl first met Nordau in Paris in 1892, as indicated in his note: 'The physician Max Nordau will be our general practitioner!'. Nordau, the vice-president of the Zionist organization until 1904, consequently supported Herzl and his political diplomatic course and until his own death in 1923 he remained committed to political Zionism. Several of his speeches were highlights of Zionist congresses. Even journalists were impressed by Nordau's appearances:

'After Dr. Herzl had tended to appeal to the emotive feelings in his warm speech, Dr. Nordau from Paris showed himself to be a speaker who, armed with the sharpest weapons of dialectics, turned his attention

1 Max Nordau [1849–1923], cultural and social commentator and proponent of political Zionism.

more toward appealing to the intellect. The striking features of this man are well known in the literary world.'[1]

In the Zionist iconography of the first decade, Nordau's portrait was second in the ranking of importance after that of Herzl with whom he is often seen together in pictures. As early as 1898 he created the term 'Muskeljudentum' (muscle jewry), which was to lead to a new Zionist identity of the Jews in Eastern and Western Europe. At the time of the bitter Uganda Debate of 1903 Nordau, who considered the area which had been proposed by England to be unsuitable, nevertheless came to the assistance of Herzl with the term 'Nachtasyl' (night asylum), which could serve as a sanctuary for impoverished and threatened Jews. Although Herzl wanted Nordau to be his successor, the latter declined the office. From 1905 to 1911 he was president of the congress. After the First World War he remained one of the spiritual leaders of the political opposition against Chaim Weizmann and his 'synthetic Zionism'. Although Weizmann tried to convince him of his ideas, Nordau was not to be won over.

[1] Basler Nachrichten of 31 August 1897.

Nadia Guth Biasini

Arthur Cohn, Rabbi of Basel's Jewish Community

Arthur Cohn, who was born in 1862, was the first permanently employed rabbi in Basel's Jewish community. Shortly before taking office in 1885, he had received his diploma at the rabbinical seminary of Azriel Hildesheimer in Berlin, whose orientation can be characterized as 'neo-orthodox' and thus stood in opposition to 'reform Judaism'. Parallel to his training as a rabbi, he had completed his studies in history and philology, and in 1884 he obtained a doctorate with distinction under the tutelage of Theodor Mommsen. The combination of traditional Judaism and European culture corresponded completely with the programme offered at the rabbinical seminary in Berlin and later was also a feature of his work as a rabbi in Basel.

Impressed by the distinguished figures of Theodor Herzl and Max Nordau and by the Zionists from Russia, in 1897 Rabbi Cohn changed from initially being a skeptic to an enthusiastic supporter of Zionism. In this way he differed noticeably from his German colleagues. During the first congresses, various Zionists visited him at his house. In the article he wrote about the First Congress, which appeared in the orthodox magazine 'Der Israelit' and which the editorial office supplemented by adding a statement concerning anti-Zionism, Cohn supported the view that the settling in the Holy Land was consistent with the Messianic hopes. Cohn's statement signified a breakthrough and made it possible for many other rabbis to support Zionism as well. Even before the First Congress took place, Rabbi Cohn acted as mediator between the Zionist movement and Basel's Jewish community.

1   Arthur Cohn [1862–1926].

In 1911 Cohn became convinced that the official statements of the Zionists were no longer compatible with a religious view of the world. For this reason he participated in establishing the 'Agudat Israel' in Katowice in 1912, a non-Zionist, orthodox organization that was supposed to represent the interests of Jews all over the world.

During his period in office in Basel, differences emerged from time to time with the community leaders. Thus, in 1917 without consulting them the rabbi asked the military authorities to allow Jewish soldiers to go on leave so that they could attend the Passover celebration. Representatives of the community did not support this petition because it contradicted their views. In his work and in his writings, Arthur Cohn, who died in 1926, fought throughout his whole life to strengthen orthodox Judaism.

Simone Berger

David Farbstein: A Pioneer of Swiss Zionism

1 David Farbstein [1868–1953].

David Farbstein was born in Warsaw in 1868. His upbringing was 'religious, but not fanatic'.[1] As was so often the case in these times, the library of his father contained the Jewish religious books, while his mother preferred the German classics. He retained a lasting impression from his Talmud teacher Rabbi Chaim Eliezer Wachs, a follower of Hovevei Zion. Farbstein started Zionist activities very early; at the age of twenty, he and his brother Joshua Heshel founded the Zionist youth organization 'Doreshei Zion'. Also during his years at the university – at the age of 24, he began his studies at the law faculty in Berlin and went to Zurich in 1894 – he was an active member of pro-Zionist associations. Together with Victor Jacobson, Leo Motzkin, Joseph Lurie, Marcus Ehrenpreis and Osias Thon he was an active member of the 'Jung-Israel' (Young Israel) organization.

Farbstein wrote his doctorate in Berne. In 1897 he became a Swiss citizen. Seven years later he was elected as social democrat to the city council of Zurich. In this capacity he approached the Jewish question twice, both times in connection to new laws about Eastern Jewish refugees looking for asylum. In the internal Jewish framework he also stood up for the Eastern European Jews:

'The Eastern European Jews are poor, but honest people. Most of them work very hard for their daily bread and possibly even an Eastern European usury Jew stands above a Western European Mr. Arton.'[2]

'We were Zionists before Herzl' is how Farbstein summarized his early Zionist activity. In the first year of the monthly news magazine 'Ha-Shiloach' published by Ahad Haam, he discussed Herzl's 'Jewish state'. He made a clear distinction between his attitude and that of Herzl:

'Herzl wants the release from national hatred, so his chief issue is the Jewish state, while I see economical reasons as the main point for the hatred of the Jews. A change of the economical living conditions is the main thing, and because this change can only happen in a Jewish state, the Jewish state is the principal prerequisite for the solution of the Jewish question. Not by buying a land but by cultivating its soil can the living conditions

---

[1] David Farbstein: Aus meinem Leben. In: Schweizerischer Israelitischer Gemeindebund 1904–1954. Festschrift zum 50jährigen Bestehen. Basel 1954, p. 197.

[2] David Farbstein: Der Zionismus und die Judenfrage ökonomisch und ethisch. Bern 1988, p. 18 (special edition of the speech at the First Zionist Congress).

of our people be improved. "Rome and Jerusalem" was the beginning of the utopian period of the national movement and the "Jewish state" is the beginning of the end of the utopian movement, which has to be followed by a scientific period.'[3]

Thereupon he was engaged by Herzl as an employee of 'Die Welt'. He organized that Basel should become the location for the First Zionist Congress, where he held a well-received speech about the economic and social-political necessity of Zionism. After the Congress, Farbstein founded in Zurich the 'Zionistische Ortsgruppe' (the local Zionists), of which he became chairman. The foundation of the Zionist students' association 'Hessiana', named after Moses Hess, took place at around the same time. For a long time Farbstein was head of the 'Zionistische Ortsgruppe', was delegate at the Zionist congresses and wrote energetically about Zionism in the press.

Farbstein worked as an attorney for a long time and was often called upon to defend criminal cases at jury court. He was involved in many political trials, also as defence attorney at the military court. His work as a lawyer was not satisfying for him in the long term, however. Furthermore, in those days it was

'impossible for a Jew to be elected district judge. I was supported by the social-democratic party for the position of district judge, but I was not elected.'

Farbstein could not become a private lecturer, because he did not have the financial means. So he taught himself several further fields of jurisprudence.

In 1922, Farbstein was one of the first Jews ever elected to the national council, where he remained until 1938 and was mainly active in judicial commissions. In 1929 his party nominated Farbstein for the position of federal judge at the Federal Assembly. Farbstein himself was of the opinion that he would have been elected if he had not declined the candidacy from the beginning. Although Farbstein was brought up in an orthodox fashion, it can be seen from his personal notes that he participated in meetings on Saturday afternoons and that he met with his colleagues afterwards in cafés. But he always remained true to his Talmudic knowledge:

'The biggest influence on my judicial works were my Talmudic upbringing and my knowledge of the Talmud.'

Farbstein tended to want to intercede between two different systems. In this way he tried to bring Zionism closer to non-Jews, but also published an article, in which he recommended the democratic system of Switzerland and the system of referenda and the citizens' initiative to the Israeli government as a model worthy of imitation. He placed emphasis on his good relationships to the national councils of other parties and according to an anecdote chuckled about the meeting of the banker Julius Bär for talks with the Social Democrats.

He was full of praise for the understanding of the Swiss people for the Jews:

'The people of Switzerland are an intelligent people. They can see that Jews, who have suffered so much in the past and to some extent still do, are linked by a strong bond.'

The 'double identity' of being a Swiss and a Jew does not seem to have been a cause for concern for him.

'The Swiss Jew should acquire the high cultural values of the Swiss, their honest character, their democratic ideas, he should think and feel in a Swiss way. But none the less he should stay an upright Jew.'[4]

Although Farbstein did not define the 'upright' Jew, we can assume, by looking at his personal character and behaviour, that he saw his life as a realization of this ideal. Farbstein died in Zurich in 1953.

---

[3] Berliner Büro der Zionistischen Organisation (ed.): Warum gingen wir zum ersten Zionistenkongress? Berlin 1922, p. 33, 34.

[4] Farbstein: Aus meinem Leben, pp. 219, 220, 224, 223.

Verena von Planta

Ahad Haam

1 Ahad Haam [1856–1927].

Asher Ginzberg, who later called himself Ahad Haam – 'one of the people' – was born on August 18, 1856, in Skvira, in the Kiev district. He studied philosophy in various European cities and lived in Odessa from 1885, and then in London from 1907 on. His first travels to Palestine were in 1891 and 1893. His name is closely associated with cultural Zionism, which came into being not least as a result of the criticism at the First Zionist Congress. Already in his first articles in the journal 'Ha-Meliz' Ahad Haam criticized the lack of orientation of the cultural and spiritual values of Judaism, for example, the Hovevei Zion movement, of which he initially was a member, or the settlers in Palestine. The Hebrew journal 'Ha-Shiloah', the editor of which he was from 1896 to 1903, intended to promote knowledge and understanding of Judaism in different ways, to describe the 'inner' life of the Jewish people, as well as to provide the new Hebrew literature with a forum. Ahad Haam himself made a significant contribution to the revival of modern Hebrew with his essays. His aim was to unite the scattered people with a unifying cultural bond. The plans for a Jewish encyclopaedia in Hebrew, which he hoped would have a great 'educational effect', aimed in the same direction.

Ahad Haam was deeply disappointed with the results of the First Zionist Congress, since in his opinion it did not deal with cultural but only with political and diplomatic issues. He found Herzl's objectives unrealistic and overhasty. In his view the Jews that had been assimilated to the Western world had already surrendered their identity and no longer knew about 'Jewish nature and values', so that in the end the Jewish state 'would be a state of Germans or French of Jewish descent' without charisma. Ahad Haam wanted Zionism to be the quest for a spiritual national centre which might be able to have an effect on the Diaspora. For him the founding of 'a true *Jewish* state' was only possible on the basis of a living Jewish culture. With his ideas he exerted a great influence on younger Zionists such as Martin Buber and Chaim Weizmann. During the war Ahad Haam kept in close contact with Weizmann. When the Balfour Declaration was being drawn up, Ahad Haam warned against exaggerated expectations and drew the attention to the justified claims of the Arab inhabitants of Palestine. He died on January 2, 1927, in Tel Aviv, where he had been living since 1922.

Almut Bonhage

Nathan Birnbaum

1   Nathan Birnbaum [1864–1937].

Nathan Birnbaum's life was shaped by the idea of unifying the Jewish people as a nation. Even though the forms of this concept changed – Zionism, Diaspora nationalism or orthodoxy – his aim always remained the same: to cultivate the independence and individuality of the Jewish people and to guarantee its survival. Right from the beginning he was one of the pioneers in supporting the renewal of Judaism.

Birnbaum was born in Vienna on May 16, 1864. He grew up in an environment of assimilated Jews. From 1881 the migration of the Eastern Jews to the west increased in its scope. They fled because of the pogroms and the poverty in the Russian empire. Often they were entirely unfamiliar with German culture. Many established Jews in Vienna feared that this would give rise to a disturbance of the German-Jewish dialogue and an increase in anti-Semitism. Their reaction to this was to put more effort into their assimilation. Birnbaum was strictly opposed to using assimilation as a tool to solve the 'Jewish Question'. He considered this as a shameful hypocrisy and an insipid imitation of German culture. He called upon his people to mould an independent Jewish self-awareness.

In 1882 – at the age of eighteen – Birnbaum founded the students' association 'Kadimah' in Vienna. From 1885 onwards he published the newspaper 'Selbst-Emancipation' (Self-Emancipation) in which he coined the term 'Zionism' in 1890. He was also probably the first person to publicly use the term 'Eastern Jew'. In 1893 he published the essay 'The National Rebirth of the Jewish People as a Means of Solving the "Jewish Question"; an Appeal to the Good and Noble of all Nations'. In contrast to Herzl, Birnbaum did not see Zionism as a mobilization of Western European powers to save the Eastern Jews. For him, Zionism was a cultural movement which should help the Western Jews to find their 'ethnic identity' and urge the Eastern Jews to modernize. Zionism was supposed to reunify the Jewish people in this way.

Disappointed after the second Zionist Congress, Birnbaum turned from Zionism and dedicated himself to Eastern Judaism. He committed himself to having Jews accepted as an independent nation in the Diaspora. In the multinational empire of Austria and Hungary he put all his efforts into the acceptance of Yiddish as an offical language and of the Jewish people as an independent cultural group. In 1908 he organized the World Convention for the Yiddish Language in Czernowitz.

Later he became more and more of the opinion that the only values on which Judaism could base itself were God and the Torah. Thus he became one of the leaders of the orthodox 'Agudat Israel'. Birnbaum died on April 2, 1937, in Scheveningen.

Patrick Marcolli

Israel Zangwill

The English author Israel Zangwill participated in the First Zionist Congress as a more or less sceptical listener. Another participant later recalled that he 'demonstratively took a seat on the last chair of the hall as a kind of observer'.[1] This attitude towards Zionism is typical for the man that Herzl, upon his first visit to London in 1895, met with the words:

'I am Theodor Herzl. Help me to rebuild the Jewish state.'

Zangwill's first biographer, who was otherwise well disposed towards him, describes Zangwill's position towards the question of the Jewish Diaspora and the problems connected with it as 'consistently inconsistent'.[2] And indeed his attitude does seem contradictory at first glance. Looking at it more closely, a direction is discernable. Israel Zangwill was born in London in 1864 as the son of Jewish immigrants from Galicia. During his work as author, journalist, Zionist and territorialist he tried to deal with Jews in the Diaspora and the consequences of their persecution in two different ways. He gave priority to alleviating the situation of Eastern Jewish refugees, which is why in 1905 he promoted the Uganda proposal of the English government and inspired the Territorial Organization. At the same time for Zangwill there also existed a philosophical-spiritual level, which he often tried to unify with pragmatical steps, thus getting entangled in apparent contradictions and complications which gave fuel to his critics.

The first phase of Zangwill's thoughts can be traced to approximately 1895, when he published his book 'Children of the Ghetto', with which he enjoyed considerable literary success. In this book he dealt with the Jewish community of London. He formulated for the first time his view of historic-positive Judaism which in his opinion had universal significance, and was the real religion of mankind, so that the Jews would be the forerunner in unifying the whole of mankind. Zangwill never lost contact with this stream of thoughts, not even as he fully committed himself to Herzl's Zionism a short time later. In 1899 he wrote an essay entitled 'Zionism', in which he named four possibilities for the future of the Jews: '(1) national renewal, (2) religious renewal, (3) disappearance and (4) no solution.'[3] Under the conditions of the time, he believed that a religious regeneration was only possible by founding a Jewish state. Consequently there were only two real alternatives for Judaism: Jewish nationalism or complete dissolution.

Until 1905 Zangwill participated in several Zionist congresses as an official English delegate. The offer of the English government to provide

---

[1] R. Gottheil to L. Wolf, 17 November 1926. Quoted in: Stuart A. Cohen: English Zionists and British Jews. Princeton 1982, p. 33.
[2] Maurice Wohlgelernter: Israel Zangwill. A Study. New York, London 1964, p. ix.
[3] Maurice Simon (ed.): Speeches, Articles and Letters of Israel Zangwill. London 1937, p. 155.

1 Israel Zangwill at the Seventh Zionist Congress in Basel in 1905.

the territory around Uganda as a Jewish 'homestead' led to his breaking with the official Zionist politics. Zangwill founded the 'Jewish Territorial Organization'. Later, mainly between the end of the First World War and his death in 1926, as it became clear that projects of this type had failed, the United States became the focus of his interest. In his stage play 'The Melting Pot' in the year 1909, he took up this idea and from then on the United States became the country where the multi-ethnical 'new Hebrew people' could originate. Zangwill tried to teach the universal truth of Hebrewism to the Americans, always bearing in mind the aim of unifying mankind.

Jews in Basel and the Region: Their Situation and the Beginnings of Zionism

Werner Meyer

Jews in Medieval Basel

As far as can be ascertained, the Jews of Basel moved there from the Alsace and from the cities of the central Rhine area around 1200. In the Middle Ages, Basel was, culturally and economically speaking, part of the Alsace. In addition to this the city had relationships to the Burgundian area as it was placed under the suzerainty of the archbishopric of Besançon and had belonged to the kingdom of Upper Burgundy. There were also orientations to the Breisgau. All of these facts influenced the migrationary directions of the Jews. Around 1300, as the expulsion of the Jews from France gave rise to new waves of immigration into the Alsace, at least some of the expellees probably ended up in Basel. Perhaps the 56 French coins which stem from the time before 1305 found in the older Jewish cemetery in 1937 may be connected to these events.

In Basel, the Jews formed a firmly organized community, similar to their settlements in other Alsatian cities, under the leadership of directors and rabbis, not only as a religious community but also as a commercial association. This showed certain similarities with the guilds which began forming in the 13th century. These, however, were formed under the patronage of the episcopal head of the city, whereas the Jews, as 'servants of the court' enjoyed the protection of the Emperor. The relative size of the Basel Jewish community could be seen in the imperial tax of 40 marks which, around 1240, corresponded to that of the Jews of Colmar. The Strasbourg Jews, on the other hand, paid 200 marks. The synagogue, the central focus of the Jewish community, stood at the former cattle market near today's Gerbergasse. As did most of the Jewish houses, it stood in the area of the St. Leonhard diocese which took taxes from the individual residences. Inasmuch as the houses can be localized – to a certain extent they were probably built by the Jews and partially bought from Christian owners – they were spread around the craftsmen's quarter between today's Barfüsserplatz and Marktplatz. Even though they were all close to the synagogue, they did not form a ghetto but could be found amongst the estates of the trading members of the guilds. Unfortunately, no archaeological remains of these Jewish buildings have been found so far. On the other hand, there have been a number of findings in the Jewish cemetery. The cemetery was outside the city walls, in the area around the 'Kollegiengebäude' (today's main building of the University) at Petersplatz. After burial places had already been discovered in 1885, but unfortunately were not documented, further graves containing around 150 skeletons were discovered in 1937. Documented are children and adults as well as two coin deposits from around 1300, one with French coins and the other with pfennigs from the region. This cemetery also possessed the largest number of gravestones, which had been used as construction material and were repeatedly found in the city.

The Jews were well integrated in the economic life of the city. They were active as money-changers and – often in grand dimensions – as money-lenders. Among their debitors was also the bishop, who pawned the cathedral treasure

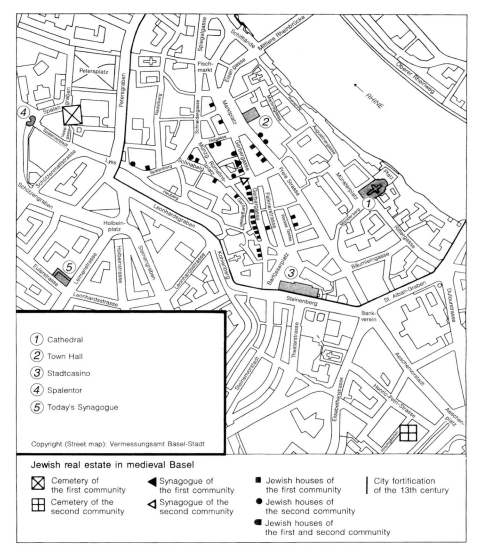

1 The city map shows the real estate that could be clearly identified. Not marked are the houses that appeared in documents but could not be located. They were mainly situated in the area of the houses marked on the map. In some cases, Jews also had houses on the right bank of the Rhine in the city of Kleinbasel.

around 1223, presumably to finance the construction of the Rhine bridge. The Jews received competition from the Lampartians from northern Italy and the Cavertians from southern France who forced their way into the credit business in Basel around 1300. The Basel Jews were apparently not affected by the unrests and persecutions at the end of the 13th century and the early 14th century which the Alsatian Jews suffered from. In 1345 Basel joined a peace alliance of Alsatian cities

2 Gravestone of Rabbi Jacob, who was assassinated and burried on August 19, 1330. The stone was found in the cloister of the cathedral where it was used as a base-plate. Now in the yard of the Jewish Museum in Basel.

and lords which was directed against the persecution of Jews by gangs of farmers. And in 1347/48 the city banned a number of noblemen who had attacked and robbed Jews in order to get rid of their debts.

As in many other cities, for the Basel Jewish community disaster struck in 1349. However, the exact reasons and processes cannot be reconstructed from the sources with any certainty. Frightened by the horrible rumours of the plague, the people of Basel seem to have succumbed to a mass hysteria, and to have pressed their rulers into using violence against the Jews which served as scapegoats. On January 16, 1349, all Jews the people could get hold of were burnt on an island in the Rhine. Others, who had hoped to save themselves by being baptized, were later charged with the old accusation of poisoning food and wells and tortured into making a confession, which also led to their execution. This version of the pogrom, solely based on official sources, remains implausible. Presumably, the council itself which was under the strong influence of the nobles, deeply indebted to the Jews, and the Christian money-lenders was behind the violence and the persecution. By blaming the population for it, the council wanted to justify itself to the emperor and to hide the fact that the infamous act of extermination was aimed at eliminating stubborn creditors and troublesome competitors. In any case, by the end of 1349, the Jewish community was exterminated, its cemetery destroyed, and all debts were declared liquidated. Basel swore not to admit any Jews for the next 200 years.

Jews who had escaped from the massacre found sanctuary in the surrounding districts with the landed gentry, namely in territory under Austrian rule. As early as 1360, Alsatian cities began again to grant Jews the right of domicile. Jews were needed for the loan business and it was considered desirable to have them under control within the city walls, for under Austrian protection they represented a political risk factor as creditors. There is evidence of Jewish presence in Basel again after 1362. After 1365, as emperor Charles IV – even though revocably – gave up his protection and tax collecting right to the city, there was a real wave of immigration from the Alsace. This made the formation of a new community possible which concentrated around Gerbergasse and Rümelinsplatz, although the new dwellings are only partially identical with the houses of the first community that could be documented. The synagogue was located in Grünpfahlgässlein, at the place of today's building of a branch of 'Crédit Suisse'. From 1394 on, the Jewish community had a cemetery on the unoccupied land within the new city walls in Hirschgässlein, close to today's Historical Seminar. Included in the jurisdiction of the city, the Jews were now under the protection of the Basel council. Molesting of Jews, such as stone throwing, was punished with a ban from the city. On the

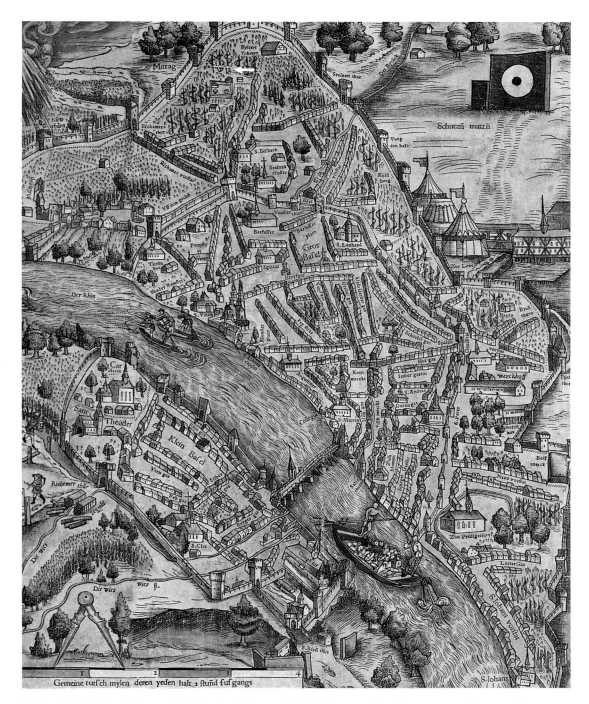

3 Detail of the Basel city map by Sebastian Münster of 1538. The newer Jewish cemetery of the second community, known as the *Garden of Eden* (in Hebrew letters), is visible (white arrow) at the upper edge of the map.

Jews in Medieval Basel

other hand, Jews were also banned by the authorities when they disregarded the pleas for fairness – for example when violently collecting their debts. Wealthy Jews, however, did have the opportunity of buying themselves out of their ban by paying a large amount of money.

The circumstances of the end of the second Jewish community in Basel remain unclear. After 1390 it appears that a renewed anti-Jewish sentiment arose in the Alsace due to plagues and unrests, which might have reminded the Jews of the terrible events in 1349. In Basel, where the question of the political patronage – city or Austria – had not yet been decided upon finally and threatened to break out into a conflict between pro- and anti-Austrian parties, most Jews chose to leave the city and to settle in territories under Austrian rule, especially in the Sundgau. Attempts by the council to stop this exodus failed. So the Jewish community disappeared shortly before 1400 but still, a number of questions remain unanswered. For instance, we do not know how long the cemetery in Hirschgässlein, which was also used by communities from outside the city and which was still referred to as 'Garden of Eden' written in Hebrew on Sebastian Münster's map of the city in the 16th century, was still needed. But most of all it is uncertain when and why the decision was taken in Basel after 1397 not to allow any more Jews to live in the city. What is certain is that no Jews lived in Basel any longer shortly after 1400 and that this remained so until around 1800, while the other Alsatian cities did not expel their Jews until around 1500. Presumably they had no need for Jews anymore: in the 15th century, the Basel loaning business was increasingly dominated by wealthy merchants who were also members of the council.

The Jews were also forced out of another professional sector, medicine. The very last Jewish doctor in Basel was Master Gutleben, who worked as an appointed surgeon between 1398 and 1406.

From then on, the Jews lived in the country surrounding Basel, under the protection of Austria, the bishop of Basel and of smaller lords. Their presence is proven by the multitude of duties which travelling Jews and their belongings were subjected to, and especially their dead, who often had to be transported to distant burial grounds. Attempts by the city to have the Jews expelled from the villages near the city failed to a large extent. As Pope Felix was crowned in 1440 during the council, to which the traditional hommage of the Jews also belonged, the city council issued an appeal to the public which was designed to protect the Jews that came from the surroundings from molestations by the population. Perhaps the increase in Jewish christenings in the 15th century can be explained by the lack of support that would have been offered by a strong Jewish community.

After 1500, Basel developed into a centre for academic studies dealing with Jewish culture. The upholding of the Hebrew language at the university and the – censored – printing of Jewish works by Basel printers are no reason to assume that Basel had a particularly favourable attitude towards Jews. Although this would correspond with Basel's self-complacent representation of its past. But when one considers the stubbornness with which the city fought against the presence of Jews within its walls and in the nearby villages of the bishop, between the 16th and 18th century the open-mindedness of a small group of academics should not be overestimated.

Nadia Guth Biasini

The Jewish Community in Basel

The history of the third Jewish community in Basel around the turn of the century begins with the immigration of Jewish men and women from the Alsace around 1800, after Switzerland had introduced the Helvetian constitution in 1798, which in many respects was influenced by France. The year 1805 can be regarded as the date when the community was established. With the defeat of France and the order created by the Congress of Vienna, the situation of the Jews in Basel changed to their disadvantage. They were now only allowed to receive residence permits that were limited to a temporary period of time. Attempts to expel them totally from the city could only be prevented by the Eidgenössische Tagsatzung (Swiss Confederate Diet). This restrictive policy proved to be effective: whereas in 1815 35 Jewish families were living in Basel, in 1847 the number of families with residence permits had been reduced to eleven. In 1849 the situation of the Jewish families improved again inasmuch as the revision of the law regulating the right of domicile – after several attempts – granted all sons born or raised in Basel the right of domicile. From this time on the continuity of the community appeared assured. The community in Basel gained the right of establishment and the freedom of trade through the partial revision of the federal constitution of 1866, and freedom of religion through the new federal constitution of 1874. Moreover, this late emancipation of the Jewish population in Basel, compared to Switzerland as well as to Europe, originated from demands made by France, Holland, England and the US, which linked the finalization of bilateral trade agreements with a call for equal rights for all citizens in Switzerland. Compared to other cantons in Switzerland, Basel was not really progressive: Geneva first accepted Jews as citizens in 1843 and Bern granted them the freedom of domicile in 1846.

The Jewish community in Basel – as were the other Jewish communities throughout Switzerland – was confronted with huge tasks in the decades which followed the emancipation of 1866/74. The most important matter was the necessity to deal with a rapid increase in the Jewish population. Between 1880 and 1900, the number of people rose from 830 to 1,897, and by 1910 it had reached 2,452. In the same period of time, the total number of people living in the city increased from 65,101 to 135,918. The general demographic change was linked to drastic changes in the economic, social and political life. Basel also began to transform itself: after the walls of the city were pulled down in 1860, the radius of the city had enlarged considerably, and in the 1880s Marktplatz had been redesigned. Between 1891 and 1913, the small streets in the city centre were widened, the first tram line in Basel began to operate in 1895, and the wooden bridge over the Rhine was rebuilt in stone at the beginning of the century.

The Jewish men and women living in Basel first immigrated mainly from the Alsace – which belonged to Germany after 1871 – and from France. In addition, between 1880 and 1910, numerous Jews moved to the city from Aargau and

1 The day before the old Rhine bridge was torn down on May 27, 1903.

some from Zurich and the countryside around Basel. Toward the end of the 1880s, immigrants came in increasing numbers from Baden and other parts of Germany. A larger number of Jews stemming from Eastern Europe were first recorded in 1900. In 1910 they represented between 20 and 25 percent of the Jewish population.

The growth of the Jewish population caused the community to commission an architect in 1888 to enlarge the synagogue designed at one time by Hermann Gauss, which had only been inaugurated twenty years before. The community's request for a public contribution for the renovation work was rejected, because only a few months before – on December 2, 1889 – the cantonal parliament had revised the position of the state to the effect

2 The synagogue by Hermann Gauss (1868). As seen from the south-east.

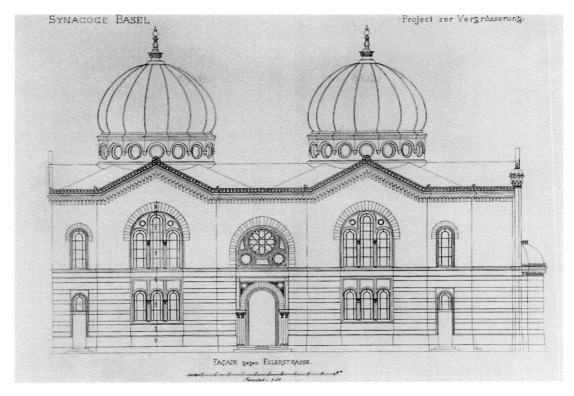

3   The plan of Paul Reber: Façade on Eulerstrasse.

'that it would finance exclusively the cultural needs of the Reformed Church and the Roman Catholic Church.'[1]

The enlargement of the synagogue, which basically amounted to doubling the size of the building at a cost of about 145,000 Swiss francs, was thus carried out by the architect Paul Reber [1835–1908] without public funds. As in 1868, two members of the city council of the Canton Basel-Stadt as well as other representatives of the authorities took part in the official dedication, which took place on September 15, 1892. The synagogue's Romanesque façade, which was designed by Gauss and adopted by Paul Reber, fitted easily into the surroundings and can thus be viewed as the expression of the willingness to integrate into the existing Christian society. The striking cupola and the dominance of the elements of Moorish style in the interior indicate, on the other hand, that the architect and the community decided in favour of a mixture of various oriental styles, which at that time was gaining acceptance in Europe as an architectural style for building synagogues and was intended to give expression to the Jewish identity. In addition to this, Reber had a special gallery furnished in the western part of the building to accommodate the organ; however, none was ever bought. In 1900 the members of the community agreed to introduce choir singing and a chancel for the purpose of holding sermons in the German language,

[1]   StABS, Kirchenakten Q1, 1 January 1890.

The Jewish Community in Basel

4 Theodor Herzl in front of the Synagogue in Basel, 1903.

dox' school of thought; however, in Berlin he had also received a doctorate in history and philology. The work he did in Basel and in Switzerland was focused on his attempts to strengthen a Jewry loyal to the Torah, but he was also prepared to make certain compromises.

In the last decade of the 19th century, all of the Jewish communities in Switzerland had to come to terms with the anti-Semitic campaign which emerged within the scope of an initiative to prohibit kosher slaughtering, which was adopted by the people and the Stände (cantons) in August 1893 – against the recommendation of the Executive Federal Council and the National Council. When the results of the vote were announced, a distinct anti-Semitic atmosphere arose in Basel, as was recorded in a statement made by the community's president to the police and in the accompanying administrative report.[2]

Around the turn of the century, the Jewish population in Basel was mainly engaged in trade. The majority of their businesses were in the textile branch – ranging from the trade in wool, silk and waste silk, the 'schappe', to silk ribbons and fabrics to the sale of linen, hats and clothing. Because Basel had been a centre for the silk ribbon industry and silk processing since the 18th century, it was clear that many became active in this field. In addition, many were involved in the food and wine business. The number of cattle dealers in Basel, on the other hand, was quite small. Some members of the community traded in furs, leather and leather goods. Of the two Jewish banking establishments in Basel during those years, one developed to one of the leading private banks in the city, and also achieved importance in the whole of Switzerland. After the turn of the century, there were no fundamental changes in the occupational and business structure for a while. The number of those working in professions rose gradually as well as the degree of academic training.

which was adopted by the reform movement. The city did not grant the Jewish community the right to have a separate cemetery until 1902. Up to that time the deceased had been transported to Hegenheim in the Alsace.

The community's first permanently appointed rabbi was Arthur Cohn, who took office in 1885 at the age of twenty-three. On the basis of his rabbinical training, he belonged to the 'neo-ortho-

[2] StABS, Kirchenakten Q1, 8 August 1893.

Patrick Kury

'First the Return Home, Then the Conversion'

Christian Zionism and Philo-Semitism in Basel at the Time of the First Zionist Congress

'I think it is fair to say the first and the subsequent Zionist congresses in Basel had a profound effect on the relationship between Jews and Christians in Basel, and the deep feelings which the Christians of Basel had for the participants in the congresses had an effect on the direct relationship between the Jewish and non-Jewish population of Basel. The practising Protestant Christians in Basel believed in the fulfilment of the prophecy that promised to return the Jews the "Holy Land" that they once lost.'[1]

Theodor Nordemann's statement is an example for the positive evaluation of the relationship between Jews and Christians in Basel. Without doubt the ten congresses strengthened the understanding between the two religions and enriched the city of Basel. In the memories of participants of the congresses there is much praise for and happiness about the uncomplicated and warm welcome that they received in that city. However some sources from the environment surrounding the First Zionist Congress do darken this harmonious picture.

Especially from the Christian community disconcerting voices could be heard. The closing words of a comment in the 'Basler Volksblatt' – the official organ of the Catholics – about the First Zionist Congress were as follows:

'We know from the Bible that the Jews of the Old Testament worked in the fields, grew wine, had orchards; that there were professionals amongst them goes without saying. But what would the farms and handicraft workshops of the Jews look like today! These things require hands to *work*, and all of Europe knows only trading Jews, not working Jews. It is possible that the Zionists instruct their sons in time! In this and in other respects, the Zionist Congress appeared to the dispassionate observer to be somewhat utopian and for a large section of the Zionists the "return home" only seems to be clear from the outside, from the inside it still seems to be very obscure. We must concur with Dr. Herzl here, when he says that in order to return to Palestine, it is first necessary to return to Judaism, i.e. to Moses, the Prophets and the Jewish laws. But we would like to go one step further and say that a Jewish return home only makes sense if it is done with the recognition of the Messiah who was prophecied by the Prophets and long awaited by the Jews but who was then not accepted and maliciously crucified by them! Other prophecies have been fulfilled, this prophecy will also be fulfilled. How? When? God's ways are not our ways, but *He* will continue to find ways and means of leading his people to salvation. First the return home, then the conversion. Thus the efforts of Zionism are of interest to us Christians and they are attractive to us because we have the same focus: the Messiah!'[2]

For us today this kind of arrogant style and the reproaches against Judaism seem very strange. Besides anti-Semitic expressions one can hear sympathy and agreement with the aims of the Zionist movement. At the turn of the century the 'Basler Volksblatt' was one of the newspapers

---

[1] Theodor Nordemann: Zur Geschichte der Juden in Basel. Jubiläumsschrift der israelitischen Gemeinde Basel, aus Anlass ihres 150jährigen Bestehens 5565–5715, 1805–1955. No place, no date, p. 131.

[2] Basler Volksblatt, 2 September 1897.

1. Bernhard Collin-Bernoulli [1824–1899], Protestant and committed social philanthropist. Co-Founder of the «Allgemeine Consumverein».

with rather mistrusting and disapproving attitudes towards Judaism. On the question of ritual-religious equality of Jews and Christians on the other hand, the Jewish community of Basel found a reliable partner in this newspaper, which had not forgotten the experiences of the 'Kulturkampf' (cultural struggle). This contradictory behaviour can also be explained by the social position of the Catholics in the Protestant-dominated city of Basel. More tolerated than accepted, the Catholics – most of whom belonged to the lower class and were excluded from the city's informal course of decision making – fought for social acceptance. The time of the First Zionist Congress was only eleven years after the Catholics of Basel were allowed to consecrate their first new church after the Reformation. Jews and Catholics were the minorities of the city, but with enormous numeric differences. Like so often in history, instead of the minorities joining together to be stronger against the majority, the numerically larger group also developed discriminating practices against the 'smaller' group in a kind of minority hierarchy. Besides these 'pecking order struggles' of the religious minorities, 'proselytism' played an important role, and was widespread in the 19th century.

In the argumentation pattern of the author – following a precapitalistic understanding of the term work – a criticism of Jewish trading activities as something 'unproductive' is connected with numerous anti-Jewish stereotypes, especially the 'Christ's or God's murder accusation'. Since antiquity, this unfounded accusation was continually made and in the late Middle Ages and in the early modern times reached its sad climax. Not until the Second Vatican Council was this attitude finally dropped by the Catholics. This, the oldest anti-Jewish stereotype of Christian origin together with other ideas were the fundament for Christian attempts to convert Jews, as they are also emphasized at the end of the article. In the 19th century mainly Protestant-Pietist theologians wanted to accelerate the 'conversion of Israel'. It is not always clear, however, whether the comprehensive Christianization of the Jews, the 'acceleration of the return of the Heavenly Redeemer' by returning the Jews to Palestine or the escorting of 'Israel on its way to self-realization in the face of its God' was meant.[3] Here Pietists of Basel were of tremendous importance.

Several times it is indicated that Bernhard Collin-Bernoulli [1824–1899], Paul Kober-Gobat [1842–1898] and Carl Friedrich Heman [1839–1919] were very helpful in preparing the First Zionist Congress. Not only were these three men of German background, but they were also deeply anchored in Pietist Protestantism and the Basel society.

The businessman Bernhard Collin-Bernoulli, a typical Christian social philanthropist of the 19th century, came to Basel in 1848 converted from Judaism to Christianity and joined the wholesale ribbon business of Emanuel Bernoulli.

---

[3] Thomas Willi: Der Verein der Freunde Israels 150 Jahre. Schweizerische Evangelische Judenmission, Stiftung für Kirche und Judentum. Festschrift zum 150jährigen Bestehen. Basel 1980, p. 32.

In 1857 Collin married the daughter of the principal. One of his main concerns was the renewal of society based on religion. Allegedly in his inheritance fragments of a society novel were to be found, which dealt with the colonizing of early Christian areas. His name is irreversibly linked to the foundation of the 'Allgemeine Consumverein' in 1865 of which he was the president for some years.

Paul Kober was born in Württemberg in 1842. He was also a businessman and in 1861 he joined the Christian-religious book-selling business of his great uncle Friedrich Spittler in Basel. In 1863 Kober took over the branch office of Spittler in Jerusalem. There he got to know Maria Gobat, daughter of the Protestant bishop of Jerusalem, Samuel Gobat, from Switzerland. They married in 1869 and Paul Kober-Gobat took over the Spittler bookshop. The strict Pietist-Protestant atmosphere in the Kober family was described by Saul Landau and David Farbstein, both of whom stayed at Kober's house during the Zionist Congress:

'The Kober family treated its guests with particular attention and we were witness to an extremely patriarchal family life. The two daily meals, lunch and dinner were always preceded by a reading from the Psalms by the head of the family, which the servants were also allowed to listen to while seated.'[4]

Kober was especially successful in publishing religious scripts. In 1898 he died on his way to Jerusalem, where he wanted to participate in the consecration of the Church of the Redemption by Kaiser Wilhelm II.

Probably the most interesting and for the Zionist movement most important personality was the theologian and philosopher Carl Friedrich Heman, who was born in 1839. He was the son of David Heman, who converted to Christianity in 1833. Since 1842 father Heman ran the 'House of Proselytism', in the name of the society 'Der Freund Israels' (Friend of Israel), for newly converted Jews at the 'Gemsberg' in Basel. This society saw itself as 'Israel's lawyer', and had the aim of representing the Jewish case 'before God and within Christianity'.[5] One of the most important duties, which they saw for themselves, was the care of the proselytes. For this reason the teacher David Heman from Baden was engaged.

In the earlier days of this society, we are confronted with a famous 'Christian Zionist': Samuel Preiswerk [1799–1871]. Preiswerk, a former teacher in the Missionshaus (Missionary Centre) in Basel, professor for Hebrew and the interpretation of the Old Testament in Geneva and then once again a cathedral priest in Basel, was the first Christian to use again in 1838 the term 'Erez Israel', and who was committed to the founding of a Jewish state. For many years he decisively influenced the society 'Der Freund Israels'.

Surprisingly we can find anti-Semitic allusions in statements of the society, although they maintained that the contrary was true:

'But, one may say, should we allow the Jews to wheel and deal as they please amongst us? Should we stand by and watch them exploit the goodwill of people and impoverish the people for their own monetary gain as their power and influence grow and they force themselves to the top in every field? Should we allow the Christian faith and Christian values to be ridiculed and destroyed? Do they always lead the way whenever there is a possibility to damage and displace Christianity? Or should we even be philo-Semites who support, promote and protect them while they are doing this? Oh no, dear friends, that would be far from correct. Nor should we be the protective front for the Jews and Judaism. No coherently thinking Christian would promote or agree to that. No, we must fight and defend ourselves, but as Christians and with the weapons that behove a Christian and which are the only weapons with which a Christian can

---

[4] Saul Raphael Landau: Sturm und Drang im Zionismus. Rückblicke eines Zionisten vor, mit und um Theodor Herzl. Vienna 1937, p. 93.

[5] Willi: Der Verein der Freunde Israels 150 Jahre, p. 12.

2 Carl Friedrich Heman [1839–1919], well-known 'Christian Zionist'.

successfully battle. Anti-Semitism is a poor, blunt weapon for Christians against the Jews. The Christian has but one weapon that he may carry and that will allow him to be victorious "our belief", says John, "is the victory that has conquered the world"; and it is also the victory over the power of the Jews.'[6]

Which tendencies did Carl Friedrich Heman, the presumed author of these lines, follow? For almost forty years he had been the secretary of this society. During his term of office the decision was made to participate in proselytizing Jews.[7] Professionally, Heman was teacher at the Protestant Preacher's School and later a lecturer in Philosophy and the theory of education at the University of Basel. In his scientific and publicistic scripts he often dealt with the history of Judaism and its special position in Christian soci-ety. In 1897 Heman wrote down his impressions of the First Zionist Congress under the very irritating title: 'Das Erwachen der jüdischen Nation. Der Weg zur endgültigen Lösung der Judenfrage' (The awakening of the Jewish nation. The way to a final solution of the Jewish question). In his introductory comments, he points out that he had already hinted at the importance of the return of the Jews to Palestine fifteen years ago. He was happy about the fact that the Jewish side also recognized this now. Indeed Heman had had early contact with Zionists, he even had contact with Herzl. His motivation, however, differed from those of the 'Fathers' of the Zionist movement.

'The Zionist movement must not be only political, it must also become religious if it is to succeed. It does not have to become like that, simply because otherwise God's blessing, which is what it is all for, would be absent but also because otherwise the movement would be lacking the firm ground under its feet, and the centre that holds it all together, and the force which is the only thing that can fill hearts with enthusiasm and overcome difficulties.'[8]

In addition to that, Heman realized the attractive power of Zionism as an alternative to socialism.

'The great and good effects that Zionism is capable of having on the Jewish people are shown by the fact that a large number of Jewish workers and writers who had already joined the social democratic movement are now turning away from it and toward Zionism.'[9]

According to Heman, Jewish culture, even the Jews themselves were doomed. The biggest threat was the secularization of religion and assimilation to the surrounding society.

---

[6] Freund Israels, 62. Jahresbericht, 20 (1893) 4, pp. 73–92, here p. 78.
[7] The foundation for church and Judaism, the successor of 'Vereins der Freunde Israels' explicitly rejects the missionizing of Jews in its concept: 'Jewish mission, in the sense of a conversion of Jews to Christianity, is not a suitable posture for the Church with regard to Judaism, nor is it a solution for the tense relationship between the Christians and the Jews.' In: Stiftung für Kirche und Judentum. Circular 24 August 1995.
[8] Freund Israels, 67. Jahresbericht des Vereins der Freunde Israels zu Basel, vorgetragen am Jahresfest 1898 von Prof. C.F. Heman, 25 (1898), p. 59.
[9] Freund Israels, ibid., pp. 74 f.

3 Missionaries among Jews in Lodz.

'What is to become of such a Judaism that wants to assimilate in all things of the peoples of the world, that even gives up and denies its nationality and wishes to keep only this mundane, spiritually dead, shadow religion? Is this Judaism not facing spiritual bankruptcy and downfall?'[10]

Instead of assimilating he suggested reflecting on Jewishness. The history of his own family might have influenced him:

'You want to be Germans, but they will always call you Jews. Give up these hopeless efforts and choose to be true Jews again! Can you not see that your desire for assimilation only has the effect that the movement away from Judaism is constantly growing and the number of Jews is constantly becoming smaller? This is what the Zionists preach. The return to Jerusalem is the only medicine for the damage and wounds of the daughter Zion, the only saving glory from the downfall and almighty destruction of Judaism and the Jewish people.'[11]

Heman saw his purpose in strengthening and accompanying the 'people of Israel' on their way to their own identity. But at the end of this path was supposed to be the conversion of the Jewish community:

'Until now, the Jewish people is much too unfamiliar with Jesus and the Gospel of Jesus; they have no idea at all about the spirit of Christ and the life-giving power of his Gospel. Until now it has adamantly refused to look more closely at the Gospel of Jesus Christ and to get to know it more closely. But this is just the reason why we Christians must not stop trying to bear witness to them of Christ and his Gospel; and as experience shows us, it is not without sense and success. Our association considers, in its evangelical work, that it is most important to point to the person of Jesus Christ not simply as their

---

[10] Freund Israels, ibid., p. 55.

[11] Freund Israels, ibid., p. 56.

Messiah, but also as the only one who is the way, the truth and the life for all people. The unforgettably high importance of Jesus for all people and every single soul has to be made apparent to them. We want to bring them to a stage that they see Jesus, whom they have always hated and despised, finally as theirs, as the Saviour and Redeemer of themselves and their people.'[12]

This sympathy for the fate of the Jewish people was characterized by Christian eagerness to help. The new Zionist movement seemed to be putting it on the right track. That is why there were so many enthusiastic 'Christian Zionists' like Heman. But they were never free of the anti-Semitic stereotypes of the time. After all, they were not unselfish in their engagement for the Jews. They believed that after the Jews had returned to Zion, it would be easier to convince them that Jesus was the real Messiah, and convert them to Christianity.

---

[12] Freund Israels, ibid., pp. 61 f.

Patrick Kury

The Other Side of the Coin: Anti-Semitism in Basel at the Turn of the Century

The notion that the status of Jews in Basel in modern history has always been particularly good is widespread in the collective memory of the population. This perception was reinforced by an awareness of the very friendly relationship which exists between Israel and Basel and to which the innumerable Zionist congresses have perhaps contributed and the fact that the Basel government during the Second World War had a more humane refugee policy than Berne. Hardly anyone remembers the alienating stubbornness with which the city's citizenry tried, in the middle of the 19th century, to hinder the settlement of Jews or even to withdraw this right. In 1859 the American envoy Theodore S. Fay included the city of Basel and its neighbouring canton in his list of seven cantons which confronted Jews with open enmity. Also the city of Basel, unlike other Swiss cities, made almost no effort to accommodate the Jewish community until the end of the 19th century. Laws affecting the Jewish population were moderated because of political and socio-economic pressure rather than because of a change of heart. Thus, Basel can in no way be seen as being unambiguously friendly towards Jews at the end of the 19th century.

Intellectual Life in Basel and 'Der Samstag'

In order to track down anti-Jewish tendencies in Basel, special attention must be paid to the satirical cultural magazine 'Der Samstag' (Saturday) which was aimed at 'intellectuals in Basel'. In its first edition on New Year's Eve of 1904 the publishers stated that:

'As an organ for intellectual debate and art culture "Der Samstag" aims at being a forum in which the representatives of different areas of life can meet to speak freely.'[1]

This magazine was published fortnightly between 1904 and 1914 and then was brought out again in the early thirties by the person who had earlier played a dominant role, Dr. Paul Schmitz, better known by his pseudonym Dominik Müller, operating independently. Other authors apart from him were intellectuals from the university and the artistic-literary world. The publishers were not afraid of printing an increasing number of anti-Semitic articles within the course of the years. In addition to numerous articles on 'eugenics', written by Dr. Albert Graeter, the authors managed to write something anti-Jewish on every subject. As a rule, the authors did not express their anti-Jewish sentiments in the obvious vocabulary of 'hooligan anti-Semitism', but central elements of their style consisted of irony and innuendo rather

---

[1] Der Samstag No. 1, 31 December 1904, p. 1.

Der Samstag

Basler Wochenschrift

Inhalt dieser Nummer

Geleitwort. — Basel als Concilstadt, I., von Rudolf Wackernagel. — Rassenhygienisches vom zahnärztlichen Kongreß, von K. G. — Richard Strauß und die „Symphonia Domestica", von Kapellmeister Hermann Suter. — Eindrücke von der Weihnachtsausstellung der Basler Künstler, von Dr. H. Kienzle. — Berliner Brief, von C. A. Bernoulli. — Baslerisches, von Gottlieb Krähenbühl. — Rundschau: Zwei Keller-Bücher, die „Revue Germanique", Süddeutsche Monatshefte, Russische Expedition. — Feuilleton: Krono's Wagen, von Carl Spitteler. — Eine Geschichte zum Jahreswechsel, von Anatole France. — Autobiographisches, von Anatole France. — Bücherliste.

Abonnementspreise:

Vierteljährlich Fr. 3.—, halbjährlich Fr. 6.—, jährlich Fr. 12.—

(für das Ausland mit entsprechendem Portozuschlag)

Basel 1904
31. Dezember

Preis 25 Cts

Verlag und Druck von Gasser & Cie

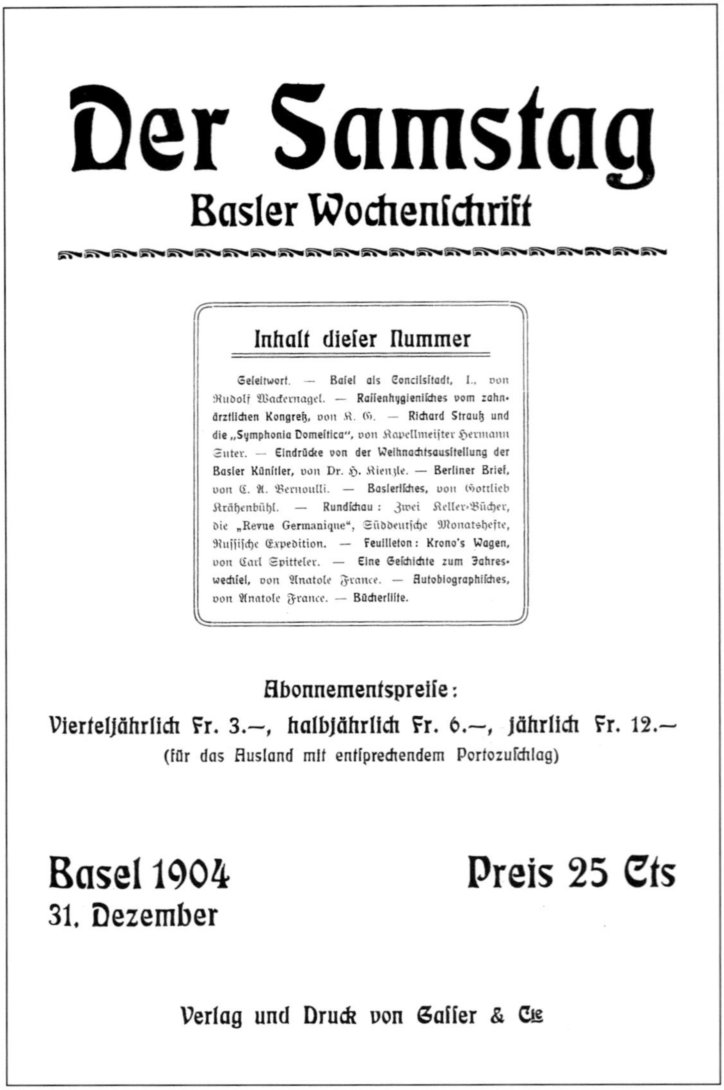

1 First front page of the Basel weekly 'Der Samstag' (New Year's Eve 1904), in which anti-Semitic articles were to be found again and again.

than explicit allegations or the naming of names. Other texts had supposedly scientific contents. One special example of how anti-Semitism was openly exhibited is given by the article written as a satirical report in 1909:

'The "mauscholeum" (mauscheln = to talk Yiddish or to mumble or to cheat), also known as the Basel Stadtcasino, was subjected once again to a thorough airing and maintenance check! This fact is all the more disconcerting and worthy of notice as about 2 years ago the entire floor was torn up and replaced. And now the floor is already once again in a state of decay. If one regards the guests who sit in the "mauscholeum" every day, how they drool, spit and gamble, how they consume a 1/4 litre of fluid and belch a whole litre of fluid back onto the floor, the whole thing has a rather more obvious explanation. Of particularly wood-corroding pungency would appear to be the sweat of the flat feet of Russian Jews.'[2]

The writer of these lines, most probably Paul Schmitz, uses the entire range of anti-Semitic stereotypes: supposed lust for power, conspiratorial theories, certain physical difference, accusations of deceptiveness and impurity are combined with fears about the unknown to stir up racist, anti-Jewish feeling. The author refers to the Basel Stadtcasino, in which by 1909 six Zionist congresses had taken place, as a 'mauscholeum', thus implying that the casino had passed into Jewish hands completely: the Jews sit everywhere and display their power for all to see. If we believe the author, these 'holders of power' are people who 'mauscheln', that is – according to the ideas of that time – speak an incomprehensible language which enables to bargain and even cheat, a language of a small clique which wants nothing more than to exploit the majority. This group of people that only sits around, plays cards, excretes more fluid than it consumes, has no manners but is obsessively miserly, greedy and egoistical, embodies the antithesis of the industrious, well-mannered, diligent and honestly working citizen. Their sitting around and card playing also stand for unproductiveness and parasitism, behaviour which damages the entire society. This lack of productivity is cleverly combined with the external appearance of racial stereotypes: the 'flatfoot' – this deformation of the feet that could have been caused by a lack of physical exercise, by excessive weight and by unsuitable shoes, which corresponds with the stereotypes mentioned above. Thus the author paints a new anti-Jewish picture: by combining the image of the gambling lounge Jew, the man of leisure, who is not burdened with having to work for a living, with that of the proletarian Eastern Jew.

It is not known whether 'intellectual circles in Basel' distanced themselves from articles of this type. Among the founders of the 'Samstag' were the theologian, dramatist, Nietzsche and Bachofen scholar Carl A. Bernoulli, the scientist Albert Graeter, the orientalist Adam Mez and the journalist Eduard Behrens. The philologist Paul Schmitz (alias Dominik Müller) who was to become a celebrated dialect poet during the first decades of this century, was, for a short period, the representative of the people's party in the cantonal council and became the 'private poet' of well-known Basel families. As the first and only man of letters of the city, he was given an 'honorarium', a kind of pension in the thirties. As he made no secret of his support for National Socialist Germany and agitated in his poetry in favour of annexation to the Reich, he was stripped of this pension in 1939. Angry, he left his hometown, probably not aware of why he had so suddenly fallen out of favour: after all, he had not changed his convictions. Under the auspices of Dominik Müller 'Der Samstag' developed into a polemic against Judaism, the freemasonry and also against parts of the city establishment. Why his comrades-in-arms had not distanced themselves earlier from him or from the racial-theoretical essays of Albert Graeter remains a mystery – unless of course they shared the same opinions. In 1909 Carl A. Bernoulli took over the publishing of the magazine temporarily, at a time when anti-Jewish statements were printed on a regular basis. Obviously the tolerance of anti-Semitic statements was quite high at the turn of the century. It was considered socially acceptable or even desirable in Basel's social circles to make anti-Jewish fibs in conversation. In respected daily newspapers – such as the 'Basler Nachrichten' – such remarks could also be found, albeit in a somewhat more moderate form.

---

[2]   Der Samstag, Zweite Traum-Nummer, 4 September 1909, pp. 6 f.

2 Poster for the plebiscite on the 'ritual slaughter ban initiative' of April 20, 1893. Those in favour of the ban – 'der Zentralverband der Schweizerischen Tierschutzvereine' (Central Board of the Swiss Animal Protection Societies) – supported a 'humane' slaughtering with the slogan: 'It conflicts with common sense to view slaughtering as a religious matter and a butcher's shop as a house of God.'

The Ritual Slaughter Ban Initiative of 1893

No other question burdened the relationship between Christians and Jews in Switzerland between 1890 and 1930 to the same extent as the banning of ritual slaughter. In the plebiscite of August 20, 1893, the antislaughter initiative was accepted, against the will of both the Federal Council and parliament, with an impressive people's majority of 191,527 to 127,101 votes and a small majority of the cantons of 11.5 to 10.5.[3] In Basel the banning of ritual slaughter was also approved with 3,480 votes for and only 1,058

[3] Oswald Georg Sigg: Die eidgenössischen Volksinitiativen 1892–1939. Ph.D. dissertation, Einsiedeln 1978, pp. 92 ff.

against. Even Theodor Nordemann, who was otherwise known for his careful thought in such matters and who wrote the commemorative publication for the 150th jubilee of the Israeli community in Basel in 1955, commented upon the vote:

> 'It was probably a general wave of anti-Semitic thought which propagated this statute article under the guise of the protection of animals, and in the plebiscite of August 20, 1893 achieved its goal [...] The author of the commemorative address himself remembers the events at the marketplace on that Sunday evening and the celebrations of the people. The atmosphere was at the time certainly against the Jews, and one could hear, among other shouts, calls such as: "down with the Jews!" and "death to the Jews!". This childhood experience had left an indelible impression on the author of this publication.'[4]

Other sources confirm Nordemann's childhood recollection. In the arguments of the advocates of the initiative of 1893, 'Christian empathy' was appealed to and 'humane slaughter' was called for.[5] At the same time there were innumerable attacks against the Jewish religion and against Jewish business dealings. Stereotypical accusations such as that of wanting to rule the world were raised. In Basel on the other hand, all of the daily newspapers, with the exception of the 'Allgemeine Schweizer Zeitung', were clearly against the ban. Even the organ of Basel's Catholics, the 'Basler Volksblatt', in which at the time anti-Jewish statements could often be found, sided with those who were against the ban. The Catholic-dominated press, whose wounds had not yet healed after the 'cultural struggle' was, in questions of religious independence, on the side of the minorities. On the Sunday of the vote, the 'Allgemeine Schweizer Zeitung' wrote 'One Last Word about the Plebiscite on the Question of Ritual Slaughter'. In it they criticized above all the Catholic press and the Catholic national councillors, who had opposed the initiative and quoted a certain Dr. Otto Pestalozzi from Zurich:

> 'If the Israelite who lives in our country wishes to adhere rigidly to this law [the slaughter ritual], the significance of which is to isolate the Jewish people from all other groups who are considered to be impure, he should quite simply refrain from acquiring Swiss citizenship. He belongs to a foreign people, who only have the rights of a guest here and which should leave us if our laws don't appeal to him.'[6]

Even during the interim period when ritual slaughter was authorized by the Federal Government by emergency decree due to the restricted import availability of ritually slaughtered meat during and in the period immediately following the First World War, there were repeated polemics against the Jewry. A declaration to the Federal Council written by members of a right-wing local group 'Vereinigung Schweizerischer Republikaner' (Association of Swiss Republicans) and published in the 'Basler Nachrichten' on January 13, 1920, triggered off a debate in this newspaper. The president of the 'deutschschweizerische Tierschutzvereine' (Animal Protection Societies in German-speaking Switzerland) Keller replied to an article by Rabbi Arthur Cohn as follows:

> 'So, dear Rabbi Cohn, we have no reason to be hostile towards the Jewish people, but we certainly do have reason to oppose you and your colleagues, because you refuse to agree to the humane slaughter of these beasts without any grounds whatsoever and speak up for a barbaric practice which only serves to strengthen your position of power by allowing you to lead your people around in the dark and, against our better knowledge, to stubbornly defend as being in the service of God a practice which is thousands of years old and which makes a mockery of human decency. We are certain that we can count on our humanitarian Swiss people!'[7]

---

[4] Theodor Nordemann: Zur Geschichte der Juden in Basel. Jubiläumsschrift der Israelitischen Gemeinde Basel aus Anlass ihres 150jährigen Bestehens 5565–5715, 1805–1955. No year, p. 125.
[5] cf. Friedrich Traugott Külling: Antisemitismus in der Schweiz zwischen 1866 und 1900. Ph.D. dissertation, Zurich 1977, pp. 319–350.
[6] Allgemeine Schweizer Zeitung of 20 August 1893, No. 194, p. 1.
[7] Basler Nachrichten of 9 March 1920, 2nd supplement to No. 105, p. 1.

3 The fight of David against Goliath and legends of ritual murders are combined by the 'Nebelspalter' for anti-Jewish propaganda.

The pattern of argumentation becomes very clear: accusations were made indirectly and in a more or less factual form. Helvetian virtues were to be defended. Authors often used quotes so as not to make themselves liable. Their own anti-Semitic leanings were denied by stating that one only objected to the orthodox Jews, to the rabbis, to those Jews who spoke up, to those who did not hold themselves to the 'customs of the land' and thus had to bear the guilt for the ban of the slaughter themselves. Anti-Jewish and xenophobian thoughts were hidden under the guise of so-called Helvetian values.

Patrick Kury

'Foreign and Backward': Eastern Jews in Basel around 1900

'The administration of the Basel community has, just like the Zurich community and many others, always been of the opinion up till now, that as a rule, co-religionists, at least those immigrating from Eastern Europe, should not be accepted as citizens, and has recently denied an application for an admission of this kind in the exercising of this practice [...] The reasons for the refusal were less of a personal than of a cultural, economic and social nature. It had been said that these people, who constitute approximately 1/5 of the Jewish people in Basel, are at odds with Western European Jewry in their entire being. Their religious outlook deviates crucially from that of the majority; a deep chasm separates them from the established population due to their upbringing and ways of life. If these new arrivals were to be granted a decisive influence through the voting slips of the members of the community, this can only occur at the cost of the healthy and rapid development, in other words, by accepting the immigration of such a large percentage of foreign, backward elements we will be returning to conditions as they were 150 years ago at the time of Mendelssohn and which were overcome because of Western Jewry.'[1]

This excerpt from an article in the 'Israelitische Wochenblatt' of 1904 does not represent the official opinion of the board of the Basel Jewish community; it is merely the published opinion of a member of the community who is not mentioned by name. The statement was apparently subject to controversy, the editorial office declared itself to be prepared to print opposing opinions.

Nevertheless, or perhaps precisely because of this, we can draw an astonishing detailed picture of the difficulties created by the juxtaposition of Eastern and Western Jews. We are given information as to the proportional make-up of the Jewish community in Basel at the turn of the century, although the number of Eastern Jews would seem to be somewhat exaggerated for the time. It is particularly noteworthy that the cultural, economic and social differences were considered to be insurmountable. Culture appears to be defined according to criteria informed by the individual's own religiousness, customs and level of education. The derogatory, often hostile tone attracts attention. The author fears having to accept 'cultural backwardness' when allowing Eastern Jews into the community. This is based on the serious concern that the Eastern Jews could jeopardize the fragile process of integrating Western Jews into society. Not only in his own individual perception was the Eastern Jew the antithesis of the assimilated, emancipated Jew. The sections of the article which report on the admission practices turn the concept of a supposedly simple integration of Eastern Jewish immigrants upside down. On the contrary, an integration into the Jewish community was more or less hindered by them for a long time. Such an exclusion of Eastern Jews was practiced, if we are to believe the author, not only in Basel but in many communities in Switzerland.

---

[1] Israelitisches Wochenblatt No. 2, 8 January 1904, pp. 2 f.

The immigration of Eastern Jews began between 1888 and 1900.[2] According to official statistics, only one Russian or Russian-Polish man of Jewish faith lived in Basel in 1888. In 1900 there were 179 and in 1910 as many as 454 Jews of Russian or Russian-Polish origin in the canton. The share of Galician Jews can only be estimated. A notable increase in the people from the countries of the Danube monarchy, and this probably means mainly Galicia, also took place after 1888 and continued until 1910. Thus a modest estimate has around 600 Eastern Jews living in the city after 1910. This was more than one quarter of the Jewish population – a ratio which was to remain stable for quite some time. Reasons for the immigration were the fear of pogroms, poverty and congestion in the shtetl.

In addition to these immigrants who found a second, often only temporary home in Basel, several thousand refugees and around a thousand transients stayed for a few days in the city every year. The fluctuations in the numbers of people passing through were a reflection of the pogrom waves in Eastern Europe. These were people who were not granted long-term permission to stay, as they often did not possess the necessary papers, or who did not intend to stay and lived instead as traveling vagabonds. These poor people were fed by the Jewish community, which saw itself confronted with considerable financial and infrastructural problems. The travelers passing through around the turn of the century had very little to do with the traditional scrounging of the 19th century. Much more, this increase in the number of Jews looking for a new home was the consequence of dramatically worsening living conditions in the East. The following note gives evidence of the Odyssey-like existence of these people:

1   Jews in front of the Stadtcasino, around 1900.

'A young Russian married couple, he was a painter, she a cigarette maker, came to us and asked for assistance in getting to Zurich where they had acquaintances. We fulfilled their wish. From Zurich, where they were unable to find work, they went to Berne where they were advised to go to Basel, where there was work to be found. They followed this advice and did not realize, until they saw the train station in Basel that they had been here before already!'[3]

A cause of even larger difficulties for the Jewish community were the emigrants from Eastern Europe who stopped over for a few days in Switzerland on their way westwards. As the

[2]   cf. Patrick Kury: 'Man akzeptierte uns nicht, man tolerierte uns!' Ostjudenmigration nach Basel 1890–1930. Umfang – Wahrnehmungen – Erfahrungen. Unveröffentlichte Lizentiatsarbeit, Basel 1994, pp. 20–39 (based on the published data provided by the censuses of the Basel City Canton between 1870 and 1930).

[3]   Staatsarchiv Basel-Stadt (StABS), IGB-REG, H1, Soziales 183 (old signature), Jahresbericht der Israelitischen Armenkasse pro 1905, p. 6.

2   Basel around 1885. View from Gross- to Kleinbasel.

emigrants, coming from Buchs, were generally waiting to continue their travels to the French Atlantic harbours, Basel became a centre of transit. For this reason, members of the community formed the advisory centre for Jewish emigrants from Eastern Europe in 1906.[4] The main bulk of this refugee movement was borne by the Jewish community under its own steam. Especially after the First World War, as the emigration increased once again, the emigration office had to continue taking care of and paying for the further travels of the emigrants from Eastern European states due to their weak currency. A description from this time clearly shows the regrettable situation of the refugees:

'Two travelers, who belonged to the intelligentsia, wanted to order a decent breakfast in Buchs, after a 36-hour journey there from Vienna. The waitress gave them a bill for 7 francs, which was equivalent to about 350 crowns. The two gentlemen decided to order a tea and to eat the dry bread from their backpacks instead. [...] A father with four children wanted to treat his young ones and himself to something warm to eat in Buchs and ordered five teas with bread. When the bill came and he had no Swiss currency, he was charged 250 crowns, which he paid crying bitterly, and complaining that everything that he had saved up for the journey was gone and he had only just begun his long trip [...] One woman had to be taken to hospital with a fever. There it was noted that the woman, who was traveling with three children, had nothing on beneath the rags which represented her clothing, and that this and especially the lack of nourishment during as well as before the journey were the cause of her breakdown. When asked why she had begun such a journey with the certainty of catching a cold as such an illness was inevitable due to the change in climate in the mountains of Tyrol and Switzerland, she replied that if she hadn't left home she would have starved to death.'[5]

In contrast to the Eastern European refugees, the number of students in Basel was negligable, unlike in Zurich, Berne and Geneva. As at the

---

[4]   cf. StABS, IGB-REG, Dossier S 4-591, Auskunftsbureau für jüdische Auswanderer 1905–1911.

[5]   StABS, IGB-REG, H1, Soziales 76e, Memorandum in Sachen..., written by Dr. M.W. Rapaport, 20 February 1920. The memorandum was written for the 'Joint Distribution Committee' in London.

3 The Claraplatz – the centre of Kleinbasel. Several Eastern Jews were living in Kleinbasel; in the Florastrasse was one of their prayer rooms.

turn of the century most of the Eastern Europeans studying in Switzerland were women, they had the status of pioneers among women students. The preference for other university towns can be explained by the considerably more restrictive conditions of admission for foreign students at the university in Basel.

The first generation of Eastern Jews, who had fled from everyday discrimination and social need in Eastern Europe and who settled in Basel, belonged to the lower classes in the city and were often dependent on the 'Israelitische Armenkasse' (Jewish Aid for the Poor). In 1911 almost half of the Eastern Jewish population received financial assistance at least once a year from the community. This poverty separated the Jews from a large section of the population of Basel, but also from the established Western Jews. The districts with low rents were not in the immediate proximity of the synagogue. This is why the Eastern Jews formed their own prayer rooms: on the corner of Birmannsgasse/Spalenring, later Thannerstrasse, in the Hegenheimerstrasse, later Schützenmattstrasse, and in the Florastrasse in Kleinbasel. Religious considerations also played a part in this autonomy, which also determined the selection of professions. So as not to violate Sabbath, they were dependent on positions in companies run by Jews or they had to work independently. As money and education were generally insufficient only jobs such as travelling salesman remained. In addition to these salesmen and a few involved with retail – coal, junk and used clothing traders, there were a large number of craftsmen, plumbers, watchmakers, tailors, seamstresses, turners and carpenters. Thus the Eastern and Western Jews also differed in the professions which they pursued.

With the passing years many managed to rise socially, which simplified their integration. As early as the second generation there were numerous lawyers and doctors to be found. But many, however, did not succeed in managing to earn a living. In extreme cases they even fled the city, leaving wife and children behind. In a report written in 1912, the extremely sarcastic tone of the chronicler is obvious, which reveals a lot about his 'image' of the Eastern Jews:

'It was always considered to be a radical solution for their regrettable family situation by those from the east, to go to another country and to leave their wife and children in the care and under the auspices of the community there. This, certainly very practical method, has been used in Basel for quite some time now and for years we have had to deal with such disappearances and their consequences which have made deep cuts in our finances. In the year of this report, these flights have become an epidemic, and 4 fathers, some from extremely large families, have left for Canada, leaving behind them debts and other dishonourable souvenirs in the unmistakable expectation that the Jewish community would care for their wife and children.'[6]

Varying interpretations of religious life and education also led to additional tensions between Eastern and Western Jews. The maintenance of their own religious-cultural identity could not be reconciled with acculturation. Although the Eastern Jews were not the founders of the 'Israelitische Religionsgesellschaft' (Jewish Religion Society) which opened the second synagogue in Basel in 1929, many did find an institutional framework here which reinforced their autonomy and enabled them to keep their Judaism alive.

There were also other problems hindering a rapid integration. Many had a great fear of all authorities as a result of the discrimination they had experienced in Eastern Europe. This resulted in behaviour, as a kind of self-protection, which did not allow them to appear self-confident in public and made it difficult to gain social recognition. Furthermore, increasing anti-Semitism also worsened the conditions for the Eastern European Jewish population in Switzerland, especially during the First World War and in the post-war period. Eastern Jews suffered because of the banning of peddlers and of food profiteering court cases. A number of newspapers and weekly journals fanned the flames of hostility toward Eastern Jews, who at the same time were used for political purposes. The Eastern Jewish population lived for a long time in a kind of 'double emigration'. Not until the second generation did they receive some recognition and social advancement, through institutions such as the gymnastic club, the sport and theatre club or through social integration via religious instruction. However, the eventual successful social integration of refugees also teaches us that such a process is only possible if we acknowledge differences and eschew egalitarianism, and that this process takes several decades.

---

[6] StABS, IGB–REG, H1 Soziales 183, Jahresbericht der Armenpflege pro 1912, p. 6.

Bettina Zeugin

The Beginnings of Zionism in Basel and in Switzerland: 1897–1918

The history of the Zionist movement in Switzerland begins with the First Zionist Congress. Prior to 1897 only the efforts of 'Christian Zionists' and the activities of Jewish students from Eastern Europe in Zurich can be found. Depending on the sources, between twelve and twenty-three people from Switzerland took part in the First Congress – including one woman from Zurich – whose journey did not cost much. This is why many came who had not yet formed a clear opinion regarding the Zionist ideas. Immediately after the Congress, local and national groups formed all over the world. Until the Second Congress in 1898 six local groups were founded in Switzerland.

The Basel Local Group and Its Ideas

Just a few days or weeks after the Congress – the exact date is not known – a few followers of the movement founded a local group in Basel as a branch association of the newly founded World Zionist Organization. Among the several known members were the Head Cantor of the Jewish community, Sigmund Drujan as well as Joël J. Weil, the owner of a distillery for kirsch and absinthe; both were also participants in the Congress. The rest of the members were largely employed in manufacturing and trade. In November 1897 the initiators of this group wrote a first informative brochure with the title: 'An die Israeliten Basels'[1] (to the Israelites of Basel), in which they advertised their new group. In addition to the reproduction of the 'Basle Program' they stated as the main goal of the Basel local group

'to help the Jews living in inhuman conditions in Eastern Europe, North Africa and Persia to a life worthy of human beings in Palestine'.

Zionism, they said, served mainly to support the impoverished, deprived and persecuted Jewish brothers and sisters who should be granted a 'sanctuary' in Palestine. The vision of a Jewish state played no part at all in the plans of the Basel Zionists. They wanted above all to provide material support for the development work in Palestine. An emigration of the Swiss Jews was beyond their imagination:

'[...] those Jews who already enjoy equality with their fellow citizens and who have a homestead secured by public law where they reside, [should] take part in the rescue work by offering intellectual and financial support.'

The writers of this brochure took their view even further by also describing the relationship between Zionism and assimilation differently for Eastern and Western Europe:

---

[1] This and the following quotes are from the: Staatsarchiv Basel-Stadt (StABS), IGB-Reg, U 1, Zionisten.

1 Charity campaign of the Swiss Zionist Association for the Jewish National Fund.

'Zionism does not want to hinder the assimilation, and not only does it not forbid its followers interacting with the members of other ideologies, but even consideres it desirable, as is explicitly emphasized from the authoritative Zionist side. Nevertheless, Zionism does reject the merging of the Jewish people with the other peoples in the spiritually still unfree countries. In culturally advanced countries, where there is no compulsion to gag the spirit and the flesh, Zionism does not object a fusion.'

This is truly a very particular interpretation of the 'Basle Program'. Many were of the opinion that the 'homestead' in Palestine was conceived for the oppressed and impoverished Jews of Eastern Europe, but at the same time they agreed to a large extent on the fact that Zionism aimed at 'the strengthening of the Jewish feeling and identity as a people' as formulated by the programme. Obviously the Basel Zionists saw no contradiction between 'merging' with other cultures and retaining their own Jewish culture. Perhaps this tightrope walking, hardly possible in reality, is connected to the fact that its authors expressly emphasize that Zionism did not reduce the patriotism of the Jews in the western countries and thus not in Switzerland either. Thus the reproach of a 'double loyalty' was faced from the very beginning. This anticipated response to anti-Jewish attacks reached its peak when Zionism was referred to as a general, i.e. also non-Jewish, philanthropical money-collecting organization:

> 'Zionism is thus a work which deserves the support of all friends of humanity; for us Jews in particular it is *a duty of honour* to be involved in it.'

On the basis of the informative brochure of the Basel Zionists we can therefore imagine just how uncertain at least a part of the Jews here felt, how fragile the integration into the population of the city was seen and how strongly the subliminal anti-Semitic feeling was perceived, which a short time previously, on the occasion of the anti-slaughter initiative in 1893, had turned into public demonstrations. This is why many Jews – not only in Basel, but also on a much broader basis – tried to adapt to the conditions by attracting as little attention as possible in order not to jeopardize the integration. Zionism, seen as an open expression of a Jewish consciousness and Jewish culture as well as an open support of their own polity, could therefore not expect to meet with great enthusiasm.

The statutes of the Basel Zionist Association drawn up in January 1898 by a 'comité' reveal the same attitude toward Zionism as the information brochure. They were also sent out with the request that people should join the group. The comité, so it said, would not force its members to emigrate to Palestine at a later stage and appealed to the 'old Jewish virtue' of the ability to make sacrifices, the religiously founded benevolence of Basel's Jewish population and to the pioneering role of Basel in being host to the First Zionist Congress:

> 'In Basel, where the Zionist Congress was held, it is actually unnecessary to want to justify Zionism.'

After the somewhat arbitrary interpretation of the 'Basle Program' this statement did not necessarily seem convincing.

2 Congress participants in front of the Basel Stadtcasino, around 1900.

The Gradual Consolidation of Swiss Zionism

Although shortly after the Congress, local groups formed in several Swiss cities, the movement developed slowly afterwards. As early as 1901 the president of the Basel group at that time, Joël Weil, complained in a letter to the 'Actions Comité' in Vienna:

> 'Zionism in our country is sadly in regression – in fact there is no national organization – we do have statutes but not one of the associations shows any sign of life. The associations themselves have great trouble in maintaining themselves.'[2]

According to Weil, the number of members of the Basel local group had fallen to one hundred people; we do not, however, know how many members it had beforehand and in Berne, Geneva, Lausanne and Biel there were groups but no

[2] Central Zionist Archives (CZA), Z 1 277.

actual associations. Weil was of the opinion that the 'indifference' of the Swiss Jews was the biggest enemy of the movement. Nevertheless, devoted Zionists founded the 'Swiss Zionist Association' in Zurich in the autumn of the same year. Among the initiators were, in addition to Joël Weil from Basel also David Farbstein from Zurich – founder of the local group there – as well as others who came to be of great importance for Zionism in Switzerland. At this point, Chaim Weizmann also has to be mentioned; he later became the president of the Zionist Organization and the first president of the state of Israel and also took part in the first delegates' meeting of the association. Weizmann had participated in the development of the Zionist movement in Switzerland since 1899 as president of the local group in Geneva. Soon after, however, he lost interest in these local activities and devoted himself to 'greater' tasks.

As early as 1901, the association succeeded in winning over the weekly newspaper 'Israelitisches Wochenblatt' as its official organ. Since this date, the activities of the association can be followed in great detail. The advertising effect achieved with publications in the 'Israelitische Wochenblatt' could already be seen in the following year: in 1902 there were thirteen groups in Switzerland with 710 'shekel' payers.

Up until the First World War, there were relatively few Jews in Switzerland involved in Zionism. The movement was well received mainly among students and emigrants from Eastern Europe. They met sometimes in the National Jewish Student Associations or were active in the local groups. Gradually, however, as the example of the Basel local group shows, local Jews also began to become involved in Zionism. An important part was played by the social aspect of the groups. In addition to the local Zionist groups, new subgroups continued to be formed on a regular basis, representing Zionist interests. Among these was the influential 'Komitee für Erez Jisroël' (Erez Israel Committee), which was founded in Basel in 1909. This organization promoted the humanitarian and cultural efforts of the colonization of Palestine. Furthermore, different smaller groups existed such as 'Zion' in Basel, which was largely directed at Eastern Jews, and the 'Zionistische Verein Theodor Herzl' which was founded in 1917. This busy club life pointed to the fact that also in Switzerland – just as in the rest of the World Zionist Organization – there was a splitting of the Zionists into individual ideological directions. The religious 'Mizrachi groups' had been active in Switzerland since 1902 and in 1912 the local 'Poalei Zion' formed. But fierce conflicts between the different directions did not really escalate until after the First World War. The moderate groups as well as the Mizrachi were – typically for the situation in Switzerland – always the largest groups right into the postwar period. But at least due to the Balfour Declaration of 1917 and the related support of the British government for the project of a Jewish 'homestead', Zionism had become 'presentable'[3] and was joined by an increasing number of followers.

---

[3] Dominique Shaul Ferrero: Le Sionisme et la Suisse 1897–1947. Mémoire de prédoctorat. Genève 1993, pp. 13 and 19.

Dominique Shaul Ferrero

Chaim Weizmann and Switzerland

The great Zionist leader Chaim Weizmann, born in Belorussia in 1874, who was head of the Zionist World Organization after the First World War and later became the first President of the State of Israel, had a special relationship to Switzerland, a country that he first visited in 1898. First he followed his mentor, Prof. Augustin Bistrzycki, to Freiburg to finish his thesis. In spring 1899 he settled in Geneva where he taught chemistry as privat-dozent at the university. Besides his scientific research, he dedicated himself intensively to Zionist work. At this time, many Russian Jews were studying at Swiss universities, especially in Geneva, Berne and Zurich. Vehement debates occurred between militant members of different groups of political refugees. Far from Russia and czarist oppression, revolutionary parties opposed each other fiercely, on the one side, the Communists and members of the 'Bund', and on the other side the Zionists. Weizmann participated passionately in these discussions and later boasted about having convinced a number of students to leave the revolutionary agitators.

At the beginning of his stay in Switzerland, Weizmann showed interest in the local Zionist activities. He was soon elected to the head of the newly founded Zionist Society of Geneva. In February 1902 he founded a new Zionist students' association, 'Ha-Schachar'. At the end of the same year he participated in the first 'Delegates' Day' of the 'Swiss Zionist Association' in Biel, that had been founded on October 27, 1901. However, Weizmann soon turned away from local interests. He did not think much of Western Zionists and reproached them for having turned away too far from authentic Judaism. As an 'Eastern Jew' he

1 Chaim Weizmann, drawn by Wladimir Sagal.

always stayed true to his Russian 'Landsmannschaft' (Association of students or refugees from the same country). In contrast to other Eastern Zionists, such as Daniel Pasmanik and Zevi Aberson, Weizmann always represented Russian Zionism at the congresses. This was particularly noticeable at the Sixth Congress in Basel in 1903. He firmly opposed the Uganda Scheme – also in contrast to Swiss Zionists such as David Farbstein.

During his stay in Geneva, Weizmann opened in 1902 a 'Bureau of the Jewish University' in his own residence, a first tangible step towards a Hebrew University in Jerusalem. He also was one of the founders of the 'Jüdischer Verlag' (Jewish Publishing House), the first Zionist publisher. It was connected to the newly formed 'Demokratische Fraktion' (Democratic Fraction), a group of mainly young Eastern Jewish intellectuals who were opposed to Herzl's cultural policy – or rather the non-existence of a cultural policy. During his Geneva years, Weizmann neglected his scientific career in favour of an active combat for Zionism. At this time he was torn between the two important poles of his life. Later he wrote:

'The deep inner conflict in my life, a perhaps even structural duality, became irrepressibly apparent during the four years that I spent in Geneva. Already in Berlin it had become clear to me that I would have to work twice as hard, on the one hand for science and on the other for the Zionist movement in public. Up to this point I had been able to fulfil these tasks equally well; in Fribourg it was also possible, while I was writing my thesis. In Geneva, however, the balance was disturbed, my scientific work suffered from this'.[1]

In Geneva Weizmann also met his future wife, Vera Chatzman, who was his junior by seven years. She was studying medicine and also came from Russia. But this is not the only reason why Weizmann considered this period in Geneva to have been decisive in showing him the direction:

'It could be said that the outline of my future became clearer in Geneva, for it was here that I made the most important acquaintances of my life [...] My youth ended in Geneva; not if one counts the years – in that respect it had actually gone long ago – but in my mind. The end of my time in Geneva coincided with the dismal period of Jewish life in Russia, with the shock and the disappointment connected with the Uganda Project and with Herzl's death. I did not part with my youth, it is the events that caused it to part from me.'[2]

In 1904 Weizmann left Switzerland and travelled to Great Britain. He later returned several times to Switzerland for personal reasons or for the Zionist cause. After the First World War he periodically came to Geneva, the home of the League of Nations, to ensure that the Palestine Mandate, including the 'Balfour Declaration', was being strictly observed by Great Britain. In May 1922 he was in Geneva to watch the establishment of the British Mandate in Palestine, which had to be confirmed by the 18th session of the Council of the League of Nations. Weizmann also made friends with Prof. William Rappart. He was the secretary of the Mandate Commission between 1920 and 1924; this commission met until 1939. Rappart founded the 'Institut des Hautes Etudes Internationales' and represented the University of Geneva at the opening celebration of the Hebrew University of Jerusalem in 1925. Also in Switzerland, on the occasion of the Sixteenth Zionist Congress in Zurich in 1929, Weizmann achieved the extension of the 'Jewish Agency' by also accepting non-Zionists. Of course, he also participated in all the other congresses that were held in Switzerland.

From 1898 until his death in 1952, Weizmann had a close relationship to Switzerland, where he spent some of the most important years of his life, and where he returned nearly every year whether for work or privately. Although he remained closely affiliated to East European Judaism and although he despised the philanthropic Zionism of the assimilated Western Jews, he felt a deep affinity for Switzerland. He enjoyed spending time in the mountains or at the lakes. Even after being elected President of the State of Israel, he often spent his holidays in Switzerland, where he also finished his autobiography. For him, Switzerland had always been the model for independence, democratic virtue and industriousness, the living proof that a small country, can not only survive without natural resources but indeed flourish, due to the efforts of its population. He often used Switzerland as an example, hoping that the Jewish State would find inspiration through it.

---

[1] Chaim Weizmann: Memoiren. Das Werden des Staates Israel. Zürich 1955, p. 89.
[2] Ibid., pp. 112 and 117.

Dominique Shaul Ferrero # Henri Dunant and Zionism

Henri Dunant was born in Geneva and is one of the best-known forerunners of Zionism. In 1897 at the First Zionist Congress in Basel, it was important to all the participants, especially Herzl and Nordau, to emphasize Dunant's efforts to support the aims of Zionism. In reality Dunant's 'Zionist' activities can be limited to two periods, each of which lasted only a few years. Outside these periods it is not easy to find activities benefiting Zionism in Dunant's biography.

In the years between 1866 and 1870, when he was living in exile in Paris, due to unsuccessful business transactions with Algeria, he launched the project 'Société internationale universelle pour la rénovation de l'Orient'.[1] Several versions of this project developed, but the main points remained the same. The main impulse was, just as in the Algeria project, the peaceful conquest of the Middle East by the Western civilization. This should be realized by founding a large, worldwide society, where the most important European powers, mainly France and England, were to unify, and by the request, especially to Jewish groups, to provide money. Agriculture, industry, trade and construction works were to be promoted in the Orient, especially in Palestine; privileges and monopolies were to be negotiated with the Turkish government, especially land concessions and the gradual handing over of territories in Palestine; these estates were to be apportioned for money and the most fertile valleys colonized.

1 Henri Dunant [1828–1910].

In this context, Dunant advocated the foundation of colonies by prosperous 'Jewish' families, who would pave the way for their less fortunate co-religionists from Eastern Europe and Northern Africa to come to the Holy Land. He was sure that the Hebrew people would rise as a nation with its own territory. This grand enterprise should then be put under the highest patronage of Napoleon III, 'the leader of the Roman Empire', 'the mighty genius of the century'.

Dunant transferred his disappointed colonial dreams from North Africa to the Middle East, while the main idea remained the same. The new aspect was the 'Zionist' dimension. Although Dunant was bankrupt from his Algerian adventure, he hoped to obtain wealth and respect again by

---

[1] Bibliothèque Publique et Universitaire de Genève (BPU), E 2246.

way of mixing Saint-Simonian colonial business with a pro-Jewish philanthropism fueled by his evangelical religious conviction. The only obvious result was the fusion with the 'Gesellschaft der Templer' (Templer Association), an evangelical sect from Württemberg, the members of which wanted to found colonies in Palestine in the expectation of Christ's return. They founded the first modern district in Haifa ('German Colony'). Attracted by his reputation they asked Dunant, if he would be prepared, against payment, to try to negotiate with the Turkish authorities to obtain a land concession for them. Dunant took the money, without producing any concrete results. In 1870 the German-French War stopped his Palestine projects for the time being.

Between 1874 and 1876 Dunant took up his Zionist activities again in London. A cry for help from the 'Württemberg Templers', who had managed to settle in Palestine, but had fallen into financial problems made Dunant act. Under the auspices of the 'Universal Alliance of Order and Civilization', which he had founded in 1871, Dunant tried to form a committee – the 'International Palestine and Syrian Committee' – later a society – 'The Syrian and Palestine Colonization Society' – to speed up the colonization of Palestine and Syria.[2] The Jewish problems were not of any importance. The 'Templer' colonies were to be mainly financed by subscriptions. Dunant got the support of Colonel Gawler, a former British Governor in Australia who had become administrator of the Crown Jewels and who wanted to do business in the Middle East by building railway lines. Dunant additionally addressed a group from England, who considered themselves to be descendants of the ten missing tribes of Israel. But this enterprise had little success. The 'Templers' rejected the patronizing treatment by the English, suggested by Dunant. They wanted to keep their freedom of action and did not believe that the English were really descendants of the ten tribes.

After this, Dunant left London to retire to Stuttgart and later to Heiden. He gave up his activities for Zionism although he kept in contact with the 'Templers' and in manuscripts, which were never published due to a lack of money, he expressed his conviction that the Jews would return to Zion. Although several authors – for example Nahum Sokolów and Alexis François – are of a different opinion, it is almost certain that Dunant never left Heiden, to go to the First Zionist Congress. He merely sent a message to express his 'warmest and most heartfelt sympathy'.[3]

Dunant's idea of rebuilding a Jewish state in Palestine was by no means new. A large number of authors had expressed similar thoughts before him (for example Hess, Laharanne, Salvador, Kalischer, George Eliot, Daudet). Dunant, however, never mentioned these authors, as if he were the first and only person to express this idea. It also appears that he did not even know of the first Jewish enterprises in Palestine, such as the agricultural school of Mikveh Israel, founded in 1870 by the 'Alliance Israélite Universelle'. Dunant only knew little about the Jewish world; what he did know was based on the visits of a few Jewish notables, with whom he was in contact for a while due to his reputation as the initiator of international aid for disabled war veterans in Paris, London and Brussels. Dunant's perception of Jews was not unequivocal. He seemed to be convinced that the Jews were the 'kings of the age'[4] because of the enormous wealth which they had gathered. Unlike the anti-Semites, he interpreted this fact positively, as he had been taught at a young age by the ex-pastor Gaussen, founder of the 'Société évangélique de Genève', that this was

---

[2] BPU, GF 3524.

[3] Schweizer Stimmen zum Zionismus. Schriftenreihe des Schweizerischen Zionistenverbandes. Vol. 13, Geneva 1944, p. 5, and Bernhard Weinert: 'J. Heinrich Dunants Bestrebungen für Palästina'. Annuaire Israélite Suisse, 1929, p. 144.

[4] BPU, Ms.fr. 4507, Ms.fr. 4508.

a sign that the Jews would be given their rights once again and that the Day of Judgement was approaching. He acknowledged the injustices that they had suffered, 'which our forefathers were guilty of perpetrating' and was of the opinion that it was now important to compensate for them.

Why then, should the Zionists offer him a place in the pantheon of the fathers of their movement? Most certainly because his rehabilitation as the founder of the Red Cross and the origin of the myth related to it coincided with the assembly of the First Zionist Congress and the foundation of the Zionist World Organization in 1897. Political Zionism, which initially got off the ground slowly, was glad to profit from such a famous Christian philanthropist, who also received the Nobel Peace Prize in 1901. Dunant in return could also be happy that he was additionally granted a philanthropic title by the Zionists.

Patrick Kury

Veit Wyler

Veit Wyler is one of those personalities in the Swiss history of the 20th century whose achievements have hardly been honoured to this day and whose work is more likely to be known overseas than in his own country. Being a lawyer, who as a subsidiary subject studied philosophy, he made it his task 'to save people from the machinery of state bureaucracy'. His mother supported his social and political engagement. She was one of the first persons who, during the First World War, had children brought to Switzerland for a holiday. Immediately after the war, his parents organized projects to save children from Vienna and Hungary.

Veit Wyler was born in 1908 in Baden (Aargau), where he attended the primary and secondary schools. After his time at the gymnasium, which he partly spent living with his uncle, a rabbi in Wiesbaden, he studied law and philosophy in Zurich, Vienna, Hamburg and Leipzig, where he graduated before he reached the age of 22. During the thirties, he became known in Switzerland as a result of two trials that both caused a sensation. In 1934 he prevented the extradition to National Socialist Germany of one of the most famous representatives of the 'Kommunistische Internationale', the German Heinz Neumann. Two years later, Wyler, who now had his own lawyer's office, defended the Yugoslavian Jew David Frankfurter. On February 4, 1936, in Davos he had shot dead the National Socialist leader of Switzerland Wilhelm Gustloff for political reasons. The trial started in December 1936 under very tense conditions. The Third Reich put heavy

1   Veit Wyler in his study, summer 1996.

pressure on Switzerland, so that there was fear of a German invasion and the Swiss Jewish community considered it thoughtless that a Jew defended Frankfurter. But Wyler was not to be pushed into a corner, and at the wish of David Frankfurter's family – together with the main defender Dr. Eugen Curti – he courageously defended Frankfurter. The two lawyers intentionally drew attention to the persecution of the Jews and the activities of the Nazis in Switzerland, which led to the banning of the National Socialist German Workers' Party in Switzerland. But given the political situation of the time, it was not in their power to prevent Frankfurter from being sent to prison for 18 years. After the end of the war, Frankfurter was pardoned.

Although he never wanted to be politically linked to a party, despite his attraction to left wing politics, Wyler joined the Zionist group in Zurich in 1939, which was then hardly active. Later he headed the Swiss presidium for many years. During the Second World War he put all his efforts into bringing refugees, legally or illegally, into Switzerland and to make their emigration possible. He organized their entry into any country whose diplomatic representatives co-operated. Together with Samuel Scheps, leader of the 'Palestine Office' in Geneva, Nathan Schwalb, Heini Bornstein, Benjamin Sagalowitz and some others, he organized financial means, passports, visas and transit permits and maintained a refugee organization. After the war Wyler continued to dedicate himself to Jewish affairs.

Between 1949 and 1986 he published the magazine 'Das Neue Israel', where the policy of the young State of Israel was independently discussed. Veit Wyler who called himself an internationalist especially focused on the Israeli-Arab relationship. As a supporter of a binational state he was one of the few who placed great importance on reconciliation. Accordingly he received in the eighties the title of 'Honorary Fellow' from the 'International Center for Peace in the Middle East' and in 1995 the 'Weizmann Institute of Science' presented him with the 'Weizmann Award' for his various achievements above all for those during the Shoah. In 1980 the same institute had already appointed him honorary doctor in philosophy. Veit Wyler has been living and working in Zurich since the thirties.

Patrick Kury

Wladimir Sagal and Benjamin Sagalowitz

The lives of the two brothers Wladimir and Benjamin Sagalowitz are a vivid example showing that people are not powerlessly at the mercy of fate, but can fight against the problems of everyday life and against injustices, and remain strong, even under the most adverse conditions. Expulsion, exile, financial ruin and the loss of material security, the fight against fascism and escape from enemies are all stations in the life of the brothers. This may have something to do with the fact that both of them were attracted to a socialist Zionism which combined the strategies of a Jewish and a social solidarity.

Benjamin Sagalowitz was born in 1901, three years after his brother, in the same city, in Vitebsk in Russia and grew up in a wealthy family. Po-

1 Benjamin Sagalowitz [1901–1970] studying files; painted by his brother Wladimir Sagal in 1962.

groms associated with the Russian-Japanese war forced the family to leave the czarian empire in 1905. The parents took their five sons to Wiesbaden via Königsberg and as the First World War broke out they finally moved to Zurich, where Wladimir and Benjamin finished high school. In Zurich, their father, an enthusiastic Zionist, supported numerous leading personalities of the Zionist movement. Their mother became the cofounder and president of the Eastern Jewish Women's Association. For financial reasons the family moved to Germany in 1917. Only Benjamin Sagalowitz, who studied law and later obtained a doctorate, remained in Zurich.

During the time of the great inflation, the family lost its entire fortune. It was not even possible for them to return to Soviet Russia. Wladimir Sagalowitz, who later called himself Sagal, had to give up his medical studies. Nevertheless he was able to attend the school of art in Berlin for a brief period of time and made a living as a painter of advertisements and posters, as an anatomical painter for Professor Sauerbruch and most of all as a press and portrait artist. In this function he worked at a number of different Zionist congresses and visited Switzerland several times before 1939. He painted the portraits of the most important representatives of Zionism as well as atmospheric sketches of what happened at the congress. In 1933 he fled to France where he voluntarily joined the French army in 1939. In 1943 he succeeded in effecting a daring escape to Switzerland over the French Alps. After a brief internment, he married his childhood sweetheart Lucie Aus der Au in the following year. Although married to a Swiss woman, a refugee of Eastern Jewish origin was still not welcome after the Second World War; he was repeatedly put under pressure to leave Switzerland. But Wladimir Sagal stayed until his death in 1969. After getting the Swiss citizenship he could work in peace. In addition to his regular work as a press artist and portraitist for the 'Tagesanzeiger' and the 'Volksrecht' newspapers he also produced pictures of

2   Wladimir Sagal [1898–1969] at work in front of the Congress Building in Lucerne during the 19th Zionist Congress in 1935, photographed by Tim Nahum Gidal.

famous people, figure compositions, landscapes as well as innumerable sketches of everyday life in Zurich.

The life of his brother Benjamin Sagalowitz was similarly dramatic, although he was able to live in Switzerland during the entire period of National Socialism. The socialist Zionist Sagalowitz fought National Socialism with all his might. He recognized that the persecution of the Jews would soon mean the end of freedom for all if nothing was done to stop it. He repeatedly appeared in public as an admonisher and criticized the refugee policy of the government as heartless and scandalous. In 1933/34 the Swiss-Israeli community alliance created an office through which all anti-Semitic attacks could be warded off publicly and Jewish activities could be elucidated. As the situation came to a head during the course of the thirties Benjamin Sagalowitz took over the leadership of this Jewish news agency (Juna) in 1938 and developed it into a courageous journalistic instrument of defence. The first opportunity for the archive to prove itself in the fight against anti-Semitism came during the Berne trial about the 'Protocols of the Learned Elders of Zion'. After the Second World War too, the Juna archive, which is unique in what it did, was for a long time the most important source for investigating the fate of refugees, in Switzerland. It was Sagalowitz' task to collect material from already published reports, to compile them and pass them on to foreign subscribers in the form of press reviews. Thanks to this method, Juna could never be accused of publishing untrue commentaries. It was also Sagalowitz who was responsible for the fact that as early as 1942 the 'Jewish World Congress' and via it the United States and England received information about the extermination of the Jews which was beginning in the 'German Reich'. After checking himself the credibility of the German informer, the German industrialist Eduard Schulte, Sagalowitz established the contact between him and Gerhart Riegner of the Jewish World Congress in Geneva.

After the Second World War Sagalowitz was concerned with the organization of the Juna archive until his death in 1970. He was also active as a reporter during the most varied trials of war crime in Germany and Israel for the 'Neue Zürcher Zeitung' newspaper. His friend and companion Veit Wyler honoured the work of Benjamin Sagalowitz on the occasion of his sixtieth birthday as follows:

'The time of inhuman activities in politics and of a clear conscience in times of dishonourable actions in those years which confronted Switzerland with a great humane task have found in Benjamin Sagalowitz a registrar and admonisher who, as "Rocher de bronze" rose far above his surroundings imbued by opportunism and lack of direction [...] If the non-Jewish democrats in the political life of those years had heeded the warnings of Sagalowitz and very few others, they may have been able to save some people, but most certainly they could have saved the belief in humanity of those who were humiliated; perhaps even the section of the European civilization which was capable of surviving may have remained intact – but certainly more pride in human dignity.'[1]

[1] Veit Wyler: Dr. Benjamin Sagalowitz sechzigjährig. In: Das Neue Israel, June 1961, p. 717.

Heiko Haumann

Samuel Scheps

Samuel Scheps is one of the outstanding personalities of both Swiss and international Zionism. He was born in Lodz on May 19, 1904. He probably comes from a Sabbatanian-Frankish family as the name is a distorted version of 'Shabbetai'. He started his studies at the Jagiellonen University of Cracow. In 1924 he moved to Basel, where he studied economics and sociology, mainly under Edgar Salin and Robert Michels and wrote his thesis on the monetary and central bank policy of the Republic of Poland. At this time Samuel Scheps was already a dedicated Zionist. In Basel he contributed to the finding of a consensus between the two Zionist organizations – one for Western and one for Eastern Jews – and thus to the integration of the Eastern Jews. Furthermore he founded a club for the cultivation of the Hebrew language and by giving many lectures increased the awareness of the Jewish culture. For this reason the famous Hebrew poet Chaim Bialik [1873–1934] from Volhynia visited Basel several times. On the occasion of the foundation of the Hebrew University of Jerusalem in 1925, he spoke, alongside Marcus Cohn and Moshe Neviaski, at a meeting of the Jewish Students' Association of Basel about the ideas of this university and he was engaged in founding committees of the 'Friends of the Hebrew University of Jerusalem'; up to this day he is closely connected to it. In the thirties Scheps travelled to Palestine, where he was shown around by his friend Yaakov Zur.[1] Other Zionists such as Jacob Klatzkin [1882–1948]

1 Samuel Scheps. Drawing by Sagal, 1963.

or Menahem Ussishkin [1863–1941] were also among his friends.

As after Austria's 'annexation' to the Third Reich in 1938, yet another wave of Jewish refugees fled to Switzerland in the hope of finding protection, Scheps found the mission of his life. In 1928 he was already an active member of the central committee of the Swiss Zionist Association as well as chairman of the Jewish National Fund in Switzerland. In 1937 he succeeded Neviaski as

---

[1] Zur later became Israeli ambassador to Argentine and France. Today he is a historian; cf. his contribution in this publication.

one of the directors of the Palestine office, initially in Basel, then in Geneva where he still lives. This office, a branch of the Jewish Agency, organized emigrations to Palestine and had many branch offices in several countries. During the time of the genocide of the Jews he was in a key position as regards assisting the refugees. At times he saw at least fifty people a day to help them getting their certificates and money for their entry into Palestine. He organized five rescue ships and personally accompanied the last transport during the war. He also made it possible through written certification pledges to acquire limited residence permits in Switzerland for innumerable refugees. Geneva became the centre of the Aliyah during these years. Risking his own life, Samuel Scheps travelled several times to Berlin, Vienna and Bucharest to negotiate emigration possibilities. The necessary documents could often only be organized with greatest difficulties and venturesome actions. In addition, Samuel Scheps was a leading employee of the Jewish National Fund – Keren Kayemet Le Israel. In 1942 he was one of the first to learn about the beginning of the 'final solution' through information given by the German businessman Eduard Schulte. His father and many members of his family were victims of this annihilation policy, his elder brother was killed as a Polish officer in Katyn.

After the end of the war, he tirelessly searched for survivors of the Shoah, to give them assistance. Originally he planned to move to Israel himself, but was then convinced by his contemporaries that his help was needed more in Switzerland. After the foundation of the State of Israel, he established a company and organized the export of Israeli products to Switzerland and all over Europe. Later he supported the spreading of the Jewish and Polish culture and history by giving lectures and by writing numerous essays and he is still active today. Beside various other awards, he was elected in 1994 to be the first honorary president of the Swiss Zionist Association.[2]

---

[2] This summary is based on a conversation with Samuel Scheps on 8 July 1996, as well as on numerous essays and publications by and concerning Scheps which were made available to me. I would like to express my thanks for his helpful assistance.

Nathalie Meyrat

From the City to the Country: Jews in the Alsace

The first evidence for Judaism in the Alsace can be found in Benjamin Tudela. In the middle of the 12th century, this Hispano-Jewish world traveller described the Strasbourg community as one of the largest and most flourishing in all of Germany. In the Middle Ages, Jewry in the Alsace was, as in the rest of Europe, an urban Jewry. At this time, the Jews were allowed neither to own land nor to employ workers. In the cities, on the other hand, they were allowed to buy houses. The urban Jews were mainly active in the money and interest business which was forbidden to the Christians by the canonical ban on charging interest. During the time of the Black Death in 1348/49, the Jewish urban communities disappeared all but completely. The Jews were accused of having caused the plagues by poisoning the wells. There were anti-Jewish pogroms and a large number of Alsatian Jews were murdered.

At the beginning of the 17th century, only about 500 Jewish families lived in the Alsace. After the Thirty Year War from 1618 to 1648, the largest part of the Alsace became French. After this time the Jewish population grew anew. According to the census ordered by Louis XVI in France, 20,000 Jews were residing in the Alsace again. Jews from the Canton Basel-Land also settled in the Alsace at this time. Thus most Jews of Allschwil moved to the neighbouring Hegenheim, as they had been expelled from the Swiss border area in 1694 due to reasons of professional competition. Most Jews lived in the countryside, because after the pogroms in the 14th century they had been forbidden to settle in the cities of the Alsace. This situation did not change much as the French Jews – the first in Europe – were granted full human and civil rights by the Revolution of 1789 and the Constitution of 1791. In the Alsace, the rural Jewry remained characteristic for a long time.

The majority of the rural Jews were poor and had many children. They were mainly pedlars, haberdashers, fabric, cattle and wheat dealers or money lenders. Travelling a great deal due to their professions, the rural Alsatian Jews fulfilled the role of middlemen which was so typical for the Jewish people:

'They were middlemen between the rural world and that of the administration, notaries, dignitaries. They took on commercial transactions related to purchase and sale of cattle and horses, from lending money to dealing with houses, land and property.'[1]

Due to their strict religious beliefs, everyday life of the Alsatian Jews as well as the flow of weeks and years were dominated by religious prescriptions and customs and by the innumerable holidays.

Although the civil rights, which incidentally had been restricted once again under Napoleon I and had not become completely effective until the revolutionary constitution of 1848, facilitated the integration of the Jews, it by no means caused

---

[1] Freddy Raphaël: Der Viehhändler, Symbolgestalt des elsässischen Judentums. In: Jüdisches Museum der Schweiz, Basel und Schweizerisches Museum für Volkskunde, Basel (ed.): Juden im Elsass. Basel 1992, pp. 14–15, here p. 14.

1 Revolt against the Jews in Durmenach on February 28, 1848. Lithography by L. Simon, in the possession of the Jewish Museum of Switzerland.

anti-Jewish ideas to disappear. They were especially manifest in times of crisis and transition. Thus, in the context of the French Revolution of 1789 anti-Jewish pogroms broke out in the Alsace and the revolution of 1848 was accompanied by similar unrest. Seligmann Brunschwig of Durmenach described his experience of the understated so-called 'Jewish Rumpus':

'In 1848 there was a revolution. On Monday evening a non-Jew was shot near Steinsoultz. So we all fled, the entire community. I and Aaron Ruf, a sender of blessed remembrance, went to Bouxwiller for the night and stayed with Schumacher(s); they looked after us well. In the same night, the Durmenachers had already stolen everywhere. In the morning we sent a young non-Jew to have a look and see how things were; he came back and brought with him a 'nachtele' and a pincase. He said the shop had been completely emptied. So we went home, but we did not dare to look inside [...] Everything was broken and no house was left completely standing. I had absolutely nothing left, no household, no clothing, absolutely nothing. I had hidden some wares, but not much, and I was given back a few. So I was forced to start anew. God helped again and he will continue to help.'[2]

The Upper Alsatian communities of Hegenheim and Durmenach were the worst hit. Just as after 1789, many Jewish families fled to Switzerland and were offered temporary asylum in the

[2] Astrid Starck: Jiddische Lebensbeschreibung. Von Seligmann Brunschwig von Dürmenach mit Schilderung des 'Judenrumpels' von 1848. In: Jüdisches Museum der Schweiz, Basel und Schweizerisches Museum für Volkskunde, Basel (ed.): Juden im Elsass. Basel 1992, pp. 16–19, here p. 18 f.

From the City to the Country: Jews in the Alsace

two semi-cantons of Basel – where the Jews had not yet been given equality of rights. The solidarity of part of the Basel-Land population with the displaced Jews was great. Although the expelled Jews were not offered the right to stay, several Jewish families remained in the Canton Basel-Land, where they were mainly active in trade. In 1851, however, the canton government ordered their expulsion because of pressure of Christian dealers. A protest on the part of France in favour of its citizens effected only a moderation of the decision. After the emancipation of the Jews in Switzerland in 1866, numerous Alsatian Jews moved to Basel.

In the course of the 19th century, the agricultural and industrial changes influenced the position of the Jews in the Alsace. Due to the foundation of credit institutes for farmers, they were partially pushed out of the small-scale credit business. In addition, the improvement of travelling conditions made the Jewish travelling salesmen unnecessary in some places. In the second half of the century, many Jews decided to emigrate. In contrast to this was the social rise of several Jewish families who achieved a certain prosperity as shop owners, trading agents, merchants, manufacturers, physicians or lawyers, especially in the cities – mainly Strasbourg and Mulhouse. Military careers also made it possible to enter the bourgeoisie. Connected to this was the assimilation process of part of the Alsatian Jews which was to last till the 20th century. Traditional values were lost. The religious customs were increasingly ignored, Sabbath often no longer upheld. The social net became looser and looser: the solidarity among Jews – a characteristic of the rural communities – disappeared rapidly. This 'process of normalization' also led to Yiddish being spoken lesser and lesser at official events. Out of gratitude to the French state, certain Alsatian Jews became fanatic patriots, whose chauvinism peaked in their despising and rejecting the Eastern Jews who immigrated to Alsace in the second half of the 19th century. They did not want to have anything to do with those 'Polacks' who reminded them of their own, poor past.

After its victory over France in the war of 1870/71, the German Empire annexed the Alsace. Now it became evident that for the majority of the Jews the possibilities that France had offered them outweighed the anti-Jewish events. They exhibited great allegiance to France and put great efforts into having the Alsace returned to it. A large number emigrated to France.

However, after 1918, as the Alsace became French again, the Jews were forced to admit that their hopes that anti-Semitism had been overcome were premature. It found more and more open sympathizers, and it was a traumatic experience when after the defeat of France in the Second World War, in 1940, in the European country that had first granted the Jews full emancipation, the French took part in their persecution by the Nazis.

Despite all this there are once again Jewish communities in the Alsace today, mainly in the cities. The largest growth took place in the fifties and sixties, as many Jews immigrated from Algeria, Marocco and Tunisia.

Barbara Lüthi
Sabine Strebel

Rural Jewry in the Alsace: Stories of the Past?

'We can describe incidents, but we cannot describe an epoch. We can describe things from an epoch, but how can we describe an era? We can report on events, incidents or facts [...], but we cannot describe the atmosphere of a time. This is how I feel about it.'[1]

January 17, 1996, a winter afternoon: A first meeting with our interview partner from Basel who is to tell us about her life in the Alsace. We hope that through this talk we will obtain a different access to the history of rural Jewry in the Alsace. Someone telling the story of his or her life can elucidate the diversity of the forms of life and the subjective perceptions. Mrs. F. is a small, lively lady who gives us a warm welcome. She invites us into her bright, spacious living-room and – without being asked many questions – she unfolds her life before us. A second interview takes place three weeks later. With her narrative talent she involves us in the story of her life in such a way that the individual fragments fall into place like pieces of a mosaic and form a picture. She tells us about the life in the country, about Jewish traditions and the Alsatian specialities such as 'Bibbelekäs' (cottage cheese), 'grüner Karpfen' (green catfish), 'Flammeküeche' (onion pie).

More than eighty years of reminiscences: She was born in Hirsingen in 1908, which at that time was part of Germany. At the outbreak of World War I she moved first to Delsberg and then to Basel. After the war she returned to the Alsace which, in the meantime, had become French. She recalls: 'In 1919 I came to Durmenach and there I had a really nice time. And I'll never forget it. A sheltered time with my parents [...] and with my grandmothers.' Life in the village and in the family becomes the focus of our interview. In 1930 she got married, moved to Basel and gave birth to a son. In World War II her husband was taken prisoner of war by Germany. After a short time, all Alsatians, who were regarded as Germans, were released – except for the Jews. But finally her husband was able to flee to Switzerland. In the meantime she continued to run his wine and liquor store. She was in contact with refugees, the Swiss bureaucracy and the authorities. These were years of uncertainty, of fear resulting from the awareness of the situation of her Jewish fellow citizens. In the ensuing years, which were marked by war, she was active in the refugee aid, later in Zionist organizations and assisted in the Zionist congress of 1946. From 1951 onwards she got to know Israel, where she kept returning.

March 10, 1996: We visited Durmenach, hoping to get an idea of the 'atmosphere which cannot be described'. In our mind the stories seen from the perspective of an 88-year-old woman who lived in the village as a child. We were looking for traces of the world she had told us about. The houses were built close to one another, a few old houses were being renovated at great cost, some farms were still in operation. It was Sunday, the farming village was deserted and quiet. Only the 'rue de la Synagogue' reminded us that there was once a synagogue not far from the church.

---

[1] We would like to thank Mrs. F. for her interviews.

Mrs. F. was brought up on a large farm close to the church. Her father was a cattle dealer – at the beginning of the 20th century it was still a typical occupation of rural Jews. This also dictated the life of the family and relatives. Since they had a large number of cattle, her brothers had to work in the barn before they went to school, whereas she only helped when one of the cows was ill. She much rather helped her mother who had to run the household: they did needlework, got her father's clothes ready, planted vegetables in the garden and had 14 hens. As a cattle dealer her father had close contact with various groups of the population: 'Yes, during the day my father used to visit the villages and buy cattle or he asked those farmers who wanted to buy cattle to come round.' The Christian and the Jewish populations shared a confined living space in the small village. Two cultures which time and time again came into contact. But a feeling of distance, a perception of 'being different', remained. Mrs. F.'s descriptions of the coexistence between Jews and non-Jews changed between the first and the second interview. The first time she spoke of the 'quite normal Jewish life' that existed, of the cantor of the synagogue, the Jewish holidays and the Christian people with whom 'they were friends, they lived of course among all the others. There were Jews and there were others'. The 'Judenrumpel'[2], 'that took place much earlier [...] This is of no interest to you now. It does not fit into your period.' During the second interview a more differentiated picture evolved: contacts between the Jewish and the Christian population developed in various ways. The former participated in the lives of the latter, they felt responsible for each other, for example, 'Mum used to cook meat soup every Friday [...] And when the soup was ready, there were three old Christian women in the area who were ill, who could not cook for themselves. And we had these bowls into which mum used to fill the finished soup, and on Friday I had to bring soup [...] to the three houses [...] This is just another memory that remains [...] She even sent them milk, but that was natural, we had so much milk, but that they got some of Saturday's soup was not all that natural.'

But Mrs. F. also remembers less harmonious episodes. Meetings between children that apparently expressed naivety and ignorance, but also the relation between the 'familiar' and 'foreign' at the same time: 'Songs were sung in the blueberry woods, there were lots of blueberries. And then the Christian children began to sing (original sung in Swiss dialect; rough translation): "Pick the blueberries, leave the stems, drown the Jews, let the Christians go" and then we sang: "Pick the blueberries, leave the stems, drown the Christians, let the Jews go." Repeat [...] Yes. But they started it, and our parents said, so that it wouldn't do us any harm, we should sing it as well.'

Mrs. F.'s childhood in the village was spent in a very religious, Jewish environment. Her father's day was dictated by the Jewish laws of religion. He 'did not leave the house without saying the morning prayer, and my father was kosher. And he had a pan hanging in the kitchen of a farmer and apparently [...] he had made some sort of sign on it with a pencil. So that they would not use the pan, so that it remained kosher. And then he heated up either a sausage or whatever he had brought with him and he ate it at Theres' place [...] This is typical of Alsatian Jews.' The Jewish atmosphere in the house was based on prayer, the observance of the Sabbath, the Torah readings and holidays such as Purim and Hanukkah. The children were given some religious education – however not very profoundly – by the cantor of the synagogue. When she moved to Basel, her contacts to Durmenach gradually diminished. But it remains a chapter in her life that has not faded from her memory. 'The Alsace is there where I have my connections to it', and it still means home to her.

---

[2] Riots against the Jews in the Alsace in 1848.

In an area where those in power had changed back and forth for decades and with them the language, the laws, the authorities, Mrs. F. identified with concrete, everday factors: the family, the landscape, the language, religion, the people around her. Moving from one place to another, crossing borders, fluctuating between Jewish and Christian cultures while being deeply rooted in Judaism, her role as a daughter, child, mother, Jew, mediator, liquor dealer, Zionist and much more – all this is proof of an eventful biography which flows from her memory to us as listeners. Perhaps the atmosphere of a bygone era cannot be recaptured completely. But it becomes clear 'that the people do not only make stories out of their lives but also their lives out of stories' (Marcel Reich-Ranicki).

Daniel Gerson

Zionism in the Alsace

When on September 27, 1791, the French National Assembly emancipated the Alsatian Jews, the legal equality was accompanied by the demand that the Jews had to give up their identity as a people and see themselves only as a religious community. The 'nation juive en Alsace' should become the 'israélites français'. The integration into the French national state, encouraged by economic and social changes, made it possible for the Alsatian Jews to see themselves as a part of a state with universal, humanistic principles despite anti-Semitic riots. These were less than perfect conditions for Zionism.

In 1826 Charles Netter was born in Strasbourg. He had an urban middle-class background which was nevertheless still strongly linked to Jewish traditions. He founded the agricultural school 'Mikveh Israel' in Palestine in 1869 which he ran until his death in 1882. Netter did not pursue 'Zionist' ambitions with his school in the sense of intending to settle Jews in Palestine on a large scale. As one of the co-founders of the French-Jewish relief and education organization 'Alliance Israélite Universelle', spreading a secular education under French influence among Oriental Jews since 1860, he was not thinking of Jewish national self-determination. His project remained within the conventional scope of 'making poor Jews more productive', as supported by the Jewish upper class not only in Palestine. Nevertheless, the Holy Land was of enormous importance for his identity as a Jew. Many Alsatian Jews made donations to their less wealthy fellow believers. The tie to Palestine was also maintained by adding a little earth from the Holy Land to the grave of the dead at their burial. The small 'Mizrach board', showing the direction to Jerusalem for prayer, which hung on the wall of every traditional household, was a reminder of the tie to the far-away country of origin.

The 'Dreyfus Affair', the conviction of a Jewish-Alsatian captain, accompanied by waves of anti-Semitism and which was based on forged evidence, shocked the French patriotism of the Alsatian Jews from 1894 onwards. While the majority did, however, not give up their hopes of integration into the French society, a group of young Jewish intellectuals in the cities were receptive to the Zionist ideas. Insecure in their national orientation anyhow, as since 1871 they were no longer allowed to be French and generally they did not want to be German, they had received sufficient secular education to absorb the ideas of political Zionism; at the same time they were influenced strongly enough by Judaism to comprehend and to affirm the Messianic background of the Zionist idea. These Zionist 'pioneers' were not met with enormous enthusiasm in the Alsace, but they were heard to a certain extent. In Mulhouse in 1899, Alfred Elias founded the first local Zionist group, which was followed by a group in Strasbourg in 1902.

The rabbis in the Alsace, who at the beginning of the century were mainly conservatively oriented in religious matters, saw in Zionism an ideology which could lead the young generation, otherwise indifferent towards religious matters, back to Judaism. The middle class also pursued the development of Zionism with an increasing benevolence, even if they continued nationally to be French-oriented. Because of the affiliation of the Alsace to the German Reich, many important impulses came from there. For example when in 1912 the Zionist Youth and Wanderer movement 'Blau-Weiss' was founded in Berlin, one of its first local branches was founded in Mulhouse. Furthermore, the Alsatian Jews spoke German, which was the most important official language of the Zionist organizations until the First World War. For the French Jews, however, Zionism was not easily accessible because it was mainly orientated toward the German language and culture. After the re-affiliation of the province to France at the end of the First World War, the Jews of Alsace-Lorraine retained their organizational autonomy in the 'Union régionale des sionistes de l'Est de la France'.

Various different organizations covered the broad spectrum of the Zionist movement. The Jewish boy scout movement, originally a non-Zionist middle-class liberal organization, became, in the time between the wars, the biggest Zionist-influenced youth organization with close connections to the Jewish National Fund 'Keren Kayemet Le Israel'. At the same time there were religious groups, like the 'Berit ha-Noar', which joined the international religious-Zionist 'Bnai Akiwa' youth movement. The left wing had its own organization, 'Poalei Zion Hitahdut', in which Eastern Jewish immigrants in Strasbourg were active. Young people thinking about emigrating to Palestine and preparing for the Aliyah met in a youth group called 'Hatikvah'. Women were often involved in the 'Ghalei', supporting social projects in Palestine and organizing Hebrew courses. Altogether these organizations had no more than one thousand members concentrated in the cities of Colmar, Mulhouse and Strasbourg. Nevertheless the Alsatian Jewry was the Zionist stronghold in France between 1918 and 1939. Regularly the Alsatian Zionist organizations collected more than 50% of all French

1 Synagogue in Ingwiller.

donations for the development of Palestine. Several Zionist newspapers and magazines were also published during this time: 'Le Juif', 'La Terre Promise' and 'La Terre Retrouvée'. Only a few Jews, however, considered emigrating to Palestine. From 1933 to 1937 there was a 'Hachsharah' in Altwies near Metz. On this farm approximately 100 pioneers-to-be were given an agricultural training, to prepare them for their lives in a kibbutz. In 1939 this institution had to be closed because of a lack of candidates and finances.

Due to the Nazi threat and an increasing anti-Semitic attitude among the Alsatian population in the thirties, Zionist organizations increasingly attracted sympathizers. However, shortly before the beginning of the Second World War not even in the Alsace was there an incrased readiness to give anything more than money for the Zionist ideal. The threat represented by the German National Socialism, which was more noticeable in the Alsace than in the rest of France due to the geographical proximity and family relationships to the Jews of southern Germany, did not lead to an increased Aliyah.

After the traumatic events of the Second World War, temporary expulsion from the Alsace and the murdering of a large part of the community by the Nazis and their accomplices, only a few Jews remained, who would not have spoken in favour of the Zionist ideas. Most of the Jewish survivors returned to the Alsace. Even the foundation of the state of Israel seldom made them think about leaving their homeland.

Until the end of the sixties, official representatives of the Alsatian Jews held back in public with open statements of solidarity towards Israel, so as not to come into conflict with the large group of pro-Arab French politicians such as de Gaulle. But when Israel won the Six-Day War in 1967, many Jews made no secret of their enthusiasm. The pronounced pro-Israel politics of president Mitterrand made the frictionless co-existence of French patriotism and Zionist engagement seem possible. Today, an 'israélite français' can at the same time regard himself as a member of the 'nation juive'.

Astrid Starck

Alfred Elias

1   Alfred Elias [1865–1940].

One of the first and most dedicated Alsatian Zionists was Alfred Benjamin Elias. He was born in Mulhouse in the Alsace on July 11, 1865, six years before the annexation of Alsace-Lorraine by the German Reich. The leading role that Mulhouse played in Zionist matters is shown by the fact that the first Zionist association in Alsace-Lorraine was founded there in 1899; Elias became its first president. Not until three years later, in 1902, was such an organization founded in Strasbourg. Elias was a physician. All his life he was active in his hometown: he took care of the Jewish trade school – an achievement from the 19th century – which gave Mulhouse a special position, and founded the 'Weisse Kreuz' (White Cross) that helped in case of accidents.

His tendency towards Zionism brought him into contact with the Zionist leaders of the time at the Zionist Congress in Basel, most notably Theodor Herzl, Max Nordau, David Wolffsohn and Max Isidor Bodenheimer. Elias' letters to them still exist, just as Herzl's correspondence with him. He organized lectures about Palestine in Mulhouse and invited Max Nordau and the brothers Alexander and Oscar Marmorek to participate. Due to the Dreyfus Affair, Elias and a few other Alsatian Jews turned towards German Zionism. The majority remained Francophile, however, so these events produced only a small resonance. Elias published a number of articles in the newspaper 'Die Welt' between 1901 and 1905. He wrote about the situation of Alsatian Judaism between emancipation and assimilation and discussed the French assimilation policy of the Jews. He was a member of the 'Alliance Israélite Universelle' and fought its leadership because wherever it was established it put the interests of France before those of Zionism.

His philosophy and his activities were shaped by Zionism. He dealt with the 'upholding and improving of (Jewish) characteristics' in Alsace, on economic, social and literary levels, and demanded a return to the Promised Land at the same time. He helped found the Jewish Colonial Bank and supported the Jewish National Fund. He wrote scripts about the Jewish trade school, the savings bank in Mulhouse and the history of Zionism. With the help of the Heymann & Co. Bank, which was responsible for the real-estate company 'Palestine', he purchased an estate near the technical college in Haifa, which he later gave up. Shortly before the outbreak of the Second World War he got his family to safety. He himself remained in Mulhouse to care for sick people. When the Nazis marched into Alsace on June 10, 1940, Elias committed suicide.

Ulrich Baumann

Zionism and the Changes in the Patterns of Life in the Rural Jewry of Southern Baden around 1900

The rural regions of Hesse, Franconia and Baden were represented above average at the early foundations of local Zionist groups in Germany. The percentage of 'shekel' payers, i.e. Jews who paid their annual membership fee to the World Zionist Organization, was also far higher in the small communities than in the large cities. There are records of an almost unanimous joining of a Jewish community from Müllheim/Baden. With the support of a former inhabitant of the small town, two students who made propaganda for Zionism here, were looked at

'initially somewhat shy and wary [...] like foreign intruders'.

During the lively discussion that ensued, they were then able to present such convincing arguments, that

'there was soon great enthusiasm at the meeting and ultimately all persons present paid their shekel in addition to the regional fee [...] We were not allowed to leave the same night, we celebrated the evening with an excellent Margrave wine and in the morning we were invited for breakfast by the chairman. The Müllheim local group had been founded.'[1]

An explanation for the success of the Zionist ideas, which did not meet with acceptance everywhere and in some cases lasted only briefly, can be found in the strong Jewish group identity that existed in rural communities. It was not possible in a village to conceal from the non-Jewish environment the fact that one was a Jew. The proximity also made it necessary to personally confront violent anti-Semitic criminals, as Jews in southern Baden had done over and over again in a self-assured and in some cases militant way. Zionist agitation had chances of success particularly if it was able to attract a respectable public figure – or a 'belligerent opposer'.[2] Political developments within the group of rural Jews thus combined with the old social structures of the 'kehillot', the Jewish communities.

The cultural and community life of the 'rural kehillot' did not experience as much renewal up until 1900 as did those in municipal communities. The reforms of the 1850s and 1860s had permitted German prayers and prescribed new rules of conduct: 'loud, discordant praying together' during the service or staying in the synagogue after the end of the service should cease.[3] More far-

---

[1] Max Jungmann: Memoires of a Zionist. Jerusalem 1959, p. 38, also printed in: Yehuda Eloni: Zionismus in Deutschland. Von den Anfängen bis 1914. Schriftenreihe des Institutes für Deutsche Geschichte, University of Tel Aviv. Vol. 10. Gerlingen 1987, p. 129. The exact year of joining cannot be determined. The context in Eloni and the dates of Jungmann's birth and death [1875–1975] infer the first decade after the turn of the century.

[2] Eloni: Zionismus, p. 128.
[3] See Church Service Rules of the Eichstetten Jewish community (1862) as well as the notice of the Eichstetten Synagogue Council (1851). In: Central Archives for the History of the Jewish People, Jerusalem (CAHJP), Eichstetten, p. 221/1 (loose pages).

1 Breisach, former Judengasse, after a service in the synagogue (first quarter of the 20th century). Breisach was among the most important Jewish communities in Southern Baden. Photograph taken by David H. Blum (today New York).

reaching changes, however, did not follow. The local traditions in rites and prayer melodies and their respective 'minhagim' – 'the customs' – continued to exist anyway. In the domestic sphere, the women ensured that the household adhered to kosher standards; in some cases, they had learned modern housekeeping from relatives that lived in the city. The Sabbath was observed by most Jews well into the 1930s. In Gailingen, the 'Eruv' was observed on the Sabbath and holidays: it identifies private and public space by cordoning them off with a 'Sabbath rope' and thus serves to observe the bans in force on these days, one of which forbids to carry objects from the private into the public area. At the same time, the Jewish merchants in Gailingen endeavoured to modernize the infrastructure of the village. They wanted to remain in the traditional religious community. The Upper Rhine community evolved into a village with a municipal flair into which the Jewish women brought city fashions, a 'kaff', the Yiddish term for 'village', became jokingly Francophone 'Gélangé' (Gailingen).

Although the combination of tradition and the modern succeeded here – and in some cases elsewhere as well – several thousand rural Jews left their communities in Baden and moved to the cities in the decades after 1862, the date of the emancipation and the unrestricted permission to settle anywhere. Among these were wealthy families who were searching for further social advancement, as well as many who were no longer able to earn their keep by rural trade. Other impoverished traders, small merchants and real estate agents continued to live in the village. One large group of Jewish villagers, however, did succeed in organizing a business with travellers by employing staff and in opening a store in the village and making use of new technical achievements such as the telephone and automobile. Stores and shops made it possible for Jewish women to benefit from new occupational possibilities as (co)owners or employees. Based on the bourgeois way of life, the rural Jews now adopted many ways of city life which also included a higher secular education. Before 1900, for example, the number of Jewish pupils from nearby village communities in the 'Höhere Bürgerschule' (Secondary School) in Ettenheim exceeded that of the Christian pupils, although the Jewish children belonged to a demographic minority in these communities.

Relationships between the rural Jews and their relatives in the cities appear to have continued to exist, at least in some cases. Similarly, the rural kehillot reacted open-mindedly when former villagers suggested an extension of charity. At the beginning of 1872, for instance, a few councillors of the synagogues in southern Baden prepared the establishment of a supraregional burial fund which had been suggested by Jonas Weil from New York who originally came from Emmendingen. According to information provided by the initiators, Weil was a 'member of a similar American society "Bené Beris" in New York', which was probably the lodge of the Bnai B'rith order there.[4] The project planned a one-off financial support for the survivors which was to be paid from a fund into which the members had to pay their membership fee; this form of cooperative organization did not correspond to the traditional assistance of Jewish brotherhoods.

That the rural kehillot did take part in important inner-Jewish and social questions is shown by its participation in organized defensive actions against the political anti-Semitism which had also started to spread in Baden from 1890 on. The 'Union of Israelites of Baden', a parallel organization of the 'Central Society of German Citizens of the Jewish Faith' that existed for some years, was also supported in the country.[5] The commitment of virtually all heads of Jewish families in Eichstetten to the 'Alliance Israélite Universelle', however, demonstrates that even the concerns of Jewish communities outside Europe were perceived. Similar to the situation when the local Zionist group was founded in Müllheim, it was probably the promotion by a respected member of the community that laid the foundation for such a large membership. The membership expresses yet again the influence of traditional family and community structures as well as the solidarity and willingness to act together which is typical of rural Jewish communities despite major social problems and a considerable weakening due to the departure of many families around 1900.

---

[4] CAHJP, Breisach, GA/p. 153.12.
[5] Report of the managing committee of the Vereinigung Badischer Israeliten on its activities until January 1, 1895, Karlsruhe 1895.

Manfred Bosch

'... and I Said to Myself, There Is Something Great in Zionism'

On the Reception of Zionism in Rural Alemannic Jewry, Based Largely on the Example of the Poet Jacob Picard

As Martin Buber discussed the question 'What does Palestine have to do with us?' at the Jewish school in Stuttgart in the late 1920s he met with only little interest. In contrast to 1933, as 'Palestine' was already a regular part of the curriculum, he was then confronted with the statement that 'for us Jews from Württemberg' this country 'was out of the question'. The voice of another member of the community transferred this unshakable feeling of attachment to his home country into a remarkable image of memory:

'What our teacher Max Meyer told us in his vigorous language about the judges and prophets fitted perfectly into what we had learned in the nearby grammar-school about Ludwig Uhland and Friedrich Schiller. It seemed to us as if the prophets had never spoken anything but Swabian at all. And we precisely knew the spot in the Neckar where the children of Israel had crossed the Jordan, while there was no better spot than Bopserwald for Gideon's attack of the Philistines.'

And the two worlds were even closer in a comment made by Rabbi Maier on the occasion of the inauguration of the Stuttgart synagogue on May 3, 1861:

'Yes hail to you dear Stuttgart, our Jerusalem!'[1]

If this 'superposition' of places of Jewish salvation with their own surroundings express how the largely assimilated Jews of Stuttgart must have felt about their city as their home, this is even more so for the Swabian and Alemannic rural Jews. In their communities near the Lake of Constance and in Hegau, along the Rhine and the Neckar, in the Markgräflerland, in the Ortenau and in the Breisgau, in the Vorarlberg and in the Alsace, the Jews and Christians lived together in harmony and mutual respect until the first years of National Socialism. The ghetto was an unheard of concept here and – in contrast to cities – a Jew did not have to fearfully deny his identity. Quite to the contrary, he earned the respect of the non-Jews by exactly professing his faith. A christened Jew, which was no longer unusual in cities, would have been held in contempt here – by both parts of the population.

The rural Alemannic Jews were thus largely protected against assimilation and Jewish self-denial. Due to this living together, although not always free of conflict, of the Jewish and Christian populations, they also lacked experience with anti-Semitism, a decisive factor in the concept and movement of Zionism.

'It is useless, therefore, for us to be loyal patriots [...] If we could only be left in peace [...] But I think we shall not be left in peace'[2]

– such certainty from Herzl's 'Judenstaat' did not fall on listening ears among the rural Alemannic Jews, so that the idea of a Jewish national state derived from it must have appeared to them as

---

[1] Quoted in: Maria Zelzer: Weg und Schicksal der Stuttgarter Juden. Stuttgart n. d. [1964], pp. 87, 88, 46.

[2] Theodor Herzl: Der Judenstaat. 9th ed. Vienna 1933, here quoted from the English version, New York 1988, p. 76.

'imported from the East'. 'How easy and peaceful our life was in contrast', wrote the poet of the rural Alemannic Jews, Jacob Picard [1883–1967], with regard to the historical persecutions, and he was certain

> 'Never would such things happen ever again, just as the other things that had been done to the Jews in earlier centuries would never occur again.'[3]

For the community of Gailingen, possibly the largest rural Jewish community in Germany, it was found that 'before 1933 [...] hardly anyone was interested in Zionism'.[4] Investigations in other communities seem to confirm this. The idea of a Jewish state or even emigration was unfamiliar to the rural Jews. However, in rural Jewry a collective consciousness existed, at the centre of which was the faith and a permanent relationship to the Holy Land. Jacob Picard described this determination as a devotion to Erez Israel and its holy places in his 'Erinnerung eigenen Lebens' (Recollections of My Own Life).

> 'He [his grandfather] always thought of Erez Israel. Things were often sent from there, carved wooden paper weights or pressed flowers from the Holy Land as frames for the pictures of the holy places, and in return he sent donations. But sometimes grandmother did not give him the things and the letters which came from there, because she considered this donations to be "a waste of good money".'[5]

Picard himself was first confronted with Zionism as a twenty-year-old. In 1903, as every year, he spent the summer holidays at his grandparents' place in Tiengen, from where the new high-school graduate, who had moved to Constance when he was ten, travelled to the nearby Basel for several days to the Zionist Congress. In unpublished autobiographical scripts he recorded the strong impression that this meeting had left on him:

1 Caucasian mountain Jews at Barfüsserplatz in Basel, Sixth Congress, 1903.

> 'I saw Herzl sitting amongst the others, although I did not hear him speak, but I heard Max Nordau with his square beard and his shrill, high-pitched voice. And how exciting I found the large statures of the Caucasian mountain Jews, very masculine and warlike with their ammunition belts slung diagonally across their breasts.'[6]

If the optically exotic aspect is the focus of this passage which was recorded much later, the immediate experience must have had a much deeper effect. Still in Tiengen, Picard wrote to his mother:

> 'If I were to try to write to you about the Congress, the letter would be too long. But I can tell you this much: although I went there with the intention of seeing the lives and actions and the different types of people represented there – if only for this reason – I was somehow captivated by this whole Zionism thing; in some instances, depending on the speaker, touched and even enthusiastic. And I said to myself: there is something great in this movement, even if it does not entirely reach its goal.'[7]

---

3 Leo Beack Institute New York, unpublished writings of Jacob Picard, Box III.
4 Regina Schmid: Verlorene Heimat. Gailingen – ein Dorf und seine jüdische Gemeinde in der Weimarer Zeit. Constance 1988, p. 92. Cf. Yehuda Eloni: Zionismus in Deutschland. Von den Anfängen bis 1914. Gerlingen 1987, p. 129, note 56.
5 Manfred Bosch (ed.): Jacob Picard: Werke in zwei Bänden. Konstanz 1991, vol. 2, p. 203.
6 Unpublished writings of Jacob Picard.
7 Tiengen, 26. August 1903. Unpublished writings of Jacob Picard.

The obvious fascination for the Zionist movement cannot be understood without the anti-Semitic experiences which also Picard had after moving to the Gymnasium in Constance. According to his own statement, he was deprived of the prize for history because of his religion, and the rejection by a girl for the same reason would later be the subject of his story 'Wie ich Hölderlin entdeckte' (How I discovered Hölderlin). The experience of the Congress was directly reflected in his poem characteristically called 'Pariah' which came to Picard's mind soon afterwards on Yom Kippur in the synagogue and which was subsequently published in the Zionist magazine 'Ost und West':

'Pariah

Wenn sie es auch nicht offen zeigen
Ich fühle doch das herbe Wort
Und sehe fahle Totenreigen
Aus schwarzen Nebeln aufwärts steigen
Das treibt von manchem Fest mich fort

Und hab' doch auch ein heiss' Verlangen
Nach Heimatfreude, Bruderhand
Wie alle, die mit mir den langen
so glücklich-wirren Weg gegangen
Durch ein verträumtes Jugendland'

(Even if they do not show it openly
yet I can feel the harsh word
and see pale dances of death
rise up out of black mists
which drive me away from many a festivity

And I also have a strong desire
for the joy of my home, for the brotherly hand
as do all those who travelled with me
that long, happy, confused journey
through the dreamy land of my youth)

Even though Picard did not become a Zionist – it was not for want of consideration of Zionism. He discussed the national Jewish movement with the husband of his cousin, the paediatrician from Constance Gustav Meinrath who belonged to the leading garde of Zionism in Baden, or in the house of the Zionist poet Johanna Simon-Fried-

2   Jacob Picard [1883–1967] in Long Island, around 1955.

berg, which he frequented while he was studying in Heidelberg and where he even met Chaim Weizmann around 1912.

'So I was confronted with the Zionist ideals at an early age', Picard summarizes in his 'Erinnerung eigenen Lebens', 'and many an attempt was made to win me over to the idea, me, the ever conscious Jew.'[8]

But these efforts were not completely in vain, as Picard was certainly open to the concept of the 'Jewish gathering'. Of course, he saw it considerably less politically than as a possibility for an existential renewal within assimilated Jewry. If Picard remained a representative of the 'Jewish Diaspora' though, it was only because he was much too German, and as a German much too much bounded to the Lake of Constance[9] and as such much too influenced by the experience of rural Jewish-German symbiosis. With his narratives, this poet not only dedicated a monument to

[8]   Manfred Bosch (ed.): Jacob Picard, p. 238.
[9]   Coined by Picard's friend and poet Ernst Blass.

this symbiosis – in understanding rural Jewry as a third possibility between ghetto and assimilation –, he also raised it to a small 'model' of Jewish self-assertion, which for him retained its validity beyond the Shoah and which he still remembered and of which he assured himself even in American exile as being his very own.

Picard also held on so tightly to his own world because it had been subjected to a great deal of injustice, not least of all from the Jewry itself, which was caused by ignorance and misunderstanding but which also had to do with repression. Even Jews who had their roots in the rural communities often looked upon rural Jewry full of undisclosed contempt as an obsolete and lower form of life. Picard wrote around 1937:

'In fact, some people pretended to be surprised by the fact that elsewhere there were Jews too who were still faithfully religious right up to our times and were proud of being able to profess this to the world around them [...] Oh and with what condescending arrogance these unknowing people from the big cities, mostly only educated by the newspapers, accepted these materials from the villages and small towns of the south and looked at those people who, in their own way, were sure of themselves!'[10]

A great deal of this disrespect also came from the Zionist perspective, which demanded Hebraicization and which was, therefore, reserved towards, if not to say disapproving of Yiddish, the language of the Galut. Thus Picard, after the publication of his book 'Der Gezeichnete' (The Marked One) in 1936 had to face the criticism that his characters spoke too much Yiddish – as if the use of such elements typical for the region did not add to the specific charm and authenticity of his prose.

Even if one could recognize an antithesis to Zionism in Picard's committed defence and characterization of the rural Jewish Diaspora, his cousin Leo Picard provides the rare example of an early Zionist in the western area of the Lake of Constance. As Jacob Picard, he also came from Wangen and joined the Zionist youth movement 'Blau-Weiss' as a young man due to the many anti-Semitic experiences he had had at school in Constance. Just how difficult it was for this organization, which was comparable to the 'Wandervogel', to compete with the German nationalistically oriented Jewry in Constance, already became apparent to Picard as leader of the youth movement:

'During the war years 1916–1918 it was not easy to activate the dozen or so boys – there were no girls due to the fact that a leader for them could not be found – of the Blau-Weiss group to take part in the Sunday walks, as their parents were largely opposed to Zionism. Many of the children were forbidden to take part in the trips with Leo Picard who was often referred to as a "traitor to the fatherland". Just consider the sacrilege of the "Blau-Weiss" children singing Hebrew songs on a steamboat journey from Meersburg to Constance in the middle of the World War!'[11]

In the autumn of 1919, right at the beginning of his university studies in geology, Leo Picard made himself known to Prof. Wilhelm Deecke as a Jew and asked:

'Mr. Privy Councillor, I am a Zionist, please prepare me for Palestine.'[12] 'I could', Picard said in an interview, 'speak for hours about those days at school and at university, how I came to the decision already at the age of 15: You do not want me and I do not need you! That was my principle ... My decision was clear: Building up Palestine in order to give the Jews a home!'[13]

In 1924 Picard emigrated to Palestine as one of the first Halutzim of Baden – and probably as the first rural Jew of the Höri. He was to become an internationally renowned geologist and hydrologist and was offered a professorship at the University of Jerusalem founded in 1925. Leo Picard used to be greated mockingly by the Jews of Con-

---

[10] 'Jetzt erst heisst es, sich bekennen, wie der Landjude es immer getan hat.' In: Manfred Bosch and Jost Grosspietsch: Jacob Picard 1883–1967. Dichter des deutschen Landjudentums. Katalog zur Ausstellung in der ehemaligen Synagoge Sulzburg. Freiburg 1992, p. 8.

[11] Leo Picard: Water for Israel. Pioneering in Geology. German Description. Jerusalem 1992, p. 26.
[12] Ibid., p. 21.
[13] Quoted in: Abraham P. Kustermann and Dieter R. Bauer (ed.): Jüdisches Leben im Bodenseeraum. Ostfildern 1994, p. 215.

3 Tea party in Horn: Jacob Picard with pipe, Erich Bloch standing by the tree.

stance upon his visits home with the words: 'Well isn't it lovely to be here again?!'[14]

Zionist activities in Freiburg or even Mannheim apparently did not have much influence beyond these centres. In Gailingen there is evidence of a youth association at the end of the twenties, which among others saw its task in arousing interest for Palestine. On the other hand, one of the speakers of the Jewish National Fund had to accept that, in an open confrontation, the rabbi drew his listeners away from him. Particularly after 1933, Zionist groups and working teams were formed in Constance, as under the conditions of the ghetto 'once more Jewish cultural life' developed. Now, at the latest, the rural Alemannic Jewry had to occupy itself with the emigration to Palestine and Zionism. Erich Bloch, who was able to develop and expand his country estate with a gardening business in Horn in relative peace until 1938, also trained people wanting to emigrate to Palestine as gardeners and farmers before he himself emigrated to Palestine. But even then he longed for his home near the Lake of Constance. In his poem 'Bodensee und Heiliges Land' (The Lake of Constance and the Holy Land) he conjured up memories of the 'little bridge from the Lake of Constance to the Holy Land', which he finally crossed upon his return in the sixties:

'Bodensee und Heiliges Land

Vertrieben aus dem Paradies der Heimat –
   zur Hölle geworden –
Auferstanden in Zions göttlichem Bereich.

Dissonanzen der Roheit zerrissen das Herz,
Aber Harmonien der Versöhnung beseelen
   die Zukunft.

Der Feind von Gestern heilt Wunden, die er
   geschlagen;
In Israels Angesicht leuchten einmal die
   Herzen aller Völker.

Die kleine Brücke vom Bodensee zum
   Heiligen Land
Hält stand gestörtem Gleichgewicht und
   friedlichem Ausgleich.'[15]

(Lake of Constance and the Holy Land)

Driven from the paradise of home – turned to hell –
Risen again in Zion's heavenly realm.

Dissonances of rawness tore the heart,
But harmonies of reconciliation breathe life into the
   future.

Yesterday's enemy heals wounds which he had
   caused;
Once in the face of Israel the hearts of all people
   will light up.

The little bridge from the lake of Constance to the
   Holy Land
withstands the disturbed balance and peaceful
   reconciliation.)

---

[14] Erhard R. Wiehn: Novemberpogrom 1938. Die 'Reichskristallnacht' in den Erinnerungen jüdischer Zeitzeugen der Kehilla Kedoscha Constance 50 Jahre danach als Dokument des Gedenkens. Constance 1988, p. 18.

[15] Stadtarchiv Konstanz, unpublished writings of Erich Bloch. My thanks to Else Levi-Mühsam, Jerusalem, for drawing my attention to this poem.

Ariane Dannacher Brand

The Acceptance of Zionism among the 'Rural Jews'

Three Examples

Not all Jewish rural communities accepted Zionism as openly as was often the case in South Baden.

Bruno Stern was born and brought up in Niederstetten, a little village in Württemberg, as the son of a businessman in 1912. Under the pressure of the social conditions he emigrated to the United States of America in 1937. In 1920 his hometown had approximately 1,700 inhabitants. His parents owned a shop with a wide range of goods on sale. At the same time the Sterns ran an agricultural business. After the First World War the father restructured his business and started trading with hides and skins. Before 1933 Zionism had no importance in Niederstetten at all, as Stern describes. As he began attending Secondary School in Bad Mergentheim in 1925 he came across a teacher who was an enthusiastic Zionist. He persuaded his pupil to put collection boxes for the Zionist youth organization 'Blue White' in every house of his hometown. Such advertising methods existed only since the Zionist Congress in Basel, where the Jewish National Fund was set up. The aim was to purchase land in Palestine and Syria. In 1910/11 38,000 boxes were handed out: 8,000 to Russia, 10,000 to the USA and 20,000 to all other countries. As the teacher of the Israeli primary school heard of Stern's activities he rebuked the 'wrongdoer' and asked him, if he was not aware that this actions were contrary to the spirit of the religion: Palestine was not supposed to be founded until after the arrival of the Messiah. Bruno Stern promised to stop his actions. On the following Sabbath this topic was discussed in great detail in the synagogue and the boxes were never emptied. For several years Zionism found no support in this village. Until the twenties many inhabitants of this comunity were, as the author reports, members of the 'Central Association of German Citizens of the Jewish Faith' (Centralverein deutscher Staatsbürger jüdischen Glaubens).[1]

Talking about Zionism also caused a stir in Manfred Sturmann's family. Sturmann was born in Königsberg in 1903. He studied German. Working at a publishing house in Munich, he started publishing poems and stories in 1923. In 1938 he emigrated to Palestine because of the Nazis. In his childhood memories he describes his visits during holidays to the residence of his grandfather Jacob Akiba Sturmann [1838–1917], an orthodox teacher and preacher in the East Prussian village Osterode. One day, during one of his visits, he found a grey booklet titled 'In the German Reich'. It contained an essay written by his grandfather: 'Are the Jews Able to Be a Modern People in Our Time?'. He read the book and recognized that his grandfather was a passionate opponent of the Jewish national renewal idea. During his childhood he had already learned about Zionism. In his home there lived a lady whom they called Aunt Martha, and who was a Zionist. In her room hung the famous picture of Herzl with the old

[1] Bruno Stern: So war es. Sigmaringen 1985.

bridge across the Rhine in Basel in the background and by the picture stood a box from the Jewish National Fund. Through Aunt Martha he had learned about Zionism long before he went to school and this influence lasted for the rest of his life, giving him strength after Hitler's takeover. Manfred's parents had anti-Zionist attitudes which was fuel for a lot of disputes at the dinner table. Zionism seemed to be the magic word for a new life for the young man. Later he received the Zionist youth magazine 'Young Israel'. This helped his concept of Zionism to take on a more conscious form. Palestine became a concrete concept.

'It was the wonderland of deliverance. The country of wine, palm trees and Jews tilling the soil under the rising sun.'[2]

In his first year in school, the teacher asked the pupils to sing a song of their choice. When it was Manfred's turn he sang, of course, Theodor Zlocistic's song 'Wohlan, lasst das Sinnen und Sorgen' the Zionist battle song of the time. He had learned the song from Aunt Martha and her friend Ilk. He sang it with the chorus: 'Onwards hedad, hedad, our path is clear!' which was incomprehensible for his teacher. Their teacher Mr. Raffel asked about the meaning of the word 'hedad'. Manfred answered, surprised that it was unknown to him – 'It is an old Jewish battle cry!'. Later on Manfred must have smiled to himself about this episode because hedad means nothing more than 'Hurray'. One day Ilk was sent to the province as the first Zionist speaker ever. He came to Osterode where the grandfather welcomed him very reservedly and advised him not to convene a Zionist meeting. The young man did not pay much attention to this piece of advice and rented a conference room in a local restaurant. Aunt Bella, youngest daughter of the house, and her friend Paula were his first followers in Osterode. They spread tremendous propaganda for the meeting while at the same time the grandfather prohibited anyone to visit this meeting, both privately and from his pulpit. Grandfather and Aunt Bella argued energetically on this subject but her recalcitrance was too much for the old man.

1 Box from the Jewish National Fund with a map of Palestine.

'The fatherly, virtually completely ineffective discouragement only caused Bella's enthusiasm to grow. She enjoyed playing the part of the martyr for Zionism and her activities for the meeting became more and more intense.'[3]

---

[2] Monika Richarz (ed.): Jüdisches Leben in Deutschland. Selbstzeugnisse zur Sozialgeschichte im Kaiserreich. Vol. 2. Stuttgart 1979, p. 201 ff.

[3] Ibid., p. 212.

The Acceptance of Zionism among the 'Rural Jews'

Eleven Jews, including the youngsters, visited the lecture in Osterode. Ilk stood in front of them spreading Zionistic ideas and demands. He was as enthusiastic as if he had been standing in front of thousands of listeners. He departed from Osterode with unshaken optimism. Aunt Bella and her friend were left behind as passionate followers who in the future succeeded in placing six collection boxes of the National Fund in the town. One was placed – hidden – in the grandfather's house.

Another example: Isaak Lucas was born in Hoengen near Jülich in 1878. He and his wife were killed in a concentration camp in Eastern Europe some time between 1942 and 1943. His son Eric, who succeeded in emigrating to Palestine in 1939, said of his father that when he was twenty years old he moved to the countryside near Aachen and became a successful cattle trader. One day a friend dragged him to a Zionist meeting. Isaak Lucas was against assimilation, he listened to the speaker and decided to become a Zionist.

'He joined up and from that day on he dreamt of having his farm and his cattle in the land of the Jews where he could walk upon his own land as a free man. But his work took so much of his time and energy that he forgot Zionism.'[4]

These examples can, of course, not be generalized. But they do show how varied the reactions to Zionism were and how important it is to systematically examine different life stories for their particular point of view.

---

[4] Eric Lucas: Jüdisches Leben auf dem Lande. Eine Familienchronik. Frankfurt a. M. 1991, p. 66.

Ruben Frankenstein

Zionism in Freiburg im Breisgau

1   Kurt Blumenfeld [1885–1963].

Students Take the Initiative

While German protest rabbis helped Basel achieve its status as the 'capital of Zionism', Freiburg profited from its favourable geographical position and the reputation of its university. Students of philosophy and law, in particular, enjoyed coming to the 'summer university' in Freiburg for one or two semesters. As early as the First Zionist Congress in 1897 Freiburg was represented by one participant, Markus Braude [1869–1949], the then student of philosophy and later rabbi, educator and leader of the Zionists in Galicia. One of the first local groups of Zionists was subsequently established in Freiburg, made up in particular of students and young university graduates. The physician Max Kaufmann [1858–1911] was the founder and first chairman of this local group. From the very beginning he was one of the most important political agitators in southern Germany, had participated in the congress since 1899 and was a long-standing member in the central committee of the Zionist Association for Germany. He was also a member of the representative delegation which was given an audience with Friedrich I, Grand Duke of Baden, on the occasion of the anniversary of his reign in 1902. This was something to which Herzl attached great importance, as he intended to avail himself of the good offices of the Grand Duke when conducting negotiations with his nephew, Kaiser Wilhelm II, or the Russian czar. Kaufmann's son, Richard, was involved in Zionist students' organizations and was later recognized as an outstanding city planner; since 1920 he had been working in Palestine.

Three personalities came to Freiburg in the summer term of 1905, became friends and devoted themselves to Zionism there. Of the approximately 30 members of the Association of Jewish Students, which was influenced by Zionism and existed from 1903 to 1914 they stood out. Soon they were to hold leading positions in the German Zionist movement: Richard Lichtheim [1885–1963], an eloquent journalist, was the first historian of German Zionism. Felix Rosenblüth [1887–1978], president of the Zionist Association for Germany from 1920 to 1923, founder of the Progressive and Independent Liberal Party in Israel, became known as the first Minister of Justice and was therefore the main architect of the judicial system in the State of Israel. The third, Kurt Blumenfeld [1885–1963] was one of the most important heads of the Zionist movement and one of its leading theorists. He was leader of the Zionist Association for Germany from 1924 to 1933. In his memories of Freiburg, he describes a conversation he had as a young student with Professor Heinrich Rosin, whom his father befriended in his youth. Professor Rosin tried to talk him out of Zionism in favour of which he had just decided. An encounter of two Jews could not have been more contradictory – the young, nationally minded radical Zionist on the one hand, and a Jew completely acculturated, who had access to all positions from which Jews had up to then been excluded, on the other. The distinguished professor for public and administrative law and founder of the seminar for industrial law was the first practising Jew to be elected vice-chancellor of the university in the same year. So what could Zionism mean to him?

At any rate, he was having trouble with the Zionists. Two of their representatives in the Supreme Council of the Jews in Baden together with the strictly orthodox group defeated both Rosin's draft constitution for the 'Jewish community' as well as the reformed prayer book which he propagated; the book was to no longer contain prayers about a return to Zion and the building of Jerusalem.

As one of the first in Germany, the Zionist students' fraternity 'Ivria' emerged in 1907 drawing its membership in part from the Association of Jewish Students. Richard Lichtheim, who had switched to economics, and Hans Jonas [1903–1993], later a philosopher of religion, were two of the main activists in this group. Ernst Lehmann, Hans Rubin and Alfred Wittkowski were further personalities in the public life in Israel which was at that time in the process of formation to emerge

2   Zalman Shazar [1889–1974], third president of Israel. Drawing by Wladimir Sagalowitz, 1935.

from this group. As was the case with all other Jewish associations, it was disbanded once the National Socialists had assumed power on July 6, 1933. A further Zionist association – 'Maccabi' – existed only in the summer semester of 1928. The short-lived Association of Jewish Students from Russia is more remarkable, as it was after all able to register two dozen medical students for the winter semester 1912/13. Among them was Zalman Rubashov [1889–1974], student of philosophy and history, who even at the time was an activist of the 'Poalei Zion' (Workers of Zion) and who, as Zalman Shazar, later became leader of the trade union, first Minister of Education and third president of Israel.

Decision for Palestine – the Freiburg Conference

The situation on the eve of the Seventh Zionist Congress at the end of July 1905 was highly dramatic. The question of leadership had to be clarified at this congress, the first after Herzl's death.

The news of bloody pogroms in Russia required fast rescue operations for the threatened Jews there. Finally, they had to decide on the offer made by the British government to provide a territory in East Africa for an autonomous Jewish settlement. And the Russian Zionists in particular, even those who had come from places where pogroms had taken place, flatly refused this offer and any other solution outside Palestine. This question split the German Zionists. As the Congress in Basel approached, the most resolute opponents of the Uganda Scheme gathered in Freiburg for a three-day conference from July 21 to July 23, 1905, to discuss the strategy and approach to take at the upcoming congress. The local Zionist group was entrusted with the technicalities of preparing the assembly hall and looking after the guests. The conference took place in the Kornhaus at the Münsterplatz where some of the delegates also lodged. There were approximately 200 delegates, which was about half of the total number of participants at the ensuing congress. The majority of the participants, who came predominantly from Russia, were members of the 'Zione Zion' – 'Zionists of Zion' – associated with Menahem Ussishkin and the 'Democratic Faction' associated with Chaim Weizmann. Ussishkin was the conference chairman and Victor Jacobson, Simon Rosenbaum, Menahem Sheinkin and Hillel Zlatopolsky acted as his deputies. Chaim Weizmann, the rising star of the Zionist movement, and three other members were responsible for the secretariat.

On the whole, the members at the conference agreed that the offer of a settlement region in East Africa had to be refused flatly, but nonetheless with politeness and gratitude, just like any other offer outside of Palestine. How this aim could be attained without sending the territorialists associated with Israel Zangwill off in a huff was debated, sometimes even fiercely and vehemently. Some pleaded for a moderate approach to avoid a schism, while others – like Ussishkin – were not afraid of breaking with the Uganda backers whom they regarded as anti-Zionists. As the name of the group indicated, Ussishkin and his supporters considered themselves to be the true, 'pure' Zionists. At this conference, Felix Rosenblüth and Kurt Blumenfeld, the future presidents of the Zionist Association for Germany, as well as their fellow students had to contend themselves with the role of observers, organizers and ushers. They could hardly follow the negotiations, anyway, since they were conducted in Russian or Yiddish. After the conclusion of the conference in Freiburg, as everybody was moving to the nearby city of Basel, the strategy was clearly outlined for the congress. They did not want a homestead just anywhere, not even as an interim solution, as a 'temporary safe harbour', but solely and uncompromisingly they demanded a homestead in Palestine. This guideline, originally drafted in Freiburg, was eventually approved with a clear majority at the Congress in Basel. This historic decision became an important step on the way to the creation of the 'Jewish state'.

Hachsharah in Breisgau – the Training Farm Markenhof

The training farm of Markenhof-Burg existed from 1919 to 1925 close to the city of Freiburg, in what is today Kirchzarten. It was one of the first and most successful training farms for preparing students for occupations in agriculture called 'Hachsharah'. Many such training farms existed in Germany far into the Nazi era. They were aimed at retraining young people from the bourgeoisie, among them high school graduates, students and young university graduates, and providing them with a background in various agricultural occupations and trades and training them so that they would be capable of making a living in agricultural settlements in Palestine. Markenhof was established and financed by Konrad Goldmann [1872–1942] from Kurland, an engineer and manufacturer – co-owner of the Wego

Wire and Cable Works in Freiburg. He bought the training farm, employed the instructors and even provided a small, stylish synagogue. The trainees – from throughout Germany as well as Eastern European countries – came predominantly from the 'Young Judah' circle associated with Gershom Scholem, and partly from 'Blau-Weiss' – an organization that imitated the 'Wandervogel' youth movement and had similar objectives, which, however, had failed to a large extent. Some 20 to 30 students were trained for a period of one to two years in various agricultural fields, mainly in cattle and pig breeding. The students later formed the nucleus that established one of the first kibbutzim of German Jews in Palestine, the kibbutz of Bejat Sera in the Jordan valley, which after some initial difficulties and changes of name – Kwutza Markenhof, Kefar Agun, Kefar Nathan – began to prosper. Today in the kibbutz of Beitha-Emek in Western Galilee near Nahariyah three wooden pillars that were rescued from the synagogue serve as reminders of the Markenhof as well as a commemorative plaque to Goldmann who fell into the hands of the Nazis after his forced emigration to France and died in the concentration camp in Drancy was put up.

The Consequences of the First Zionist Congress up to the Founding of Israel

Bettina Zeugin

The 22 Zionist Congresses before the Foundation of the State of Israel

A Brief Summary

The history of the Zionist congresses can be roughly broken down into four phases:

The *first* phase is the group of congresses which took place during the life of Theodor Herzl, from the First Congress in 1897 to the Sixth Congress in 1903. During this time, the Organization constitutes itself and the fundamental objectives are set.

In the *second* phase, which starts after Herzl's death and spans from the Seventh to the Eleventh Congress, the inner struggles between the different groups about the direction of the movement are the main concern.

Until the twenty-second meeting, the congress develops into the parliamentary stage of the movement in the *third* phase. The 'Balfour Declaration' is seen as the first success, which, however, is dampened by the conflicts in Palestine with the Arab population and the mandate power. Until the beginning of the Second World War, struggles take place within the movement with regard to how to deal with the problems in Palestine.

The *fourth* phase concerns the time after the foundation of the State of Israel, and the congresses only take place in Jerusalem.

Of the 22 congresses that were held until the foundation of the State of Israel, 14 took place in Switzerland. This country, and in particular Basel, appeared ideal due to their central location and neutrality.

1. 1897   Basel

For the first time, members of Eastern and Western Jewish Zionist groups as well as individual personalities participate in the Congress to decide upon the 'Basle Program', which defines the basic objectives of the Zionist Organization that formed itself in Basel under the leadership of Theodor Herzl, who acts as an integrative figure.

2. 1898   Basel

The foundation of the first financial instrument, the 'Jewish Colonial Trust', is decided upon at the Second Congress. The Socialist Zionists attend for the first time as an independent group. The conflict between followers of a 'practical' Zionism and those advocating a 'political' Zionism increasingly becomes the centre of discussion.[1]

---

[1] The individual directions are discussed in the section on trends in Zionism.

3. 1899 Basel

The significance of a 'Charta' – as proposed by Theodor Herzl in his book 'The Jewish State' – is discussed. Herzl himself campaigns for an agreement with the Ottoman Empire. The Congress decides that practical objectives in Palestine can only be envisaged once the Turkish government has given certain guarantees.

4. 1900 London

This meeting takes place under the impression of the pogroms in Romania which prove the urgency of the Zionist objectives and lead to a major wave of emigration to Palestine.

5. 1901 Basel

The most significant event at this Congress is the foundation of the 'Jewish National Fund', which had been discussed as early as the First Congress, to facilitate the purchase of land in Palestine. In parallel to this, a 'Democratic Fraction' comes into being which defines the ideological objective more in the cultural field, in a 'Jewish renaissance', instead of in a political orientation.

6. 1903 Basel

Under the shock of the pogroms in Kishinev, the offer of the British government to place land in East Africa at the disposal of the Jewish people for settlement meets with approval. But the Russian Zionists themselves will not let go of the idea that only a colonization of Palestine can be considered. Only with difficulty does Herzl succeed in hindering a splitting of the organization in view of the varying positions concerning the 'Uganda Question'.

1 'It was during the Second Zionist Congress in Basel (August 1898). The people of Basel were returning from the festivities of St. Jakob's Day, and as they passed the Congress hall, where banners greeted them, enthusiastically the people of Basel cheered: "Hurray for the Jews! Hurray for the Jews!"' Drawing by an unknown artist.

7. 1905 Basel

The commemoration of Theodor Herzl, who died in 1904, accompanies the meetings. A heated argument develops between 'Territorialists' and followers of the 'Zionist ideal'. Toward the end of the Congress, the Uganda Scheme is finally rejected and the Congress decides to concentrate the settlement activities on Palestine from now on. David Wolffsohn [1856–1914] is elected President of the Zionist Organization as the successor of Theodor Herzl.

8. 1907 *The Hague*

This Congress is largely concerned with practical development in Erez Israel. The setting up of the 'Palestine Office' is agreed upon and begins its work in 1908 in Jaffa.

Chaim Weizmann [1874–1952] helps the term 'synthetic Zionism', which was coined by Menahem Ussishkin [1863–1941], to its breakthrough. It is supposed to overcome the quarrels between the political and the more practically oriented followers by driving both directions at the same time.

9. 1909 *Hamburg*

The representatives of the workers in Erez Israel appear at the Congress for the first time in a political capacity and sharply criticize the presidency of Wolffsohn, and notably the economic-pragmatic orientation of the settlement projects. The political Zionists also reject Wolffsohn because in their opinion he has distanced himself too much from Herzl's original direction.

10. 1911 *Basel*

This Congress bears the title 'Peace Congress', for synthetic Zionism has permeated the Organization since 1907 and has been accepted. The speeches mainly deal with the activities in Erez Israel and with the promotion of Hebrew culture. The Congress is significant because for the first time a meeting is held in Hebrew and the problems of co-existence with the Arab population in Palestine are discussed in depth. David Wolffsohn resigns from his position as President and Otto Warburg becomes his successor [1859–1938].

11. 1913 *Vienna*

The reports on the previous settlement activities in Erez Israel are evidence of the advantages of gradual and small waves of immigration. The president receives the order to make preparations for the foundation of a Hebrew university in Jerusalem.

12. 1921 *Karlsbad*

The first post-war Congress takes place in Karlsbad. In 1920 Chaim Weizmann was elected president at the London Conference. Important events such as the 'Balfour Declaration' of 1917 and the conquest of Palestine by Great Britain are discussed for the first time since the war in the context of a Congress. This raises hopes of a good relationship between Jews and Arabs.

13. 1923 *Karlsbad*

The League of Nations declares its acceptance of the Great Britain mandate over Palestine before the Congress and from among the Zionist Organization the official Jewish representation in Erez Israel, the 'Jewish Agency for Palestine', is designated. The Congress concerns itself largely with the economic development of Palestine and the problems of co-existence with the native Arab population. The proposal to open the Jewish Agency for non-Zionists as well is rejected at this time. Different groups heavily criticize the too 'lenient' position of the leadership with regard to Great Britain.

2 'Meeting of the congress court. From the left to the right: Senator Dr. Ringel, member of the congress court, the lawyer Dr. S. Gronemann, chairman of the congress court, Dr. O. Wolfsberg, memb. of the congr. court, Dr. A. Barth, representative of the prosecution, Felix Rosenblüth, representative of the Zionist Organization, the president of the Zionist Organization Prof. Dr. Ch. Weizmann as witness, M. Gorssmann, defendant, V. Jabotinsky, counsel for the defence. Drawn for the "Jüdische Pressezentrale" by W. Sagalowitz, 1931.'

14. 1925 Vienna

This Congress takes place under the impression of the boost given by the Fourth Aliyah, which is dominated by a strong independent initiative of the mainly Polish immigrants. Vladimir Jabotinsky [1880–1940] and his followers, who have been united since 1925 in the 'Union of Zionist Revisionists', demand increased immigration in order for the Jews to become the preponderant population in Palestine and the creation of a state within the 'historical borders' on both banks of the Jordan.

15. 1927 Basel

The thirtieth anniversary of the First Zionist Congress stands in the shadow of the economic crisis in Palestine. The high unemployment diminishes the hope of a rapid and successful development. The possibilities of the future policies are discussed in a controversial manner.

16. 1929 Zurich

After years of arguments and despite violent protests from the Union of Zionist Revisionists, the Congress decides to allow non-Zionists to take part in the Jewish Agency. While the Organization rebuilds itself politically – forming a new Executive with the participation for the first time of two representatives of the 'Mizrachi' and one of the workers' parties – there are riots in Israel which will cause any reconciliation of Jewish and Arab views to recede into the distance.

3 Impressions from the Nineteenth Zionist Congress. Drawing by W. Sagalowitz, 1935.

17. 1931 Basel

The 'Passfield White Paper' passed by the British government before the Congress puts severe restrictions on Jewish immigration. The opposition within the movement to the policy of Weizmann, which is criticized as being too weak with regard to England, demands to proclaim the creation of the Jewish state as an official goal. The majority rejects this proposal due to the tenseness of the situation. Nevertheless, Weizmann, who had already temporarily resigned once in 1930 in order to protest against the politics of Great Britain and the White Paper, is not re-elected. Nahum Sokolów [1861–1937] replaces him.

18. 1933 Prague

The Congress assembles under the impression of three different events: the success of the National Socialists in Germany, the inflation in Palestine and the assassination of Chaim Arlosoroff [1899–1933], one of the leading representatives of the Zionist workers' movement. The conflict between the direction of the majority and the Revisionists reaches its climax as the Revisionists are associated with the assassination. The arguments lead to the official resignation of the Revisionists from the Zionist Organization in 1935.

19. 1935 Lucerne

The focus of this Congress is the question of how the persecuted European Jews can be saved. Weizmann is once again elected President and Sokolów to the position of Honorary President. The workers' parties now represent the strongest force within the Zionist Organization.

20. 1937 Zurich

This Congress has to deal with one of the most difficult problems since the Uganda Scheme. Under the impression of the riots of 1936, the report

4 Departure of the special train for the celebration of the 40th anniversary of the First Zionist Congress.

of the British 'Peel Commission' proposes the partition of Palestine into an Arab and a Jewish state. Advocates and opponents of this plan are at loggerheads. In a compromise, the given draft is rejected, but the Zionist Executive is empowered to enter into further negotiations.

21. 1939 *Geneva*

On the eve of the Second World War, the British government announces a further restriction on Jewish immigration in a new 'White Paper' and the step-by-step authorization of an independent state under Palestinian leadership. The Congress rejects this idea. David Ben Gurion [1886–1973] proposes to stop co-operating with Great Britain. The options for illegal immigration to Palestine are discussed.

22. 1946 *Basel*

The first Congress after the Second World War and the Shoah explicitly demands an independent state and an end of the oppression by the mandate power. The Congress turns to the United Nations for support. The Revisionists rejoin the Zionist Organization. The Congress is deeply torn by the position towards a partition of Palestine and about the further procedure with regard to Great Britain. Weizmann is not re-elected President, but no successor can be agreed upon.

Patrick Marcolli
Erik Petry
Bettina Zeugin

Trends in Zionism

Zionism is not a uniform theory of Jewish nationalism. For this reason, the Zionist movement can be subdivided into many different groupings. This is not surprising if one calls to mind the circumstances and conditions under which Zionism evolved: on the one hand, the longing for Zion, the historical connection of the Jewish people with Erez Israel, and the hope of Messianic redemption, and on the other hand, the far-reaching socio-economic and cultural upheaval in Eastern and Western Europe during the 19th century and the resulting crisis of confidence and identity manifesting itself in various ways, the influence of feelings of national identity and the nationalism within individual European countries, and last but not least the growing danger of anti-Semitism. In addition, there was the division of the Jewish people in the population of the 'Yishuv' in Palestine and in those in the countries of the Diaspora. To this extent, Zionism constituted just one of several national movements in the 19th century, but it does exhibit specific characteristics that led to a number of different conceptions. What was important was whether the creation of a state and thus the participation in competitive national power politics or whether the strengthening of Erez Israel as a cultural centre of Jewry should play the most important role and to what extent the individual state or the colonization of Palestine and the promotion of a national identity within the lands of the Diaspora should be prioritized with regard to autonomy. Ultimately, an answer also had to be found to the question of the role religion should play and what stance should be adopted towards political movements in Jewry which themselves were also a reaction to conditions in the 19th century.

The Zionist Organization was structured along both geographical and conceptual lines. The local groups and regional groups included all members without regard to ideological differences. Besides these, there were different groupings that represented special interests that were also represented at the local and regional level. Those chapters that recruited a minimum of 20,000 members could, with the approval of the action committee, be registered as 'special chapters' in the statutes of the Zionist Organization. Since the Second Zionist Congress, the members of the movement had been organizing themselves in fractions which in some cases ultimately formed parties. These fractions made progress at the congresses difficult. Again and again the danger of a rift arose and with it the possibility that a group would split off.

Political, Practical, Synthetic, General and Religious Zionism

Shortly after the death of Theodor Herzl, two principal trends formed within the Zionist Organization which stood for opposing views concerning the strategy and tactics of Zionist policy. The one movement considered itself to be 'political Zionism' aimed at achieving a political safeguard in the form of a 'charter' prior to any effort to

1 A group of Mizrachi delegates together with the Basel Rabbi Arthur Cohn. Standing, from left to right: Rabbi Pinchas Rasowsky (Shwintzan), Rabbi Cohn. Sitting, from left to right: Rabbi Mordechai Yaakow Rabbinowitz (Liverpool), Rabbi Abraham Aba Werner (London).

building settlements. The advocates of 'practical Zionism', on the other hand, who were predominantly Eastern Europeans, insisted on the immediate colonization of Palestine without any previous political safeguards. A special school of thought of this movement was the group that called itself the 'Zione Zion' – 'Zionists of Zion' – who rejected any discussion whatsoever about settlement regions outside Palestine. Both schools of thought gradually moved closer together. Chaim Weizmann adopted the term 'synthetic Zionism' that Menahem Ussishkin had coined for the combination of political and practical Zionism. A significant number of Zionists were able to identify with this. Prior to World War I, the idea of the 'General Zionists' arose, which being politically in the centre attracted those Zionists who had not joined any special chapter and expressed moderate views. The 'General Zionists' simultaneously called for efforts in the building up of Palestine and for equal rights for the Jewish population in the Diaspora with national autonomy. The political centre did not succeed, however, in uniting all ideological currents. The fraction and party structure remained splintered and unclear. Time and again, subgroups, splinter groups and alliances, separate left-wing and right-wing movements were formed.

It was against this background that the orthodox religious Zionists banded together. Their strongest grouping was the 'Mizrachi' (a shortened form of 'Merkaz Ruchani', 'spiritual centre') which was established during 1902 in Vilnius. The religious Zionists declared their support neither for political nor for practical Zionism, but spoke out instead for the fulfillment of the 'Basle Program' on the basis of the Torah and in the spirit of traditional Jewry. Because the ideology of the Mizrachi was principally based on religion, the party was able to enter into alliances with any other grouping within the Zionist Organization.

The Left-Wing Parties

It is certainly problematical to attempt to classify Zionist and later Israeli policy as being 'left' or 'right' in the sense of the European party system. However, since the respective groupings considered themselves to be such, they will be discussed in these terms below. Socialist Zionism evolved in Eastern Europe at the end of the 19th century. Inspired by the Jewish religion and modern socialist theory, it aimed at establishing a Jewish society in Palestine based on social and economic equality. Instead of continuing to live as before – something bourgeois Zionists were accused of doing –, the individual had to change, and till the soil with his own hands as well as build the new society. Greatly influenced by Marxism, socialist Zionism split into groups with a social-democratic as well as a communist orientation.

Not until the years after Herzl's death did the actual parties of the Zionist left form. Whereas the 'Poalei Zion' – 'Workers of Zion' – after precursors arose in Eastern Europe in 1906 and then expanded into the United States and to Palestine, the 'Hapoel Hazair' – 'The Young Worker' – party initially took shape in Palestine from 1906 on. The Poalei Zion had a Marxist orientation and hoped for a redemption of the Jewish proletariat by means of socialist revolution. The Hapoel Hazair, on the other hand, rejected the class struggle and directed the main thrust of its activities towards training the Diaspora Jews to be farmers. National and socialist elements banded together after World War I in the pioneer movement, the 'Halutziyyut'. In 1920 – the labour union organization, the 'Histadrut' was founded. This was followed in 1930 by the founding of the 'Mapai' (abbreviation for 'Mifleget Poalei Erez Israel', 'Workers' Party of the Land of Israel') which incorporated the Hapoel Hazair. The Mapai did not have a religious orientation and was moderately socialistic. During the 1930s it became the strongest party in the Yishuv. The leftwing parties were particularly badly fragmented. New groupings kept forming from splinter groups or alliances that were formed. The Zionist-socialist youth movement, which was based on the model of the European left and which propagated the emigration of the Jewish youth to Palestine, was particularly significant after World War I. The Zionist left when viewed as a comprehensive movement represented a strong power factor within the World Zionist Organization and played an important role in establishing the State of Israel.

The Right-Wing Parties

The last ideological orientation to form was the Zionist right in the middle of the 1920s. Unlike the left, it was represented by more or less one party for a prolonged period of time. The 'Union of Zionist Revisionists' which was founded by Vladimir Zeev Jabotinsky in 1925 declared open war on the Zionist executive council which it considered to be too moderate and defensive and wanted instead to establish a Jewish state to the east and west of the River Jordan. The word 'Revision' was intended to express the will to return to Herzl's political Zionism with his idea of a Jewish state. The aims of this party represented the most pronounced form of a Jewish nationalism. Revisionism spread quickly to become a mass movement. In particular in Eastern Europe, Jews flocked to join the Union, whereas it was met with reservations in Palestine and the countries of the West. During the 1920s and 1930s, the Union of Zionist Revisionists opposed the policies and tactics of the Zionist Organization as well as the presidency of Chaim Weizmann. Violent fighting between the left-wing parties and the revisionist party set the tone of the disputes that arose at this time. Even during the 1920s, the revisionists were reproached by the socialist parties for being closely associated with fascism in Italy and Germany. In 1933, the more moderate wing of the party split away and founded the 'Jewish State Party' which existed until 1946.

At the end of the 1920s and in particular in the early 1930s, various underground organizations formed in Palestine, some of which were influenced by the revisionists. This applied in particular to the 'Irgun Zevai Leummi' – the 'National Military Organization' – which rejected British mandate sovereignty. The relations between the Union and the Zionist Organization continued to deteriorate until 1935, and the Revisionist Party, which had had the status of a special chapter since 1932, left the World Organization. Jabotinsky and his supporters founded the 'New Zionist Organization'. This rejoined the Zionist Organization in 1946 after World War II and formed the 'Herut' (Freedom) Party in 1948 which also had strong nationalistic leanings.

At the Second World Conference of the Union of Zionist Revisionists in 1926, the youth organization 'Berit Trumpeldor' – 'Union Trumpeldor', abbreviated as 'Betar', that had existed mainly in Eastern Europe since 1923, was named the centre of youth education of the movement. The Betar espoused less an ideology than it did an attitude towards life. The supporters championed a Palestine which was also to include Transjordan. In addition, they wanted to promote Jewish culture and the Hebrew language. The Betar was intended to be a spiritual and cultural centre in the Diaspora for its members as well as a military and organizational training camp for those who would lead the future political fight in Palestine. The Betar troops usually appeared in uniform, thus cultivating a fascist image. To a large extent independent of the Revisionist Party the Betar was more militant in achieving the aim of a Jewish state. Menahem Begin, later Prime Minister of Israel, belonged to the Revisionist Party since 1929 and commanded the Betar in Poland. Prior to and during World War II, he was involved in the 'illegal immigration' to Palestine which had been organized to a significant extent by Betar members. In the fighting against the British mandate power during World War II and on the eve of the foundation of the state, Betar members, the Irgun commanded by Begin since 1943 and its splinter group 'Lekhi' ('Lokhame Harut Israel', 'Fighters for the Freedom of Israel') carried out numerous acts of sabotage and terror.

Cultural Zionism

Only a few conflicts within the Zionist movement demonstrate their inner disunity at the beginning of the 20th century as clearly as the debates about cultural Zionism. The spiritual father of this movement is considered to be Ahad Haam [1856–1927]. He wanted to turn Palestine into the spiritual centre in order to remedy the poor and confused Jewish self-image. This centre was to be an emerging force in bringing about a revival of national Jewish culture. With his many essays Ahad Haam acted to encourage and stimulate a generation of young Eastern European Zionists who took up his concept of a Hebrew Renaissance, a culture linking all Jews, and introduced it into discussion in 1896.

The contrast to most Western European Zionists became quickly apparent. The latter were convinced that a cultural debate was neither necessary nor beneficial for achieving the immediate aims of Zionism. It was necessary to first of all redress the 'Jewish misery' by providing a 'safeguarded homestead' in Palestine, before beginning any debate about culture. During the earliest congresses, Theodor Herzl consciously ignored the cultural discussion because he feared, not without some justification, that the few Eastern European rabbis close to Zionism would be scared off by such discussions and might close their minds to Zionism. He had placed his hopes on the influence of exactly these rabbis to help spread Zionism throughout Eastern Europe. As far as the young Eastern European Zionists were concerned, however, this was the wrong approach. None of the other problems could be solved before a national Jewish, even secularly established, culture had been incorporated into the Zionist programme. They did not consider the rabbis to be very influential and therefore refused to accept a cultural concept determined only by traditional religion.

All of these discussions, however, were overshadowed by the question of how the term national Jewish culture was to be understood. Ahad Haam had left the issue shrouded in vague definitions. The young Martin Buber [1878–1965] became more specific in 1899 at the Third Zionist Congress. He called upon the Zionist Organization to become involved in all facets of society and to found cultural, literary and academic societies as well as gymnastic clubs and choral societies. Buber became one of the leading persons in the 'Democratic Fraction' which was established in 1901 as an opposition congress group prior to the Fifth Congress. There were other important public figures in addition to Buber, in particular Berthold Feiwel [1875–1937], Chaim Weizmann [1874–1952] and Leo Motzkin [1867–1933], who demanded the incorporation of Jewish culture not only in theoretical discussions, but who also spoke up in practice for a Jewish education as well as the promotion of Jewish literature and the Hebrew language. The visible sign of cultural Zionist activities was the foundation of the Jewish Publishing House in 1902 in Germany and in Palestine the founding of the first Hebrew Gymnasium in Jaffa in 1906. Ahad Haam did not himself get involved in the work. Martin Buber, on the other hand, exercised considerable influence on the Zionist youth during his early years as an active representative of the Democratic Fraction and perhaps as the first cultural philosopher of Zionism. Incidentally, he regarded the Diaspora as a force that promoted culture, that was capable of surviving and that was necessary for survival. This brought him sharp criticism. In particular, writers such as Micha Josef Berdyczewski [1865–1921] and Jacob Klatzkin [1882–1948] accused Buber – and cultural Zionism in general – of being seclusive and unaware of the terminally ill state of the Diaspora. As far as they were concerned, a renewal of Jewish culture could only take place in Palestine.

Although the cultural debates made the difference in opinions between East and West obvious, they never caused a rift. During the years leading up to the First World War, as synthetic Zionism brought about a symbiosis between politics and practice, cultural topics increasingly became an integral part of Zionism. Whereas German had originally been the principal language at the congresses, Hebrew gradually superseded it. In 1913/14 there was again a dispute about whether German or Hebrew should be the language of instruction at the Technion that was founded in Haifa in 1912. The decision in favour of Hebrew also meant the final breakthrough of Hebrew as the official language in the 'New Yishuv'. The cultural debate lost its vehemency completely after 1918, since other problems had by then come to the fore. An influence of cultural Zionism can still be seen in the establishment in 1926 of the 'Peace Alliance' – 'Berit Shalom' – which aspired to a binational state in Palestine in which Jews and Arabs were to have equal rights.

2   Israel Zangwill with his wife Edith Ayrton on the balcony of the Hotel 'Drei Könige' in Basel.

Territorialism

The roots of territorialism can be traced back to the year 1903 when once again bloody pogroms occurred in Russia, above all in Kishinev. After this infamous riot, Joseph Chamberlain, the British conservative Minister of Colonial Affairs, proposed establishing a semi-autonomous Jewish colony on the Gwas-Ngishu plateau in British East Africa to Theodor Herzl. This has gone down in the annals of history as the 'Uganda Scheme', although the region near Nairobi – approximately 300 kilometres long and only thinly populated – is located in what is now Kenya. The offer was presented to the delegates in Basel for the first time at the Sixth Zionist Congress in August 1903. A Jewish administrator was to head the local administration, although the final say remained with the British government. Fierce resistance to the project was voiced within the Zionist movement, above all from Eastern European circles. When a schism threatened to occur, the congress voted to appoint a commission empowered to gather more detailed information with respect to the suitability of the region. While the resistance continued to grow in English Jewry and among the British settlers in Kenya, the British writer and Zionist, Israel Zangwill, voiced his enthusiasm about the offer submitted by the British government. He termed it a 'triumph for Zionism, a moral triumph for England and a victory for humanity'.[1] He considered the prospect of a Jewish state, at least partially independent, as a possibility that ought not to be rejected, even if only on humanitarian grounds. Zangwill viewed the plan as being a quick way of offering Jewish refugees from Eastern Europe a shelter and a new home. And this, in turn, meant for him a first step in reviving the Jewish culture that he dreamed of. In response to the antagonists of the 'Uganda Scheme', he summed up his position in

---

[1]   Maurice Simon (ed.): Speeches, Articles and Letters of Israel Zangwill. London 1937, p. 182.

the sentence: 'Zionism would be practicable but for Zion.'[2]

Zangwill thus demanded a breach with the majority of delegates at the Sevenths Zionist Congress in Basel in 1905 who had proved to be unyielding themselves. After a clear rejection of the East Africa offer, Zangwill and his followers left the venue greatly upset and shortly thereafter called the 'Jewish Territorial Organization' into being in the Basel 'Safranzunft'. The basic tenet of this organization was 'to procure a territory upon an autonomous basis for those Jews who cannot, or will not, remain in the lands in which they at present live'.[3] Here once again the fundamental difference to the now official policy of the Zionists becomes clear. Whereas they saw no other alternative to Palestine as the location of the Jewish state, Zangwill and his supporters extended the territorial possibilities without restriction. For them, the 'Palestine' possibility was still in the far too distant future, whereas the problems of the Jewish refugees from the East were so critical that they could not wait for more favourable political circumstances. A number of different critics – mostly Zionists – accused Zangwill of having acted out of pure stubbornness and for the purpose of enhancing his personal image, so as to finally emerge from Herzl's shadow, who in the meantime had passed away.

The Jewish Territorial Organization had its heyday in the years prior to the Balfour Declaration of 1917. Just in England, at times it alone had more than 5,000 members. Their activities, however, did not produce any concrete results. Although Zangwill and his supporters envisioned a number of possible locations for a Jewish autonomous territory, e.g. regions in Australia, Canada and Mesopotamia, all attempts were thwarted by the political circumstances of the time. Only the Galveston Project, initiated by the American financier and philanthropist Jacob Schiff and supported by Zangwill's Jewish Territorial Organization, proved to be at least partially successful. A few thousand Jewish immigrants were brought to Galveston, Texas, from 1906 on and were allowed to build up a new existence in the Midwest, far away from New York, a magnet for Jewish immigrants.

But this was all that was accomplished. Zangwill, embittered by the postwar agreements about a Jewish mandate in Palestine, disbanded the Jewish Territorial Organization, which had only existed on paper during its last few years, in 1925 shortly before his death.

---

[2] Simon: Zangwill, p. 160.
[3] ITO Pamphlet No. 1. London 1905.

Erik Petry

Martin Buber

Martin Buber was born in Vienna on February 8, 1878. He grew up in Lemberg in Hassidic surroundings. He studied philosophy under the tutorship of Wilhelm Dilthey and Georg Simmel. During his life, his activities as a journalist, author, theologian and social philosopher formed Martin Buber and he became the leading representative of the school of thought which he called 'Hebrew Humanism'. This can be seen in all stages of his philosophical development, of his search for a Jewish self-image, the task of Judaism in the world. He wrote in 1916, linking his philosophy with the demands of Zionism: 'We don't want Palestine for the Jews: we want it for all mankind, for we want it for the fulfilment of Judaism.'[1] The realization of Judaism, was for Buber the realization of a unity to be aspired by mankind, in the form of an ideal community of human beings, the true community. To keep up the dialogue despite all the contrary positions, Buber introduced the concept of 'I and Thou'. It is based on the true conversation that accepts the other side, despite all differences and disagreements, thereby divulging all contrary standpoints and finally making it possible to overcome them. This approach strongly engaged Buber in the Jewish-Arab dialogue in Palestine.

Buber joined the Zionist movement as early as 1898. Following his ideas of a necessary spiritual renewal of Judaism, he joined the cultural Zionists of Ahad Haam. He was one of the founding members of the 'Jüdische Verlag' (Jewish Pub-

1 Martin Buber [1878–1965].

lishing House) and temporarily he acted as the publisher of the weekly Zionist paper 'Die Welt' (The World). He also taught at the 'Jüdische Lehrhaus' (Jewish School), at the University of Frankfurt a.M., and from 1938 on, after his emigration, at the Hebrew University of Jerusalem. His work as a writer was mainly dedicated to topics of Jewish mysticism and Hassidism.

Especially in Germany, Buber is still to this day seen as the initiator and facilitator of a Jewish–Christian dialogue in the sense of his interpretation of Judaism, which however was bitterly criticized by the historically standardized Judaism. Despite these attacks and especially because of his literal translation of the Bible together with Franz Rosenzweig, Buber remains one of the most important Jewish theologians. He died in Jerusalem on June 13, 1965.

---

[1] Martin Buber: Völker, Staaten und Zion. In: Martin Buber: Der Jude und sein Judentum. Gesammelte Aufsätze und Reden. Cologne 1963, pp. 280–308, here p. 290.

Monika Häfliger

Zionism in the USA

Non-Jewish Zionism

Zionism has a long tradition in the United States of America – among non-Jews. It was founded on the notion which had been predominant among the Protestants in the Anglo-Saxon world since the 16th century that in accordance with the correct interpretation of the Bible, the end of the Jewish Diaspora and the territorial concentration of the Jews in Palestine were a preparation for the return of Christ. Many of the pilgrims that had emigrated to America then adapted this idea to their own intentions and compared their own experiences as settlers to those of their biblical forefathers. They regarded themselves as 'Children of Israel' on the way to the Promised Land. Thus America became the 'new Canaan', to which they had fled from the 'Land of Egypt' – i.e. England – under the rule of its 'Pharaoh' King James I.[1] They learned Hebrew and saw themselves as the spiritual descendants of the old Israelites, who were now building a new Zion in the wilderness. Thomas Jefferson even suggested using the picture of Jews fleeing from Egypt as the official seal of the United States.

Against this background Zionism, understood as the return of the Jews to Palestine, became a popular topic in the Christian society. This spiritual trend among the non-Jewish settlers might also have contributed to the awakening of Zionist longings among some Jews. At any rate, from the middle of the 19th century on, several American 'fundamentalists' settled in the Holy Land, to witness the resurrection of the Jewish state and the return of God's son. However, most of these projects failed after only a short time.

On March 5, 1891, six years before the First Zionist Congress in Basel, the priest William E. Blackstone [1841–1935] sent a petition to President Benjamin Harrison titled 'Palestine for the Jews' which had been signed by 413 famous public figures of America, including at least 175 Christians. In this petition Blackstone urged the President to think about the situation of the Jews in the Diaspora and their demands for an independent state in Palestine. The government reacted with great reserve, however. Altogether this early non-Jewish Zionist tendency contributed to the fact that later many Americans immediately accepted the modern State of Israel.

On the other hand, this attitude could – and still can – quickly change to anti-Semitism: for example if Jews preferred living in the USA to moving to Palestine or if they refused to convert to Christianity and thus posed an obstacle to the return of Christ – according to the view of many 'fundamentalists'.

Even today, Israel still fits the image that many Americans have of themselves:

'America, which saw itself as the New Jerusalem, identified with the evolution of the old. Far more than in Europe, the American Christianity celebrated the geography of the Holy Land and the experience of the Old Testament. America's vibrant Jewish community was

---

[1] John Bunzl: Zwischen Washington und Jerusalem. Vienna 1992, p. 31.

1 Members of the Poalei Zion as immigrants to the United States in a play about the history of the Jewish people. Milwaukee, 1919.

politically more active and socially more accepted than its European counterparts ever were ... The people's culture (literature, media, movies – especially "Exodus" strengthened the affection for the Israeli David, fighting against the Arab Goliath. Israeli heroes – Ben Gurion, Golda Meir, Moshe Dayan – became American heroes.'[2]

Jewish Zionism

Despite the popularity of Zionism in the Christian society of the USA and also of some Jewish state projects – the most important stemmed from Mordecai Manuel Noah [1785–1851] – it was initially not well received by the Jewish community. The first reactions to Theodor Herzl's appearance were not enthusiastic at all. Jacob Schiff [1847–1920], a financier from New York and one of the most powerful men of the Jewish society in America at the turn of the century, said after his first meeting with Herzl that Zionism was 'a sentimental theory without future'.[3] The reactions to the First Zionist Congress were also mainly negative.

For most Jews their assimilation and acculturation to American society had first priority; in addition they feared the accusation of divided loyalty. Especially the already assimilated, prosperous Jews of German origin fought a bitter struggle against Zionism and called themselves Americans of Mosaic belief, just as there were Americans of Christian belief. They dissociated themselves to a large extent from the Eastern European Jews, among whom supporters of the Zionist movements were most likely to be found, because they considered them to be ' "unwashed", unassimilated, Yiddish-speaking, often religiously orthodox, *Ostjuden*'.[4] Last but not least – and this is where the 'American dream' of the Protestant immigrants maybe had its effect – a large part of the Jews equated America with Israel, with Zion.

From 1897 up until the thirties of the 20th century Reform Judaism in America, which saw the Jews exclusively as a religious community, rejected the idea of an independent state and of any Zionist activities. They were proud of their Universalism and their Americanization. For several years orthodox Judaism also took a negative stance towards Zionism. Their leaders looked at Zionists as 'going against God's will' and they were of the opinion that if God 'wanted us to have Zion again, He would restore it without the help of so-called Zionists'.[5] Only those conservative Jews who observed the tradition, but who were more open-minded regarding progressive ideas than the orthodox were prepared to commit themselves to the cause of Jewish nationalism and Zionism. During the First World War, the organized political Zionism – in 1898 the 'Federation of American Zionists' had been founded – became more influential. In 1914 there were – according to various sources – 12,000 to 20,000 registered Zionists of a total of approximately three million Jews living in the USA. By 1919 their number increased to 150,000 or four percent of the Jewish population which had by then grown to 3.5 million. This success can mainly be attributed to the outstanding personality of Louis D. Brandeis [1856–1941] who had exceptional organizational skills and above all offensively countered the accusation of divided loyalty. He argued that it was in keeping with the American ideals to stand up for a better life also for human beings in other countries, and therefore the loyalty of each and every Jew towards America necessitated it to become a Zionist. His Zionism was first of all culturally and socially orientated. The threat towards Jews in

---

[2] Steven L. Spiegel: Amerika and Israel. In: The National Interest. Winter 1990/91, p. 15.
[3] Edward Tivnan: The Lobby. New York 1987, p. 14.
[4] Edward B. Glick: The Triangular Connection. London e.g. 1982, p. 36.

[5] Gerald Sorin: A Time for Building. Baltimore, London 1992, p. 223.

Palestine through the years of war made many American Jews help and become involved in the Zionist movement. In 1916 the foundation stone for the 'American Jewish Congress' was laid. President Woodrow Wilson's advocacy of the Balfour Declaration increased the number of new followers of Zionism. In 1916 Brandeis was nominated judge at the Supreme Court by Wilson and was elected despite bitter opposition. This meant that now he had to refrain from openly supporting Zionism. The Federation of American Zionists which in 1918 became the 'Zionist Organization of America' once again began losing influence and members. In addition the cultural orientation of the American Zionists time and again led to conflicts with the World Zionist Organization. In 1921 a large number of important members left the Zionist movement, without, however, giving up their support of projects in Palestine.

This attitude also remained characteristic after Zionism had become an important movement in the USA because of the Second World War and the ensuing changes in the structure of the Jewish society. It made it possible, to choose between assimilation and the survival of the Jewish culture because it places great value on Jewish history, tradition and culture. For American Jews it did not mean an obligation to emigrate to Palestine. Since 1948, especially since 1967, the Jewish organizations have made Israel to the centre of public Jewish life in the USA. But still, only 15 percent of the Jews have at least once thought about living in Israel. The State of Israel is certainly of great importance for the American Jews and their identity, but only of little attraction.

Monika Häfliger

Henrietta Szold

Henrietta Szold was born in Baltimore on December 21, 1860, as the oldest daughter of the well-known Hungarian Rabbi Benjamin Szold who was a member of the Hovevei Zion movement and an advocate of conservative Judaism. She dedicated all her life and her talents to the Jewish society in America and that in Palestine. The home of Benjamin Szold developed very early on into a meeting place for many Russian intellectuals, and this is where Henrietta first came into contact with the Haskalah. She learned about the latest works of Hebrew and Jewish literature and was confronted with the problems of the East European immigrants. Her family and she herself remained faithful to traditional Judaism. Thus she fully accepted the traditional role of the Jewish woman in the family, although it remained a role that to her regret she never had the chance to play. Her father made it possible for her to get a solid, Jewish-religious and secular education. Later she taught at several schools, where she also looked after Jewish immigrants from Eastern Europe. Because of this and due to her journalistic and literary work she came into contact with the ideas of Zionism to which she dedicated her life from 1895 onwards. The return of the persecuted Jews to Palestine, especially from Eastern Europe, seemed to her to be the only possible solution. In 1897 she became a member of the Hovevei Zion in Baltimore, in those days one of the most active groups in Palestine. In 1903 after the death of her father, she moved together with her mother to New York where she was the first woman ever to receive permission to attend the

1 Henrietta Szold [1860–1945].

'Jewish Theological Seminary', on the condition that she did not intend to be ordained a rabbi.

After a personal crisis Henrietta Szold visited Palestine in 1909. Shocked by the terrible quality of healthcare for Jews in Palestine, she turned her attention mainly to the practical aspect of Zionism. In 1910 she became the honorary secretary of the 'Federation of American Zionists' where she tried to sort out the chaotic organization and administration. On February 24, 1912, Henrietta and forty other women founded a new national Zionist women's organization, the 'Hadassah Chapter of Daughters of Zion' with the express aim of improving the hygienic and medical care in Palestine as well as promoting Zionist education and an awareness of Judaism in America. They chose their motto from the biblical quotation 'aruhath bat ami' – 'Why does the wound of the daughter of my people not heal?' (Jeremiah 8:22). Henrietta Szold was elected national president of this group which abridged its name to 'Hadassah' two years later and eventually was to become the largest Zionist organization in the USA and the largest Jewish women's organization worldwide. In 1920 they added 'Junior Hadassah' for women aged between 18 and 21 years. Henrietta Szold, supported especially by Louis D. Brandeis, developed an effective healthcare system for the Jews in Palestine, on the basis of which the Israeli healthcare system today is considered to be one of the best in the world. Due to her initiative the Hadassah was able to keep to a large extent its independence from the Federation of American Zionists and its successor organizations.

Because of several administrative problems of the 'American Zionist Medical Unit' in Palestine which was led by her and which in the meantime had grown into an institution with 400 employees and a budget of nearly one million dollars, Henrietta Szold set out for Palestine in 1920 at the age of almost 60 years. Originally she planned to stay there for only two years, but she remained in Jerusalem, except for a number of breaks, until her death. In 1927 she was elected to the three-person 'shadow cabinet' of the World Zionist Organization, the 'Palestine Zionist Executive', as the member responsible for the sectors 'health' and 'education'. Later she withdrew as president of the 'Hadassah' and was appointed as its honorary president. In 1931 she was elected to the 'Vaad Leummi', a national council board founded by the British mandate administration. This was in connection with the foundation of the Ministry of Social Welfare, which she took over after her election. Several other awards followed. From 1934 on she was responsible for youth immigration from Germany, the 'Youth Aliyah', which saved tens of thousands of Jewish children and youths from the Nazi terror. Most of the money and the most intensive support came from the 'Hadassah'. Until 1945 about 13,000 children and until 1948 another 17,000 were taken to Palestine by the Youth Aliyah. In spite of her old age and weakened health, Henrietta Szold personally welcomed every arriving ship and supervised the accommodation of the children in settlements, schools and institutions according to their religious origins. Henrietta Szold died on February 12, 1945. In her will she bequeathed all her money to a charitable foundation for children, which was to become a centre of research and publications and was also to co-ordinate the national youth activities. After her death the administration body for children was called 'Mosad Szold' in her memory. Her unorthodox Zionism always contained an element of pacifism connected with philanthropical social work, but excluded ideological or political aspects. Although she was a Zionist by conviction, she recognized very early that the co-operation with the Arab population would be a big problem for Palestine. For this reason, she had opened the doors of the Hadassah institutions to Palestinians from the very beginning and committed herself all her life to a mutual and peaceful co-existence.

Barbara Lüthi

One's Personal Traits in Another Person: First Encounters of Zionists with the Arab Culture

Reflections on Zionism and the Arabs Seen in Historical Perspective Based on a Book by Yosef Gorny[1]

'We abroad are accustomed to believe that the Arabs are all desert savages, asses, who neither perceive nor understand what goes on around them. That is a serious mistake. Like all Semites, the Arabs are of sharp intellect and full of cunning. In all the cities of Syria and Palestine, there are many Arab merchants who know how to exploit the masses and deceive their customers just as is done in Europe. The Arabs, and I am referring particularly to the town dwellers, see and understand what we are doing and what our aspirations are in Palestine, but they keep their silence and pretend not to know, because at present they do not perceive our actions as a threat to their future [...]'[2]

This passage was written by Ahad Haam, the spiritual father of cultural Zionism, after his first trip to Palestine in 1891.

Every encounter with a foreign culture goes hand in hand with a projective imagination, with inner spiritual pictures that originate from our own culture, but also from concrete expectations. The description of foreigners – their conduct, their appearance and their way of life – at the same time provides the means to visualize and ensure one's own identity. The images and projections of the Zionists originated in their European background and often in a resultant feeling of cultural superiority. The expectations were reflected in the hope of creating a Jewish state and a Jewish cultural renaissance in Palestine.

Today – after conflict-ridden decades between the Jewish and Arab population in Israel – the justified, but frequently forgotten question arises concerning the attitudes and judgements of the first Zionists with respect to the Arabs in the land of Palestine at the turn of the century. In 1880, there were only 24,000 Jews living in Palestine out of a total population of 525,000 people. The creation of a Jewish state could not yet be predicted. The Zionist Jews were convinced of their nationality, strove to achieve a state of their own and bring about a renaissance of Jewish culture in Palestine, although they had not yet gained a foothold in the country owing to their long tradition of exile. The Arab population on the other hand had not yet banded together to form a national unit, but nonetheless lived on the land. In the following it will be shown with the examples of Ahad Haam, Theodor Herzl and Max Nordau, of whom only the first two travelled through Palestine gathering impressions of the Arab population, how diverse the attitudes to the Arabs were.

In his article published in 1891 and entitled 'The Truth from Palestine', Ahad Haam intended to make clear the negative developments of the

[1] Yosef Gorny: Zionism and the Arabs 1882–1948. A Study of Ideology. Oxford 1987. Chapter 1.
[2] Ahad Haam: Die Wahrheit aus Palästina. In: Ahad Haam: Am Scheidewege. Gesammelte Aufsätze. Vol. 1. Berlin 1923, p. 87.

Zionist movement and show that the previous conceptions did not agree with the reality there. He saw in the picture which European Jews had of the Arabs the potential for conflict between the two peoples. The Arabs profited from the Jewish settlers, as long as they continued to bring work and money into the country.

'But there will come a time when the life of our people in Palestine will have developed to such an extent that the rural population will feel more or less cramped. Then they will not make way for us just like that.'[3]

And he warned the Jewish settlers in the country,

'not to incite the anger of the rural population by repugnant acts; how cautious we must be in our relations with a foreign people in whose midst we wish to settle; how important it is to show friendliness and respect and of course propriety and honesty towards them'.

But instead, with a feeling of endless freedom, the Jewish settlers developed inclinations to despotism, treated the Arabs hostilely and cruelly, infringed their rights and offended them: conduct often found when 'the slaves become masters'.

While above Ahad Haam's text reads like a moral protest, he also adopted the views shared by the Jewish settlers, namely that

'the Arabs only respect those who display strength and courage; but this only applies when they are aware that the law is on the side of their adversaries; this is not so when they have good reason to think that the conduct of their adversaries is unjust and oppressive. Then, even if they keep silent until their time has come hatred burns in their hearts and they harbour a strong grudge'.

Although Ahad Haam respected the existence of an Arab society with its own national characteristics, at the same time he also pointed out the potential for future confrontation with reference to the 'collective Arab character'. It is striking that he always described the Arabs and Jews as a collective abstract. His personal experiences which he had gathered during the course of his travels turned into a generalizing view of Arab-Jewish problems.

Around the turn of the century, a number of European Zionists were of the widely publicized opinion propagated by Western colonizers that the achievements and progress made by the European civilization would bring Eastern countries political, economic and cultural advantages. Theodor Herzl also shared this view. Whereas cleanliness, tidiness and outward beauty had molded his view of the world, he was shocked by the decay and filth he saw in Jerusalem during his visit to Palestine in 1898. He imagined a new, clean and generous Jerusalem with fresh air and sanitation. The projection of Western values into his vision of a future Jewish state in Palestine already took shape at this time.[4]

Although his book 'Altneuland' (Oldnewland) has a purely utopian character, it nevertheless reveals some essential features of Herzl's thinking and vision. Of a total of three hundred pages, a mere seven are devoted to the Arab problem. Despite its paternalistic-missionary tone, the book also reveals an awareness of the complex cultural and psychological problems that exist between both peoples. When the protagonist in the book, a Jew named David, in his capacity as leader of the 'new Jewish society' invites guests to take a tour through the village and his Arab friend Rashid Bey joins the party, there is an exchange of words which is characteristic of Herzl's sensitivity to the potential for conflict, but also to possible solutions between the two groups of people. When one of the Jewish companions says triumphantly:

'We Jews have brought culture here', Rashid Bey replies: 'Forgive me, my friend! This culture was already

---

[3] Haam: Wahrheit aus Palästina, pp. 87 f. The following quotations from pp. 107–108.

[4] Gorny: Zionism, p. 30.

1 Arab farmers in the Jesreel plain, around 1900.

here before, in any event its beginnings. My father already planted large numbers of oranges here.'

The Arab's response illustrates Herzl's awareness that the local population might feel beset by the paternalistic attitude of the emissaries of Western culture. At the same time, however, he conveys through the speaker Rashid Bey that the situation of the Arabs has improved considerably:

'[...] they now make a respectable living, their children are healthier and are studying. Nobody has raised a hand against their religion or their customs – they have only benefited from increased welfare.'[5]

Based on this and other evidence, Herzl attests his belief in a possible Arab acculturation towards Western civilization. The Arabs, with whom the Jews are supposed to live in friendship, in his opinion, could profit individually in material terms while at the same time maintaining their own culture. The new Jewish society should therefore be a reflection of Western European civilization which would allow room for individual cultural characteristics.

Max Nordau reveals a pronounced Eurocentric way of thinking. He emphasized in front of critics that he would never agree

'that the return of the Jews to the land of their forefathers should constitute a retreat to barbarism as our enemies and slanderers claim. The Jewish people will envolve their unique essence within the framework of general Western culture, like every other cultured people, but not outside it. Not among Asians despising culture as Ahad Haam seems to be in favour of.'[6]

At the Eighth Zionist Congress in 1907, where he spoke about the cultural superiority of the

---

[5] Theodor Herzl: Altneuland. In: Gesammelte Zionistische Werke. In fünf Bänden. Vol. 5. Tel Aviv 1935, pp. 245 ff.

[6] English text from Gorny, as footnote 1, p. 34.

Jews over the indigenous population, Nordau again demonstrated that the emphasis on the 'Europeanism' of the Jews plays an important role as contrasted with 'Asianism':

> 'We will not become Asiatics from the point of view of anthropological and cultural inferiority any more than the Anglo-Saxons became redskins in North America, Hottentots in South Africa or Papuas in Australia.'

He thus represented the belief in a cultural mission of the Jews:

> 'We intend to come to Palestine as the emissaries of culture and to expand the moral boundaries of Europe to the Euphrates.'[7]

In so doing, he made no reference whatsoever to the potential for conflict between Jews and Arabs, promising that the cultural mission of the European Jews would have a positive effect. This biased theory had little to do with reality.

The different views held by Zionist public figures were not only based on individual impressions, but they also varied by virtue of their social and national conceptions of Zionism. Nordau had a superior Jewish nation in mind to which other peoples were supposed to submit. Herzl understood Zionism as a dynamic mass undertaking in which the Arab problem was primarily a 'quantitative' factor: the strong and open future Jewish society in Palestine would absorb the Arabs in its midst. The representatives of Hovevei Zion, on the other hand, saw the problem in a 'qualitative' light, since for them Zionism was a slowly developing enterprise involving individual participants. Adherence to Jewish values and traditions therefore appeared to them to be indispensable and consequently the complete integration of both cultures undesirable; they merely aspired to the peaceful co-existence with mutual recognition of the respective cultures. The views with respect to the 'foreign' Arabs, therefore, reveal a lot about how the Zionists saw themselves. The concept that created the greatest distance between the two peoples, thus making it almost impossible to settle the conflict, was the one that ultimately gained acceptance.

---

[7] Max Nordau: VIII. Kongressrede. Quoted after: Zionistisches Aktionskomitee (ed.): Max Nordau's Zionistische Schriften. Cologne, Leipzig 1909, here p. 176.

Erik Petry

Immigration Movements from 1904–1948

At the beginning of the 20th century, the rural settlements had achieved a modest but stable standard of living. However, the immigration itself had almost come to a standstill. According to Herzl's doctrine, the Zionist Organization had badly neglected the colonization. The development in Palestine seemed to be going on without it. New immigrants were needed, new ideas and new initiatives on the part of the 'practical Zionists', to breathe new life into the dying settlement movement. But first, organizational prerequisites had to be met.

In order to solve the problems of the purchase of land and of the building of new settlements while simultaneously acquiring land as inalienable property for the Jewish people, the 'Jewish National Fund' – Keren Kayemet Le Israel – was founded in 1901 and the 'Palestine Land Development Company' in 1908. As early as 1899, the Zionist Organization had created its own financing instrument, the 'Jewish Colonial Trust', in London. It was joined in 1903 by the 'Anglo-Palestine Company', which was designed to support the Yishuv in Palestine as a creditor and subsidizer. For the co-ordination of its work in Palestine, the Zionist Organization created the 'Palestine Office' in Jaffa in 1908 which was responsible for the rural settlements as well as for the urbanization.

Regarding immigration, the period from 1904 to the foundation of the state in 1948 can be divided into different phases, clearly separated from each other. During the Second Aliyah, from 1904 to 1914, particularly Jews from Eastern Europe, who were mostly followers of the leftist Zionist movements 'Hapoel Hazair' and 'Poalei Zion', emigrated to Palestine. During this time, the first structures were created which were to become the basis for the State of Israel beyond the British mandate.

Those immigrants founded the first kibbutzim, but also the privately run Moshavot, although co-operatively organized, experienced an unexpected boom. Working as day labourers in the settlements, the 'Halutzim' – 'pioneers' – attempted to 'conquer the work' – 'Kibbush Ha-Avodah' – which had previously been carried out almost exclusively by Arabs. They founded self-help organizations such as the 'Ha-Shomer' – 'the watchman' – to guard the colonies and laid the foundation for a new Hebrew press. But the Jewish communities flourished in the cities as well. The economic possibilities were improved, new quarters were built. The most striking example among these was Tel Aviv in 1909, which remains a symbol for the idea of a new Jewish urbanization of Erez Israel. By 1914 almost 40,000 people had immigrated: this movement was interrupted abruptly by the First World War.

The years of war brought with them considerable setbacks for the Yishuv, the economy stagnated, the population went hungry, and the Turkish authorities expelled Jewish citizens from Palestine who were troublesome for them. The Balfour Declaration of 1917 had raised Zionists hope of facilitated immigration conditions and thus of a prosperous development in the country, but the British mandate between 1919 and 1948

1 Jewish pioneers in the colony Merchavia, 1917/18.

was to be characterized by a constant see-sawing of the British government between Jewish and Arab interests in Palestine. The six 'White Papers', the statements of the British government regarding its Palestine policies, which were published between 1922 and 1939, continually issued new regulations for immigration, quotas were set and then abolished, decrees made and not held. That this procedure did not contribute to stability and a peaceful development between Jews and Arabs is reflected by the Arab uprisings of 1920/21, 1929 and 1936 as well as the violent riots by the Jews.

The immigrations of the Third Aliyah set in with the beginning of the mandate, and lasted from 1919 to 1923 continuing almost without interruption the Second Aliyah in regard of its structure and the intentions of the immigrants. Once again 35,000 immigrants came, more than half of them from Poland. They particularly helped the kibbutz movement to its upswing, founded new moshavim, created union structures and began to form a Jewish army, the 'Haganah' from the Hashomer organization.

Not until the Fourth Aliyah from 1924 to 1931 did entrepreneurially oriented immigrants arrive in Palestine in larger numbers, most of whom were Jews from the Polish bourgeoisie. About 80 percent of the 80,000 immigrants settled in the cities and mainly gave the construction industry the decisive commercial shove.

The municipal economy flourished as never before. Workshops and small factories were founded. This upswing, however, was stopped again as early as 1927/28 by a massive economic crisis. The Fifth Aliyah, which lasted from 1932 to 1939, was to be the last before the outbreak of the Second World War and brought 235,000 legal and at least 12,000 illegal immigrants from Central Europe to Palestine. The somewhat euphemistic

2 Tel Aviv at the beginning of the 1930s, crossing of Allenby and Carmel Street.

term 'immigrants' can no longer be used for this Aliyah: these were refugees. Among them, the German Jews occupied a special position. Driven out of the Nazi Reich, they contributed, with their urban way of life and the partially saved capital, to a further urbanization of the country. Even if they were not more than 55,000 in number, these 'Jeckes' played an important part in the development of political, economic and judicial structures in the State of Israel.

The development of the rural settlements, especially of the kibbutzim between the Second and Fifth Aliyah, is closely linked to the name of a man who, in the historiography of Zionism, is very seldom given the acknowledgement he deserves: Dr. Arthur Ruppin. Born in 1876 in Rawicz (Poznán), he devoted himself to sociology and demography after having studied law and economics. His book 'Die Juden der Gegenwart' (The Contemporary Jews), which was published in 1904, attracted great attention in the Jewish world and brought Ruppin into contact with the Zionists, who sent him to Palestine in 1907 to check the development and working opportunities of the Zionist Organization in the Yishuv. In 1908, he then became the head of the newly created Palestine Office in Jaffa and remained in this position until his death in 1943. Ruppin did not come to Zionism via romantic ideals of the Jewish tradition or via the Hebrew culture, he was much more interested in the development of the economy, in the investigation of sociological backgrounds and the construction of a humane social order in Palestine. This required the transformation of the idealist political Zionism into a practical, creative and social movement. Ruppin was the man who attempted this transformation.

His life's work in Palestine can be divided into four phases, which partially correspond to the four Aliyot. Until the beginning of the First World War, Ruppin's entire interest was based on the foundations for a Zionist colonization of Palestine. This phase coincided with the foundation of Tel Aviv and the first kibbutzim. During the First World War, he made all efforts to keep the Yishuv alive at all. The Turkish authorities in Palestine, however, considered this work to be a threat to their already highly endangered position and expelled Ruppin in 1916. Not until 1920 was he able to return and strove to renew the structures

3   Arrival of the refugee ship 'Haganah Ship Theodor Herzl' in the harbour of Tel Aviv, photograph taken by George Goldstein.

which had been built up before the war, to strengthen the rural and urban settlements and to lead the economy of the Yishuv through the great economic crises of the twenties. The dramatically increasing threat to the Jews in Europe as from 1933 also forced the Yishuv to deal with the new conditions. Ruppin again assumed a leading role in this by successfully advocating the integration of the European refugees.

Apart from his outstanding significance for the economic development of the rural and urban Yishuv, Ruppin also committed himself to a mutual understanding between Jews and Arabs. To this end he founded the 'Berit Shalom' – the 'Peace Alliance' – in 1925. Toward the end of his life, however, he somewhat moved away from the idea of a binational state in Palestine as aimed for by this alliance, perhaps out of resignation, perhaps because he had recognized that such a state was utopic at the end of the thirties. From the middle of the twenties on he also taught the 'Sociology of the Jews' founded by him at the Hebrew University in Jerusalem.

Historiography has often not recognized the decisive importance of Ruppin for the development of a practically oriented Zionism, although Ruppin is one of the greatest leaders in Zionism along with Herzl, Weizmann and Ben Gurion. His contemporaries, who are until this day still more famous, saw this much more clearly than the posterity. Chaim Weizmann said of him:

'The man, who during the years before World War I and indeed throughout the quarter century following the First World War, played a decisive part in the colonization of Palestine was Arthur Ruppin [...] and when he differed with me – as for example in 1922 on the question of the minimum of costs of colonization – he was usually right.'[1]

[1]   Chaim Weizmann: Trial and Error. London 1949, p. 129.

Kathrin Ringger

'An English Adventure': Diplomatic Efforts for a Home for the Jewish People 1897–1922

'Let the sovereignty be granted to us over a portion of the globe large enough to satisfy the rightful requirements of a nation; the rest we shall manage for ourselves [...] The governments of all countries surged by anti-Semitism will be keenly interested in assisting us to obtain the sovereignty we want.'

This was how Theodor Herzl optimistically spelled out his vision of the future in his programmatic work 'The Jewish State' in 1896. He did not refer to a particular geographical region, but did draw attention to the historical bonds linking the Jewish people and Palestine:

'Palestine is our ever-memorable historic home [...] If His Majesty the Sultan were to give us Palestine, we could in return undertake to regulate the whole finances of Turkey. We should there form portion of a rampart of Europe against Asia [...] We should as a neutral State remain in contact with all of Europe, which would have to guarantee our existence.'[1]

Herzl and the later Zionists longed both for the recognition of their organization as a negotiating partner in the name of the Jewish people and for international protection for their vision of a 'Jewish state'. Partners in Europe had to be found for this purpose. Consequently, once the Zionist Organization had been founded at the First Zionist Congress, official negotiations were initiated with the governments of the major European powers.

Even if it had not been the case previously, following this congress, the Zionists and Herzl in particular saw themselves as being to all intents and purposes the advocates of the Jews and took charge of the negotiations with governmental representatives in the name of the Jewish people. Although Zionism was merely one of several currents in Jewry, Herzl and those who were later to become leading Zionists were recognized as the representatives of the Jewish community, since they alone sought to form a state: they were given the opportunity to present their demands to governmental representatives. In accordance with the customs of the law of nations at the turn of the century, this approach was problematical. The doctrine of international law at that time assumed that only states were subjects under international law – the law of nations was the legal system that was valid among states. According to more modern teachings, international organizations can also be accorded the status of a subject under international law. The Zionist Organization, however, was not an intergovernmental institution, but rather an association under private law whose regional chapters were registered in the individual states. Moreover, the recognition of an international organization required – and even today still requires – recognition by the community of states. To a certain extent, such a community existed in Europe at the turn of the century only in the limited form of the 'European Concert'. The aim of this community was the consultation and co-operation of the great European

---

[1] Theodor Herzl: Der Judenstaat. Zurich 1946, quoted here from the English version New York 1988, pp. 92, 93, 96.

powers in settling and contending with international crises and the conclusion or prevention of wars. The 'Concert', however, was not a permanent international organization; periodical meetings were not planned. Although up until the outbreak of World War I, several conferences and congresses had taken place, they never dealt with the demands made by the Zionists, but instead merely considered the situation of the Jews in individual states. There can be no question whatsoever of any official recognition of the Zionist Organization on the part of this organ or by individual member states.

The 'Basle Program' and Its Implementation

'Zionism seeks to establish a home for the Jewish people in Palestine secured under public law.'[2]

This deliberately vague wording was chosen in order not to overly restrict the scope of negotiations and not to challenge the sovereignty of the Ottoman Empire. In Constantinople, the term 'under public law' could be interpreted as meaning 'under public Ottoman law', whereas in London, Paris or Berlin, the same term could be interpreted as meaning 'under international law'. This made it possible for the European powers to support a 'Jewish home'. After the conclusion of the congress, Herzl, now the official president of the newly founded Zionist Organization, began to implement the programme. His attention had been focused right from the outset on Germany from which he hoped to receive the greatest support. Approximately a year before the First Congress, William Hechler succeeded in arranging a meeting between Grand Duke Friedrich I of Baden and Herzl. Friedrich I suggested 'infiltrating' Jews into Palestine and only subsequently searching for a solution at the political level in the course of time. Herzl rejected this unreasonable request. The Grand Duke promised Herzl to arrange for an audience with the Kaiser Wilhelm II. This took place in October 1898 in Constantinople during the Kaiser's visit to the Ottoman Empire. During this meeting, the Kaiser made assurances about his support to the Zionists and declared himself prepared to protect the Jewish migration, if the Sultan agreed to the colonization of Palestine. A 'chartered company – under German protection'[3] was to be set up. German interests in Zionism were probably largely economic – Germany hoped to participate in possible profits from Jewish settlement projects. Moreover many advocates – including the basically anti-Semitic Kaiser – thought that the 'unloved Jews' would then leave Germany.

A conversation along these lines between the Kaiser and Sultan Abdul Hamid did not, however, produce any results. Nevlinski, a political agent and journalist, suggested that the initiative failed because the Kaiser remarked 'that the Zionists were "not dangerous to Turkey, but everywhere the Jews are a nuisance" of whom one "should like to get rid"'[4], which had met with disapproval. Turkey did not appreciate anti-Semitic remarks. Moreover, Abdul Hamid could not have been expected to grant shelter to persons the German Kaiser considered undesirable. This description of the circumstances is not reliable, but the Kaiser was known to frequently take a rather dilettante approach with diplomatic affairs. After the resistance of the Sultan, it was in any case impossible for him to stick to his proposal in order not to upset his important foreign allies. And even the chief rabbi of Jerusalem took pains not to meet Herzl during his visit to Palestine in 1898.

---

[2] Zionisten-Congress in Basel (29, 30 and 31 August 1897). Officielles Protocoll. Vienna 1898, p. 119.

[3] Theodor Herzl: Briefe und Tagebücher. Ed. by Alex Bein et al. Vol. 2. Berlin, Frankfurt a.M., Vienna 1983, p. 670.

[4] Quoted in: Isaiah Friedman: Germany, Turkey and Zionism 1897–1918. Oxford 1977, p. 77.

1 Kaiser Wilhelm II in Palestine. The only parts of Theodor Herzl that can be seen in this photograph made by David Wolffsohn on October 28, 1898, are one leg and his pith helmet at the right margin of the picture.

The Sultan's reservations with respect to the Zionist idea become clear when one considers the position of the Ottoman Empire at the time. Since the Congress of Paris in 1856, at which the 'sick man of the Bosporus' became involved in the European Concert, the influence of the great powers on Constantinople had increased. They also exerted mutual control on one another to prevent individual governments from being able to acquire territory prior or subsequent to the expected collapse of the empire. France, Germany, Russia, Great Britain, and the Habsburg monarchy had been active within the empire as protectorate powers of the non-Moslem population for quite a long time. Against this background, it is not surprising that the Zionist movement and its idea of the return of the Jews to Palestine was a welcome opportunity for the European powers to expand their influence in the Ottoman Empire under the pretext of a protectorate. The new Jewish settlers were mainly Ashkenazim and, unlike the Sephardic Jews who had long settled in Palestine, they hesitated to become Ottoman citizens and preferred instead to be subject to the authority of a protectorate power. The Ottoman government assumed – quite rightly so – that the commitment of the Europeans was guided much less by humanitarian motives than by the desire to expand their sphere of influence in the Middle East. After all, the protectorate powers included governments who had in no way put an end to the discrimination and persecution of Jews in their own countries. In spite of the unsuccessful mediation efforts on the part of Wilhelm II, Herzl nevertheless succeeded in being received by the Sultan in 1901, not as a Zionist, but rather as a leading representative of Jews and an influential journalist. But even this meeting did nothing to change Abdul Hamid's stance – Palestine remained closed for larger streams of Jewish immigrants.

In August 1903, Herzl travelled to St. Petersburg to meet the Minister of the Interior Pleve. The idea of negotiating with a governmental representative who had been held responsible for the pogrom in Kishinev did not appeal to Herzl – and also widened the gap to many Russian Jews, but it was clear to him that he required the diplomatic support of Russia in the face of the Sublime Porte in order to make it possible for Russian Jews to safely enter Palestine. After the first conference of Russian Zionists in Minsk in 1902, all Zionist activities had been forbidden. In particular, the 'cultural Zionism' that had been discussed there and the nationalist Jewry which advocated the recognition of Jewish nationality were in conflict with the Russian objective of inducing the Jewish population to either assimilate or emigrate. The czarist government feared the emergence of a state within the state which would create a new nationality problem:

'We liked your Zionist movement earlier as long as it was working toward emigration [...] But ever since the Congress in Minsk, we have noticed un changement des gros bonnets. Mention is made less of Palestinian Zionism than of culture, organization and Jewish nationality.'[5]

Pleve did not acquiesce until Herzl gave assurances that the ultimate goal of Russian Jews was emigration. In a letter, the Minister of the Interior pledged the support of the Russian government for the creation of an independent Jewish state in Palestine. The motives of Russia were clear: it was possible in this way not only to resolve the 'Jewish question' but also to weaken the Ottoman Empire from within at the same time.

By continuing the negotiations with Austria-Hungary and Italy, Herzl intended to induce the other great European powers to bring concerted pressure to bear on the Ottoman Empire. But

[5] Herzl: Tagebücher, Vol. 3, p. 590.

2   Kaiser Wilhelm II and Theodor Herzl in Palestine. This is a composite picture, since the photograph made by David Wolffsohn turned out to be a failure.

such an interest group never came about; the individual governments were much too involved with more important questions involving foreign and domestic policy. Only Great Britain appeared to be interested in promoting the Zionist cause. Unlike France, Russia and even Germany, England's presence in the Middle East was weak. Whereas France had taken over the protection of all Catholic and Maronite Christians in Lebanon and Russia had assumed protection of the orthodox Christians as well as most Jewish settlers from the East, Great Britain, together with Germany, acted only as the protectorate power for

Protestant Christians. A union with the Zionist Organization would be able to offset this disadvantage.

The Zionist Organization did not begin negotiations with London until 1902. Palestine was not considered a homestead at that time due to the intransigent position taken by the Sublime Porte. The Zionist leadership therefore strove to acquire territory immediately nearby. The plans to colonize the Sinai Peninsula in the vicinity of El Arish supported by England, however, met with the Sultan's disapproval as well as that of the Egyptian government. In the spring of 1903, Chamberlain offered a region in East Africa in the name of the British government. This concrete proposal, known as the 'Uganda Scheme', meant great political success for the Zionists and was interpreted as a commitment by England to help establish a Jewish home. Leopold Greenberg, publisher of the 'Jewish Chronicle' and the 'Jewish World', wrote to Herzl:

> 'It seems to me that intrinsically there is no great value in East Africa. It will not form a great attraction to our people for it has no moral or historical claim. But the value of the proposal of Chamberlain is politically immense *if we use it to its full* [...] It matters not if East Africa is afterwards refused by us – we shall have obtained from the British Government a recognition that it cannot ever go back and which no other British Government will ever be able to upset. Everything after that will have to start from that point – the point of recognition of us as a Nation. It also follows naturally that ... if it is found that East Africa is no good they will have to make a further suggestion and this it is possible will gradually and surely lead us to Palestine.'[6]

As was to be expected, the 'Uganda Scheme' failed – due to its rejection by the Seventh Zionist Congress in 1905 and due to the controversy about this plan that had arisen in Great Britain. Nonetheless, the British government was to remain the main partner to whom the concerns and interests of the Zionist Organization could be addressed.

After the death of Theodor Herzl, diplomatic negotiations came to a halt. He was difficult to replace and, what's more, the Zionist Organization became languid during the ensuing years due to internal strife and the formation of splinter groups. After the beginning of World War I, Chaim Weizmann and Nahum Sokolów took over the leadership of diplomatic activities. They had become somewhat pressing because, as the demise of the Ottoman Empire continued, the allies began dividing it up and setting out their war objectives in a series of secret negotiations. Great Britain concluded the 'Sykes-Picot Agreement' with France in October 1916 which provided for the subdivision of the Arab regions into five parts. France was to get all of Syria including Lebanon and parts of Palestine; the rest of Palestine would be internationalized and Great Britain was to obtain parts of Mesopotamia. Furthermore, France and Great Britain emerged in this agreement as protectorate powers of the Arab states and declared that they would not permit a third power to acquire territorial rights in the Arab peninsula. To achieve these aims, the British government also attempted to undermine the Ottoman Empire from within. It was the British High Commissioner in Cairo, McMahon, who won over Sharif Hussein of Mecca, the highest dignitary of the Arab world, to the idea of leading the Arabs in an uprising against the government in Constantinople. He in return expected concessions from the British. In a letter dated October 24, 1915, McMahon outlined the region in which Great Britain was prepared to acknowledge and support Arab independence. During the ensuing period, England never contested the contractual character of these agreements, thus warding off France's claims to Syria which had been anchored in the 'Sykes-Picot Agreement'. Hussein was accepted by Great Britain as the representative of all Arabs, just as the

---

[6] Quoted in: Friedman: Germany, p. 104 f.

Zionists had been recognized as the representatives of the Jewish community. Although not all Arabs stood behind Hussein, they subsequently quoted this correspondence in an effort to support their claims about the obligations Britain had towards them.

The British government, however, was in no way relying solely on its Arab card, and decided to play its Zionist trump card as well. By 1917 in particular, the Zionists were regarded as an important factor in achieving the allied war objectives and were used for this purpose. It was thought that if Great Britain were to make a declaration for the benefit of the Zionist idea, the Zionists should in turn support the allies. Lloyd George, Prime Minister at the time, wrote about this aspect in his memoirs:

> 'The actual timing of the declaration was determined by consideration of war policy [...] the launching [...] was due to propagandist reasons [...] Public opnion in Russia and America played a great part, and we had every reason at that time to believe that in both countries the friendliness or hostility of the Jewish race might make a considerable difference.'[7]

In the United States, the Jewish community was to exert pressure to induce Wilson to enter the war. The Russian Jews were expected to try to prevent Russia from abandoning the allied front after the February Revolution. Furthermore, an attempt was made to forestall a promise to the Zionists on the part of the German government. Although the reactions among the Zionists in the United States and Russia to the subsequent declaration were overwhelming, their influence in politics was greatly overestimated.

Great Britain was pursuing other aims as well. As the guarantor of the Jewish home, it was able to entrench itself not only in Egypt, but also on the other side of the Suez Canal, thus obtaining an important land connection on the way to India. At the same time, a British protectorate was able to keep the French and the Germans out of Palestine. And finally, anti-Semitic motives probably played an important role as well. After the incidents in Russia in 1917, the British government feared the influence of Russian Jews on the revolutionary movements in England. The spectre of a 'global Jewish conspiracy' was in the minds of many politicians synonymous with the 'socialist world revolution'.

The Zionist Organizations from Great Britain and the United States together with the British and American governments drafted a declaration intended to assure the Zionists of a home in Palestine. By way of Claude Montefiore and Sir Edwin Montagu, the only Jew in the British Cabinet of the day, also vehement anti-Zionists among England's Jews brought their influence to bear on the wording of the declaration. Montagu in particular was instrumental in incorporating protective clauses into the final wording and missed no opportunity to draw the attention of the British government to the problematic nature of such a declaration. The declaration was sent to Lord Rothschild on November 2, 1917.

The Meaning of the Balfour Declaration in Light of International Law

Although the final wording of the declaration named after the then British Foreign Minister, Lord Balfour, only constitutes a toned-down version of the original Zionist proposal, the Zionists nonetheless drew fundamental conclusions from it. First and foremost, they interpreted the declaration as bringing recognition of the Jewish people as subjects under international law. This interpretation is not unproblematic in terms of international law. The term 'people' under international law is understood to be only a nation organized under constitutional law. This means that according to the generally accepted principle of international law there can be neither a

---

[7] Quoted in: Sharman Kadish: Bolsheviks and British Jews. The Anglo-Jewish Community, Britain and the Russian Revolution. London 1992, p. 145.

> Foreign Office,
> November 2nd, 1917.
>
> Dear Lord Rothschild,
>
> I have much pleasure in conveying to you, on behalf of His Majesty's Government, the following declaration of sympathy with Jewish Zionist aspirations which has been submitted to, and approved by, the Cabinet.
>
> "His Majesty's Government view with favour the establishment in Palestine of a national home for the Jewish people, and will use their best endeavours to facilitate the achievement of this object, it being clearly understood that nothing shall be done which may prejudice the civil and religious rights of existing non-Jewish communities in Palestine, or the rights and political status enjoyed by Jews in any other country"
>
> I should be grateful if you would bring this declaration to the knowledge of the Zionist Federation.

3 Facsimile of the Balfour Declaration.

Jewish people nor an Arab people. Attempts after World War I to define people in an ethnic sense as subjects of international law failed to arrive at a generally accepted definition. As a rule, the expansion of the concept encompassed only international organizations such as the League of Nations and later the United Nations. On the basis of the Balfour Declaration, the Zionist Organization was not recognized by the community of states, but only by the British as a public authority. This 'political alliance' subsequently made it possible for the Zionist Organization to participate in the Paris Peace Conference in 1919. Moreover, the Zionists read out of the declaration the obligation of Great Britain under the law of nations to create a 'national home' or at least to actively promote it. The relevant wording, however, is hardly convincing. Only the two surrounding clauses clearly commit the British to protect the rights cited. The

4   Share certificate of the 'Jewish Colonial Trust'.

declaration can only be construed to be a demonstration of political sympathy in favour of the Zionist movement or as expressing a moral obligation on the part of Great Britain. The declaration was definitely on rather shaky ground from a legal point of view.

The Palestine Mandate

In February 1919, US President Wilson read 'the programme of global peace' in a plenary assembly of the Paris Peace Conference. He outlined in 14 points how lasting peace could be

5 Jewish National Fund – olive tree donation.

achieved. He made the following proposal to dissolve the Ottoman Empire:

'The Turkish part of the *Ottoman Empire* shall be granted a secured sovereignty, the other nationalities shall be guaranteed [...] an absolute and undisturbed uninterrupted possibility of their *autonomous development.*'[8]

In order to be able to realize the aims of his programme, Wilson sought to create a League of Nations which was to create a new lasting order in international politics. The statute of the League of Nations that was passed on April 28, 1919, laid down the basis for the creation of mandates, in which 'more developed States' would take over 'the mandate in the name of the League' over

'colonies and territories that in the course of the war have gained their independence but are not yet able to govern themselves [...]'.[9]

[8] Konferenzen und Verträge. Vertrags-Ploetz. Ein Handbuch geschichtlich bedeutsamer Zusammenkünfte und Vereinbarungen. Teil II, Vol. 4: Neueste Zeit 1914–1958. Würzburg 1959, p. 24.
[9] Ibid., p. 39.

The Zionists succeeded in becoming fully involved in the conference proceedings. They resisted an internationalization of Palestine and demanded a sole mandate for Palestine with reference to the promises made in the Balfour Declaration. The American Zionists dispatched competent lawyers who submitted new proposals in the proper legal form over and over again. The Arab camp, on the other hand, was poorly represented, as a pan-Arab representation had not yet come about at this time.

The mandate was subsequently transferred to Great Britain in 1920 and, in so doing, the Balfour Declaration was included in the agreement of July 24, 1922. 'The mandatory will be responsible for putting into effect the declaration made on November 2, 1917, by the British Government and adopted by the other allied powers in favour of a national home for the Jewish people, it being clearly understood that nothing shall be done that may prejudice the civil and religious rights of existing non-Jewish communities in Palestine or the rights and political status enjoyed by Jews in any other country.'[10] After being incorporated into the Mandate Agreement, the Balfour Declaration gained multilateral recognition and became a binding document unchallengeable under international law, although this changed nothing with respect to the uncertainties in its legal interpretation. For the Zionists, the mandate had to be regarded as a success, since it had achieved the creation of a national home for the Jewish people in Palestine and the recognition of the Zionist Organization as a public authority. For the time being, this mandate was the end of the efforts of the Zionist Organization to implement parts of the 'Basle Program'.

There were many voices in Great Britain who criticized the commitment to implement the Balfour Declaration, making reference to the difficulties associated with the relocation of large groups of immigrants in an already populated region. Montagu, for instance, feared that the creation of a homestead in Palestine could further worsen the situation of the Jewish population in Europe. Nonetheless, the advocates of the Balfour Declaration prevailed. The Arab side was ignored at that time, thus creating unexpected problems with the Arab world for the British. During the ensuing period, the British were constantly busy trying to reconcile the two sides, but were at best able to satisfy one side only at a time. The Arabs felt they had been cheated out of their right of self-determination, and the Zionists demanded unrestricted immigration rights with reference to the commitment to implement the Balfour Declaration. In view of the resultant tension that developed between the Jewish and Arab population and its impact, which is still felt today, the words of Lord Balfour, replying to persons criticizing his declaration, take on an almost cynical tone: 'Zionism may fail [...] this is an adventure [...] Are we never to have adventures? Are we never to try new experiments?'[11]

---

[10] Quoted in: Heinz Wagner: Der Arabisch-Israelische Konflikt im Völkerrecht. Berlin 1971, p. 142.

[11] Quoted in: Henry Cattan: Palestine and International Law. The Legal Aspect of the Arab-Israeli Conflict. London 1973, p. 13.

Kathrin Ringger

The Palestine Mandate 1923–1948: The Institutionalization of the Conflict

A Chronology

1923

The Palestine Mandate came into operation on May 29, 1923. The mandate that Great Britain was entrusted with by the League of Nations was on the one hand designed to promote the creation of a Jewish 'national home' and on the other to protect the rights of the Arabs in Palestine and to bring about the national independence of Palestine. The thus arising 'dual commitment' for Great Britain was hardly feasible from a political point of view and resulted in innumerable decrees, boards of enquiry and 'White Papers'. It was the aim of the British to affront neither the Arabs nor the Zionists.

Jewish emigration to Palestine was of major significance for the creation of a national home. The number of immigrants was limited, but immigration was unorganized and caused considerable tension in Palestine itself. There had been bloody unrests in Jaffa in May 1921 with people dead and injured among Jews and Arabs alike. The official board of enquiry cited an increasingly anti-Zionist mood in the Palestinian population as the principal reason for the insurrection. Immigration regulations were therefore revised. However, the new restrictions that were then passed were successfully contested by the Jewish Agency.

In the White Paper of 1922, Winston Churchill, the Authorized Representative of the Colonial Office at the time, confirmed that the Jewish immigration was essential to the development of Palestine, but he emphasized that consideration must be given to the economic situation of the country. Immigration should not occur at the expense of the resident population. The statements made in the White Paper subsequently formed the basis of the British Palestine policy.

1929

In September 1929, there were renewed clashes between Jews and Arabs, triggered by disputes concerning the Wailing Wall in Jerusalem. Jews were murdered in several locations. More than 60 Jews were the victims of a massacre in Hebron – a shock which can still be felt today. Although the appointed Shaw Commission placed responsibility for the unrest on the Arabs, it also concluded that the settlement policy of the Jewish immigrants had to undergo fundamental revision. The immigrants were to be forbidden to acquire more land for settlement, acquisition of land would have to be subject to more stringent guidelines.

1 The British mandatory power advancing against Arab freedom fighters towards the end of the 1930s. This photograph was taken by Georg Goldstein, German physician and photographer, who worked in Palestine and Israel between 1936 and 1953. Goldstein worked for the 'Jüdische Rundschau' until it was closed.

1930

The Passfield White Paper adopted the conclusions of the Shaw Report. The dual commitment of the mandatory power was maintained and the Palestinian and Zionist interests were declared equal and mutually compatible. The White Paper, however, essentially meant a revision of the policy with respect to Jewish immigration and the Zionist Organization. The latter attempted to bring its influence to bear and persuade the British government to revoke the report.

1931

The White Paper remained officially in force. In a letter to Chaim Weizmann, who had resigned in protest from his position as president of the World Zionist Organization and Head of the Jewish Agency, Prime Minister MacDonald explained the intentions of the British government and allayed the statements made in the White Paper so as to reassure the Zionists. The Arab side termed this letter the 'Black Letter'. They saw their suspicions confirmed that the British government was conducting a see-saw policy and that the Zionists would succeed time and time again in obstructing statements that were made by the commission meeting in Palestine in favour of the Arab population.

1936

Renewed disturbances that lasted until 1939 and that were directed against the mandatory rule in Palestine resulted in yet a further board of examiners. Although the Peel Report did support the Balfour Declaration, it also recognized the demands of the Palestinian population for independence. The report arrived at the conclusion that it was impossible to fulfil the dual commitment: 'The answer to the question: "Which of the two will govern Palestine after all?" can only be: Neither of them [...] Partition at least appears to offer an opportunity for permanent peace. We cannot see an opportunity in any other plan.'[1]

[1] Arnold Harttung (Ed.): Ursprung und Entwicklung des arabisch-israelischen Konflikts und der Palästina-Teilungsplan der Vereinten Nationen. Berlin 1993, p. 71.

1937

In a new White Paper of July 1937, the British government accepted the radical demand of the Peel Commission for a partition of Palestine. The government 'had come to the conclusion that between the efforts of the Arabs and the Jews in Palestine there was an irreconcilable antagonism' and that the idea of partitioning Palestine is 'the best and most promising solution in this inextricable situation'[2]. Different models for partitioning the region were worked out during the ensuing period but were ultimately rejected either by the Arab or by the Zionist side. The mandatory power therefore reverted to the policy outlined by the Churchill White Paper.

1939

Since the unrest in Palestine had not stopped, new solutions were called for. In a White Paper published in May, the mandatory power rescinded its intention to create a Jewish state. The mandate was to be terminated in 1949. An independent Palestine was envisaged for the period afterwards in which Jews and Arabs would share government based on their mutual interests. Until that time, the White Paper suggested, the number of immigrants should be restricted during the next five years to 75,000 and the provisions for the acquisition of land should be tightened. This new policy was rejected by both Jews and Palestinians. The Zionist side referred to the mandatory obligations and to the situation of the Jewish population in Germany. The standing Mandatory Commission of the League of Nations also considered the White Paper to be an inadmissible change in the mandatory obligations. This meant an interference with the rights of the League of Nations. Due to the outbreak of the war on September 1, 1939, however, the League of Nations never assembled to debate this question. Great Britain nonetheless continued to pursue the course outlined in the White Paper and noticeably restricted the number of immigrants.

1942

A conference of American and foreign Zionists and representatives of other Jewish organizations was held in the 'Biltmore' Hotel in New York in May. The White Paper of 1939 was denied all moral and legal validity and the 'Biltmore Program' decided. In this decision, the groups present demanded 'an opening of the doors of Palestine' as well as the transfer of control on immigration and land distribution to the Jewish Agency. Palestine was to become a sovereign Jewish 'commonwealth'. This was the first time that the official demand was made, not for a national home, but for a state for the Jewish people.

1945

As a reflection of the change that had taken place in the balance of forces in international politics, the American commitment in the Palestine question grew after World War II. Great Britain decided to retain the mandate only until a solution was forthcoming that would be approved by the United Nations. This gave rise to an Anglo-American Committee of Inquiry. It proposed the immediate issuance of 100,000 immigration permits. What in fact would have meant the annulment of the White Paper of 1939. The British government was not prepared to do this. Several proposals for partition were subsequently drafted and submitted to the various parties, but an agreement could not be reached.

---

[2] Ibid., p. 71.

1946/47

Starting in September 1946 and continuing well into February 1947, various conferences convened in London, initially without the participation of the Palestinian Arabs and Jews. The governmental representatives of the Arab states submitted a counterproposal to the plans for partition: Palestine was to be given its independence as a centralized state with a guaranteed Arab majority. This proposal was rejected at the Twenty-Second Zionist Congress in Basel in December 1946, since it was not in conformity with the mandatory agreements. The Zionists continued to demand a Jewish 'commonwealth' in Palestine. When it became clear that no compromise would be forthcoming, Great Britain decided to lay down its mandate on February 18, 1947, and announced the final withdrawal of its troops for May 15, 1948. The British government failed to recommend to the United Nations any solution to the Palestine problem. On November 29, 1947, the organization then voted to partition Palestine. Both the Arab and the Jewish sides immediately responded with military actions. The rapidly expanding war was only to be contained in 1949.

1948

On May 14, 1948, David Ben Gurion proclaimed the independence of the new State of Israel. The United States of America recognized it 'de facto' the same day. The Soviet Union followed on May 17, 1948. Great Britain did not decide to follow suit until April 27, 1950.

Attila Novák

'There Is a Community of Interests Here ...'

Contacts between the Hungarian and Zionist Diplomacy in the Thirties

In the peace treaty of Trianon in June 1920 Hungary had to hand over more than two thirds of its territory to the victorious powers. More than three million Magyars now lived as members of a minority under the rule of a foreign sovereignty. Since March 1920 Miklós Horthy, regent of Hungary, had the fate of the country in his hands; in the second half of the twenties, his politics became increasingly authoritarian and anti-liberal. In 1932, Horthy appointed Gyula Gömbös, from the revisionist nationalist camp, minister president. Within the scope of a facist axis between Germany, Italy and Hungary, Gömbös hoped to be able to revise the Treaty of Trianon and, especially from 1935 on, intensified the contacts to Italy and the German Reich.

For the Hungarian Jews, the situation had become visibly worse. Many formerly liberal politicians and large portions of the population seemed to be convinced that the policy of assimilation had failed and that the Hungarian-Jewish symbiosis would not be able to function. The reason for this change of heart was, on the one hand, the unsolved 'question of the Eastern Jews' – that is, the undiminished immigration of innumerable Jews from Eastern Europe – and on the other hand, the participation of numerous Jews in the failed left-wing 'Republic of Soviets' in November 1918. Since the beginning of the twenties the various governments practiced a political stance of dissimilation, that is the exclusion of the Jews from the political and social life of the country. This started in September 1920 with a 'numerus clausus law' which restricted admission to university for Jews.

In its efforts in favour of the Hungarian minorities abroad, the Hungarian diplomatic service received unexpected support in the second half of the thirties: namely from the 'international' Zionist diplomacy. How did this unusual cooperation come into being?

For a long period of time, both the Zionist organizations in Hungary 'Magyar Cionista Szövetség' – 'Hungarian Zionist Association' – and 'Magyar Zsidók Pro-Palesztina Szövetség' – 'Pro Palestine Association of Hungarian Jews' – had been able to collect money thanks to a special authorization from the Ministry of the Interior. On December 31, 1935, this authorization expired and was not renewed by the relevant organs in the Ministry of the Interior. As the reason for this, the authorities advanced the charitable collections being made by Miklós Horthy's, wife, in order to reduce the need and poverty of the people. Each additional collection, thus the authorities argued, would reduce the success of this campaign. With respect to the Shekel collection, this argumentation was ridiculous inasmuch as the money collected by the Zionists was invested with the assistance of the Hungarian national bank and taking into account Hungarian interests, to ensure that Hungarian goods found a market in Palestine.

The fact that the national office of the Hungarian Jews and the Pest Jewish community were opposed to Zionism contributed to the conflicts.

The leaders of the religious community, notably Samu Stern, considered the 'national' Jews to be traitors and were of the opinion that the Zionists destroyed the structure of their assimilation policy. Thus they took every opportunity to hinder the Zionist movement, also using their contacts to the government, especially to the ministries of culture and of the interior.

In 1936, the infringements increased mainly of left wing Zionist groups. Several groups and organizations informed the Jewish Agency about these disturbances. The dramatically worsening situation in Hungary activated the foreign centres of the Zionist movement for instance in Jerusalem, London and in Geneva. The main protagonists on the part of the Jewish Agency were Nahum Goldmann, a delegate of the agency at the League of Nations in Geneva, Arthur Lourie, their political secretary and Selig Brodetsky, a member of the executive committee. In Geneva on June 22, 1936, Goldmann presented a memorandum to the Hungarian representative László Velics. In his letter he asked the Hungarian authorities to hinder the work of the Hungarian Zionists no longer. He declared his willingness to travel to Budapest immediately if this proved to be necessary. In December 1936, in a letter to the political department of the Jewish Agency, the Jewish National Fund 'Keren Kayemet Le Israel' reported that contact had been made with Goldmann in Geneva and that he had been requested to co-operate. In this letter, the Keren Kayemet Le Israel mentioned for the first time the possibility of boycotting Hungarian products in Palestine. Goldmann too advocated this option. But the idea of a boycott was rejected in Jerusalem at the beginning of 1937 as it was feared that the affected products would not be able to be replaced and that the importers might therefore refuse to yield to the pressure of the Jewish Agency.

In January 1937, the Budapest Jewish community founded an alternative Palestine organization. From the beginning this association enjoyed the trust of the Ministry of Culture which wanted

1   Nahum Goldmann [1895–1982].

to concentrate the collections in one hand – regardless of the fact that the immigration permits for Palestine which were confirmed by the British authorities were only allowed to be distributed by the Jewish Agency. These permits were sent to the local Zionist organizations who in turn were independent of the institutions of the community.

Goldmann's suggestion to travel to Hungary was accepted and he arrived in Budapest on February 12, 1937. On the very next day he held negotiations in the Ministry of Foreign Affairs. His interlocutor there was Gábor Apor, the extraordinary envoy and authorized ministerial representative with the rank of a vice foreign minister. During this friendly discussion, Apor – according to his own notes – was 'receptive'[1]. Goldmann on the other hand spoke about the 'community of interests' of the Hungarian and Zionist foreign policy. But did mutual interests really exist? In fact, the 'community of interests' of both parties was that the national rhetoric on both sides – in

---

[1]   From Gábor Apor's 'daily report', in which he writes about his negotiations with Nahum Goldmann: Országos Levéltár (state archive) Budapest, K 63 1939–43, Budapest, February 13, 1937.

Hungary and Palestine – included the notion of 'mother states' and that in addition there were respective 'regions outside the borders' with Magyar or Jewish minorities. Each national state, even if it is only just developing, has an interest in protecting the rights of those belonging to the nation who live beyond its national frontiers. The national state considers these people, as Goldmann stated in several letters, not to be an ethnic part of the state in which they live. Hungarians in Slovakia, therefore, did not belong to Slovakia but to the Hungarian nation, the Jews in Hungary, on the other hand, to the Jewish nation. This example shows that two national movements can sympathize with each other if there are no competing interests between them. At this meeting, which took place on the mutual basis of the notion of 'national', the option for a foreign political deal was formulated which would be advantageous for both parties. Apor and Goldmann wanted to enter into a proper deal: Goldmann would support the Hungarian delegation at the League of Nations in minority questions, if the work of the Zionists in Hungary was facilitated. In the meantime, the London group started moving as well: in March, Lourie and Brodetsky visited the Hungarian Embassy and, at the request of the ambassador, Szilárd Masirevich, recorded Goldmann's proposals. They succeeded in winning Masirevich for their cause.

The collections in Hungary remained forbidden and the pressure of the police against the Zionist movement continued to increase. In November 1937, the Budapest police summoned more than thirty Zionists, and in the country incidents also occurred. In February 1938 Goldmann negotiated once again in Budapest. According to his report, the atmosphere was quite good. Goldmann praised the Hungarian foreign policy, but criticized the leadership of the Jewish community in Budapest several times. In 1939, the Ministry of the Interior finally granted the Pro Palestine Association as well as the 'pseudo Zionist' association of the Jewish community the right to collect money. The illusion of a Hungarian-Jewish community of interests was, however, destroyed soon after for several reasons: the Hungarian 'Jewish laws' played a part, as well as the clash of interests within the Hungarian government, furthermore the attitude of the 'official' Jewish establishment and last but not least the outbreak of the Second World War. The leaders of the Jewish Agency had to accept with regret that in Hungary the influence of Samu Stern and of the Jewish community was greater than that of the Zionist organizations with their numerous international contacts.

After 1939, the Jewish Agency changed its policy. After the second 'Jewish law' was passed, it no longer showed any interest in the situation of the Hungarian minorities outside Hungary. For the Hungarian diplomacy, on the other hand, the relations with Goldmann were still useful to test the international reactions to the 'Jewish laws'. All in all, the basis for a community of interests proved to be too narrow.

Heiko Haumann

Shoah and Zionism

At the end of July 1942, Eduard Schulte, a major industrialist from Germany, arrived in Zurich. He got in touch with his old business associate Isidor Koppelman, director of an international investment company in Basel. Schulte told him that by virtue of his economic connections he had heard from sources close to the highest ranking German command that the systematic extermination of the Jews, the 'Final Solution of the Jewish Question', by gassing them in special camps, was being discussed or had already been decided. Koppelman, who knew Schulte's anti-National Socialist stance, did not doubt his words for a moment. He called his friend Samuel Scheps in Geneva and then Benjamin Sagalowitz who, as head of the Jewish news agency 'JUNA', had the necessary connections. Sagalowitz informed Gerhart Riegner, the representative of the Jewish World Congress in Switzerland, who, in turn, notified the American embassy. Despite urgent request, the US State Department did not pass on the message to Stephen Wise, the president of the Jewish World Congress, who only later found out by indirect routes of communication. After additional reports about the 'Final Solution' had leaked out, the allied governments protested against the intended genocide in a solemn declaration on December 17, 1942. Little more happened. In 1988, Eduard Schulte, who had died in 1966, was posthumously given the honour of a 'righteous person' by Yad Vashem.

In connection with these events, the reproach was made that 'the Zionists' could have done more to prevent or at least mitigate the Shoah, the extermination of the Jews. Above all, they had not made use of their influence on the allied governments. Here, however, it is necessary to distinguish between various levels. In Eastern Europe, Zionists – besides members of other Jewish groups – helped at the front position in enabling Jews to escape, to organize resistance in the ghettos, or to form partisan units against the Germans and their accomplices. In Western countries, as well, we again and again find Zionists among those who, since the beginning of the Nazi regime in Germany, had tried to provide means to the threatened people to help them leave or escape, and who had done all they could to make states agree to accept further immigrants. They did not give up, although it had become clear at the latest after the conference at Evian-les-Bains in July 1938 and with the onset of the work of the 'Intergovernmental Committee on Political Refugees', established at that conference, that the governments of the world were not willing to open the borders for the threatened Jews – quite to the contrary, border regulations had become even more stringent.

Exemplarily one should mention some operations carried out in Switzerland, which also closed its border and turned back numerous Jewish refugees. In 1938/39, the Zionist Markus Löffel illegally organized refugee transports to Palestine via a 'Palestine Information Service' and an 'Emigration Office'. Therefore Paul Grüninger – the St. Gallen police inspector – also illegally issued Löffel a passport which enabled him to leave and re-enter Switzerland. Heini Born-

1 In the Palestine Office in Geneva, 1942. Mrs. Scheps standing on the right side, Samuel Scheps sitting next to her.

stein, representative of the 'Hashomer Hazair', Veit Wyler, George Brunschvig and others helped to smuggle refugees into Switzerland and to improve their situation. The Palestine Office in Basel, and later in Geneva – in particular under Samuel Scheps' leadership between 1937 and 1946 – did everything to provide refugees with permission for a limited stay in Switzerland and for the continuation of their journey to Palestine – first via Trieste, later via Istanbul. Thousands were rescued in this way. Together with other Jewish organizations, the Office also participated in attempts to 'pay for the release' of the threatened Jews in negotiations with Nazi authorities. They also supported the efforts undertaken by Henrietta Szold and her companions of the Hadassah to protect as many children and young people from death as possible with the help of the Youth Aliyah.

The behaviour of some of the leading Zionists or of the Yishuv politicians in Palestine was less straightforward. Here the concern about the fate of the Jews in Europe was just one of the central issues – the confrontation with the British mandate authorities and their restrictions on the number of immigrants, the conflict with the Arabs and the fear that the German armies supported by the Arabs could also conquer Palestine via North Africa and Egypt were also of concern for the Jewish population. The group 'Al Domi' – 'Don't be quiet!' – had made public appearances since the end of 1942. Martin Buber, Samuel Joseph Agnon, a poet from Galicia [1888–1970], and other famous intellectuals were members of this group. In a desperate attempt, they appealed to the Yishuv to do more for the rescue of the Jews threatened by the Nazis. One of the requests was to urge the Allies to bomb the extermination camps and the access roads leading to these camps.

Just as the other proposals, this plan was not implemented either. Many Jews could have been rescued. The reason given by the Allies to explain why they had not intervened – the military action would have been hampered and thus the war protracted excessively – has in the meantime turned out to be a mere pretext. Both actions could easily have been coordinated. It was conspicuous, however, that the leading Zionist politicians had not tried more earnestly to bring their influence to bear. One should remember though that for a long time it had been difficult to imagine the full extent of the persecution of Jews. The Shoah was inconceivable.

But more has to be considered. Fierce debates about the future ways and even hostile struggles for power had flared up within the Zionist leadership. It was controversial whether or not they were allowed to negotiate with the Nazis. Some were in favour of the idea: if the fascists wanted to expel the Jews, the Zionists could take the opportunity to bring them to Palestine – a basis for agreements which had applied before the 'Final Solution' began and which applied once more during the final phase of the war when Nazi leaders such as Himmler wanted to maneuver themselves into a favourable position for the period after the military defeat. Some 'right-wing' Zionists even saw common ideological positions with the Nazis. Others, however, such as Jabotinsky, refused to enter into any contact.

Some of the Zionist politicians, on the other hand, were already so entrenched in diplomatic and quasi-state actions that they were unable to speak frankly out of consideration for the Allies. Under no circumstance did they wish to risk losing the Allies' support for the creation of a state after the war nor give momentum to anti-Semitic clichés by exerting excessive pressure. In addition, it was a shock for them that the Zionist movement had failed to a certain extent: despite the insight that anti-Semitism would have to end in a catastrophe, the movement had not succeeded in inducing the threatened Jews to leave in time. How was the State of Israel to be legitimized and built? Some politicians thus felt induced to work to rescue primarily those Jews that could be of use in the construction of the state. Others regarded the Allies' failure to open their borders to Jewish immigrants and to do everything during the war to prevent genocide as an argument to finally gain allied consent to create a Jewish state.

With their behaviour, Zionists were caught in the horns of a dilemma because most members of their families had also fallen victims to the Shoah. Perhaps this was a contributory factor to explain why more often the unspoken as well as open reproach was heard that the European Jews should have listened to the Zionists and emigrated to Palestine. But instead they had let themselves be led 'to the slaughter like lambs'. These words, following Isaiah, that had led the residents of the Vilna ghetto to revolt[1] towards the end of 1941, were now being used more and more to justify their own actions and later were even used against those that had survived. In conjunction with the image of the 'muscle Jew', as model of the man who was to build the State of Israel, this led to a certain contempt for the non-Zionist pattern of life while at the same time to the mystical transfiguration of the heroic ghetto fighter and pioneer in Erez Israel.

The Shoah thus blended together all Jews of the world, making them understand the necessity of creating a state of their own and standing up for it. At the same time, the Shoah also triggered processes of repression within the Zionist movement and in Israel, which burdened the memory and rendered the orientation of Zionism more difficult once the state had been created.

---

[1] Tom Segev: Die siebte Million. Der Holocaust und Israels Politik der Erinnerung. Reinbek 1995, p. 152.

Priska Gmür

'It Is Not up to Us Women to Solve Great Problems'

The Duty of the Zionist Woman in the Context of the First Ten Zionist Congresses

'The ladies are of course very honoured guests, but will not take part in the vote.'[1]

Thus reads the response of Theodor Herzl to a question by the congress participant Dr. Moriz Kornblüh, as to whether or not women attending the First Zionist Congress in 1897 were eligible to vote as well. At the Second Congress in 1898 thus, the sources reveal clearly, women were able to be elected as delegates and were fully entitled to vote at the meeting.

Even though at this point in time, the issue of women's suffrage was a very topical and much discussed issue in many countries, it was not undisputed even amongst advocates of women's rights. At the international level, women were only fully enfranchised in New Zealand and in some states in the United States, and enjoyed a limited suffrage in Spain. In religious communities, equal rights for women with respect to votes and voting was by no means a matter of course. In Germany, for example, women were granted suffrage both in Protestant as well as in the first Jewish communities in 1919, at the same time as it was introduced at the federal level in the Weimar Republic. The question therefore arises as to how female Zionists were able to obtain such formal equality at such an early date and what impact this had on the participation of women at the subsequent congresses as well as on the cooperation of women and their ranking in the Zionist movement.

Miriam Schach [1867–1956], a Zionist born in Lithuania but especially active in France and a professor of modern languages and art, interpreted in her speech before the Tenth Congress in 1911 women's suffrage as a present that men had given women,

'without our striving for it, without quarrel or controversy, whereas elsewhere it has to be fought for so bitterly and harshly, up to now, with only questionable success.'[2]

When looked at from this perspective, the gratitude shown toward male Zionists and the passivity attributed to the women are striking. In point of fact, no major confrontations or conflicts are known. Nonetheless, an interpretation of Zionist women's suffrage merely as 'a present from the men' might fall too short of the mark. The Zionist Organization was at that time a young movement with insignificant numbers, particularly in western Europe and as such reliant on each and every member. The equality of women thus also served to boost membership. In addition, the cultural Zionist approach placed great importance on the revival of the Jewish tradition as part of a strong Jewish national consciousness. Hence, it was virtually impossible to bypass women in their capacity as the traditional 'guardian of the Jewish

---

[1] Zionisten-Congress in Basel (29., 30. und 31. August 1897). Officielles Protocoll. Vienna 1898, p. 115.

[2] Stenographisches Protokoll der Verhandlungen des X. Zionisten-Congresses in Basel vom 9. bis inklusive 15. August 1911. Berlin, Leipzig 1911, p. 220.

house'. Zionist suffrage thus proves to be at least a Janus-faced present: exceptional rights for this time on the one hand and – more or less consciously – taking women into service for the Jewish cause on the other. Perhaps the entire issue was also influenced by the fact that particularly women deeply felt the crisis of the Jewish self-image and saw a possibility in Zionism to combine the reflection upon the core of Jewry with modern perspectives. It was possible to utilize this attitude for the Zionist cause.

There are no reliable records about the number of female delegates who attended the congresses, since not all minutes were accompanied by a list of participants and even the lists that do exist are only relatively informative. The proportion of women among the delegates can be estimated at two to five percent for the first ten congresses that took place between 1897 and 1911. Based on the total number of delegates, which fluctuated between 250 and 500, the absolute number of women in attendance was thus very low. The minutes that cover the female representatives in committees and boards appointed by the congress do provide more detailed information. For instance, the American Zionist Emma Gottheil was elected to the cultural committee at the Second Congress in 1898, although only at her own insistence,

'that she had found it only right that a woman had a seat and vote in the commission that was responsible for dealing with Jewish national education'.[3]

In addition, the Romanian Zionist Rozia Ellmann was a member of the scrutiny committee. Although the number of positions held by women doubled in 1899, it soon dropped again shortly thereafter. One or even no female representative was the rule. In the larger and the restricted Action Committees, the actual leadership bodies of the Zionist Organization, there were no female representatives during the observed period. These were male committees that were always composed in similar ways, into which it was extremely difficult for women to intrude and most likely they did not even strive for it.

With the exception of the Fifth Congress, all minutes contain requests from women for leave to speak. However, the motions mostly turned out to be very brief: the proportion of female votes usually amounted to less than one percent based on the extent of the minutes. Women spoke relatively frequently on topics which arose directly in the course of the congress. Comments on general Zionist issues, by contrast, were less frequent, although they were characterized by a very cogent and self-assured argumentation. The longest contributions were made on topics pertaining to women themselves and their roles and duties within the Zionist movement. This included the speech given by Miriam Schach at the Tenth Congress in 1911, which caused the Zionist women's work to appear as an official topic on the congress agenda. But even before that time, women and sporadically also men had spoken again and again on this topic. One of the first recorded sources is a proclamation read by Rozia Ellmann and signed by twelve women, delegates and guests at the Second Congress in 1898. This proclamation clearly displayed the second side of the 'donated' women's suffrage, that is the duty of women 'to devote all their strength to promote this great work' expressly derived from the suffrage issue. Jewish women were also able to see their husbands and children suffer. It was the 'good Jewish way [...] practiced by our forefathers [...]' for her to stand by her husband without a moment's hesitation.[4] The ideal female Zionist thus appears as the true companion of the man on whose side she fights for the common Jewish

---

[3] Stenographisches Protokoll der Verhandlungen des II. Zionisten-Congresses gehalten zu Basel vom 28. bis 31. August 1898. Vienna 1898, p. 36.

[4] Protokoll des II. Zionisten-Congresses, p. 239.

1 Group picture with women in front of the Stadtcasino, probably taken at the Sixth Zionist Congress in 1903.

cause, thus for an almost familial cause, as she maternally empathizes with the suffering and selflessly feels solidary with them – a pattern of argumentation which is encountered over and over again in the voting of other women. After an initial – rather euphoric – phase between the Second and Fourth Congress, there was silence, which was only broken after the Eighth Congress in 1907 when both men and women agreed that women had done too little for Zionism. Only Theodor Herzl had already criticized the passivity of women as early as 1901 in a speech held at the Vienna Women's Club:

'What are women for Zionism? I will not say: nothing. What could they be, what should they be? Perhaps everything. And if our agitation finds the right paths, then this is also what it will have to come to.'[5]

The consistency with which the demand for the foundation and networking of Zionist women's associations appears at the congresses seems to confirm this analysis. The women who had signed the proclamation of 1898 regarded themselves as 'a provisional committee for creating Zionist women's associations wherever there are Jewish communities'[6] and called upon all Jewish women to join these associations. In a motion made by Emma Gottheil at the Fourth Congress, a similar concern was expressed, underscored by the desire for an international exchange of information. At the Tenth Congress, finally, the women's association that had convened there reiterated the same demand, combined with an appeal for moral and financial support on the part of the congress and the desire to establish a central

[5] Theodor Herzl: Die Frauen und der Zionismus. In: Leon Keller (ed.): Theodor Herzl's gesammelte Schriften. Berlin 1905, p. 195.

[6] Protokoll des II. Zionisten-Congresses, p. 240.

headquarter for Zionist women's work. Besides similar demands, all of these motions had in common that the women preferred to set up an organizational network of their own rather than intensifying their work in already existing, male-dominated Zionist groups. The efforts of the Zionist women were not entirely unsuccessful. In 1907 the 'association' was founded at the Eighth Congress, and in 1912 the 'Hadassah' was called into being as an international Zionist women's organization in the United States. The 'Women's International Zionist Organization', which included women's organizations from all over Europe, Australia and Canada, was established in London in 1920, and was certainly delayed by World War I.

The proclamation of 1898 had circumscribed the responsibilities of the Zionist women in four principal areas: youth education in the Jewish spirit and Jewish religion, co-operation on the 'restoration and conservation of our national heritage'[4], watching over Zionist ideals within the family as well as the convincing of 'anti-Zionists'. Therefore the Zionist woman should be first and foremost a mother and teacher of her children and thus also conveyor and guardian of Jewish religion and tradition. This implied, as was frequently demanded, that Zionist women should learn Hebrew. In a speech given during the Fourth Congress in 1900, Emma Gottheil also called upon women as cultural ambassadors and guardians, and sharply demarcated women's duties from those of men:

'I hope that we will make the old traditions the centre of our lives again. Yet we know that it is not up to us women to solve the great problems, we leave this to our husbands and brothers, but as long as we maintain the atmosphere, the religious atmosphere, that cannot be separated from our nationality, our duty is perhaps no less important than that of men.'[7]

Emma Gottheil restricted women's activities to the religious and domestic areas even more strongly than the proclamation of 1898. However, this division into private as being the sphere of women and public as that of men has an absoluteness about it that makes it an upper middle class rather than a traditional Jewish notion of male and female roles. Theodor Herzl said something similar in his aforementioned speech. He argued – without giving any concrete reasons – that it was worthwhile for women to become involved with Zionism because this was in the interest of their children's future. In addition to this traditional maternal-domestic function, Zionist women were repeatedly made responsible for acquiring the financial means. The leading role of women in collecting bank subscriptions for the National Fund was thus willingly emphasized, and in an article bearing the title 'Jewish Women' that appeared in the Zionist newspaper 'Die Welt' in 1903, the author J. Upřmny concluded:

'The Jews of the Golus purchased Palestinian soil so as to rest their heads on it when they died. The National Fund intends to purchase the same soil so that Jews can tread on it in order to live. There is the workplace of our women.'[8]

While the respective roles did not change, the assessment of the work done by Zionist women did change in the course of time. The criticism of female passivity and inactivity became louder and even female voices joined in. In the introduction to her paper on Zionist women's work, Miriam Schach, for example, commented in 1911 that women had not done too much so far and what little they had done was hardly obvious. However, she did not spare male Zionists from criticism either:

[7] Stenographisches Protokoll der Verhandlungen des IV. Zionisten-Congresses in London. 13., 14., 15. August 1900. Vienna 1900, p. 55.

[8] Die Welt, 11. Dezember 1903, p. 3.

'If you, gentlemen, ask: What have Zionist women accomplished?, then I would like to return the question: What have you, Zionist men, who should have been our initiators, done to allow us to become more efficient?'⁹

Moreover, she stigmatized the male condescension concerning female issues:

'If we want to be serious about women's work, then I must ask you gentlemen to wipe those smiles off your faces and stop taxing your wives with inefficiency.'¹⁰

Four years earlier, at the Eight Congress in 1907, women had already voiced similar criticism when the Eastern European Zionist Kritshevsky denounced the gaping void that frequently emerged at the congress when cultural questions were to be discussed. By combining cultural and women's issues, she demanded:

'You will just have to give us some attention. You must first win women over to Zionism and create for them a new relationship to culture [...] I also protest in the name of our children: They are withdrawing from us, since we have lost the right words to talk to them or perhaps we have not even found them yet.'¹¹

The claim to leadership of men was never questioned, not even by active female Zionists. Rather, they criticized that the men had not proved equal to this role and had not taken the women seriously enough or supported them. Nor was the clear division of roles between the sexes called into question either. The principal responsibility of the Zionist woman remained her own Jewish household and the care of the children. In particular, the argumentation presented by Miriam Schach seems at first glance to contradict her biography and the behaviour of this very self-assured, professionally active and successful, unmarried woman. The question arises as to how many tactics might have been concealed behind the argumentation and role patterns of many female Zionists. And the supposedly contradictory nature resolves at least in part when we set aside our current conceptions of equality and emancipation that have been molded by the new women's rights movement at the end of the 20th century and consider values like domesticity and motherliness from that time and in those surroundings and not regard them as negative concepts from the very outset.

---

[9] Protokoll des X. Zionisten-Kongresses, p. 224.
[10] Protokoll des X. Zionisten-Kongresses, p. 227.
[11] Stenographisches Protokoll der Verhandlungen des VIII. Zionisten-Kongresses im Haag vom 14. bis inklusive 21. August 1907. Cologne 1907, pp. 335–336.

Ruben Frankenstein

Zionism: Only Something for Men?

The Forgotten Contribution of Zionist Women: The Example of Betty Frankenstein

Although Zionism viewed itself as an emancipatory movement, it was just as unwilling to allow women to participate in decision-making bodies as was every other institution around the turn of the century. A look at the picture gallery of the Zionist Congresses makes it clear – the few women there stand out with their broad, fashionable hats. Particularly revealing is the picture of the delegates who attended the First Zionist Congress, which was done after the conference: on which women are depicted in the bottom row, as if they only served the purpose of decoration.

Sholem Aleichem, the well-known Yiddish-writing humorist, who attended the Eighth Zionist Congress in The Hague in 1907 as a delegate from the US, described the situation exactly:

'The Jewish parliament would be poorer without the presence of these fine, truly Jewish women, these trustworthy ladies of the daughters of Zion, whom the goyim would cast an envious look at if they could. God created them (the women, not the goyim) to adorn and sweeten our lives. Dressed in a simple but tasteful manner, they looked like lovely flowers in a Jewish garden and imparted to the whole congress a special charm. It is a pity that not one of them can or would like to stand up on the podium and speak ...'[1]

Competent and capable women, who sought to achieve self-fulfilment in Zionism, had to restrict themselves merely to those fields typically assigned to women, such as social work, working with the youth or charitable activities, and this also was to be done in women's organizations specially established for this purpose, the most important of which were 'Wizo' and 'Hadassah'. Recha Freier, who initiated the 'Aliyat Hanoar' for the transportation and deliverance of Jewish youth to Palestine, stands out as an example and at the same time as an exception.

Betty Frankenstein went another way. She was the daughter of a teacher and school principal and was born on March 7, 1882, in Krone on the Brahe near Bydgoszcz (Poznán). In 1900 she went to Berlin where her older brother had already set up a medical practice. When Dr. Arthur Hantke established the central office of the Zionist Association for Germany in the spring of 1904, the 22-year-old Betty Frankenstein applied for the position of the first and for the time being only secretary. Although somewhat physically disabled, with an iron will she lent her support to the Zionist idea – against her family's wish – which filled her with enthusiasm. For nearly 35 years she was the right arm of different presidents: Arthur Hantke, Alfred Klee, Felix Rosenblüth, Alfred Landsberg, Kurt Blumenfeld and Siegfried Moses.

'Officially she was the administrator of the central office of the Zionist Association for Germany and the director of the publishing house which issued the "Jüdische Rundschau". But she was much more than an "office employee". With profound interest she followed the development of the movement and its trends. She had very definite views of her own and used her expert knowledge in judging people and opinions. However,

---

[1] Scholem Alejchem: Ajndrukn fun zionistishn kongress, 1907. Translated from: Oyf wos badarfn jidn a land? Tel Aviv 1978, p. 254.

like her esteemed boss Hantke she knew that the cause stood above people and opinions, a cause which everyone was committed to serving.'[2]

'Chairmen and presidents came and went, but Betty remained. For decades all circulars bore her signature. She knew what a good organization should look like, and she acted accordingly. The men often discussed and analyzed until the early hours of the morning. Betty ran the organization with a firm hand and outstretched arms. That was why Meinekestrasse in Berlin, where she and the offices moved to from Sächsische Strasse, was called a matriarchate.'[3]

In October 1910 she additionally took over the administration of the 'National Fund' and of the publishing house of the 'Jüdische Rundschau', which together with the editor Robert Weltsch she developed with great ability. She was the hub of a complicated organizational apparatus. She participated in a lively exchange of ideas with the active members of the Zionist movement in Germany, and at the same time for numerous people she was a person to confide in, with an open heart and an open ear. Thus, for over 15 years she maintained a close friendship with Ernst Toller, whom she served, so to speak, as a sister confessor.[4]

In the years of the impending catastrophe Betty Frankenstein was besieged from all sides by people in distress. She did everything she could, but after the Zionist Association for Germany was dissolved in the wake of the pogrom night of 1938, she herself was powerless to act and was not able to save three of her four siblings, whom she had warned in the previous years, from the closing trap of Nazi terror. When she bid farewell to her desk at Meinekestrasse 10 in Berlin and moved to

1   Betty Frankenstein together with Robert Weltsch (middle), the editor of the 'Jüdische Rundschau', and Arthur Hantke, the president of the Zionist Association for Germany.

Palestine herself, the history of Zionism in Germany came to an end as well. Having reached the actual objective of her work, in Erez Israel, because of her forced retirement she was now condemned to an idleness that was foreign to her and difficult to cope with. She spent the last 22 years of her life in Jerusalem, where she was sustained by her memories of the past, which unfortunately she never divulged. She died on July 5, 1960, on a flight from Tel Aviv to Munich.

---

[2]   Richard Lichtheim: Die Geschichte des deutschen Zionismus. Jerusalem 1954, p. 155.
[3]   From the obituary of Benno Cohn. In: Mitteilungsblatt. Wochenzeitung des Irgun Olej Merkas Europa, Nr. 29 of 15 July 1960, p. 3.
[4]   About one hundred of his very personal and in part very detailed letters to her can be found in the Deutsche Literaturarchiv, Marbach. This is the most intensive correspondence that was left by the expressionist dramatist and radical socialist.

Claudia Prestel

'Strong, Courageous Women and Loyal Jewesses!'

Image and Role of Women Zionists in the Early Years of the Building-Up of Palestine

When Theodor Herzl asserted that the Zionist movement was the first major political movement that granted women complete equality, he created a myth which has endured until today. There is no doubt that the Zionist movement adopted a different attitude towards women than had previously been customary; after all the Second Zionist Congress of 1898 introduced the vote for women. This, however, by no means meant that the emancipation of women had been achieved. On the contrary, the myth of emancipation was misused to blame women for the failures of the movement, and they were accused of being interested only in rights without showing the willingness to acknowledge the duties associated with these rights.

The few women who joined the Zionist movement in the early years did so for a variety of reasons. In the cases of Emma Gottheil and Rebekah Kohut Herzl's personality was decisive. The sociocultural origins played an important part. Women as different in both character and background such as Henrietta Szold, the founder of the 'Hadassah', the Women's Zionist Organization of America, or Manya Shochat, pioneer of the Second Aliyah, did not feel drawn to Zionism for the same reasons. For many women the liberation of the Jewish people came first and not their personal liberation. Women who emigrated to Erez Israel, above all those of the Second and Third Aliyah from 1904 to 1914 and 1919 to 1923, had already ceased to fit into the traditional women's role model in their countries of origin, Russia and Poland, but were confronted with it after their immigration.

Women Zionists were principally active in women's movements. Even female members of the socialist 'Hapoel Hazair' – 'The Young Worker' – justified this with, in their opinion, different domains for men and women. Male members, they thought, had to fulfil important political duties, while work within the microcosm of the home was the task of women. If feminist research stresses that women's organizations were an expression of female autonomy, this argument does not necessarily stand up to close examination in the case of Zionist women's organizations, since the women here considered their own work to be less important than the Zionist men's enterprises. As far as the male leadership was concerned, there was certainly a lack of understanding for the 'special female [...] tasks for the reconstruction of Palestine'.[1] The Zionist women's associations can be defined as organizations which, although they extended the domain of women, nonetheless never questioned the traditional division into domains of men and women. In the official ideology, however, the domain of women was really of considerable importance. For this reason several Zionist women felt that the success of the movement was dependent on the woman's role. Miriam Schach, for example, wrote:

---

[1] Jüdische Rundschau, No. 2, 1925, p. 16.

1 Women building a road.

'The woman will either make her house – as also your house, gentlemen – into a Jewish house, or its Jewishness will diminish. Either a woman will make her children thorough Jews, or they will sooner or later become non-Jews.'[2]

The tasks of Zionist women's organizations included the social and cultural work. The 'Association of Jewish Women for Cultural Work in Palestine' – 'Cultural Association', which was founded in 1907 – set up schools teaching how to make lace in Jaffa, Jerusalem, Tiberias and Safed as well as workshops for embroidery. They were meant to give women and girls, most of whom were Sephardic, a source of income and at the same time an understanding of European culture. In general the training of women played an important part in preparing for the migration to Palestine. The first attempts of the Cultural Association to open up agriculture as a profession for women were continued by the 'Women's International Zionist Organization' – 'Wizo' – founded in 1920, for which the regeneration of the Jewish nation depended on Jewish women turning to agriculture. The women engaged in social work were members of the middle class, and only very few of them thought of emigrating to Palestine themselves. With practical work for Palestine – such as the founding and supporting of schools of domestic science, girls' farms, embroidery workshops – women in the Diaspora could also claim a share in the building up of Palestine. This was declared to be their pioneering work and defined their identity. For the women living in Palestine, on the other hand, this help seemed essential in order for them to be able to work in agriculture – the dream of all the women pioneers of the Second and Third Aliyah. The financial support created jobs and a basis for their livelihood, which made it possible for the immigrants to remain in the country. The women's organizations could hardly count on the help of the Zionist organizations. People smiled at the attempts made by the Cultural Association in agricultural training – such as the creation of the agricultural training farm for girls in Kinneret in 1911. When, during the First World War, the farm in Kinneret, which had meanwhile become successful, was threatened with closure, the Jewish National Fund even refused help, in spite of a resolution of the

---

[2] Stenographisches Protokoll der Verhandlungen des X. Zionisten-Kongresses in Basel vom 9. bis inklusive 15. August 1911. Berlin, Leipzig 1911, pp. 225–229.

2   Washday at the agricultural training farm for girls in Kinneret.

Tenth Zionist Congress to support the Cultural Association's work.

Although training in agricultural work was a step to make women do a job that was consistent with the Zionist ideology, it was not planned to allow them to work as independent farmers. They were rather intended to support their future husbands. The undertaking was thus in the interest of men and the new society and was less thought of as part of women's new independence. Moreover, the training farms did not only give women training in agriculture, but over the course of the years instruction in housework and cooking gained priority. Even a pioneer like Hanna Maisel-Schochat, the founder of the agricultural training farm for girls at Kinneret, defined the girls' main task as 'principally housekeeping'.[5] The training in housekeeping did, of course, not promote equality, but reinforced the gender division of work. This met with vehement opposition from most of the pioneers of the Second and Third Aliyah, who came from Eastern Europe. They protested against a gender-specific division of work and tried to earn their livings in 'men's' jobs – in agriculture, road construction and house building. After the first attempts had failed, the women joined together in 'Kwutzot', in 'groups', and refused men's help. They understood all too well that physical – so-called productive work – was the prime condition to be an equal member in this new society. And finally the country's leaders were also recruited from the productive group. Those who were occupied with unproductive work such as housekeeping and child rearing on the other hand could not claim the same share in the building up of the country.

Various methods were selected to convince the pioneers that the gender-specific division of work was the right thing. Otto Warburg, for example, maintained that to work as a home help, a maid, a cook or a nanny honoured the young women just as much as to work in agriculture or road building, and for Salman Schocken the economic upturn in the country was dependent on the willingness of the women to accept the role attributed to them. He argued that only if women were prepared to use their energy in the workers' kitchens would Jewish workers be in a position to compete with the cheaper Arab labourers. Some socialists, on the other hand, put forward ideological arguments. For real 'halutzim' – 'pioneers' –

---

5   Das Jüdische Echo, 1918, p. 495.

the benefit of the cause was more important than personal interests. The community thus decided on the fate of the individual. In the case of women this meant that they only served the Jewish people most effectively in the domain of women. The division of labour according to gender-specific principles thus appeared to be also a socialist conviction. The women's attempt to find new areas of work was criticized as being egoistic, and they were accused of lacking the 'true' halutz spirit. Entering into the men's world was considered to be unnecessary, as sufficient work was available for women within their own domains. It was not necessary for women to find personal satisfaction in the work itself but in bearing in mind the results. Women should create the atmosphere which would make it possible for the 'halutz' to build up the country and to find satisfaction in his work. The ideal pioneer was felt to be the one who did not go beyond the 'natural' boundaries, was 'intelligent, serene, industrious, expert in her work, serious' and dedicated herself 'lovingly and devotedly' to gender-specific tasks.[4] Women, on the other hand, who wanted to force their way into the so-called productive areas of men's work were felt to be obstacles on the way to the building-up of the country, since they caused an 'unnecessary sacrifice of money and people'.[5]

Several reasons can be found for this attitude. In the new society work associated with the land was the entrance ticket to this society and its leaders – and women were to be excluded from it. Furthermore, the unpopularity of 'unproductive' occupations resulted in a lack of workers, since the idea never occurred of sharing the yoke of the 'unproductive' tasks in the household, kitchen, laundry and kindergarten between the sexes. With the increase of immigration the leaders of the Yishuv saw themselves obliged to find a solution regarding feeding the workers. Workers' kitchens were to provide healthy and warm meals at reasonable prices. Thus the slogan 'the building-up of Palestine begins in the kitchen' became popular, which might have been true, but under the conditions of the time was used to restrict women to their traditional role.

Finally, the ideal of masculinity of the Zionist ideology played a considerable part. The transformation of people was an important condition for the creation of a new society. Thus Jewish masculinity also had to be redefined. Since in the anti-Jewish environment the Jews were thought to be weak, unproductive and feminine, in the new society the Jew or the Hebrew – thus the new terminology – was to be strong as well as productive and the masculine element. A masculinization of the whole society was, however, to be avoided. Women therefore were to continue to play the feminine part assigned to them. Men incorporated the active and intellectual element, women the passive and emotional element. Women often tried to contrast the glorification of masculine virtues with the ideal of the Jewish mother – a function that only they could fulfil – or they propagated the return to traditional values: to be the man's helpmate, as a young woman in the 'Blue-White' youth organization argued:

'We want to become women! Strong, courageous women and loyal Jewesses! And when [...] the time of our people's liberation does come again, then it will find us awake and ready. When you fight, we will soothe your battle wounds.'[6]

The right to do any work – and with it the possibility of taking up any social position in the new society – still had to be fought for.

---

[4] Die Arbeit, 31 May 1919, p. 127.
[5] Hanna Biram: In: Das Jüdische Echo, 1925, p. 820.
[6] Blau-Weiss-Blätter, January 1915, p. 16.

Simon Erlanger

The Zionist Youth Movements

Since the beginning of the Zionist movement, it has been carried and decisively influenced by young people. Zionism strived for changes in traditional Jewish life, or even its abandonment. 2000 years of Diaspora were regarded as the wrong approach. 'Shilat Hagola', the denial of the Diaspora and its culture, was the slogan. Against the spiritual and cultural values of the Diaspora the Zionists emphasized a return to a strong bond between people and country. Influenced by romantic, social revolutionary and socialist ideas from the turn of the century they revolted against existing attitudes, values and the ways of life of the time. More than just 'returning to Zion', they wanted to build up a new society and to create a 'new kind of Jew'. Often the Zionists looked at their Jewish brothers as if they were alienated, unproductive, facing the threat like cowards and without pride, as not actively resisting but passively suffering. Somehow they reflected the anti-Semitic stereotypes of their surroundings. Returning to productive work as farmers and workers, breaking down old structures, the Zionists hoped for a healing of the social evil. Such a movement based on revolutionary changes attracted mainly the enthusiasm of the youngsters, especially in Eastern Europe where standards of living were low because of poverty and persecution of the masses. Many looked for radical solutions.

One of the first Zionist groups was the 'Bilu'. This organization was founded after the pogrom in 1881. They subsequently left czarian Russia and went to Palestine, where they started building up agricultural settlements. The members were aged between 15 and 25 years and it is with them that the history of the First Aliyah, the modern Jewish settlement of Palestine, begins. Influenced by the romantic and idealistic youth culture of the fin de siècle, expressed in works such as 'Wandervogel', many Zionist youth movements were called into being after 1897. Their aim was to give youth a feeling of belonging, educating and moulding them, spreading and teaching the Zionistic philosophy. From this time on, the youth organizations played an important role in all kinds of groups and parties of the Zionist movement, some were even founded on the basis of them. No Jewish community in Eastern or Western Europe was without a large number of opposing and ideologically rivalling youth associations.

The model of the youth association, similar to that of a sport club, was also preferred by non- or anti-Zionist-orientated Jewish groups. The social democratic 'Bund', which was against the immediate return to Zion and approved a Yiddish speaking autonomy in Poland and Russia, had, in 'Future' and 'Skif', two of the biggest youth movements in Poland in the time between the wars. The ultraorthodox and anti-Zionist 'Agudat Israel' was in charge of another major youth movement 'Zeire Agudat Israel'.

The different youth groups had distinguishing characteristics such as their own symbols and items of clothing, for example shirts and scarfs. Sometimes they even chose uniforms as in the revisionist youth movement 'Betar' with paramilitary elements. Every youth movement developed its own forms, hierarchy and greetings, even its own slang which was intentionally taken from new Hebrew and not from Yiddish. By doing so they wanted to express their individuality and differ from their ideological rivals. All of the groups were hierarchically organized into several sections according to country, city and age groups. Youth leaders, the 'Madrikhim', and often even people sent from Palestine, the 'Shlichim', were the head of the organizations. Nevertheless the forms were quite relaxed so that the contours of the different groups mixed. There were fusions, splittings and dispersals or even, due to severe ideological disagreements, refoundations. The scene of Jewish youth groups was constantly fluctuating although certain ideological groups could easily be defined such as the left wing Zionists, the Revisionists and the Religious.

All Zionist youth organizations were supporters of an active and practical Zionism. They preached the emigration to Palestine. Sometimes the members had to contract for emigration. Nearly all groups in Europe had 'Hachsharot' – model farms – to train their members for their work in their old new home. Especially in those Zionist youth movements influenced by socialism only life in the collective co-operative of the kibbutz was acceptable. The aim was to rebuild a new society free of the obligations and fears of the Diaspora.

The youthful, idealistic motivation, the ideology, the political consciousness and the high level of organization led to the fact that during the Shoah the majority of Jewish partisans, resistance and ghetto fighters were recruited from the youth movements. The resistance groups of the ghettos of Warsaw, Vilnius and Bialystok comprised mainly fighting groups of the youth groups of the 'Bund', the 'Hashomer', the Revisionists and other youth organizations of mainly Zionist persuasion. Some of the more important youth groups are listed in the following.

1 Cover of the programme of the 'Vereinigte Übungsstätten jüdischer Sportverbände' (United training sites of Jewish sports clubs), 1925.

Hechalutz

The 'Hechalutz', 'the Pioneer', was founded in 1904. This organization emerged from several precursor organizations such as 'Zeirei Zion', the young people of Zion, or 'Ha-poel Hazair' (Young Worker), and functioned as parent organization. It preached the ideal of the agricultural pioneer life in Erez Israel based on co-operative and socialistic concepts and promoted the founding of agricultural settlements. Like most of the youth groups they prepared their members with agricultural training courses for the work as pioneers in the marshes and deserts of Palestine. They were ideologically influenced by the social revolutionary theories of Aaron David Gordon [1856–1922], who stressed redemption by way of physical work. Famous members of the Hechalutz were mainly involved in the Second Aliyah, such as David Ben Gurion – leader of the Yishuv and first prime minister of Israel – or Jizhak Ben Zwi [1884–1963], later president of Israel. The influence of the Hechalutz can be seen in the year 1927 when 43% of all Jewish workers in Palestine and 80% of the members of kibbutzim had been trained by the Hechalutz and were members of it. The ideological base was exemplary for many years, also for the direction which subsequently became the 'Mapai', the core of today's Labour party. In 1939 the Hechalutz in Europe had 100,000 members.

Ihud Habonim

In 1958 the 'Ihud Habonim' was refounded in Israel as the parent organization of many social democratic youth groups. The 'Ihud' was closely related to the Mapai. Mainly 'Habonim' belonged to it, the 'Bauleute' (the Builders), a youth group originally founded in Germany, originating from three other youth groups, 'Berit ha-Olim' – the 'Alliance of Immigrants' – founded in 1925, 'Kadimah' – 'Forward' – and 'Blau-Weiss' (Blue-White) founded in 1912. Today Ihud Habonim is officially connected to the social democratic 'Kibbutz ha-Meuhad' movement, one of the biggest kibbutz movements in Israel. The official youth organization of the labour party founded in 1926 'Ha-Noar Ha-Oved ve-ha-Lomed' (Working and Learning Youth) also joined the Hechalutz. The suborganization 'Habonim-Drer' is still active in Great Britain, Canada, Australia, South Africa and South America.

Gordonia

In 1923 the 'Gordonia' was founded in Galicia. They supported the establishment of Erez Israel through 'self-commitment'. Their aims were education on the basis of humanistic values and the renaissance of the Hebrew culture. They mainly focused on the lower classes of Jewish society based on the works of Aaron David Gordon. With 'Kwutzot' – 'groups' – the Gordonia also founded settlements in Palestine under British mandate. Later they were absorbed by the Habonim group. In 1939 the Gordonia still had 40,000 members, mainly in Eastern Europe. Members of the Gordonia had leading positions during various ghetto revolts.

Hashomer Hazair

The 'Hashomer Hazair' – the 'Young Guardian' – was established in 1916 through a fusion of the youth groups 'Zeire Zion' and 'Hashomer'. It was also influenced by the ideology and theory of Gordon, Josef Trumpeldor [1880–1920] and Josef Chaim Brenner [1881–1921] – a workers' poet from the Ukraine who wrote in Hebrew. He died as the victim of an Arab attack in Jaffa. The group was also influenced by German youth movements and revolutionary Russian movements. Hashomer Hazair joined Zionism with a pronounced socialism. With its enthusiastic idealism it affected mainly pupils and students. Its members were to be educated for a life in a kibbutz in the state of Israel. The 'Kibbutz ha-Arzi' movement was and is deeply obliged to Hashomer Hazair. The leftist socialist 'Mapam' party, which as part of the 'Merez' alliance occupied a place in the Israeli government until 1984, originated from it. In 1939 the Hashomer Hazair had more than 70,000 members. During the Shoah some of the main organizers of the Jewish resistance emerged from it. The elite troops 'Palmah' also emerged mainly from the Hashomer in the British mandate Palestine long before the foundation of the State of Israel. Apart from Israel, the Hashomer is still active in North and South America and Western Europe.

Betar

The 'Betar' was founded in Riga in 1923 by Zeev Jabotinsky as a revisionist organization. The leader in Poland before the war was Menahem Begin, later prime minister of Israel. The underground fighters of the 'Irgun' and the 'Lekhi', which later formed the party of the 'Herut', the main part of today's 'Likud', were members of this youth movement of the Revisionists. The Betar was antisocialist and was a strong rival of the Hashomer Hazair. The offical aims of the Betar were free immigration to Palestine, self-defending pioneers and Jewish homes on both sides of the river Jordan. In accordance with its ideas the Betar was quite militant. In 1938 the Betar had 90,000 members worldwide. Today it is active in Israel, the USA and above all in France.

2 Flyer for the creation of a training site for Jewish sports clubs, 1925.

Bnai Akiwa

The 'Bnai Akiwa' – 'Sons of Akiwa' – was founded in Jerusalem in 1929 with the involvement of Raw Abraham Isaak Kook [1865–1935], the chief rabbi at the time, as the youth organization of the religious Zionist Mizrachi group. Bnai Akiwa emerged from the 'Bachad' – 'Berit Halutzim Datiyyim', the 'Alliance of Religious Pioneers'. The name came from the famous rabbi of the time of the Bar-Kokhba revolution, whose interpretation of the Torah formed the fundament for the teachings of the Mishna, one part of the Talmud. The structure of the Bnai Akiwa is similar to that of Hashomer Hazair but it stands for a religious ideology according to the teachings of Raw Kook. Originally influenced by socialist ideas and connected to the religious kibbutz, 'Kibbutz ha-Dati', it has constantly drifted towards the right wing over the last decades. In Israel today they are politically closely related to the settlers' movement. The Bnai Akiwa exercises great influence on the state religious education system in Israel and has a network of schools and Talmud high schools ('Yeshivot Bnai Akiwa', 'Yeshivot Hesder') closely affiliated to it. The Bnai Akiwa involves 35% of all Jewish youngsters today in Israel and has more than 100,000 members worldwide.

3 '... your sons come from afar... ' (Isaiah 60:4). 'Aliyah. Immigration to Erez Israel! This is the aim thousands of homeless Jews strive for and which they with reach, despite all obstacles!' Quoted from the Erez Israel calendar of 1939/40.

Youth Movements as Innovation

The youth movements represented an innovation in the Jewish communities with their many charitable and religious societies and associations. In the West they were similiar to the non-Jewish youth groups, where Jewish children could not or did not want to be members, so they returned to their roots as an alternative. In the East they were the bearers and ambassadors of the changes which questioned the traditional Jewish life. Youth movements still exist today. They are well established and it is difficult to imagine an active community life without them. From an instrument of ideological innovation they have turned into an instrument of Jewish education, Jewish socialization, the upholding of Jewish identity in a shrinking Diaspora which is constantly suffering from a loss of substance. For tens of thousands of Jewish youths in Europe, America and also in Israel they are often the only link to Jewish culture or the only place to meet their Jewish peers. In former times the Zionist youth movements were mainly strictly political and bearers of the Zionist ideology, but nowadays things have changed. Emigration to Israel and working as a pioneer in a kibbutz are no longer the main aims. The groups are content with the joint experience in Jewish surroundings, supporting the involvement in the Jewish way of life within the respective communities and the identity-promoting emotional tie to Judaism and to the State of Israel.

Inka Bertz

Culture and Politics in the Zionist Movement

Even before 1897 the question of a Jewish national culture was discussed in Jewish students' associations in Vienna and Berlin or in – little known – magazines such as 'Selbst-Emancipation' (Self-Emancipation), 'Serubabel' or 'Zion'. At the beginning it was not a political, but an ideological and literary subject. The First Zionist Congress changed the institutional framework of this debate. Now their leaders found themselves confronted with the politics of an organized national movement. As this group wanted to represent the entire Jewish people, a new problem arose for the cultural ambitions of Zionism: the question of culture was no longer 'purely theoretical' but a subject of internal party policy. The objects and personalities associated with the 'political cult'– the flag, the person of Herzl or National Fund stamps – produced far less controversy than did the cultural policy. It was the third item on the 'Basle Program' and it was this issue which the movement decided to concentrate on and which promoted, vaguely expressed, the 'strengthening and fostering of Jewish national sentiment and national consciousness'.

To this end, two 'lectures about culture' were held at the First Zionist Congress. Late in the evening Marcus Ehrenpreis talked about modern Hebrew literature and Nathan Birnbaum about 'Zionism as Cultural Movement'. Admittedly the records show that culture was not at all a central concern of the movement, perhaps because they were aware of the potential for conflict which surrounded this subject. Secular Zionists such as Ehrenpreis, Birnbaum and their companions from the student associations 'Young Israel' and 'Kadimah' were influenced by European nationalism. For them, culture was a constituent of the nation. On the other side were the orthodox Zionists motivated by a religious love for Zion. For them culture was part of religion, and a secular Jewish culture was unthinkable. In the following years this conflict recurred at Zionist congresses despite the efforts of the political Zionists to make peace between the parties. They had a neutral attitude towards the culture question and their main concern was the unity of the movement.

These circumstances formed the background for the scandal at the Fifth Zionist Congress, at the end of December 1901 in Basel. The 'cultural Zionists' – the opposition around Leo Motzkin, Martin Buber, Chaim Weizmann, Berthold Feiwel and Ephraim Moses Lilien – had meanwhile formed the 'Democratic Zionist Fraction'. They hoped to find support for their endeavours at the conference. Buber and the illustrator Lilien, authorized to draw postcards of the congress, had organized an exhibition of Jewish artists for the Zionist congress. Martin Buber gave a lecture about Jewish art and Chaim Weizmann spoke about a Jewish university. The fraction filed a petition to the Zionist Organization to provide funding for the establishment of the planned Jewish publishing house. After an argument about the agenda and the scheduling of the voting on their proposal, the 37 members of the fraction temporarily left the assembly room. In the continued process the Congress agreed to all parts of

1 'The Jewish May' by Ephraim Moses Lilien [1874–1925]. Lilien, who depicted here the longing for Zion, was a famous Art Nouveau (Jungendstil) graphic artist and book designer as well as a dedicated Zionist and a cofounder of the 'Democratic Zionist Fraction' at the Fifth Congress in 1901. The Democratic Fraction worked mainly for the strengthening of cultural elements in Zionism.

the petition which did not give rise to any direct expenses for the movement, but did not approve funding for the setting-up of the foundation. The Democratic Zionist Fraction not only criticized Herzl's autocratic leadership style – also as the president of the congress – but was afraid that its demands were rejected because of disproportionate considerations being paid to the small orthodox group.

A development, occurring at this time at the periphery of the Zionist movement, and for which Martin Buber had coined the term 'Jewish Renaissance' was merely touched upon at the congress. Their most important organ was the magazine 'Ost und West', published since January 1901 in Berlin, and whose illustrious circle of editors included Zionists as well as liberal Jews, who were willing to be assimilated. In this publication, besides scientific essays, prose and lyric poetry, 'young Jewish' poetry, translations of Hebrew and Yiddish literature, new Jewish art was also propagated. The first publication of the newly founded 'Jüdische Verlag' (Jewish Publishing House), the 'Jewish Almanac 5663' [1902/03] was aesthetically pleasing and the contents of high quality. This proved that there were many Jewish artists and authors, who although not politically active members of the Zionist movement, were still sympathetic to its cause or at least its cultural ambitions, such as Stefan Zweig, Karl Wolfskehl, Richard Beer Hofmann and Max Liebermann.

The representatives of cultural Zionism demanded an active culture policy using the slogan 'Gegenwartsarbeit' (contemporary work). In their 'educating' bearing, dress and taste, they were closely related to modern artistical movements and the bourgeois reform movements. At the beginning, political Zionists were less than enthusiastic, but also not totally opposed to the ambitions of the cultural Zionists. The conflicts of the year 1903 changed this constellation completely. They undermined even further relations between the two movements which had already been troubled since the Congress in 1901. The cultural Zionists joined Ahad Haam during the debate about Herzl's novel 'Altneuland' (Oldnewland) and were also aligned to the oppositional 'Zione Zionists' during the Uganda conflict. In the years after Herzl's death, power struggles occured, during which the 'practical Zionists' – arising mainly from the Russian 'Zione Zionists' –

2 'Mother Israel' distributing charity to the needy Jews in Palestine. Allegory, around 1910.

gradually gained the upper hand. In contrast to the political Zionists, they demanded the immediate initiation of the colonization of Palestine, independent of achieving 'public law' security, as set out in the 'Basle Program'. During the years until the beginning of the First World War, several projects in educational and cultural fields were realized: a Hebrew gymnasium in Tel Aviv, the Technion in Haifa and the Bezalel Academy of Arts in Jerusalem; other projects, such as the Jewish National Library or the Jewish University were about to be realized in the near future. Many of these activities were realized through close co-operation with non-Zionist organizations.

Since 1910 a younger, more radical generation started to doubt the practical pragmatic orientation of the leading functionaries of the movement. In the Prague student association 'Bar Kokhba', Martin Buber supplied the new orientation for the movement in his 'Three Speeches on Judaism': every individual was asked to make up his mind about the value of the cultural elements himself, and thus be one of the group of 'choosers' rather than one of the passive 'let-it-happen' members and also to overcome the 'duality' of Judaism and 'European culture', by a new 'unity'. Kurt Blumenfeld demanded that every single Zionist should be prepared to personally commit himself, and to develop a 'personal interest' in Palestine. This ideological radicalization and the notion of creating a 'distance' (Kurt Blumenfeld) towards German society was also a reaction born of a general perception of crisis, resulting from the aggressive foreign and internal policies and the increasing anti-Semitic climate, even in intellectual circles. There was also a relationship between the followers of Buber's 'expérience mystique' – as Paul Mendes-Flohr called it – and the contemporary neo-religious, neo-mystical movements which could be found in literary and artistic expressionism.

The subjectification of 'Jewishness', the ideological framework of which had been set out by Buber and Blumenfeld, also had consequences for an aesthetic theory of a Jewish art. The literary debates of 1912/13 made it clear that it was no longer a question of the definition of the term Jewish art but rather of the location of Jewish artists which Arnold Zweig defined as the 'Problems of the Jewish Poet in Germany'. In the discussion between Julius Bab and Ludwig

Strauss in the magazine 'Die Freistatt' (The Refuge) it became clear that the differences of opinion did not only involve the relationship of 'Judaism and Germanism' but were also a question of aesthetic convictions. Because of liberalism Strauss had lost his faith in human culture and a language of art which would be both comprehensible to and an obligation for all. Expressionism had broken up with the same expectations as those which had informed impressionism and parts of Art Deco. Jewish authors of this generation now published their works in 'Freistatt', besides Ludwig Strauss, these included Else Lasker-Schüler, Albert Ehrenstein, Gustav Landauer and Arnold Zweig. Just as around the turn of the century, many young Jewish intellectuals commented on Jewish questions in Jewish magazines without being affiliated to Zionism as a party or even standing close to non-Zionist Jewish national positions as represented by the 'Galut nationalism' of the 'Freistatt'. Representatives of 'old' Jewish liberalism, such as Julius Bab, were forced to take a back seat.

The First World War and the events which followed reinforced this development. Increasing anti-Semitism, 'Jew counting' – 'Judenzählung' – in the armed forces, encounters with Jews in the Eastern war zones, the international recognition of the Zionist Organization and its objectives by the Balfour Declaration, all led to a new orientation of their self-image among German Jews and was the personal turning point for many for whom Buber and Blumenfeld had spoken in 1910. After the war, the revolution and economic crises, the 'ideas of 1910' were linked with political, social and cultural utopias of the time to mould a new Jewish 'community'. The youth movement, the Jewish hostel in Berlin or the 'Jüdische Lehrhaus' (Jewish House of Learning) in Frankfurt,

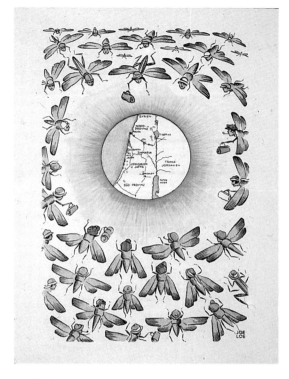

3 'To Swarm out to Palestine', painted between 1925 and 1930.

were organized according to this new plan. This cultural process of change is documented in the magazine 'Der Jude', published by Martin Buber. The huge number of books published in the early twenties also reflects the general re-awakening of interest in Judaism. Now – and without the programmatic emphasis that was prominent in 1900 – it was much more self-evident that literature, theatre, music, architecture and art were integrated into the creation of a modern Jewish culture.

Erik Petry
Kathrin Ringger

Iconographic Aspects of Zionism

Looking at the official postcards of the first eleven congresses, it is possible to recognize some exceptional iconographic features, which can be explained on the one hand by the development of the Zionist world of ideas, and on the other by the design created by different artists. However, whereas biographical information about the artists and the graphic designers is often incomplete – with the exception of Hermann Struck, Heinrich York-Steiner and Ephraim Moses Lilien –

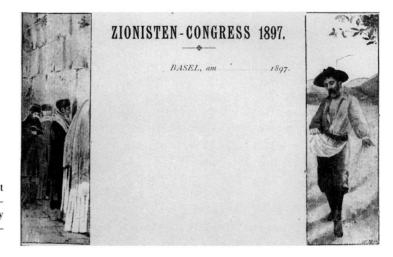

1   Official postcard of the First Zionist Congress, 1897. Drawing by Carl Pollak. Design by Heinrich York-Steiner [1859–1934].

2   Delegates' card of the Second Zionist Congress, 1898. The official postcard has the same motif. Drawing by Menahem Okin.

3 Official postcard of the Third Zionist Congress, 1899. Drawing by Menahem Okin.

4 Official postcard of the Fourth Zionist Congress, 1900.

5 Official postcard of the Fifth Zionist Congress, 1901. Drawing by Moses Ephraim Lilien.

Iconographic Aspects of Zionism

6 Official postcard of the Sixth Zionist Congress, 1903. Drawing by Ranzenhoffer.

7 Official postcard of the Seventh Zionist Congress, 1905. Drawing by Carl Pollak.

continuity and change can be demonstrated by means of the symbolism that was used. This can be illustrated by looking at a few examples.[1]

On the postcards up to the Sixth Congress the motif of the farm worker is kept up, who under the sun of Erez Israel has thrown off the shackles of the Golus and in a freely determined present is working for a better future. Not seldom does the sun form the focal point of the picture. In addition, the depiction of the scene from Erez Israel is always on a higher plane compared with the other motifs in the picture, corresponding with the Jewish idea of a 'going upward', of an 'elevation' – which is the literal translation of the Hebrew

[1] For more detailed analyses compare Michael Berkowitz: Zionist Culture and West European Jewry before the First World War. Cambridge 1993.

8 Official postcard of the Eighth Zionist Congress, 1907. Drawing by Hermann Struck [1876–1944].

9 Official postcard of the Eleventh Zionist Congress, 1913. Drawing by Hermann Struck.

word 'Aliyah' – of life through the immigration to Erez Israel.

Until the Fifth Congress, the religion, symbolized by the supporters of the orthodoxy, also plays a key role, though in a contradictory way, partly still adhering to urban life and the ghetto, but in a way already being in the process of departing. This is particularly clear on the postcards of the Third and Fourth Congress.

After the death of Herzl in 1904, a fundamental change can be observed. The era of the almost mystical symbolism is replaced by depictions focusing on concrete persons and places. Herzl himself is now often used as a motif, and included are also pictures of other Zionist leaders or photographs of the cities in which the particular congress took place. Only the postcard of the Eighth Congress, a stylized view of the city of Jerusalem seems to diverge somewhat from this trend, but only this one time there is an interruption of the general tendency toward personification and concretization.

Jerzy Malinowski

A Jewish National Art
The Ideas of Zionism in the Art of the Polish Jews[1]

Early signs of the Zionist idea appeared in the works of art by Maurycy Gottlieb, the creator of modern Jewish art in Poland. The first fantastic depictions of Jerusalem and Palestine can be seen in his paintings showing scenes from the Old Testament and in the illustrations of Lessing's 'Nathan der Weise'. When painting his self-portrait Gottlieb picked up the thread of the symbolism of Ahasuerus: he depicted himself as the 'eternal Jew'. This artist, who came from Lvov, had connections to the Jewish organization 'Shomer Israel' – Israel's Guardian – founded there in 1868, which linked up with the ideas of the Haskalah, of the enlightenment.

In the eighties of the 19th century Lvov became the centre of Zionist ideas. In organizations and journals, namely the society 'Sjon', the Zionists discussed how an independent national policy was to be implemented. Its most radical advocates included the writer and sculptor Alfred Nossig. His tragedy 'Król Syjonu' – 'The King of Zion' –, performed in 1885, was devoted to the revolt of Bar Kokhba. Martin Buber, Zygfryd Naumberg, Arieh Weinstock, S.B. Buchstab and Eleazar Byk also belonged to this circle. Closely connected with them were the then best-known Jewish Polish artists, such as Samuel Hirszenberg, Ephraim Moses Lilien, Wilhelm Wachtel, Leopold Gottlieb, Boris Schatz, Jakub Weinles and Leopold Pilichowski. They published their paintings and drawings in the Lvov Year Book 'Rocznik Żydowski' ('Jewish Year Book').

In the nineties the symbolic motifs of homelessness and the wandering life of the Jews appeared in the work of these artists – but also of others, such as Henryk Glicenstein, Lesser Ury and Maurycy Minkowski. Besides this they frequently depicted well-known biblical prophets and national heroes. Nossig, for example, created a sculpture 'Ahasuerus', which shows the hero at the moment when he ascended Mount Carmel and saw the land of his ancestors. Other motifs of Zionist iconography depict the Torah and the Holy Book and symbolically express the preservation of the religious national tradition and its passing on to the next generation. In the depiction of scenes the subject of which was the pogroms of Jews some artists – including Pilichowski, Wachtel and Jakob Steinhardt – alluded to Christ as a Jew.

At the same time an attempt was made to develop a national Jewish style in art. Here Lilien performed pioneering work. He developed a graphic style in which he combined Jewish decorative motifs – which were known from synagogues, medieval manuscripts, graves and also from the ancient art of the Middle East – with ancient Hebraic or modern political themes. In doing so he introduced new motifs which symbolically expressed and spread Zionist ideas, for example the star of David or the Menorah.

Zionist congresses were attended not only by politicians but also by well-known artists. The first exhibition in the history of Jewish art took

---

[1] The term 'Poland' refers to the 'old' Poland before the partitions independent of the state borders at the time.

1 Samuel Hirszenberg [1865–1908]: 'News from Argentine', painted 1890.

2 Card designed by Ephraim Moses Lilien for the Fifth Zionist Congress in Basel, 1901.

place in 1901 during the Fifth Congress in Basel. The artists associated with Eastern European Jews who took part were Lilien, Nossig, Ury, Hermann Struck[2], a graphic artist from Germany who felt attracted by the milieu of Polish Jews and also exhibited his work in Poland, Mark Antokolski and Josef Israels. Lilien, who together with Buber was one of the co-founders of the 'Democratic Fraction', published the well-known drawing 'From the Ghetto to Zion' in memory of this Congress. It shows an exhausted wanderer, possibly Ahasuerus, to whom an angel appears with the star of David on its chest pointing out to him the figure of a Jewish farmer ploughing a field

[2] Hermann Struck designed the official postcards of the Eighth and Eleventh Zionist Congress. The cards are shown in the article 'Iconographic Aspects of Zionism' by Erik Petry and Kathrin Ringger.

A Jewish National Art

over which the sun is rising. In this period, the artist also depicted Moses to whom the sun appears with the inscription of 'Zion' in an illustration for Börries von Münchausen's 'Juda'. As early as the 1901 Congress Glicenstein gave the sculpture 'Messiah' to the 'Jewish people' as a present. At this Congress Buber stated in his talk on 'Jewish Art' that although 'special features of the people' could be noticed in the artistic activities only 'the national rebirth' and Zionist ideology could gradually create an independent Jewish art that would contribute to the people's aesthetic education. Buber sought Jewish features in the expressive Oriental colouring and the monumental style of the pictures by Lesser Ury, such as 'Jeremiah'.

The discussions conducted during the congresses influenced the works of many Jewish artists from Poland. One of the first works was the triptych 'Israel' by Maurycy Trebacz: 'Past – Jeremiah Laments the Destruction of Jerusalem', 'Present – Atonement', 'Future – the Dream'. The depiction of the angel with a palm branch in the third scene was meant to symbolize the return to the Promised Land. Wachtel, one of the creators of the visual propaganda of Zionism, painted a picture for David Malz's essay 'Zionism' in the 'Rocznik Żydowski' of 1902 in which Solomon's throne, the Menorah and the Book appear to a young Jew. In the picture 'The Vow' – with Jerusalem in the background – the left hand of a Jew is resting on the Torah and in his right hand he is holding the sword. Wachtel propagated the 'ideology of the deed' and accompanied the development of national symbolism with an active defence of the people's interests, for example in 'Saying Farewell to the Golus'. In a painting by Pilichowski a group of Jews who have returned from the Diaspora gathers around the 'Tree of Liberty' which was planted near Jerusalem.

On account of the discrimination and persecution of the Jewish society in Eastern Europe, namely in the czar's empire, Berlin became the major centre of Jewish art. It is there that the

3   Wilhelm Wachtel [1875–1942]: 'Farewell to the Golus'. Lithography, 1935.

'Association of Jewish Publishers' was formed in 1902, which Lilien, Buber and Nossig also joined. It published a study book entitled 'Jewish Artists'. In 1906 Nossig and Pilichowski mounted the first large exhibition in Berlin, in which over 50 Jewish artists participated, about half of them coming from Poland. Since this time Jewish art has appeared to be an independent theme within art.

The Seventh Congress held in Basel in 1905 accepted the proposal to found the school of fine and applied arts 'Bezalel' in Jerusalem. In the following year the founder of the school, Boris Schatz, went to Palestine accompanied by Lilien. The lecturers of this school included Polish Jews, among them Samuel Hirszenberg, Leopold Gottlieb, Joseph Budko and Jakob Steinhardt. Many

4 'At the Railway Station' painted by Leopold Pilichowski [1867–1933].

Jewish artists from Poland visited Jerusalem and the school. After their return they exhibited views of the city and the Wailing Wall as well as scenes of the life of the Jews and the Arabs. Since 1914 Nossig had been designing the 'religious national' monument 'The Holy Mountain', which was to be erected on Mount Carmel as a symbol of the Jews' return to the land of the fathers. Pilichowski painted not only portraits of well-known politicians – such as Herzl, Nordau, Sokołów or Ahad Haam – but also a great work 'The Opening of the University in Jerusalem'. After the twenties this kind of symbolic representation was replaced by the depiction of scenes of the life of the pioneers in Jewish settlements in Palestine, praising their activities and field work and emphasizing their ethos.

Chaim Weizmann, the president of the Zionist World Organization for many years and later the first president of Israel, said about the participants at one of the Basel congresses that although they represented 30 states their roots and their energy stemmed in the end from Polish Jewry. This statement certainly applies to Jewish art.

Monica Rüthers

'Muscle Jews' and 'Effeminate Jews'

Originally a macho ideal was foreign to the Jewish culture. In the Christian world Jews did not have the right to have a say in political matters and since the Middle Ages usually had no right to bear arms. Consequently physical strength did not have any cultural value. The men's religious erudition, that is spiritual strength, guaranteed the continued existence of the Jewish people. This explains why initially the contrast between the strong, emotionally controlled man and the weak, emotional woman did not arise. Jewish men could be emotional, Jewish women could be physically strong, adroit and efficient. The head was the most important part of the male body, as spiritual strength was the most important feature of Jewish manliness. Men were expected to be pale and lean to show that they studied the Talmud every day. In those days it was regarded as especially distinguished to demonstrate withdrawnness, clumsiness and naiveté in material matters of everyday life. A popular description of a scholar was that he could not tell the difference between the front and the back of a coin.

The wave of modernization in the 19th century also cast its spell on the Jews. Religion became less important in everyday life whereas the significance of commercial success increased. This not only applied to Western Europe but also to enlightened urban Jewish circles in Eastern Europe, which since 1860 had begun to move closer to the centres of the bourgeois culture as a result of the construction of the railways. Although the process of secularization was not concerted, it could not be stopped. The middle-class culture, especially in Germany, had become the Jews' 'target culture', even for Eastern Jewish patterns of life. Admission to the bourgeois society had to be 'earned' by adopting the respective standards. Any hope that integration would come about quickly as a result – especially as equality before the law had been achieved in many countries – proved to be illusory, however. Since the second half of the 19th century, nationalism and anti-Semitism had increasingly dissociated society from the outside but also excluded the 'other' within the society itself. This mainly applied to sexually 'diverging' habits and clashed with the bourgeois image of masculinity based on the body ideal of the ancient world, the 'chivalry' and the military as a domain of men proving their worth. Against this image the pious cerebral Jewish male was deemed to be unmanly, even 'effeminate'. In Prussia, a state that accorded the highest symbolic prestige to the military, Jews were denied access to the officer corps. National and bourgeois ideals were attended to in shooting clubs, fraternities and gymnastics clubs, all 'men's unions' in which men proved to each other their courage and bourgeois ability to fight. In 1896 the German Fraternity Congress passed a resolution that Jews should no longer be admitted to the fraternities, and Max Nordau remarked in his speech at the First Zionist Congress that the Jew 'was still allowed to vote at the election of the people's representatives, but he found himself gently or roughly excluded from the associations and assemblies of his Christian fellow countrymen'.[1]

Jews were thus excluded from the most important arenas of male self-portrayal and the forming of a bourgeois identity.

Medicine and racial anthropology attributed to the male Jew the negative 'female' characteristics of fickleness and weakness, which involve dishonesty, simulation, irrationality and certain 'ugly' physical features: unhealthy paleness, a weak constitution, flat feet and a hooked nose. 'Effeminate' men like the Jews were particularly prone to 'female' illnesses, first and foremost to hysteria.

The experience of being ostracized, despite their having an equal legal status, was distressing and finally led to an identity crisis. One reason why especially assimilated Jews did not necessarily reject certain 'scientific' insinuations was to be found in their identification with middle-class values: as part of the middle-class discourse the images of the Jews were after all a part of the culture to which they ascribed themselves. Hence many endeavoured to integrate these images of the 'Jewish character' into their own ideas. The German Jews, for example, solved the problem in their own way. As 'Western Jews' they put the blame for the negative image of the Jew on the allegedly backward and wild 'Eastern Jews'. Thus they excluded themselves. They considered themselves to be civilized and acculturated Germans of Mosaic faith. The 'Polish' Jews, however, who had fled to the West from the pogroms in the czarist realm since the eighties of the 19th century, seemed to them to be unwashed barbarians in caftans, who spoke an incomprehensible dialect and whose religiousness was considered by them to be irrational. In a dangerous way they personified the German Jews' own past and they were a threat to the Jewish image and the attempts to gain respectability.

The Jews – like other 'minorities' – reacted to the exclusion from the bourgeois 'men's associations' by founding their own associations in which they internalized middle-class values. In 1886 a group of Breslau students founded one of the first Jewish student fraternities, the 'Viadrina', which aimed to impart a new feeling of Jewish self-confidence to its members. Physical training was given priority, as a declared intention was to prove the courage and manliness of young Jews. The ideals and the life-style of the German educated bourgeoisie were held as an example. In other places too, Jewish duelling students' societies were founded which either attempted to outdo the German national student fraternities by imitating 'Germanic' drinking customs and ways of settling affairs of honour or emphasized their Jewish national character. The Jewish students defended their honour:

'It was a rule for our members to return anti-Semitic insults, i.e. to slap the offender.'[2]

The adversary who had his insult returned in such a way then had to ask for satisfaction, which gave the Jew the advantage of the choice of weapon. The Jews were eventually generally excluded from the duelling culture. Physical prowess was also very popular outside student circles. Around the turn of the century the Jewish gymnastics club 'Bar Kokhba' was founded in Berlin, the name of which was directly associated with the bellicose traditions of the Jewish uprising against the Romans and underlined the link between manliness and arms:

---

[1] Zionisten-Congress in Basel (29., 30. und 31. August 1897). Officielles Protocoll. Vienna 1898, p. 16.

[2] Friedrich Solon: Mein Leben in Deutschland vor und nach dem 30. Januar 1933. London 1940. In: Monika Richarz (ed.): Jüdisches Leben in Deutschland. Selbstzeugnisse zur Sozialgeschichte im Kaiserreich. Stuttgart 1979, pp. 435–444, here p. 436.

'Bar Kokhba is the last embodiment of war-hardened, weapon-embracing Jewry.'[3]

An article by Walther Rathenau published under a nom de plume in 1897, in which he describes the Jews as shrill upstarts among the 'genuine' Teutons, provides evidence of hurt self-esteem.

'In the middle of German life an isolated, strange tribe of people, glossily and conspicuously dressed up, of hot-blooded, volatile behaviour. An Asiatic horde on the sand of Mark Brandenburg!'

They should 'take care that in the middle of a militarily strictly educated and reared race' they do not make of themselves 'a laughing stock by walking along in a careless, bent and undisciplined fashion'. He demanded a 'racial accommodation', the aim of which, however, should 'not' be 'imitated Germans, but Jews with a German nature and education'.[4] In 1903 the theses of the 'effeminate Jew' came to their sad and popular climax in Otto Weininger's book 'Geschlecht und Character' (Sex and Character). Weininger placed women and Jews on the same level, denying both of them the dignity of their own personality. In the Jewish gymnastics journal, 'Jüdische Turnzeitung', Max Nordau pointed out that the Jews allowed themselves to be too strongly influenced by the way they were viewed. It was

'for many, even proud Jews a fact requiring no proof that the Jew is physically clumsy, lamentably awkward, deplorably puny, that he had two left hands and was constantly stumbling over his own legs, preferring to stand crooked and bent rather than erect, etc.'

Max Nordau regarded these blemishes as mainly imaginary features and, when they ex-

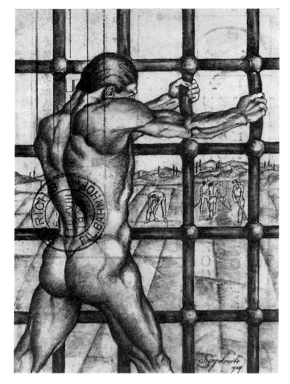

1 Official postcard of the Sixteenth Congress by Wladimir Sagalowitz, Zurich 1929.

isted, as surmountable. He demanded a new 'muscle Jew':

'It is up to every Jew who sees himself as weak or who is indeed weak to develop the muscular body of an athlete.'[5]

The idea was that having a muscular body would lead to the corresponding self-confidence. Neither Walther Rathenau nor Max Nordau succeeded in breaking away from the logic of the 'ef-

---

[3] Max Nordau: Muskeljudentum. In: Jüdische Turnzeitung, June 1900. Quoted from: Zionistisches Aktionskomitee (ed.): Max Nordau's Zionistische Schriften. Vienna, Leipzig 1909, pp. 379–381, here p. 380.

[4] Walther Rathenau: Höre, Israel! In: Die Zukunft, 6 March 1897, pp. 454–462.

[5] Max Nordau: Was bedeutet das Turnen für uns Juden? In: Jüdische Turnzeitung, June 1900. Quoted from: Max Nordau's Zionistische Schriften, pp. 382–388, here p. 385.

feminate Jew' argument and from the evolutionary biological discourse that evaluated people according to their body. The 'muscle Jew', who was to revive the heroism of the Maccabi, became the ideal of both the Zionists and the advocates of assimilation.

The concepts of body and clod, and blood and soil were symbolically joined. The real nation, the healthy people, was at home in the country and in the village. Anti-urban and anti-modernistic impulses run parallel to the history of nationalism. The decadence movement and the homosexual associations at the fin de siècle were said to be at home in the cities that in any case were considered to be unhealthy, and in the dark corners of which all outsiders abandoned themselves to their promiscuous excesses that were a threat to the health of the nation. City life was associated with nervousness, weakness, weariness and mental illness and was a stronghold of degeneration for which the cultural critic and evolutionist Max Nordau coined the term 'Entartung' (degeneration) that was to become popular.[6] The reform movement with its vegetarianism, nudism and the garden towns opposed decadence just as did the youth movement. Out in the country, in the bosom of nature the sinewy, tanned male body was linked to the soil.

The survival strategy of the Jewish people in exile consisted in maintaining their spiritual and scriptural links with the past. The physical body had always been despised. Now it was given a new value. Intellectual, scriptural and religious realms receded into the background. It seems as if the cult associated with the body expressed the longing for a new 'homestead' outside of scripture. The discussion about rendering 'more productive' Jews mainly working in intellectual professions also points in this direction. The 'Garden Town of Palestine' would also make an escape from the town possible and give the 'air people' some ground under its feet.

---

[6] Max Nordau: Entartung. 2 vols. Berlin 1892.

Anatol Schenker

Zionist Press and Publishing Houses in German-Speaking Countries

A Survey from the Beginnings up to the Second World War

The Pre-Zionist and Early Zionist Period

The 'Zeitung aus India', written in Yiddish and published in Amsterdam in 1667, is considered to be the first specifically Jewish newspaper. It appeared only a short time after the earliest general journalistic works and like these developed from irregularly published leaflets. It was published for only a short time. Nearly a hundred years later, a significant impulse emanated from the progressive newspaper 'Kohelet Mussar' – 'The Moralizer', which was founded by Moses Mendelssohn in Berlin in 1750. In the middle of the nineteenth century numerous journals were directed at an orthodox readership. However, most of these newspapers and periodicals were short-lived. The liberal-religious 'Allgemeine Zeitung des Judentums', which was published in Berlin from 1837 to 1922, became a particularly influential newspaper.

The establishment of the first 'Hovevei Zion' societies in the German-speaking countries in the 1880s marked the beginning of a phase during which a large number of newspapers that were orientated towards early Zionism were established but most were short-lived. The periodical 'Der Colonist' (The Colonist), which was edited in Katowice in 1882, is regarded as the earliest publication with a recognizably Zionist background. In 1885 Nathan Birnbaum published the national-Jewish newspaper 'Selbst-Emancipation' (Self-Emancipation) in Vienna which appeared as a monthly publication for eight years. The monthly 'Serubabel', which was founded in Berlin, appeared from 1886 to 1889. Heinrich Loewe, born in 1869 and one of the most-important early Zionists in Germany, established the monthly periodical 'Zion' in Berlin in 1895, which was able to last until 1899 and became an important forum for early discussions on methods and content of the Zionist idea. Reports on the colonies in Palestine alternated with articles of a theoretical nature, as well as with detailed information about the activities of the local Zionist groups that were forming. 'Zion' was one of the most influential predecessors of the two leading Zionist newspapers in the German-speaking countries.

'Die Welt'

In 1897 Theodor Herzl founded the weekly publication 'Die Welt' (the World) in Vienna. In a short period of time it developed to become the outstanding news organ of the early congress Zionism. In order to avoid confrontation with his employer, the 'Neue Freie Presse', Herzl rarely appeared openly in the 'Welt'. He nevertheless maintained a firm hold on things and during the first years monitored the editing as well as the production. Conflicts with the staff editors, who replaced each other in rapid succession were therefore inevitable. Despite this, 'Die Welt' maintained a high standard of journalism in the early phase of publication, judging from the articles which were contributed by the most well-known Zionists of the time. In addition to detailed cover-

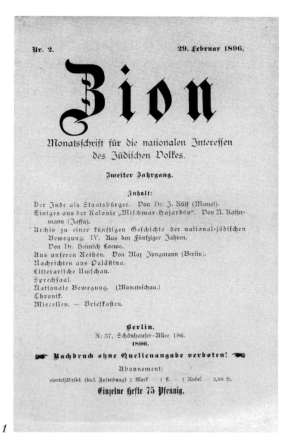

1   Front page of the monthly magazine 'Zion', 1896.
2   On October 17, 1910, 'Die Welt' published a Palestine edition.

age of the congresses, the periodical included articles on the state of colonization in Palestine, as well as on the activities of Zionist groups in the German-speaking countries. Together with a change in the location of the organization 'Die Welt' was also published in Cologne from 1906 to 1911. During these years 'Die Welt' entered into productive competition with the 'Jüdische Rundschau'. After the Zionist organization had moved once more, this time to Berlin, both newspapers were finally published in the German capital after 1911. The last years of 'Die Welt' proved that, in spite of the growth of the movement, the market for two newspapers with a nearly identical orientation was too small. Until the publication of its last issue on July 13, 1914, however, 'Die Welt' maintained its high standard of journalism.

The 'Jüdische Rundschau'

The 'Israelitische Rundschau', which was founded in Berlin in 1895, at first eked out a shadowy existence and compared to the 'Welt' was only able to survive with difficulty. The turnabout was initiated by Heinrich Loewe, who took over the editorial office in 1902 and remained its head until 1910. After the name had been changed to 'Jüdische Rundschau', the publication began to expand and soon became the most important Zionist newspaper in Germany. In the beginning, however, it was critical of Herzl and his ideas. Although both papers focused on similar topics, in time the 'Jüdische Rundschau' proved to be more liberal and modern than 'Die Welt'. Above all it was able to address – mainly by including regular supplements on a variety of subjects related to Jewish-Zionist life – a younger reading public.

At the outbreak of the First World War, the 'Jüdische Rundschau', which now dominated the market, found itself in a difficult situation. Under its new chief editor, Leo Herrmann, the newspaper did not entirely succeed in placing Zionist convictions above the ecstatic euphoria brought about by the war. When the new chief editor Robert Weltsch started in 1919, he took over a difficult job. But within only a few years he managed to give the 'Jüdische Rundschau' back its former glory and guide it to new qualitative heights. During the Weimar Republic the newspaper shaped the image of Zionism in Germany. In these years Weltsch's journalistic far-sightedness gained great respect for the 'Jüdische Rundschau' amongst many non-Zionists and it was even appreciated in non-Jewish circles. After the National Socialists took power, he courageously continued to run the newspaper until November 1938 – despite threats of closure and temporary bans on publication. In that last phase the size of the 'Jüdische Rundschau' was greatly increased, and in the end it even appeared twice a week. Numerous leading articles written by Robert Weltsch were among the most outstanding journalistic works during these years of darkness. His famous essay of April 4, 1933, 'Wear It with Pride, the Yellow Patch', impressed a Jewish reading public, which at that time was feeling extremely insecure and intimidated.

A Survey of Other Zionist Newspapers and Periodicals

Between the First Zionist Congress and the Second World War a vast number of additional newspapers with a Zionist orientation was published. For the German-speaking region particularly the 'Selbstwehr' (Self-Defence) which had appeared in Prague since 1907, and the 'Jüdische Volksstimme' (Jewish People's Voice) which had already been published six years earlier in Brno were of considerable quality. After the First World

3 Special edition of the 'Jüdische Rundschau' commemorating Herzl's death on July 3, 1904.

War both papers focused primarily on the German-speaking minorities in the Central and Eastern European countries which had come into being following the collapse of the Habsburg monarchy. The editors and staff writers included many of the most well-known journalists and writers, such as Robert Weltsch, Siegmund Kaznelson, Franz Kafka, Max Brod and Oskar Baum. The intellectually demanding cultural Zionist monthly 'Ost und West' (East and West) published from 1901 to 1922, and the colonialist 'Altneuland' (Oldnewland) which was later renamed 'Palästina' (Palestine) were some of the most important periodicals but today are hardly known anymore.

Zionist Book Publishers

Numerous books and brochures with a Zionist content appeared in the publishing houses of the newspapers and periodicals mentioned. The most important independent publisher of books focusing on Zionism was the 'Jüdische Verlag', which was founded in Berlin in 1902. The idea for this developed among the supporters of the 'cultural fraction', a group of young dissidents within the Zionist movement who met during the Fifth Zionist Congress in Basel in 1901. Convinced that, because of the priority given to the political work of those associated with Herzl, the cultural element of Zionism was being neglected, the group around Martin Buber resolved to set up a publishing house that would provide a basis for achieving their objectives. In spite of their modest financial means and lack of organizational skills, the 'Jüdische Verlag' managed to publish a number of remarkable books within a short period of time, of which the 'Jüdische Almanach' which first appeared in 1902 was the most significant one from today's point of view. A short while later the publishing house was only able to meet its financial obligations with the help of massive subsidies from the Zionist organization. This caused the founders of the publishing house to leave and led to a restructuring of the programme. Owned in effect by the organization until the beginning of the twenties, the 'Jüdische Verlag' published a series of standard works of early Zionist literature such as various editions of the writings of Herzl, Nordau or Ahad Haam. Later the 'Jüdische Verlag' passed over into private hands but maintained rather close ties to the Zionist executive office, which itself had some important works published by the publishing company as well. The five-volume 'Jüdische Lexikon' and Simon Dubnow's 'Weltgeschichte des jüdischen Volkes' (World History of the Jewish People), both of which were published during the twenties, are regarded as the most important works produced by the 'Jüdische Verlag', which despite censorship by the National Socialists continued to operate in Berlin until 1938.

Other Jewish publishing companies had also been publishing a great deal of Zionist literature since the end of the 19th century. Something which has received very little attention but which is worth noting is the number of small publishing companies, some of which were very tiny, that were primarily engaged in producing brochures and leaflets as a means of stimulating inner-Zionist debate. Youth and student organizations, local groups, dissident fractions and individuals made use of these instruments of propaganda for disseminating their ideas and their concerns. As a rule, established book publishers restricted themselves to publications of general accounts, biographies of prominent Zionist figures and in particular to literature about Palestine and the colonizational work. Among the larger companies were the 'Orient Verlag' and the 'Welt Verlag', the publishing houses 'Benjamin Harz' and 'Siegfried Scholem', as well as the well-known 'Schocken Verlag', all of which by no means restricted themselves to publishing works which were Zionist per se.

Of particular interest to these publishing houses were the accounts of the history of Zionism. The earliest attempt to put together a comprehensive treatment of this topic is the work 'Der Zionismus' written by Joseph B. Sapir and published in Brno in 1903, which has been largely forgotten but is nonetheless still worth reading.

Five years later a 'Zionistisches A-B-C Buch' appeared in Berlin, which was published by the 'Zionist Association for Germany' and which drew considerable attention in many circles. Shortly after the First World War, other important studies followed, of which the works of Adolf Böhm (1920/21) and Nahum Sokolów (1918 in English and 1921 in German) should be mentioned here. In the German-speaking countries Böhm's two-volume work 'Die Zionistische Bewegung' (The Zionist Movement), which was last published in 1935 and 1937 in a greatly expanded and supplemented form, has up to the present remained of great value for doing research on the history of Zionism.

Silke Schaeper

'From Zwickau to Jerusalem': The Cultural Zionist Salman Schocken

1 Salman Schocken [1877–1959], drawing by Wladimir Sagal, 1947.

Historians studying the history of Zionism are familiar with the Central Zionist Archives, which were established in Berlin in 1919 and transferred to Jerusalem in 1933/34 and represent the most extensive collection of source material on the history of Zionism. Not many people know that in the part of Jerusalem called Talbyieh, in the 'Schocken Institute for Jewish Research', there is another important collection of source material on Zionism, in particular on the history of cultural Zionism in Germany. This collection goes back to Salman Schocken [1877–1959]. Born in the village of Margonin, which was located in the former Prussian province of Poznán, Schocken grew up in a large, traditionally religious family in which German was spoken. As a child he attended the heder and learned Hebrew, and after his Bar Mitzvah, he was a cantor in the local synagogue. After only a few years at school, the fourteen-year-old with a hunger for reading and knowledge was forced to enter a training programme in the retail trade against his will, first in small towns in the province of Poznán, and later in Berlin and Leipzig. In his leisure time young Schocken read works on economics, politics and philosophy and became enthusiastic about German literature; his literary taste was influenced by the educational ideal of the German bourgeoisie. Increasingly removed from the Jewish tradition and culture, in 1897 he read Herzl's 'Judenstaat', which was published the year before, and the reports of the First Zionist Congress, both of which made no impression on him. Schocken began a successful business career in partnership with his brother operating a department store in the industrial city of Zwickau in 1901. Increasing affluence made it possible for him to dedicate himself to building up a private book collection, which at the time of his emigration from Germany in 1933 numbered approximately 20,000 volumes.[1]

1 Under the supervision of Dr. Dov Schidorsky of the School of Library, Archive and Information Science at the Hebrew University in Jerusalem, I wrote a Master's thesis entitled 'The History of the Book Collection of Salman Schocken [1877–1959] with Special Emphasis on the Development of the Collection of Hebrew Books' (Hebr.). See also my publications on the subject: Silke Schaeper: Bibliophilie als kultureller Auf-

Around the age of thirty Schocken began to undergo a spiritual return to Judaism, which in the end brought him into contact with Zionism and its special variant – 'cultural Zionism'. Like many other German Jews of his generation, Schocken discovered Hassidism through the works of Martin Buber, which opened up for him the up to then incomprehensible world of the devoutness of ordinary Jewish people, and thus the culture of Eastern Jewry. Schocken joined the congregations of several synagogues in Zwickau and again began to take Hebrew lessons regularly from various private teachers. In 1911 he was one of the founders of the Zionist Committee of Zwickau, which for the first time sent him to a delegates' conference of the 'Zionist Association for Germany' as a representative in 1912. On the occasion of the tenth anniversary of Theodor Herzl's death in 1914, Schocken provided the participants at the delegates' conference of the Zionist Association for Germany in Leipzig with copies of the first bibliophile edition, Theodor Herzl's 'Sechs Kongressreden', which he had printed privately. He organized lectures on Zionism in the region of Saxony, at which he himself was also a speaker. From 1913 to 1931 Schocken took part in all Zionist World Congresses. In Berlin in 1914 he met the Hebrew writer Samuel Joseph Agnon, and became his life-long patron and publisher. In 1915 Schocken was one of the founders of the periodical entitled 'Der Jude', which was published from 1916 on by Martin Buber with his financial support. Imbued with educational ideals, he established a cultural committee at the delegates' conference of the Zionist Association for Germany in Berlin in 1916, with Martin Buber, Moses Calvary, Kurt Blumenthal, Max Brod and Hugo Bergmann on the executive

2   Front page of the first issue designed by Emil Rudolf Weiss [1875–1942].

trag – Die Geschichte der Schocken Bibliothek bis 1939. In Saskia Schreuder, Claude Weber (ed.): Der Schocken Verlag/ Berlin – Jüdische Selbstbehauptung in Deutschland 1931– 1938. Berlin 1994, pp. 347–359; Silke Schaeper: Goldadern wertvollen jüdischen Lebens – Salman Schocken und seine Hebraica-Sammlung. In: Jüdischer Almanach 1995. Frankfurt a. M. 1994, pp. 121–135.

board. As chairman and the driving force of the committee, Schocken undertook his first publishing experiments, among them the publication of textbooks for learning Hebrew for adults and children. At the Twelfth Zionist Congress in Karlovy Vary (Karlsbad) in 1921, Schocken was elected to the newly established Financial and Economic Council and was given a seat on the executive committee of the Zionist Organization. In addition, he became a member of the directorate of the Keren Kayemet Le Israel. In the spring of 1922 Schocken embarked on his first journey to Palestine, which he reported on before various Zionist groups in Germany. He also encouraged emigration to Palestine; thus, the family ran one of the most important agricultural training sites, the farming estate Winkel in Spreehagen near Berlin. In 1925 he took part in the opening ceremony of the Hebrew University in Jerusalem, the development of which he strongly supported in Germany until he emigrated to Palestine in 1933/34. Until moving to the United States in 1940, Schocken remained an active member of the administrative board of the university.

During his life Schocken established three publishing houses: the 'Schocken Verlag' in Berlin in 1931, 'Hozaat Schocken' in Tel Aviv in 1937 and 'Schocken Books' in New York in 1945. The liberal Hebrew daily newspaper 'Haaretz', to which today a number of local publications with a high circulation is affiliated, has been owned by the Schocken family since 1935. Salman Schocken regarded his activity as a publisher as his most important life's work:

> 'If someone were to ask me: "What did you make the best business deal with in your life?" I'm a businessman, I don't know whether I would answer "with the 100 million marks that I earn for selling merchandise each year", or "with the 20 department stores I have built" – perhaps however "with my Jewish writers". I think I would do it.'[2]

Schocken's cultural Zionist ideals are reflected both in the programmes of his publishing companies as well as in his role as an important collector of books, manuscripts and autographs. He opened his Hebrew collections to selected academics, and in conjunction with his library he established his own research institutes – in 1931 the 'Forschungsinstitut für Hebräische Dichtung' (Research Institute for Hebrew Literature) in Berlin, and in 1939 the 'Institut für die Erforschung der Jüdischen Mystik' (Institute for the Study of Jewish Mysticism) in Jerusalem and provided their academic staff members with financial and publishing support.

From 1934 to 1937 Schocken commissioned the world-famous Jewish architect, Erich Mendelsohn [1887–1953], to put up a residential building and a separate library in the heart of Jerusalem. Mendelsohn, whose work in Palestine was strongly supported by Schocken, had already erected department store buildings for him in Nuremberg, Chemnitz and Stuttgart. Today, the library building, with its intact façade, the unmodified layout of the rooms and the original furnishings, is registered as a historical monument, and constitutes the only complete work of art of Mendelsohn that has remained unaltered up to today. Salman Schocken died in 1959. In 1961 the Jewish Theological Seminary of America took over the administration of the library building, together with its 20,000-volume collection of Jewish and Hebrew writings and in 1976 ownership was transferred to them.[3] Schocken's German library containing 30,000 volumes and several hundred of the most valuable printed Hebrew writings of his collection were sold by his heirs mostly at auctions and so distributed all over the world.

---

[2] Speech held by Salman Schocken on the issue of Martin Buber's appointment, at a curators' meeting of the Hebrew University, Lucerne, 8/9 September 1935, Schocken Archives 332/22.

[3] Information about the Zionist material in the Schocken Institute for Jewish Research can be found in the bibliography located in the appendix.

Heiko Haumann

'A Jewish Switzerland Built on Shares?'

Inner Jewish Opposition to Zionism

On June 30, 1924, the Dutch-Jewish writer, politician and lawyer Jacob Israel de Haan was shot dead at close range as he left a synagogue in Jerusalem. De Haan, born on December 31, 1881, was originally a religious socialist and Zionist, before joining the orthodox 'Agudat Israel'. Together with Rabbi Joseph Chaim Sonnenfeld [1849–1932], leader of that organization, he had begun to combat Zionism. He had made contacts with Arab public figures and had attempted to reconcile Palestinians and Jews. He had been not too choosy about his methods or the comments he made in public. The Zionist side had responded with commensurate hostility as they felt their political objectives and their authority to represent all Jews before the British High Commissioner to be endangered. The 'Jüdische Rundschau' had called him a 'betrayer of the people'.[1] What initially no one wanted to believe soon proved to be right: the murder had been committed by two Jews, two newly arrived young Zionist immigrants. A taboo had been broken. It was only much later that it was discovered that the Zionist self-defence organization 'Haganah', established in 1920, had given the order to have de Haan killed, presumably because he intended to disclose their illegal activities. While orthodox newspapers termed him the 'victim of Jewish national fascism', the Zionists succeeded in depoliticizing the issue by pointing to de Haan's homoerotic inclinations; the murderers were never arraigned in court.[2]

During his visit to Palestine in 1932, Arnold Zweig, himself a Zionist, learned more details about the incident and was deeply shocked, although in all likelihood he probably never learned of the execution order put out by Haganah. This is clearly expressed in a letter of January 16, 1933, addressed to Max Brod:

'For sensitive persons in Palestine, it is as Hugo Bergmann wrote to me a few weeks ago: de Haan's murder has at the same time also murdered *our* Zionism.'[3]

---

[1] Quoted from: Hans-Albert Walter: Ein Fall von Vatermord oder Bilanz der palästinensischen Judenheit anno 1932. Eine Interpretation. In: Arnold Zweig: De Vriendt kehrt heim. Roman. Frankfurt a. M. 1995, pp. 265–427, here p. 286.

[2] Walter: Ein Fall, pp. 291–294; Manuel Wiznitzer: Arnold Zweig. Das Leben eines deutsch-jüdischen Schriftstellers. Frankfurt a. M. 1987, pp. 44–48.

[3] Margarita Pazi: Ideologie und Einflüsse in den frühen Schriften Arnold Zweigs und ihr Echo in den Jahren nach 1930. In: David Midgley et al. (ed.): Arnold Zweig. Psyche, Politik und Literatur. Akten des II. Internationalen Arnold-Zweig-Symposiums Gent 1991. Bern et al. 1993, pp. 49–69 here p. 59 (from the Brod Archives). The philosopher Hugo Bergmann [1883–1975] hailed from the 'Prague line of Zionism' and built up the National Library in Palestine starting after 1920. He later became Professor of Philosophy at the Hebrew University in Jerusalem and temporarily also assumed the office of vice-chancellor of the university (Julius H. Schoeps [ed.]: Neues Lexikon des Judentums. Gütersloh, München 1992, p. 68).

Zweig considered the views that had made the murder possible as being also responsible for the bloody clashes that occurred between Jews and Arabs in 1929 and which – particularly after the shock about the massacre of unarmed Jews in Hebron – caused all hopes of reconciliation and peaceful co-existence between the two nations to fade. In his novel 'De Vriendt kehrt heim' (De Vriendt Returns Home), published at the end of 1932, he dealt with the murder in 1924 and the unrest in 1929, and portrayed both events within the same time frame. The representatives of Zionism did not receive the novel well.

The dealing with the events of 1924 and 1929 in Zweig's novel indicates the differences of opinion that existed within the Zionist movement itself. The extremist Zionist Revisionists opposed with increasing vehemence Chaim Weizmann's centristic orientation because this was too moderate for them and not nearly aggressive enough. Chaim Arlosoroff [born 1899], one of the leaders of the Zionist Workers' Party, fell victim to an assassination attempt on June 16, 1933. He had been at pains to reconcile the Jews and Arabs while at the same time anxious to rescue German Jews. There is much evidence to indicate that members of the Zionist Revisionists were responsible, but they too had to be acquitted of the charges due to a lack of evidence. Zweig, on the other hand, alludes to the criticism encountered by those Zionists who espoused reconciliation with the Arab population of Palestine. That applied, for example, to Arthur Ruppin [1876–1943], Hugo Bergmann [1883–1975], Hans Kohn [1891–1971] and Georg Landauer [1897–1954], and others who founded the 'Berit Shalom' – the 'Peace Alliance' – in 1925/26 which championed a binational state of Palestine with equal rights for Jews and Arabs. Many of the 'cultural Zionists' viewed these efforts with sympathy. It is therefore not surprising that Martin Buber and Judah Leon Magnes [1877–1948] continued the work of the Berit Shalom, even though it had become the target of violent criticism owing to the unrest of 1929 and had been forced to dissolve in 1933, and called the successor organization 'Ihud' – 'Unity' – into being in 1942. Although many supporters of this movement held official functions within the Zionist movement, they were marginalized by mainstream Zionism because of their views.[4] Ultimately, these Zionists who not only wanted to carry out mutual developement work with the Arabs, but also tried to realize a social utopia showed their dismay at the turn their movement had taken. Once again, Arnold Zweig is typical of this movement when drawing on Gustav Landauer [1870–1919], he described a

'pure socialism [...] – in small settlements, without a state, emerging from a social, antipolitical spirit, living a life in the socialist spirit with the common possession of land and property and crucial means of production, in a Jewish land, the land of our work and fulfillment [...]'

The future society would resemble a 'leftwing Switzerland' – pacifist, classless, with a variety of cultures, a textbook example for the peoples of Europe who were held captive by nationalist madness and capitalist class schism.[5]

The murder in 1924 also demonstrated how deep the gulf between Zionists and their antagonists in religious Jewry had become. From the very beginning, Hassidim in Eastern Europe had opposed Zionist endeavours, particularly the direction they took after 1881: through them secular tendencies in Jewry became increasingly strengthened and the coming of the Messiah was being delayed. They used sermons and excommunication, and even reports to the czarist au-

---

[4] Arthur Ruppin: Briefe, Tagebücher, Erinnerungen. Ed. by Schlomo Krolik. Königstein 1985, pp. 17–18, 378–422, 435, 464–468, 580; Peter Freimark: Zum Selbstverständnis jüdischer Nationalität und Staatlichkeit in Palästina. In: Helmut Mejcher, Alexander Schölch (ed.): Die Palästina–Frage 1917–1948. Historische Ursprünge und internationale Dimensionen eines Nationenkonflikts. Paderborn 1981, pp. 47–72, here pp. 51–52, 54–55, 58, 67–68.

[5] Quoted from: Walter: Ein Fall, p. 363. See also: Arnold Zweig: Das Neue Kanaan. Eine Untersuchung über Land und Geist. Berlin 1925, section 8.

thorities in an attempt to contain the expansion of Zionism. Numerous orthodox Jews in Eastern and Western Europe reacted just as disapprovingly. In 1897 this attitude found expression in the 'protest' of the liberal and orthodox rabbis organized by the 'General Association of Rabbis in Germany' against the convention of the Zionist congress. This declaration viewed Zionism as being opposed to the 'Messianic promise of Jewry' and the 'sources of religion'.[6]

A number of orthodox Jews did not share this opinion. For them Zionism was as ancient as the ardent desire of the Jews to return to their ancestral home from which the Romans had driven them. In order to strengthen Jewry and to prepare for the return to Zion, a consolidation of all Jews as a nation and a fortification of Jewish identity were exactly what was needed. Zionism would also contribute to bringing back to the fold those who had turned their backs on the faith. The Basel Rabbi Arthur Cohn who belonged to the orthodox tradition was transformed from a sceptic to a conscious Zionist through his contacts with leading Zionists and his participation at the First Congress and through his publications he ensured that the resistance of the orthodox Jews began to crumble. However, he withdrew again in 1911 because for him Zionist politics had become too secular and no longer appeared to be consistent with religious tenets. He joined the 'Agudat Israel' – the 'Union of Israel' – which had been founded in Katowice in 1912 and which was strictly religiously oriented. Only God could revoke the banishment of the Jews and lead them back to Israel. The Agudat Israel tried to unite all orthodox groupings in Eastern and Western Europe against Zionism including the Mizrachi movement. It itself became politically active in various countries and sought recognition as an independent Jewish community. The centres of

1   Rabbi Joseph Chaim Sonnenfeld [1849–1932], one of the main representatives of anti-Zionist orthodoxy in Jerusalem.

the movement were located in Germany, Poland and Hungary. It had also started to become active in Palestine in 1921. Here, the ultraorthodox line gained more and more influence as it was represented by Chaim Sonnenfeld who – in return – was influenced by the work of Chatam Sofer [1763–1839] who had been particularly active in Hungary and had given expression to the quasinational identity of the Jewish people and their aspiration to return to Zion. Because of their very strict interpretation of the Torah, innovation of whatever type was strictly forbidden. The ultraorthodox Jews regarded Zionism – just like emancipation, enlightenment and assimilation – as a mortal danger to Jewry.

After the Shoah, the Agudat Israel decided to participate in the building up of the new state and became involved in many different coalitions. In 1987/88 the orthodox Jews separated from this organization which thus became the party of the

---

6   Yaakov Zur: Die deutschen Rabbiner und der Frühzionismus. In: Julius Carlebach (ed.): Das aschkenasische Rabbinat. Berlin 1995, pp. 205–217. See also his article in this book.

Hassidim. The ultraorthodox Jews remained estranged from Zionism and formed their own separate groupings such as the 'Neturei Karta' – the 'Guardians of the City'. For them, the State of Israel is blasphemy. To do away with it, some of the members were even prepared to co-operate with Palestinian organizations.

In their attempt to fight Zionism, orthodox Jews often joined forces with those whom they actually despised: with liberal Jews who were willing to be assimilated. The 'protest' of the rabbis of 1897 had already made clear that this faction feared that their integration into the existing state would be endangered and their commitment to its national concerns would be called into question. As patriots, they did not want the 'reliability of their national allegiance' to be doubted and did not want to have to endure the accusation – raised again and again until today – of a 'Janus-faced loyalty' between their homeland and the Zionist world movement or the State of Israel. The assimilated Jews reacted not only defensively, but even openly attacked Zionism as being the wrong path. The philologist Victor Klemperer, for instance, who was 'so certain "of his Germanism" [...]', felt disgusted by the 'affinity' and the 'linguistic harmony' he perceived to exist between Herzl and Hitler – despite all basic 'dissimilarities' – as expressed in their demagogy and in the 'kitschy romanticism' of the 'common mental and stylistic bonds of the two leaders'. For this reason, Zionism was no solution for German Jews.[7] As early as 1896, Anton Bettelheim, author and literary critic, had set out the fundamental critical position of assimilated Jews with regard to Zionism in his review of Herzl's book 'Judenstaat'. According to Bettelheim, Herzl's concept would not overcome anti-Semitism and would not resolve the 'Jewish question'. What was important was to combat anti-Semitism wherever one lived and whatever the country was where one felt at home. The path of emancipation would ultimately prove to be right and no insult could possibly rob him of his love for his country. Herzl's project, on the other hand, suffered in Bettelheim's eyes from a 'paucity of ideas' and was 'rich in foolishness', was nothing other than a 'prospectus' for 'a Jewish Switzerland built on shares'.[8]

---

[7] Victor Klemperer: LTI. Notizbuch eines Philologen. 13th ed. Leipzig 1995, pp. 217, 220, 223, 224.

[8] Anton Bettelheim: Der Gründerprospect einer jüdischen Schweiz. In: Beilage zur Allgemeinen Zeitung (München) No. 52 of 3 March 1896, pp. 4–6. I would like to express my gratitude to Dr. Edith Schipper at the Bavarian State Library in Munich for having made this article available to me, as well as to the staff at the Munich Municipal Archives and at the Austrian National Library in Vienna for their help with research.

Zionism Today – An Outlook

Michael Hagemeister

The 'Protocols of the Learned Elders of Zion' and the Basel Zionist Congress of 1897

In January 1917, only a few weeks before the downfall of the Russian monarchy, a book was published in the famous cloister of the Holy Trinity of the Holy Sergei, not far from Moscow, with the apocalyptian title '"It is very near". About that which we do not want to believe but which is so close'. The book had been written by Sergei Nilus [1862–1929], a former land-owner and lawyer, who had spent years in Russian cloisters and made a name for himself as a religiously fanatic author.[1] The book told of ascetics and saints, their visions and prophecies about the end of the world and about their struggle against the powers of darkness. Most of all, however, it told of the conspiracy of the 'church of Satan', the 'Jewish free masonry', against Russia and all of Christianity and of the ever-increasing signs that pointed to the impending arrival of the false Messiah of the Jews, the Anti-Christ. The text, which Nilus had not written himself but which rather had been given to him for publication, covered about 70 pages and appeared to confirm all of the dark prophecies of his book. This were the 'Protocols of the Learned Elders of Zion'.

Nilus was not the first to publish the 'Protocols'. As early as 1903 they had appeared in a right-wing extremist newspaper in Petersburg under the title 'Programme for conquering the world by the Jews'. As the editorial office reported, this was the translation of the minutes of meetings held by the 'World Association of Free Masons and Learned Elders of Zion' in France. They went on to say that the exact origin of these minutes was unknown, but that there be no doubt whatsoever as to their authenticity, as they dealt with the plan to take over the world in a tone typical of the 'megalomania of the "chosen people"'. The intention of Zionism, 'to unite the Jews of the world in one alliance', which would be 'even more strictly run and more dangerous' than the order of the Jesuites, was thus made obvious in all its threatening character.[2]

The 'Protocols of the Learned Elders of Zion', as they are generally called, quote the virtually confessional speech of the chairman – or a member – of the Jewish secret government, in which the methods and aims of the Jewish conspiracy for the destruction of the Christian orders and the building up of the Jewish rule of the world are explained in great detail: in the struggle against throne and altar, the conspirators manipulate the masses, stir up political arguments and labour unrest, spread liberal ideas, corrupt morals and provoke terror and war. The Jewish Empire will grow out of the ruins of the old order with a king from the House of David at its head. He will rule as a benevolent despot over a united, perfectly controlled, organized and contented world.

Between 1905 and 1907, several other editions of the 'Protocols' appeared in Russia. Sergei Nilus

---

[1] Michael Hagemeister: Wer war Sergej Nilus? Versuch einer bio-bibliographischen Skizze. In: Ostkirchliche Studien 40 (1991) 1, pp. 49–63. Ibid. extended: Qui était Sergueï Nilus? In: Politica Hermetica 9. Paris 1995, pp. 141–158.

[2] Programa zavoevanija mira evrejami. In: Znamja, 28 August/10 September 1903, p. 2. Also in: Neizvestnyj Nilus. Vol. 2 Moskva 1995, p. 474.

published them for the first time in 1905 in the second edition of his book 'The Large in the Small and the Anti-Christ as an Apparent Political Option. Notes of an Orthodox Man'. He had supposedly been given them in 1901 by a friend who had died in the meantime. The manuscript, as Nilus stated, came from one of the most influential leaders of free masonry in France; a woman had managed to steal it from him.[3] Even though Nilus' book was widely read in pious circles and was published in several editions, the 'Protocols' did not show any effect initially.

This changed with the edition of 1917, in which Nilus made a new statement regarding the origin of the 'Protocols', which was to determine their reception in the years to come:

> '[...] not until now have I found out, from reliable, Jewish sources, that these "Protocols" are nothing more than the strategic plan to take over the world in order to place it under the yoke of Israel, that fighter against God; a plan which had been elaborated by the leaders of the Jewish people during the many centuries of their dispersion and which was finally presented to the council of elders by the "Prince of Exile", Theodor (?) Herzl, during the First Zionist Congress, which he had called in Basel in August 1897.'[4]

After the October Revolution and the victory of the Bolsheviks, Russian emigrants brought the 'Protocols' to Germany. Soon they appeared in racial and anti-Semitic circles in Berlin and Munich. In January 1920, the first German version appeared with the title 'Die Geheimnisse der Weisen von Zion' (The Secrets of the Learned Elders of Zion). The publisher Gottfried zur Beek (i.e. Ludwig Müller, called von Hausen) was involved with anti-Bolshevik Russian emigrants, among whom there were also Nilus' son and niece. With the aid of the German Embassy in

1 Front page of the 'Zionistischen Protokolle' (Zionist Minutes), reprint of the 1980s.

Moscow, they tried to get Nilus out of Soviet Russia, but they failed; instead his archive was brought to Berlin in the embassy dispatch bag.

The German edition of the 'Protocols' proved to be a success. At the end of 1920, six editions had already been sold. In 1924 they were published by Theodor Fritsch, the 'grand master of German anti-Semitism', under the title 'The Zionist Protocols. The Programme of the International Secret Government'. In 1920, translations appeared in France, England and the USA. The London 'Times' gave them a positive review and in the USA they probably found their most prominent advocate in the industrialist Henry Ford.

---

[3] Sergei Nilus: Velikoe v malom i antichrist, kak blizkaja politicheskaja vozmozhnost'. Zapiski pravoslavnogo. Izdanie vtoroe, ispravlennoe i dopolnennoe. Carskoe Selo 1905, pp. 321 f.

[4] Sergei Nilus: 'Bliz est', pri dverech.' O tom, chemu ne zhelajut verit' i chto tak blizko. Sergiev Posad 1917, pp. 88 f. A whole chapter of this book is dedicated to Herzl and the Zionist movement.

2 Front page of Alfred Rosenbergs' 'Weltverschwörerkongress zu Basel' (Congress of the world conspirators in Basel), 1927.

The triumphal progress of the 'Protocols' had begun. They 'uncovered' the Jews as the secret rulers of the world and 'unveiled' the motives and machinations behind the First World War, the Russian Revolution and the downfall of the monarchies.

Some publishers of the 'Protocols' took over Nilus' reference to Herzl and the Basel Zionist Congress and sometimes varied it adventurously. Zur Beek even came up with a 'scout' of the Russian government who had succeeded in bribing a Jew into taking the French 'reports of the secret meetings' from Basel to the 'Jewish lodge' 'Zur aufgehenden Morgenröte' in Frankfurt. On this journey 'where the Russian was waiting for him with a troop of clerks' in a small town, the Jew supposedly gave him the documents to copy: ' ... the clerks copied all they could in one night!' The copy was then sent to the 'scholar Nilus' who 'translated them into Russian'. According to zur Beek, the 'Protocols' revealed, that the 'Jewish covetousness' was not restricted to the 'Promised Land'. Herzl's Jewish state, he said, was only a means of achieving the domination of the world which they had been promised for thousands of years:

'The world allowed itself to be led astray by the Zionist method of war; only the minutes of the meeting of the learned Elders of Zion provided the key to the great war plans of the Jewish leaders.'[5]

Soon the 'Protocols' fell into the sight of the National Socialists. Their 'head ideologist' Alfred Rosenberg, who had supposedly brought with him a copy from Moscow to Germany in December 1918, published extracts that were commented on in great detail in 1923 with the title 'The Minutes of the Learned Elders of Zion and the Jewish World Policy', and in 1927 his work 'Congress of the World Conspirators in Basel' appeared, in which he left no room for doubt that the plan for the conquest of the world had been discussed and documented in Basel in 1897. As to the authenticity of the spread text of the 'Protocols', his declaration was rather non-committal, of course:

'The way things look today', he already wrote in 1923, 'neither a conclusive *legal* proof for the absolute authenticity nor for a forgery can be found. Part of the leaders of the congress of 1897 have died and the rest will beware of admitting the truth. And also the Russians who had it copied might be long dead by now.'[6]

---

[5] Gottfried zur Beek [d.i. Ludwig Müller, gen. von Hausen]: Zur Einführung. In: Die Geheimnisse der Weisen von Zion. 3rd ed. Charlottenburg 1919 [recte 1920], pp. 8–9.
[6] Alfred Rosenberg: Die Protokolle der Weisen von Zion und die jüdische Weltpolitik. Munich 1923, p. 9 (emphasized in the original).

In Hitler's speeches the 'learned Elders of Zion' appeared for the first time in 1921. Although Hitler used the well-known fable of the Jewish world conspiracy as an effective weapon of propaganda he – like the other leading members of the party – avoided referring directly to the 'Protocols'. They were only an additional confirmation, but not the 'proof' of a Jewish conspiracy. Thus the 'Protocols' were mentioned in the Nazi propaganda and also repeatedly published in large numbers during the Third Reich, but the authorities never got involved in discussions concerning their historical authenticity. They even remained passive in the famous Berne lawsuit.

From 1933 to 1935, a lawsuit took place in front of the district court of Berne against the distributors of the 'Protocols' in the Canton of Berne. The petitioners, the Swiss-Jewish communities association and the Berne Jewish Community, turned the court case referred to as the 'Zionist lawsuit' by the Nazi press but also by Swiss usage into a globally observed tribunal against the 'Protocols' and the legend of its origins. The court experts Carl Albert Loosli, a writer and journalist, and Arthur Baumgarten, professor at the Law Faculty of the University of Basel, confirmed that the work was a forgery. Innumerable participants and observers of the Basel Zionist Congress of 1897 confirmed on the stand that all meetings had taken place in public so that there could be no secret minutes. Straight away, the conspiracy expert who had come from Germany then declared them to be the minutes from a Jewish-Masonic parallel congress. In August 1897 – he said – a 'congress of the order of Bnai B'rith and Jewish high lodges' had taken place as well.[7] Nilus, on whose statement the identification of the 'Protocols' as Zionist programme was based, had thus been misled himself: 'As his only proof', he had relied 'on the declaration of a Jew'. 'This Jewish information was false.'[8] The statement now was that: 'The Protocols are a *Masonic document,* and have nothing to do with the official Basel Zionist Congress.'[9] The judge from Berne, however, came to the conclusion that the 'Protocols' were a plagiarism and probably also a forgery and banned as 'trashy literature'. In second instance in 1937, however, this judgement was rescinded because the 'Protocols' were to be categorized as a means of political competition and could, therefore, not be forbidden.

The publishers and defendants of the 'Protocols' have made very varying and contradictory comments on their origin, character and age. They were not only brought into connection with the Basel Zionist Congress, but also with the important free masons, the Bnai B'rith Lodges, the Alliance Israélite Universelle, the 'Illuminaten' or the mysterious 'Central Office of Zion'. Theodor Herzl, Asher Ginzberg (Ahad Haam), Adam Weishaupt or the 12 or 13 or 300 mysterious 'learned Elders of Zion' were named as authors, Alfred Nossig served as the alleged witness that the original document had been written in French or Hebrew. Finally, there was the version – which of course was soon dropped – according to which the 'Protocols' had already been written in 929 BCE in Jerusalem under Salomon. And since 1982, an international bestseller proclaims that they document – although 'fundamentally altered' – a worldwide conspiracy with the aim of restoring the dynasty of the Merovingians![10]

To this day the origin of the 'Protocols' has not been clarified. There are many things which point to Russian agents and members of the czarian secret police in France being involved in its writing just before the turn of the century, but it

---

[7] Ulrich Fleischhauer: Die echten Protokolle der Weisen von Zion. Sachverständigengutachten, erstattet im Auftrage des Richteramtes V in Bern. Erfurt 1935, p. 73.

[8] Stephan Vász: Das Berner Fehlurteil über die Protokolle der Weisen von Zion. Erfurt 1935, p. 131.

[9] Ibid. (Emphasized in the original).

[10] Michael Baigent, Richard Leigh, Henry Lincoln: The Holy Blood and the Holy Grail. 16th ed. London 1990, p. 203.

was never possible to clarifiy the manner and scope of this participation let alone to prove it. Nevertheless only very few researchers have tried to penetrate into the thicket of lies, intrigues, adventure stories and secret dealings which surround the origin of the 'Protocols' and none of them has managed to do more than formulate hypotheses.[11]

But whoever it was who wrote the 'Protocols' and for whatever reason, one thing is clear: they are a forgery – or more precisely a plagiarism: The 'Protocols' were compiled from a range of literary documents, which had been known to a certain extent for many years. The main source is a polemic of the liberal French author Maurice Joly, which had been published anonymously in Brussels in 1864 under the title 'Dialogue aux enfers entre Machiavel et Montesquieu, ou la politique de Machiavel au XIXe siècle' and which was directed against the regime of the Second Empire in France. In this book, Machiavelli – who embodied Napoleon III – developed the programme for a modern dictatorship, down to the smallest detail: populistically legitimized, it is based on the manipulation of the masses, on bribery, spying and a charismatic leader. In total, more the 160 excerpts of the 'Protocols', around two fifth of the text, are clearly based on the book by Joly.[12] This book in turn made reference to the contemporary popular literature, and the description of a Jesuit conspiracy to take over the world was in part literally taken from the novel by Eugène Sue 'Les mystères du peuple', which was published between 1849 and 1857 in his 'Dialogues'.[13]

But not only the contents of the 'Protocols', its framework too, the secret meeting of the 'learned Elders of Zion' and the speech held there originated in trivial fiction. In the novel 'Biarritz' which was published in 1868 in Berlin under the pseudonym 'Sir John Retcliffe' the sensationalist author Herrmann Goedsche depicts, using the stylistic device of a gothic story, a secret nightly meeting at the Jewish cemetery in Prague, in which the representatives of the twelve tribes of Israel report to the devil of their successful infiltration and subjugation of the Christian world and discuss their further procedure. To this purpose, Goedsche had copied the introductory scene of the novel 'Joseph Balsamo' by Alexandre Dumas père, in which the conspiracy of the 'Illuminaten' with Cagliostro is represented. Later on, the chapter 'At the Jewish cemetery in Prague' of Goedsche's novel was repeatedly published independently and finally rewritten as a major 'speech of the rabbi' which was then spread throughout the world as an alleged document of the Jewish world conspiracy and which gave the forgers of the 'Protocols' their plot.

To this day, the 'Protocols' are still being published and used all over the world, by the 'Christian Patriots' as well as by the extremists of the 'Nation of Islam', by the nationalists of the Russian 'Pamjat' movement, as well as by the communists, who have replaced the 'enemy of the working classes' with the 'world conspirators'.[14] A plagiarism from dubious sources, the 'Protocols' prove to be a work, 'the infamy of which is only surpassed by its success'.[15]

---

[11] Michael Hagemeister: Sergei Nilus und die 'Protokolle der Weisen von Zion'. Überlegungen zur Forschungslage. In: Jahrbuch für Antisemitismusforschung 5 (1996), pp. 127–147.

[12] Norman Cohn: Die Protokolle der Weisen von Zion. Der Mythos von der jüdischen Weltverschwörung. Cologne, Berlin 1969, p. 94.

[13] Umberto Eco: Im Wald der Fiktionen. Sechs Streifzüge durch die Literatur. Munich 1994, pp. 177 f.

[14] Michael Hagemeister: Die 'Protokolle der Weisen von Zion'. Einige Bemerkungen zur Herkunft und zur aktuellen Rezeption. In: Russland und Europa. Historische und kulturelle Aspekte eines Jahrhundertproblems. Leipzig 1995, pp. 195–206.

[15] Ulrich Raulff: Die Libido des Polizeistaats. In: Frankfurter Allgemeine Zeitung, 10 August 1991, p. 25.

Moshe Zimmermann

Zionism and Anti-Semitism

Theodor Herzl and Wilhelm Marr both died in 1904. Herzl – the patriarch of Zionism – Marr – the patriarch of anti-Semitism. The close temporal proximity of their deaths can be a starting point for considerations concerning the relationship between Zionism and anti-Semitism. Further dates in the lives of Herzl and Marr are also significant. Herzl was born in 1860, 41 years after Wilhelm Marr. Herzl founded his 'Zionist movement' in 1897, 18 years after the foundation of the 'Anti-Semitic league' by Marr. Herzl's programmatic pamphlet 'Der Judenstaat' (The Jewish State) appeared 16 years after the publication of Marr's book 'Der Sieg des Judentums über das Germanentum' (The Victory of Judaism Over Germanism). The word 'anti-Semitism' coined in 1879 preceded the term 'Zionism' by eleven years. And even if Herzl cannot claim to be the inventor of the term 'Zionism', it is just as firmly connected to Herzl as anti-Semitism is to Marr. Anti-Semitism is thus – at least conceptually – somewhat older than Zionism. Historians are forced to investigate the relationship between Zionism and anti-Semitism and examine whether it is causal or of a different nature.

Up to the foundation of the State of Israel in 1948, the question of the relationship between Zionism and anti-Semitism seemed to have been clearly answered: the rise of anti-Semitism at the end of the 19th century and the terror that was connected to it had caused the Jewish people to found their own nationalist movement. Hence, the Jews in Western and Central Europe, who were emancipated in a legal sense, had been convinced of the ineffectiveness of this emancipation in the face of growing anti-Semitism and as a consequence had turned back to their national origins. The Jews in Eastern Europe, however, who had not yet been emancipated had seen that the struggle for emancipation was senseless and had also supported the idea of a Jewish nation. Of course, not all Jews had come to the conclusion of swapping the Diaspora for the land of Israel. Nevertheless, the relationship between Zionism and anti-Semitism was represented as causal, yes, even as monocausal. In the course of time, an ideological, as well as professionally-historical objection to this interpretation arose.

The ideological objection arose in the State of Israel immediately after its foundation and especially after the Six-Day War in 1967. In Israel, Zionism was declared to be a movement which had continuously been alive in the Jewish people ever since the destruction of the Second Temple in the year 70 CE. The collective longing for Zion as a consequence of the destruction of the temple and the continuation of the Jewish people in exile became, in this ideological interpretation, a Zionist movement. And just as this explanation left no room for a historical development of Zionism, it was also presumed that the enmity against the Jewish people and anti-Semitism had not historically developed either, but had been unchangeable factors of destiny which had accompanied this Zionism throughout the centuries. The dehistorization of Zionism does not, however, answer the question why the politically organized

Zionist movement had not come into being until 1800 years after the destruction of the Second Temple. Furthermore, this explanation suppressed the predominant worldly, non-religious character of this movement since Herzl. And finally, this approach also abolished the necessity of searching for the historical reasons which had triggered the hostility towards the Jewish people or had nourished it – here, anti-Semitism is reduced to a term which serves the description of the 'eternal' phenomenon of the hatred of Jews and which is exclusively employed to explain the relationship between Jews and non-Jews for 2000 years.

Along with this ideological objection, the original meaning of the term became less clear. The term 'Zionism' was selected 100 years ago because of its 'neutrality' as the name for the organized Jewish national movement. As the 'Nationaljüdische Vereinigung für Deutschland' (National Jewish Association for Germany) in Cologne was renamed 'Zionist Association', it mainly wanted to fight the statement from Jews and non-Jews alike that the term 'national Jewish' allowed the presumption of a double loyalty, of a betrayal of the fatherland. The neutral term 'Zionism' avoided the term 'Jewish nationalism' and disguised the circumstance that the nationalist Jewish organization was an innovation of the late 19th century.

A similar confusion surrounded the term 'anti-Semitism', which was coined to give new meaning to the negative attitude towards the Jews. According to Marr it was necessary to give up the religiously founded hatred of Jews and to develop a modern, scientific and worldly interpretation for the relationship between Jews and non-Jews. But this was not the reason why this term was generally accepted. Just as later on the term 'Zionism', it was successful because it was regarded to be much more neutral and scientific than the terms 'hatred of Jews' or 'Jew eater'. The word 'anti-Semitism' lost its 'innocence' largely only due to the radicalization of anti-Semitic actions in the Third Reich. The term 'Zionism' on the other hand lost its neutrality as Zionism was increasingly identified with the State of Israel and its power policy. Therefore both terms called for distancing through their increasingly associative burdens.

'Zionism' and 'anti-Semitism' were terms of the late 19th century and served to designate new tendencies. But the fate of these terms in the 20th century and the separation between the old and the new terminology which mutually excluded each other – i.e. the opinion that anti-Semitism was entirely different from the hatred of Jews, whereas Zionism was the opposite of what the Diaspora Jewry had engendered up to the present time – had to provoke critical statements. In contrast to many historians, the ideologists came to an extreme conclusion: they ignored the difference between the old and new terms, between past and present and believed to have recognized that the history of the Jewish people ran in two parallel paths – eternal anti-Semitism and eternal Zionism.

The professional-historical objection was also aimed against the usual interpretation of the connection between Zionism and anti-Semitism: historians dealing with crises and revolutions know that developments do not proceed in simple opposites but dialectically. In our context, this means that: anti-Semitism was not necessarily the opposite of the hatred of the Jews that had been known until that time, nor was Zionism against everything the Diaspora Jewry had produced so far. But despite all the existing elements of continuity, both movements also exhibited entirely new elements and a change of character.

Although anti-Semitism did succeed in releasing itself to a certain extent from the religiously motivated old hatred of the Jews, this was not because it had intentionally meant to do so but rather because of the social circumstances surrounding its beginning. As a consequence of the industrial revolution and the progress of liberal democracy, the Jews could be identified with the new 'social question' which threatened those social groups which suffered under the new order. In this context, the religious argumentation had lost its central role, even if the influence of faith and religious education on the language and attitudes of anti-Semitism did not disappear. Anti-Semitism referred to the reality of an industrialized and more liberal society in which the emancipation of the Jews was the most important new element. If one searches for a causal connection between anti-Semitism and Zionism, one finds it here: against the background of the new hatred of the Jews one came to a new reaction on the part of the Jews, which had not been necessary before. The new Jewish national movement, Zionism, was thus partially an answer to the new elements of modern anti-Semitism. Thus we escape the downward spiral which allows neither renewal nor change, but only eternal enmity and eternal reaction.

However, this is only part of the complex correlation. The causal connection is also rooted in the mutual, modern roots of both movements: in nationalism. The hatred of Jews in its anti-Semitic form and Zionism are products of the development of nationalism since the time of the revolutions. The national component has replaced the religious component in the rejection of the Jews by the non-Jewish society in the 19th century. Nationalism had to confront the principles of secularization, of enlightment and of liberalism which had also led to the emancipation of the Jews. If someone wanted to annul the emancipation of the Jews, he would have to resort to nationalism, not religion. And those who wanted to solve the 'social question' could no longer limit themselves to religious arguments but had to give preference to an explanation which promised the solution of the problem by solving the 'Jewish question'. Thus, anti-Semitism and Zionism dialectically stepped out together of the origins of modern nationalism. Here too, the vicious circle is broken: nationalism led to a new form of hatred of the Jews, without which the longing for

1 Contemporary illustration of the degradation of captain Dreyfus. The shock of the anti-Semitic wave in France in connection with the Dreyfus Affair motivated Herzl to write the 'Judenstaat', the programmatic pamphlet of Zionism.

Zion, which was only expressed in the prayer books – and in a limited immigration to the Holy Land – would have remained the only form of expression of 'Zionism'. Moreover this dialectical relationship also implies, however, that the new aspects brought about by Zionism did not depend exclusively on anti-Semitism but would also have been possible without it.

The connection between Zionism and anti-Semitism is therefore transient, not only causal. Because both of these ideological movements arose in the same societies and under the same conditions, a mutual stimulation and joint fundamental prerequisites can also be recognized. Here, above all, the definition of the Jews as a nation and people, not as a religious community should be mentioned. When the Hebrew Bible refers to Jews as a people and a nation, this was meaningless as long as these two terms did not yet possess the signification they would have in the 18th century. At the very moment at which these terms became identity-defining factors, the opinion that the Jews were a nation as well took on a revolutionary meaning. The majority of the Jews – the orthodox Jews in Eastern Europe and the liberal Jews in Western Europe and America alike – protested strongly against this conception. For some it was a break with tradition and for the others a threat to their emancipation and integration in the new national state. Jew haters concentrated on this aspect with the increasing importance of the nation since the French Revolution, increasingly, however, with the intensification of the national discussion as a whole toward the end of the 19th century. Parallel to this process, the idea of national self-determination also 'matured' amongst the Jews, as is reflected in Moses Hess's reaction to the unification of Italy. Anti-Semites and Zionists thus found themselves on the same ground with their interpretation of nation and national struggles as the focus of the historical events when they defined the Jews as a nation like all others, and what is more: both sides were of the same opinion that the situation of the Diaspora Jewry was not 'normal'. And Zionists and anti-Semites could also agree on the solution to the problem – the founding of a state for the Jews in their historical territory.

Two restrictions must be made here: many anti-Semites believed, however, as a consequence of their anti-Semitic posture, that the Jews were not capable of building up a state, or that this state would be nothing more than the centre of 'international Jewish conspiracy'. Furthermore, not every Jew who recognized the existence of a Jewish nation was also convinced of the necessity of a territorial concentration in a Jewish state. The autonomists, led by the historian Simon Dubnow, believed in a Jewish national solution in exile.

A clear dialectical connection between both movements had existed since the beginning of the Zionist movement, alone due to the attention which they paid to each other. Not only Zionism was a reaction to the anti-Semitic argumentation and policy from the very beginning; one must also realize how anti-Semites, whether alone or as parties, replied to the developments in Zionism. Wilhelm Marr immediately gave his opinion on the Zionist ideas. He considered that the anti-Semites themselves had to provide funds to bring the Jews to Palestine. But at the same time he doubted whether the Jews would be prepared to be banned to a country such as Palestine. Even at the first Zionist Congresses organized by Herzl, Marr reacted in a way which was typical for him: The idea was ideal but impossible to realize.

Even Hitler pointed to a relationship between his anti-Semitism and Zionism in 'Mein Kampf'. He stated that he found confirmation in the Zionist movement in Vienna that the Jews were truly a nation of their own, which was distinguishable from the German people. The National Socialist ideologist Alfred Rosenberg also made it to the main issue in his book 'Der staatsfeindliche Zionismus' (The Anti-State Zionism). The German Zionists knew about these positions and expected that the 'Third Reich' would also share the opinion of the Zionists that the Jews were a nation and support their Zionist activities. The basic ideas were quickly turned into practice: within the national socialist movement there was not only the slogan 'Jews to Palestine', but there were also initiatives which led to a co-operation with the Zionists to bring Jews to Palestine after 1933.

A further important realization by Marr, which was pivotal for the relationship between anti-Semitism and Zionism as a whole, has to be taken into account: Marr supported the idea of the Jews leaving Europe but could not understand – in 1898! – how Zionism could solve the Jewish question via a national territorial concentration of the Jews in one country in which Arabs were already living. Marr's attention was drawn here to a circumstance of which the Zionists were still largely unaware: the threatening confrontation between Jews and Arabs and between the Jewish and Arab nations. The Jewish nationalist movement was certainly also one of the reasons for the foundation of the Arab nationalist movement and for the conflict in the Middle East, and what is more: this conflict 'carried' the European anti-Semitism 'over' into a region in which is had not been known previously – at least in its modern, racist form. Herzl was convinced that the medicine for the anti-Semitic disease was the emigration of the Jews out of Europe. This was also the belief of the anti-Semites, although of course, the other way round. Herzl, however, did not expect that his theory about the connection between Jewish presence and anti-Semitism would also be confirmed in his new Jewish state. The appearance of Zionism in the Middle East and the foundation of the state of Israel not only introduced the European terminology to the conflict with the Arabs, but also allowed the paradox of the emergence of an anti-Semitism in a 'Semitic' society, which had not been crucial in this form in the Moslem society of the Middle East before. To fight against Zionism, the Arab nationalist movement took on positions imported from Europe. And this is where the ends tie up: the relationship between Zionism and anti-Semitism changed under new historical conditions. On the one hand, the epoch of the realization of Zionism in Israel became an epoch in which anti-Semitism in the western, Christian societies of Europe lost its overall importance, but on the other hand, to an epoch in which anti-Semitism entered into a region which had developed into the centre of Zionism.

Daniel Gerson

Zionism, Anti-Zionism, Anti-Semitism

Organized Zionism was the culmination of a Jewish political movement of the 19th century which assumed that without an independent national consciousness, without autonomy or even without an independent state, a dignified life was not possible. In its opinion, emancipation had brought legal equality in the Western European countries but did not minimize the discrimination in daily life and it even hindered the development of Jewish culture. Furthermore the foundation of nation states, growing nationalism and problems of industrialization had an added impetus to 'racially' based anti-Semitism. In Eastern Europe, where the legal situation of the Jews was worse, an improvement of their conditions seemed to be even less probable.

The demand of the 'Basle Program' adopted at the First Zionist Congress to create a 'Homestead in Palestine' for 'the Jewish People' certainly did not meet only with approval amongst the Jewish people. Initially there were more anti-Zionists: religious Jews opposed the secularization of the concept of deliverance; Jews that were willing to assimilate and acculturate denounced Jewish nationalism as an anti-Enlightenment ideology and were afraid it would place at risk the emancipation achieved in the belief that it had prospects despite anti-Semitism and the social status that they had attained. For the Jewish socialists, the nation state was a bourgeois-capitalist phenomenon, which had to be overcome by class struggle and worldwide revolution. At the beginning non-Jewish circles accepted the objectives of a 'Jewish state' quite positively. Pro-Zionism was, however, partly connected with anti-Jewish tendencies. Some 'Christian Zionists' hoped for the second coming of Jesus after the return of the Jews to Zion, and for the conversion of the Jews to Christianity. Others, politicians and supporters of anti-Semitism, thought that the emigration of the Jews to Palestine would solve the 'Jewish question' in European countries.

In the twenties a new situation developed. The Arab population of Palestine and their representatives did not accept the Jewish immigration and their own treatment as manipulable puppets in an international power game. More and more the Zionists were seen as vanguards of an anti-Islamic and anti-Arabic imperialism, which aimed to destroy the Arabic culture and take possession of the holy places in Jerusalem. Jewish nationalism was followed by Arab nationalism. At the climax of the conflict, the Arabic argumentation fell back on anti-Semitic clichés, which until this time had been connected to the European cultures.

In order not to lose their influence over the Arabs and to be able to continue to pursue their international political interests, the powers involved in the Middle East, especially Great Britain, took on anti-Zionist ideas when they considered them to be necessary. The Zionist movement was temporarily faced with a front of disapproval. But anti-Zionist reservations about the international confederation of states which had failed in protecting the European Jews stopped after the Shoah. The survivors of the German Holocaust could not be denied a national home.

1 Cover of the publication 'The Jewish World Supremacy over the Ruins of the Nations' from the Propaganda-Verlag of Paul Hochmuth, Berlin 1933.

However anti-Zionism did not subside after the foundation of the State of Israel in 1948. Arabic countries and the Palestinians did not want to accept the new conditions. Internationally, a new constellation arose, when the Soviet Union, which initially immediately recognized the State of Israel hoping for a good relationship, denounced Israel as an outpost of 'US imperialism' during the heightening East-West conflict and allied with Arabic countries, to gain influence in that region. The denunciations often made use of classical anti-Semitic stereotypes. This combined with internal struggles in the Soviet-controlled areas of Eastern Europe where their enemies were often denounced as 'Zionist' and soon every Jew was in danger of suffering negative consequences due to being seen as a 'Zionist'. Anti-Zionism and anti-Semitism, officially frowned upon, blended into one. On an international level this process of becoming one was repeated more and more at an often subliminal level. The climax of this international anti-Zionist campaign was the UN resolution, in November 1975 which equated Zionism with racism.

2 Iraqi anti-Zionist propaganda from the newspaper 'Al-Manar', June 8, 1967.

A unique special form of anti-Semitism was formed by the Western European left wing, not least by the student movements of the sixties and seventies, and was most prevalent in West Germany. The one-sided partisanship for the Palestinians, especially after the Six-Day War in 1967, can be explained by the fact that they were seen as the oppressed and the exploited who deserved help in the worldwide struggle against imperialism. Furthermore, the attempt to come to terms with the 'Third Reich' and the behaviour of the older generation played an important role. The abhorrence about the genocide of the Jews, in which many parents had been involved or which they at least had watched without putting up any resistance, was combined with the often morally judged shock that now the same Jews were using violence and presenting themselves as conquerors. Some scientists point to the fact that psychologically speaking, this behaviour could have been partly based on repressed feelings of guilt: every German was responsible for the extermination and expulsion of the Jews from Europe and therefore as a consequence for the expulsion of the Palestinians from their country.

Only a success in the Arab-Israeli peace process will make it possible to break down the ideological barriers and loosen the problem-ridden link between anti-Zionism and anti-Semitism.

Patrick Kury
Kathrin Ringger

Unsolved Questions

'The Israeli Jews must recognize the fact that the Palestinian Arabs as a people have the right to live in peace in their country, in Palestine. The Palestinian Arabs have to recognize the fact that there is an Israeli people with the right to live in peace in the country which it considers to be its home.'[1]

As representatives of a secular national movement, the Zionists pursued the aim of seeking a 'secured home' for the Jewish people. A hundred years later this seems to have been achieved by way of peace treaties with most of the neighbouring countries. Largely unsolved on the other hand are the questions of a peaceful co-existence of two nations in one country. The democratic way of mutual acknowledgement requires the communication with the Palestinians in Israel as well as the restitution of the occupied regions. This is the approach described by Said Hammami, who was one of the first PLO representatives to try to come to a dialogue with the Israelis and who paid for his co-operation with his life in 1978. But the Zionist-Israeli policy has created conditions which impede this process of understanding, or which even run counter to it, for many Palestinians still live in misery and partly without political rights.

The hopes of the Palestinian population for self-determination were destroyed soon after the end of the Second World War. Under the impression of the Shoah and the knowledge of having been partially guiltily entangled in the murdering of millions of European Jews, an internationally organized increased immigration of survivors began after 1945. When all efforts to mediate between the Arab and Jewish parts of the population had failed, the British decided to lay down the mandate and to leave the solution of the conflict to the UN. The commission which it constituted proposed a partition of the country, which was accepted by the General Assembly of the UN on November 29, 1947. The Palestinian national movement and the Arab League declared the splitting of the country to be illegal, while the Jewish Agency viewed it quite favourably but found fault with the partition. After Britain had resigned from the mandate, a civil war broke out in which the Jews, thanks to their military supremacy, soon gained the upper hand. After the proclamation of the State of Israel on May 14, 1948, by David Ben Gurion, this permanent conflict triggered the first Arab-Israeli war which was only ended in 1949. For the Palestinian population the war brought with it expulsion and flight from their homes. They consider the year 1948 as the year of the catastrophe. In Israeli historiography the 'departure' of the Palestinians had been presented as a voluntary act for a long time. Recent research has proven this to be false. With the 'exodus' of the Palestinians from Israel, a time of wandering began for them, a time of life in refugee camps and of an uncertain future. Their old social structures had been destroyed, respected families found themselves to be without power or influence, the intellectual and econom-

---

[1] Der Dialog geht weiter. Interview mit Said Hammami, held by James Dorsey. In: John Bunzl (ed.): Der Nahostkonflikt. Analysen und Dokumente. Vienna, Frankfurt 1981, pp. 129–142, here p. 129.

1 The market bustling with activity in Jerusalem, around 1900. Co-existence of Arabs and Jews.

ic elite was in exile. The refugees met again in a new dependency, this time on the governments of Arabian countries. A struggle for survival as a minority set in, a struggle, not only against external enemies but also against the loss of their own identity.

The Six-Day War of 1967 finally dramatically worsened the position of the Palestinian population. The Israeli army conquered the remaining parts of Palestine as well as the Golan Heights. Gaza, Jerusalem and the West Bank came under Israeli (military) administration, more than 150,000 Palestinians fled from Cisjordan to Jordan and from then on hundreds of thousands lived under the rule of the occupying power.

The state policy created an actual three-class society in Israel and the occupied territories, consisting of Jewish Israelis, Palestinian Israelis and the 'occupied'. Although the approximately 800,000 Palestinian Israelis have enjoyed equality of rights on paper since 1966, they have remained 'second-class people'. The discriminatory politics continued in the selective application of individual laws, in the unjust allocation of state support as well as in the discrimination at work. The occupation, which has lasted for more than two decades, led to devastating socio-economic conditions in the occupied territories.

2   Juvenile Palestinians in Hebron hoisting their flag at the end of Ramadan, March 1994.

'The situation of the approximately 1,800,000 Palestinians in the Gaza Strip and in the West Bank proves to be full of conflict. This population has no political rights and even the Geneva Conventions, which promised them passive protection from attacks, are only partially observed by Israel. This fact has not been fundamentally changed by the peace process.'[2]

The long history of suffering of the Jewish people thus finds its continuation in the story of suffering of the Palestinian people. This also has consequences for the emotional state of the Palestinians:

'The Palestinians are subject to the danger of alienation even in their own home country. Strangers in foreign countries and threatened by alienation in their own home they are trapped in a severe nostalgia. Everyday life is tainted by a feeling of loss and sorrow, because everything that has anything to do with our identity, and everything that gives our lives a sense of importance and meaning is in danger.'[3]

[2] Arnold Hottinger: Der Leidensweg des palästinensischen Volkes. In: Sumaya Farhat-Naser: Thymian und Steine. Eine palästinensische Lebensgeschichte. Ed. by Rosmarie Kurz and Chudi Bürgi. Basel 1995, pp. 207–226, here p. 213.
[3] Ali H. Qleibo: Wenn die Berge verschwinden. Die Palästinenser im Schatten der israelischen Besatzung. Heidelberg 1993, p. 16.

Also the ideologization of the Israeli-Palestinian conflict which set in after the founding of the state and especially after the Six-Day War was mainly carried out at the expense of the Palestinian population. The Six-Day War marks a turning point. The political discussion polarized. While the Israelis were seen as the successors of European colonialists, only representing the interests of the West in the Middle East, particularly of the United States of America, the Arab world – and with it the Palestinians – were seen as allies of the USSR. UN Resolutions were hardly able to change anything in this situation. Thus Resolution 242 of November 22, 1967, stated that the conquest of territories could not be accepted by international law. Israel was requested to withdraw from the occupied territories and to recognize the integrity and the political independency of the Palestinian people. In 1970, Israel accepted this Resolution, but this had virtually no political consequences.

After decades of violence, both sides, the Palestinian and the Israeli, were finally forced to look for new approaches. Due to the situation in the occupied territories, which was becoming increasingly difficult to control, but also due to the

Unsolved Questions

growing public pressure within Israel itself, political as well as military circles increasingly came to realize that the 'Intifada' – the Palestinian struggle against the occupation policy of Israel – could never be brought to an end by repression. Thus a partial agreement was surprisingly signed in Oslo on September 13, 1993, which was based on UN Resolution 242. For the interim renunciation of a sovereign state and for the acknowledgement of the existence of Israel, the Palestinians obtained further autonomy in Gaza and parts of Cisjordan as well as the international recognition of their status as a people with national interests. Difficult unsolved questions, such as the status of Jerusalem and of the Jewish settlers in Hebron, are to be attended to at a later date. The concern as to whether the strengthening of the fragile peace will be successful, moved the Israeli writer Amos Oz to the following summary in October 1996:

'The peace cannot last as long as Israel continues to nibble away at what is left of Palestine. Peace means most of all that the other is seen as a partner and not as a plague. The Palestinians will not win back a home for themselves if they continue to spill even more Israeli blood; they have already tried this several times before. The Israelis on the other hand, will never live in peace if they do not stop turning Palestinian land into Israeli land.'[4]

---

[4] Amos Oz: Ein neuer Krieg um heilige Stätten? In: Die Zeit No. 42 of 11 October 1996, p. 8.

Sumaya Farhat-Naser

One Hundred Years of Zionism – Associations of a Palestinian Woman

One hundred years of Zionism – seen through the eyes of a Palestinian woman, born in 1948, the year of the foundation of the State of Israel, the story of Zionism is inextricably linked to the history of her people's suffering.

No Room for Palestinians

In contrast to other national movements which emerged to free a country from the yoke of foreign rule or an oppressing political system, Zionism emerged as a movement that would gather people of the European Diaspora, mainly as an answer to European anti-Semitism and the ever-recurring persecutions.

From a Palestinian point of view, however, the basis of the Zionist idea, as it was articulated in Basel one hundred years ago, is a colonial conception of the world. In contrast to other national movements, the objective of Zionism had never been to free a country and its population; it wanted to reshape a persecuted ethnic-religious community into a nation by acquiring a territory for it. The aim of building up a home for the Jewish people, of settling in a country and of supporting the creation of an Israeli national culture ignored the existence of an inborn population. The Zionist concept of an ethnically defined Jewish state never had any room for the Palestinians living in Palestine. This is why this conception could only be realized with violence and at the expense of the Palestinians. The Jewish state with its values and orientations was not aimed at its Arabic surroundings but at the West, at Europe and the USA. This is why it is still perceived as a strategic outpost of the West. In the future, however, the security of Israel will largely depend on a successful integration into the Arabic world.

Nationalism Hinders Co-Existence

The time of the British Mandate brought about the development of national Jewish structures in the country. With circumspection, organization, determination and also with violence the Zionist organizations worked on bringing the largest possible areas of the land under their control. The Palestinians reacted in a hostile manner to these endeavours: why should they share their home country with foreign people, people coming from Europe whose politics, culture and language were unfamiliar to them? Thus the nationalism of the Jewish people gave rise to the Palestinian nationalism. But the Palestinians were not successful in their struggle against the settlers and the mandate authorities. They had no organizational background and no unified strategy; they also never really thought it possible that they could actually lose their home country.

The catastrophe of the Jewish people, the Shoah, accelerated and legitimized the foundation of the Jewish State of Israel. At the same time, this state caused the catastrophe of the Palestinian people. And until today it determines the discussion in Europe about the Israeli-Palestinian conflict. The topic is burdened, the talks are tense, the participants trapped in feelings of guilt. This makes a rational criticism of Israel's actions even more difficult and leads to rash justifications of every measure undertaken by the Israeli in the name of security and the existence of the Israeli population. For many years, it was not possible for the western public to extend their solidarity with Israel to large parts of the Palestinians and concede them the same rights.

Polarizing Information

During my studies in Germany between 1966 and 1974 I personally experienced this bias. The experience that in Germany one was generally informed one-sidedly and almost exclusively by Israeli news sources, and that the Palestinian standpoint was thus faced with many prejudices constantly put me into a position of defence, of fear and of impotence, but it also opened my eyes to the importance of public relations, of political education as a precondition for communication. Step by step I realized the mechanisms of a selective information policy: whoever possessed the information channels had control over the media, spread the selected information, if need be changed injustice into justice, broadcast what should be seen and concealed what was not desirable, reinforced the foe image and influenced judgements based on one-sided interests.

I also came to understand that the Palestinian-Israeli history was part of the German-Jewish history. To burden the Middle-Eastern problem with the question of who was at fault made a normal and realistic evaluation in Europe very difficult. To stand behind Israel without restaint to some extent became a question of confession.

The East-West conflict complicated our problems even more. The Palestinians were generally looked upon as allies of the East and consequently met with suspicion and hostility. This conflict was also reflected in our people: splits, conflicts of interest as well as dependencies were the consequence. The East as well as the West took advantage of this conflict for their own interests.

Religion as a Political Tool

One of the unique aspects of Zionism as a national movement is that religion and people are one within it. It is the national movement of a religious group. This also characterizes the contemporary State of Israel and its relationship to the Palestinians, as can be seen particularly clearly in the case of East Jerusalem. Tens of thousands of housing units, which Israel has built there in the years since 1967, are only available for Jews but not for Moslems or Christians. And while Jews from all over the world have the right to take residence in East Jerusalem whenever they wish, local Palestinians have to fulfil strict criteria to be able to maintain the right of residence. A woman, for example, loses this right if she marries a man from the West Bank. A newborn child only receives the right of residence if both parents are from Jerusalem and if it can be proven that also its grandparents were born in Jerusalem and were living there in 1967. But at that time there was no reliable registration system, thus many cannot prove their claim. Who has been living outside the city for seven years cannot come back; this affects many Palestinians because since 1967 the building of 'Arab' apartment buildings in the city has only seldom been authorized.

The Palestinians consider this policy as a kind of ethnic purification with administrative means. They are powerlessly subjected to it and thus are losing their belief in law and justice. People who feel threatend tend to isolate themselves, they define their cultural and religious identity strictly and exclusively in order to be able to assert themselves in the face of the unknown. Religious fanatism then has an easy task. Our people do not – as would be rational – aim their anger only towards the State of Israel but also increasingly against the Jewish religion and culture itself. More and more they tend to interpret the conflict as a fight of religions, and their hatred also includes the Christians. They see a Western, Christian-Jewish coalition at work fighting worldwide against Islam and threatening their existence. Religious motives and religious groups have gained more and more influence in the Middle-East conflict – both on the Jewish and the Palestinian sides. This development is cause for great concern on my part because it reduces the chances for a rational solution to the conflict and because it threatens to draw the whole Middle East into our conflict. With whom and about what should one then be able to negotiate? For years, I and many people around me have pushed this danger from our thoughts and avoided talking about it. In the future this will become increasingly impossible.

Compromised Peace

The 'Palestinian National Authority' has inherited a difficult legacy. A country with a completely destroyed infrastructure is to be socially and economically developed. A society, which has for so long been oppressed and humiliated, is now to be changed from the chaos of revolution into a civil, democratic society. The legal prerequisites have not yet been met and the necessary structures, financial means and experience are still missing. The Palestinian National Authority thus rightly regards the strengthening of its own security forces and the demonstration of public order as its first priority. Israel asks the Palestinian National Authority to neutralize the radical Palestinians – a task which the occupying forces did not succeed in for decades although they had incomparably more powerful means. Some of these radical groups – by the way – are forces which were originally able to establish themselves as the counter-movement to the PLO with the assistance of Israeli policy. The Palestinian police opposes the radical groups with all severity. Arrests, disarmaments and convictions have been lasting for months. A course of action which the Palestinian people needs to learn and to accept, as in the times of violent confrontations attacks against the oppressors were regarded as heroic deeds.

Out of true desire the Palestinian leaders have chosen the way of peace and have no other option left today. In the polls of January 1996, the population in the occupied territories clearly voted in favour of their leaders and, therefore, in favour of the peace process, prepared to sustain the building up of the new state system. The blockade of the peace process and the latest experiences have, however, undermined this positive attitude and led more and more Palestinians to equate the word 'peace' with 'voluntary subjection' and 'capitulation'. Was it not the peace process that legitimated and simplified the unchanged politics of occupation by using Palestinian police instead of Israeli soldiers to suppress protests? In everyday life, the peace has brought small relief, but all in all the conditions remain the same as during the occupation. This situation threatens to compromise the Palestinian authorities.

Prerequisites for Peace

Since the summer of 1996, a party coalition is in power in Israel which is not only opposed to the peace process, but has constitued with the explicit objective of hindering the implementation of the existing treaties. The government though claims to be in favour of the peace process. But in effect it is blocking the realization of the existing agreements. It constantly questions the basis of the Oslo Agreements and tries to start new negotiations without fixing a time frame or concrete aims. Only after long hesitation and under international pressure, was Prime Minister Benjamin Netanjahu willing to talk to Yassir Arafat, Chairman of the Palestinian National Authority, and he even managed to refer to this meeting as a 'concession'. Meanwhile, new facts are being created in the occupied territories which undermine the peace process. Closures mark and burden our daily life like a nightmare. Check points to Israel and to Jerusalem are closed. The traffic of people and of goods is heavily hindered. And even within the occupied territories, barriers restrict any freedom of movement. This government is not willing to accept the Palestinians as equal partners with equal rights, but instead it is trying to obtain further concessions by force. Once again we are confronted with the arrogant mentality of an occupying power. How shall and how can hope and trust ever develop?

But in Israel too, concern about the progress of the peace process seems to be growing, as well as the dissatisfaction with the current political course. It is imperative that all who share this concern join together in finding a way out of this dead-end street. One example for this is the declaration by Israeli and Palestinian women of the 'Bat Shalom' (Daughters of Peace) and the 'Jerusalem Center for Women' united in the 'Jerusalem Link', which was published on August 2, 1996.

If we do not want to suffocate we need hope again. We have to be able to dream again that real peace is possible. In order to be able to do this we need the willingness for mutual recognition, for equality in our dealings with each other and in our co-existence. Peace is only possible when occupation ends, when the right for both sides to a state and home within the borders of 1967 is respected and when both countries work together for their economic development as well as for the building up of a civil, democratic and lawful society.

The Jerusalem Link Declaration

'Jerusalem Link' is an institution in Jerusalem financed by the European Union uniting the Israeli 'Bat Shalom' and the Palestinian 'Jerusalem Center for Women'. The following declaration of August 2, 1996, is the result of dialogues that had been held for many years, striving for the development of a future together based on democracy.

'We, Palestinian and Israeli women, united in a joint effort to bring about a just and lasting peace between our two peoples, affirm our commitment to working together, within the framework of the Jerusalem Link, for the rapid realization of our common vision of peace based on the following principles:

(1) Recognition of the right to self-determination of both peoples in the land, through the creation of a Palestinian state alongside Israel.

(2) The city of Jerusalem: two capitals for two states.

(3) The Oslo Declaration of Principles, signed on September 13, 1993, and all subsequent agreements, must be implemented in their entirety and should serve as the basis for negotiations of the permanent settlement.

(4) The permanent settlement negotiations must resume immediately, the terms of reference being UN Resolutions 242 and 338, and the Oslo Agreements.

(5) The settlements and their ongoing expansion constitute a severe impediment to peace.

(6) Respect for international conventions, and the active involvement of the international community in the peace process, is crucial to its success.

(7) The realization of political peace will pave the way for peace, mutual trust, and good neighbourly relations on the basis of equality and respect for the national and human rights of each community.

(8) Women are central partners in the peace process – their involvement in negotiation and in government is crucial to the fulfilment of an open and just peace.

(9) We women are opposed to the use of violence and are committed to the promotion of democratic norms and civil society for the realization of an enduring peace.

We call on women in the region and elsewhere to join in making our vision of peace a reality.

August 2, 1996'

Christian Hofer

The Use of Historical Myths in the Creation of the State of Israel

Similarly to the 'invention of the nations' during the 'Peoples' Spring' in the 19th century, intellectuals, mainly writers and historians, created myths in the course of the development of Zionism which were designed to derive behaviours wished for in the present from the past and to promote a national identity. These myths were based on historical events of which selected parts were presented and interpreted according to the desired effect.

Sabra – The New Jew

The resistance or defence myth was already expressed before the foundation of the State of Israel in the efforts to promote the Aliyah to the 'Oldnewland' and to create an individual different from that of the Diaspora. The image of the intellectual, 'top-heavy' Jew, whose pale face was evidence of the steady reading in the study, did not fit into the concept of the Zionist founders.

'The Diaspora was associated with weakness, defencelessness and persecution. Now the people were demonstrating strength and a willingness to fight.'[1]

The Shoah led to this aim being pursued all the more intensively. The physically weak Diaspora Jew, was thus argued, had allowed himself to be led to his own killing like a lamb to the slaughtering bank. The future was to belong to a new generation of strong and able-bodied people in the State of Israel, the future was to create the 'new Jew'.

'To the old concept of the "People of the book" the concept of the "people of the book and the sword" was added in Israel's self-image.'[2]

The negation of the exile became the negation of the 'old religion' and of the 'old Jew'. This strengthened the tendencies towards secularization and Hebraicization which had already begun before the Shoah. With the introduction of Hebrew, the names of the Jewish immigrants from the Diaspora were also turned into Hebrew: Simon Persky became Shimon Peres, Golda Meirsson Golda Meir, David Gruen became David Ben Gurion. Many old, Jewish-biblical names were combined with the post-biblical heroic period: 'Maccabi' (as a synonym for 'resistance' and 'struggle'), 'Barak' ('lightning'), 'Arie' ('lion'), 'Dov' ('bear'), 'Eitan' ('strong'), 'Oz' ('brave') or 'Zeev' ('wolf'). For the building of the 'Mamlahtiut' – the 'statehood' – the young state needed a political, secular identity which was nourished by the work ethic and the love for weapons. This pioneer generation of strong Jews born in Israel was called the 'Sabra' generation. 'Sabra' – the Hebrew term for the cactus fruit: hard and prickly on the outside, soft and sweet inside. This new cactus was supposed to defend itself with its

---

[1] Michael Wolffsohn and Douglas Bokovoy: Israel. Grundwissen – Länderkunde. Geschichte, Politik, Gesellschaft, Wirtschaft (1882–1994). Opladen 1995, p. 49.

[2] Yossi Beilin: Israel. A Concise Political History. New York 1992, p. 144.

thorns against the outside and therefore hold together the inside and prevent it from being wounded. The new immigrants had to adjust to this pioneer ideal.

Ghetto Fighters

The Israeli historian Tom Segev speaks of the 'myth of invulnerability'.³ This is based on the heroic interpretation of the Shoah. In Israel it was for a long time almost exclusively dealt with in connection with the history of the resistance fighters in the European ghettos. The identification of the Jewish Israelis with the Jewish victims of Europe was, of course, self evident – and also an instrument of power in foreign policy – but in domestic politics it has long remained incapable of triggering a feeling of identity. Yad Vashem, the national memorial for the victims and heroes of the Shoah in Jerusalem has embodied this contradiction ever since its foundation in 1953.

'Every non-Jewish guest who comes to visit us naturally feels obliged to visit Yad Vashem [...] to get into the right mood and to feel the appropriate feelings of guilt which are expected of him.'⁴

But in the Jewish visitor, on the other hand, feelings of resistance were to be wakened. The memory of the Shoah, therefore, had a double function: it was to point out to the international community of states that they had failed to give assistance in fighting the genocide of the Jews and to convince it to support the State of Israel as the only legitimate alternative to the continued suffering of the European Jews. In the opinion of the government under Ben Gurion, for the Jews in Palestine the memory of the Shoah, merely

1 Commemorative plaque for the 50th memorial day of the uprising in the Warsaw ghetto.

represented by the heroic ghetto fighter, should enable the conquest of as much territory as possible on both sides of the Jordan:

'Let us create a Jewish state immediately, even if this does not encompass the entire country. The rest will come with time. It has to.'⁵

To achieve this, a generation of warriors, a nation under arms was needed. The glorification of the ghetto fighter was designed to motivate the Israelis for the fight against the Arabs. The mani-

---

3   Tom Segev: Die Siebte Million. Der Holocaust und Israels Politik der Erinnerung. Reinbeck 1995, p. 518.
4   Benjamin Beit-Hallahmi: Schmutzige Geschäfte. Die geheimen Geschäfte Israels. Munich 1989, p. 9.

5   David Ben Gurion, in a letter to his wife Paula, 1938, quoted in: Benny Morris: 1948 and After. Israel and the Palestinians. New York 1990, p. 9. Morris uses further quotes which point to the fact that Ben-Gurion's acceptance of the partition plan of the Peel Commission 1937 and the acceptance of the UN apportionment plan of 1947 were merely a tactical decision and not a modification of the Zionist dream (settlement of both banks of the Jordan).

2 The gun barrels carry the names of the states Sudan, Algeria, Egypt, Saudi Arabia, Jordan, Iraq, Syria, Lebanon. From the Lebanese daily newspaper 'Al Djarida', May 31, 1967.

fold motives of attack of the Arab armies were deliberately reduced to the banal formula 'the Arabs want to throw us into the sea'. The danger of a 'second Shoah', this time caused by the Arabs, was evoked and determined the defence mentality of the Israelis. Still in 1993, on the 50th memorial day of the ghetto uprising in Warsaw, Rabin spoke of the exemplary function of the ghetto fighters:

'We have risen from the ashes of the martyrs and will live on. The courage of the ghetto fighters was the basis for the foundation of Israel.'[6]

But in fact, during the Shoah the Yishuv had not so much cared about the horror in Europe than about the building-up of their own state in Palestine. Neither militarily nor financially had the Yishuv contributed anything notable to the saving of the Jews in Europe. Nor has the mandate region of Palestine been the main destination of the Jews freed from the concentration camps after the war. Most of them wanted to go to other countries and only when this proved impossible did they choose the civil-war-ridden country of Palestine as an alternative. Therefore neither the victims nor the heroes of the Shoah were really the foundation pillar of the State of Israel.

Massada

A further element of the resistance myth was the politically extremely effective use of the 'Massada complex': the celebration of a historical legend in the form of a nationalistic ritual. In the fifties and sixties, bands of Israeli youth went on pilgrimage to Massada, a fortress situated on the top of an isolated rock in the Negev desert, the symbol of Hebrew resistance and pride. The ancient stones had 'political meaning'.[7] According to the official Israeli tradition, 960 Jewish 'fanatics' – 'zealots', had entrenched themselves there after the destruction of the temple and the fall of Jerusalem. In order not to have to surrender to the Romans, all but a few had committed suicide. The Romans of yesterday are the Arabs of today:

[6] Yitzhak Rabin: Speech on 17 April 1993 on the occasion of the 50th memorial day of the ghetto uprising in Warsaw. Foreign Ministry of Israel Information Service.

[7] Amos Elon: Interview, Jerusalem 20 March 1995. Wolffsohn and Bokovoy: Israel. Opladen 1995, p. 45.

'Massada represents the realization of the threat which had been present over all the centuries of Jewish history.'[8]

It had become popular in Israel as early as the thirties but was not excavated until 1963. Massada symbolized the possibility of a repeat of the killing, it represented the concept of a people that was totally alone and dependent on itself. In brief, Massada means that Esau always hated Jacob and always will, and this is the reason for the prayer: 'Massada should not fall a second time.' This element of the resistance mythos lost somewhat of its significance only after the conquest of Jerusalem during the Six-Day War in 1967 and with the reduction of the 'Mamlahiut' in the early seventies. The conquest and excavation of the Wailing Wall in 1967 meant that the national symbol had moved from the desert into the heart of the new Israel, to the centre of the 'eternal' capital Jerusalem.

Simon Bar Kokhba

More and more legends were added to the resistance identity of the Sabra, which were based on fragmentarily handed down incidents from antiquity. 'For the glorification of the Jewish resistance', the Maccabis were produced, who had defeated the Hellenic-Seleukidic Syrians and founded a Jewish state in the second century BCE. But the Zionist thinkers found the prototype of the self-defending Jew in the war hero Simon Bar Kokhba. Between 132 and 135 CE he had led the last Jewish revolt against the Romans. The 'Bar Kokhba syndrome' is defined as 'the admiration of a rebelliousness and heroism entirely liberated from the responsibility for the consequences'.[9] The resistance had cost the lives of hundreds of thousands of Jews and driven the Jewish people into exile. Nevertheless, this act of collective suicide is idealized in Israel. Poems were written about Bar Kokhba, streets, public places and buildings named after him and even a national, secular holiday, the Lag Ba-Omer, has been associated with the revolt due to his not clearly definable origin.

Josef Trumpeldor

The Trumpeldor legend is 'the defence mythos par excellence'.[10] Josef Trumpeldor was a one-armed, Jewish-Russian officer, who was killed in 1920 while defending a settlement in the north of Israel. He became the model for the Jewish settlers: he had presumably been killed by Arabs, not as a battle-tested regular soldier but as a righteous peaceful farmer. The place of his murder, the Moshaw Tel-Hai, where a huge statue of a lion had been erected, became an annual place of pilgrimage for generations of schoolchildren from all over Israel. 'Tel-Hai' was what the youth movement of the rightist Zionist revisionists chose as its motto, 'Betar' (Berit Josef Trumpeldor) as its name. The day of Trumpeldor's and of his comrades' death was declared a national day of commemoration by the Yishuv. The suspiciously heroic last words of a dying hero: 'Tov laamud behad laaretz' – 'It is good to die for the fatherland', which were celebrated in blood and soil rituals by the father of Revisionism, Vladimir (Zeev) Jabotinsky, were also attributed to Trumpeldor.

The heroic myths fulfilled their objective of promoting a militant mentality for the foundation of the state. Still today, they have their place in the 'collective memory' of the Jewish Israelis, even though they are increasingly questioned in public discussion.

---

[8] Barry Schwartz, Yael Zerubavel et al.: The Recovery of Massada: A Study in Collective Memory. In: Eyal Ben-Ari (ed.): Defining Israeli Culture: An Anthropological Approach. Jerusalem 1995, pp. 158–167, here p. 160.

[9] Harkabi, Yehoschafat, quoted in: Susan Hattis Rolef: The Political Dictionary of the State of Israel. Jerusalem 1993, p. 53.

[10] Beilin: Israel, p. 139.

Barbara Lüthi

The Variability of History: Israel's Historian Debate

Myth and History

'Culture' can be conceived as a term for collective meanings which social groups produce together, share and express symbolically and from which a specific way of thinking and behaving follows. In each period of history, a limited and changeable supply of central themes exist which are expressed symbolically by myths and rituals and which contain the most important values and goals of the community. Cultures are not produced, upheld and changed in a vacuum, rather they exist in a specific social, economic and political constellation by which they are formed and which they also form in a dialectic interchange.

In this process, myths can be understood as a 'narrative', as a 'story-telling element' which seeks to anchor the present in the past and give it a specific meaning. From this perspective, they can give us clues as to how a nation or social group produces its collective memory. If one sees myths, not simply as false belief or dogmas, despite contradicting historical facts, they can be a legitimate and necessary means for understanding long-term processes.

Since the eighties of our century, there has been an on-going public debate in the sciences and media in Israel which questions the self-image of Israel as a Zionist state. Part of the challenge is reflected in the criticism by a largely younger generation of historians of the 'official historical version' of Zionism, understood as the histography which was determined by the Labor Zionist Movement. Since the inception of the State of Israel, Zionism represents the leading pattern of Israeli political culture. Up to this day, it has had an important influence on its identity. The formation of a Jewish nation was accompanied by mythical resort to motifs such as the

'ingathering of the exiled, the upbuilding of Zion as a model Society, the creation of a new Jewish type and an overarching vision of national redemption'.[1]

The stressing of national security, unity, rootedness, pioneer spirit and military virtues apparently represented an indispensability in the creation of the state for the Zionists. The prerequisites of a land with poor natural resources and surrounded by a foreign culture required a high level of motivation and collective willpower.

The 'new historians' see their task in a 'demythologizing' of the existing official version of history. In a comparison of 'old' and 'new' history, Benny Morris as a representative of the new generation, paraphrased the problem in 1988 as follows, especially with respect to the year of the foundation of the state:

'The essence of the old history is that Zionism was a beneficent and well-meaning progressive rational movement; that Isreal was born pure into an uncharitable, predatory world; that Zionist efforts at compromise and conciliation were rejected by the Arabs, and in their wake the surrounding Arab states, for reasons of innate selfishness, xenophobia, and downright cussedness, re-

[1] Robert Wistrich and David Ohana: The Shaping of Israeli Identity. Myth, Memory and Trauma. London 1995, p. X.

fused to accede to the burgeoning Zionist presence and in 1947 to 1949 launched a war to extirpate the foreign plant [...] The old historians offered a simplistic and consciously pro-Israel interpretation of the past, and they deliberately avoided mentioning anything that would reflect badly on Israel [...] Blackening Israel's image, it was argued, would ultimately weaken Israel in its ongoing war for survival. In short, raisons d'état often took precedence over telling the truth. The past few years have witnessed the emergence of a new generation of Israeli scholars and a "new" history. These historians, some of them living abroad, have looked and are looking afresh at the Israeli historical experience, and their conclusions, by and large, are at odds with those of the old historians.'[2]

'Rewriting Zionism'

The challenge for historiography has existed, from a political point of view, ever since the creation of the State of Israel in 1948. Not only the Palestinian side had an alternative view. Within the Israeli radical left wing, led by the Communist party, and the right wing, Herut and Likud, just as from feminist circles and the Arab Israelis, criticism was directed at the existing historiography: their history had been excluded from it. Through literature, lyricism, and political events they tried to change this. Not until the seventies and then increasingly in the eighties did mainly Israeli academics, by no means a homogeneous group, begin to include some of the views of these groups in their academic work. In addition to the historians, sociologists, anthropologists, political scientists and other specialists, but also exponents of cultural life joined in. The emergence of this academic debate could be traced back to a number of clearly recognizable reasons. At the beginning of the eighties, after the opening of various archives, academics were offered access to previously unknown state documents. Furthermore, a generation of historians had now come of age which had a background of experience different from that of older historians who were still influenced by the initial stage of the foundation of the state. Finally, a new source of problems had its effect: the Six-Day War of 1967 with its territorial expansion into Palestinian areas, the Yom-Kippur War of 1973, the reinforcement of the Sephardic political group in favour of the Likud, the escalation of violence in the Palestinian zones, the criticism and condemnation of the Israeli politics by foreign countries, the effects of the Lebanon war and the ever-increasing contrasts betwen the religious and secular groups of the society supported a re-evaluation of history and the Zionist ideology. In addition, the 'de-ideologization' and westernization of the Israeli society which took place in the eighties played a major role: materialism, individualism and consume orientation supported a pluralistic way of life and thinking. Major ideological syntheses were increasingly rejected. The society of the nineties split more and more into different ethnic groups, into local references, and in a cultivation of the Diaspora roots.

The beginning of the peace negotiations and the altered consciousness which went with it promoted the publicness of this debate.

'What we're doing is rewriting Zionism. Of course, it's because the Zionist project has won that we can do what we're doing.'[3]

One of the central questions of the debate rotated around the problems of the foundation stage of the state. Various 'myths' were questioned critically and the events shown in a new light: that the Zionist movement agreed less enthusiastically to the UN partition plan for Palestine in 1947 than previously suggested; that the surrounding Arab states did not unite to form a closed front with the Palestinians in order to destroy the growing Jewish state; that in the

---

[2] Benny Morris: The New Historiography. Israel Confronts its Past. In: Tikkun 3 (Nov./Dec. 1988) 6, p. 20.

[3] Ethan Bronner: Rewriting Zionism. In: Boston Globe, 27 November 1994, Sunday Magazine, p. 22.

war, it was not a militarily weak David facing a strong Arab Goliath; that the Palestinian Arabs did not flee as ordered by the Arab states and that Israel did not truly make efforts to reach peace at the end of the war. In a re-evaluation of the Palestinian refugee problem of the years 1947 to 1949, Benny Morris criticized the existing attitude that the flight of the Palestinian Arabs was mainly an immediate consequence of an appeal from the Arab governments and leaders by radio, through which those living in the country were requested to evacuate the area due to the state of war and not to return until the victory of the Arab armies was secure. In this view, the fleeing of the war zone was voluntary and not due to Jewish pressure. During his research, Morris found no evidence to support these statements. Much more, he believed in a 'multi-causal multi-staged model', in which the flight was a result of various coinciding factors: fear of attacks, orders from the Palestinian leaders and reactions to attacks of the Jewish military. Further issues, which were subjected to criticism and re-evaluation, reach from relationships between the Yishuv and Nazi Germany through to the denunciation of Zionism as a 'colonialist phenomenon'. Even the once untouched personalities such as Ben Gurion were subjected to critical analysis.

The consciousness of existing tensions in the country, not only between Israelis and Palestinians, but also within the Israeli society itself, now makes it clear that the state was not fulfilling all Zionist ideals. The generation of new historians views the Zionist movement as merely one out of several elements in a dynamic field of events and movements in the region. The viewpoint of the non-Zionist groups in the country has to be taken into consideration. With increasing clarity, the debate showed that the production of knowledge – of supposed historical realities – takes place within the scope of power struggles which privileges one historical perspective over another. History is an 'always problematic and incomplete reconstruction of what no longer exists'.[4]

Critical Voices

And it is just this of which the new historians are now being accused: 'to read history backwards' and to project 'the present into the past'.[5] The statement of Benny Morris, is being critized, namely that the new history

'may also in some obscure way serve the purposes of peace and reconciliation between the warring tribes of that land'.[6]

The aims are no longer academic, but the political standpoint of the academic is decisive. This is the accusation formulated by the new historians that the old historians had placed their interpretation of history in the service of Zionism. However, the newness of the debate is denied: the notion of a historical original sin, the dispossession of the Palestinian Arabs, is considered to be as old as Zionism itself. Furthermore a tendency towards the re-evaluation of history can also be observed in many countries such as Germany, France and Japan. Here too, the new research refers to the traumatic events of the respective country. However, the debate must be considered as 'Israel centred' inasmuch as exclusively Jewish, Israeli and most of all Zionist subjects are at the focus.

In addition to the political aims of the new historians, methodological and content-related procedures that distort the image of the past are also being attacked. Following the words of the author Aharon Megged every historian selects from the

---

[4] Pierre Nora: Zwischen Geschichte und Gedächtnis. Berlin 1990, pp. 12 f.
[5] Shlomo Slonim: The 'New Historians' and the Establishment of Israel. In: Studies in Contemporary Jewry 7 (1991) p. 306.
[6] Shabtai Teveth: Charging Israel with Original Sin. In: Commentary 88 (Sept. 1989) 3, pp. 24 ff.

garbage heap of facts of the past, facts that fit his purpose, and ignores others.

'[...] It is possible to write the history of WW II focusing on the suffering of the German people from Allied bombings and invasions, and it will all be based on facts – for indeed the Germans suffered terribly [...] Similarly, some Israeli historians now "prove", with great pleasure, that our self-defense wars were really wars to destroy another people, and they attribute to Israeli soldiers, our own flesh and blood, the face and mentality of Nazi stormer troopers'.[7]

The accusation of not regarding the events appropriately in their surroundings and of having selected one-sided sources comes from the right-wing political spectrum, but also from the Palestinian camp. Megged demands that history shall not only be written on the basis of written documents, the researchers should also 'talk with those who were there at the time'. The Palestinians see things similarly, when it is emphasized that neither Palestinian research approaches nor Arab sources nor the orally acquired statements of the Palestinian refugees are taken into account.

'History and historiography ought not necessarily be written, exclusively or mainly, by the victors. They should be used as tools for initiating dialogue or even cooperation across the national divide.'[8]

1 Jerusalem, May 1996: Women of the 'right wing' demonstrate after an assault by Palestinians on Jewish settlers in Ramallah with masks and pictures of Yassir Arafat and Shimon Peres against the policy of the then Israeli prime minister. Photograph: Menahem Kahana.

The debate still reflects the conditions of the Israeli-Palestinian conflict.

The debate is far from being finished. It represents not only a purely academic dispute but also a changing society in a new process of struggle with its Arab neighbours and its own minorities in the country. In Israel an era has begun in which one day, the national consensus may no longer be produced via the danger of destruction and the resulting security policies, but the agreement about a new face of the society and its culture will have to be negotiated. Possibly the conclusion of an Israeli scientist is still valid for the historiography to date when he states that

'more perspective is needed but, beyond that, a new generation of researchers is needed, a generation that not only was not personally involved in the events of the time, but that can free itself of one obligation or another to support one of the sides which participated in the history of the period. The time of seeing that period in pure-

---

[7] David Bar-Illan in: Jerusalem Post, 17 June 1994, see also Aharon Megged: Haaretz, 10 June 1994, pp. 27 ff.
[8] Nur Mashala: '1948 and After' Revisited. In: Journal of Palestine Studies 24 (Summer 1995) 4, p. 95.

ly historical terms has not yet begun; we are still at war over that war.'⁹

The newer historiography in Israel is not less confronted with the problem of subjectivity and myth than the old one. Yet, the identity of a country, and the problems associated with it, can depend on how past events are viewed: on what is seen as the own and as foreign, on what collective images this is anchored in the heads of the people and symbolically expressed, how eventually the social ability to conceive and memory can be translated into action and thus influence the social reality.

---

⁹ Bronner: Rewriting Zionism, p. 22.

Simon Erlanger

Topicality of Zionism

The annual general meeting of the 'World Jewish Congress' took place in Jerusalem in January 1996. The World Jewish Congress is one of the most important parent organizations of all Jewish groups from all over the world. At this meeting all eyes were turned to the future and the question of Jewish continuity, which seems more and more threatened in the Diaspora. What is left for the Jewish organizations to do, now that after the fall of the USSR, the Jews may practise their religion and culture freely, in the countries of the CIS and can emigrate any time without hindrance? How will the relationship between the Jewish Diaspora, the 'Gola', and the Jewish state turn out in an epoch which is no longer characterized by mutual aims? What influence does the peace process have on the solidarity between Gola and Israel? How can a common Jewish identity be defined, after the smallest common denominator – the existential threat – seems to have become obsolete? Can we succeed in building up an identity that is based on positive Jewish traditions and values and not only on the memory of former isolation, persecution and extermination, or the mutual defence against present-day threats? Can the threat of the demographic disappearance of the Gola due to assimilation, declining birth rates and the superannuation be stopped at all? And finally: Is there anything at all that still connects the different parts of Jewish society? Is there any mutuality left at all?

Demands for Normalization

One of the best known guest speakers at the conference in Jerusalem was the Israeli author Abraham B. Jehoshua. His words: 'We don't need your money anymore!' shocked the audience.[1] According to Jehoshua, since the Second World War the identity of the Jews of the Gola had centred on the following focal points: As today most Jews were wordly minded and thus had drifted away from traditional Jewish culture, until recently, Jewish identity, besides the memory of the Shoah, the fight against anti-Semitism and the help to the Jews in the USSR, was mainly based on the identification with Israel – by way of donations, political support and moral pressure to join the Aliyah.

All of these identification factors had become invalid because of the peace process. In the times of the 'dividends of peace', which are accompanied by an extraordinarily high rate of economic growth, Israel was no longer dependent on donations. Today Israel was politically accepted by the world, had broken out of isolation and was maintaining relations with the former Eastern bloc as well as most parts of the Arabic world. And finally, after the mass immigration from the CIS, the

---

[1] A copy of the thesis, which Jehoshua later wrote, was kindly handed over to the author of this essay by Prof. Dr. Jakob Hessing from the Hebrew University Jerusalem: Abraham B. Jehoshua: Elementim Hadashim WeDialog Hadash (New elements and new dialog). Typoscript. Jerusalem, February 1996.

problem of the Aliyah was also settled, as no major waves of immigration are to be expected anymore from the democratic and prosperous West. Thus the financial and political support of the Gola was no longer needed. This, however, leads to a loosening of the relationship between the Diaspora and the State of Israel, to a vacuum in the identity of the Diaspora Jews and finally to an increasing distance between Israel and the Jews of the Gola. According to Jehoshua, this development could be remedied by spreading the Hebrew language as 'lingua franca' of the Jews, by creating common aims for Israel and the Diaspora in their efforts for the 'Third World', and by establishing organizations which think about the future and work out concepts, as well as by the magic word 'Jewish education'. But: 'There is nothing to be done. We have to get used to the fact that an Israel in misery can no longer be the source of identity for Jews for the simple reason that Israel is getting out of this misery more and more.' As early as 1984, Jehoshua had already expressed similiar ideas.[2] He was obviously looking for indications of what Israel should look like in the future. Should it be a 'Jewish State'? This would have consequences for the right to immigrate and the immediate award of citizenship to the Jews of the Diaspora as well as for the non-Jewish minorities which after all make up 18 percent of the population. Or should Israel become a 'normal' state, a 'state of all its citizens', that would abondon its specific Jewish character and would 'simply' be concerned with the welfare of all its citizens?

Zionism after the Foundation of the State in 1948

With the proclamation of the State of Israel, the Zionist movement had achieved its most important objective. But through the creation of firm state structures and the foundation of an own Israeli identity, it somehow became superfluous. Its institutions lost its quasi-governmental functions. Thus the activities of the 'Jewish Agency', which during the time of the British Mandate in Palestine had served as some kind of official government and representative of the Jewish part of the population, the 'Yishuv', were reduced to dealing with immigration, education and raising money. Other institutions, such as the 'Jewish National Fund', which were concerned with buying, cultivating and reafforesting land, were accepted and integrated into the state with only little difficulty. Until today, the Zionist movement so rich in traditions is still looking for its own area of responsibility and its own profile. Today, political decisions concerning the 'Jewish state' are no longer made at the still regularly held Zionist congresses with delegates from all over the world, but rather by representative institutions of the sovereign State of Israel.

The idea remains. But even here changes were unavoidable: from a broadly based movement, Zionism developed after 1948 into a state-bearing ideology. Here the 'Mapai' party, today the main part of the 'Maarach' – the labour party – played an important role. It had led and decisively formed the Yishuv during the development of the state in the thirties and forties and during the War of Independence 1948/49. With its socialistic pioneer ethos, the Mapai substantially contributed to the building of the country and created the basis for the independence and the economic and social developments which followed. On the other hand, this party ruled Israel from 1948 until 1977, virtually uncontested, together with its coalition partners, forming a closely knit, yes, even corrupt establishment. The economy, the unions and medical insurances, the media, positions of power and influential positions were practically monopolized by the Mapai. Although Israel always had a multi-party system, a functioning parliament and an independent judiciary, over the

[2] Abraham B. Jehochua: BiShut HaNormaliut (In the Name of Normality). Jerusalem, Tel Aviv 1984.

years, especially in the economic sector, it showed traits of a one-party system with various abuses, inefficiencies and multiplying scandals.

Realization of Zionism in the New State

Even if the Zionists were right with their analyses of the deadly danger for the Jews in Europe at the beginning of the 20th century, they could not possibly have conceived the extent of the Shoah. They even found an answer to this threat: the 'Jewish state'. However, its foundation came too late to save the Jewish population of Europe from persecution and extermination, but by 1948 more than 600,000 Jews had found refuge in Israel.

The young state made it its duty to guarantee that in the future Jews would always have a refuge and that they would have the means to defend themselves. From this point of view, Zionism was and is successful. Israel has become an established state. Until today, its Jewish population has increased up to 4.5 million people. Now as before, the support of immigration is one of the fundamental aims of the Israeli state. This can be seen especially in the so-called 'law of return' which grants every person of Jewish origin the right to immigrate and the immediate right to Israeli citizenship. In practice, however, problems arise as it is controversial who can be regarded as a Jew. Zionism was not successful in keeping promise that with the creation of a state, anti-Semitism would disappear. In Europe it is still alive and the Arabic national movement has bluntly adopted it in dealing with the Zionists. In an atmosphere of periodically recurring wars and terror, the Zionist visions of harmony and of a state of Israel playing the role of the 'light of people' as fulfilment of the prophetic demand seemed to be a misappreciation of bitter realities. The problem seemed to have shifted from an individual to a national level: 'Israel had become the "Jew of the nations", the "Pariah people", had become the "Pariah nation".'[3] The climax of this development was reached with a UN resolution, which has meanwhile been abrogated again, that equated Zionism with racism in the mid seventies.

Social and Ethnic Conflicts

In a state that in such a short time, under such unfavourable conditions had absorbed so many immigrants from the most different countries and cultures, social and ethnic conflicts were almost inevitable. They first arose in the fifties and sixties particularly with the immigration of oriental Jews from Jemen, Iraq, India, Morocco, Tunisia and Algeria. Great tensions arose between the Oriental and the European Jews due to socio-cultural differences, a justified feeling of being neglected, of being discriminated and of being culturally dominated by the Israeli establishment. The Oriental Jews formed a 'second Israel' in the slums of the big cities and the 'developing cities' were hastily built. This had not been foreseen by the utopia of classical Zionism as a movement which also promised to solve the social problems of Jews from all over the world.

Thus the term Zionism grew increasingly hollow in Israeli reality. The positive achievements of Zionism, the state, the immigrations, were already taken for granted by a younger generation, were assumed and faded in the face of the bitter reality of daily life, of the continuous external conflicts with war and terror and of the social crisis. The blame for this misery was increasingly put on Zionism as the state-supporting ideology. Though it did remain a basic value shared by most people, it was now more often met with ambivalent emotions. Thus 'LeDaber Zionut' – talking Zionism – is a familiar expression which means 'to talk with empty pathos'.

---

[3] Conor Cruise O'Brien: Belagerungszustand. Die Geschichte des Zionismus und des Staates Israel. Munich 1991, p. 212.

'In its hour of triumph, Zionism became an alien element, an anachronism in the new state. All those who had led the fight for independence were Zionists. Zionism was the ruling ideology. In modern Israeli literature though, one can easily detect the widespread feeling of the young Israelis that high-flown ideas and the choice of words of the old Zionists have no meaning in the world in which the youth has to grow up. Life and people have become more complicated because there is a discrepancy [...] between the language and the reality of the past on the one hand and the reality of the present on the other.'[4]

1967 as Turnabout

The Six-Day War of June 1967 decisively changed this situation. Until then, Zionism, despite all of its problems, had been the naturally accepted main consensus of the Israeli society. Anyone who was not a Zionist – like the ultra-orthodox of the 'Neturei Karta', the 'Guardians of the City' in Jerusalem, who considered political Zionism to be a religious sin, because only the Messiah was allowed to build up a Jewish state – excluded himself from Israeli society. After 1967, different tendencies gained in importance besides the predominant school of thought in Zionism. The victory fundamentally changed Israeli politics. For the first time since the destruction of the Second Temple, Jerusalem and large parts of the biblical land of Israel with an extremely high percentage of the Palestinian population were under Jewish control.

As early as 1968, the then ruling Labour Party, the Maarach, tried to give back the conquered territories in exchange for peace and recognition. After the triple no of the Arab League at the conference of Khartum – no to negotiations, no to peace, no to recognition – the Maarach tried to strengthen the unification of Jerusalem and to get safe, defensible borders by building up settlements in the Jordan valley, on the Golan heights and in other strategic positions in the Westbank and Gaza. This objective was quite pragmatic: most Palestinian territories were not claimed. These were to be returned to Jordan as enclaves.

In this situation, other forms of Zionism, which had hardly been noticed before by the public at large, suddenly gained attention: on the one hand a strict nationalist interpretation of Zionism in the tradition of the Revisionism of Vladimir Zeev Jabotinski and, on the other hand, a strict religious and Messianic-oriented form in the tradition of Rabbi Abraham Isaak Kook. Both traditions have given rise to numerous groups ranging from moderate to extreme and fanatic. Most of them entertain maximalistic territorial claims. And only some of them are willing to accept the idea of a territorial compromise and the realities created in recent times by the Oslo agreements.

Messianism

Immediately after the end of the Six-Day War, the 'Land of Israel Movement' was founded by prominent politicians, academics and cultural public figures to protest against the intentions of the government to exchange conquered territories for peace. In this movement, representatives of the Labour Party, who wanted nothing more than strategically secure, militarily defensible borders, came together with Revisionists and right-wing activists who demanded the entire biblical land of Israel for nationalist reasons. After the negotiations had broken down, a return of the occupied territories was no longer in question. Only in 1978 when the autonomy agreement was signed in Camp David was the future of the territories discussed again. At this time, many members of the 'Land of Israel Movement' had already become spokesmen of a third group of young activists, representing a particular tendency of religious Zionism. It has ideologically influenced the settlement policy in the occupied

---

[4] O'Brien: Belagerungszustand, p. 211.

1 'Jerusalem Day 1994.' National religious juveniles celebrate the anniversary of the capture of Jerusalem in the Six-Day War in 1967.

territories. From among its ranks the settlement activists of the 'Gusch Emunim' – the 'Block of the Believers' – were recruited. With its Messianic demands, this group goes far beyond classical Zionism, even to the extent of questioning it.

In 1902 the religious wing of the Zionist movement had united in the group called 'Mizrachi'. Although the religious aspect of the return to Zion was always more important to this wing than the creation of a mere place of refuge, the Mizrachi had always remained moderate. For Rav Izhak Reines, one of the founders of the Mizrachi, Zionism was less the beginning of Messianic redemption than an answer to the burning problems of the persecuted Jews of his time. Thus it was only logical that the 'Mafdal', the political wing of the party of the Mizrachi, had been a member of the coalition and reliable junior partner in every government of the Labour Party since 1948, whose policy it shared and among which it was a moderate power representing the interests of the religious tendencies.

Under the influence of the teachings of Rav Kook, the first chief rabbi of the Yishuv, this attitude slowly began to change. For to Rav Kook, the Zionist venture was the 'Atchalta DiGeula' – 'the beginning of redemption' –, the beginning of the Messianic age, which according to tradition was connected with the return of the Jewish people to Zion. According to Kook's mystical point of view, the secular Zionists, in spite of their alienation from traditional Judaism, were the unwitting agents of God's will, Herzl the forerunner of the actual Messiah. The philosophy of Rav Kook 'sanctified' the secular Zionist movement to a certain extent and conferred upon it a religious importance. Therefore Kook did not in the least consider himself to be in opposition to it, did not found a political movement, and did not raise politically motivated demands.

This changed with the Six-Day War. The tremendous and fast victory, with the conquest of the old city of Jerusalem and the Temple Mount, was seen by many as a miracle, as a divine sign. Kook's students, who after his death gathered round his son Rav Zevi Judah Kook, considered themselves to be confirmed. They were living in the Messianic age. This victory was another step on the way to deliverance. Consequently, political actions had to be taken. The whole country of Israel was holy, not another inch must be given up during the negotiations. Their slogan was: 'The land of Israel for the people of Israel based on the Torah of Israel'. This no longer corresponded with the pragmatic attitude of traditional political Zionism. Activities set in that turned a religious philosophical trend which had previously played only a minor role into one of the most influential political powers in Israel, that no government could ignore any longer. This movement succeeded in finding a large base of support, especially among the youth. In addition, it now dominates the 'Mafdal', which today is part of the right wing. Followers of this trend have taken on considerable influence in Israeli society and increasingly fill positions which in the past had rather been reserved for the left-oriented elite of the kibbutzniks. The representatives of the Messianic-oriented Zionism are now divided into a dozen groups, which, however, range from quite liberal and conditionally prepared to compromise, right through to radical extremists and fanatics.

'Normalization?'

But besides Messianism there is also a peace movement. Formed after the Lebanon war of 1982, its core is a group called 'Shalom Ahshav' – 'Peace Now'. In contrast to the 'Berit Shalom' – the 'Peace Alliance' – in the twenties and thirties and the 'Ihud' – the 'Unity' – of the forties, who have striven for a binational Jewish-Arab state with an administration on equal terms, the new movement is working towards a historical compromise with the Palestinians on the basis of 'land for peace'. They advocate the formation of a Palestinian polity or even state besides Israel. Many of its supporters are deeply rooted in classical Zionism. They stand for a variety of traditional, territorially compromising Zionist policy and for political and moral reasons disapprove of the continued occupation of the territories. Fears for the Jewish character of the state are often expressed. 'Rather a Jewish state in a part of the country of Israel, than a binational state in the whole country of Israel' is increasingly heard.

In addition there is a wing, which though small in number, is intellectually highly influential, and which speaks in support of a normalization that neutralizes the classical Zionist concept of normalization. According to these 'post-Zionists', Israel should become a 'normal' state that existed as an integral part of the Middle East and denounced its Jewish character. Israel is to be reconstructed as the 'state of its inhabitants'. The Jewish and Arabic inhabitants, thus the most extreme supporters of this movement, are to be blended into a new independent Israeli culture and identity. The specific Jewish symbols – such as the flag and the anthem – are to be changed. Furthermore, the manifold spiritual and material connections to the Jewish Diaspora are to be discontinued. Jehoshua's thoughts as mentioned in the beginning also go in this direction, although he is not که radical and still wants to preserve the Jewish character of Israel. All of the groups in this camp have as their common interest the

2   Passers-by mourn for Yitzak Rabin, November 1995.

claim for a separation of church and state, for the total secularization of legislation and social and cultural life.

In Israel today both Messianism and normalization have minority positions, even if they are partially influential and loud. The majority – by no means unified – is somewhere between these extreme positions. Second-hand ideologies are of diminishing importance to them. If Israel was an island under siege until recently, the peace process has now allowed a cautious opening, above all in thinking. Borders fell, enemies became potential allies, even in this region Israel is now accepted as a valuable partner. Still nothing is final, a lot is fragile, the right path has not yet been found. For most Israelis, Zionism is an uncritical basic outlook which determines the attitude towards the complex of problems of state and society, Israel and the Diaspora. Thus for most of them it goes without saying that the

Jewish character of the state should be upheld. But now that the light of organized classical Zionism starts to fade and the traditional Zionist values, such as self-sacrifice and collectivism are being replaced by values of the western consumer society, a search for new orientations has started. Demands to emphasize Jewish sources are growing louder, even when leaving the paths of traditional religiousness. Also in the Jewish education, the reflection upon the sources of Jewish culture is to be given more importance. In the future a new Israeli and therefore ultimately also a new Jewish identity will probably develop out of the tense relationships between Zionism, traditional sources and normalization.

Appendix

Desanka Schwara

Glossary

Acculturation Encounter of one's own culture with another culture in the hope of achieving a synthesis.

Agudat Israel 'The Union of Israel' (Hebrew). Association of orthodox Jews who live by their religious laws, notably from Germany and Eastern Europe. Founded in Katowice in 1912 with the aim of combating the spread of endeavours to assimilate and Zionist ambitions in Western and Eastern Europe. An agreement of the religious →*Mapai* and other Zionist parties with the Agudat Israel in 1947 is held to be the unwritten constitution governing religious policy. Extensive concessions were made to orthodoxy in state life and social life in order to secure their co-operation.

Agunah Agunah (Hebrew 'the abandoned') describes a woman who is committed to her missing husband and is not allowed to remarry until evidence of his death is produced. However the obligation to furnish proof has been alleviated over the centuries, and credible circumstantial evidence will suffice to release the wife from her commitment to a deceased man. But in traditional Judaism a woman who has been abandoned cannot dissolve her marriage and therefore cannot enter into a new marriage. According to Jewish law, there can be no divorce without the co-operation of the husband, and at the very least a divorce letter personally signed by him remains necessary. A husband who is left by his wife without being divorced is called Agun.

Ahasuerus A legendary figure, 'The eternal Jew', who is forbidden from resting anywhere and has to wander around restlessly through the world as a punishment for beating Christ and supposedly refusing him a brief rest. This legend which can be traced back to several sources and has been chronicled several times since the mid 13th century, enjoyed great popularity since it reinforced the widespread hostility towards Jews and served as evidence of Christian salvation. Its best-known form was found in the 'Volksbuch' (Popular Book) dating from 1602. Since that time it has repeatedly been taken up as a literary theme and also been reworked by Jewish authors, not least by Zionists. The creator of the Ahasuerus legend must have been ignorant of Jewish issues and cannot have been acquainted with Jewish life. In 'Ahasuerus' he chose a name which cannot be found in Jewish literature and was also not in common everyday use. It is likely that he was recalling the non-Jewish husband of Esther, Ahasuerus (which is of old Persian or Babylonian origin).

Ahavath Zion 'Love of Zion' (Hebrew). Austrian association for the colonization of Palestine which was founded in Vienna in 1882 as a reaction to the Russian pogroms. Its objectives were largely the same as those of the →*Hibbat Zion*. However, it was dissolved a year later. In 1899 an association with this name was established again, this time in Pressburg, from the →*Shiur* set up in 1897, the →*Talmud* course for young business people.

Alliance Israélite Universelle An international aid organization founded in Paris in 1860. The principle conviction of the Alliance was that all Jews should have to stand up for one another. An end had to be put to the special laws for Jews, despotism, violence and suppression. The Alliance championed the cause of Jews in all countries where help was necessary. In addition to political work it rendered humanitarian assistance where there was famine, typhoid, pogroms and in areas ravaged by war. It took care of Jewish orphans and organized emigration to America. It set up schools and apprentice workshops for boys and girls throughout the world, for example an agricultural school in Palestine in 1870 →*Mikveh Israel*.

Aliyah / Aliyot The 'ascent' (Hebrew). Aliyah describes a process which is associated with a spiritual enhancement of the personality, such as the pilgrimage to the temple in Jerusalem and being called to read the →*Torah*. Since Zionist ideas from 1882 onwards demanded the resettlement of Palestine by the Jews, Aliyah has explicitly meant the immigration of Jews to Palestine. At the same time the various waves of immigrants bear witness to the persecution and suppression of the Jewish population in other countries. After the five Aliyot prior to the creation of the State of Israel, survivors of the →*Shoah* and Jewish immigrants from Arab countries immigrated from 1948 onwards. To date, the last large-scale immigration waves have been from Ethiopia and Russia.

Assimilation The surrender to a large extent of an individual's own culture by adapting to another culture.

Bar Mitzvah 'Son of the law' (Hebrew). A Jewish boy becomes a Bar Mitzvah by undergoing a religious ritual at the age of thirteen. From this point onwards he has to fulfil all the religious duties of an adult man. Girls reach the age of majority in a religious sense at the age of twelve. There has been a 'Bat Mitzvah' since the 19th century, principally in Reform Judaism.

Bet ha-Midrash 'House of study' (Hebrew). House of prayer in which communal study is undertaken of the →*Torah*, the →*Talmud* and other religious texts before and after prayer in the synagogue in the morning and in the evening. These houses of prayer with their collections of books existed in all Jewish communities. The Hassidic houses of prayer in Eastern Europe were called 'Shtibl' (Yiddish), 'little room'.

Betar Abbreviation for 'Berit Trumpeldor', the 'Trumpeldor Union', the Jewish youth organization founded in Riga by the →*Zionist Revisionists* named after Joseph Trumpeldor who was killed fighting the Arabs in 1920. Betar campaigned on behalf of colonization and self-defence in Palestine by militant means and trained young people accordingly. Members of Betar fought in the Warsaw Ghetto revolt in 1943 and in the underground organizations before the foundation of the State of Israel. At the same time the name is evocative of a fortress in Israel which was the last one to be captured by the Romans in the year 135 CE during the revolt led by Bar Kokhba.

Bilu/Biluim Abbreviation for 'Beit Yaakov Lekhu ve-Nelkhah', 'House of Jacob come ye and let us go' (Isaiah 2:5). The student organization was founded in Kharkov in January 1882 as a reaction to the pogroms of 1881 with the objective of settling in Palestine. The first Jewish students were able to emigrate to Palestine as early as summer 1882 with the assistance of →*Hovevei Zion*. The Bilu movement was an influential role model for the first →*Aliyah*.

Bnai Akiwa 'Sons of Akiwa' (Hebrew). A youth group of the religious Zionist →*Mizrachi* movement founded in Jerusalem in 1929. Originally influenced by socialist ideas and associated with the →*Kibbutz* movement, in Israel today it is politically close to the settler movement (→*Gush Emunim*). Their name originated from the Jewish martyr and important scholar Rabbi Akiwa [50–135 CE].

Bnai B'rith 'Sons of the Covenant' (Hebrew). Association of Jewish lodges, since Jews were in most cases not accepted in Christian lodges in spite of their humanistically worded objectives. They set themselves the task of bringing together Jews to promote high humanitarian aims. Pursuing the principles of philanthropy, they wanted to support the sciences and arts, provide relief for the destitution of the poor and needy, visit and take care of the ill (→*Hevrot*) and help the victims of persecutions. These objectives were not supposed to be restricted to individual confessions, but were intended to be all-embracing, spanning political and religious conflicts with the aim of achieving understanding among people. Founded in America by German Jewish immigrants, Bnai B'rith was able in the course of time to win over supporters for its aims in many countries in Europe, the Americas, Asia, and Africa. The association also played a very active part in the struggle against anti-Semitism and racism.

Bnai Moshe 'Sons of Moses' (Hebrew). Secret national Jewish league formed in Odessa in 1889 by Ahad Haam. Bnai Moshe advocated the cultural renewal of the Jewish people. With its conviction that a sense of national identity and the rebirth of Jewish self-confidence were necessary preconditions, it began its cultural work in the →*Diaspora*. It greatly influenced the →*Hibbat Zion* movement.

Bund Abbreviation for 'General Jewish Workers' Alliance in Lithuania, Poland, and Russia'. Founded in Vilnius in 1897, it was strongly influenced by Marxism. In 1898 it joined the Russian Social Democratic Workers' Party as an autonomous group. It advocated a non-territorial autonomy of the Jewish population in the countries in which it lived, social revolution and the recognition of Yiddish as a national language. The Bund proved to be a committed opponent of Zionism and exerted a considerable influence on the masses, although there were interconnections via socialist Zionist groups.

Central Association of German Nationals of the Jewish Faith This association was founded in Berlin in 1893 with the objective of protecting the civil and national equality of German nationals of Jewish faith regardless of their religious and political stance, endorsing the adoption of a German mentality and an identification with the German people at the same time as it tried to fight anti-Semitism. It rejected any kind of Jewish nationalism. It adopted a liberal stance with regard to Jewish settlements, whether in Palestine or elsewhere, as long as they were not established out of national motives.

Diaspora 'Dispersion' (Greek). Life amongst peoples of another belief or non-believers. Since the destruction of the Temple the term →*Galut* (Hebrew) or →*Golus* (Yiddish) is often used: 'leading away, banishment'. A forced Diaspora already existed in the days of old Israel. The largest dispersion, the actual 'exile' (Latin) itself, began after the destruction of the Second Temple in the year 70 CE. Most settlements were located on the one hand in Spain (which were therefore known as 'Sephardim' according to the Hebrew term), Portugal, and after they were driven out in 1492, North Africa and South Eastern Europe, and on the other hand in Germany (which was known as 'Ashkenazim') and Eastern Europe. Since the end of the 19th century the USA has developed into a new focal point for Jewish emigration. As a result of Zionism and the establishment of the State of Israel, a discussion has begun regarding the issue of a reassessment of the Diaspora.

Erez Israel 'Land of Israel' (Hebrew). Often known simply as Erez or Haaretz, biblical term for the Promised Land for the Jews.

Galut See Diaspora.

Ghetto (Italian) Already in the Middle Ages the Jewish population lived in specific parts of towns. The term 'Ghetto' used to refer to these areas has however only been in existence since 1516. This was the name of the residential quarter allocated to the Jews in Venice. Since then it has been the term for designated Jewish residential districts, which are both officially enforced and restricted to confined areas.

Goi / Goiim 'Non-Jew' (Hebrew). Actually means people, peoples. In antiquity this term therefore referred to heathen peoples, however the term was also used sometimes for Israel. Later the term became firmly accepted for 'non-Jews' in Yiddish as well. On principle the word has no contemptuous overtones, but often in its secondary meaning it approximates something incomprehensible, and strange to Jewish nature.

Golus See Diaspora.

Gush Emunim 'Block of the Faithful' (Hebrew). National and radical orthodox religious movement founded in 1974, which attempts to force the Jewish settlement of Judea and Samaria with demonstrations and illegal settlements. Although insignificant in terms of numbers, the Gush Emunim receives great attention in the international media on account of the radical nature of its demands and its campaigns. Its strong counterbalance is the 'Shalom-Ahshav' or 'Peace Now!' movement, which is to a large extent prepared to abandon the occupied territories and hopes as a result to lay the foundations for permanent peace.

Hachsharah 'Preparation' (Hebrew). What is meant is the organized preparation for a life and work in Palestine by the →*Halutzim* movement. In many countries there were farms where groups which wanted to emigrate to Palestine (Kwuzot) were prepared for the new and unusual demands. Occasionally Jews entered service with farmers. The training for tradesmen was organized in a similar manner. In addition to this the future colonists learned Hebrew.

Hadassah A Zionist women's organization in America founded in 1912, and named after the original name of Queen Esther. The first lady president was Henrietta Szold. Hadassah primarily organized medical aid for Palestine and after the First World War built up a model health system for the Jewish and Arab population. It also supported the youth Aliyah and as a result saved numerous children and youngsters from being murdered during the National Socialist era. Today Hadassah is the largest Zionist women's organization in the world.

Haganah 'Protection, defence' (Hebrew). Zionist underground self-defence organization in Palestine founded in 1920 to protect Jewish settlements. In 1948 the Haganah was integrated into the Israeli armed forces.

Halukkah 'Distribution' (Hebrew). General support distributed according to certain rules predominantly among needy and pious Jews of the old →*Yishuv* in Palestine by the Jews in the →*Diaspora*.

Halutziyyut / Halutzim 'Pioneering, pioneers' (Hebrew). Since the First World War this term has been used to describe young people who have emigrated to Palestine with the firm intention of making a contribution to the recovery of the country with physical labour. Their own life was to be renewed by work and agriculture was to reunite those uprooted for centuries with the soil of Palestine. Numerous groups of young Halutzim came into being in Russia and in the Ukraine during the First World War. Their ideas and aims – elements of nationalism and socialism were combined in the 'pioneering'– were soon able to establish themselves in other countries as well. In many cases the Halutzim were prepared in a →*Hachsharah*, and the climax was the entry into a →*Kibbutz*. For a long time the Halutziyyut was held to be the predominant Zionist ideal.

Hanukkah 'Consecration' (Hebrew). An eight-day-long festival of light which is celebrated in remembrance of the reconsecration of the Temple by the liberator Judah Maccabee (2nd century BCE), after the temple had previously been desecrated by the Seleucid garrison. The Jews were supposed to have found a small bottle of oil that, as a result of a miracle, burned for eight days, although the oil inside it was actually sufficient for only one day.

Hapoel Hazair 'The young worker' (Hebrew). Non-Marxist Jewish Socialist Workers' Party, founded in Palestine in 1906. The members of Hapoel Hazair were convinced that the Jewish immigrants had to develop the colonies by their own efforts and had to be physically active in all other spheres of economic life. Mere administration and management of the work of others contradicted not only their political stance but also their basic attitude towards life. In 1950 the party was merged into the →*Mapai*.

Hashomer Hazair 'Young watchman' (Hebrew). A left-wing socialist Zionist youth movement founded in 1913 which combined Zionist ideology with revolutionary tendencies in Eastern Europe. After the First World War the demand was voiced, particularly amongst the younger generation, that Zionism should be achieved actively, by the individual moving to Palestine himself.

Haskalah 'Enlightenment' (Hebrew). Movement in the 18th and 19th century in Central and Eastern Europe as part of the European Enlightenment. The adherents of Haskalah wanted to break with the religious way of life handed down for centuries and demanded that Jewry adopt secular tendencies. They spread general knowledge amongst the Jews and initially supported →*Acculturation* or even →*Assimilation*, but soon realized the danger concealed by them: the disintegration of the Jewish people. They continued to demand secularization, but on a Jewish national basis. The Hebrew language was resurrected in connection with this. There were far-reaching differences between Haskalah in Western Europe and in Eastern Europe.

Hassidim / Hassidism The 'pious' (Hebrew). Mystical religious trend which came into being in the 18th century and initially spread mainly throughout Volhynia and Podolia, thereafter throughout large parts of Eastern Europe. Hassidim strived for a loving relationship with all life, happiness and fraternity, a new joyful approach to nature prevailed. The explanations of the scholastic Talmud rabbis for the ravages of the time were no longer sufficient for this pious people's movement, and it also questioned the traditional community organization. If it was originally shaped by the direct relationship of the pious ones with God, the person of the →*Zaddik*, the 'righteous man', gradually came into the foreground more and more as a mediator between mankind and God. Claims to power and the formation of dynasties by many of these Zaddikim led to an atmosphere of paralysis. But until today Hassidism has proven its powers of renewal.

Heder 'Room' (Hebrew). Primary school for boys, where from the age of roughly three or four they learned biblical Hebrew often up until the →*Bar Mitzvah*, studied the →*Torah* and the →*Talmud* and received fundamental instruction in Jewish morals as well as basic mathematics.

Hevrot 'Brotherhoods' (Hebrew, singular form Hevra 'association, alliance'). Such associations have been in existence in all Jewish communities for centuries. Their members look after the ill, assume responsibility for burials when people pass away, and support the surviving dependants ('Hevra Kaddisha', 'burial brotherhood'). Other Hevrot look after members who find themselves destitute and develop other forms of charitable work. Since the second half of the 19th century brotherhoods also came into being as self-help organizations, or to represent interests.

Hevrot Bnai Israel 'Brotherhood of the Sons of Israel' (Hebrew) with the English name 'Federation of Synagogues', a federation of synagogues that took place in England in 1887 as a counterbalance to the 'United Synagogue' which was unacceptable for most Eastern European immigrants on account of its service, which was reformist in outlook, and its high membership subscriptions. The Hevrot Bnai Israel wanted to win over the immigrants to join it by founding synagogues which followed a strictly orthodox line, and assured them a large degree of religious self-determination. There was a fear that the socialist influence of the Eastern Jews might permeate English Jewry and the attempt was made to gain social control over them by these means.

Hibbat Zion The 'Love of Zion' (Hebrew). Zionist movement in Eastern Europe. Its supporters called themselves →*Hovevei Zion*.

Hovevei Zion 'Love of Zion' (Hebrew). Supporters of the concept of Zion in Eastern Europe, members of the →*Hibbat Zion* movement, founded in Russia in 1881 and 1882 as a result of the pogroms. Hovevei Zion campaigned for the immediate colonization of Palestine and rejected suggestions which designated other areas as a possible homeland for the Jewish people.

Holocaust 'Burnt offering' (Greek). See Shoah.

Jewish Agency Institution of the World Zionist Organization formed in 1922 on the basis of Article 4 of the Mandate for Palestine, and recognized as an organization representing the Jews. The Jewish Agency advised the British government in Palestine and worked together with it on social and economic issues. Above and beyond this it represented the interests of the Jewish population at the League of Nations (at the United Nations from 1947 onwards). In 1923 the Palestinian government offered to allow the Arabs to have their interests represented by an Arab Agency. The Arabs rejected this offer. The Jewish Agency built up an extensive administration system in Palestine and became the real government of →*Yishuv*. The Jewish Agency grew rapidly in 1929 after intense internal strife. It now became necessary for the membership of all institutions to be drawn from 50% Zionists and 50% non-Zionists. Since the foundation of the State of Israel in 1948, the Jewish Agency has campaigned primarily for immigration to Israel, and also endeavours to ensure the protection of human rights for Jews throughout the world. In this way it has become a link between the Jews in Israel and the Diaspora.

Jewish Colonial Trust Jewish Colonial Bank, created in 1899 at the initiative of Herzl, and under the supervision of the Zionist Organization. With its funds collected by means of public people's subscriptions, its aim was to finance colonization in Palestine.

Kabbalah 'Received, tradition' (Hebrew). Secret tradition, doctrine passed on orally. From the 13th century onwards it was a term used to denote Jewish mysticism. The 'Zohar', the most important text of the Kabbalah, appeared in the 13th/14th century in Spain.

Kahal 'Community' (Hebrew, also 'Kehilla'). It was responsible for the organization and administration of the Jewish community. The Kahal was already in existence in antiquity, but developed with specific responsibilities in Germany in the 14th century and above all in the 16th century in Poland, since it was here that the Jews were granted their greatest measure of autonomy. The Kahal was responsible for the administration and the collecting of taxes, preserving Jewish culture and education, jurisdiction amongst the Jewish community, and the representation of the members of the community externally and was largely responsible for the provision of Jewish welfare. Initially democratic, a Kahal oligarchy gradually developed. Officially the Kahal was successively abolished in Eastern Europe from the end of the 18th century onwards but continued to exist in other forms.

Keren Hajesod Zionist Palestine fund set up in London in 1920 to finance immigration into Palestine and for the establishment of agricultural colonies.

Keren Kayemet Le Israel 'Jewish National Fund' (Hebrew). Organization for the purchase of land and property in Israel. Proposed as early as the First Zionist Congress in 1897, the National Fund took up its work in 1901.

Kibbutz / Kibbutzim Agricultural settlement which is based on the principles of a co-operative and democracy. All possessions are the communal property of the members of the kibbutz and are managed centrally. Educating children, looking after the ill and other social tasks are carried out jointly. There is a communal kitchen, a library, and leisure pursuits and activities are open to all. The kibbutz ideas have remained up to date, however new forms of kibbutz life have developed as well. In many kibbutzim many children no longer share their rooms with other children of the same age, but live with their parents.

Kosher 'Suited' (Hebrew). This term is applied above all to foodstuffs and means food which complies with the food law.

Luftmenschen (Air people) Those unskilled people without specific profession who suffered as a result of the process of impoverishment in Eastern Europe in the 19th century, who had nothing left to live on but the air. They tried to keep their head above water by going into service as day labourers where they could, or by acting as middlemen for business deals. Mostly they relied on the charity of their fellow Jews.

Mamlahtiut Derived from 'Mamlaha' (Hebrew), 'Kingdom', a term used to denote statehood.

Mapai Abbreviation for 'Mifleget Poalei Erez Israel' (Hebrew), 'Workers' Party of the Land of Israel'. Zionist social democratic party founded in Palestine in 1930 as the result of a merger of →*Hapoel Hazair* and 'Ahdat Haavoda' – 'Unity of Labour'. Amongst the founders were David Ben Gurion, Berl Katznelson, and Zalman Shazar (Rubashow). The Mapai became the strongest party in the →*Yishuv* and in the World Zionist Organization. The Prime Ministers of Israel from 1948 to 1977 also came from amongst their ranks. In 1968 the 'Israeli Workers' Party' was formed out of the Mapai and a splinter group.

Maskil / Maskilim 'The reasonable, thinker' (Hebrew). Supporter of the Jewish enlightenment, of the →*Haskalah*.

Menorah 'Candelabra' (Hebrew). Seven-branched, for →*Hanukkah* eight-branched candelabra, a ninth branch carries the light to light up the other branches. Originally the Menorah stood in the temple, and during the →*Diaspora* it stood in the synagogues and was a part of every Jewish household. The Menorah became the symbol of Judaism per se. Since 1948 the Menorah has been the official emblem of the State of Israel. However, it also stands for movements which are open to all Jewish opinions (such as the 'Menorah Movement' founded in 1906 at Harvard University).

Mikveh Israel 'Hope of Israel' (Hebrew). The first Jewish agricultural school in Palestine founded in 1870 by Charles Netter on behalf of the →*Alliance Israélite Universelle.*

Minjan 'Count' (Hebrew). Ten men who are older than thirteen years, and who may therefore fulfil all religious duties, form the minimum number which is necessary for a religious service to be held. Women are also included in →*Reform Judaism.*

Misnagdim / Mitnaggedim 'Opponents, protesters' (Hebrew). This is what the →*Hassidim* called their orthodox opponents.

Mizrachi 'Spiritual Centre' (Abbreviation for Hebrew 'Merkas Ruhani'). Association of Zionists faithful to the →*Torah* founded in Vilnius in 1902, which wanted to put the 'Basle Program' into effect on the basis of the →*Torah* and in accordance with traditional Judaism. The members of Mizrachi turned against the anti-Zionism of Jewish orthodoxy, but also against antireligious trends in Zionism, particularly in 'Cultural Zionism'. A part went over to the →*Agudat Israel* after 1912 out of disappointment with the Zionist movement. Mizrachi made an important contribution to the religious revival and to reconstruction work in Palestine. In 1956 the members of Mizrachi united with other groupings to form the 'National Religious Party'. This represents the claim, justified on religious grounds, to the territories conquered in 1967 and a legislation with a religious outlook.

Mizura / Mitzvot 'Commandment' (Hebrew). Religious duties.

Moshav / Moshavim 'Settlement' (Hebrew). Agricultural settlements in Palestine, which are founded on a co-operative basis, but consist of separate sole proprietorships. The land is owned by the state, the most important means of production are jointly owned property. Purchases and sales are effected centrally in accordance with co-operative principles. Every settler family however runs its own business, has its own house and is responsible for its own affairs, although there is also a duty to provide mutual assistance.

Neo-Orthodoxy A trend within Jewish orthodoxy, which, grappling with attempts at reform, sought to combine the strictest adherence to the →*Torah* with an openness towards secular education and a renewal of liturgical practice. The most significant theoretician was the Rabbi Samson Raphael Hirsch.

Pale of Settlement The 'cherta osedlosti evreev' (Russian) was a territory in Russia between the Baltic Sea and the Black Sea allocated in various stages to the Jews from 1791 onwards. Jews were only allowed to stay outside the settlement belt with special authorization.

Pamjat' 'Remembrance, memory, commemoration' (Russian). A movement that arose during the Soviet era from endeavours to preserve traditional Russian culture, and which developed into an extremely nationalist grouping with strong anti-Semitic tendencies.

Parnosse 'Living, earnings' (Yiddish) derived from 'parnassa' (Hebrew), 'living, maintenance'.

Pessah 'To pass over' (Hebrew), exact meaning is disputed. Celebration in commemoration of the flight from Egypt prior to which the angel of death, which had killed the Egyptian first-borns, 'passed over' Jewish houses.

Poalei Zion 'Workers of Zion' (Hebrew). Socialist Zionist party founded in Eastern Europe in 1906 and as a global organization in 1907 following various precursor groupings that had been in existence since 1901. It held that a concentration of the Jewish proletariat in Palestine was necessary for the class struggle to develop and for the social revolution to be possible. This view, greatly influenced by Marxism and essentially drawn up by Ber Borochov, was moderated in the 1920s in favour of settlement work and an outlook that was primarily nationalistic. As a result of this the movement split up into several factions.

Pogrom 'Devastation' (Russian). Riots, looting, and massacres, against the Jewish population.

Purim Festival of joy in commemoration of the rescue of the Jews of Persia from the plans for their annihilation drawn up by the minister Haman as narrated in the book of Esther. Esther, the Jewish wife of King Ahasuerus (Xerxes), was able to save her fellow Jews by having an audience with the king. Haman and his ten sons were hanged. This story is read out at the festival of joy, in the synagogues from the Megillat-Esther – the Esther scroll. Children dress up, everybody is in high spirits and there is merry-making, with various sweet dishes to eat.

Rabbi / Rav / Rebbe Since the early →*Talmud* era this has been an honorary title for leading religious scholars (derived from Rav, 'Master' and Rabbi 'My Master'). The office of the rabbi (Rebbe in Yiddish) as a community employee with the functions of judge, teacher, preacher, specialist in religious laws, and leader of the community only dates from the Middle Ages.

Reform Judaism A Jewish movement which spread from Germany and which from the end of the 18th century onwards sought to integrate the Jewish religion into its cultural environment and to take on board the ideas of enlightenment and emancipation. The external forms of worship were partly adapted to that of other confessions, especially that of the Protestants. In some ways this also applied to the position of women or the desire to return to Israel. Reform Judaism has most of its followers in the USA.

Shekel 'Coin' (Hebrew). Originally a biblical monetary unit. At the First Zionist Congress in 1897 the annual subscription fee was called a Shekel as a declaration of faith in the 'Basle Program' and as a sign of membership of the Zionist Organization. Paying the Shekel enabled one to take part in the reconstruction of Palestine even if one did not personally emigrate. The Israeli national unit of currency has been called Shekel since 1970.

Shiur 'Measure' (Hebrew). →*Talmud* course, syllabus of a student of the →*Talmud*.

Shoah 'Destruction, annihilation, catastrophe' (Hebrew). Planned, systematic and bureaucratically administered mass murder of Jews in the sphere of power of the National Socialist Third Reich. The reason for this state-implemented act of genocide was ideological and the result of continual propaganda; after legal discrimination, the destruction of the economic and social existence as well as numerous riots and pogroms, after being committed to concentration camps and having been put under pressure to emigrate, the 'Final Solution of the Jewish Question' was decided upon in 1941 in several stages and then implemented. The death camps in Eastern Europe were the centres of this genocide. Auschwitz near Cracow has become a synonym for Shoah.

Shomer Israel 'Watchmen of Israel' (Hebrew) was the name given to the watchmen of the Jewish colonies in Palestine. Shomer Israel was an organization founded in Lvov in 1868 which took up the ideas of the →*Haskalah* and demanded equality for Jews, at the same time as it emphasized its loyalty to the House of Habsburg and was orientated towards German culture.

Shtetl 'Little town' (Yiddish). Typical Jewish residential districts in Eastern Europe with a considerable, sometimes almost exclusively Jewish population.

Talmud 'Instruction, teaching' (Hebrew). Compendium of very varied supplements to the →*Torah*, consisting of doctrine (Mishnah) and commentaries (Gemarah) which were initially handed down orally and then written down up to the year 500 CE. In addition to discourses on the law and discussions about it (Halachah) the Talmud also contains traditional popular tales and legends (Agadah) which are both elevating and didactic. It has been handed down in two versions, the Jerusalem and the Babylon Talmud.

Territorialism Term used for the movement within Zionism, the aim of which was not to create a state in Palestine, but which gave precedence to the rapid establishment of settlements in a territory – wherever possible and appropriate – in order to assist impoverished and threatened Jews. This movement found its most important organizational expression in the 'Jewish Territorial Organization' founded by Israel Zangwill in Basel in 1905.

Torah 'Teaching, instruction, law' (Hebrew). Term used for the five books of Moses.

Wizo 'Women's International Zionist Organization', worldwide organization of Zionist women, established in London in 1920, managed the Zionist work of women and called organizations into being in Palestine which made it possible for Jewish women to play an active part in the reconstruction of Palestine. WIZO was able to establish itself in almost all European countries as well as Canada and Australia, but not in the USA, since there Zionist women had joined the →*Hadassah* organization.

Yeshiva → *Talmud* high school for training scholars and rabbis.

Yichus 'Origin' (Hebrew). Yichus is a term used to describe the distinguished lineage of a Jew. Distinguished primarily meant learnedness, and not worldly possessions or influence. Yichus means being descended from great scholars and important rabbis, however, it only has value if the person concerned proves that he is worthy of his forbears. Every Jew can achieve Yichus for himself and his offspring if he has the spiritual and moral qualities, by distinguishing himself through 'Yichus acmo' – 'personal nobility'.

Yishuv 'Settlement' (Hebrew). Term used to describe the Jewish population in Palestine. The 'old Yishuv' was formed by those Jews already living in Palestine before 1882 and those who, although they came to Palestine during or after the waves of immigration established by Zionists, nevertheless came for religious reasons. The 'new Yishuv' consisted of immigrants from the →*Aliyot* after 1882. Whereas the old Yishuv mostly lived in the four holy cities (Jerusalem, Safad, Tiberias, Hebron) and was dependent upon the →*Halukkah*, the new Yishuv established agricultural settlements and economic centres such as Tel Aviv or Haifa. A self-government system at community level was set up especially from the 1920s onwards.

Zaddik / Zaddikim 'Righteous man, holy man' (Hebrew). See Hassidism.

Zionist Revisionists The union of the Zionist revisionists was formed in 1925 under the leadership of Zeev Jabotinsky as a party within the Zionist organization which regarded itself as being in opposition to the prevalent movement. It strove to return to Herzl's idea of a Jewish state and held the view that settlement in Palestine could only succeed if the path ahead had been politically prepared for the Jews. They advocated 'pure' Zionism without the admixture of socialism or other ideas as an ideal, and also the military training of Jewish youth, Jewish self-defence, and an aggressive policy towards the great powers and the Arabs. In 1915 the Union left the World Zionist Organization, but returned to it in 1946.

Silke Schaeper

Library and Private Archive of Salman Schocken
The 'Schocken Institute for Jewish Research' in Jerusalem

This library today holds around 55,000 books in several languages, numerous magazines, Hebrew manuscripts, photographs of Genisa fragments, reproductions of Hebrew codices (liturgy and Kabbalah), Hebrew and Yiddish autographs as well as smaller special collections. Since 1996, it has been possible to access the magazines via the catalogue of the Israeli Scientific Libraries (Aleph) on the Internet. The Zionist primary literature contains publications of the Hebrew University, works by Theodor Herzl and Max Nordau as well as articles about them. There are also texts covering not only Zionist ideology, history and politics, but also Palestine and the Jewish settlements there, publications of Zionist institutions, Zionist periodicals and compendia.

Furthermore, the Schocken Institute also houses the manuscript of Moses Hess' 'Rom and Jerusalem' and various unpublished autographs and typewritten texts of Zionist personalities such as Shmarya Levin. A collection of Palestine photographs from the estate of the Zionist artist Ephraim Moses Lilien was 'rediscovered' in the Schocken library a few years ago and since then it can be found in the Tel Aviv Museum of Art.

The archive contains works on the following subjects:

Education and agricultural training in Germany (inter alia Gut Winkel, Gross-Glagow, Ahlem)
Zionistische Vereinigung für Deutschland, local Zionist groups (inter alia Berlin, Chemnitz, Dresden, Plauen)
German Aliyah (inter alia emigration assistance, settlement organizations, Haavarah, youth Aliyah)
Youth work (Hechalutz, Blau-Weiss, Maccabi, Kadimam, Jungjüdischer Wanderbund, religious organizations, sport and student associations)
Kulturausschuss der Zionistischen Organisation (administration, publishing activities, Hebrew schoolbooks, projects and manuscripts)
Cultural work in Germany (Beth Am Ivri, Histadrut Ivrit, Berit Ivrit Olamit and others)
Cultural work for Palestine (inter alia Ben Shemen, Bezalel, Verein der Freunde der Hebräischen Realschule Haifa, Bialik Preis)
Zionist parties and organizations (inter alia Herzl Bund, Jüdische Volkspartei, Arbeitsgemeinschaft für Zionistische Realpolitik)
Zionist press (inter alia 'Die Welt', 'Jüdische Rundschau', 'Jerubaal', 'J.T.A.', 'Der Jude')
Zionist World Organization (administration and organization, Jewish Agency, financial administration and financial institutes, commerce, colonization, immigration, transport, cultural work, medical services, political parties and groups)
Keren Kayemet Le Israel (administration and organization, propaganda, finances, acquiring real estate [inter alia Haifa-Bay, Hule Concession], institutes, projects, maps)
Keren Hajesod (correspondence, circulars, reports, finances, loans)

Furthermore, the thematically and alphabetically organized correspondence files of Salman Schocken are stored here. On the subject of 'Zionism' alone there is correspondence with more than 60 people, including Felix Rosenblüth, Chaim Weizmann, Martin Buber, Arthur Ruppin, Arthur Hantke and Moses Calvary, and on the subject of 'Palestine' there is correspondence with about 40 people including Moses Smoira and Meir Dizengoff.

Even the subjects of the archive which are not related to the topic of 'Zionism' document Schocken's commitment to cultural Zionism. Examples of this are his initiative to find reading material for Jewish prisoners of war during the First World War as well as the promotion of books on Jewish issues in the department stores of the Schocken Group. Chronological data card indices and registers which Salman Schocken had systematically compiled in the last years of his life – using his library and archive – show that he was preparing to write his autobiography.

Schocken Institute for Jewish Research of The Jewish Theological Seminary of America, Balfour Street 6, 92102 Jerusalem (Israel)
Tel: 00972-2-5631288, Fax: 00972-2-5636875, E-mail: JTSLIB@vms.huji.ac.il

Selected Bibliography and Further Reading*

General Literature and Reference Books

Almog, Shmuel: Zionism and History: The Rise of a New Jewish Consciousness. New York, Jerusalem 1987.
Antonius, George: The Arab Awakening. Beirut 1969 (Reprint).
Avineri, Shlomo: Die Krise der jüdischen Identität und die Anfänge des Zionismus. In: Geschichte in Wissenschaft und Unterricht 31 (1980) pp. 531–540.
Avineri, Shlomo: The Making of Modern Zionism. The Intellectual Origins of the Jewish State. London 1981.
Barnavi, Eli (ed.): Universalgeschichte der Juden. Von den Ursprüngen bis zur Gegenwart. Ein historischer Atlas. Vienna 1993.
Baron, Salo: A Social and Religious History of the Jews. New York 1952.
Bein, Alex: Die Judenfrage: Biographie eines Weltproblems. 2 vols. Stuttgart 1980.
Bein, Alex: Theodor Herzl. Vienna 1934. New edition Frankfurt a. M., Berlin, Vienna 1983.
Beller, Steven: Herzl. Vienna 1996.
Ben-Sasson, Haim Hillel (ed.): Geschichte des jüdischen Volkes. Von den Anfängen bis zur Gegenwart. Munich 1992.
Böhm, Adolf: Die zionistische Bewegung bis zum Ende des Weltkrieges. 2 vols. Tel Aviv 1935, Jerusalem 1937.
Dinse, Helmut and Sol Liptzin: Einführung in die jiddische Literatur. Stuttgart 1978.
Dubnow, Simon: Weltgeschichte des jüdischen Volkes. 10 vols. Berlin 1925–1929.
Eisenstadt, Shmuel N.: Die Transformation der israelischen Gesellschaft. Frankfurt a. M. 1992.
Elon, Amos: Herzl. New York 1975.
Elon, Amos: The Israelis. Founders and Sons. New York 1981.
Gelber, Nathan Michael: Zur Vorgeschichte des Zionismus. Judenstaatsprojekte in den Jahren 1695–1845. London, Vienna 1927.
Gorny, Yosef: Utopian Elements in Zionist Thought. In: Studies in Zionism 5 (1984) pp. 19–27.
Gorny, Yosef: Zionism and the Arabs, 1882–1948. A Study of Ideology. Oxford 1987.
Grözinger, Karl E. (ed.): Judentum im deutschen Sprachraum. Frankfurt a.M. 1991.
Halpern, Ben: The Idea of the Jewish State. Cambridge 1961.
Haumann, Heiko: Geschichte der Ostjuden. 3rd ed. München 1991.
Hertzberg, Arthur: The Zionist Idea. New York 1969.
Herzl, Theodor: Der Judenstaat. Versuch einer modernen Lösung der Judenfrage. Vienna, Leipzig 1896.
Herzl, Theodor: Altneuland. In: Julius H. Schoeps (ed.): Wenn ihr wollt, ist es kein Märchen. Kronberg im Taunus 1978, First edition Leipzig 1902.
Herzl, Theodor: Gesammelte Zionistische Werke in fünf Bänden. Tel Aviv 1934/35.
Herzl, Theodor: Briefe und Tagebücher. Ed. by Alex Bein, Hermann Greive, Moshe Schaerf, Julius H. Schoeps. 7 vols. Frankfurt a. M., Berlin 1983 ff.
Hess, Moses: Philosophische und sozialistische Schriften 1837–1850: eine Auswahl. 2nd ed. Vaduz 1980.
Kessler, Mario: Antisemitismus, Zionismus und Sozialismus. Arbeiterbewegung und jüdische Frage im 20. Jahrhundert. Mainz 1993.
Laqueur, Walter: Der Weg zum Staat Israel. Geschichte des Zionismus. Vienna 1975.
Leibowitz, Jeshajahu (with Michael Shashar): Gespräche über Gott und die Welt. Frankfurt a. M. 1990.
Mandel, Neville: The Arabs and Zionism before World War I. Berkeley 1976.
Meyer, Michael A.: Jüdische Identität in der Moderne. Frankfurt a.M. 1992.
Morris, Benjamin: The Birth of the Palestinian Refugee Problem, 1947–1949. Cambridge 1987.
Mosès, Stéphane: Der Engel der Geschichte. Franz Rosenzweig, Walter Benjamin, Gershom Scholem. Frankfurt a. M. 1994.
Reinharz, Jehuda: Fatherland or Promised Land. The Dilemma of the German Jews, 1893-1914. Ann Arbor 1975.
Reinharz, Jehuda and Paul Mendes-Flohr: The Jew in the Modern World: A Documentary History. New York 1980.
Reinharz, Jehuda and Anita Shapira (ed.): Essential Papers on Zionism. London, New York 1996.
Richarz, Monika (ed.): Jüdisches Leben in Deutschland. Selbstzeugnisse zur Sozialgeschichte im Kaiserreich. Vol. 2. Stuttgart 1979.
Rürup, Reinhard: Emanzipation und Antisemitismus. Studien zur «Judenfrage» der bürgerlichen Gesellschaft. Frankfurt a. M. 1987.
Sachar, Howard M.: A History of Israel. From the Rise of Zionism to Our Time. New York 1982.

---

* Bibliographical references are given according to the German way of citation.

Sapir, Joseph B.: Der Zionismus. Eine populär-wissenschaftliche Darlegung des Wesens und der Geschichte der zionistischen Bewegung. Brno 1903.
Scholem, Gershom: Judaica I. Frankfurt a. M. 1963.
Scholem, Gershom: Die jüdische Mystik in ihren Haupströmungen. 5th ed. Frankfurt a. M. 1993.
Shapira, Anita: Land and Power. The Zionist Resort to Force, 1881–1948. New York, Oxford 1992.
Sokolow, Nahum: History of Zionism, 1600–1918. London 1919.
Stegemann, Ekkehard W. and Wolfgang Stegemann: Urchristliche Sozialgeschichte. Die Anfänge im Judentum und die Christusgemeinden in der mediterranen Welt. Stuttgart et al. 1995.
Stein, Leonhard: The Balfour-Declaration. London 1961.
Vital, David: The Origins of Zionism. Oxford 1975.
Vital, David: Zionism: The Formative Years. Oxford 1982.
Vital, David: Zionism: The Crucial Phase. Oxford 1987.
Warnke, Kerstin: Lord Rothschild und seine armen Brüder: Osteuropäische Juden in London 1880–1906. In: Georg Heuberger (ed.): Die Rothschilds. Beiträge zur Geschichte einer europäischen Familie. 2 vols. Frankfurt a. M. 1994, pp. 117–132.
Weizmann, Chaim: Trial and Error. London 1949 (Germ.: Memoiren. Das Werden des Staates Israel. Zurich 1953).
Wheatcroft, Geoffrey: The Controversy of Zion. Jewish Nationalism, the Jewish State, and the Unresolved Jewish Dilemma. Reading et al. 1996.
Wolffsohn, Michael and Douglas Bokovoy: Israel. Grundwissen – Länderkunde. Geschichte, Politik, Gesellschaft, Wirtschaft (1882–1994). Opladen 1995.
Yerushalmi, Yosef Hayim: Zachor: Erinnere Dich! Jüdische Geschichte und jüdisches Gedächtnis. Berlin 1988.
Zweig, Arnold: Jüdischer Ausdruckswille. Publizistik aus vier Jahrzehnten. Ed. by Detlev Claussen. Berlin 1991.

Reference Books

Encyclopaedia Judaica. 17 vols. Jerusalem 1972–1981.
Evrejskaja Ènciklopedija. St. Peterburg 1908–1913.
Herlitz, Georg and Bruno Kirschner: Jüdisches Lexikon. Ein enzyklopädisches Handbuch des jüdischen Wissens in vier Bänden. Berlin 1927.
Schoeps, Julius H. (ed.): Neues Lexikon des Judentums. Gütersloh, Munich 1992.
Ujvári, Péter (ed.): Zsidó Lexikon. Budapest 1929, Reprint 1987.
Walk, Joseph (ed.): Pinkas hakehilot. Encyclopaedia of Jewish Communities from their Foundation till after the Holocaust. Vol. II, Germany: Württemberg – Hohenzollern – Baden. Jerusalem 1986.

Preconditions and Beginnings of Zionism

Aaronsohn, Ran: Ha-Baron we-ha-Moschawot 1882–1890. Jerusalem 1990.
Abeken, Heinrich J. W. R.: Das evangelische Bistum in Jerusalem. Geschichtliche Darlegung mit Urkunden. Berlin 1842.
Achad Haam: Am Scheidewege. Gesammelte Aufsätze. 4 vols. (only 2 were published). Berlin 1923.
Adler, E. N.: Von Ghetto zu Ghetto. Reisen und Beobachtungen. Stuttgart 1909.
Alderman, Geoffrey: Modern British Jewry. Oxford 1992.
Alejchem, Scholem: Eisenbahngeschichten. Ed. by Gernot Jonas. Frankfurt a. M. 1995.
Andlauer, Teresa: Hindernisse des Wandels. Juden in Österreichisch-Galizien und im Russischen Reich am Ende des 19. und zu Beginn des 20. Jahrhunderts. In: Heiko Haumann and Stefan Plaggenborg (ed.): Aufbruch der Gesellschaft im verordneten Staat. Russland in der Spätphase des Zarenreiches (= Menschen und Strukturen 6). Frankfurt a. M. et al. 1994, pp. 71–97.
Andlauer, Teresa: Die jüdische Bevölkerung im Modernisierungsprozess Galiziens (1880–1914). Unpublished manuscript. Freiburg i. Br. 1995.
Bányai, László, László Csorba et al.: Hét évtized a hazai zsidóság életében (= Vallástudományi tanulmányok 4/5). 2 vols. Budapest 1990.
Barnai, Jacob: On the History of the Jews in the Ottoman Empire. In: Esther Juhasz (ed.): Sephardi Jews in the Ottoman Empire. Aspects of Material Culture. Jerusalem 1990, pp. 19–35.
Bein, Alex: Erinnerungen und Dokumente über Herzls Begegnung mit Wilhelm II. In: Zeitschrift für die Geschichte der Juden. Tel Aviv, pp. 35–52.
Bein, Alex: Von der Zionssehnsucht zum politischen Zionismus. In: Hans Tramer and Kurt Loewenstein (ed.): Robert Weltsch zum 70. Geburtstag von seinen Freunden. 20. Juni 1961. Tel Aviv 1961, pp. 33–68.
Benbassa, Esther and Aron Rodrigue: Juifs des balkans. Espaces judéo-ibériques, XIVe–XXe siècles. Paris 1993.
Bihl, Wolfdieter: Das Judentum Ungarns 1780–1914. In: Studia Judaica Austriaca 3 (1976) pp. 17–32.
Birnbaum, Nathan: Ausgewählte Schriften zur jüdischen Frage. Czernowitz 1910.
Birnbaum, Nathan: Die jüdische Moderne. Frühe zionistische Schriften. Augsburg 1989.
Bitton, Livia E.: Zionism in Hungary. The First Twenty-Five Years. In: Raphael Patai (ed.): Herzl Year Book. Essays in Zionist History and Thought 7 (1971) pp. 285–320.
Blumberg, Arnold: Zion before Zionism 1858–1880. Syracuse 1985.
Blumberger, Jakab: Natonek József rabbi a szentföldi gyarmatositás elsö magyar propagálója életrajza. n.p. 1910.
Bodenheimer, Henriette Hannah: Im Anfang der zionistischen Bewegung. Eine Dokumentation auf der Grundlage des Briefwechsels zwischen Theodor Herzl und Max Bodenheimer von 1896–1905. Frankfurt a. M. 1965.
Bodenheimer, Max: So wurde Israel. Aus der Geschichte der zionistischen Bewegung. Ed. by Henriette Hannah Bodenheimer. Frankfurt a. M. 1958.
Bristow, Edward: Prostitution and Prejudice. The Jewish Fight against White Slavery 1870–1939. Oxford 1982.
Bristow, Edward: The German-Jewish Fight against White Slavery. In: Leo Baeck Institute Year Book 28 (1983) pp. 301–328.
Brocke, Michael (ed.): Beter und Rebellen. Aus 1000 Jahren Judentum in Polen. Frankfurt a.M. 1983.
Budde, Hendrick and Andreas Nachama (ed.): Die Reise nach Jerusalem. Eine kulturhistorische Exkursion in die Stadt der Städte. 3'000 Jahre Davidsstadt. Eine Ausstellung der 9. Jüdischen Kulturtage in der Grossen Orangerie, Schloss Charlottenburg Berlin. Berlin 1995.

Bunzl, John: Klassenkampf in der Diaspora. Zur Geschichte der jüdischen Arbeiterbewegung. Vienna 1975.

Burstyn, Ruth: Zionismus und Wien von seinen Anfängen (1882) bis zum Auftreten Theodor Herzls (1896). In: Kairos 30 (1988/89) pp. 105–120.

Cała, Alina: Asymilacja Żydów w Królestwie Polskim (1864–1897). Postawy, Konflikty, Stereotypy. Warsaw 1989.

Carmel, Alex: Die Siedlungen der württembergischen Templer in Palästina 1868–1918. Stuttgart 1973.

Carmel, Alex: Christen als Pioniere im Heiligen Land. Ein Beitrag zur Geschichte der Pilgermission und des Wiederaufbaus Palästinas im 19. Jahrhundert. Basel 1981.

Cohen, Stuart A.: English Zionists and British Jews. Princeton 1982.

Dawidowicz, Lucy S. (ed.): The Golden Tradition. Jewish Life and Thought in Eastern Europe. New York et al. 1967.

Diederichs, Ulf (ed.): Dein aschenes Haar Sulamith. Ostjüdische Geschichten. Düsseldorf, Cologne 1981.

Doron, Joachim: Social Concepts Prevalent in German Zionism: 1883–1914. In: Studies in Zionism 5 (1982) pp. 1–31.

Doron, Joachim: Jüdischer Nationalismus bei Nathan Birnbaum (1883–1897). In: Walter Grab (ed.): Jüdische Integration und Identität in Deutschland und Österreich 1848–1918 (= Jahrbuch des Instituts für deutsche Geschichte, Beiheft 6). Tel Aviv 1984, pp. 199–227.

Drouin, Michel (ed.): L' affaire Dreyfus de A à Z. Paris 1994.

Duclert, Vincent: Die Dreyfus-Affäre – Militärwahn, Republikfeindschaft, Judenhass. Berlin 1994.

Duvernoy, Claude: Le prince et le prophète. Jerusalem 1966.

Edinger, Dora: Bertha Pappenheim (1859–1936). A German Feminist. In: Jewish Social Studies 20 (1958) pp. 180–186.

Eisenbach, Artur: Emancypacja Żydów na ziemiach polskich 1785–1870 na tle europejskim. Warsaw 1988.

Eliav, Mordechai: Sefer ha-Alija ha-Rischona. 2 vols. Jerusalem 1981.

Ellern, Hermann (ed.): Herzl, Hechler, the Grand Duke of Baden and the German Emperor 1896–1904. Tel Aviv 1961.

Eloni, Yehuda: Zionismus in Deutschland. Von den Anfängen bis 1914 (= Schriftenreihe des Instituts für Deutsche Geschichte, Universität Tel Aviv 10). Gerlingen 1987.

Ertel, Rachel: Le Shtetl. La bourgade juive de Pologne de la tradition à la modernité. Paris 1986.

Ettinger, Shmuel: The Jewish Labor Movement in Eastern Europe. In: Tamar Manor-Friedman (ed.): Workers and Revolutionaries. The Jewish Labor Movement. Tel Aviv 1994, pp. 32–75.

Falk, Avner: Herzl – King of the Jews. A Psychoanalytic Biography of Theodor Herzl. Lanham 1993.

Feldman, David: Englishmen and Jews. Social Relations and Political Culture 1840–1914. New Haven, London 1994.

Fieseler, Beate: Frauen auf dem Weg in die russische Sozialdemokratie, 1890–1917. Eine kollektive Biographie. Stuttgart 1995.

Fischer, Rolf: Entwicklungsstufen des Antisemitismus in Ungarn 1867–1939. Die Zerstörung der magyarisch-jüdischen Symbiose (= Südosteuropäische Arbeiten 85). Munich 1988.

Fishman, Joshua A.: Ideology, Society and Language. The Odyssey of Nathan Birnbaum. Ann Arbor 1987.

Frankel, Jonathan: Prophecy and Politics: Socialism, Nationalism, and the Russian Jews, 1862–1917. Cambridge 1981.

Frenkel, Bernát: Natonek József. Az első politikai cionista élete és müvei. Válogatott fejezetek Messiás címü müvéből. Tel Aviv 1953.

Friedman, Isaiah: The Austro-Hungarian Government and Zionism 1897–1918. In: Jewish Social Studies 27 (1965) pp. 147–167 and 236–224.

Fuchs, W. P.: Studien zu Grossherzog Friedrich I. von Baden. Stuttgart 1995.

Gaisbauer, Adolf: Davidstern und Doppeladler. Zionismus und jüdischer Nationalismus in Österreich 1882–1918 (= Veröffentlichungen der Kommission für Neuere Geschichte Österreichs 78). Vienna et al. 1988.

Gessen, Yulii I.: Iuda Makkavej. Istoričeskij očerk. St. Peterburg 1901.

Gessen, Yulii I.: Istorija evreev v Rossii. St. Peterburg 1914.

Gessen, Yulii I.: Istorija evrejskogo naroda v Rossii. 2 vols. Leningrad 1925/27.

Gidrey, W.T.: The History of the London Society for Promoting Christianity amongst the Jews from 1809 to 1908. London 1908.

Gold, Hugo (ed.): Die Juden und die Judengemeinde Bratislava in Vergangenheit und Gegenwart. Ein Sammelwerk. Brno 1932.

Goldstein, Joseph: The Beginnings of the Zionist Movement in Congress Poland: The Victory of the Hasidim over the Zionists? In: Polin 5 (1990) pp. 114–130.

Goldstein, Jossi: An der Zeitenwende. Achad Ha'am in historischer Perspektive. In: Jakob Hessing (ed.): Jüdischer Almanach 1995/5755. Frankfurt a. M. 1994, pp. 81–90.

Gonda, László: A Zsidóság Magyarországon 1526–1945. Budapest 1992.

Guesnet, François: Minderer Status, Organisation und Autonomie: Der Weg der Juden in Kongresspolen 1862 bis 1905. Unpublished Ph.D. diss. Freiburg i. Br. 1996.

Gutwein, Daniel: The Divided Elite. Economics, Politics and Anglo-Jewry 1882–1917. Leiden et al. 1992.

Halevi, Jehuda: Zionslieder. Aus dem Hebräischen von Franz Rosenzweig. Berlin 1933.

Häusler, Wolfgang: Assimilation und Emanzipation des ungarischen Judentums um die Mitte des 19. Jahrhunderts. In: Studia Judaica Austriaca 3 (1976) pp. 33–79.

Heimann-Jelinek, Felicitas: Die sephardische Diaspora. In: Felicitas Heimann-Jelinek und Kurt Schubert (ed.): Spharadim – Spaniolen. Die Juden in Spanien – die sephardische Diaspora (= Studia Judaica Austriaca 13). Eisenstadt 1992, pp. 185–241.

Heller, Klaus: Revolutionärer Sozialismus und nationale Frage. Das Problem des Nationalismus bei russischen und jüdischen Sozialdemokraten und Sozialrevolutionären im Russischen Reich bis zur Revolution 1905–1907. Frankfurt a.M. et al. 1977.

Hess, Moses: Rom und Jerusalem. Die letzte Nationalitätenfrage. 1862. Published in: Moses Hess: Ausgewählte Schriften. Ed. by Horst Lademacher. Cologne 1962.

Heubach, Helga (ed.): Bertha Pappenheim, die Anna O. Sisyphus: Gegen den Mädchenhandel – Galizien. Freiburg i. Br. 1992.

Hödl, Klaus: Als Bettler in die Leopoldstadt: Galizische Juden auf dem Weg nach Wien. Vienna 1994.

Holzer, Jerzy: Zur Frage der Akkulturation der Juden in Galizien im 19. und 20. Jahrhundert. In: Jahrbücher für Geschichte Osteuropas 37 (1989) pp. 217–226.

Holzer, Jerzy: «Vom Orient die Fantasie, und in der Brust der Slawen Feuer...» Jüdisches Leben und Akkulturation im Lemberg des 19. und 20. Jahrhunderts. In: Peter Fässler, Thomas Held und Dirk Sawitzki (ed.): Lemberg – Lwow – Lviv. Eine Stadt im Schnittpunkt europäischer Kulturen. Cologne et al. 1993, pp. 75–91.

The Jewish Publication Society of America (ed.): The Jews of Czechoslovakia. Historical Studies and Surveys. 3 vols. Philadelphia, New York 1968–1984.

Kaiser, Wolf: Palästina – Erez Israel. Deutschsprachige Reisebeschreibungen jüdischer Autoren von der Jahrhundertwende bis zum Zweiten Weltkrieg. Hildesheim et al. 1992.

Kaplan, A.E. and Max Landau (ed.): Vom Sinn des Judentums. Ein Sammelbuch zu Ehren Nathan Birnbaums. Frankfurt a. M. 1924.

Kaplan, Marion A.: Die jüdische Frauenbewegung in Deutschland. Organisation und Ziele des Jüdischen Frauenbundes 1904–1938 (= Hamburger Beiträge zur Geschichte der deutschen Juden 7). Hamburg 1981.

Katz, Jacob: Zwischen Messianismus und Zionismus. Zur jüdischen Sozialgeschichte. Frankfurt a. M. 1993.

Kirshenblatt-Gimblett, Barbara: The Concept and Varieties of Narrative Performance in East European Jewish Culture. In: R. Bauman and J. Sherzer: Explorations in the Ethnography of Speaking. Cambridge et al. 1974, 2nd ed. 1989, pp. 283–308.

Kłanska, Maria: Aus dem Schtetl in die Welt, 1772–1938. Ostjüdische Autobiographien in deutscher Sprache (= Literatur und Leben 45). Vienna et al. 1994.

Kleeblatt, Norman (ed.): The Dreyfus-Affair: Art, Truth and Justice. Berkeley 1987.

Laharanne, Ernest: La nouvelle question d'orient. Empire d'Égypte et d'Arabie. Reconstitution de la nationalité juive. Paris 1860.

Lamberti, Marjorie: Jewish Activism in Imperial Germany. The Struggle for Civil Equality. New Haven, London 1978.

Landau, Moses: Geschichte des Zionismus in Österreich-Ungarn. Unpublished Ph.D. diss. Vienna 1932.

Levin, Nora: Jewish Socialist Movements, 1871–1917: While Messiah Tarried. London 1978.

Levy, Avigdor: The Sephardim in the Ottoman Empire. Princeton 1992.

Lichtheim, Richard: Geschichte des deutschen Zionismus. Jerusalem 1954.

Linner, Barbara: Die Entwicklung der frühen nationalen Theorien im osteuropäischen Judentum des 19. Jahrhunderts. Eine Studie zur Theorie und geistesgeschichtlichen Entwicklung des nationaljüdischen Gedankens in seinem Zusammenhang mit der Haskalah (= Europäische Hochschulschriften, Reihe 3, Geschichte und ihre Hilfswissenschaften 238). Frankfurt a. M. et al. 1984.

Manor-Friedman, Tamar (ed.): Workers and Revolutionaries. The Jewish Labor Mouvement. Exhibition catalogue. Beth Hatefutsoth, The Museum of the Jewish Diaspora. Tel Aviv 1994.

Ma'oz, Moshe (ed.): Studies on Palestine during the Ottoman Period. Jerusalem 1975.

Margalith, Israel: Le Baron Edmond de Rothschild et la colonisation juive en Palestine 1882–1899. Paris 1957.

Mayorek, Yoram: Zwischen Ost und West: Edmond de Rothschild und Palästina. In: Heuberger, Georg (ed.): Die Rothschilds. Beiträge zur Geschichte einer europäischen Familie. Frankfurt a. M. 1994, pp. 133–150.

Mendelsohn, Ezra: Class Struggle in the Pale. The Formative Years of the Jewish Worker's Movement in Tsarist Russia. Cambridge 1970.

Mendelsohn, Ezra: From Assimilation to Zionism in Lvov: The Case of Alfred Nossig. In: The Slavonic and East European Review 49 (1971) pp. 521–534.

Mendelsohn, Ezra: Zionism in Poland. The Formative Years, 1915–1926. New Haven, London 1981.

Minczeles, Henri: Histoire générale du Bund. Un mouvement révolutionnaire juif. Paris 1995.

Mirbach, E. von (ed.): Das deutsche Kaiserpaar im Heiligen Lande. Berlin 1899.

Mishkinsky, Moshe: Regional Factors in the Development of the Jewish Labor Movement in Tsarist Russia. In: YIVO Annual of Jewish Social Science 14 (1969) pp. 27–53.

Mishkinsky, Moshe: Die spezifischen historischen Bedingungen der Entstehung der jüdischen Arbeiterbewegung in Russland. In: Helmut Konrad (ed.): Probleme der Herausbildung und politischen Formierung der Arbeiterklasse. Internationale Tagung der Historiker der Arbeiterbewegung, 24. Linzer Konferenz 1988. Vienna, Zurich 1989, pp. 52–63.

Molho, Michael (ed.): Israelitische Gemeinde Thessalonikis in memoriam gewidmet dem Andenken an die jüdischen Opfer der Naziherrschaft in Griechenland. Essen 1981.

Moser, Jonny: Antisemitismus und Zionismus im Wien des Fin de siècle. In: Traum und Wirklichkeit. Wien 1870–1930. Vienna 1985, pp. 260–274.

Myers, Jody Elizabeth: The Messianic Idea and Zionist Ideologies. In: Jonathan Frankel (ed.): Jews and Messianism in the Modern Era: Metaphor and Meaning (= Studies in Contemporary Jewry 7). New York, Oxford 1991, pp. 3–13.

Nicault, Cathérine: Theodor Herzl et l'affaire Dreyfus. In: Les Archives juives 27 (1994) 1, pp. 15–25.

Nicault, Cathérine: Theodor Herzl et le sionisme. In: Michel Drouin (ed.): L'affaire Dreyfus de A à Z. Paris 1994, pp. 503–507.

Patai, Raphael: The Jews of Hungary. History, Culture, Psychology. Detroit 1996.

Pawel, Ernst: Herzl: The Labyrinth of Exile. New York 1989.

Penkower, Monty Noam: The Emergence of Zionist Thought. New York et al. 1991.

Penslar, Derek J.: Zionism and Technocracy. The Engineering of Jewish Settlement in Palestine, 1870–1918. Bloomington 1991.

Perry, Yaron: «Mount Hope». Deutsch-Amerikanische Siedlung in Jaffa 1850–1858 (= Abhandlungen des Gottlieb-Schumacher-Instituts 1). Haifa 1995.

Pięćdziesiąt lat sjonizmu. 1884–1934. Jubileuszowa księga pamiątkowa. Tarnów 1934.

Pietsch, Walter: Die jüdische Einwanderung aus Galizien und das Judentum in Ungarn. In: Gotthold Rhode (ed.): Juden in Ostmitteleuropa. Von der Emanzipation bis zum Ersten Weltkrieg. Marburg 1989, pp. 271–293.

Pietsch, Walter: Von Chatam Sofer zu Theodor Herzl. Zum Verhältnis von Orthodoxie und Frühzionismus im Königreich Ungarn im 19. Jahrhundert. In: Heiko Haumann (ed.): 100 Jahre politischer Zionismus – Neue Forschungen zu Voraussetzungen und Folgen des Ersten Zionistenkongresses 1897 (Arbeitstitel). Weinheim 1997 [in print].

Pinsker, Leon: Autoemancipation. Ein Mahnruf an seine Stammesgenossen von einem russischen Juden. Berlin 1882.

Poppel, Stephen M.: Zionism in Germany. 1897–1933. The Shaping of a Jewish Identity. Philadelphia 1977.

Preiswerk, Samuel: Stand der Dinge im Morgenlande. In: Das Morgenland. Altes und Neues für Freunde der heiligen Schrift, No. 9, September 1839.

Rahe, Thomas: Frühzionismus und Judentum. Untersuchungen zu Programmatik und historischem Kontext des frühen Zionismus bis 1897 (= Judentum und Umwelt 21). Frankfurt a. M. et al. 1988.

Rahe, Thomas: Religiöse Zionstradition, säkularer Nationalismus und die Anfänge des Zionismus. In: Geschichte in Wissenschaft und Unterricht 39 (1988) pp. 413–426.

Reinharz, Jehuda: Dokumente zur Geschichte des deutschen Zionismus, 1882–1933. Tübingen 1987.

Rhode, Gotthold (ed.): Juden in Ostmitteleuropa von der Emanzipation bis zum Ersten Weltkrieg (= Historische und Landeskundliche Ostmitteleuropa-Studien 3). Marburg 1989.

Riedl, Joachim (ed.): Versunkene Welt. 2nd ed. Vienna 1984.

Rüthers, Monica: Tewjes Töchter. Lebensentwürfe ostjüdischer Frauen im 19. Jahrhundert (= Lebenswelten osteuropäischer Juden 2). Cologne et al. 1996.

Schölch, Alexander: Palästina im Umbruch 1856–1882. Untersuchungen zur wirtschaftlichen und sozio-politischen Entwicklung. Stuttgart 1986.

Scholem, Gershom: Zum Verständnis der messianischen Idee im Judentum. In: Gershom Scholem: Judaica I. Frankfurt a. M. 1963, pp. 7–74.

Schonebohm, Dieter: Ostjuden in London. Der 'Jewish Chronicle' und die Arbeiterbewegung der jüdischen Immigranten im Londoner East End, 1881–1900. Frankfurt a.M. et al. 1987.

Schramm, Gottfried: Wilna und die Entstehung eines ostjüdischen Sozialismus 1870–1900. In: Shulamit Volkov (ed.): Deutsche Juden und die Moderne (= Schriften des Historischen Kollegs, Kolloquien 25). Munich 1994, pp. 129–140.

Schwara, Desanka: Humor und Toleranz. Ostjüdische Anekdoten als historische Quelle (= Lebenswelten osteuropäischer Juden 1). Cologne et al. 1996.

Schweitzer, Gábor: Miért nem kellett Herzl a magyar zsidóknak? A politikai cionizmus kezdetei és a magyarországi zsidó közvélemény. In: Budapesti Negyed (1994) nyár pp. 42–55.

Seroussi, Edwin: Die sephardische Gemeinde in Wien: Geschichte einer orientalisch-jüdischen Enklave in Mitteleuropa. In: Felicitas Heimann-Jelinek und Kurt Schubert (ed.): Spharadim – Spaniolen. Die Juden in Spanien – die sephardische Diaspora (= Studia Judaica Austriaca 13). Eisenstadt 1992, pp. 145–153.

Shafir, Gershon: Land, Labor and the Origins of the Israeli-Palestinian Conflict 1882–1914. Cambridge et al. 1989.

Silberner, Edmund: Moses Hess. Geschichte seines Lebens. Leiden 1966.

Simon, Maurice (ed.): Speeches, Articles and Letters of Israel Zangwill. London 1937.

Somogyi, Tamar: Die Schejnen und die Prosten. Untersuchungen zum Schönheitsideal der Ostjuden in Bezug auf Körper und Kleidung unter besonderer Berücksichtigung des Chassidismus (= Kölner Ethnologische Studien 2). Berlin 1982.

Sternhell, Zeev: La droite révolutionnaire 1885–1914. Paris 1978.

Tamir, Vicky: Bulgaria and Her Jews. The History of a Dubious Symbiosis. New York 1979.

Tobias, Henry J.: The Jewish Bund in Russia. From its Origins to 1905. Stanford 1972.

Tomaszewski, Jerzy (ed.): Najnowsze dzieje Żydów w Polsce w zarysie (do 1950 roku). Warsaw 1993.

Trančik, Martin: Zwischen Alt- und Neuland. Die Geschichte der Buchhändlerfamilie Steiner in Pressburg. Ein mikrohistorischer Versuch. Bratislava 1996.

Verete, Mayir: The Restoration of the Jews in English Protestant Thought. In: Middle Eastern Studies 8 (1972) pp. 3–50.

Wawrzyn, Heidemarie: Unerhört, Fräulein Pappenheim! Protest einer jüdischen Frauenrechtlerin. In: Jüdischer Almanach (1997/5757) pp. 67–78.

Wigoder, Geoffrey: The Sephardi World in the 19th and 20th Centuries. In: Ruth Porter and Sarah Harel-Hoshen (ed.): Odyssey of the Exiles. The Sephardi Jews 1492–1992. Tel Aviv 1992, pp. 127–166.

Wilcher, Asher: Ivan Franko and Theodor Herzl: To the Genesis of Franko's «Mojsej». In: Harvard Ukrainian Studies 6 (1982) pp. 233–243.

Wilson, Stephen: Ideology and Experience. Antisemitism in France at the Time of the Dreyfus Affair. London, Toronto 1977.

Winock, Michel: Edouard Drumont et Cie. Antisémitisme et fascisme en France. Paris 1982.

Winock, Michel: Nationalisme, antisémitisme et fascisme en France. Paris 1991.

Wohlgelernter, Maurice: Israel Zangwill. A Study. New York, London 1964.

Wrobel, Piotr: The Jews of Galicia under Austrian-Polish Rule, 1869–1918. In: Austrian History Yearbook 25 (1994) pp. 97–128.

Zborowski, Mark and Elizabeth Herzog: Das Schtetl. Die untergegangene Welt der osteuropäischen Juden. 3rd ed. Munich 1992.

Zipperstein, Steven J.: Elusive Prophet. Achad Ha'am and the Origins of Zionism. Berkeley, Los Angeles 1993.

The First Zionist Congress in Basel in 1897

Allerhand, Jakob: Messianische Elemente im Denken und Wirken Theodor Herzls. In: Norbert Leser (ed.): Theodor Herzl und das Wien des Fin de siècle. Vienna et al. 1987, pp. 61–75.

Berliner Büro der Zionistischen Organisation (ed.): Warum gingen wir zum Ersten Zionistenkongress? Berlin 1922.

Cohn, Arthur: Von Israels Lehre und Leben. Reden und Aufsätze. Basel 1928.

Cohn, Marcus: Erinnerungen eines Baslers an den ersten Zionistenkongress. In: Schweizerischer Israelitischer Gemeindebund. Festschrift zum 50-jährigen Bestehen 1904–1954. Basel 1954, pp. 225–236.

Farbstein, David: Zionismus und die Judenfrage ökonomisch und ethisch (Sonderausgabe der Rede am Ersten Zionistenkongress). Berne 1898.

Farbstein, David: Aus meinem Leben. In: Schweizerischer Israelitischer Gemeindebund. Festschrift zum 50-jährigen Bestehen 1904–1954. Basel 1954, pp. 197–224.

Ferrero, Dominique Shaul: La Suisse «berceau du sionisme politique». Aperçu sur les relations entre le sionisme et la Suisse (1897–1947). In: Equinoxe. Revue romande des sciences humaines 13 (1995) pp. 95–111.

Fraenkel, Josef: Mathias Achers Kampf um die «Zionskrone». Basel 1959.

Heman, Friedrich: Das Erwachen der jüdischen Nation. Der Weg zur endgültigen Lösung der Judenfrage. Basel 1897.

Herzl, Theodor: Neues von der Venus. Plaudereien und Geschichten. Leipzig 1887.

Herzl, Theodor: Das lenkbare Luftschiff. In: Klaus Dethloff (ed.): Theodor Herzl oder der Moses des Fin de siècle. Vienna 1986, pp. 178–185.

Kolatt, Israel: A Jewish National Assembly or the Foundation of the State of Israel? The First Zionist Congress. In: Dispension and Unity 17/18 (1973) pp. 67–77.

Landau, Saul Raphael: Sturm und Drang im Zionismus. Rückblicke eines Zionisten vor, mit und um Theodor Herzl. Vienna 1937.

Orlan, Haiyim: The Participants in the First Zionist Congress. In: Herzl Year Book 6 (1964–65) pp. 133–152.

Preiswerk, Samuel: Die Juden und ihr Vaterland. In: Das Morgenland. Altes und Neues für Freunde der heiligen Schrift. August 1840.

Sokolow, Florian: Nahum Sokolow. Life and Legend. London 1975.

Wachten, Johannes: Theodor Herzl als Literat. In: Norbert Leser (ed.): Theodor Herzl und das Wien des Fin de Siècle. Vienna et al. 1987, pp. 139–158.

Zionistisches Aktionskomitee (ed.): Max Nordau's Zionistische Schriften. Cologne, Leipzig 1909.

Zur, Yaakov: Die deutsch-jüdische Orthodoxie und ihr Verhältnis zur inneren Organisation und zum Zionismus (1896–1911). Unpublished Ph.D. diss. (hebr.). Tel Aviv 1982.

Zur, Yaakov: Die deutschen Rabbiner und der Frühzionismus. In: Julius Carlebach (ed.): Das aschkenasische Rabbinat. Berlin 1995, pp. 205–217.

Jews in Basel and the Region: Their Situation and the Beginnings of Zionism

Abitbol, Michel: Les deux terres promises. Les juifs de France et le sionisme. Paris 1989.

Assal, Paul: Zwischen den Welten, die sich vereinen. Juden im Elsass. In: Allmende. Eine alemannische Zeitschrift 2 (1981) pp. 51–64.

Assal, Paul: Juden im Elsass. Bühl-Moos 1984.

Avneri, Zvi, Arye Maimon et al. (ed.): Germania Judaica. Vols. 1, 2/1, 2/2, 3/1, 3/2. Tübingen 1963–1995.

Baer, Jizchak Fritz: Galut. Berlin 1936.

Baumann, Ulrich: Die sozialen Beziehungen zwischen Christen und Juden in südbadischen Landgemeinden 1862–1940. Unpublished M.A. thesis. Freiburg i. Br. 1995.

Bloch, Erich: Das verlorene Paradies. Sigmaringen 1992.

Blumenfeld, Kurt: Erlebte Judenfrage. Ein Vierteljahrhundert deutscher Zionismus. Stuttgart 1962.

Blumenkranz, Bernard and Albert Soboul (ed.): Les juifs et la Révolution Française. Toulouse 1976.

Boll, Günter: Dokumente zur Geschichte der Juden in Vorderösterreich und im Fürstbistum Basel (1526–1578). In: Zeitschrift des Breisgau-Geschichtsvereins «Schau-ins-Land» 115 (1996) pp. 19–44.

Bondy, Ruth: Felix Pinchas Rosen and His Time. Tel Aviv 1990.

Bosch, Manfred (ed.): Jacob Picard: Werke in zwei Bänden. Constance 1991.

Bosch, Manfred and Jost Grosspietsch (ed.): Jacob Picard 1883–1967. Dichter des deutschen Landjudentums. Katalog zur Ausstellung in der ehemaligen Synagoge Sulzburg. Freiburg 1992.

Burckhardt, August: Die Eberler genannt Grünenzwig. In: Basler Zeitschrift für Geschichte und Altertumskunde 4 (1905) pp. 246–275.

Caron, Vicki: Between France and Germany. The Jews of Alsace-Lorraine, 1871–1918. Stanford 1988.

Cohen, Phyliss A.: The Modernization of French Jewry. Hanover 1977.

Dreifuss, Emil: Ein Genfer tritt für Palästina ein. Henri Dunants Einsatz für die Wiederbelebung der alten Heimat des jüdischen Volkes. In: Der Bund, No. 201, 29 August 1983.

Elias, Alfred: Die jüdische Handwerkerschule in Mühlhausen. Brno 1904.

Elias, Alfred: Histoire du sionisme. Unpublished manuscript 1940.

Fischer, Herbert: Die verfassungsrechtliche Stellung der Juden in den deutschen Städten während des 13. Jahrhunderts. Breslau 1931.

François, Alexis: Aspects d'Henri Dunant, le bonapartiste, l'affairiste, le sioniste. Genève 1948.

Gerson, Daniel: Zwischen Selbstbehauptung und Assimilation: Die elsässischen Juden im 19. Jahrhundert. In: Jüdisches Museum der Schweiz, Basel und Schweizerisches Museum für Volkskunde, Basel (ed.): Juden im Elsass. Basel 1992, pp. 9–13.

Gilman, L. Sander: Jüdischer Selbsthass – Antisemitismus und die verborgene Sprache der Juden. Frankfurt a. M. 1993.

Ginsburger, M.: Die Juden in Basel. In: Basler Zeitschrift für Geschichte und Altertumskunde 8 (1909) pp. 315–436.

Graetz, Michael: Les juifs en France au XIXe siècle. De la Révolution Française à l'Alliance Israélite Universelle. Paris 1989.

Graus, Frantisek: Pest – Geissler – Judenmorde. Das 14. Jahrhundert als Krisenzeit (= Veröffentlichungen des Max-Planck-Institutes für Geschichte 86). 2nd ed. Göttingen 1988.

Guth, Nadia: Synagoge und Juden in Basel. Ed. by the Israelitische Gemeinde Basel. Zurich 1988.

Guth-Dreyfus, Katia: 175 Jahre Israelitische Gemeinde Basel. In: Basler Stadtbuch 1980, pp. 153–162.

Haas, Gaston: «Wenn man gewusst hätte, was sich drüben im Reich abspielte...» 1941–1943. Was man in der Schweiz von der Judenvernichtung wusste. Ed. by the Schweizerische Israelitische Gemeindebund (= Beiträge zur Geschichte und Kultur der Juden in der Schweiz 4). Basel, Frankfurt a. M. 1994.

Haumann, Heiko and Hans Schadek (ed.): Geschichte der Stadt Freiburg im Breisgau. 3 vols. Stuttgart 1992–1996.

Haverkamp, Alfred: The Jewish Quarters in German Towns during the Late Middle Ages. In: R. Po-chia Hsia and H. Lehmann (ed.): In and Out of the Ghetto: Jewish-Gentile Relations in Late Medieval and Early Modern Germany. New York 1995, pp. 13–28.

Haverkamp, Alfred: Zur Siedlungs- und Migrationsgeschichte der Juden in den deutschen Altsiedellanden während des Mittelalters. In: Michael Matheus (ed.): Juden in Deutschland (= Mainzer Vorträge 1). Stuttgart 1995, pp. 9–32.

Haverkamp, Alfred and Franz-Josef Ziwes (ed.): Juden in der christlichen Umwelt während des späten Mittelalters (= Zeitschrift für Historische Forschung, Beiheft 13). Berlin 1992.

Historischer Verein Mittelbaden (ed.): Schicksal und Geschichte der jüdischen Gemeinden: 1938–1988: Ettenheim, Altdorf, Kippenheim, Schmieheim, Rust, Orschweier. Ein Gedenkbuch. Ettenheim 1988.

Janner, Sara: Aus dem Archiv der Stiftung für Kirche und Judentum I: Briefe von frühen Zionistinnen und Zionisten an Carl Friedrich Heman. In: Der Freund Israels 156 (1993).

Janner, Sara: Aus dem Archiv der Stiftung für Kirche und Judentum II: Das Archiv der Stiftung für Kirche und Judentum als Depositum im Staatsarchiv des Kantons Basel-Stadt. In: Der Freund Israels 157 (1994).

Janner, Sara: Aus dem Archiv der Stiftung für Kirche und Judentum III: Das Reisejournal von Karl Brenner-Sulger aus dem Jahre 1833. In: Der Freund Israels 158 (1995).

Jungmann, Max: Erinnerungen eines Zionisten. Jerusalem 1959.

Kamis-Müller, Aron: Antisemitismus in der Schweiz 1900–1930. Ph.D. diss. Zurich 1990.

Külling, Friedrich Traugott: Antisemitismus in der Schweiz zwischen 1866 und 1900. Ph.D. diss. Zurich 1977.

Kury, Patrick: «Man akzeptierte uns nicht, man tolerierte uns!» Ostjudenmigration nach Basel. Umfang – Wahrnehmungen – Erfahrungen. Unpublished M.A. thesis. Basel 1994.

Kustermann, Abraham P. and Dieter R. Bauer (ed.): Jüdisches Leben im Bodenseeraum. Ostfildern 1994.

Leuenberger, Martin: Ein kurzer Sommer des Asyls. Juden aus dem Elsass als Flüchtlinge in Baselland. In: Fremd?! Baselbieter Heimatbuch vol. 20. Liestal 1995, pp. 65–78.

Leuenberger, Martin: Frei und gleich ... und fremd: Flüchtlinge im Baselbiet zwischen 1830 und 1880. Liestal 1996.

Lichtheim, Richard: Rückkehr. Lebenserinnerungen aus der Frühzeit des deutschen Zionismus. Stuttgart 1970.

Lucas, Eric: Jüdisches Leben auf dem Lande. Eine Familienchronik. Frankfurt a. M. 1991.

Mentgen, Gerd: Studien zur Geschichte der Juden im mittelalterlichen Elsass. Hanover 1995.

Mercanton, Daisy: Henri Dunant: essai bio-bibliographique. Lausanne 1971.

Nordemann, Theodor: Judenwohnungen im mittelalterlichen Basel. In: Basler Jahrbuch (1929) pp. 172–201.

Nordemann, Theodor: Zur Geschichte der Juden in Basel. Jubiläumsschrift der Israelitischen Gemeinde Basel aus Anlass ihres 150jährigen Bestehens 5565–5715, 1805–1955. Basel n.d.

Nordmann, Achilles: Über den Judenfriedhof in Zwingen und Judenniederlassungen im Fürstbistum Basel. In: Basler Zeitschrift für Geschichte und Altertumskunde 6 (1907) pp. 120–151.

Nordmann, Achilles: Geschichte der Juden in Basel seit Ende der zweiten Gemeinde bis zur Einführung der Glaubens- und Gewissensfreiheit 1397–1875. In: Basler Zeitschrift für Geschichte und Altertumskunde 13 (1914) pp. 1–190.

Picard, Leo: Water for Israel. Pioneering in Geology. German Description. Jerusalem 1992.

Pous, Jacques: Henri Dunant l'Algérien ou le mirage colonial. Genève 1979.

Raphaël, Freddy: Catholiques, protestants, juifs en Alsace. Alsatia 1992.

Raphaël, Freddy: Der Viehhändler. Symbolgestalt des elsässischen Judentums. In: Jüdisches Museum der Schweiz, Basel und Schweizerisches Museum für Volkskunde, Basel (ed.): Juden im Elsass. Basel 1992, pp. 14–15.

Raphaël, Freddy: Esprit du Judaïsme d'Alsace. In: Allmende 13 (1993) 36/37, pp. 54–65.

Raphaël, Freddy and Robert Weyl: Juifs en Alsace. Culture, société, histoire. Toulouse 1977.

Raphaël, Freddy and Robert Weyl: Regards nouveaux sur les juifs d'Alsace. Strasbourg 1980.

Rappard, William E.: A la mémoire de Chaïm Weizmann. Principal fondateur et premier président de l'Etat d'Israël, Ami de la Suisse. Neuchâtel 1953.

Reinharz, Jehuda: Chaïm Weizmann. The Making of a Statesman. New York, London 1993.

Rieger, Paul: Ein Vierteljahrhundert Kampf um das Reich und die Zukunft der deutschen Juden. Ein Rückblick auf die Geschichte des Centralvereins deutscher Staatsbürger jüdischen Glaubens in den Jahren 1890–1918. Berlin 1918.

Schär, Arnold: Das Werk von Bernhard Collin-Bernoulli. Ein Beitrag zu den Anfängen der Basler Sozialpolitik. Basel 1935.

Schilling, Konrad (ed.): Monumenta Judaica. 2 vols. 2nd ed. Cologne 1964.

Schmid, Regina: Verlorene Heimat. Gailingen – ein Dorf und seine jüdische Gemeinde in der Weimarer Zeit. Constance 1988.

Sigg, Oswald Georg: Die eidgenössischen Volksinitiativen 1892–1939. Ph.D. diss. Einsiedeln 1978.

Starck, Astrid: Jiddische Lebensbeschreibung von Seligmann Brunschwig von Dürmenach mit der Schilderung des «Judenrumpels» von 1848. In: Jüdisches Museum der Schweiz, Basel und Schweizerisches Museum für Volkskunde, Basel (ed.): Juden im Elsass. Basel 1992, pp. 16–19.

Steinberg, Augusta: Studien zur Geschichte der Juden in der Schweiz während des Mittelalters. Ph.D. diss. Zurich 1922.

Tromm, Ulrich: Der Markenhof bei Freiburg im Breisgau als zionistisches Auswandererlehrgut 1919–1925. In: Geschichtswerkstatt 15 (1988) pp. 23–32.

Utz, Jeggle: Judendörfer in Württemberg (= Untersuchungen des Ludwig-Uhland-Institutes der Universität Tübingen 23). Tübingen 1969.

Wackernagel, Rudolf: Geschichte der Stadt Basel. 4 vols. Basel 1907–1954.

Warndorf, Paul: Gailingen am Hochrhein. Beitrag zur soziokulturellen Geschichte des Judendorfes. Constance 1985.

Wecker, Regina: Basel und die Russinnen. Exkurs über eine nicht zustandegekommene Beziehung. In: 100 Jahre Frauen an der Uni Basel: «d'Studäntin kunnt!» Katalog zur Ausstellung von HistorikerInnen und StudentInnen des Historischen Seminars der Universität Basel. Basel 1991, pp. 84–91.

Weill, Georges: Charles Netter et les oranges de Jaffa. In: Nouveaux Cahiers 21 (1970) pp. 2–37.

Weizmann, Vera: The Impossible Takes Longer. London 1967.

Weldler-Steinberg, Augusta: Geschichte der Juden in der Schweiz. Vom 16. Jahrhundert bis nach der Emanzipation. Revised and supplemented by Florence Guggenheim-Grünberg. 2 vols. Zurich 1966.

Willi, Thomas: Der Verein der Freunde Israels 150 Jahre. Schweizerische Evangelische Judenmission, Stiftung für Kirche und Judentum. Festschrift zum 150-jährigen Bestehen. Basel 1980.

Wyler, Veit: Dr. Benjamin Sagalowitz sechzigjährig. In: Das Neue Israel (Juni 1961).

Wyler, Veit: Erinnerungen eines zionistischen Schweizer Juden. Vortrag gehalten am 11. Juli 1990. Bandübertragung Februar 1991.

Zelzer, Maria: Weg und Schicksal der Stuttgarter Juden. Stuttgart n.d. [possibly 1964].

The Consequences of the First Zionist Congress up to the Founding of Israel

Agnon, S. J. and Salman Schocken: Chilufei Igrot 1916–1959. Tel Aviv 1991.
Avneri, Arieh: The Claims of Dispossession. Jewish Settlements and the Arabs 1878–1940. Tel Aviv 1982.
Bar Am, Micha and Orna Bar Am: Painting with Light. The Photographic Aspect in the Work of E. M. Lilien. Tel Aviv 1991.
Bauer, Yehuda: Freikauf von Juden? Verhandlungen zwischen dem nationalsozialistischen Deutschland und jüdischen Repräsentanten von 1933 bis 1945. Frankfurt a. M. 1996.
Berkowitz, Michael: Zionist Culture and West European Jewry before the First World War. Cambridge 1993.
Berkowitz, Michael: Western Jewry and the Zionist Project, 1914–1933. Cambridge et al. 1997.
Bertisch, Abraham Maurice: A Study of the Political-Economic Philosophy of Arthur Ruppin and His Role in the Economic Development of the Zionist Settlement in Palestine from 1907–1943. New York 1980.
Bertz, Inka: «Eine neue Kunst für ein altes Volk.» Die Jüdische Renaissance in Berlin 1900 bis 1924. Ausstellungsmagazin. Berlin 1991.
Bertz, Inka: Politischer Zionismus und Jüdische Renaissance in Berlin vor 1914. In: Reinhard Rürup (ed.): Jüdische Geschichte in Berlin. Essays und Studien. Berlin 1995, pp. 149–180.
Biale, David: Zionism as an Erotic Revolution. In: Howard Eilberg-Schwartz (ed.): People of the Body. Jews and Judaism from an Embodied Perspective. New York 1992, pp. 283–307.
Brenner, Michael: The Renaissance of Jewish Culture in Weimar Germany. New Haven 1995.
Brinkmann, Brigitte: Konfliktstrukturbildende Elemente in der Entwicklung des arabisch-israelischen Konflikts 1915/16–1948. Frankfurt a. M. et al. 1996.
Browning, Christopher R.: A Final Decision for the 'Final Solution'? The Riegner Telegram Reconsidered. In: Holocaust and Genocide Studies 10 (1996) pp. 3–10.
Buber, Martin: Israel und Palästina. Zurich 1950.
Buber, Martin: Werke. 3 vols. Munich, Heidelberg 1962–1964.
Buber, Martin: Ich und Du. 11th ed. Heidelberg 1983.
Buber, Martin: Der Jude und sein Judentum. Gesammelte Reden und Aufsätze. Köln 1963, 2nd ed. Gerlingen 1993.
Bunzl, John: Zwischen Washington und Jerusalem: Nahost-Lobbies in den USA. Vienna 1992.
Cattan, Henry: Palestine and International Law. London 1973.
Dahm, Volker: Das jüdische Buch im Dritten Reich. Part II: Salman Schocken und sein Verlag. Frankfurt 1982.
Dash, Joan: Summoned to Jerusalem. The Life of Henrietta Szold. New York 1979.
Deutsch-Israelische Gesellschaft, Arbeitsgemeinschaft Bonn (ed.): Die «Jeckes» in Israel. Der Beitrag der deutschsprachigen Einwanderer zum Aufbau Israels. Katalog zur Ausstellung. Bonn 1995.
Doron, Joachim: Rassenbewusstsein und naturwissenschaftliches Denken im deutschen Zionismus während der wilhelminischen Ära. In: Jahrbuch des Instituts für deutsche Geschichte 9 (1980) pp. 389–427.
Eichler, Hava: Zionism and Youth in Hungary between the Two World Wars. Ph.D. thesis (Hebr.). Ramat Gan 1982.
Eichler, Hava: Rescue Operations of the Halutz Underground in Hungary. In: Asher Cohen and Yehoyakim Cochavi (ed.): Zionist Youth Movement during the Shoah (= Studies on the Shoah 4). New York et al. 1995, pp. 265–288.
Eisen, George: Zionism, Nationalism and the Emergence of the Jüdische Turnerschaft. In: Leo Baeck Institute Year Book 28 (1983) pp. 247–262.
El Sayed, Adel: Palästina in der Mandatszeit. Der palästinensische Kampf um politische Unabhängigkeit und das zionistische Projekt. Zur Dynamik eines Interessenkonflikts – vom Zerfall des Osmanischen Reiches bis zur Gründung des Staates Israel im Jahre 1948. Frankfurt a. M. et al. 1996.
Friedman, Isaiah: Germany, Turkey and Zionism 1897–1918. Oxford 1977.
Fuchs, Konrad: Ein Konzern aus Sachsen – Das Kaufhaus Schocken als Spiegelbild deutscher Wirtschaft und Politik 1901 bis 1953. Stuttgart 1990.
Gilman, Sander L.: The Jew's Body. New York et al. 1991.
Glick, Edward B.: The Triangular Connection: America, Israel, and American Jews. London et al. 1982.
Gonen, Jay: A Psychohistory of Zionism. New York 1975.
Greive, Hermann: Zionism and Jewish Orthodoxy. In: Leo Baeck Institute Year Book 25 (1980) pp. 173–195 and 28 (1983) pp. 241–246.
Gvati, Chaim: A Hundred Years of Settlement. Jerusalem 1985.
Harttung, Arnold (ed.): Ursprung und Entwicklung des arabisch-israelischen Konflikts und der Palästina-Teilungsplan der Vereinten Nationen. Berlin 1993.
Hermand, Jost: Judentum und deutsche Kultur. Beispiele einer schmerzhaften Symbiose. Cologne et al. 1996.
Herzog, Andreas (ed.): Ost und West. Jüdische Publizistik 1901–1928. Leipzig 1996.
Heymann, Michael (ed.): The Uganda Controversy. The Minutes of the Zionist Central Council. 2 vols. Jerusalem 1970, 1977.
Hirschfeld, Ariel: Schocken und Agnon. Münz und Masal. In: Saskia Schreuder und Claude Weber (ed.): Der Schocken Verlag, Berlin. Jüdische Selbstbehauptung in Deutschland 1931–1938. Essayband zur Ausstellung «Dem suchenden Leser unserer Tage» der Nationalbibliothek Luxemburg. Berlin 1994, pp. 191–199.
Hoberman, John M.: Weininger and the Critique of Jewish Masculinity. In: Nancy A. Harrowitz and Barbara Hyams (ed.): Jews and Gender. Responses to Otto Weininger. Philadelphia 1995, pp.141–154.
Hodes, Aubrey: Encounter with Martin Buber. Harmondsworth 1975.
Kadish, Sharman: Bolsheviks and British Jews. The Anglo-Jewish Community, Britain and the Russian Revolution. London 1992.
Kagedan, Allan Laine: Soviet Zion. The Quest for a Russian Jewish Homeland. Houndmills, London 1994.
Kaplan, Marion A.: The Making of the Jewish Middle Class: Women, Family and Identity in Imperial Germany. New York 1991.
Katznelson-Shazar, Rachel (ed.): The Plough Woman. Memoirs of the Pioneer Women of Palestina. 2nd ed. New York 1975.
Keller, Stefan: Grüningers Fall. Geschichten von Flucht und Hilfe. 3rd ed. Zurich 1994.
Kessler, Mario: Zionismus und internationale Arbeiterbewegung 1897 bis 1933. Berlin 1994.
Klemperer, Viktor: LTI [Lingua Tertii Imperii]. Notizbuch eines Philologen. 13th ed. Leipzig 1995.
Kohn, Hans: Martin Buber – sein Werk und seine Zeit. Cologne 1961.
Konferenzen und Verträge. Vertrags-Ploetz. Ein Handbuch geschichtlich bedeutsamer Zusammenkünfte und Vereinbarungen. Part II, vol. 4: Neueste Zeit 1914–1959. Würzburg 1959.
Laor, Dan: Bechanuto shel mar Schocken. In: Haaretz, 5 July 1991.
Laqueur, Walter: Was niemand wissen wollte. Die Unterdrückung der Nachrichten über Hitlers «Endlösung». Frankfurt a. M., Berlin 1981.

Laqueur, Walter and Richard Breitman: Der Mann, der das Schweigen brach. Wie die Welt vom Holocaust erfuhr. Frankfurt a. M., Berlin 1986.

Luz, Ehud: Parallels Meet. Religion and Nationalism in the Early Zionist Movement, 1882–1904. Philadelphia et al. 1988.

Mallison, W. Thomas and Sally V. Mallison: An International Law Analysis of the Mayor United Nations Resolutions Concerning the Palestine Question. New York 1979.

Marcus, Jacob Rader: The American Jewish Woman 1654–1980. New York, Cincinnati 1981.

Meier-Cronemeyer, Hermann: Kibbuzim. Geschichte, Geist und Gestalt. 1st part. Hanover 1969.

Mejcher, Helmut and Alexander Schölch (ed.): Die Palästina-Frage 1917–1948. Historische Ursprünge und internationale Dimensionen eines Nationalkonflikts. Paderborn 1981.

Mendes-Flohr, Paul: Von der Mystik zum Dialog. Martin Bubers geistige Entwicklung bis hin zu «Ich und Du». Königstein i. Ts. 1979.

Midgley, David R.: Arnold Zweig. Eine Einführung in Leben und Werk. Frankfurt a. M. 1987.

Mintz, Matityahu: Ber Borokhov. In: Studies in Zionism 5 (1982) pp. 33–53.

Moses, Siegfried: Salman Schocken – His Economic and Zionist Activities. In: Leo Baeck Institute Year Book 5 (1960) pp. 73–104. The same essay was published in German in the bulletin of the Leo Baeck Institute 13 (1961) pp. 1–43.

Nordau, Max: Entartung. 2 vols. Berlin 1892.

Nordau, Max: Muskeljudentum. In: Jüdische Turnzeitung, Juni 1900. Published in: Zionistisches Aktionskomitee (ed.): Max Nordau's Zionistische Schriften. Cologne, Leipzig 1909, pp. 379–381.

Nordau, Max: Was bedeutet das Turnen für uns Juden? In: Jüdische Turnzeitung, Juni 1900. Published in: Zionistisches Aktionskomitee (ed.): Max Nordau's Zionistische Schriften. Cologne, Leipzig 1909, pp. 382–388.

Novák, Attila: Cionisták, baloldaliak, államrezon. Cionizmus és államhatalom a 30-as évek Magyarországán. In: Századok 130 (1996) 6, pp. 1341–1392.

Penslar, Derek Jonathan: Engineering Utopia: The World Zionist Organization and the Settlement of Palestine, 1897–1914. Ann Arbor 1987.

Picard, Jacques: Die Schweiz und die Juden 1933–1945. Schweizerischer Antisemitismus, jüdische Abwehr und internationale Migrations- und Flüchtlingspolitik. Zurich 1994.

Pietsch, Walter: Über die Wurzeln der Ultra-Orthodoxie im ungarischen Judentum. Gestalt und Wirken von Rabbi Chaim Josef Sonnenfeld. Will soon be published in: Aschkenas.

Prestel, Claudia T.: Frauen und die Zionistische Bewegung (1897–1933). Tradition oder Revolution? In: Historische Zeitschrift 158 (1994) 1, pp. 29–71.

Prestel, Claudia T.: Zur Stellung der Frau in jüdischen Organisationen und Gemeinden vor und nach dem Ersten Weltkrieg. In: Inge Stephan, Sabine Schilling and Sigrid Weigel (ed.): Jüdische Kultur und Weiblichkeit in der Moderne. Cologne 1994, pp. 245–258.

Reichmann, Eva G.: Der Bewusstseinswandel der deutschen Juden. In: Werner E. Mosse (ed.): Deutsches Judentum in Krieg und Revolution 1916–1923. Tübingen 1971, pp. 511–612.

Reinharz, Jehuda: The Zionist Response to Antisemitism in Germany. In: Leo Baeck Institute Year Book 30 (1985) pp. 105–140.

Roth, M. A.: Der Zionismus vom Standpunkte der jüdischen Orthodoxie. 2nd ed. Nagytapolcsany 1904.

Rudavsky, T. M. (ed.): Gender and Judaism. The Transformation of Tradition. New York, London 1995.

Ruppin, Arthur: Die Juden der Gegenwart. Berlin 1904.

Ruppin, Arthur: Der Aufbau des Landes Israel. Berlin 1919.

Ruppin, Arthur: Soziologie der Juden. 2 vols. Berlin 1930.

Ruppin, Arthur: Dreissig Jahre Aufbau in Palästina. Berlin 1937.

Ruppin, Arthur: Briefe, Tagebücher, Erinnerungen. Ed. by Schlomo Krolik. Königstein 1985.

Schaeper, Silke: Bibliophilie als kultureller Auftrag. Die Geschichte der Schocken Bibliothek bis 1939. In: Der Schocken Verlag, Berlin. Jüdische Selbstbehauptung in Deutschland 1931–1938. Essayband zur Ausstellung 'Dem suchenden Leser unserer Tage' der Nationalbibliothek Luxemburg. Berlin 1994, pp. 347–359.

Schaeper, Silke: Goldadern wertvollen jüdischen Lebens. Salman Schocken und seine Hebraica-Sammlung. In: Jüdischer Almanach 1995. Frankfurt a. M. 1994, pp. 121–135.

Scheps, Samuel: Bâle, Genève et Istanbul. Centres de sauvetage et d'aliyah 1933–1946. In: Society for the Study of International Problems (SSIP) Bulletin No. 43 (1976) pp. 109–121.

Schocken, Salman: Palästinensische Wirtschaftspolitik (= Zionistische Broschüren Bibliothek). Berlin 1922.

Schoeps, Julius H. (ed.): Zionismus. Vierunddreissig Aufsätze. Texte von Kalischer / Pinsker / Herzl / Nordau / Buber / Rathenau / Borochow / Weizmann / Jabotinsky u.a. (= Nymphenburger Texte zur Wissenschaft 16). Munich 1973.

Schoeps, Julius H.: Theodor Herzl 1860–1904. Wenn Ihr wollt, ist es kein Märchen. Eine Text-Bild-Monographie. Vienna 1995.

Shilo, Margalith: Nisjanot be-Hitjaschwut. Jerusalem 1988.

Shimoni, Gideon: The Zionist Ideology. Hanover, London 1995.

Sorin, Gerald: A Time for Building. The Third Migration, 1880–1920. Baltimore, London 1992.

Tivnan, Edward: The Lobby. Jewish Political Power and American Foreign Policy. New York 1987.

Volkov, Shulamit: Die Verbürgerlichung der Juden als Paradigma. In: Volkov, Shulamit: Jüdisches Leben und Antisemitismus im 19. und 20. Jahrhundert. Zehn Essays. Munich 1990, pp. 111–130.

Wagner, Heinz: Der Arabisch-Israelische Konflikt im Völkerrecht. Berlin 1971.

Weingarten, Ralph: Die Hilfeleistung der westlichen Welt bei der Endlösung der deutschen Judenfrage. Das «Intergovernmental Committee on Political Refugees» (IGC) 1938–1939. 2nd ed. Berne et al. 1983.

Wells, Leon Weliczker: Und sie machten Politik. Die amerikanischen Zionisten und der Holocaust. Munich 1989.

Wiznitzer, Manuel: Arnold Zweig. Das Leben eines deutsch-jüdischen Schriftstellers. Frankfurt a. M. 1987.

Wolf, Lucien: Notes on the Diplomatic History of the Jewish Question. London 1919.

Wyman, David S.: Das unerwünschte Volk. Amerika und die Vernichtung der europäischen Juden. Ismaning near Munich 1986.

Yago-Jung, Ilse Elisabeth Veronika: Die nationale Frage in der jüdischen Arbeiterbewegung in Russland, Polen und Palästina bis 1929. Frankfurt a. M. 1976.

Zimmermann, Moshe: Jewish Nationalism and Zionism in German-Jewish Students' Organisations. In: Leo Baeck Institute Year Book 27 (1982) pp. 129–153.

Zimmermann, Moshe: Das Gesellschaftsbild der deutschen Zionisten vor dem 1. Weltkrieg. In: Trumah 1 (1987) pp. 139–158.

Zweig, Arnold: Das neue Kanaan. Eine Untersuchung über Land und Geist. Berlin 1925.

Zweig, Arnold: De Vrient kehrt heim. Roman. Frankfurt a. M. 1995.

Zionism Today – An Outlook

Abbas, Mazen: Le Chemin d'Oslo. Paris 1994.
Ashrawi, Hanan: This Side of Peace. New York 1995.
Avineri, Shlomo: Politische und soziale Aspekte des israelischen und arabischen Nationalismus. In: Heinrich August Winkler (ed.): Nationalismus. 2nd ed. Königstein 1985, pp. 232–251.
Avnery, Uri: Zwei Völker – zwei Staaten. Hamburg 1995.
Beilin, Yossi: Israel. A Concise Political History. New York 1993.
Beit-Hallahmi, Benjamin: Schmutzige Geschäfte. Die geheimen Geschäfte Israels. Munich 1989.
Bodenheimer, Aron Ronald: Rabins Tod. Ein Essay. Zurich 1996.
Bunzl, John (ed.): Der Nahostkonflikt. Analysen und Dokumente. Vienna, Frankfurt a. M. 1981.
Christlicher Friedensdienst (ed.): Welcher Dialog? Standpunkte von AktivistInnen in der Schweiz, in Israel und Palästina. Berne 1996.
Claussen, Detlev: Ein neuer kategorischer Imperativ. Die politische Linke und ihr Verhältnis zum Staat Israel. In: Micha Brumlik (ed.): Jüdisches Leben in Deutschland seit 1945. Frankfurt a. M. 1986, pp. 230–242.
Claussen, Detlev: Grenzen der Aufklärung. Zur gesellschaftlichen Geschichte des modernen Antisemitismus. Frankfurt a. M. 1987.
Cohn, Norman: Die Protokolle der Weisen von Zion. Der Mythos von der jüdischen Weltverschwörung. Cologne, Berlin 1969.
Cruise O'Brien, Conor: Belagerungszustand. Die Geschichte des Zionismus und des Staates Israel. Munich 1991.
Darwish, Khalil: Sozioökonomische Struktur und sozialer Wandel der palästinensischen Gesellschaft nach 1948. Eine empirische Untersuchung am Beispiel zweier Flüchtlingslager. Pfaffenweiler 1985.
Diner, Dan: Individualität und Nationalität. Wandlungen im israelischen Geschichtsbewusstsein. In: Babylon 15 (1995) pp. 5–27.
Farhat-Naser, Sumaya: Thymian und Steine. Eine palästinensische Lebensgeschichte. Ed. by Rosmarie Kurz and Chudi Bürgi. Basel 1995.
Flapan, Simcha: Zionism and the Palestinians. London, New York 1979.
Flapan, Simcha: Die Geburt Israels, Mythos und Wirklichkeit. Munich 1988.
Grossmann, David: Der geteilte Israeli. Munich 1992.
Habibi, Emil: Das Tal der Dschinnen. Basel 1993.
Hagemeister, Michael: Sergej Nilus und die «Protokolle der Weisen von Zion». Überlegungen zur Forschungslage. In: Jahrbuch für Antisemitismusforschung 5 (1996) pp. 127–147.
Hattis Rolef, Susan: The Political Dictionary of the State of Israel. Jerusalem 1993.
History and Memory. Studies in Representation of the Past. Special Issue: Israeli Historiography Revisited. Vol. 7/1 (1995).
Hunziker, Ernst: Zwischen Allah und Arafat. Palästinenser und die Versöhnung. Osnabrück 1996.
Kanafani, Ghassan: Das Land der traurigen Orangen. Palästinensische Erzählungen. Basel 1983.
Liebmann, Charles S. and Eliezer Don-Yehiya: Civil Religion in Israel. Traditional Judaism and Political Culture in the Jewish State. Berkeley 1983.
Löwy, Michael: Redemption and Utopia. Jewish Libertarian Thought in Central Europe. A Study in Elective Affinity. London 1992.
Lüthi, Urs: Der Mythos von der Weltverschwörung. Die Hetze der Schweizer Frontisten gegen Juden und Freimaurer – am Beispiel des Berner Prozesses um die 'Protokolle der Weisen von Zion' (= Beiträge zur Geschichte und Kultur der Juden in der Schweiz 1). Basel, Frankfurt a. M. 1992.
Mallison, W. Thomas and Sally V. Mallison: The Palestine Problem in International Law and World Order. Essex 1986.
Mashala, Nur: «1948 and After» Revisited. In: Journal of Palestine Studies 24 (1995) 4, pp. 90–95.
Morris, Benjamin: The New Historiography. Israel Confronts Its Past. In: Tikkun 3 (1988) 6.
Morris, Benjamin: 1948 and After. Israel and the Palestinians. New York 1990.
Myers, David N.: Re-Inventing the Jewish Past. European Jewish Intellectuals and the Zionist Return to History. New York, Oxford 1995.
Nora, Pierre: Zwischen Geschichte und Gedächtnis. Berlin 1990.
Oz, Amos: Bericht zur Lage des Staates Israel. Frankfurt a. M. 1992.
Palästina-Komitee: Die Palästinensische Revolution nach dem Oktoberkrieg 1973. Hamburg 1974.
Qleibo, Ali H.: Wenn die Berge verschwinden. Die Palästinenser im Schatten der israelischen Besatzung. Heidelberg 1993.
Ram, Uri: Narration, Erziehung und die Erfindung des jüdischen Nationalismus. Ben-Zion Dinur und seine Zeit. In: Österreichische Zeitschrift für Geschichtswissenschaft 5 (1994) 2, pp. 151–177.
Rollin, Henri: L'apocalypse de notre temps. Les dessous de la propagande allemande d'après des documents inédits. Paris 1939, new ed. Paris 1991.
Sacks, Jonathan: Will We Have Jewish Grandchildren? Jewish Continuity and How to Achieve It. London 1994.
Sarkowicz, Hans: Die Protokolle der Weisen von Zion. In: Karl Corino (ed.): Gefälscht! Betrug in Literatur, Kunst, Musik, Wissenschaft und Politik. Nördlingen 1988, pp. 56–73.
Schiff, Ze'ev and Ehud Ya'ari: Intifada: The Palestinian Uprising: Israel's Third Front. New York 1990.
Schwartz, Barry, Yael Zerubavel et al.: The Recovery of Massada: A Study in Collective Memory. In: Eyal Ben-Ari (ed.): Defining Israeli Culture: An Anthropological Approach. Jerusalem 1995, pp. 158–167.
Schweid, Eliezer: Likrat Tarbut Yehudit Modernit. Tel Aviv 1996.
Segev, Tom: Die siebte Million. Der Holocaust und Israels Politik der Erinnerung. Reinbek 1995.
Silberstein, Laurence J. (ed.): New Perspectives on Israeli History. The Early Years of the State. New York, London 1991.
Slonim, Shlomo: The «New Historians» and the Establishment of Israel. In: Studies in Contemporary Jewry 7 (1991) pp. 306–316.
Smith, Pamela Ann: Palestine and Palestinians: 1876–1983. London, Sydney 1985.
Spehl, Helmut: Die Fortzeugung des Behemoth. Freiburg 1978.
Sprinzak, Ehud: The Ascendance of Israel's Radical Right. New York, Oxford 1991.
Taguieff, Pierre-André: Les Protocoles des Sages de Sion. Vol. 1: Introduction à l'étude des Protocoles, un faux et ses usages dans le siècle. Vol. 2: Etudes et documents. Paris 1992.
Teveth, Shabtai: Charging Israel with Original Sin. In: Commentary 88 (1989) 3, pp. 24–33.
Wasserstein, Bernard: Vanishing Diaspora. The Jews in Europe since 1945. London 1996.
Wistrich, Robert and David Ohana: Between Redemption und Perdition. Modern Antisemitism and Jewish Identity. London 1990.
Wistrich, Robert and David Ohana: The Shaping of Israeli Identity. Myth, Memory and Trauma. London 1995.
Zimmermann, Moshe: Wende in Israel. Zwischen Nation und Religion. Berlin 1996.

Acknowledgement of Illustrations

Basler Denkmalpflege 182 bottom
Bayerisches Hauptstaatsarchiv, Munich 269
Benzian (photo archive), Tel Aviv 371, 373
Beth Hatefutsoth, The Nahum Goldmann Museum of the Jewish Diaspora, Tel Aviv 97, 98, 103, 125, 259
B.J. (private collection), Warsaw 7, 8, 60, 61, 62, 65, 67, 75, 76, 77, 78, 80, 81, 84, 93, 119, 120
Blum (private collection), New York 229
Bosch (private collection), Rheinfelden 233, 235
Bund Archives, New York 94

Carmel (private collection), Haifa 3, 35, 37, 39, 40, 44, 46, 47, top and bottom, 49 top, 50, 266, 350
Central Zionist Archives, Jerusalem 13, 22, 30 left and right, 88, 89, 111, 113, 114, 122, 132, 133, 138, 140, 141, 142, 145, 150, 151, 152, 153, 155, 162, 164, 165, 166, 167, 168, 169, 171, 172, 174, 184, 198, 203, 204, 232, 245, 255, 257, 262, 270, 274, 275, 280, 294, 300, 301, 311, 312, top and bottom, 313 top, middle, bottom, 314 top and bottom, 315 top and bottom, 317 bottom, 343

Frankenstein (private collection), Freiburg im Breisgau 239, 298
Frenkel (private collection), Haifa 32

Gessen (private collection), St. Petersburg 86

Hagemeister (private collection), Marburg 337

JPFO Archives, America's Aggressive Civil Rights Organization, Milwaukee 359
Jüdisches Museum der Schweiz, Basel 178, 219
Jüdisches Museum der Stadt Wien 237

Keystone International, Zurich 351, 365
Kiscelli-Múzeum, Budapest 107
Kore-Verlag, Freiburg im Breisgau 70

Metzger (private collection), Basel 249
Meyer (private collection), Basel 179
Moshé Raviv-Vorobeichic (Moï-Ver)© (private collection), Tel Aviv 9, 16, 17
Muzeum Historyczne Warszawy 54, 56, 57
Muzeum Narodowe w Krakowie 318
Muzeum Sztuki w Łodzi 317 top, 319

Sch. (private collection), Basel 115, 279, 304, 306, 307, 325 left and right, 326, 347
Scheps (private collection), Geneva 290
Schweizerische Nationalbibliothek, Berne 196
Staatsarchiv Basel-Stadt 136 (Kirchenakten Q1), 143 (Photoarchiv Höflinger), 183, 194 (IGB-REG, G 4.1.), 199
  Sammlung Müry im Staatsarchiv 12, 134, 182 top, 199, 200
Starck (private collection), Mulhouse 227
Steiner (private collection), Bratislava 102
Steinheim-Archiv, Duisburg 271, 283
Stiftung Kirche und Judentum, Basel 189

Universitätsbibliothek Basel 192, 338
  Porträtsammlung der Universitätsbibliothek 135, 137, 187, 188

Verlag Neue Kritik, Frankfurt a.M. 72
Vermessungsamt Basel-Stadt 177

Wyler (private collection), Zurich 211

Zafran-Sagal (private collection), Herrliberg 66, 206, 213, 214, 216, 240, 247, 248, 309, 322, 328
Zangen-Cohn (private collection), Haifa 310
Zydowski Instytut Historyczny, Warsaw 27

Illustrations for which no legal successor could be found 26, 48, 49 bottom, 82, 109, 158, 208, 225, 251, 278, 287, 329, 333, 348, 360

Index of Persons

Aberson, Zevi 206
Adler, E.N. 79
Adler, Nathan 118
Agnon, Samuel Joseph 74, 290, 329
Aleichem, Sholem (pseudonym for Shalom Rabinowitsch) 55, 64–67, 297
Alexander I (Czar) 52
Alexander II (Czar) 7
Alexander, Michael Solomon 38, 46, 49
Alkalai, Judah ben 5, 29, 30, 137
Amieli, Abir → Natonek, Josef
Antokolski, Mark 317
Apor, Gábor 287, 288
Arafat, Yassir 356
Arlosoroff, Chaim 18, 248, 332
Atatürk, Kemal 126
Auerbach, Selig 128, 129
Aus der Au, Lucie 214
Ausländer, Rose 74

Bab, Julius 310, 311
Bachofen, Johann Jakob 193
Balfour, Lord Arthur J. 277, 281
Bär, Julius 170
Bar Kokhba, Simon 361, 377
Baruch, Joseph Marcou 126
Baum, Oskar 326
Baumgarten, Arthur 339
Bayezid II (Sultan) 124
Beek, Gottfried zur (i.e. Ludwig Müller, called von Hausen) 337, 338
Beer Hofmann, Richard 309
Begin, Menahem 253, 306
Behrens, Eduard 193
Benedikt, Moritz 151, 152
Ben Gurion, David (Gruen, David) 2, 249, 260, 271, 285, 305, 349, 358, 359, 364, 380

Ben Zwi, Jizhak 305
Berdyczewski, Micha Josef 254
Berend, Bernhard 5
Bergmann, Hugo 99, 329, 331, 332
Bergner, Hinde 74
Bergson, Henri 123
Bernoulli, Carl A. 193
Bernoulli, Emanuel 186
Bettelheim, Anton 19, 334
Bettelheim, Samuel 109
Bezruch, Petr 98
Bialik, Chaim 216
Bierer, Ruben 110
Birnbaum, Nathan 11, 12, 31, 66, 110, 145, 146, 172, 308, 324
Bistrzycki, Augustin 206
Blackstone, William E. 258
Bloch, Elsa 139
Bloch, Erich 235
Blumenfeld, Kurt 240, 241, 297, 310, 311
Blumenthal, Kurt 329
Bodenheimer, Max Isidor 14, 112–114, 147, 166, 227
Böhm, Adolf 327
Bornstein, Heini 212, 289, 290
Borochov, Ber 14, 381
Brandeis, Louis D. 260, 261, 263
Braude, Markus 239
Braudo, Aleksandr I. 85
Brenner, Josef Chaim 305
Brod, Max 99, 326, 329, 331
Brodetsky, Selig 287, 288
Bromberg-Bytkowski, Sigmund 77
Brunschvig, George 290
Brunschwig, Seligmann 219
Buber, Martin 15, 25, 99, 153, 171, 231, 254, 257, 290, 308–311, 316–318, 327, 329, 332, 384
Buchstab, S.B. 316

Budko, Joseph 318
Byk, Eleazar 316

Calvary, Moses 329, 384
Chamberlain, Joseph 255, 276
Charles IV (Emperor) 178
Chatzman, Vera 207
Chech, Svatopluk 97
Chernyshevskij, Nikolai 91
Churchill, Winston 282
Cinberg, Sergei L. 85
Cohn, Arthur 12, 18, 130, 137–139, 143, 144, 168, 184, 195, 333
Cohn, Marcus 139, 144, 216
Collin-Bernoulli, Bernhard 186, 187
Cundelevich, Aaron 91
Curti, Eugen 211

Daudet 209
David, Heinrich IX, 135
Dayan, Moshe 260
Deecke, Wilhelm 234
Dilthey, Wilhelm 257
Dizengoff, Meir 384
Dreyfus, Alfred 11, 121–123, 152, 224, 227
Dreyfus-Brodski, Julius 139
Drujan, Sigmund 139, 202
Drumont, Edouard 121
Dryander, Ernst von 43
Dubnow, Simon 15, 327, 344
Dühring, Eugen 151
Dumas, Alexandre père 340
Dunant, Henri 208–210
Durkheim, Emile 123

Ebner, Mayer 76
Ehrenpreis, Marcus (Mordechai) 126, 147, 169, 308
Ehrenstein, Albert 311
Elias, Alfred Benjamin 224, 227

Eliezer, Israel ben 4, 51
Eliot, George 209
Ellmann, Rozia 293
Engels, Friedrich 31, 92
Eulenburg, Philipp Count of 44

Farbstein, David 12, 57, 131, 137, 138, 145, 169, 170, 187, 205, 206
Farbstein, Joshua Heschel 57, 169
Fay, Theodore S. 191
Feinberg, H. 139
Feiwel, Berthold 254, 308
Felix (Pope) 180
Finkelstein, Jakub 91
Ford, Henry 337
Fourier, Charles 163
François, Alexis 209
Frank, Jacob 3, 4, 51
Frankenstein, Betty 297, 298
Frankfurter, David 211, 212
Frankl, Ludwig August 47
Franzos, Karl Emil 74
Freier, Recha 297
Friedrich I of Baden (Grand Duke) 42–44, 239, 273
Friedrich III (Emperor) 42, 43
Friedrich Wilhelm (Crown Prince) 42
Friedrich Wilhelm IV (King) 36, 42
Fritsch, Theodor 337
Frutiger, Johannes 41, 46

Gaulle, Charles de 226
Gauss, Hermann 182, 183
Gaussen (ex-pastor) 209
Gawler (colonel) 209
George, Lloyd 277
Gessen, Adel' Iosifovna 85
Gessen, Yulii 85, 86
Ginzberg, Asher → Haam, Ahad
Glicenstein, Henryk 316, 318
Gobat, Maria → Kober-Gobat, Maria
Gobat, Samuel 38, 46, 187
Goedsche, Herrmann (pseudonym Sir John Retcliffe) 340
Goldberger, Rudolf 104
Goldberger, Selma 101
Goldmann, Konrad 241, 242
Goldmann, Nahum 287, 288
Goldsmid, Albert 43
Gömbös, Gyula 286
Gordon, Aaron David 113, 305
Gordon, Judah Leib 79

Gorny, Yosef 264
Gottheil, Emma 293–295, 299
Gottlieb, Leopold 316, 318
Gottlieb, Maurycy 316
Gozhanskii, Samuel 92
Graeter, Albert 191, 193
Granach, Alexander 74
Greenberg, Leopold 276
Gruen, David → Ben Gurion, David
Grüninger, Paul 289
Güdemann, Moritz 152
Gumplowicz, Ludwig 19
Günther, Hans F.K. 19
Gustloff, Wilhelm 211
Gutleben (master) 180

Haam, Ahad (Ginzberg, Asher) 15, 31, 80, 83–85, 99, 134, 169, 171, 253, 254, 264, 265, 309, 319, 327, 339, 377
Haan, Jacob Israel de 18, 331
Halevi, Judah 25
Hamid, Abdul (Sultan) 273, 274
Hammami, Said 349
Hantke, Arthur 114, 297, 298, 384
Harrison, Benjamin 258
Hausen von → Beek, Gottfried zur
Hausmann, Alexander 10, 76
Hechler, Dietrich 43
Hechler, William Henry 42–45, 137, 273
Helfand, Chaim Yankel (pseudonym Litvak, A.) 92
Heman, Carl Friedrich 137, 186–190
Heman, David 187
Herrmann, Leo 326
Herz, Elise 47
Herzen, Aleksander 91
Herzl, Hans 151
Herzl, Theodor IX, 2, 10–12, 14, 19, 20, 27, 28, 30, 32, 41–45, 50, 76, 77, 80, 83, 85, 103, 104, 109–111, 113, 120–122, 126, 129–132, 134, 135, 137, 139–144, 146–173, 185, 188, 205, 207, 208, 227, 231, 232, 236, 239, 240, 244–246, 250, 252, 254–256, 260, 264–268, 271–276, 292, 294, 295, 299, 308, 309, 315, 319, 324, 325, 327–329, 334, 337–339, 341, 342, 344, 345, 372, 380, 383

Hess, Moses 5, 30, 31, 33, 150, 170, 209, 344, 384
Hildesheimer, Azriel 168
Himmler, Heinrich 291
Hirsch, Baron Maurice de 149, 157
Hirsch, Samson Raphael 101, 381
Hirszenberg, Samuel 316, 318
Hitler, Adolf 237, 334, 339, 344
Horovitz, Marcus 128–130
Horthy, Miklós 286
Hussein (Sharif of Mecca) 276, 277

Ibrahim Pasha 34
Ilk (referendar) 237, 238
Israels, Josef 317

Jabotinsky, Zeev (Zhabotinskii, Vladimir) 15, 247, 252, 253, 291, 306, 361, 370, 383
Jacobsohn, M. 139
Jacobson, Victor 169, 241
James I. (King) 258
Jefferson, Thomas 258
Jehoshua, Abraham B. 367, 368, 372
Joly, Maurice 340
Jonas, Hans 240
Joseph II (Emperor) 96
Judah, Eliezer ben 65, 79

Kafka, Franz 99, 326
Kalischer, Zevi Hirsch 5, 30, 33, 209
Katznelson, Berl 380
Kaufmann, Max 239
Kaufmann, Richard 239
Kaznelson, Siegmund 326
Keller (president of Animal Protection Societies in German-Speaking Switzerland) 195
Klatzkin, Jacob 216, 254
Klee, Alfred 297
Klemperer, Victor 334
Kober-Gobat, Maria 144, 187
Kober-Gobat, Paul 131, 137, 186, 187
Kohn, Hans 99, 100, 332
Kohn, Samuel 107
Kohut, Rebekah 299
König, Hermann 101
König-Bendiner, Josephine 101
Kook, Abraham Isaak (Izhak) 26, 28, 306, 370, 371, 372
Kook, Zevi Judah 372
Koppelman, Isidor 289

Kornblüh, Moriz 142, 292
Korngold, Liber 156
Kremer, Arkadii 92, 93

Laharanne, Ernest 29, 30, 122, 209
Lämel, Simon Edler von 47
Landau, Saul 187
Landauer, Georg 332
Landauer, Gustav 311, 332
Landsberg, Alfred 297
Lasker-Schüler, Else 311
Lassalle, Ferdinand 31
Lehmann, Ernst 240
Lenin, Wladimir Iljitch 93, 95
Lessing, Gotthold Ephraim 316
Levin, Shmarya 384
Levinson (pseudonym Kosovskii), Nahum Mendel 93
Lévy, Lazar 122
Lichtheim, Richard 239, 240
Liebermann, Aaron Samuel 91
Liebermann, Max 309
Lilien, Ephraim Moses 308, 312, 316–318, 384
Lilienblum, Moses Leib 79
Lippe, Karpel 144
Litvak, A. → Helfand, Chaim Yankel
Loewe, Heinrich 115, 166, 324, 325
Löffel, Markus 289
Loosli, Carl Albert 339
Lorje, Chaim 30
Louis XVI (King) 218
Lourie, Arthur 287, 288
Lucas, Eric 238
Lucas, Isaak 238
Lurie, Joseph 169

Maccabee, Judah 85
MacDonald, James Ramsay 283
Machar, Joseph Svatopluk 98
McMahon, Henry 276
Magnes, Judah Leon 332
Maier (Rabbi) 231
Maisel-Schochat, Hanna 301
Malz, David 318
Markus, Aron 141
Marmorek, Alexander 227
Marmorek, Oscar 132, 227
Marr, Wilhelm 341, 342, 344, 345
Martov → Zederbaum Yulii O.
Marx, Karl 31, 92

Masaryk, Tomáš 98
Masirevich, Szilárd 288
Maybaum, Sigmund 128, 129
Mazzini, Giuseppe 150, 163
Megged, Aharon 364, 365
Meinrath, Gustav 233
Meir, Golda (Meirsson) 260, 358
Meirsson, Golda → Meir, Golda
Meisel, Dov Berush 54
Mendelsohn, Erich 330
Mendelssohn, Moses 65, 197, 324
Mendes-Flohr, Paul 310
Meyer, Max 231
Meyer, Oscar 139
Mez, Adam 193
Mezei, Ernö 109
Michels, Robert 216
Mickiewicz, Adam 4, 75
Minkowski, Maurycy 316
Minor, Clorinda 48
Mitterrand, François 226
Mitterwurzer, Friedrich 149
Moltke, Helmuth von 36
Mommsen, Theodor 168
Monson, Sir Edmund 43
Montagu, Sir Edwin 277, 281
Montagu, Sir Samuel 119
Montefiore, Claude 277
Montefiore, Sir Moses 29, 46
Morgenstern, Soma 74
Morris, Benny 362, 364
Moses, Siegfried 297
Motzkin, Leo 89, 146, 169, 254, 308
Muhammed Ali (King) 34, 36
Müller, Dominik → Schmitz, Paul
Müller, Ludwig → Beek, Gottfried zur
Münchausen, Börries von 318
Münster, Sebastian 180
Mussolini, Benito 15
Mutnikovich (pseudonymes Gleb, Mutnik), Abram 93

Napoleon I 218
Napoleon III 29, 122, 208, 340
Naschauer(-Herzl), Julie 149
Natonek, Josef (pseudonym Abir Amieli) 5, 32, 33
Naumberg, Zygfryd 316
Neruda, Jan 97

Netanjahu, Benjamin 356
Netter, Charles 50, 224, 381
Neumann, Heinz 211
Neviaski, Moshe 216
Nevlinski (journalist) 273
Nicholas I (Czar) 52, 156
Nietzsche, Friedrich 193
Nikolayson, John 34, 38
Nilus, Sergei 336–339
Noah, Mordecai Manuel 5, 260
Nordau, Max 12, 15, 139, 141, 145, 146, 153, 159, 167, 168, 208, 227, 232, 264, 266, 267, 319, 320, 322, 323, 327, 384
Nordemann, Theodor 185, 195
Nossig, Alfred 75, 316–319, 339

Oesterreicher, Béla 109
Omar (Calif) 43
Oppenheimer, Franz 163
Orlan, Haiyim 142
Oz, Amos 352

Palmerston, Lord Henry 29, 36
Pappenheim, Bertha 69–73
Pasmanik, Daniel 206
Peltin, Samuel Zevi 155
Peltinowa, Salomea 155
Peres, Shimon (Persky, Simon) 358
Peretz, Isaac Leib 58, 66, 92
Persky, Simon → Peres, Shimon
Pestalozzi, Otto 195
Picard, Jacob 231–234
Picard, Leo 234
Pickard, J. 139
Pilichowski, Leopold 316, 318, 319
Pinsker, Leon (actually Judah Leib) 8, 31, 79, 85
Pinski, David 92
Pisarev, Dimitrii 91
Pleve (czarian minister of Interior) 10, 81, 275
Preiswerk, Samuel 137, 187

Rabin, Yitzak 360
Rabinowitsch, Sara 69
Rabinowitsch, Shalom → Aleichem, Sholem
Raffel (teacher) 237
Rappart, William 207
Rathenau, Walther 322
Reber, Paul 183

Reich-Ranicki, Marcel 223
Reines, Izhak 371
Retcliffe, Sir John → Goedsche, Herrmann
Riegner, Gerhart 215, 289
Rohling, August 99
Rónai, János 108, 109
Rosenbaum, Simon 241
Rosenberg, Alfred 338, 344
Rosenblüth, Felix 115, 239, 241, 297, 384
Rosenzweig, Franz 257
Rosin, Heinrich 240
Roth, Joseph 74
Rothschild (family) 150
Rothschild, Alfons 48
Rothschild, Baron Edmond de 10, 11, 89, 153
Rothschild, James Jacob 48
Rothschild, Lionel de 117
Rothschild, Lord 277
Rothschild, Mayer Amschel 5, 30, 48, 89
Rubashow (Rubashow), Zalman → Shasar, Zalman
Rubeni, David 3
Rubin, Hans 240
Ruf, Aaron 219
Ruge, Arnold 31
Rülf, Isaak 113, 129, 166
Ruppin, Arthur 19, 270, 271, 332, 384

Sacher-Masoch, Leopold von 74
Sagal, Wladimir → Sagalowitz, Wladimir
Sagalowitz, Benjamin 212–215, 289
Sagalowitz (Sagal), Wladimir 213, 214
Salin, Edgar 216
Salvador, Joseph 121, 209
Salz, Abraham 76, 77
Sandel, Theodor 47, 50
Sapir, Joseph B. 327
Sauerbruch, Ferdinand 214
Schach, Miriam 292, 293, 295, 296, 299
Schatz, Boris 316, 318
Scheps, Samuel 212, 216, 217, 289, 290
Schick, Conrad 41
Schiff, Friedrich 164

Schiff, Jacob 256, 260
Schiller, Friedrich von 231
Schmitz, Paul (alias Dominik Müller) 191, 193
Schocken, Salman 301, 328–330, 384
Scholem, Gershom 27, 242
Schreiber, Moses → Sofer, Chatam
Schulte, Eduard 215, 217, 289
Schulz, Bruno 74
Schwalb, Nathan 212
Seforim, Mendele Mokher 55, 62, 66
Segev, Tom 359
Shaftesbury, Lord Anthony Ashley 29
Shasar, Zalman (Rubashow) 240, 380
Sheinkin, Menahem 241
Shochat, Manya 299
Simmel, Georg 257
Simon-Friedberg, Johanna 233
Smoira, Moses 384
Smolenskin, Peretz 31, 79, 110
Sofer, Chatam (Schreiber, Moses) 32, 101, 333
Sokolów (Sokolow), Nahum 55, 155–160, 209, 248, 276, 319, 327
Sokolów, Regina 157
Sonnenfeld, Joseph Chaim 331, 333
Speiser, Paul IX, 134, 144
Spektor, Mordechaj 56
Sperber, Manès 74
Spittler, Christian Friedrich 41, 46, 187
Spitzer, Salomon 110
Stalin, Josif Vissarionovitch 95
Steinbeck, Friedrich 48
Steinbeck, Johann 48
Steinbeck, John 48
Steiner, David Sigmund 105
Steiner, Gustav 103, 104
Steiner, Hermann 101–104
Steiner, Josephine 103
Steiner, Józsi 103
Steiner, Lily 104
Steiner, Margit 104
Steiner, Max 103–105
Steiner, Moritz 102
Steiner, Nelly 103

Steiner, Reline 105
Steiner, Selma 105
Steiner, Siegfried 102–104
Steiner, Sigmund 101
Steiner, Wilhelm 102–105
Steinhardt, Jakob 316, 318
Stern, Bruno 236
Stern, Samu 287, 288
Strauss, Ludwig 310, 311
Struck, Hermann 312, 317
Sturmann, Jacob Akiba 236
Sturmann, Manfred 236, 237
Südfeld, Gabriel 167
Sue, Eugène 340
Swidrichsen, M. 139
Syrkin, Nachman 14
Szold, Benjamin 262
Szold, Henrietta 262, 263, 290, 299, 378

Thon, Osias 169
Tobler, Titus 38
Toller, Ernst 298
Trebacz, Maurycy 318
Trumpeldor, Josef 16, 305, 361, 377
Tudela, Benjamin 218

Uhland, Ludwig 231
Uprmny, J. 295
Ury, Lesser 316–318
Ussishkin (Usyshkin), Abraham Menahem 83, 216, 241, 246, 251

Velics, László 287
Victoria (Queen) 29, 43, 117
Vrchlický, Jaroslav 98

Wachs, Chaim Eliezer 169
Wachtel, Wilhelm 316, 318
Warburg, Otto 246, 301
Wechsler, Hile 112
Weil, Joe 139
Weil, Joël J. 202, 204, 205
Weil, Jonas 230
Weininger, Otto 322
Weinles, Jakub 316
Weinstock, Arieh 316
Weishaupt, Adam 339
Weizmann, Chaim 14, 83, 119, 167, 171, 205–207, 233, 241, 246, 248, 249, 251, 253, 254, 271, 276, 283, 308, 319, 332, 384

Weltsch, Felix 99
Weltsch, Robert 99, 100, 298, 326
Werner (Rabbi) 128, 129
Wielopolski, Aleksander 54
Wilhelm I (King/Emperor) 42, 43
Wilhelm II (Emperor) 42–44, 50, 187, 239, 273, 274
Wilson, Woodrow 261, 277, 279, 280
Wise, Stephen 289
Wittes, B.L. 139
Wittkowski, Alfred 240
Wittmann, Hugo 149
Wolffsohn, David 113, 114, 132, 141, 166, 227, 246
Wolfskehl, Karl 309
Wollestonecraft, Mary 69
Wyler, Veit 211, 212, 215, 290

York-Steiner, Heinrich 312

Zangwill, Israel 14, 161, 162, 173, 174, 241, 255, 256, 382
Zederbaum, Yulii O. (pseudonym Martov) 94
Zevi, Shabbetai 3, 4, 26, 51
Zlatopolsky, Hillel 241
Zlocistic, Theodor 237
Zur, Yaakov 216
Zutt, Richard (president of the government) 135
Zweig, Arnold 18, 310, 331, 332
Zweig, Stefan 309

Acknowledgements and Thanks

Archiv für Zeitgeschichte an der ETH Zürich

Basel Tourismus
Basler Kunstverein: Roda, Hortensia; Soiron, Alicia
Basler Mission
Bayerische Staatsbibliothek München: Schipper, Edith
Berta-Hess-Cohn-Stiftung
Bessermann, Max
Beth Hatefutsoth, The Nahum Goldman Museum of the Jewish Diaspora, Tel Aviv
Bornstein, Heini
Brańska, Joanna
Broder, Henryk M.
Bund Archives, New York
Burckhardt, Leonhard

Carmel, Alex
Central Archives for the History of the Jewish People, Jerusalem: Assouline, Hadassah
Central Zionist Archives, Jerusalem: Mayorek, Yoram; Koffler, Reuven; Bar-Tikva, Gitta; Rubinstein, Rachel; Kanner, Nechama
Cesarani, David
Cohn, Arthur

Deutsch, Helga Ayala
Dreifuss, Emil

Frenkel, Mordecai

Gesellschaft für das Gute und Gemeinnützige
Gessen, Valerii Jul'evich
Gierowski, Józef
Goldschmidt, Erich
Goldschmidt, Victor
Gorny, Yosef
Guggenheim-Weil, Susi
Guttmann, Max

Hartley Library, University of Southhampton: Woolgar, C.M.
Herzig, Willi
Historisches Museum Basel: Schärli, Beatrice
Hońdo, Leszek
Hunziker, Ernst

Israelitische Cultusgemeinde Zürich: Domhardt, Yvonne
Israelitische Gemeinde Basel
Israel Museum, Jerusalem

Janner, Sara
Jewish Museum, London: Baumann, Ricki; Marin, Jennifer

Jewish Museum, New York: Kauskamp, Jessica; Kleeblatt, Norman; Chevlowe, Susan; Treitel, Barbara
Jüdisches Museum der Schweiz: Guth-Dreyfus, Katia
Jüdisches Museum der Stadt Frankfurt a. M.: Wachten, Johannes
Jüdisches Museum der Stadt Wien: Schoeps, Julius H.; Albrecht-Weinberger, Karl; Sulzenbacher, Hannes; Milchram, Gerhard

Katz, Paul
Kaufmann, Uri
Kieser, Hans-Lukas
Kolatt, Israel
Kurz, Rosmarie

Lehmann, Thomas
Leo Baeck Institute, New York
Liatowitsch, Marcel
Liebe, Klaus
Link-Lenczowski, Andrzej K.
Lokshin, Aleksandr

Magyar Zsidó Múzeum/Magyar Zsidó Levéltár, Budapest: Toronyi, Zsuzsanna; Turán, Robert B.
Maier, David
Meles, Brigitte
Metzger, Leopold
Monderer, Simon
Moscati, Gianfranco
Museum der Kulturen, Basel
Muzeum Historii Miasta Łodzi
Muzeum Historyczne m. Krakowa
Muzeum Historyczne m. st. Warszawy: Janusz Durko
Muzeum Narodowe w Krakowie
Muzeum Narodowe w Warszawie
Muzeum Sztuki w Łodzi

Nittenberg, Joanna
Novartis

Pugatsch, Leo

Raviv-Vorobeichic, Maya and Ruth
Reinhardt Druck, Basel

Salomon-Ludwig-Steinheim-Institut, Duisburg
Schenker, Anatol
Scheps, Samuel
Seewann, Harald
Shimoni, Gideon
Silbiger, Freimette
Staatsarchiv Basel-Stadt: Baur Sarasin, Esther; Meneghetti, Franco; Wichers, Hermann; Zwicker, Josef
Stegemann, Ekkehard

Steven Spielberg Jewish Film Archives, Jerusalem: Koolik, Marilyn; Tryster, Hillel
Stiftung für Kirche und Judentum: Rubeli Guthauser, Nico
Stiftung Irene Bollag-Herzheimer

Tomaszewski, Jerzy

Universitätsbibliothek Basel

Vestermanis, Margers

Wahl, Edouard
Weill, Ralph
Weingarten, Ralph
Westdeutscher Rundfunk, Köln
Wohlmann, Herbert
World Zionist Organization, Jerusalem: Eyal, Eli; Kornblum, Rami; Rodan, Martin; Wolf, Arie; Livne, Arie
Wyler, Veit

Yivo Institute, New York

Zafran-Sagal, Nina
Zangen-Cohn, Esther
Zimmermann, Moshe
Żydowski Instytut Historyczny, Warszawa: Tych, Feliks

In addition to the persons and organizations mentioned above a number of authors and colleagues have also made material available.

We would furthermore like to express our gratitude to all those who have given us permission to reproduce material to which they hold the copyright.

Herzl-Jubiläum
Basel
1897·1997

UNI
BASEL
Historisches Seminar